An Introduction to Property Law in Australia

HEAD OFFICE: 100 Harris Street PYRMONT NSW 2009
Tel: (02) 8587 7000 Fax: (02) 8587 7100
For all sales inquiries please ring 1800 650 522
(for calls within Australia only)

INTERNATIONAL AGENTS & DISTRIBUTORS

CANADA
Carswell Co
Ontario, Montreal,
Vancouver, Calgary

HONG KONG
Sweet & Maxwell Asia
Hennessy Road, Wanchai

Bloomsbury Books Ltd
Chater Road, Central

MALAYSIA
Sweet & Maxwell Asia
Petaling Jaya, Selangor

NEW ZEALAND
Brooker's Ltd
Wellington

SINGAPORE
Sweet & Maxwell Asia
Albert Street

UNITED KINGDOM & EUROPE
Sweet & Maxwell Ltd
London

UNITED STATES
Wm W Gaunt & Sons, Inc
Holmes Beach, Florida

William S Hein Co Inc
Buffalo, New York

JAPAN
Maruzen Company Ltd
Tokyo

An Introduction to Property Law in Australia

by

ROBERT CHAMBERS

BEd, LLB (Alberta), DPhil (Oxford)
Associate Professor, University of Alberta Faculty of Law
Formerly Senior Lecturer, University of Melbourne Law School

LBC INFORMATION SERVICES 2001

Published in Sydney by

LBC Information Services
  100 Harris Street, Pyrmont, NSW

First edition 2001

National Library of Australia
   Cataloguing-in-Publication entry.

Chambers, Robert, 1957– .
An introduction to property law in Australia.

   Bibliography.
   Includes index.
   ISBN 0 455 21692 4.

1. Property — Australia. I. Title.

   346.9404

© LBC Information Services
   a part of Thomson Legal & Regulatory Group Asia Pacific Limited 2001
   ABN 64 058 914 668

   This publication is copyright. Other than for the
   purposes of and subject to the conditions prescribed under
   the Copyright Act, no part of it may in any form or by any
   means (electronic, mechanical, microcopying, photocopying,
   recording or otherwise) be reproduced, stored in a retrieval
   system or transmitted without prior written permission.
   Inquiries should be addressed to the publishers.

Product Developer: Catherine Dunk
Senior Editor: Jessica Perini
Internal Design: 1 Bluedog Design

Typeset in 9 on 11 point Stone Sans and Stone Serif by RE Typesetting, Woy Woy, NSW

Printed by Ligare Pty Ltd, Riverwood, NSW

PREFACE

This book is an introduction to the law of property in Australia. It is written for property law students and teachers, lawyers and judges, and others who may want (or need) to learn something of the subject. You may wonder how a relatively small book on a big subject could appeal to such a broad range of readers. It approaches property law differently than other books. First, it is not a reference work. There are several excellent books which fill that role and all members of the public can now use the internet to search for and find current legal materials. Secondly, this book is not a summary of property law. There are several books, aimed at property law students, which provide a condensed description of its basic rules.

This book is designed to help the reader gain a deeper understanding of property law by explaining (in plain language) the analytical framework of the subject. There are two major obstacles which it seeks to overcome: property law can be very difficult to learn and is often isolated from other subjects. The solution (I believe) is to organise the subject in a way which makes it accessible both to someone approaching it for the first time and to those working in other areas of law.

Learning Property Law

There are two things which lawyers and law students often say about their first encounter with property law: it was the most difficult subject they studied in law school and they never really understood it until the end of an entire year of study. This is not just an Australian phenomenon. I had the same experience studying law in Canada. The language was arcane and each class introduced something which seemed wholly unrelated to everything else I had encountered previously in property law, other law subjects, and life in general. This is a pity, because property law is a fascinating subject which ought to engage the interest of students from the outset.

As a teacher of property law, I was determined to do something about these problems. The inspiration came from my tennis coach in Melbourne. He was able to break down the complex skills needed to play the game into a sequence of components which could be learned by someone coming to the game for the first time (later in life and with little athletic ability). Each lesson was enjoyable and built on skills acquired in previous lessons. Surely this could be done for the law of property. What is the first thing a student needs to know about the subject? What should come next? This book attempts to do just that. Although not completely free of "chicken and egg" problems (what should come first if A depends on B and B depends on A?), it aims to introduce the subject in a sequence which is pedagogically sound.

Integrating Property Law

The second and more serious problem with property law is its isolation, both from other areas of the law and among its component parts. Specialisation among lawyers, while necessary, tends to impede communication. Solutions to legal problems in one field need to be understood and considered by lawyers in other fields. Otherwise, there is a risk of duplication, wasted effort, and inconsistency.

The law of property is one of the oldest branches of Australian law and it continues to use a language and organisation developed centuries ago in England. This exacerbates the problems created by specialisation. A concept of property law may be essentially similar to another legal concept and yet the similarity is disguised by differences in the terminology and structure of different branches of the law. This means that the solution to a legal problem may depend on how that problem is classified.

For example, suppose that an elderly couple mortgage their home to a bank to guarantee a loan to their daughter's business. If this transaction later becomes a legal problem, the solution will depend on whether it is identified as a problem of contract law, equity, trade practices, property, or unjust enrichment. Surprisingly, it is likely that the mortgage will be set aside if the daughter unduly influenced her parents to grant it, but not if she forged it without their knowledge. This is because cases of undue influence are handled by equity lawyers, cases of forged mortgages by property lawyers, and those two groups will approach the problem in different ways using different language. The former will talk of "unconscionability", while the latter speak of "indefeasibility", and yet the problem is the same in both cases: the parents did not really want to mortgage their home and the bank relied upon the apparent validity of the mortgage when it advanced money to their daughter.

It is important that inconsistencies like these be uncovered and eliminated. Similar legal problems must receive similar treatment, unless there is a coherent and defensible reason for treating them differently. A lack of communication within the legal profession does not excuse the difference.

A great deal of progress has been made in recent years. Connections among various branches of common law and equity are being discussed by judges, lawyers, and law students, in court judgments, law books and essays, and classrooms. Efforts are directed towards producing a more coherent law of obligations, which integrates contract, tort, unjust enrichment, and other areas of law. Unfortunately, these discussions tend to ignore the law of property. It is important that property lawyers participate fully in them. We have much to contribute and there is much to learn.

I hope that this book can help break down the barriers to communication which separate property law from other areas. It works toward this goal in two ways. First, property concepts are explained in plain, accessible language. Secondly, the subject is organised in a way which allows it to be compared directly with other areas of law. The book begins by looking at the nature of property rights and moves on to discuss the kinds of property rights recognised in Australian law. It then examines the ways in which property rights are created. This invites direct comparisons with the events which create other legal rights and obligations, such as contract, tort, unjust enrichment, and detrimental reliance.

This book also tries to overcome some of the isolation found within the law of property itself. The traditional law school curriculum separated land law (real property) from other aspects of property law (personal property). Today, most law schools offer a single subject called "property law". However, the mark left by the traditional approach is still plain to see. Aspects of personal property (such as the possession of wild animals or finding of lost items) are introduced, but the subject continues to be almost exclusively a study of real property.

In this book, personal property and real property are integrated as much as possible. This has two advantages. First, it is an efficient way to learn. Most core property concepts are applicable to all forms of property and there is no need to re-learn them as each new form is encountered. Secondly, the easiest way to understand property law is to identify and study those core concepts. The traditional divisions of property law obscure the framework which underlies the whole.

Another tradition, which continues in most law schools, is the complete segregation of specific aspects of property law (such as copyrights, patents, and mineral rights) from the rest. Normally, these are taught by specialists as optional subjects, such as intellectual property or natural resources law. These subjects are important features of law school curricula and need and deserve the close attention they receive from students, teachers, and researchers. However, this does not explain why they are wholly excluded from the study of the general law of property. Many students do not study those optional subjects and, therefore, leave law school with an incomplete picture of property law.

I hope that this book can help alleviate this problem by providing an introduction to the whole of the law of property. Although it does not attempt to deal with every property right, it introduces the reader to many forms of property which have been excluded from property law books in the past, such as intellectual property, mineral rights, and corporate shares. This is intended to help the reader obtain a broader understanding of the law of property and see the connections between the general body of property law and its specialised branches. Hopefully, this will prove valuable whether or not the reader goes on to further study of any of those specialised branches.

Thanks

There are many people I wish to thank for their contributions to this book. First and foremost are the staff and students of the University of Melbourne Law School. It is a wonderful place to work and study and I benefitted greatly from my years there. My colleagues were wonderfully generous, kind, and helpful. My students were also very kind and teaching them was both a pleasure and a learning experience. Attempts to compile a proper list of people to thank were unsuccessful. The list is far too long to be repeated here and the risk of omission is far too great. So, unfortunately, those who deserve the most thanks are not named here individually. They know who they are and it is to them that this book is dedicated.

I would like to thank a few other people, not included in that list, for their kindness to me in Melbourne. Thank you to Peter Birks, Michael and Nyuk Nahan, Mitchell McInnes and Alison Hughes, Francesca, Rosemary, and Michael Cann, Liz Chatham, Paul Porter, Colin Barrow and Tayneiagh Becker, Julie Evans and David Neal, Paul Ban, Elizabeth Lindell, and Karen Yeung. Thanks also to my parents, Tom and Lenore, brother, Steve, sisters, Joan and Susan, and new colleagues at the University of Alberta.

I owe an enormous debt to my immediate family, Carol, Tom, and Nigel, for their patience and sacrifice. Like me, they miss Australian friends and Australian life (especially on a cold, dark, January morning in Canada). The nomadic life of an academic lawyer has, for them, been like second-hand smoke. Their love and support around the globe is much appreciated.

Thanks are also due to Catherine Dunk, David Longfield, Elizabeth Paul, Jessica Perini, and everyone else at LBC Information Services who helped with the publication of this book.

Robert Chambers
December 2000

SUMMARY OF CONTENTS

▌▌▌

Preface v
Table of Contents xi
Table of Abbreviations xxv
Table of Cases xxvii
Table of Statutes xxxix

I   WHAT IS PROPERTY?
1   Understanding Property Law 3
2   What is Property? 7
3   What Things can be Subject to Property Rights? 13
4   Distribution of Property 31
5   Taxonomy 37

II POSSESSION
6   Possession 45
7   Competing Claims to Possession 55
8   Limitation of Actions 67

III THE VARIETY OF PROPERTY RIGHTS
9   Variety of Property Rights 75
10 Ownership 77
11 Tenure 83
12 Estates 89
13 Equitable Rights 105
14 Security Rights 117
15 Shared Rights 129
16 Non-Possessory Property Rights to Land 145
17 Property Rights to Intangible Things 175
18 Licences 205
19 Native Title 217

IV CREATION OF PROPERTY RIGHTS

20 Creating Rights 233
21 Intentional Transfers 239
22 Succession on Death 275
23 Detrimental Reliance 291
24 Unjust Enrichment 313
25 Wrongdoing 343
26 Physical Changes to Things 355

V PRIORITY OF PROPERTY RIGHTS

27 Competing Property Rights 377
28 Priority of Legal Property Rights 379
29 Priority of Equitable Property Rights 403

VI REGISTRATION OF PROPERTY RIGHTS TO LAND

30 Registration 429
31 Deeds Registration System 433
32 Torrens System 445

Bibliography 493
Index 509

TABLE OF CONTENTS

███

Preface v
Summary of Contents ix
Table of Abbreviations xxv
Table of Cases xxvii
Table of Statutes xxxix

I WHAT IS PROPERTY?
  1 Understanding Property Law 3
  2 What is Property? 7
      The Essential Characteristics of Property Rights 8
         Enforceability 8
         The Existence of Some Thing 9
         Are There Any Other Essential Characteristics? 10
  3 What Things Can be Subject to Property Rights? 13
      Human Tissue 16
         Property Rights to Living Things 16
         Property Rights to Dead Human Tissue 16
         Property Rights to Living Human Tissue 20
            Regenerating Tissues 21
            Non-regenerating Tissues 22
            Sperm, Ova, and Embryos 23
      Information 24
         Freedom of Information 25
  4 Distribution of Property 31
      Types of Property 32
      Private Property 34
  5 Taxonomy 37
      Land/Goods 38
      Real/Personal 38
      Legal/Equitable 39
      Tangible/Intangible 40
      Property Creating Events 41

II POSSESSION
  6 Possession 45
      What is Possession? 45
         Control 45
         Intention to Possess 48

6 Possession — *continued*

- Importance of Possession 49
- Ownership, Title, and Possession 50
- Obtaining Possession 51
  - Possession Acquired by Consent 52
  - Possession Acquired Without Consent 53

7 Competing Claims to Possession 55

- Breach of Duty 55
  - Trespass 55
  - Conversion 56
  - Detinue 57
  - Overlap 57
  - Other Wrongs 57
- Responses to Breach of Duty 58
  - Direct Enforcement 59
  - Compensation 59
  - Restitution 61
  - Punishment 62
- Rights to Possession 62
  - Obtaining the Right to Possession 63
  - Relativity of Property Rights 63
    - Lost and Found 65
    - Master and Servant 65

8 Limitation of Actions 67

- Limitation Statutes 67
- Adverse Possession 68
  - Possession 68
  - Permission 69
  - Successive Periods of Adverse Possession 70
  - The Right to Possession Extinguished 70

III THE VARIETY OF PROPERTY RIGHTS

9 Variety of Property Rights 75

10 Ownership 77

- Ownership and Possession 77
- Bundle of Rights 79
- Alienability 80
- Responsibilities of Ownership 80
  - Duty to Prevent Harm 81
  - Liability to Execution 82

11 Tenure 83

- Feudalism 83
- Evolution from Tenure to Ownership 84
  - Abolition of Subinfeudation 84
  - Elimination of Feudal Services 85
  - Nature of the Crown's Right to Land 86

12 Estates 89

- Freehold Estates 90
  - Fee Simple 90
  - Fee Tail 91
  - Life Estate 92

12 Estates — *continued*

- Leasehold Estates 92
  - Relationship between Landlord and Tenant 93
  - Duration 94
    - Fixed Term 94
    - Periodic 94
    - At Will 95
  - Combinations and Options 96
- Other Estates 96
- Possession 98
- Future Interests 99
  - Contingent Remainders 100
  - Rule Against Perpetuities 100
  - Waste 102

13 Equitable Rights 105

- Development of Equitable Property Rights 106
- Equity Today 107
- Trusts 108
  - Trustees 108
  - Subjects 108
  - Objects 109
  - Beneficial Ownership 110
  - Types of Trusts 111
  - Development of the Trust 111
  - Modern Uses of the Trust 113
- Nature of Equitable Property Rights 115

14 Security Rights 117

- Reasons for Taking Security Rights 118
- Types of Security Rights 118
  - Possession 118
    - Pledge 119
    - Common Law Lien 119
  - Ownership 120
    - Mortgage 120
    - Hire-Purchase and Conditional Sale 121
  - Encumbrance 121
    - Equitable Charge 121
    - Equitable Lien 122
    - Statutory Encumbrance 123
- Mortgages 124
  - Intervention of Equity 124
  - Mortgages and Trusts 125
- Substance over Form 126

15 Shared Rights 129

- Four Unities 130
  - Unity of Possession 130
    - Agreements Regarding the Use of Shared Rights 130
    - Sharing Non-Possessory Rights 130
  - Unity of Interest 131
  - Unity of Title 131
  - Unity of Time 131

15 Shared Rights — *continued*

- Sharing the Benefits and Burdens of Ownership 132
  - Wrongdoing 132
  - Unjust Enrichment 133
  - Statute 134
- Survivorship 134
  - Corporations 135
  - Order of Death 135
  - No Survivorship 136
- Creation of Shared Ownership 136
  - Common Law 137
  - Statute 138
  - Equity 139
- Severance and Partition 140
  - Severance of a Joint Tenancy 140
    - Destruction of the Four Unities 140
    - Agreement 141
    - Unilateral Declaration 141
  - Partition of a Tenancy in Common 142

16 Non-Possessory Property Rights to Land 145

- Profits à Prendre 146
  - What Things? 146
  - Profit à Prendre or Sale of Goods? 147
  - Duration 148
- Easements 149
  - Benefit to Nearby Land 149
    - Proximity of the Dominant Tenement 149
    - Benefit to the Land 150
    - Easements in Gross 150
    - Ownership of the Dominant and Servient Tenements .. 150
  - Rights which can be Easements 151
    - Positive Easements 151
    - Negative Easements 152
    - Less than Possession 152
    - Clearly Defined 153
    - Cost of Maintaining the Easement 154
  - Creation of Easements 154
    - Easement of Necessity 154
    - Easement by Prescription 154
  - Changes in Use 156
- Restrictive Covenants 156
  - Compared to Other Property Rights 156
    - Estates 156
    - Profits à Prendre and Positive Easements 157
    - Negative Easements 157
  - Privity of Contract 158
    - Benefit of the Covenant 159
    - Obligation to Perform the Covenant 159
  - Rights which can be Restrictive Covenants 160

16 Non-Possessory Property Rights to Land — *continued*

- Attaching Covenants to Land 162
  - The Burden of the Covenant 162
  - The Benefit of the Covenant. 162
  - Development Schemes 163
- Pastoral Rights 164
  - Possession. 165
  - Property 167
- Mineral Rights 168
  - The Crown's Right to Minerals 169
  - Right to Explore for Minerals 170
    - Miner's Rights 171
    - Exploration Licences 171
  - Right to Take Minerals 172

17 Property Rights to Intangible Things 175

- Intellectual Property 175
  - Forms of Expression 176
    - Copyrights 176
    - Designs. 179
    - Circuit Layouts 180
  - Scientific Advancements 181
    - Patents 181
    - Plant Breeder's Rights 183
  - Reputation 184
    - Passing Off 185
    - Trade Marks 185
    - Business Names 186
  - Confidential Information 187
    - What is Confidential Information? 187
    - Creation of a Duty of Confidence 188
    - Breach of Confidence 189
    - Responses to Breach of Confidence 190
    - Is the Right to Confidential Information Property? 191
- Corporate Shares. 193
  - What is a Corporation? 193
  - What is a Share? 194
  - Is a Share Property? 195
  - Right to Dividends 197
  - Right to Assets on Dissolution 198
  - Right to Vote 198
    - Enforcement of the Right 199
    - Lack of Control 200
    - Indirect Control 201
    - The Power of Life and Death 203

18 Licences 205

- Categories of Licences 206
  - Bare Licence 206
  - Contractual Licence 206
  - Licence Coupled with an Interest 207

18 Licences — *continued*

- Personal Right or Property?.................................. 208
  - Is the Right Recognised as Property?..................... 208
  - Steps Needed to Create Property......................... 208
  - Intention to Create Property............................. 209
- Enforcing the Licence... 210
  - Enforcing the Licence against the Grantor............... 210
  - Enforcing the Licence Against Others.................... 213

19 Native Title 217

- What is Native Title?.. 217
  - Rights to Land... 218
  - Recognised by Australian Common Law................. 218
  - Traditional Laws and Customs............................ 219
  - Indigenous Inhabitants of Australia...................... 220
  - Communal, Group, or Individual Rights................. 220
- Native Title in Australian Law................................. 221
  - Native Title and Sovereignty............................. 222
    - Acquisition of Sovereignty............................ 222
    - Recognition of Existing Property Rights.............. 222
    - Radical Title.. 224
  - Native Title and Tenure.................................. 225
  - Proof of Native Title..................................... 226
    - Native Title Today.................................... 227
    - Native Title When Britain Acquired Sovereignty...... 227
    - Transfer of Native Title.............................. 227
    - Level of Proof.. 228
    - Loss of Native Title.................................. 229
    - The Native Title Act.................................. 230

IV CREATION OF PROPERTY RIGHTS

20 Creating Rights 233

- Creation of Rights... 233
  - Wrongs... 233
  - Consent.. 234
  - Unjust Enrichment... 234
  - Other Events... 234
  - Importance of Taxonomy................................. 235
- Creation of Property Rights 236
- Creation of Trusts... 237

21 Intentional Transfers.. 239

- Legal Property Rights 240
  - Formalities 240
  - Methods of Transferring Legal Property Rights 240
  - Goods... 241
    - Delivery... 241
    - Document 242
    - Contract of Sale....................................... 243
  - Money.. 244
    - What is Money?.. 244
    - Transfer of Money 245

21 Intentional Transfers — *continued*

- Intangible Personal Property ... 246
  - Document ... 246
  - Registration ... 246
- Land ... 247
  - Livery of Seisin ... 247
  - Deed ... 248
  - Requirement of Writing ... 249
  - Registration ... 249
  - Possession ... 250
- Equitable Property Rights ... 250
  - Formalities ... 250
  - Express Trusts ... 252
    - Certainty of Intention ... 252
    - Constitution of Trusts ... 253
  - Equitable Charges ... 254
    - Intention to Create a Charge ... 254
    - Giving Effect to that Intention ... 255
    - Legal or Equitable? ... 255
  - Restrictive Covenants ... 257
- Specific Performance ... 257
  - Responses to Breach of Contract ... 258
  - Effect of Specific Performance ... 259
  - Why does the Trust Arise? ... 259
  - The Role of Intention ... 260
  - Nature of the Trust ... 261
  - Sale of Goods ... 262
  - Other Property Rights ... 263
  - Options to Purchase ... 263
  - Part Performance ... 264
    - How does Part Performance Work? ... 265
    - Oral Mortgages ... 266
- Vendors' and Purchasers' Liens ... 267
  - Common Law ... 267
    - Vendors' Liens ... 267
    - Purchasers' Liens ... 267
  - Equity ... 268
    - Vendors' Liens ... 268
    - Purchasers' Liens ... 269
    - What Things? ... 269
    - How Liens Affect a Sale ... 270
- Incomplete Gifts ... 271
  - Completion of Gifts ... 272
  - Incomplete Gifts and Express Trusts ... 272
  - Incomplete Gifts and Constructive Trusts ... 273

22 Succession on Death ... 275

- Testamentary Dispositions ... 275
  - Testamentary and Inter Vivos ... 275
  - Wills and Codicils ... 276
  - Executors and Administrators ... 276

22 Succession on Death — *continued*

    Transfer to Personal Representatives 277
        Backdating the Transfer 277
        The Public Trustee 278
        Combinations of the Two. 278
    Transfer to the Beneficiaries 278
  Intentional Testamentary Dispositions 279
    Wills and Codicils 279
        Real and Personal Property. 280
        Residuary Estate 280
        Formalities 280
        Testamentary Trusts 281
    Donationes Mortis Causa 281
        Conditional Gift. 281
        Inter Vivos or Testamentary 281
        Before Death 282
        After Death. 282
        What Things? 283
  Transfers on Death by Operation of Law. 284
    Secret Trusts 284
        Communication. 285
        Acceptance. 285
        Constitution. 285
        Inter Vivos or Testamentary 286
        Express or Constructive?. 286
    Mutual Wills. 287
        When does the Trust Arise? 287
        Why does the Trust Arise? 287
    Intestacy. 288
    Bona Vacantia. 288
    Family Provision. 289

23 Detrimental Reliance 291

  Estoppel 291
    Varieties of Estoppel 292
        Common Law Estoppel 292
        Equitable Estoppel 293
    Creation of Estoppel. 293
        Representation 293
        Detrimental Reliance 294
    Consequences of Estoppel 295
        Possible Responses to Equitable Estoppel 295
        Choosing the Appropriate Response. 295
  Family Property 297
    Ownership of Assets at the End of a Relationship. 297
    Statutes. 298
        Marriage. 298
        Other Relationships 299
    Equity. 300
        Intention to Create a Trust 301
        Contract. 302
        Unjust Enrichment. 302
        Detrimental Reliance 303
        Unconscionability 306

24 Unjust Enrichment 313
Types of Unjust Enrichment 314
   Enrichment 314
   Unjust Factors 315
      Non-Voluntary Transfer 316
      Public Policy 317
Restitution of Unjust Enrichment 317
Rescission 318
   The Act of Rescission 318
   Rescission at Common Law and in Equity 319
   Statutory Rights to Rescind 320
      Protection of Creditors 320
      Sale of Goods 320
      Fair Trading 321
   The Effect of Rescission 321
   Property Rights Created by Rescission 322
      Rescission at Common Law 322
      Statutory Rescission 323
      Rescission in Equity 323
   Property Rights Before Rescission 324
Rectification 325
   The Effect of Rectification 325
      Perfectionary Trust 326
      Restitutionary Trust 326
   When Does the Trust Arise? 326
Resulting Trusts 327
   Situations in which Resulting Trusts Arise 328
   Trusts which Fail 328
   Apparent Gifts 329
      Presumption of Resulting Trust 329
      Presumption of Advancement 330
      The Presumptions Today 330
      Contributions to the Purchase Price 331
      The Donor's Intention 332
   Unjust Enrichment in other Situations 333
      When is a Trust Appropriate? 333
      Classification of the Trust 334
Equitable Liens 335
   Connection to the Asset 335
   Trust or Lien? 336
Tracing 337
   What is Tracing? 337
   Tracing through Mixtures 339
      Presumptions Against Wrongdoers 339
      Sharing Pro Rata 340
      Clayton's Rule 340

25 Wrongdoing 343
What is Wrongdoing? 343
Responses to Wrongdoing 344
   Direct Enforcement 344
   Compensation 344
   Restitution 344
   Punishment 345

25 Wrongdoing — *continued*

- Forfeiture to the Government 345
  - Recovery of the Benefits of Wrongdoing 345
  - Things Used by Wrongdoers 346
  - Transfer of Property Rights 346
  - Restraining Orders 347
- Restitution to the Victim 347
  - Which Wrongs? 348
    - Other Wrongs 348
    - Intention 349
  - Property or Personal Right? 350
- Restitution to Others 351
  - Unlawful Killing 352
  - Loss of Rights 352
  - Constructive Trust 353
  - Relief from Forfeiture 354

26 Physical Changes to Things 355

- Creation and Destruction of Things 355
  - Goods 356
    - Making New Things 356
    - Allocating Property Rights 358
  - Land 359
    - Accretion and Erosion 359
    - Total Destruction of the Premises 361
- Accessories 362
  - Accession 362
    - Is Separation Practical? 363
    - Accessory or Principal? 363
  - Fixtures 364
    - Degree of Annexation 365
    - Object of Annexation 365
    - Tenant's Fixtures 366
    - Security Rights 369
- Mixtures 370
  - Possible Property Rights 370
  - Mixture by Consent 371
  - Mixture Without Consent 371
    - Wrongful Mixture 372
    - Nature of Property Rights to a Mixture 373

V PRIORITY OF PROPERTY RIGHTS

27 Competing Property Rights 377

28 Priority of Legal Property Rights 379

- Nemo Dat 379
  - Innocent Purchasers 379
  - Careless Owners 380
- Exceptions to Nemo Dat 381
  - Exceptional Transactions 382
    - Notice 383

28 Priority of Legal Property Rights — *continued*

- Estoppel ... 383
- Apparent Agency ... 385
- Buyers and Sellers in Possession ... 387
- Market Overt ... 389
- Less Durable Rights ... 390
  - Money ... 390
  - Option to Rescind ... 393
  - Native Title ... 395

29 Priority of Equitable Property Rights ... 403

- Nature of Equitable Property Rights ... 403
- Bona Fide Purchase ... 405
  - Effect of the Defence ... 405
  - Elements of the Defence ... 406
    - Bona Fide ... 406
    - Purchase ... 406
    - For Value ... 406
    - Without Notice ... 407
- Notice ... 408
  - Actual Notice ... 408
  - Constructive Notice ... 409
    - Nature of the Transaction ... 409
    - Facts Discovered During the Transaction ... 410
    - Failure to Search ... 411
  - Imputed Notice ... 412
  - Knowledge and Notice ... 413
- Competing Equitable Property Rights ... 414
  - First in Time ... 414
  - Postponing the Older Right ... 415
    - Reasons for Postponing the Older Right ... 415
    - Reasons for Not Postponing the Older Right ... 415
    - Similarity to Bona Fide Purchase ... 416
  - Express Trusts ... 416
  - Mere Equities ... 417
    - What are Mere Equities? ... 417
    - Priority of Mere Equities ... 420
    - What Classify Property Rights as Mere Equities? ... 421
- Resolving Priority Disputes ... 423
  - Identify the Competing Rights ... 424
  - Where the Older Right is Legal ... 424
  - Where the Older Right is Equitable ... 424
    - And the Newer Right is Legal ... 424
    - And the Newer Right is Equitable ... 424
  - Registration ... 425

VI REGISTRATION OF PROPERTY RIGHTS TO LAND

30 Registration ... 429

- Variety of Registers ... 429
- Importance of Registration ... 431

xxii | Table of Contents

31 Deeds Registration System 433
    What is a Deeds Registration System? 433
    What can be Registered? 433
        General Registration Systems 434
        Specific Registration Systems 435
    Effect of Registration 435
        Creation of Property Rights 435
        Priorities 436
            Practical Effects of Registration 436
            Order of Registration 437
            Property Rights that Cannot be Registered 439
            Entitlement to Priority 440
                Value 441
                Notice 442
                Fraud 443

32 Torrens System 445
    Introduction 445
        Limits of Deeds Registration 445
        Goals of the Torrens System 446
        Rights Created by Registration 446
        Priority over Unregistered Rights 446
        Outline of the Chapter 447
    Creation of Property Rights 448
        Registered Property Rights 448
            Bringing Land into the System 448
            Folios and Certificates of Title 449
            Dealing with Land 450
            Effect of Registration 456
        Unregistered Property Rights 456
            Rights Created without Documents 457
            Rights Created with Documents 458
    Registered Property Rights 460
        Priority Between Registered Rights 460
            Rights Attached to Different Estates 460
            Variation of Priority 461
        Priority Over Unregistered Rights (Indefeasibility) 462
            Indefeasibility Provisions 462
            Immediate and Deferred Indefeasibility 464
        Survival of Unregistered Rights
            (Exceptions to Indefeasibility) 465
            Express Exceptions 465
            Other Statutes 469
            Donees 470
            Fraud 472
        Creation of New Unregistered Rights
            (the In Personam Exception) 475
            Creation of Rights 476
            Events before Registration 477
            Restitution of Unjust Enrichment 479

32 Torrens System — *continued*

- Unregistered Property Rights 481
  - Protection of Unregistered Property Rights (Caveats) 481
    - Effect of a Caveat 482
    - Right to Lodge a Caveat 482
    - Compensation for Lodging a Caveat Improperly 486
  - Priority Between Unregistered Property Rights 486
    - Legal Rights 486
    - Equitable Rights 487
    - Caveats 487
  - Possible Reform 490

Bibliography 493
Index 509

TABLE OF ABBREVIATIONS

This table explains the standard abbreviations used in this book to refer to law reports and courts. It does not contain the abbreviations for the older English law reports that are reproduced in the English Reports (ER). When an older English law report is cited, a reference to the English Reports is also provided.

A = Atlantic Reporter (USA)
AC = Appeal Cases (Law Reports) (House of Lords and Privy Council)
ACLC = Australian Company Law Cases
ACLR = Australian Company Law Reports
ACSR = Australian Corporations and Securities Reports
All ER = All England Law Reports
All ER Rep = All England Law Reports Reprint
ALJR = Australian Law Journal Reports
ALR = Australian Law Reports
Alta LR = Alberta Law Reports (Canada)
Am Dec = American Decisions (USA)
Am Rep = American Reporter (USA)
App Cas = Appeal Cases (Law Reports) (UK)
BCLC = Butterworths Company Law Cases (UK)
BCLR = British Columbia Law Reports (Canada)
BLR = Building Law Reports (UK)
BPR = Butterworths Property Reports (New South Wales)
CA = Court of Appeal
Ch = Chancery (Law Reports) (UK)
Ch App = Chancery Appeal (Law Reports) (UK)
Ch D = Chancery Division (Law Reports) (UK)
CLR = Commonwealth Law Reports (High Court of Australia)
Conn = Connecticut Reports (USA)
CP = Common Pleas (Law Reports) (UK)
CPD = Common Pleas Division (Law Reports) (UK)
DLR = Dominion Law Reports (Canada)
Eq = Equity
Ex = Exchequer (Law Reports) (UK)
ER = English Reports
ETR = Estates and Trusts Reports (Canada)
F = Federal Reporter (USA)
Fam LR = Family Law Reports (Australia)
FCR = Federal Court Reports (Australia)
FLR = Federal Law Reports (Australia)
FSR = Fleet Street Reports (UK)

Gr = Grant's Chancery Reports (Canada)
HCA = High Court of Australia
HL = House of Lords
HLR = Housing Law Reports (UK)
IPR = Intellectual Property Reports (Australia)
IR = Irish Reports
Kans = Kansas Reports (USA)
KB = King's Bench (Law Reports) (UK)
Ky = Kentucky Reports (USA)
LJ = Law Journal (UK)
LR = Law Reports (UK)
LT = Law Times (UK)
Mass = Massachusetts Reports (USA)
NE = North Eastern Reporter (USA)
NSWLR = New South Wales Law Reports
NSWR = New South Wales Reports
NW = North Western Reporter (USA)
NYS = New York Supplement (USA)
NZLR = New Zealand Law Reports
OR = Ontario Reports (Canada)
Or = Oregon Reports (USA)
P = Pacific Reporter (USA)
P = Probate, Divorce and Admiralty (Law Reports) (UK)
P&CR = Property and Compensation Reports (UK)
PC = Privy Council
PD = Probate, Divorce and Admiralty Division (Law Reports) (UK)
QB = Queen's Bench (Law Reports) (UK)
QBD = Queen's Bench Division (Law Reports) (UK)
Qd R = Queensland Reports (Australia)
RI = Rhode Island Reporter (USA)
RPC = Reports of Patent, Design and Trade Mark Cases (UK)
SASC = South Australia Supreme Court
SASR = South Australia State Reports
SCC = Supreme Court of Canada
SCR = Supreme Court Reports (Supreme Court of Canada)
SCR (NSW) = Supreme Court Reports (New South Wales)
SE = South Eastern Reporter (USA)
SR (NSW) = State Reports, New South Wales
S Ct = Supreme Court Reporter (USA)
SW = South Western Reporter (USA)
Tas R = Tasmania Reports
TLR = Times Law Reports (UK)
US = United States Reports (US Supreme Court)
VLR = Victoria Law Reports
VR = Victoria Reports
WALR = Western Australia Law Reports
WAR = Western Australia Reports
WLR = Weekly Law Reports (UK)
WWR = Western Weekly Reports (Canada)

TABLE OF CASES

▌▌▌

Abela v Public Trustee [1983] 1 NSWLR 308 141
Abigail v Lapin [1934] AC 491, 51 CLR 58, [1934]
    All ER Rep 720 (PC) 417, 452, 490
Adamson v Hayes (1973) 130 CLR 276 .... 172, 251
Aitken Agencies Ltd v Richardson [1967] NZLR 65 .... 56, 60
Alati v Kruger (1955) 94 CLR 216 319
Allen v Snyder [1977] 2 NSWLR 685 (CA) 261
Aluminium Industrie Vaassen BV v Romalpa Aluminium Ltd [1976]
    1 WLR 676 357
Amalgamated Property Co v Texas Bank [1982] QB 84, [1981]
    3 All ER 577 (CA) 294
Anderson v Lockhart [1991] 1 Qd R 501 120
ANZ Banking Group Ltd v Curlett, Cannon & Galbell Pty Ltd [1992]
    2 VR 647 119
Arcade Hotel, Re [1962] VR 274 163
Archibald Home Pty Ltd v Commissioner of Stamp Duties (NSW)
    (1948) 77 CLR 143 196
Argyll v Argyll [1967] 1 Ch 302, [1965] 1 All ER 611 188
Armory v Delamirie (1722) 1 Str 506, 93 ER 664, [1558-1774]
    All ER Rep 121 63
Asher v Whitlock (1865) LR 1 QB 1 .... 64, 65
Assets Co Ltd v Mere Roihi [1905] AC 176 (PC) 472
Associated Alloys Pty Ltd v Metropolitan Engineering & Fabrications
    Pty Ltd (1996) 20 ACSR 205, 14 ACLC 952; affirmed as
    Associated Alloys Pty Ltd v ACN 001 452 106 Pty Ltd [2000]
    HCA 25 (11 May 2000) 356, 357
Attorney-General v Blake (27 July 2000, HL) 349
Attorney-General v Brown (1847) 2 SCR (NSW) App 30 86
Attorney-General v Guardian Newspapers (No 2) [1990] 1 AC 109 344
Attorney-General for Hong Kong v Reid [1994] 1 AC 324 (PC) 351, 478
Austin v Keele (1987) 61 ALJR 605 (PC) 303
Australian Guarantee Corp Ltd v De Jager [1984] VR 483 473
Autodesk Inc v Yee (1996) 139 ALR 735 179

Backhouse v Judd [1925] SASR 16 81
Bahr v Nicolay (1988) 164 CLR 604 .... 474, 475, 477, 480
Bailey v Barnes [1894] 1 Ch 25 (CA) 407
Barbour, Re [1967] Qd R 10 138
Barlow Clowes International Ltd v Vaughan [1992] 4 All ER 22 (CA) 341
Barnhart v Greenshields (1853) 9 Moo PC 18, 14 ER 204 411
Barry v Heider (1914) 19 CLR 197 .... 423, 458, 465, 483
Barton v Armstrong [1976] AC 104 (PC) 322
Basham, Re [1986] 1 WLR 1498, [1987] 1 ER 405 304
Baumgartner v Baumgartner (1988) 164 CLR 137 .... 307, 309, 310
Bayliss v Public Trustee (1988) 12 NSWLR 540 283
Beard v Baulkham Hills SC (1986) 7 NSWLR 273 208
Bedford Properties Pty Ltd v Surgo Pty Ltd [1981] 1 NSWLR 106 486
Belgrave Nominees Pty Ltd v Barlin-Scott Airconditioning (Aust) Pty Ltd
    [1984] VR 947 365
Bendal Pty Ltd v Mirvac Project Pty Ltd (1991) 23 NSWLR 464 59
Berry, Re (1906) 147 F 208 334
Big Rock Pty Ltd v Esanda Finance Corp Ltd (1992) 10 WAR 259 384
Biggs v McEllister (1880) 14 SALR 86 470
Birmingham v Renfrew (1937) 57 CLR 666 287
Bishopsgate Motor Finance Corp Ltd v Transport Brakes Ltd [1949]
    1 KB 322, [1949] 1 All ER 37 .... 381, 389
Black v S Freedman & Co (1910) 12 CLR 105 .... 334, 338
Blacklocks v JB Developments (Godalming) Ltd [1982] Ch 183 327
Blackwood v London Chartered Bank of Australia (1871) 10 SCR (NSW)
    (Equity) 56 438
Blackwood v London Chartered Bank of Australia (1874) LR 5 PC 92 407
Bogdanovic v Koteff (1988) 12 NSWLR 472 (CA) 442, 470, 471
Boscawen v Bajwa [1995] 4 All ER 769, [1996] 1 WLR 328 (CA) 338
Boyce v Beckman (1890) 11 LR (NSW) (L) 139 438
Boyce v Boyce (1849) 16 Sim 476, 60 ER 959 109
Boyes, Re (1884) 26 Ch D 531 .... 285, 286
Bradshaw v Toulmin (1784) Dickens 633, 21 ER 417 136
Brady v Stapleton (1952) 88 CLR 322 323
Brand v Chris Building Society Pty Ltd [1957] VR 625 336
Breen v Williams (1995) 186 CLR 71, 138 ALR 259 192
Breskvar v Wall (1971) 126 CLR 376 485

Brickwood v Young (1905) 2 CLR 387 133

Bridges v Hawkesworth (1851) 21 LJ QB 75 47

Brown v Brown (1993) 31 NSWLR 582 (CA) 332

Buckinghamshire County Council v Moran [1990] Ch 623, [1989]
    2 All ER 225 (CA) 48, 68, 70

Bunny Industries Ltd v FSW Enterprises Pty Ltd [1982] Qd R 712 259

Butler v Egg and Egg Pulp Marketing Board (1966) 114 CLR 185 ...... 36, 60

Byrne v Hoare [1965] Qd R 135 66

Byrne v Steele [1932] VLR 143 154

Calverley v Green (1984) 155 CLR 242 .... 139, 331, 337

Canadian Long Island Petroleums Ltd v Irving Industries Ltd [1975]
    2 SCR 715, 50 DLR (3d) 265 264

Canadian Pacific Railway Co Ltd v Turta [1954] SCR 427, [1954]
    3 DLR 1 .... 445, 466

Car and Universal Finance Co Ltd v Caldwell [1965] 1 QB 525, [1964]
    2 WLR 600, [1964] 1 All ER 290 (CA) 322

Case of Mines (1567) 1 Plowden 310, 75 ER 472 169

Castrol Australia Pty Ltd v Emtech Associates Pty Ltd (1980)
    33 ALR 31 .... 189, 190

Chan v Zacharia (1984) 154 CLR 178 350

Chase Manhattan Bank NA v Israel-British Bank (London) Ltd [1981]
    Ch 105 334

Cholmondeley (Marquis of) v Lord Clinton (1820) 2 Jac&W 1,
    37 ER 527 67

City Motors (1933) Pty Ltd v Southern Aerial Super Service Pty Ltd (1961)
    106 CLR 477 77

Clapman v Edwards [1938] 2 All ER 507 150

Clayton's Case (1817) 1 Mer 572, 35 ER 781, [1814-23] All ER Rep 1 340

Clem Smith Nominees Pty Ltd v Farrelly (1978) 20 SASR 227 161

Clough Mill Ltd v Martin [1985] 1 WLR 111, [1984] 3 All ER 982 (CA) 358

Coco v AN Clark (Engineers) Ltd [1969] RPC 41 189

Colbeam Palmer Ltd v Stock Affiliates Pty Ltd (1968) 122 CLR 25 .... 348, 349

Cole, Re [1964] Ch 175, [1963] 3 All ER 433 (CA) 242

Commercial Bank of Australia Ltd v Amadio (1983) 151 CLR 447 319

Commissioner of Stamp Duties (NSW) v Henry (1964) 114 CLR 322 147

Commissioner of Stamp Revenue (Vic) v Royal Insurance Australia
    Ltd (1994) 182 CLR 51 317

Commissioners of the State Savings Bank of Victoria v Permewan,
    Wright & Co Ltd (1914) 19 CLR 457 393

Commonwealth v John Fairfax & Sons Ltd (1980) 147 CLR 39 190
Commonwealth v Registrar of Titles (Vic) (1918) 24 CLR 348 .... 152, 155
Commonwealth v WMC Resources Ltd (1998) 152 ALR 1 (HCA) 172
Commonwealth Life (Amalgamated) Assurance Ltd v Anderson (1945)
    46 SR (NSW) 47 .... 94, 95
Computer Edge Pty Ltd v Apple Computer Inc (1986) 161 CLR 171 177
Cook v Hutchinson (1836) 1 Keen 42, 48 ER 222 329
Copeland v Greenhalf [1952] Ch 488, [1952] 1 All ER 809 152
Corin v Patton (1990) 169 CLR 540,
    64 ALJR 256, 92 ALR 1 .... 254, 273, 436, 459
Corporate Affairs Commission v ASC Timber Pty Ltd (1989)
    18 NSWLR 577 148
Cowell v Rosehill Racecourse Co Ltd (1937) 56 CLR 605 211
Crabb v Arun District Council [1976] 1 Ch 197, [1975] 3 All ER 865 (CA) .. 295
Craven's Estate, Re [1937] Ch 423, [1937] 3 All ER 33 282

Davidson v O'Halloran [1913] VLR 367, 19 ALR 305 442
Davies v Littlejohn (1923) 34 CLR 174 97
Davis v Commonwealth of Australia (1988) 166 CLR 79 .... 25, 26
Dee Trading Co Pty Ltd v Baldwin [1938] VLR 173 .... 57, 58
Delohery v Permanent Trust Co of New South Wales (1904) 1 CLR 283 ... 155
Deta Nominees Pty Ltd v Viscount Plastic Products Pty Ltd [1979] VR 167 . 191
Dillon, Re (1890) 44 Ch D 76, [1886-90] All ER Rep 407 (CA) 282
Dinmore Meatworks Pty Ltd v Kerr (1962) 108 CLR 628 119
Diplock, In re [1948] Ch 465 (CA); affirmed [1951] AC 251 (HL) 340
Director of Public Prosecutions, Re; Ex parte Lawler (1994)
    179 CLR 270 .... 345, 346
DKLR Holding Co (No 2) Pty Ltd v Commissioner of Stamp Duties
    (1982) 149 CLR 431 116
Dockrill v Cavanagh (1944) 45 SR (NSW) 78 .... 95, 250
Doherty v Allman (1878) 3 App Cas 709 161
Doodeward v Spence (1908) 6 CLR 406 .... 17, 19
Dougan v Ley (1946) 71 CLR 142 259
Douglas/Kwantlen Faculty Association v Douglas College [1990]
    3 SCR 570 33
Doulton Potteries Ltd v Bronotte [1971] 1 NSWLR 591 59
Duffield v Elwes (1827) 1 Bli NS 497, 4 ER 976 283
Dwyer v Kaljo (1992) 15 Fam LR 645 300
Dyer v Dyer (1788) 2 Cox Eq 92, 30 ER 42 330

E v Australian Red Cross Society (1991) 27 FCR 310, 99 ALR 601 21
Eagle Trust plc v SBC Securities Ltd [1993] 1 WLR 484 408
Eastdoro Pty Ltd (No 2), Re [1990] 1 Qd R 424 455
Edwards v Lee's Administrator (1936) 96 SW2d 1028 (Kentucky CA) . . . 89, 348
El Ajou v Dollar Land Holdings plc [1994] 2 All ER 685 (CA) 322
Ellenborough Park, Re [1956] Ch 131, [1955] 3 All ER 667 (CA) . . 152, 156, 157
Elliston v Reacher [1908] 2 Ch 374 163
Emerald Quarry Industries Pty Ltd v Commissioner of Highways (1976)
 14 SASR 486 147
Errington v Errington [1952] 1 KB 290, [1952] 1 All ER 149 (CA) 213

Falke v Scottish Imperial Insurance Co (1886) 34 Ch D 234 (CA) 133
Farquharson Brothers & Co v C King & Co [1902] AC 325, [1900-3]
 All ER Rep 120 386
Federal Commissioner of Taxation v Vegners (1989) 90 ALR 547 111
Federated Homes Ltd v Mill Lodge Properties Ltd [1980]
 1 WLR 594, [1980] 1 All ER 371 (CA) 163
Fejo v Northern Territory (1998) 195 CLR 96 . . . . 219, 395, 397
Fisher v Automobile Finance Co of Australia Ltd (1928) 41 CLR 167 120
Fisher v Deputy Federal Commissioner of Land Tax (NSW)
 (1915) 20 CLR 242 97
Fisher v Mansfield [1997] 2 NZLR 230 287
Fisher v Wigg (1700) 1 Salk 391, 91 ER 339 137
Flack v National Crime Authority (1998) 156 ALR 501 . . . . 49, 65
Foley v Hill (1848) 2 HLC 28, 9 ER 1002 11
Forgeard v Shanahan (1994) 35 NSWLR 206 134
Forrest Trust, Re [1953] VLR 246 . . . . 125, 451
Foskett v McKeown [1997] 3 All ER 392 (CA) 123
Fouche v Superannuation Fund Board (1952) 88 CLR 609 114
Franklin v Giddings [1978] Qd R 72 . . . . 189, 191
Frazer v Walker [1967] 1 AC 569, [1967] 1 All ER 649 (PC) 464, 475, 480

Gambotto v WCP Ltd (1995) 182 CLR 432 . . . . 196, 197
Garcia v National Australia Bank Ltd (1998) 194 CLR 395 480
German v Chapman (1877) 7 Ch D 271 (CA) 161
Gibbs v Messer [1891] AC 248 (PC) 464
Gillies v Keogh [1989] 2 NZLR 327 (CA) 303, 305
Gissing v Gissing [1971] AC 886 303

Giumelli v Giumelli (1999) 196 CLR 101 . . . . 293, 294, 295, 296
Glasgow (Lord Provost and Magistrates of) v Farie (1888) 13 App Cas 657 . . 168
Gollan v Nugent (1988) 166 CLR 18 . . . . 59, 62
Graham v Freer (1980) 35 SASR 424 321
Graham v KD Morris & Sons Pty Ltd [1974] Qd R 1 89
Grant v Edwards [1986] 1 Ch 638 303
Green v Green (1989) 17 NSWLR 343 305
Gulbenkian's Settlement Trusts, Re [1970] AC 508, [1968] 3 All ER 785 109

Halifax Building Society v Thomas [1996] Ch 217, [1996] 2 WLR 63 (CA) . . 348
Harper v Minister for Sea Fisheries (1989) 168 CLR 314 145
Haupiri Courts Ltd (No 2), Re [1969] NZLR 353 483
Hawkins v Minister for Lands (NSW) (1949) 78 CLR 479 97
Hayward v Chaloner [1968] 1 QB 107, [1967] 3 All ER 122 (CA) 70
Haywood v Brunswick Permanent Benefit Building Society (1881)
    8 QBD 403 160
Hedley v Roberts [1977] VR 282 152
Heid v Reliance Finance Corp Pty Ltd (1983) 154 CLR 326 . . . . 488, 489
Henderson v Radio Corp Pty Ltd (1960) 60 SR (NSW) 576 185
Hewett v Court (1983) 149 CLR 639, 46 ALR 87, 57 ALJR 211 . . . . . . 269, 270
Hills v Hills (1841) 8 M&W 401, 151 ER 1095 281
Hircock v Windsor Homes (Development No 3) Pty Ltd [1979]
    1 NSWLR 501 138
Hobson v Gorringe [1897] 1 Ch 182, [1895-9] All ER Rep 1231 (CA) 369
Holland v Hodgson (1872) LR 7 CP 328, [1861-73] All ER Rep 237 366
Holroyd v Marshall (1862) 10 HLC 191, 11 ER 999, [1861-73]
    All ER Rep 414 259
Hospital Products Ltd v United States Surgical Corp (1984) 156 CLR 41 349
Hounslow LBC v Twickenham Garden Developments Ltd [1971]
    Ch 233, [1970] 3 All ER 326 211
Hunter BNZ Finance Ltd v CG Maloney Pty Ltd (1988)
    18 NSWLR 420 . . . . 322, 325

IAC (Finance) Pty Ltd v Courtenay (1963) 110 CLR 550 471
Ilich v The Queen (1987) 162 CLR 110 . . . . 334, 390
Indian Oil Corp Ltd v Greenstone Shipping Co SA [1988] QB 345,
    [1987] 3 WLR 869, [1987] 3 All ER 893 . . . . 339, 373
International News Services v Associated Press (1918) 248 US 215 28

Interstate Parcel Express Co Pty Ltd v Time-Life International (Nederlands)
BV (1977) 138 CLR 534 179

J & H Just (Holdings) Pty Ltd v Bank of NSW (1971) 125 CLR 546 ... 483, 489
Jacobs v Platt Nominees Pty Ltd [1990] VR 146 489
Jared v Clements [1902] 2 Ch 399, [1903] 1 Ch 428 (CA) 410, 411
Jelbert v Davis [1968] 1 WLR 589, [1968] 1 All ER 1182 (CA) 156
Joly v Shoppers Drug Mart, National Post (Canada), Tuesday,
18 May 1999, page A1 16
Jones v Dodd [1999] SASC 125 .... 17, 20
Jones v Price [1965] 2 QB 618 (CA) 154
Joseph v Lyons (1884) 15 QBD 280 (CA) 409

Kay's Leasing Corp Pty Ltd v CSR Provident Fund Nominees Pty Ltd
[1962] VR 429 369
Keech v Sandford (1726) Sel Cas T King 61, 25 ER 223 .... 350, 351
Keefe v Law Society of NSW (1998) 44 NSWLR 451 (CA) 340, 341
King v David Allen & Sons Billposting Ltd [1916] 2 AC 54,
[1916-17] All ER Rep 268 210
King v Smail [1958] VR 273 470
Kirk v Sutherland [1949] VLR 33 71
Kolari, Re (1981) 36 OR (2d) 473 334
Koorootang Nominees Pty Ltd v ANZ Banking Group Ltd [1998]
3 VR 16 477

Lace v Chandler [1944] KB 368 (CA) 94
Lampton's Executors v Preston's Executors (1829) 24 Ky 455 357
Latec Investments Ltd v Hotel Terrigal Pty Ltd (1965)
113 CLR 265 .... 325, 420, 485
Leason Pty Ltd v Princes Farm Pty Ltd [1983] 2 NSWLR 381 321
Ledgerwood v Perpetual Trustee Co Ltd (1997) 41 NSWLR 532 285
Leigh v Taylor [1902] AC 157 .... 365, 367
Lester-Travers v City of Frankston [1970] VR 2 58
Lloyds Bank plc v Rosset [1991] 1 AC 107 303
Lofts v MacDonald (1974) 3 ALR 404 339
Loke Yew v Port Swettenham Rubber Co Ltd [1913] AC 491 (PC) . 473, 474, 475
Louis and the Conveyancing Act, Re [1971] 1 NSWLR 164 163
Luke v Luke (1936) 36 SR (NSW) 310 132
Lyons v Lyons [1967] VR 169 141
Lysaght v Edwards (1876) 2 Ch D 499 259

Mabo v Queensland (1989) 166 CLR 186 398
Mabo v Queensland (No 2) (1992) 175 CLR 1,
    107 ALR 1 .... 12, 86, 217, 218, 220-225, 227, 396
Mackay v Wilson (1947) 47 SR (NSW) 315 264
Macquarie Bank Ltd v Sixty-Fourth Throne Pty Ltd [1998]
    3 VR 133 (CA) 413, 481
Mallet v Mallet (1984) 156 CLR 605, 52 ALR 193 299
Margil Pty Ltd v Stegul Pastoral Pty Ltd [1984] 2 NSWLR 1 151
Mascall v Mascall (1984) 50 P&CR 119 (CA) 273
Mason v Clarke [1955] AC 778, [1955] 1 All ER 914 .... 148, 265
McKean's Caveat, Re [1988] 1 Qd R 524 486
McKeown v Cavalier Yachts Pty Ltd (1988) 13 NSWLR 303 364
McKinney v University of Guelph [1990] 3 SCR 229 33
McMahon's (Transport) Pty Ltd v Ebbage [1999] 1 Qd R 185 (CA) 368
Melms v Pabst Brewing Co (1899) 79 NW 738 103
Mercantile Credits Ltd v Shell Co of Australia Ltd (1976) 136 CLR 326 454
Midland Bank Trust Co Ltd v Green [1981] AC 513, [1981] 2 WLR 28,
    [1981] 1 All ER 153 .... 406, 442
Milirrpum v Nabalco Pty Ltd (1971) 17 FLR 141 11
Miller v Minister of Mines [1963] AC 484, [1963] NZLR 560,
    [1963] 1 All ER 109 (PC) 469
Model Dairy Pty Ltd v White (1935) 41 Argus LR 432 59
Moffett v Dillon [1999] 2 VR 480 (CA) 416, 488
Montagu's Settlement Trusts, Re [1987] Ch 264, [1992] 4 All ER 308 408
Moonking Gee v Tahos (1960) 80 WN (NSW) 1612 439
Moore v Regents of the University of California (1990) 793 P2d 479 .... 22, 23
Moorgate Tobacco Co Ltd v Philip Morris Ltd (No 2) (1984)
    156 CLR 414 .... 28, 191, 193
Motor Dealers Credit Corp Ltd v Overland (Sydney) Ltd (1931)
    31 SR (NSW) 516 56
Mumford v Stohwasser (1874) LR 18 Eq 556 408
Munro v Southern Dairies Ltd [1955] VLR 332 58
Murdoch v Attorney-General (Tas) (1992) 1 Tas R 117 110
Muschinski v Dodds (1985) 160 CLR 583 .... 307, 308

Napier v Public Trustee (WA) (1980) 32 ALR 153 (HCA) 329
National Carriers Ltd v Panalpina (Northern) Ltd [1981] AC 675 361
National Provincial Bank Ltd v Ainsworth [1965] AC 1175, [1965]
    3 WLR 1, [1965] 2 All ER 472 418

Newtons of Wembley Ltd v Williams [1965] 1 QB 560, [1964] 3 WLR 888,
  [1964] 3 All ER 532 (CA) 394
Nisbet & Potts' Contract, Re [1906] 1 Ch 386, [1904-7]
  All ER Rep 865 (CA) 406
Norbis v Norbis (1986) 161 CLR 513 299
North Ganalanja Aboriginal Corp v Queensland (1996) 185 CLR 595 230
Northern Counties of England Fire Insurance Co v Whipp (1884)
  26 Ch D 482, [1881-5] All ER Rep 941 (CA) 380, 404
Nullagine Investments Pty Ltd v Western Australian Club Inc (1993)
  177 CLR 635 143

O'Brien v O'Brien (1982) 452 NYS2d 801 15
O'Keefe v Malone [1903] AC 365 .... 166, 167, 398
O'Keefe v Williams (1910) 11 CLR 171 .... 166, 167, 398
O'Neill v O'Connell (1946) 72 CLR 101 263
Official Receiver in Bankruptcy v Schultz (1990) 170 CLR 306 278
Ogilvie v Ryan [1976] 2 NSWLR 504 .... 265, 302, 304, 305
Ohio v Shaw (1902) 65 NE 875 48
Oldham v Lawson [1976] VR 654 58
Ontario v Henson (1987) 28 ETR 121 111
Oxford Meat Co Pty Ltd v McDonald (1963) 63 SR (NSW) 423 64

Pacific Film Laboratories Pty Ltd v Federal Commissioner of Taxation (1970)
  121 CLR 154 178
Papaioannoy v Greek Orthodox Community of Melbourne (1978)
  3 ACLR 801 199
Parij v Parij (1997) 72 SASR 153 310
Parker v British Airways Board [1982] 1 QB 1004, [1982]
  1 All ER 834 (CA) 47, 49, 65
Parkinson v Braham (1961) 62 SR (NSW) 663 453
Pata Nominees Pty Ltd v Durnsford Pty Ltd [1988] WAR 365 264
Pavey & Matthews Pty Ltd v Paul (1987) 162 CLR 221 313
Penfold Wines Pty Ltd v Elliott (1946) 74 CLR 204 .... 57, 58
Perlmutter v Beth David Hospital (1954) 123 NE2d 792 21
Permanent Trustee Australia Ltd v Shand (1992) 27 NSWLR 426 146
Person-to-Person Financial Services Pty Ltd v Sharari [1984]
  1 NSWLR 745 488
Perth Construction Pty Ltd v Mount Lawley Pty Ltd (1955) 57 WALR 41 .. 162
Peter v Beblow (1993) 101 DLR (4th) 621 (SCC) 306
Peters American Delicacy Co Ltd v Heath (1939) 61 CLR 457 ...... 197, 199

Petkov v Lucerne Nominees Pty Ltd (1992) 7 WAR 163 69
Pettitt v Pettitt [1970] AC 777 330
Pettkus v Becker (1980) 117 DLR (3d) 257 334
Phillips v Phillips (1862) 4 De GF&J 208, 45 ER 1164 .... 404, 419
Phipps v Pears [1965] 1 QB 76, [1964] 2 All ER 35 (CA) 155, 157
Pierce v Proprietors of Swan Point Cemetery (1872) 10 RI 227,
    14 Am Rep 667 .... 17, 18, 28
Pilcher v Rawlins (1872) 7 Ch App 259 404
Pyramid Building Society v Scorpion Hotels Pty Ltd [1998]
    1 VR 188 (CA) 464, 481

Quach v Marrickville Municipal Council (1990) 22 NSWLR 55 470

R v Toohey (1982) 158 CLR 327 .... 167, 206
R M Hosking Properties Pty Ltd v Barnes [1971] SASR 100 473
Radaich v Smith (1959) 101 CLR 209 .... 98, 166, 213
Rasmanis v Jurewitsch (1969) 70 SR (NSW) 407 (CA) 140, 353
Rasmussen v Rasmussen [1995] 1 VR 613 470
Red House Farms (Thorndon) Ltd v Catchpole [1977]
    244 Estates Gazette 295 46
Registrar of the Accident Compensation Tribunal v Federal Commissioner
    of Taxation (1993) 178 CLR 145 111
Registrar of Titles v Spencer (1909) 9 CLR 641 367
Rendell v Associated Finance Pty Ltd [1957] VR 604 363
Rice v Rice (1854) 2 Drew 73, 61 ER 646 415
Riley v Penttila [1974] VR 547 46
Russell v Wilson (1923) 33 CLR 538 57

Sands & McDougall Pty Ltd v Robinson (1917) 23 CLR 49 178
Schemmell v Pomeroy (1989) 50 SASR 450 56
Sen v Headley [1991] Ch 425, [1991] 2 All ER 636 (CA) 283
Sharp v McNeil (1913) 15 DLR 73 334
Shaw v Foster (1872) LR 5 HL 321 260
Shelley v Kraemer (1948) 334 US 1 161
Shropshire Union Railways and Canal Co v The Queen (1875)
    LR 7 HL 496 417
Silovi Pty Ltd v Barbaro (1988) 3 NSWLR 466 (CA) 295, 296
Silsbury v McCoon (1850) 3 NY 379, 53 Am Dec 307 (CA) 358
Sinclair v Hope Investments Pty Ltd [1982] 2 NSWLR 870 486

Singer v Berghouse (1994) 181 CLR 201, 123 ALR 481, 68 ALJR 653 289
Sistrom v Urh (1992) 117 ALR 528 140
Smith v Jones [1954] 1 WLR 1089, [1954] 2 All ER 823 .... 411, 422
Smith v Tamworth City Council (1997) 41 NSWLR 680 .... 17, 207
Smith Kline and French Laboratories (Australia) Ltd v Secretary, Department
    of Community Services and Health (1991) 28 FCR 291 14
Southern Centre of Theosophy Inc v South Australia [1982] AC 706,
    [1982] 1 All ER 283, 38 ALR 587 (PC) 360, 361
Spence v Union Marine Insurance Co Ltd (1868) LR 3 CP 427 374
Spyer v Phillipson [1931] 2 Ch 183 (CA) 366
Steadman v Steadman [1976] AC 536, [1974] 2 All ER 977 266
Stoneham, Re [1919] 1 Ch 149, [1918-1919] All ER Rep 1051 .... 241, 272
Strong v Bird (1874) LR 18 Eq 315, [1874-80] All ER Rep 230 272
Swanston Mortgage Pty Ltd v Trepan Investments Pty Ltd [1994]
    1 VR 672 .... 484, 485, 486

Taitapu Gold Estates Ltd v Prouse [1916] NZLR 825 .... 326, 479
Talbot v General Television Corp Pty Ltd [1980] VR 224 189
Teck Corp v Millar (1972) 33 DLR (3d) 288, [1973] 2 WWR 385 201
Thomas v The Times Book Co Ltd [1966] 2 All ER 241,
    [1966] 1 WLR 911 241
Thomas Australia Wholesale Vehicle Trading Co Pty Ltd v Marac Finance
    Australia Ltd (1985) 3 NSWLR 452 (CA) 384
Thompson v Park [1944] KB 408, [1944] 2 All ER 477 212
Thomson v Clydesdale Bank Ltd [1893] AC 282 406
Travinto Nominees Pty Ltd v Vlattas (1973) 129 CLR 1 455
Troja v Troja (1994) 33 NSWLR 269 (CA) 352
Tubantia [1924] P 78, [1924] All ER Rep 615 47
Tulk v Moxhay (1848) 2 Ph 774, 41 ER 1143, [1843-60]
    All ER Rep 9 .... 158, 159, 160
Tutt v Doyle (1997) 42 NSWLR 10 480

Union Bank of Australia Ltd v Murray-Aynsley [1898] AC 693 (PC) 406
University of London Press Ltd v University Tutorial Press Ltd [1916]
    2 Ch 601 177
University of Manitoba v Sanderson Estate (1998) 155 DLR (4th)
    40 (BC CA) 287
USA v Motor Trucks Ltd [1924] AC 196 (PC) 326

Vadasz v Pioneer Concrete (SA) Pty Ltd (1995) 184 CLR 102 322
Vandervell v Inland Revenue Commissioners [1967] 2 AC 291 252

Vandervell's Trusts (No 2), Re [1974] Ch 269 329
Verrall v Great Yarmouth Borough Council [1981] QB 202,
    [1980] 1 All ER 839 (CA) 212
Victoria Park Racing and Recreation Grounds Co Ltd v Taylor (1937)
    58 CLR 479, 43 ALR 597 .... 26, 27, 28
Voges v Monaghan (1954) 94 CLR 231 284

Wade v NSW Rutile Mining Co Pty Ltd (1969) 121 CLR 177,
    [1969] ALR 577 .... 89, 169, 173
Wait, Re [1927] 1 Ch 606, [1926] All ER Rep 433 262
Walker v Wimborne (1976) 137 CLR 1 202
Walsh v Lonsdale (1882) 21 Ch D 9 (CA) 263
Walton Stores (Interstate) Ltd v Maher (1988)
    164 CLR 387 .... 293, 294, 296, 303
Waterloo v Hinchcliffe (1866) 5 SCR (NSW) 273 152
Watt v Westhoven [1933] VLR 458 320
Waverley BC v Fletcher [1995] 4 All ER 756 (CA) 47
Westdeutsche Landesbank Girozentrale v Islington LBC [1996]
    AC 669 .... 334, 335
Western Australia v The Commonwealth (1995) 183 CLR 373 398
Western Australia v Ward (2000) 170 ALR 159 .... 229, 396
Wham-O MFG Co v Lincoln Industries Ltd [1984] 1 NZLR 641 (CA) 176
Wheatley v Bell [1982] 2 NSWLR 544 193
White v Neaylon (1886) 11 App Cas 171 (PC) 440
Wik Peoples v Queensland (1996) 187 CLR 1, 141 ALR 129
    .... 87, 92, 97, 98, 165, 166, 167, 172, 213, 225, 395, 396, 401
Wilkes v Allington [1931] 2 Ch 104 281
Willey v Synan (1937) 57 CLR 200 66
Wilson v Lombank Ltd [1963] 1 WLR 1294, [1963] 1 All ER 740 ...... 64, 65
Wincant Pty Ltd v South Australia (1997) 69 SASR 126 368
Winkfield [1902] P 42, [1900-3] All ER Rep 346 (CA) 60
Winter Garden Theatre (London) Ltd v Millennium Productions Ltd [1948]
    AC 173, [1947] 2 All ER 331 212

XL Petroleum (NSW) Pty Ltd v Caltex Oil (Australia) Pty Ltd (1985)
    155 CLR 448 62

Yakamia Dairy Pty Ltd v Wood [1976] WAR 57 62
Yanner v Eaton (1999) 73 ALJR 1518, 166 ALR 258 .... 217, 218
Yarmirr v Northern Territory (1998) 156 ALR 370 228
Young v Hichens (1844) 6 QB 606 48

TABLE OF STATUTES

Aboriginal Land Rights (Northern Territory) Act 1976 (Cth): 167
s 3(1): 167
Aboriginal Relics Act 1975 (Tas)
s 2(3)(c): 19
s 11: 19
Administration Act 1903 (WA): 277
s 8: 277
s 14: 288, 289
Administration and Probate Act 1919 (SA): 277
s 72G: 288, 289
Administration and Probate Act 1935 (Tas): 277
s 45: 91, 289
Administration and Probate Act 1958 (Vic): 277
s 51: 288
Administration and Probate Act (NT): 277
s 52: 278
Agricultural Tenancies Act 1990 (NSW)
s 14: 367
Australian Bicentennial Authority Act 1980 (Cth): 26
s 22: 26
Bankruptcy Act 1966 (Cth): 82, 323
ss 120-122: 320
Bills of Exchange Act 1909 (Cth): 392
Bills of Sale Act 1898 (NSW)
s 4: 243
Bürgerliches Gestetzbuch (German Civil Code)
article 903: 81
Business Names Act 1962 (NSW)
s 7A: 187

Business Names Act 1996 (SA)
s 8(4): 187
s 9: 187
Charter of Rights and Freedoms (Canada): 33
Chattel Securities Act 1987 (Vic): 370
Chattel Securities Act 1987 (WA): 370
Cheques Act 1986 (Cth): 392
s 10: 391
s 40: 392
s 49: 393
s 50: 393
s 54: 393
s 55: 393
s 71: 392
s 73: 392
s 88: 392
ss 89, 90: 392
Cheques and Payment Orders Act 1986 (Cth): 392
Circuits Layout Act 1989 (Cth): 175, 180
s 17: 180
s 20: 180
Commonwealth Aluminium Corporation Pty Limited Agreement Act 1957 (Qld): 172
Companies Act 1985 (UK)
s 309(1): 202
Confiscation Act 1997 (Vic)
s 35: 347
Constitution Act 1990 (Australia)
s 51(xxxi): 14
s 109: 399
Consumer Credit Codes: 127
Contracts Review Act 1980 (NSW)
s 7: 321

Conveyancing Act 1919 (NSW): 434
  s 26(1): 138
  s 54A: 264
  s 88A: 150
  s 88AB(1): 147
  s 184G: 437, 441
Conveyancing and Law of Property Act 1884 (Tas)
  s 35: 410
Conveyancing and Law of Property Act 1898 (NSW)
  s 68: 93
  s 69: 93
Copyright Act 1968 (Cth): 25, 175, 176, 177, 179
  Pt IX: 178
  s 21(3)(a): 180
  s 116: 179
Corporations Law
  s 124: 193
  s 221: 194
  s 246AA: 199
  s 246B: 201
  s 249D: 199
  s 250A: 199
  s 254T: 197
  s 254U: 197
  s 254V: 198
  s 462: 202
  s 501: 198
  s 565: 320
  s 1085: 196
  s 1087: 196
  s 1089: 196
Crimes (Confiscation of Profits) Act 1988 (WA)
  s 11: 347
Crimes (Forfeiture of Proceeds) Act (NT): 346
Criminal Assets Confiscation Act 1996 (SA)
  s 15: 347
Criminal Code Act 1924 (Tas)
  s 11: 345
Crown Lands Act 1884 (NSW): 166
Crown Lands Act 1931 (NT): 167
Crown Lands Act 1989 (NSW)
  s 172: 360
Crown Lands Acts: 97
  s 205G: 346
  s 228: 346
  s 229: 346
  s 229A: 346
  s 243B: 346

De Donis Conditionalibus 1285 (UK): 91
De Facto Relationships Act 1996 (NT)
  s 16: 300
De Facto Relationships Act 1996 (SA)
  s 3: 299
  s 9: 300
  s 14: 320
Designs Act 1906 (Cth): 175, 180
  s 4: 179
  s 32B(2): 176
Domestic Relationships Act 1994 (ACT)
  s 3: 299
  s 15: 299
  s 19: 300
Escheat (Procedure) Act 1940 (WA): 91
Factors Act 1892 (Qld)
  s 3: 387
Fair Trading Act 1987 (WA)
  s 41: 321
Fair Trading Act 1999 (Vic)
  s 108: 321
Family Law Act 1975 (Cth): 298, 381
  s 78: 301
  s 79: 298, 301
  s 85: 320
Family Provision Act 1969 (ACT)
  s 7: 289
Family Provision Act 1982 (NSW): 320
  s 23: 289
  s 29: 289
Fences Act 1975 (SA): 154
Fisheries Act 1959 (Tas): 145
Fisheries Management Act 1991 (Cth): 346
  s 106: 346
Forestry Rights Registration Act 1990 (Tas)
  s 5(1): 147
Forfeiture Act 1991 (ACT): 354
Forfeiture Act 1995 (NSW): 354
Fossicking Act 1994 (Qld): 171
Goods Act 1928 (Vic): 320

Goods Act 1958 (Vic)
  s 30: 387
  s 31: 387
  s 100: 321
  s 101(e): 323
Goods Acts: 243, 244
Health and Safety Code (California): 23
Heritage Act 1993 (SA): 430
Hire Purchase Act 1959 (Qld, Tas, Vic, WA): 369, 388
Historic Shipwrecks Act 1981 (SA): 430
Historical Cultural Heritage Act 1995 (Tas)
  s 60: 161
Human Tissue and Transplant Act 1982 (WA)
  s 29: 22
Infertility Treatment Act 1995 (Vic)
  s 5: 24
  s 24: 24
Inheritance (Family and Dependants Provision) Act 1972 (WA)
  s 7: 289
Insurance Contracts Act 1984 (Cth)
  Pt IV: 320
Judicature Act 1873 (UK): 40
Land Acts: 97
Land Act 1910 (Qld): 165
Land Act 1962 (Qld): 165, 213
Land Act 1994 (Qld): 433, 435
  s 10: 361
  s 41(2): 110
  s 298: 443
  s 300: 441, 442
  ss 301, 302: 433, 436
Land (Planning and Environment Act) 1991 (ACT)
  s 219: 168
Land Title Act 1994 (Qld): 445, 472
  s 17: 482
  s 59(1): 141
  s 59(2): 141
  ss 86-88: 151
  s 97A: 455
  s 103: 487
  s 104: 487
  s 109: 451
  s 122: 483
  s 178: 461
  s 180: 470
  s 181: 459
  s 184: 463
  s 185: 467, 468, 478
Land Titles Act 1980 (Tas): 445
  s 14: 484
  s 40: 462, 466, 468
  s 44: 139
  s 49: 249
  s 63(1): 141
  s 64: 453
  s 102: 455
  s 132: 451
Land Titles Act 1925 (ACT): 445, 455
  s 69: 457
  s 82: 453
  s 83: 454
Land Titles Validation Act 1994 (Vic): 400
Land Transfer Act (NZ): 469
Landlord and Tenant Act 1935 (Tas)
  s 26: 367
Landlord and Tenant Act 1958 (Vic)
  s 28: 367, 368
Law of Property Act 1936 (SA)
  s 22: 155
  s 29: 251
  s 40(3): 140
  s 61: 102
  s 86: 320
  s 117: 412
Law Reform (Abolitions and Repeals) Act 1996 (ACT)
  s 3: 92
Limitation Acts: 67, 457
Limitation of Actions Acts: 67, 457
Mineral Resources Act 1989 (Qld)
  s 9: 170
  s 10: 172
  s 310: 170
Mineral Resources Acts: 168
Mineral Resources Development Act 1990 (Vic)
  s 4: 168
  s 11: 169
  s 70: 172, 436
Mineral Resources Development Act 1995 (Tas)
  s 3: 171
  s 183: 440

Mineral Resources Development Acts: 168
Mining Act 1904-1971 (WA): 172
  s 273: 172
Mining Act 1971 (SA): 171, 430
  s 16: 169, 469
  s 18: 170
Mining Act 1978 (WA)
  s 8: 168
  s 9: 169
  s 65: 172
  s 70: 171
  s 86: 173
  Mining Regulation 103: 441
Mining Act 1992 (NSW)
  s 160: 436
  s 161: 436, 441, 442
  s 232: 171
Mining Act (NT): 435
  Mining Regulation 29: 435
Mining Act (NZ): 469
Mining Acts: 168
Mining Regulations (NT)
  reg 29: 435
Mining Regulations 1981 (WA)
  reg 103: 441
Native American Grave Protection and Repatriation Act 1990 (USA): 20
Native Title Act 1993 (Cth): 230, 395, 399, 430
  s 3: 230
  s 11: 399, 469
  s 14: 400
  s 15: 400
  ss 17, 18: 400
  ss 19, 20: 400
  s 22A: 401
  s 22B: 401
  s 22F: 401
  s 56: 221
  s 223: 217
  s 228: 400
  ss 229-232: 400
  s 232A: 401
  s 232B: 401
  s 233: 401
  s 237A: 400
Native Title Act 1994 (ACT): 400
Native Title Amendment Act 1998 (Cth): 401

Native Title (New South Wales) Act 1994 (NSW): 400
Native Title (Queensland) Act 1993 (Qld): 400
Native Title (South Australia) Act 1994 (SA): 400, 430
Opal Mining Act 1995 (SA): 173, 430
  s 7: 171
Patents Act 1990 (Cth): 25, 175, 181
  Ch 8: 182
  s 7(2): 181
  s 9: 182
  s 14: 246
  s 18: 181
  s 18(1)(d): 182
  s 40(2)(a): 182
  s 67: 182
  s 68: 182
  s 123: 176
  s 133: 182
  s 134: 182
  s 173(1): 182
Penalties and Sentences Act 1992 (Qld)
  s 35: 344
Petroleum Act 1923 (Qld)
  s 9: 169
Petroleum Act 1940 (SA): 430
Petroleum Act 1998 (Vic): 171
  s 6: 168
Petroleum Acts: 168
Petroleum (Submerged Lands) Acts 1982: 168
Plant Breeders Rights Act 1994 (Cth): 175, 183
  s 19: 183
  s 27(5): 183
  s 43: 183
  s 44(10): 246
  s 53(1)(c): 183
Plant Variety Rights Act 1987 (Cth): 183
Prescription Act 1832 (WA): 155
Proceeds of Crime Act 1987 (Cth): 346
  s 20: 347
Property Law Act 1925 (UK): 248

Property Law Act 1958 (Vic): 434
  s 6: 442
  s 18A: 85
  s 28: 135
  s 28A: 134
  s 44: 410
  s 51: 248
  s 55(d): 264
  s 78: 162
  s 79: 162
  s 79A: 163
  s 84: 162
  s 187: 142
  s 285: 300
Property Law Act 1969 (WA)
  s 34: 249
  s 103: 102
  s 120(d): 136
  s 126(1): 143
Property Law Act 1974 (Qld): 434
  s 11: 251
  s 35: 138
  s 43: 134
  s 45: 248
  s 155: 367, 368
  s 198A: 155
  s 237: 410
Property (Relationships) Act 1984 (NSW)
  s 4: 300
  s 5: 300
  s 7: 301
  s 8: 301
  s 20: 300
Quia Emptores 1290 (UK): 85, 91
Racial Discrimination Act 1975 (Cth): 226, 230, 395, 398, 399, 401
  s 6: 399
  s 10(1): 398, 399
Real Property Act 1886 (SA): 430, 445, 454, 455, 469
  s 56: 461
  s 69: 467
  s 71: 471
  s 74: 138
  s 117: 454
  s 161: 451
Real Property Act 1900 (NSW): 445
  s 12: 482
  s 42: 462
  s 47(7): 151
  s 53: 453, 454
  s 74F: 455, 483
  s 88B: 163, 257

Real Property Act (NT): 445
  ss 47, 49: 455
  s 71: 471
  s 72: 472
  s 117: 454
  s 162: 450
  s 251: 457
Registration of Deeds Act 1856 (WA): 434
  s 3: 441
Registration of Deeds Act 1935 (SA): 430, 434
  s 9: 435
  s 10: 435, 437, 442
Registration of Deeds Act 1935 (Tas): 434
  s 9: 441
Registration of Deeds Act 1957 (ACT): 434
Residential Tenancies Act 1987 (NSW)
  s 27: 368
Residential Tenancies Act 1997 (Vic)
  s 64: 103, 368
Residential Tenancies Acts: 92
Sale of Goods Act 1893 (UK): 243, 262
Sale of Goods Act 1895 (SA)
  s 17: 244
  s 22: 389
  s 40: 267
  s 59(2): 321
Sale of Goods Act 1895 (WA)
  s 23: 394
  s 24: 389
Sale of Goods Act 1923 (NSW)
  s 4: 389
  s 19: 21
Sale of Goods Act 1954 (ACT)
  s 26: 383, 389
  s 62(1A): 321
Sale of Goods Acts: 243, 244, 269, 270
Settled Estates Act, 1880-1943 (SA)
  s 44: 93
Shipping Registration Act 1981 (Cth): 432
  s 36: 242
Statute of Anne 1705 (UK): 134
Statute of Frauds 1677 (UK): 249

Statute of Monopolies 1624 (UK): 181
Statute of Uses 1536 (UK): 112, 113, 248, 329
Statute of Wills 1540 (UK): 91, 280
Succession Act 1981 (Qld): 277
  s 65: 135
Supreme Court Act 1986 (Vic)
  s 29(1): 107
Tenures Abolition Act 1660 (UK): 85, 91
Testator's Family Maintenance Act 1912 (Tas)
  s 3A: 289
Titles Validation Act 1995 (WA): 400
Trade Marks Act 1995 (Cth): 176, 186
  s 124: 186
Trade Practices Act 1974 (Cth): 189, 321
  s 71: 21
  s 75A: 321, 323
Transfer of Land Act 1893 (WA): 445
  s 53: 460
  s 55: 451
  s 61: 136
  s 91: 453
  s 129A: 455
  s 134: 463
  s 136D: 455
  s 136H: 163, 257
  s 140: 486

Transfer of Land Act 1958 (Vic): 445
  s 4(1): 138
  s 40: 456
  s 42: 469
  s 43: 471
  s 44: 463
  s 66: 453
  s 74(2): 123
  s 88: 455
  s 89: 482
Transfer of Land (Single Register) Act 1998 (Vic)
  s 22: 434
Trustee Act 1893 (NT)
  s 13: 131
  s 57: 131
Trustees Act 1962 (WA)
  s 68: 413
Uniform Commercial Code (USA): 123
Validation of Titles and Actions Act 1994 (NT): 400
Warehousemen's Lien Acts: 119
Water Resources Act 1997 (SA): 430
Wills Act 1936 (SA)
  s 12: 280
Wills Act 1992 (Tas)
  s 45: 280
Wills Act 1997 (Vic)
  s 11: 280
Wills Acts: 284, 285
Wills, Probate and Administration Act 1898 (NSW): 277
  s 61B: 288

Part I
What is Property?

Chapter One

UNDERSTANDING PROPERTY LAW

▌▌▌

We all have things. If nothing else, we have the clothes on our backs, but most of us have more: food, money, a place to live, and the list goes on. We have laws regulating the use of our things. They stop others from interfering with our things without our consent. They tell us how things are bought, sold, borrowed, given, or thrown away. They provide a peaceful way of resolving disputes when two or more people claim the same thing.

Property law is the law relating to things and property rights are the legal rights that entitle people to make use of things. The *Australian Pocket Oxford Dictionary* defines "thing" as "any possible object of thought". Not every object of thought can be subject to property rights. Most tangible things can be. For example, people have property rights to coats, cats, and cars, but what about a detached human arm? Many intangible things can be subject to property rights, such as songs, inventions, and shares in a corporation. What about information and news? Property law has the difficult task of determining which things can and cannot be subject to property rights. This is an issue explored in the pages below. However, most of the law of property is concerned not so much with the things themselves as with the rights people have regarding things.

When dealing with property rights, there are three basic questions which should be asked and answered:

1)......what sort of right is it;
2)......how was it created; and
3)......what priority does it have?

The answer to one question will affect the answer to another, but it is useful to consider each question separately.

These questions are dealt with in the six parts of this book. Parts I and III are devoted to the first question. Part I (What is Property?) looks at the nature of a right to a thing. It asks, first, what is a property right and, secondly, what things can be subject to property rights. It also deals briefly with the distribution of property rights in society and the way in which the law of property is organised. Part III (The Variety of Property Rights) examines the different types of property rights recognised in

Australian law, including ownership, estates, trusts, mortgages, and native title.

The second question is the subject of Part IV (The Creation of Property Interests). It deals with the creation of property rights by intention (such as by gift, sale, or will) and also by operation of law in response to events such as unjust enrichment and wrongdoing.

Part V (Priority of Property Rights) is devoted to the third question. It looks at how the law resolves conflicts between competing claims to the same thing. Suppose, for example, that a thief steals a bicycle and sells it to an unsuspecting purchaser. Who has the better claim to that bicycle? The innocent victim of the theft or the innocent purchaser? It is the job of property law to provide rules to resolve these disputes peacefully and with certainty.

Part II (Possession) is the study of a particularly important property right. In that part, the old saying, "possession is nine tenths of the law", comes to life. In a sense, Part II provides a microcosm of the entire subject because it covers all three basic questions: the nature of possession, how it is created, and how the law deals with competing claims to possession. This is also true of Part VI (Registration of Property Rights to Land), which concerns the effect of registration on the methods of creating property rights to land, the types of rights created, and the priority between competing rights.

Property law has a reputation for being a difficult subject (which is only partly deserved). There are three main reasons for this: its vocabulary, the breadth of the subject, and a lack of organisation. First, our property law has evolved slowly over centuries and many of the words still in use, such as "chattel", were dropped from common speech a very long time ago. However, most of these strange terms identify relatively simple concepts. Secondly, most law subjects are (relatively) narrowly confined by logical or contextual boundaries. For example, tort and contract are each concerned with rights arising from one type of event (wrongdoing or agreement, respectively). Administrative and family law are concerned with rights arising in a particular context. Property law cuts across these divisions. Property rights can be created by agreement or by wrongdoing and can arise in disputes among family members or with governments. The sheer breadth of the subject can be daunting. Thirdly and most importantly, there is so much material to cover that it is easy to lose sight of the forest for the trees. The successful study of any subject requires a useful taxonomy, so that each part can be compared and contrasted with other parts and with other subjects. This is especially true of property law.

Property law is an enjoyable and worthwhile subject of study. It is a useful way to pull together and build a framework for understanding other areas of law, such as contract and tort, which tend to be studied as separate, unrelated pockets of Australian law. An understanding of property law is also an essential foundation for the study of a number of areas of law, such as trusts, restitution, intellectual property, and commercial law. More than this, property law is itself surprisingly enjoyable. It goes beyond the buying, selling, and mortgaging of houses with which it is most commonly associated. Many of the most interesting and topical aspects of law are property issues, such as the trade in body parts and genetic material, squatters and homelessness, de facto spouses and ownership of the family home, freedom of information, and tracing the proceeds of crime.

Chapter Two

WHAT IS PROPERTY?

III

Property rights are rights to things. There are two steps to understanding property rights. The first, which is the subject of this chapter, is to identify the kinds of rights which the law regards as property rights. The second is to identify the kinds of things which can be subject to those rights. That is discussed in the next chapter.

Rights can be divided into two categories: rights *in personam* and rights *in rem* (using the Latin words for person and thing). Rights *in personam* are so called because they are enforced against particular persons, without much regard to the things they might have. Rights *in rem* are rights people have concerning particular things, without much regard to the people against whom those rights might be enforced. Property law is primarily about rights *in rem*.

An example may help. If I borrow $20 from you and promise to repay it, I owe you $20. You do not expect to get the same $20 note back. Instead, I have a personal obligation to pay which corresponds to your personal right to be paid $20. This is a right *in personam* which can be enforced against me, regardless of what has become of the $20 note that I borrowed. If I give that note to a friend or spend it at a milk bar, you do not acquire any rights against my friend or the shopkeeper. You have no right to that note nor to any other $20 note that I may have.

In contrast, if I borrow your book and promise to return it, you continue to own the book. In addition to my promise, you have a right *in rem* which is enforceable against me because I have your book. The property right follows the book and, if I give your book to a friend, you can assert your right *in rem* against my friend, because he or she has your book.

The distinction between rights *in rem* and rights *in personam* is important in the law. A right *in rem* depends upon the continued existence of the thing to which the right relates. For example, if your book is destroyed, your property right is gone. The destruction may give you a right *in personam* against the person who destroyed your book or against your insurance company, but it brings to an end your right *in rem* to the book.

In contrast, a right *in personam* does not depend on the existence of any particular thing. Instead, it corresponds to some person's obligation to fulfil that right. The value of the right *in personam* depends upon the ability of the person to perform the corresponding obligation. So, for example, if I owe you $20, you have a right *in personam* which appears to be worth $20. However, if it turns out that I owe money to almost everyone I know and am unable to pay my debts, the practical value of your right may be greatly reduced. Although your right to be paid does not depend on the existence of any particular thing, my lack of sufficient assets to meet my obligations can affect the value of your right.

The Essential Characteristics of Property Rights

Property rights come in a variety of shapes and sizes. For example, the right to use a book borrowed from the library differs in many ways from a landlord's right to a home which is rented out. Despite these differences, these and all other property rights share two common characteristics which distinguish them from personal rights. The first is that a property right always relates to, and depends upon the existence of, some particular thing. The second is that a property right can be enforced not just against specific persons, but against a wide range of persons. It will be helpful to look at the second characteristic first.

Enforceability

All legal rights, whether personal or property, have correlating obligations. For example, if I owe you $20, you have a legal right to be paid $20 and I have a corresponding obligation to pay that amount. Your personal right and my personal obligation are two sides of the same coin. They form a relationship between specific persons. In this example, the relationship is called **debt**, in which I am the **debtor** who owes money to you, the **creditor**.

Property rights, like all legal rights, are also enforced against persons. However, unlike personal rights, there are no specific persons responsible for their fulfilment. Who, for example, owes the obligation which corresponds to your property right to this book? Although the book must exist for your property right to exist, it cannot fulfil that right for you. That right can only be enforced against other persons. The obligation which corresponds to your property right is owed by other members of society. They each have a duty not to interfere with your rights to your book.

In an influential essay called "Fundamental Legal Conceptions as Applied to Judicial Reasoning" (1917) 26 *Yale Law Journal* 710 at 718, Wesley Hohfeld said that the difference between rights *in rem* and rights *in personam* is simply the number of rights involved. A personal right is either a unique right enforceable against "a single person" or one of a small group of similar rights against "a few definite persons". In contrast, property rights consist of "a large class of fundamentally similar yet separate rights" which correspond to the obligations of "a very large and indefinite class of people". In other words, Hohfeld would view your property right to your book as a very large collection of rights against every member of society, each of whom is under an obligation to you not to interfere with your rights relating to your book.

Hohfeld used an example to illustrate his point. Suppose that I made a contract with Yvonne that she would keep off your land. What is the difference between my contractual, personal right against Yvonne and your property right against her? Both rights have the same content. Hohfeld would say that the only real difference is that I have only one right of that kind, whereas you have a large number of similar rights which are enforceable against an indefinite class of people (of which Yvonne is a member).

A difficulty with Hohfeld's portrayal of property rights, as equivalent to an indefinite number of personal rights, is that it devalues the role of the things which are subject to those rights. Also, it does not accord with the way property rights function in society. Property rights do not normally involve specific relationships among those who hold the rights and those around them who are obligated to respect those rights. As members of society, we are all under the same general duty not to interfere with the persons and things of others. The identity of the persons involved is irrelevant until someone interferes with the property right of another. The Hohfeldian analysis of property, as an indefinite number of one-to-one relationships of rights and corresponding obligations, is unnecessary.

Assume, for example, that I have an obligation not to trespass on land belonging to others and, therefore, act unlawfully if I walk on their lawns without their consent. As I walk along the street passing lawn after lawn, a Hohfeldian might say that I enter a legal relationship with the owners of each lawn that I pass. They have a right to keep me off their lawn which corresponds to my obligation to stay off. However, I do not know who or how many people live in the houses I pass nor whether they are at home or away. It does not matter. The identity of the property owners is irrelevant because I know that I have a general duty not to interfere with the things of others, that those are not my lawns, and that I do not have permission to tread on them. We have no legal relationship except as members of the same society bound to observe the laws of that society.

The Existence of Some Thing

An essential characteristic of property rights is that they are enforceable generally against other persons in society. However, this is not a sufficient definition of property. The law also protects people from personal injury by imposing a general duty on members of society not to injure others intentionally or negligently. These rights to personal integrity and freedom from bodily interference correspond to general duties not to touch others intentionally without their consent and to take reasonable care not to harm them. The law protects your body and your things in much the same manner. Someone who wrongly interferes with your arm is guilty of a tort and is liable to compensate you for any loss you suffer. The same is true of someone who wrongly interferes with your book.

If your right to non-interference with your person is not a property right, but a personal right, then what distinguishes these two types of rights? It is clear, using the language of Hohfeld, that both rights are enforceable against an "indefinite class of people". However, the right to be free from bodily interference is not a property right because our bodies are not "things". Property rights must relate to things which are separate and apart from ourselves. As James Penner said, in "The 'Bundle of Rights' Picture of Property" (1996) 43 *UCLA Law Review* 711 at 807, "'Thing' here is a term of art which restricts the application of property to those items in the world which are contingently related to us, and this contingency will change given the surrounding circumstances, including our personal, cultural or technological circumstances."

Things which are intrinsically connected to us, such as our bodies and reputations, cannot be subject to property rights. Although they are valuable to us and protected by laws, such as the rules against assault and defamation, they are not protected by property law. It is possible that the intrinsic connection to some things might be severed and reduced to a contingent connection. For example, a lock of hair could be cut off and transformed from being a part of a person into a thing which a person owns. The same is true, perhaps, of a kidney. However, unless the intrinsic connection is broken, they cannot be subject to property rights: see Radin, "Property and Personhood" (1982) 34 *Stanford Law Review* 957 at 966.

Are There Any Other Essential Characteristics?

So far, a property right has been identified as a right to a thing, which corresponds to a general duty placed on other members of society not to interfere with that right. Although basic, this definition identifies the two characteristics which separate all property rights from personal rights. Given the wide variety of property rights (discussed in Part III), it is unlikely that anything further can be added to this basic definition. There are several characteristics which the majority of property rights share, such as alienability, excludability, and value. However, as discussed below, not all property rights have these traits, while many personal rights do. Therefore, they are not useful as defining characteristics of property rights.

First, it is sometimes said that property rights are **alienable**, meaning that they can be sold or given away to others. However, there are property rights that cannot be sold or given away. For example, a non-assignable, residential lease is certainly a property right, even though the tenants are not free to transfer that lease to others. Conversely, there are many personal rights which are alienable in this sense. For example, creditors are normally free to assign the debts which they are owed.

Property rights can be described as "alienable" if a wider definition of that term is adopted. Since property rights must relate to some thing which is only contingently connected to the right holder, it must be possible for that person to alienate the thing in the sense of severing her or his connection to it. However, that connection can be severed without transferring that right to another. For example, the tenant with a non-assignable lease can give up that lease and vacate the dwelling.

The second characteristic often attributed to property rights is **excludability**, meaning that the holder of a property right is able to exclude others from making use of the thing subject to that right. Most property rights do include this trait. For example, if you own or rent a home, you have the right to exclude others from that home. If you borrow a book from the library, you have the right to exclude others from using that book. However, there are property rights which do not allow the right holder to exclude others from the thing subject to that right. For example, a **right of way** (discussed below in Chapter 16) is a property right to cross another person's land. It meets the definition of a property right in that it relates to some thing (land) and is enforceable against other members of society (including the land owner), who are not permitted to interfere with the proper exercise of that right of way. However, the holder of a right of way is not permitted to exclude others from the land subject to that right of way.

Just as all property rights do not entitle the right holder to exclude others from the thing, some personal rights do. Hohfeld's example (discussed above) gave me a personal right to exclude Yvonne from your land. Also, sometimes in the course of a domestic dispute, one spouse might be granted the right to exclude the other spouse from the family home, even though that other spouse is the sole or part owner of that home.

Value is a third characteristic which most, but not all, property rights share. They usually have some market value. Even second-hand clothing can fetch a few dollars in a charity shop. However, value is not a necessary characteristic of property: Cohen, "Dialogue on Private Property" (1954) *Rutgers Law Review* 357 at 363-364. Many things which are subject to property rights have only sentimental value (such as my child's primary school artwork). There are other things which are completely valueless. For example, your property right to dirty motor oil drained from your car may create a liability for the cost of discarding it safely.

On the other hand, there are many personal rights that have market value, such as a contractual right to be paid a sum of money. In modern Australian society, many of the things for which we pay money are not property rights, but services, such as the right to listen to live music, have our cars washed, or receive medical advice.

Some personal rights are commonly regarded as property rights because of their value. The most familiar example is the **bank account**. Money in the bank may be a person's most valuable asset, but that does not make it property. If you deposit a $100 note in the bank, your property right to that note passes to the bank and the balance in your account increases by $100. The bank does not keep that $100 note safe for you. It belongs to the bank and is used as the bank sees fit: *Foley v Hill* (1848) 2 HLC 28 at 36, 9 ER 1002 at 1005-1006. The deposit does not give you any property rights to any other notes or assets in the bank. Your "money in the bank" does not correspond to anything but the bank's promise to pay you $100 (plus interest, less fees and taxes) on request. In other words, you have exchanged your property right to the $100 note for a personal right of similar value. You are the bank's creditor and the bank is your debtor. Your personal right is a valuable asset, not because it relates to any particular thing, but because the bank will almost certainly pay its debts.

It is important not to overstate the essential characteristics of a property right. This happened in *Milirrpum v Nabalco Pty Ltd* (1971)

17 FLR 141, and led to the dismissal of the plaintiffs' claim for native title. The plaintiffs claimed that the defendant's mining activities were wrongly interfering with their property rights to use certain land to perform ritual ceremonies. The judge, Blackburn J, said (at 272), "I think property, in its many forms, generally implies the right to use or enjoy, the right to exclude others, and the right to alienate." Since the plaintiffs were not entitled to exclude others from the land and could not sell or give their rights to others, Blackburn J decided that they did not have property rights enforceable against other members of society.

However, it is clear that the plaintiffs' rights related to a thing (the land) with which they were contingently connected. Although individual members of the plaintiffs' clan could not sell or give their rights to others, they had the power to sever their connection with the land by moving away. Also, the right to perform ritual ceremonies on the land, like a right of way, can be a property right so long as it corresponds to a general duty placed on other members of society not to interfere with the exercise of that right. The right to exclude others from the land was not required. As discussed in Chapter 19, the result in *Milirrpum* would probably be different if that case was decided today, now that native title has been recognised by the High Court of Australia in *Mabo v Queensland (No 2)* (1992) 175 CLR 1.

Chapter Three

WHAT THINGS CAN BE SUBJECT TO PROPERTY RIGHTS?

■■■

So far, the focus has been on the nature of *rights* to things. This chapter looks at the *things* which can be subject to property rights and discusses the controversial questions whether human tissue and information can be subject to property rights.

As discussed in the previous chapter, a property right must relate to something which is only contingently connected to the right holder. This means that property law excludes those things which are intrinsic to the person and requires that a distinction be drawn between the person and the thing. The study of property rights to human tissue explores this distinction. With that boundary in place, it remains necessary to ask whether everything which is external to the person can or should be subject to property rights. The possibility of property rights to information is a suitable vehicle for that discussion.

It is helpful to begin this inquiry by asking why it is important. If a person has a particular right, does it matter whether that right is personal or property? This distinction can have at least three important consequences, affecting:

1) .....access to resources;
2) .....the value of rights; and
3) .....the legal rules by which rights are created and enforced.

The first and most important consequence stems from the nature of property rights. Since, by definition, they are enforceable generally against other members of society, a decision that something may be subject to property rights means that access to that thing can be controlled by the holders of those rights. Every society has to decide whether some things, such as information, air, and water, should remain outside property law and beyond that sort of control. As Kevin Gray said, in "Property in Thin Air" (1991) 50 *Cambridge Law Journal* 252 at 256, "the refusal to propertise a given resource is absolutely critical because logically anterior to the formulation of the current regime of property law".

A secondary consequence of the distinction between personal and property rights relates to the value society places on those rights. Labelling something as property can raise or lower its value, depending on the context. In societies where property is seen as a constitutionally guaranteed right (in the same category as rights to liberty and security of the person), a property designation can be used to elevate the status of a particular right. Under section 51(xxxi) of the *Commonwealth of Australia Constitution Act* 1990, the Commonwealth Parliament may pass laws for the "acquisition of property on just terms from any State or person for any purpose in respect of which the Parliament has power to make laws". Therefore, if a particular right can be classified as a property right, the Commonwealth government can take that right only if it fairly compensates the right holder: see *Smith Kline and French Laboratories (Australia) Ltd v Secretary, Department of Community Services and Health* (1991) 28 FCR 291.

In an essay called "The New Property" (1964) 73 *Yale Law Journal* 733, Charles Reich argued that claims to assistance from the government are as important as property rights in American society and should be accorded the same status. However, the questions whether someone has a right to government assistance and whether that right should be protected constitutionally are distinct from the question whether that right is a property right. It is a claim against a specific person (the government) and does not relate to any particular thing owned by the government. As Ronald Sackville said in "Property, Rights and Social Security" (1978) 2 *UNSW Law Journal* 246 at 247-248, "Reich's argument does not depend on the redefinition of welfare benefits or other forms of government largesse, *as property*. His argument...proceeds by analogy from the protection traditionally accorded to property rights and compellingly demonstrates the need to elevate government largesse into a similar position." The property label was being used strategically to elevate the status of a personal right.

The language of property has also been used to elevate the status of our rights to personal autonomy. For example, we have been encouraged to claim ownership of our own bodies to reinforce our rights to control our own sexuality and reproduction. A similar technique has been used to promote children's rights to freedom from physical abuse: see Harris, "Who Owns my Body" (1996) 16 *Oxford Journal of Legal Studies* 55. Although these objectives are laudable and justify the manipulation of popular conceptions of property, it seems strange that the value placed on the autonomy and security of the person should be enhanced by treating the body as a thing capable of being owned. Since it is generally agreed that people are more valuable than things, the shift from person to thing would seem to be a demotion. In any event, the appeal to popular notions of property to increase our control over the decisions we make regarding our bodies does not change the right to non-interference with the person into a property right.

The treatment of intrinsic personal attributes as things can also have the opposite effect. It tends to objectify those attributes and can lower their value in society by reducing them to commodities to be bought and sold. This happens when sex industry workers are viewed as selling sex (or their bodies) or when large business enterprises view their labour forces as assets or expenses on par with their supplies or physical facilities. However, it is important to remember that the objectification of things intrinsically connected to individuals, such as their labour or sexuality, cannot sever that connection and, therefore, cannot turn them into things subject to property rights.

In Australia, the right to the personal services of another is always a personal right, never a property right. This is not a logical necessity, but a moral imperative. Some societies have allowed one person to have property rights to another person. Since people are only contingently connected to each other, it is possible to create a coherent and sophisticated body of property law which included living human beings in the list of things subject to property rights. For example, see Birks, "An Unacceptable Face of Human Property" in Birks, *New Perspectives in the Roman Law of Property: Essays for Barry Nicholas* (1989) 61, for a discussion of the early Roman answer to the question of who owned a child born to a woman in slavery.

Thirdly, the classification of a legal right as personal or property affects the legal rules which govern the creation and enforcement of that right. For example, in most jurisdictions, when a relationship between married or de facto spouses comes to an end, each spouse is entitled to share the property rights acquired by the other spouse during the relationship. This creates a powerful incentive to classify rights as property and thereby allow spouses to share the value of those rights at the end of the relationship.

There are American states which treat professional qualifications, such as medical or law degrees, as property rights which can be shared by spouses: see, eg, *O'Brien v O'Brien* (1982) 452 NYS2d 801. It is easy to appreciate why a court would want to do so. For many couples, their earning capacities are far more valuable than all their other assets combined. As Claudia Wendrich said, in "Who Should Profit from an Academic Degree Upon Marital Breakdown?" (1997) 25 *Manitoba Law Journal* 267 at 269, "If the most valuable asset is excluded from sharing, the purpose of the deferred community property regime, *viz*, the equal sharing of all assets acquired during the marriage, has not been achieved."

There are cases where one spouse worked long hours and lived frugally for years helping the other spouse obtain an expensive university education. The relationship ended when the other spouse obtained the professional qualification and started to earn a high income. The benefit of that education should be shared by the spouse who sacrificed to make it possible. However, that does not make it property. The certificate which represents the degree is a thing subject to property rights, but the degree itself is not. The degree is a recognition of the training, knowledge, and attributes of its holder. It is intrinsically connected to that individual and cannot be shared or used by others.

In societies like Australia, where slavery is not permitted, it is not possible to own any aspect of another (living) human being. A declaration that a professional qualification is property gives the court the power to order professionals to pay their former spouses for benefits obtained at their expense. It is done strategically, to fill a gap in a legal system which does not allow spouses to claim personal rights to be paid for benefits conferred during the relationship, but does not convert the professional qualification into a property right.

Human Tissue

As discussed above, Australian law does not allow one person to have property rights to another living person. However, as discussed below, it is possible to have property rights to other living things, such as plants and animals. A difficult question is whether it is possible to have property rights to human tissue which is no longer part of a living person. Two categories of human tissue are discussed below: dead human tissue (such as a corpse) and living human tissue (such as an organ removed for transplant).

Property Rights to Living Things

There are important differences between my property rights to my book and my property rights to my cat. The latter rights are less extensive and coupled with obligations to the thing itself. For example, I am entitled to throw my book on the fire, but would be prosecuted and disdained if I attempted to do the same with my cat.

There are many who believe that some living things should not be subject to property rights. It has been argued that dolphins, whales, and primates are too intelligent to be treated as things which may be owned, but should be treated as beings with rights of their own: see Roger Fouts, *Next of Kin: What Chimpanzees have Taught Me about Intelligence, Compassion, and Being Human* (1997); reviewed by Michael Doherty, (1998) 77 *Canadian Bar Review* 291.

The law draws a fundamental distinction between persons and things. Persons have rights and things are subject to rights. A recent Canadian case illustrates this point: *Joly v Shoppers Drug Mart*, National Post, Tuesday, 18 May 1999, page A1. The plaintiff claimed to be from Mars and sued several defendants, alleging that they had conspired to conceal his Martian origins. The judge ruled that, since the plaintiff was neither human nor corporation, he was not a person and did not have the right to sue. The status of being a person and the capacity to hold rights are legal concepts. Corporations are persons with legal rights. Animals (and extraterrestrials) do not have that status. There are laws to protect animals, just as there are laws to protect buildings with historical significance, but animals do not hold those rights themselves.

Property Rights to Dead Human Tissue

The law seems confused about whether a human corpse is a thing which should be subject to property rights: see Roger Magnusson, "Proprietary Rights in Human Tissue", in Palmer & McKendrick, *Interests in Goods* (2nd ed, 1998) p 25. At common law, the executor (or administrator) of a deceased person has several duties to perform (discussed in Chapter 22), including the duty to deal with the body according to law. He or she has a right to custody of the body for that purpose. This looks like a property right, since it relates to an external thing and is enforceable generally against others in society. However, courts have been reluctant to say that a human corpse is a thing capable of being subject to property rights.

Early English cases suggested that there could be no property rights to a human corpse. This may be the product of a jurisdictional division of the time, rather than a considered decision that human bodies ought not to be considered as things subject to property rights. In that country, ecclesiastic courts had exclusive jurisdiction over legal questions concerning the burial of a corpse. Therefore, a refusal by a common law court to recognise property rights to a corpse may mean nothing more than that the legal action was commenced in the wrong court. There were no separate ecclesiastic courts in America and Australia. Therefore, questions concerning the disposal of human remains are answered by the superior courts which have jurisdiction over personal and property rights generally: see *Smith v Tamworth City Council* (1997) 41 NSWLR 680.

In *Jones v Dodd* [1999] SASC 125, the Supreme Court of South Australia was asked to decide whether the father or the former de facto spouse of a deceased person was entitled to his body for the purpose of burial. Relying on English authority, Perry J said, "There is no property in a dead body, that is to say, it is incapable of being owned by anyone." However, he went on to say "that in certain circumstances the law would protect lawful possession of a corpse or body parts" and that the issue before the court was "who has the right to possession of the body for the purpose of burial". As discussed in Chapters 6 and 7, a right to possession of a thing, enforceable in a court of law, is a property right. How is this apparent inconsistency to be resolved? There are two solutions:

1) .....recognise that it is possible to have a property right to a human corpse, which is usually far more limited than full ownership; or
2) .....decide that a human corpse is not a thing which can be subject to property rights and that rights to the corpse must exist outside the law of property.

The first solution is simpler than the second. The law of property contains a sophisticated body of rules governing the creation and enforcement of rights to things, which is the product of centuries of development. There seems little point trying to "reinvent the wheel" in relation to the human corpse. The reluctance to acknowledge property rights to a corpse seems to be caused by the fairly common mistake of equating property and ownership. As discussed in Chapter 10, there are many property rights which are less extensive than the right to the full use and enjoyment of things which we call "ownership". The right to possess something for a limited time or for a limited purpose is not ownership, but is nevertheless a property right.

In *Doodeward v Spence* (1908) 6 CLR 406 at 418, Higgins J referred to the right to the human corpse as "special property". In *Pierce v Proprietors of Swan Point Cemetery* (1872) 14 Am Rep 667 at 681, Potter J called it "quasi property":

> "Although...the body is not property in the usually recognized sense of the word, yet we may consider it as a sort of *quasi* property, to which certain persons may have rights, as they have duties to perform toward it, arising out of our common humanity. But the person having charge of it cannot be considered as the owner of it in any sense whatever; he holds it only as a sacred trust for the benefit of all who may from family or friendship have an interest in it, and we think that

a court of equity may well regulate it as such, and change the custody if improperly managed."

The adjectives "special" and "quasi" seem chosen to indicate that the executor's right to the body is not created and enforced for her or his own benefit, but for the purpose of ensuring that the body receives a proper burial or cremation. However, this qualification on the right does not take it outside the realm of property. It can be compared with the right of a trustee: see Chapter 13. It is clear that trustees have legally enforceable property rights to things held in trust, even though they are not permitted to use those rights for their own benefit. Is there a compelling reason why executors cannot have a similar property right?

As discussed above, Australian law chooses to exclude living human beings from the list of things which can be subject to property rights. It could also choose to exclude dead human beings. Our concern for life, liberty, and security of the person makes slavery unacceptable. The exclusion of the corpse from the law of property would require a different justification, such as our respect for the dignity of the person. Our methods of disposing of human remains show that our respect for the corpse is tied to our respect for the life and memory of the deceased person. There is a fear that the formal recognition of property rights to the corpse would reduce the corpse to the status of a commodity. This creates a dilemma. The executor has a right to control the body, which is enforceable generally against other members of society, and yet we are afraid to identify that right as property.

If a moral choice drives us to the second solution of recognising the executor's right to the corpse outside the law of property, then what type of right is it? Perhaps the closest analogy is the right of a parent or guardian to custody of an infant child. This was the analogy which Potter J used in the *Pierce* case, above, at 681. When the child is very young, the parents have almost complete control. They decide how and where the child will live and who he or she can visit. Of course, they are not permitted to mistreat the child and may lose their parental rights and be guilty of a crime if they do. However, similar things could be said about a pet owner's right to a dog or cat. Why is one a property right but not the other? It is because we choose to exclude children (and other living human beings) from the law of property.

Parental rights are enforceable generally against other members of society, but they exist for the benefit of the child: see Bryan, "Parents as Fiduciaries: A Special Place in Equity" (1995) 3 *International Journal of Children's Rights* 227. Those rights are needed to protect children until they are able to make decisions for themselves as adults with full legal capacity. The rights to a human corpse could be regarded in a similar way. If the corpse is not a thing subject to property rights, then the executor has a right to custody as the guardian of the corpse. That right is granted, not for the executor's benefit, but to facilitate the proper treatment of the dead body. In other words, on death we cease to be legal persons, but would not become things. We would be under the care of those responsible for the disposal of our remains.

This solution may work for corpses intended for burial, but what about human remains used for medical or scientific purposes (such as a skeleton in a medical school) or for display to the public (such as an Egyptian mummy in a museum)? It is hardly conceivable that these human remains are not subject to rights and therefore freely available to anyone who dares lay hold of them. Yet, guardianship does not appear to be an appropriate concept in these situations. It is clear that these rights exist for the benefit, not of the deceased, but of the right holders. Medical schools and museums charge money to view the remains.

The Commonwealth, states, and territories of Australia have statutes dealing with objects of Aboriginal cultural significance, including human remains. For example, section 2(3)(c) of the *Aboriginal Relics Act 1975* (Tas) defines "relic" to include "the remains of the body of such an original inhabitant or of a descendant of such an inhabitant who died before the year 1876 that are not interred". Section 11 states that a relic found on Crown land is "the property of the Crown". What justifies the treatment of such remains as things subject to property rights? If all human remains are subject to property rights, the only difficulties are the questions of who should be entitled to hold those property rights and for what purpose. However, if some human remains are beyond the reach of property law, then some meaningful basis for distinction must be found.

In *Doodeward v Spence* (1908) 6 CLR 406, the High Court decided that the plaintiff had a property right to possession of the corpse of a child who had been stillborn with two heads. The police had seized the corpse from the plaintiff, who had been showing it for profit, and were required to return it. It is difficult to extract general principles from this case because the judges relied on two dubious justifications for their decision. First, since the child had been stillborn, he or she was never a legal person and therefore was not the corpse of a deceased person. This provides little guidance since most of the human remains held by laboratories, museums, and universities would not fall in this narrow exception. Secondly, a person who lawfully performs work on a corpse can thereby transform it into a thing subject to property rights. Since the stillborn child had been placed in a bottle of preserving fluid, it qualified as a thing subject to property rights. This fails to provide a useful distinction in an age when bodies are routinely embalmed in preparation for funerals.

There is no meaningful distinction between those human remains intended for burial or cremation and those used for other purposes. What one person regards as a museum artifact may be another person's ancestor in need of a proper burial. In "Maoris Claim Head" (1992) 1 *International Journal of Cultural Property* 393, Patrick O'Keefe reported the case of a preserved head of a Maori warrior which had been listed for sale in 1988 at an auction in London. After viewing the auction catalogue, the New Zealand High Court decided that the warrior had died in New Zealand in about 1820 and appointed a Maori chief as the administrator of his estate. The head was then removed from sale and returned to New Zealand for burial.

The antiquity of the remains does not provide a generally accepted basis for distinction. As Jane Hubert noted, in "Dry Bones or Living Ancestors? Conflicting Perceptions of Life, Death and the Universe" (1992) 1 *International Journal of Cultural Property* 105 at 115-117, there was considerable controversy over the status of fossilised remains that were thousands of years old and had been found in Kow Swamp, near the Murray River. Aboriginal people living in the area claimed the fossils as the remains of their ancestors. What one group regarded as a major scientific discovery, another saw as an integral part of its spiritual and cultural heritage.

Perceptions of human remains have changed in recent years. The 1989 "Vermillion Accord", produced by the World Archaeological Congress, affirms the principles that "Respect for the mortal remains of the dead shall be accorded to all irrespective of origin, race, religion, nationality, custom and tradition" and that the wishes of deceased persons, their relative, guardians, and local communities should be respected whenever possible: see Hubert, above, at 111. This change is reflected in the *Native American Grave Protection and Repatriation Act* 1990 in the United States, which requires institutions that receive federal funding to return human remains of native Americans to their descendants. It is also visible in *Jones v Dodd* [1999] SASC 125, where Perry J referred to the "right to the repatriation of human remains" found in Article 13 of the *Draft Declaration on the Rights of Indigenous Peoples* (1994) and said that "common considerations of decency and respect for human dignity should lead those responsible for the burial of a corpse to recognise, and where possible give effect to, the cultural, spiritual and religious beliefs, practices and traditions of the deceased."

Does this shift in perception mean that human artifacts and relics are no longer things subject to property rights? A right to recover human remains from a museum for the purpose of burial meets the criteria of property, since it relates to an external thing and is enforceable generally against other members of society. The change is perhaps nothing more than a recognition that, in some cases, the lineal and cultural descendants of those deceased persons have better property rights than the museums.

The problem will not be solved by excluding some human remains from the law of property and redefining the boundaries of that category. The coherent solution is to recognise that all human remains are subject to property rights and that, in most cases, those rights are given to executor, administrator, or family of the deceased person for the limited purpose of properly disposing of those remains in accordance with the cultural or religious traditions of that person. However, the law acknowledges other uses for dead bodies. People can choose to donate their bodies to science or for medical training. We do not object to people having full ownership of human remains lawfully acquired for such purposes. The problem arises when that ownership is acquired without the consent of deceased persons or those members of their families and communities who have vested interests in the proper disposition of their remains. This is not a question of whether someone should have property rights to the body but who should have those rights.

Property Rights to Living Human Tissue

Advances in technology have raised difficult moral questions concerning property rights to living human tissue. Now that medical science enables the donation of blood, sperm, ova, bone marrow, organs, and other parts of the body, the law must cope with living human tissues which are not part of a person. Tissues that were once regarded as intrinsic parts of the person (and therefore outside the realm of property law) can become only contingently connected (and potentially a thing subject to property rights).

The law has had difficulty dealing with this change and has been reluctant to recognise the possibility of property rights to living human tissue. This reluctance is derived from our desire to preserve the dignity of the human being and maintain the boundary between person and thing. We abhor the ownership of humans (following the abolition of slavery) and fear the consequences of a market for body parts. The transition is difficult.

Different types of human tissue raise different issues. The removal of regenerating tissues, like blood, leaves the donor as he or she was before (or capable of returning to that state). In contrast, the removal of non-regenerating tissues, like a kidney, diminishes the living donor. It is easier to regard something as separate from the person (and subject to property rights) if severing the connection between the person and thing does not involve a permanent subtraction from the person. Sperm and ova raise a different concern. Their removal is not perceived as a subtraction from the donor. However, the creation of embryos, with their potential to become separate legal persons, takes us back to the border between person and thing.

Regenerating Tissues

The human body produces a variety of tissues which will be replaced naturally if removed, such as blood, fingernails, hair, saliva, and urine. These things can be subject to property rights. People have been convicted of theft for taking back urine and blood samples given to the police: see Matthews, "Whose Body? People as Property" (1983) 36 *Current Legal Problems* 193 at 223-225. People sell their hair to wig makers and wigs made from that hair fetch high prices.

There are a few cases concerning blood transfusions which cast some doubt on this issue. For example, in *Perlmutter v Beth David Hospital* (1954) 123 NE2d 792, the plaintiff paid for a transfusion of blood containing harmful impurities. The New York Court of Appeals held that the supply of blood was incidental to the service provided by the hospital and not a "sale" of blood. Therefore, the transaction was not subject to the warranties regarding the quality and fitness of merchandise, found in the statute regulating the sale of goods. Similarly, in *E v Australian Red Cross Society* (1991) 27 FCR 310, the plaintiff contracted HIV from a transfusion received during surgery. The court held that the consumer protection provisions of section 71 of the *Trade Practices Act* 1974 (Cth) and section 19 of the *Sale of Goods Act* 1923 (NSW), did not apply and that, even if blood fell within the statutory definition of "goods", it had been supplied free of charge and only incidentally to the supply of medical services.

These cases say nothing about whether blood can be a thing subject to property rights. They concern consumer protection legislation which regulates the provision of goods and services to the public. The issue in these cases is regulated by the law of contract, not the law of property.

Non-regenerating Tissues

For the law of property, is there any difference between tissues that regenerate (such as blood and hair) and tissues that do not (such as a cornea or kidney)? The most significant difference is the potential effect of removal on the tissue donor. If living tissues are removed at the time of death, the issue then relates to the dignity of the corpse, as discussed above. However, the removal of non-regenerating tissue from a living donor diminishes that donor. It transforms something which was an intrinsic part of the individual into a separate thing. Should that thing be subject to property rights?

There is a fear that the recognition of property rights to transplantable tissues will open the doors to widespread abuse as wealthy people in need of treatment prey on those less fortunate. There are rumours of organs being harvested from deceased orphans and prisoners in other parts of the world and of people in poverty selling organs to maintain their families. The problem is not caused by treating living human tissues as things subject to property rights, but from an imbalance and abuse of power. It is the same problem which causes children in developing countries to take part in a sex industry aimed at tourists from developed nations. The recognition of property rights to blood has not increased the potential for abuse of blood donors. The exclusion of other tissues from the law of property would merely exacerbate the problem by pushing the trade in body parts further into the black market.

The solution is the regulation or prohibition of certain types of transactions involving human tissue, which is better accomplished if the law recognises that people can have property rights to that tissue. For example, section 29 of the *Human Tissue and Transplant Act* 1982 (WA) makes it unlawful for people to sell or make contracts to sell human tissue. This does not mean that human tissue cannot be subject to property rights. People are permitted (and encouraged) to give that tissue to others. The statute merely prohibits certain types of transactions (sales and contracts) with respect to human tissue.

In the controversial case of *Moore v Regents of the University of California* (1990) 793 P2d 479, the majority of the Supreme Court of California decided that people did not have a right to possession of tissues removed from their bodies. The defendants had removed tissue from the plaintiff and then used it to develop and patent a valuable cell line. The removal was necessary for the treatment of the plaintiff's leukaemia and had been done with his consent. However, he did not know about or consent to the use of his tissue for medical research. The court decided that the plaintiff had a claim against the doctor who removed the tissue, for breach of his **fiduciary** duty (of loyalty) to the plaintiff, his patient. The relationship of trust between doctor and patient required the doctor to make decisions regarding treatment with a view to the patient's best interests and not for the purpose of making a secret profit.

The majority of the court also decided that the defendants could not be held liable to the plaintiff for **conversion** of that tissue. As discussed in Chapter 7, the tort of conversion is the wrongful interference with another person's right to possess a thing. The majority held that the plaintiff did not have a sufficient property right in the tissue removed from his body to support a claim for conversion of that tissue. This was based, in part, on the effect of California's Health and Safety Code, which regulated the disposal of human tissue. Panelli J stated (at 492):

> "By restricting how excised cells may be used and requiring their eventual destruction, the statute eliminates so many of the rights ordinarily attached to property that one cannot simply assume that what is left amounts to 'property' or 'ownership' for purposes of conversion law."

Although the result seems correct in the particular case, the reasoning is unsatisfactory. The plaintiff had consented to the removal of his tissue and, therefore, did not have a right to possess it. The same rule would apply if the plaintiff had been duped into selling or giving away his car. The law would allow him to **rescind** the transaction and recover his right to possession (discussed in Chapter 24), but only if the parties could be restored to their original positions. If the car had been resold or destroyed in the meantime, rescission would be impossible. In the *Moore* case, the tissue had been used for scientific research and could not be returned in its original condition. Therefore, even if the court had decided that his tissue could be subject to property rights, the plaintiff would not have had a right to possession in the circumstances.

It seems strange that statutory restrictions on the use of human tissue could take it outside the law of property. Many other things are heavily regulated, such as cars, firearms, and plutonium, and yet people have property rights to them. The exclusion of living human tissues from the law of property would have bizarre consequences. Neither the plaintiff nor the defendants in the *Moore* case would have a property right to the tissue in question. The law would be helpless if the defendants' competitors managed to lay hold of it or if an organ ready for transplant was taken from a hospital. If a motorist lost an arm in an accident, he or she would have no better right to possess that arm than anyone else in society. This cannot be right.

Once tissue is removed from a living person, it takes on a separate identity as a thing which can be subject to property rights. The question is not whether property rights exist, but who is entitled to those rights at the moment of removal. As Paul Matthews said, in "Whose Body? People as Property" (1983) 36 *Current Legal Problems* 193 at 227:

> "Where parts of a living person's body are removed and that person continues to live, one would have thought that as with blood, hair and the like that person had the first and best right to possession, though presumably one might transfer that right, as blood donors transfer it to a hospital or blood bank."

Sperm, Ova, and Embryos

From the perspective of the law of property, sperm and ova do not differ from other regenerating human tissue. Although ova do not regenerate, they can be removed in a manner which leaves the woman able to function as before. Like blood, urine, and hair, they can be subject to property rights. However, when combined to produce an embryo, another consideration arises: the potential creation of another person.

In most jurisdictions, a human becomes a legal person capable of holding rights from the moment of birth. However, the law has had great difficulty determining the status of the human before birth. Do sperm and ova cease to be things subject to property rights when they combine to make embryos or does the transition from thing to pre-person happen at some later stage of development? There are no easy answers.

The National Health and Medical Research Council provides guidelines for those who conduct research on humans and human tissue. Its *Statement on Human Experimentation and Supplementary Notes* (1992), supplementary note 4, section 6, states:

> "Sperm and ova produced for IVF should be considered to belong to the respective donors. The wishes of the donors regarding the use, storage and ultimate disposal of the sperm, ova and resultant embryos should be ascertained and as far as is possible respected by the institution. In the case of the embryos, the donors' joint directions (or the directions of a single surviving donor) should be observed; in the event of disagreement between the donors the institution should be in a position to make decisions."

Although this recognises property rights to sperm and ova, it avoids the issue with regard to embryos. It seems to contemplate a guardianship arrangement, similar to the rights of a parent to a child or, possibly, the rights of an executor to a corpse. This is similar to the approach taken by the *Infertility Treatment Act* 1995 (Vic). Section 24 bans research which would harm the embryo and section 5 states that the most important principle guiding the application of the act is that "the welfare and interests of any person born or to be born as a result of a treatment procedure are paramount".

This may be suitable in the context of IVF (in vitro fertilisation), where the rights exist for the purpose of either protecting the embryo *en route* to becoming a person or disposing of it according to law. However, scientists have suggested that embryos may have other potential uses. The ability of embryonic cells to transform into different types of cells makes them potentially valuable for the treatment of neurological and other diseases. If society ever permits embryos to be used for that purpose, it will have to face the issue of property rights to the embryo. Guardianship is not an appropriate regime if people are allowed to use embryos for their own benefit, such as scientific research and medical treatment.

Information

The same question arises in regard to both human tissue and information: is this something which should be subject to property rights? However, the reason for asking is different. Our concern over property rights to human tissue is not that someone has control over that tissue, but that the recognition of property rights might degrade the human body to the level of a mere commodity. Rights to human tissue should be enforceable against other members of society, but in a manner which preserves the dignity of the person. In contrast, our concern over property rights to information is that someone might be able to control information to which the public should have free access.

Freedom of information is vital to a free and democratic society like Australia. This includes the freedom to exchange ideas, criticise the government, or simply read the news. Such information must remain outside property law and beyond the control of governments and others. On the other hand, the inability to have property rights to any type of information would be detrimental to society. Information can be valuable both to the people who produce it and to the people who consume it. The creation of information, such as new books, movies, inventions, and computer programs, can require a tremendous expenditure of time, skill, and money. If there were no property rights to that information and therefore little possibility of earning a profit from that effort, it might not get produced.

The law seeks to achieve a balance between the right to freely exchange some ideas and the right to exploit other ideas for gain. It works from the premiss that people should be free to exchange information unless there is some specific, justifiable restriction on that right. There are two types of restrictions. The first is the prohibition or restriction of certain forms of expression. For example, there are laws against pornography, hate literature, and defamation and there are film classification boards that set age restrictions on movie attendance. These rules are designed to protect the public, or segments of the public, from harm.

The second type of restriction is created indirectly by permitting people to have rights to control information. For example, a person can have a copyright to a book or computer program or a patent of an invention. The different forms of control are known generically as **intellectual property**, because they permit people to have rights to information which are enforceable against other members of society.

There are several distinct forms of intellectual property. Most were created by statute as specific rights to control information. For example, the *Copyright Act* 1968 (Cth) protects certain forms of expression, such as dramatic, literary, or musical works, by giving people the exclusive right to publish, copy, or perform those works. The *Patents Act* 1990 (Cth) enables people to obtain the exclusive rights to exploit new inventions. There are also statutes which protect rights to designs, trade marks, and new varieties of plants.

In addition to these statutory forms of protection, the courts devised other ways to protect information. Confidential information, such as a personal or trade secret, can be controlled through an action for breach of confidence. Also, people are not permitted to pass their goods and services off as being the products of, or endorsed by, others. Intellectual property is discussed further in Chapter 17.

Freedom of Information

The concern over freedom of information operates at a fundamental level. It can provide a constitutional limit on the powers of government, as it did in *Davis v Commonwealth of Australia* (1988) 166 CLR 79. This case concerned the *Australian Bicentennial Authority Act* 1980 (Cth), which created a company, called the Australian Bicentennial Authority, to help "commemorate the bicentenary in 1988 of the first European settlement in Australia". Section 22 of that act made it an offence to use certain expressions without the written permission of the authority, including the combination of "1788", "1988", or "88" with words such as "200 years", "Australia", "Sydney", and "Melbourne".

The authority refused to permit the plaintiffs to make clothing printed with a design which incorporated the words "1788", "1988", and "200 years of suppression and depression". The High Court held that the statutory right to control those expressions was unconstitutional. Mason CJ, Deane and Gaudron JJ stated (at 99-100):

> "[T]he effect of the provisions is to give the Authority an extraordinary power to regulate the use of expressions in everyday use in this country, though the circumstances of that use in countless situations could not conceivably prejudice the commemoration of the Bicentenary or the attainment by the Authority of its objects.... Although the statutory regime may be related to a constitutionally legitimate end, the provisions in question reach too far. This extraordinary intrusion into freedom of expression is not reasonably and appropriately adapted to achieve the ends that lie within the limits of constitutional power."

Although it is possible to copyright or trademark original forms of expression and thereby control their use, people are not permitted to gain control over the components of ordinary speech. As the *Davis* case demonstrates, such control could be used to stifle legitimate expressions of criticism and other ideas. Kevin Gray said, in "Property in Thin Air" (1991) 50 *Cambridge Law Journal* 252 at 280, that the law of property is limited by the "notion of moral non-excludability", by which he meant "that there are certain resources which are simply perceived to be so central or intrinsic to constructive human coexistence that it would be severely anti-social that these resources should be removed from the commons." The freedom to express ideas belongs in this category.

Just as people are generally free to speak, listen to, write, and read what they choose, they are also free to look around them. This is demonstrated by *Victoria Park Racing and Recreation Grounds Co Ltd v Taylor* (1937) 58 CLR 479. The plaintiff company operated a racecourse and the three defendants were:

1) .....a neighbour who built a raised platform on his house overlooking the racecourse;
2) .....a sports commentator who sat on the platform and described the races into a telephone; and
3) .....a radio station who broadcast those descriptions to the general public.

The plaintiff sought but was refused a court order to stop the broadcasts, which had caused a significant decline in attendance at its racecourse. Latham CJ said (at 494):

"The defendant does no wrong to the plaintiff by looking at what takes place on the plaintiff's land. Further, he does no wrong to the plaintiff by describing to other persons, to as wide an audience as he can obtain, what takes place on the plaintiff's ground. The court has not been referred to any principle of law which prevents any man from describing anything which he sees anywhere if he does not make defamatory statements, infringe the law as to offensive language, &c., break a contract, or wrongfully reveal confidential information."

In Latham CJ's words, there is no "property in a spectacle". People are not required to avert their eyes, nor must they keep silent about what they see (unless they would otherwise be in breach of confidence). There is no duty not to gaze upon a neighbour's land. Indeed the duty might flow the other way. A neighbour who wishes to perform her or his morning aerobics in a state of undress may have a duty to take care not to be visible to people passing on the street.

Of course, many people make a living from producing "spectacles", such as a circus or sporting event, but that does not make them property. Street performers simply rely on the generosity of the people they entertain. Other people make use of other property rights, such as the lease of a stadium or auditorium, to control access to the spectacle. Celebrities can exploit the spectacle of their wedding by selling the exclusive right to photograph the event to a magazine. Television companies pay huge sums for exclusive rights to broadcast sporting events. Although the event is not a thing subject to property rights, the edited combination of television pictures and commentary is a form of original expression which can be subject to copyright.

There were dissenting opinions in the *Victoria Park Racing* case, but not because the spectacle was thought to be property. Rich and Evatt JJ believed that neighbour's use of his land was a **nuisance** (discussed in Chapter 7), because it wrongly interfered with the plaintiff's use and enjoyment of its land. Evatt J said (at 516):

"The defendants' operations are conducted to the plaintiff's detriment, not casually but systematically, not temporarily but indefinitely; they use a suburban bungalow in an unreasonable and grotesque manner, and do so in the course of a gainful pursuit which strikes at the plaintiff's profitable use of its land, precisely at the point where the profit must be earned, viz., the entrance gates."

However, Evatt J also said (at 516) that:

"A photographer overlooking the course and subsequently publishing a photograph in a newspaper or elsewhere does not injure the plaintiff. Individuals who observe the racing from their own homes or those of their friends could not interfere with the plaintiff's beneficial use of its course."

If it is lawful to look upon a neighbour's land and describe what is seen, then what wrong have the defendants committed? The plaintiff can have no property right to the information the defendants collected.

The wrong seems to be the use of that information in a way which reduces the plaintiff's profits, but how does this differ from a neighbour who operates a competing business? Holding another race or some other spectacle nearby would have the same effect.

Evatt J suggested that the defendants were guilty of unfair competition, relying on the majority opinion of the United States Supreme Court in *International News Services v Associated Press* (1918) 248 US 215. The defendant in that case was using the plaintiff's newspaper reports published on the east coast to prepare its own reports for sale to newspapers published a few hours later on the west coast. The court ordered the defendant to stop this practice because, as Pitney J said (at 240), it was working "to reap where it has not sown".

This concept of a general prohibition against unfair competition was rejected by the High Court of Australia in *Moorgate Tobacco Co Ltd v Philip Morris Ltd (No 2)* (1984) 156 CLR 414 at 445. It is not surprising that different societies should have different ideas about what constitutes fair trade practices. However, the *International News* case created some confusion by referring to the plaintiff's rights to the news it reported as "quasi-property". Pitney J said (at 235-236):

> "[A]lthough we may and do assume that neither party has any remaining property interest as against the public in uncopyrighted news matter after the moment of its first publication, it by no means follows that there is no remaining property interest in it as between themselves.... Regarding the news, therefore, as but the material out of which both parties are seeking to make profits at the same time and in the same field, we hardly can fail to recognize that for this purpose, and as between them, it must be regarded as quasi property, irrespective of the rights of either as against the public."

This use of the term "quasi-property" differs from its use in *Pierce v Proprietors of Swan Point Cemetery* (1872) 14 Am Rep 667, above, in relation to the human corpse. In *Pierce*, it meant that the executor's rights were enforceable generally against other members of society, but were less extensive the full ownership. In *International News*, the adjective "quasi" is used to indicate that the right was enforceable only against specific persons. As James Penner said of this usage, in "The 'Bundle of Rights' Picture of Property" (1996) 43 *UCLA Law Review* 711 at 717:

> "The result of the property analysis is to create a mystery substance, 'quasi property,' which, applying as it does only between competitors and not between the owner and others in general, appears to strip away from the concept of property one of its few generally acknowledged attributes, *i.e.*, that it is a right an owner holds against all the world, not just against specified individuals."

In *Victoria Park Racing* (1937) 58 CLR 479 at 496, Latham CJ rejected the plaintiff's assertion that it had "a quasi-property in the spectacle" it had produced. He said:

"The vagueness of this proposition is apparent upon its face. What it really means is that there is some principle (apart from contract or confidential relationship) which prevents people in some circumstances from opening their eyes and seeing something and then describing what they see."

The use of the term "quasi property" is, in essence, a failure to properly identify the nature of the right in question and it is misleading. If a right to a thing (such as a corpse) is enforceable generally against other members of society, then there is nothing "quasi" about it. It is property. Conversely, if a right to a thing (such as information) is enforceable only against specific persons, it is not property. There is nothing in between for which "quasi property" is a suitable description.

Chapter Four

DISTRIBUTION OF PROPERTY

■■■

Jeremy Waldron wrote in "Property Law" (in Patterson, *A Companion to Philosophy of Law and Legal Theory* (1996) 3 at 3), that discussions about property law are of two different kinds: "First there are analytical issues, about the meaning and use of the most important concepts in property law, such as 'private property', 'ownership,' and 'thing.' The second type of issue is normative or justificatory." This book is of the former kind. This chapter is but a brief look at a few questions concerning the justification of property rights and the distribution of those rights in Australia.

This is not an indication of the relative importance of these two different kinds of inquiries, nor is it meant to suggest that they are wholly independent of each other. The property regime discussed in this book exists because the majority of Australians believe that this method of allocating rights to things is justified. The justification of this regime, morally and politically, is a complex and important task, which depends upon an understanding of the nature and regulation of property rights in Australian society.

Property rights, like all legal rights, require justification because they correspond to duties placed on other members of society. In "On Property: An Essay" (1990) 100 *Yale Law Journal* 127 at 139, Laura Underkuffler said that, "A right can be defined as that which fulfils an individual need or individual interest that is considered to be of sufficient moral importance to justify the generation of duties for others." Property rights are especially in need of justification because they correspond to duties imposed on everyone in society and not just on those who have consented to undertake particular duties to particular right holders.

The justification of property rights tends to be a highly contentious business. Why does one person have the right to prevent others from walking on some place on the earth? Why do police help shopkeepers protect large stores of food from the hungry? The debate is emotionally and politically charged. However, these questions concern the justification of particular types of property rights or the manner in which those rights are distributed in society. They do not address the basic question of whether property rights should exist at all. That question is relatively simple and free of controversy.

For example, we might argue about the ownership of Australia's telephone systems, but would agree that there must be at least one person with the right to prevent others from taking away or destroying the equipment needed to operate that system. In other words, we can agree that there ought to be property rights to the telephone system, without having to decide who should hold those rights.

Similarly, we might debate whether people should have free access to the beach. This is not a debate over whether there should be property rights to the beach. Each side favours a different property right: either the right to use the beach or the right to prevent others from using it. The former is a property right not to be excluded from the beach and to prevent others from using the beach in a manner which detracts from that access (for example, by building or dumping). Our debate is about the kind of property rights which should exist and who should hold them.

A society cannot function peacefully without rules regulating the use of things. As Waldron said in "Property Law" (above, at 5), "Disagreements about who is to use or control such objects are likely to be serious because resource-use matters to people, to their livelihood as well as their enjoyment. Thus any society with an interest in avoiding violent conflict will need a system of rules for pre-empting disagreements of this kind." The existence of property rights is simply part of the rule of law. The regulation of human behaviour necessarily involves the regulation of our use of things.

Types of Property

In "Property Law" (at 5), Waldron identified "three broad species of property arrangement: common property, collective (or state) property, and private property."

Common property is the right of everyone in society (or a sufficiently large segment of society) to make use of a thing. It corresponds to the general duty of others not to use the thing in a way which interferes with the common use. For example, no one is permitted to build on a public road or park, pollute a public beach, or prevent an aboriginal group from exercising its native title. No government or individual member of society is entitled to the exclusive use of a thing which is common property.

Collective property exists when decisions regarding the use of a thing are taken on behalf of society by public institutions, such as government agencies and departments and government owned corporations. In Australia, those decision-makers are ultimately responsible to all members of the particular collective (whether city, state, or Commonwealth) through the democratic process. The fact that decisions are made collectively does not mean that individual members of the collective have a right of access to that thing. For example, a government owned military installation may well be surrounded by barbed wire and guards.

The distinction between common and collective property is not always easy to draw. The collective may decide to use something, such as a freeway, museum, or zoo, in a manner which gives people relatively free access to that thing. However, decisions about the use of that thing are made by, or on behalf of, the government. Public access to it is granted by the decision-maker and does not exist independently as a common right.

Private property is the right of a private person or group of specific persons to make decisions regarding the use a thing. For example, if you own this book, you can decide whether to read it, write in it, tear the pages out, throw it on the fire, use it to play fetch with your dog, give it to a friend, etc. You cannot use your book to harm others, but the government and other members of society do not otherwise have a say in what you do with it. If you have borrowed this book from the library, your right to use the book is limited by the library's (private or collective) right to the book. However, your limited right to use the book during the period of loan is private property, because that right belongs to you and not to the collective or the common.

The distinction between collective and private property is not always easy to draw. If 51% of the voting shares of a corporation are owned by the government, is it collective property, private property, or a combination of the two? Is the property of a university collectively or privately owned? In Canada, community colleges are agents of the government and therefore subject to the *Charter of Rights and Freedoms* (which sets a constitutional limit on the powers of governments), but universities are not. Although both charge fees and receive massive amounts of government funding, universities are regarded as private institutions: see *McKinney v University of Guelph* [1990] 3 SCR 229; *Douglas/Kwantlen Faculty Association v Douglas College* [1990] 3 SCR 570.

All three types of property (common, collective, and private) exist in most, if not all, societies. One society can be distinguished from another according to the proportions of each type of property which exist within it. As Peter Birks said in "An Unacceptable Face of Human Property" in Birks, *New Perspectives in the Roman Law of Property: Essays for Barry Nicholas* (1989) 61 at 61:

> "Things either fall within the sphere of private ownership or they do not. The way in which the line is drawn goes far to determining the character of a society. Move it a little to one side, to exclude the means of production, and you have communism …"

In Australia, private property predominates, at least in terms of value. However, a huge portion of the country is owned collectively as Crown land or as common property, such as native title. Also, the different forms of property blend into one another. For example, a privately owned building may be designated a heritage site, thereby prohibiting the owner from altering the structure without government permission and imposing upon the owner positive duties to preserve it. In that situation, decisions about the use of the thing are being made privately and collectively. The private ownership of most things is limited to some extent by collective decisions, through zoning laws and other regulations.

Private Property

The debate over the evils and benefits of "property" is concerned not with the existence of property rights, but with the distribution of those rights in society. The use of valuable resources must be regulated, but by whom? When we speak of the need to justify property, meaning the right of some people to control things to the exclusion of others, we are really talking about justifications for private property.

Waldron suggested that private property is in need of justification because it can operate in ways which appear to be "morally objectionable" ("Property Law", above, at 8-9):

> "Private property involves a pledge by society that it will continue to use its moral and physical authority to uphold the rights of owners, even against those who have no employment, no food to eat, no home to go to, no land to stand on from which they are not at any time liable to be evicted."

What is sought is some moral justification for allowing one private individual to control something which is essential to the life or well-being of another.

The controversy can be narrowed further. The argument is not over the institution of private property, but over the things which should be subject to private property rights and over the distribution of those rights in society. There are some things which individuals need to maintain a basic existence, such as food, clothing, and a place to sleep. In some societies, such as a monastery, hospital, prison, or army, individuals may live without control over those things. However, most everywhere else, the right to decide when, where, and with whom we break our daily bread is an essential component of adult life. Even if we believed that the production and distribution of food should be done collectively, we would want to have the freedom to decide how to use our allotted portion. At some point between production and consumption, food would become privately owned. Certain basic freedoms, such as the rights to decide what to eat and wear, cannot exist unless people are permitted to control some things. In other words, there must be at least some private property.

Of course, personal fulfilment may depend on more than the bare essentials for survival. A meaningful or enjoyable life involves the pursuit of many different interests, such as our health, safety, and relationships with others. It also involves an interest in controlling and using certain external things. This is not to suggest that it is possible to construct a list of essentials which must available for private ownership. What we need to attain a desired quality of life will depend on our personal circumstances. As James Penner said, in *The Idea of Property in Law* (1997) p 205, "If I choose the life of contemplation, for instance, a room, regular meals, access to a good library, and the company of others who share my intellectual interests are what I *need*, not any property."

People seek personal fulfilment in a wide variety of ways, most of which depend upon the ability to control some things. For one person it may be a sailboat. For another it may be a tennis racket or a pair of hiking boots. Others may want the right use a computer or to bring flowers home to a spouse. These things are not essential for survival, but can be the ingredients of a life well lived. As Penner said (at p 204), "the interest in property, no less than our interest in anything else, is an interest in creating values and forming relationships and experiencing delights which together make for the good life."

Our concern is not that people have private property, but that some people have so much while others have so little. It is the unequal distribution of private property rights that causes anguish. However, even those with very little have an interest in the institution of private property. As Laura Underkuffler asked, in "The Perfidy of Property" (1991) 70 *Texas Law Review* 293 at 307:

> "Are the poor truly 'propertyless,' with no interest in protecting the right of property? It is impossible to imagine a class of persons, let alone a majority, who have no interest, no psychological investment of any kind, in the idea of protecting property. Every individual desires protection for his property, both now possessed and that which may, in the future, be acquired; this is true no matter how meager one's property may be. In fact, the poor might have a greater stake in, and a greater moral claim to, the protection of what little property they have. The general concept of property protection must be distinguished from the protection of existing property distributions."

The justification of private property is a debate over the allocation and use of private property rights and not whether those rights should exist at all. As Underkuffler said (at 308), "The relationship between the concept of property protection and the separate question of the protection of particular objects of property or particular property distributions could be envisioned as the relationship between a general right and particular instantiations of that right."

Every society has had to consider the list of things which are permissible objects of private ownership. Should it include living things, land, hospitals, educational institutions, news media, and the means of production, transportation or communication? There is a vigorous debate over where the lines between common, collective, and private property should be drawn: see, eg, Friedman, *Capitalism and Freedom* (1962); Laski, *A Grammar of Politics* (5th ed, 1967); Macpherson, *Property: Mainstream and Critical Positions* (1978); Posner, *Economic Analysis of Law* (5th ed, 1998); Schlatter, *Private Property: The History of an Idea* (1951). This debate is not about the nature or existence of property rights, but their allocation.

Linked to, but separate from, the issue of the things which should be privately owned is the problem of the distribution of those things in society. Again, this is not about the nature of property, nor even the nature of private property. It really concerns the rights people have to sell, lease, give, lend, or otherwise exploit their property rights. In other words, there is an important difference between the institution of private property and the existence of a free market which enables people to exchange that property for wealth.

Although a free market economy depends upon the existence of private property, private property can exist in the absence of a free market. For example, *Butler v Egg and Egg Pulp Marketing Board* (1966) 114 CLR 185, concerned the right of egg producers to sell their eggs. Although the farms, barns, equipment, feed, and laying hens were privately owned, the eggs were, by law, the property of the marketing board from the moment they were laid. Therefore, the egg producers were guilty of wrongly interfering with the board's property rights when they sold the eggs directly to consumers.

Questions about the distribution of wealth and resources in society are important. However, the focus of such questions is not on the nature and limits of property, but on the freedom to deal with property and other rights in the market place. The right to exchange property rights for value is an issue of distributive justice, but so too is the right to exchange services for value (consider, for example, the respective salaries of health care workers and movie stars). Calling into question the current distribution of property rights in society is not an attack on the institution of property, but on the regulation of exchange. As Penner said in *The Idea of Property in Law* (1997) pp 206-207:

> "The legitimacy of property rights *per se* strikes me as well nigh indisputable, for the practice of property protects a liberty, ie exclusively to determine the use of things, that has proved marvellously productive in contributing to the good life of many. Determining the justice of any distribution of property, on the other hand, should draw our attention to those distributional mechanisms themselves, such as gifts and contracts and commands, all of which distribute a much broader set of goods than property rights."

The economic, moral, philosophical, political, and religious issues concerning property and its distribution in society are fascinating and rewarding subjects of study. This book does not deal with them. However, it does seek to provide an understanding of the nature of property rights and the legal framework in which they exist. This is a useful prerequisite for the study of broader issues of justification and distribution.

The debate concerning these issues often takes place using the generic label, "property". It is important to be able to look beyond that label and isolate the particular points of debate. In most cases, the issue at hand is not the nature of property, but its distribution. More often than not, this is a debate about the freedom to exploit resources and the regulation of that freedom. Property enters into this debate about the market place as but one of the resources subject to that market.

Chapter Five

TAXONOMY

III

Peter Birks said, in "Equity in the Modern Law: An Exercise in Taxonomy" (1996) 26 *UWA Law Review* 1 at 6, "There is no department of human knowledge which can manage without taxonomy and, equally important, a continuing taxonomic debate." This is especially true of the law of property. The subject is so large and complex that it can appear to be an overwhelming mass of disorganised details. Without a meaningful system of classification, it is difficult, if not impossible, to make sense of the detail and understand how property rules relate to each other and to other areas of law.

There are a number of ways to organise the law of property. Distinctions can be drawn according to the nature of the things subject to property rights or according to the nature of the property rights to which things can be subject. These are the traditional methods of classifying property rights, but they suffer from two limitations: obsolescence and isolation. The first limitation is the product of a long history. Many of the categories into which property rights are divided were created centuries ago. Changes in law and society have rendered some of those categories obsolete and yet they persist as potential sources of confusion.

Secondly, the traditional categories of property law tend to isolate it from other areas of law. Categories based on the nature of the thing or the nature of the right have no counterparts outside the law of property. Since personal rights do not depend on the existence of a thing and differ from property rights by nature, it is difficult to make meaningful comparisons between property and other laws. As an aid to solving this problem, this book makes use of a classification system based on the events which create property rights. This provides a useful basis for comparing property and personal rights and makes it easier to understand the law of property itself. This taxonomy is introduced at the end of this chapter and forms the basis of Part IV (The Creation of Property Rights).

This chapter is only an introduction to methods of classifying property rights. The taxonomy of property law will be explored in greater detail in the chapters which follow, where distinctions are drawn between various kinds of property rights to various kinds of things and between various ways in which property rights can be created. Taxonomy is an ongoing process which is essential for the successful study, practice, or application of the law. It is an important feature of this book, which began in previous chapters as distinctions were drawn between property and personal rights, between the person and the thing, and between things which can and cannot be subject to property rights.

Land/Goods

The most important division in the law of property may be that which is drawn between land and other things. Most things other than land are referred to as **goods** (and less commonly as **chattels**). There are many things which are neither land nor goods, such as money, shares in a corporation, or copyright in a song. Goods are those things, other than land, which are tangible, such as a car, a dog, or a loaf of bread. The distinction between land and goods is a natural starting point. It is easy to understand why the law makes this distinction. Generally speaking, land is both permanent and stationary. It remains relatively constant while the people who use the land come and go. Most other things are transitory. Animals die, clothes wear out, and food gets eaten. Also, goods can be moved from one place to another. A parcel of land will always be subject to whatever laws apply to that location, while a car made in one state may become subject to the laws of several different states and territories as it is moved from place to place.

Roman law classified things as either **movable** (*res mobiles*) or **immovable** (*res immobiles*): Barry Nicholas, *An Introduction to Roman Law* (1962) p 105. Countries with civil codes, like France, Germany, and Japan, adopted this classification. Countries like Australia, which adopted the British common law, use a different system under which property is either **real** or **personal** (sometimes called **realty** and **personalty**). This corresponds roughly with the civilian categories of immovable or movable and our popular notions of the distinction between land and goods. However, it is important to know that the categories of goods/land, personal/real, and movable/immovable do not correspond to one another with precision.

Real/Personal

The distinctions between land and goods and between immovables and movables are based on the nature of the thing. In contrast, the distinction between real and personal property is based on the nature of the right. It is derived from the forms of legal actions used in 13th and 14th century England: Williams, "The Terms Real and Personal in English Law" (1888) 4 *Law Quarterly Review* 394. Certain property rights to land were classified as real property because the holder of the right could bring a real action to recover the land from someone who was wrongly in possession of it. Other property rights were classified as personal property because there was no real action available to recover the thing itself. Instead, the holder of a personal property right had a personal action to be compensated for the loss caused by the person who wrongly interfered with that right.

The categories of real and personal property continue to be used and are commonly associated with the categories of land and goods.

This is because all real property rights are rights to land, while most personal property rights are not. However, the similarity is misleading because there are property rights to land which, strictly speaking, are not real property. A lease of land (discussed in Chapter 12) was considered not to be real property because there was no real action which would allow a dispossessed tenant to recover the leased land itself. In the 15th century, another form of action, called **ejectment**, was developed to allow tenants to recover possession of leased land. Since ejectment was not a real action, leases of land were not reclassified as real property, but are sometimes found under the strange heading, **chattels real**: Simpson, *A History of the Land Law* (2nd ed, 1986) pp 74-76. Ironically, ejectment proved to be a more efficient remedy than the real actions and soon displaced them as the means of protecting real property rights: Megarry & Wade, *The Law of Real Property* (5th ed, 1984) pp 1155-1159.

The end of the real actions removed the original basis for the distinction between real and personal property. The right to recover the thing itself is no longer limited to real property. In addition to leases of land, the law allows the holders of property rights to goods which are difficult or impossible to replace (such as family heirlooms, original paintings, or made-to-order machine parts) to recover those goods from others wrongly in possession of them. So, the categories of realty and personalty no longer indicate with accuracy whether a property right entitles the holder to recover the thing itself or merely to receive compensation for its loss.

The distinction between real and personal property should not be confused with the distinction between rights *in rem* and rights *in personam*: Hohfeld, "Fundamental Legal Conceptions as Applied to Judicial Reasoning" (1917) 26 *Yale Law Journal* 710 at 752-753. Personal property rights are not personal rights. They are property rights because they relate to external things and are enforceable generally against other members of society. However, they are normally enforced by means of personal rights. For example, a thief who steals your car commits an actionable wrong (the tort of conversion, discussed in Chapter 7) and is liable to compensate you for your loss. Your right to your car is a property right, while your right to be compensated is a personal right against the specific person who wrongly interfered with your property right.

Legal/Equitable

Property rights can also be divided into **legal** and **equitable** rights. Like real and personal property, these categories are based on the nature of the right and were created by legal conditions which have since ceased to exist. Prior to 1875, the common law of England was administered by common law courts, such as the courts of King's Bench and Common Pleas. Rights which could be enforced in those courts are called legal rights. A separate body of law, called **equity**, was administered by the court of **Chancery**. Rights which could be enforced in Chancery, but not in the common law courts, are called equitable rights.

A statute called the *Judicature Act* 1873 merged those courts into a single High Court of Justice, which continued to administer common law and equity as separate bodies of law. This process was copied in Australia. In each state and territory, the courts of common law and equity have been merged into a single superior court empowered to administer both law and equity: see Meagher, Gummow & Lehane, *Equity Doctrines and Remedies* (3rd ed, 1992) pp 37-44. So, the separate categories of legal and equitable property rights continue to exist even though the court structure which created them does not. As FW Maitland said, in *Equity* (rev ed, 1936) p 1:

> "We have no longer any courts which are merely courts of equity. Thus we are driven to say that Equity now is that body of rules administered by our ... courts of justice which, were it not for the operation of the *Judicature Acts*, would be administered only by those courts which would be known as Courts of Equity."

Although the body of law known as equity can be defined only historically, by reference to conditions which have ceased to exist, it continues to be a vital part of the law. The rules of equity were created to fill gaps in the common law and correct perceived injustices. Many of those rules were patterned after the common law and, therefore, most legal property rights have an equitable counterpart (and vice versa). For example, a lease of land can be either legal or equitable depending on whether that lease would have been recognised in a court of common law or only in a court of equity.

The nature of equitable property rights will be discussed in more detail in Chapter 13. It is sufficient at this stage to note that there are still important practical differences between legal and equitable property rights. Two main differences are the manner of their creation and their durability. First, as discussed in Part IV (The Creation of Property Rights), most equitable property rights can be created with less formality than the comparable legal property rights. Secondly, as discussed in Part V (Priority of Property Rights), they tend to be less durable than legal property rights and are more easily extinguished by competing property rights to the same thing.

Tangible/Intangible

Property rights are sometimes classified according to whether they are **tangible** or **intangible**. Other terms for these categories are **corporeal** and **incorporeal**: see Butt, *Land Law* (3rd ed, 1996) pp 400-401. All property rights are intangible in the sense that they are rights enforceable against other persons, regardless of the nature of the thing to which those rights relate. The distinction depends on whether the property right entitles the holder to possession of the thing involved. Tangible (corporeal) property rights include the right to possession of some thing, while intangible (incorporeal) property rights do not.

Possession is a legal concept which is discussed further in the next part. A thing cannot be possessed unless it is something which can be controlled physically, like a book or parcel of land. Therefore, property rights to things which cannot be possessed (such as a copyright to a song or a share in a corporation) are necessarily intangible. However, the converse is not true. It is possible to have property rights to physical things which do not entitle the holder to possession of that thing. For example, a person can have a right of way to cross another's land and not be entitled to possession of that land. A right of way (called an easement and discussed in Chapter 16) is an example of an intangible (or incorporeal) property right to a physical thing.

Personal property is often classified as tangible or intangible. A right to possession of goods is called a **chose in possession** (using the French word for thing) and a personal property right to an intangible thing is called a **chose in action**. The latter term is also used to refer to purely personal rights, such as a bank account or other rights to receive the payment of money. When used in that sense, the chose (thing) is the obligation to which the personal right corresponds.

The terms, tangible, intangible, corporeal, and incorporeal, no longer have great significance in the law of property. However, the essential distinction between the right to possession and other property rights is important. As discussed in Part II, possession is the cornerstone of much of the common law of property.

Property Creating Events

Another way to organise property rights is according to the events that create them. Peter Birks has identified four main categories ("Equity in the Modern Law: An Exercise in Taxonomy" (1996) 26 *UWA Law Review* 1 at 8): "The rights which people bear, whether in personam or in rem, derive from the following events: wrongs, consent, unjust enrichment, and others." The origins of these categories can be found in Roman law.

Most property rights are created by consent, such as a sale of goods, a bequest in a will, or a grant of a mortgage. Property rights can also be created by wrongdoing. For example, an employer may have a property right to any bribes received by her or his employees. There are property rights created by unjust enrichment, such as the right to recover land or goods transferred by mistake. The miscellany of other events includes the creation (and destruction) of property rights brought about by physical changes to things. These events and the distinctions between them are explored in Part IV.

This taxonomy of property rights is useful because it brings together and invites comparisons between different rights which tend to be studied and applied as discrete compartments of property law. For example, mortgages are often relegated to separate chapters near the end of property law textbooks (and law school subjects) and never related to, say, gifts of chattels. The same types of events create property rights regardless of whether those rights are real or personal, legal or equitable, and tangible or intangible.

An important feature of this taxonomy is that it allows comparisons to be drawn between property and personal rights. The archaic language and taxonomy of property law has inhibited this in the past.

Overcoming these obstacles will lead to greater consistency among various branches of law and make it easier for lawyers in one field to take advantage of progress in another. For example, recent developments in the law of unjust enrichment have been slow to reach the law of property. Conversely, property law has evolved to enable a fairer distribution of wealth between de facto spouses at the end of their relationships. A better understanding of the events which create legal rights in those relationships need not be limited to property law.

A taxonomy based on the events which create legal rights (and obligations) is particularly helpful because these are, perhaps, the most important legal issues affecting our lives. We want to know, for example, whether the purchase of our new home is complete or whether we are at fault in a car accident. In other words, have events in our lives produced legal consequences? The legal profession spends much of its time seeking answers to questions such as these. Solicitors help people create rights through the preparation of contracts, settlements, transfers, trusts, and wills. Barristers work to prove or disprove the existence of rights.

It is important that the law be applied consistently. Lawyers and judges must sort through the seemingly infinite variety of human affairs in search of legally significant events. Without meaningful bases for comparison, questions regarding the existence of legal rights cannot be answered with certainty. This requires an accepted taxonomy of right creating events, so that people and their legal advisors can know whether rights found to exist in one case should be applied to another. A proper taxonomy can promote the certainty we need to plan our affairs and embark on litigation only when absolutely necessary.

Part II
Possession

Chapter Six

POSSESSION

■■■

Possession is the cornerstone of the law of property. Several sophisticated property concepts, such as the estate (discussed below in Chapter 12), evolved from the more basic concept of possession. Also, most of the legal remedies available for the protection of property rights are actually remedies to protect the right to possession.

The importance which the common law places on possession accords with popular notions of fairness. These notions are learned at an early age. It is not uncommon to hear a young child defend a claim to use a chair or toy by yelling, "I had it first!" There is a well known movie character who travels the world in search of archeological treasure. On several occasions, he risks life and limb to find some priceless artifact, only to have it taken almost immediately by the bad guys. We sense wrongdoing, but what claim did he have to the treasure? There is a belief, which the law confirms, that simple possession of a thing is a property right worthy of protection.

What is Possession?

Possession is a legal concept. To have possession of a thing, a person must control that thing and intend to possess it. Both are required. For example, you might intend to possess a wild animal, but will not have possession unless you can catch and control it. Conversely, you might board a tram or train and sit down, unaware that someone left a $10 note on your seat. You are in complete control of the note (since no one else can take the note from under you without committing a tort), but do not possess it since you are unaware of its existence and have no intention to possess it.

Control

Control (sometimes called **factual possession**) means physical control. Only tangible things, such as a book, dog, or parcel of land, can be controlled in this way. Intangible things, such as a copyright to a song, can be subject to property rights, but they cannot be possessed.

How one controls a thing varies according to its nature. For example, you might control a dollar coin by placing it in your pocket or purse, but you cannot control a horse or house in that way. The methods used will be dictated by factors such as the size of the thing, its situation, and whether it is movable. The essential question is whether the person is able to control access to the thing. With some things, such as animals or fluids, there is an additional problem of preventing the thing from escaping.

To control land, steps are taken to limit access to that land. Locking doors, windows, and gates is one method of exercising control. However, locks are not required. We live in a society regulated by law and land can be controlled without taking steps to prevent forcible entry. A closed, but unlocked gate will do. It is also possible to control land without any fence at all. Many people do not have fences all the way around the yards they control. Tending the lawn and garden or otherwise making use of the space around the house is sufficient. Others know that they need permission (express or implied) to enter the land. Although there are no physical impediments to entry, this exclusion of others is sufficient to constitute control.

Conversely, it is possible to fence an area of land and not control it. In *Riley v Penttila* [1974] VR 547, the owners of homes adjoining a park had a property right (called an easement, discussed in Chapter 16) to use that park for recreation or a garden. One of the owners built a tennis court on the park and put a fence around it. However, the other owners were invited to use the tennis court as part of their right to use the park for recreation. The fence did not amount to control over the tennis court because it was used not to keep people out, but to keep tennis balls in.

The occupation of land is just one way to control it. A vacation house can be controlled even though it sits empty for most of the year. Bare vacation lots or farmers' fields can be controlled although they are used only infrequently. In such cases, fences are normally used to control the space, but perhaps a "private property" or "keep out" sign will do. The essential question is whether someone has taken sufficient steps to use or otherwise limit access to the land in question. In *Red House Farms (Thorndon) Ltd v Catchpole* [1977] 244 *Estates Gazette* 295, a person regularly used a small parcel of marsh land for shooting. This was sufficient control of the land because shooting was the only profitable use for it.

Larger chattels, such as cars, boats, and aeroplanes, are controlled in much the same way as land. This is because people use them in a similar way: by going inside them. Therefore, control is achieved by steps taken to keep people out or limit their access. Normally, this is done with keys and locks. A person with a key to a locked car has control over that car (provided no one else has a key). It is not necessary to lock a vehicle to control it (although this reduces the risk of losing control to another).

Small things are controlled somewhat differently. Less use is made of locks and keys (although many items, such diaries, desks, filing cabinets, and bicycles, are routinely locked). Instead, they are often controlled manually. People take control of pieces of fruit or books by picking them up. Coins and keys are kept in pockets and purses. Clothes are worn. This is not the only way to control smaller things. Although homeless people are often required to maintain close manual control over their possessions, most of us would be unable to keep all of our things with us at all times. Instead, we put them inside other things we control, such as a house, garage, shed, or car.

Controlling a space allows people to control the smaller things within that space. Generally speaking, things located in a private home are controlled by the people in possession of that home. This is because they can control access to those things. Of course, there are exceptions. There may be insects in the house which are not controlled by the human occupants. Also, visitors to the home will have things with them which are not controlled by their hosts. When two or more people live together in a home, it can be difficult to know who has possession of things in that home. This is discussed further at page 242.

There are places to which the public enjoys relatively free access, such as public roads and parks, shops, cafes, and airports. This raises the question whether the people who possess those places control the things found there. As a general rule, things attached to the land are controlled by the possessor of the land. In *Waverley Borough Council v Fletcher* [1995] 4 All ER 756 (CA), the defendant used a metal detector to find a medieval gold brooch nine inches beneath the surface of the plaintiff's public park. The plaintiff controlled the brooch because public access to the park did not include the right to dig in the soil.

Generally speaking, things found on (but not attached to) land to which the public enjoys access are not controlled by the possessor of that land. In *Bridges v Hawkesworth* (1851) 21 LJQB 75, the owner of a shop did not control a bundle of bank notes that had been dropped by an unknown person in the part of the shop to which the customers had access. In *Parker v British Airways Board* [1982] 1 QB 1004, the defendant did not have control over a gold bracelet found lying on the floor of its international executive lounge at Heathrow Airport. Access to the lounge was restricted to passengers who had cleared customs and held first class tickets or were members of the defendant's passenger club. However, that level of public access meant that the defendant did not have control over everything in that space.

The method of controlling a thing can be affected by the location of that thing. For example, a ship at a dock will be controlled differently than one wrecked at the bottom of the ocean. *Tubantia* [1924] P 78, concerned a steamship which sank in 1916 to a depth of 20 fathoms (37 metres). In 1922, the plaintiffs (who were not acting on behalf of the ship's owner) began salvage operations. Over 15 months, they spent 25 days trying to recover the ship's cargo. They had moored buoys to the ship and cut a hole in its side, but their divers could spend only eight minutes each day inside the ship.

Although the plaintiffs could not control access to the wreck and had spent little time there, they had sufficient control to give them legal possession. That level of control was measured against what was possible in 1924. Changes in technology might bring about changes in the control required. Would eight minutes in the ship two or three times a month be sufficient if another salvor could be there eight hours every day? The court was concerned about the peaceful, orderly exploitation of resources and the safety of the salvors. The declaration that the plaintiffs had possession of the ship prevented a dangerous free for all. However, deciding that people have control of a thing, when in fact they have very little, can lead to the sterilisation of resources. Should the first people to find a wreck acquire the legal right to exclude others from that wreck if they do not have the ability to bring any part of it to the surface? How much control should be needed before that right is acquired?

Some things have a tendency to escape, such as animals, fluids, or logs floating on a river. To control such things, a person must able to keep them from escaping. In *Young v Hichens* (1844) 6 QB 606, the plaintiff was in the process of enclosing some fish in a net. There were still 7 fathoms (13 metres) separating the ends of his net when the defendant rowed his boat through the opening and netted fish inside the plaintiff's net. Lord Denham CJ said (at 611), "It does appear almost certain that the plaintiff would have had possession of the fish but for the act of the defendant: but it is quite certain that he had not possession."

This can be compared to *Ohio v Shaw* (1902) 65 NE 875, where three men were charged with stealing fish. The defendants had removed the fish from unattended nets in Lake Eerie. The nets had a funnel-like entrance through which fish would swim. There was nothing preventing them from swimming out again (if they could find the entrance) and, in stormy weather, some fish would escape over the top of the nets. The trial judge decided that the defendants were not guilty of theft because no one had control of the fish in the nets and, therefore, they did not belong to anybody when they were taken. This was reversed on appeal. The owners of the nets had control and possession of the fish in the nets, but would lose control and all rights to fish which managed to escape into the lake.

There are some domestic animals, such as cats, homing pigeons, and honey bees, which are permitted to wander because they have a tendency to return home on their own. Although there are many times when a wandering domestic animal is beyond the control of its owner, the animal's homing instinct provides the owner with sufficient control for possession.

Once someone has obtained enough control of a thing to be in possession of it, that control can be relaxed without losing possession. For example, you can go to work or on vacation and still have possession of your home. You can go for coffee and leave your books and coat unattended in the library without losing possession of those things. Possession will be lost if you lose something or throw it away or if someone else takes possession of it.

Intention to Possess

Control is one component of possession. An intention to possess (sometimes called **animus possidendi**) is the other. All that is required is an intention to possess something for the time being. There is no need to intend to own it or possess it permanently: *Buckinghamshire County Council v Moran* [1990] Ch 623. In most cases, this requirement does not create a problem. The acts of control reveal an intention to possess. When we see a person pick up a carton of milk at the milk bar or lock up a bicycle, we do not doubt that he or she intends to possess that thing.

The intention to possess a thing is a fact. Normally, it is proved by the acts of control and surrounding circumstances. This is because a state of mind is difficult to prove. People can testify about what they intended at a relevant time, but if proof of that intention provides them with an advantage, their evidence is self serving and treated with caution. The court looks for other evidence to support that testimony. Since the intention to possess a thing is often proved by the acts of control in relation to that thing, it is easy to confuse the two components of possession.

It is possible to intend to possess something without knowing that it exists. For example, if you intend to possess a suitcase, then you intend to possess its contents, even though you do not know what it contains. The same is true of a house or flat. In *Flack v National Crime Authority* (1998) 156 ALR 501, a bag containing $433,000 in cash was seized lawfully by police from the plaintiff's home. She had never seen the bag before and did not know it was there. Its true owner was never discovered, but the police suspected that the plaintiff's son had used his key to the home to hide the bag there. The plaintiff's intention to possess her home meant that she intended to possess the things inside it, including the bag and money.

It is important to distinguish between the intention sufficient to obtain possession of a thing and the intention required to commit the crime of possessing something illegally, such as banned drugs, firearms, or stolen goods. There is nothing inconsistent with the law of property deciding that persons have possession of stolen goods placed in their garage without their knowledge and the criminal law deciding that they are not guilty of the crime of possessing of those goods. The intention to exclude others from the garage and its contents does not necessarily amount to the guilty mind of intending to possess stolen goods.

When people possess places to which the public has access, it may be difficult to know whether they intend to possess everything within those places. In *Parker v British Airways Board*, discussed above, the board did not intend to control the gold bracelet lost by a passenger in its executive lounge. However, we can assume that the board intended to possess the furniture and decorations in the lounge. If the board intended to possess only some of the things in the lounge, what sets them apart?

Clearly, the board would not want passengers to remove items placed in the lounge by the board. However, no effort was made to prevent passengers from removing other items. If the board had posted signs requesting passengers to surrender found items to the board or it had regularly checked the lounge for lost items, the result might have been different. Many people invite the public to places they possess and make it clear that they do not want possession of the things brought there by the public. For example, it is not uncommon to see a sign above the coat rack in a restaurant or cafe which disclaims responsibility for items left there.

Importance of Possession

Possession is significant in several ways. First and foremost, it is itself a property right. In other words, having possession of a thing corresponds to the general duty of other members of society not to interfere with that possession.

Secondly, possession of a thing can generate a separate right to possession. For example, when you borrow a library book, you obtain possession of that book. If you accidentally leave that book behind in a cafe and the waiter picks it up, you have lost possession. Discovering your loss, you return to the cafe to recover the book. The waiter has possession of the book, but you have a better right to possession, based on your earlier possession of the book. Competing rights to possession are discussed further in the next chapter.

Thirdly, possession provides evidence of ownership. How does anyone know, for example, whether you own the shoes you are wearing? It is unlikely that you could produce a receipt or that the shopkeeper would remember selling them to you. Absent evidence to the contrary, your possession of your shoes is sufficient proof that they belong to you. Daily commerce depends on this. When you purchased the shoes, did you ask for documentary evidence of the shopkeeper's ownership of them? Her or his possession of the shoes was sufficient.

Fourthly, as discussed in Chapter 8, possession of a thing for long enough can become ownership. The passage of time can bring to an end the owner's right to recover possession of a thing. By default, the person with possession becomes the owner since there is no one else with a better property right.

Ownership, Title, and Possession

It is helpful to distinguish possession from two other property concepts: ownership and title. **Ownership** is a concept which is familiar and generally understood. Even though we might find it difficult to define ownership, most of us would have no trouble making a list of 10 things we own and 10 things we do not own. The discussion so far has relied on that general knowledge and will continue to do so until Chapter 10, when the meaning of ownership is discussed in greater detail. Even without that detailed knowledge, we recognise the difference between ownership and possession. There are many situations in which you obtain possession of a thing, but not ownership, such as when you borrow a pen or library book or rent a car or flat.

Ownership of a thing usually includes the right to possess it. However, it is possible to own intangible things which cannot be possessed, such as copyrights and patents. Also, owners of tangible things can transfer their rights to possession to others. For example, the owners of a house can rent it to a tenant, thereby temporarily giving up their rights to possess that house.

Many students of property law are surprised to discover that the common law does not match the popular understanding of the difference between ownership and possession. The law developed clear ideas of possession and the right to possession, along with remedies to protect those rights. It did not do so with respect to ownership. This comes to the surface occasionally. For example, people often refer to the goods they own as their possessions. As discussed in the next chapter, this is a fairly accurate reflection of their legal rights to those goods.

Title is a less familiar concept. Lawyers often speak of having title to a thing. However, the word is used to describe several different concepts. First, it is sometimes used a synonym for ownership. People might say they have title to a car or parcel of land to indicate that they own that thing.

Secondly, title sometimes refers to the documentary evidence of ownership, such as the bill of sale for a car or the deed to a house. Title documents are used for the more valuable things in society, such as land, vehicles, expensive horses, and rare musical instruments. We are happy to rely on our possession as evidence of ownership of common household items, but need greater assurance when investing more money in a thing. Sometimes, title refers to a series of documents which provide evidence of ownership. The documents enable the current owner to prove her or his property right by tracing it back to someone who held it an earlier time.

Thirdly, there is registered title. Much of the land in Australia is registered under a statutory system commonly called the **Torrens system** (after Sir Robert Torrens, the politician responsible for introducing the system to South Australia). As discussed in Chapters 21 and 32, registered title under a Torrens system is more than mere evidence of ownership. The registered title is the source of property right.

Fourthly, the word title is used to denote **native title** or aboriginal title. This does not refer to documentary evidence or registration of the property right, but to the right itself. That right may be equivalent to ownership, but it can be something less, such as the rights to hunt and fish. Native title is discussed in Chapter 19.

Finally, lawyers sometimes speak of **possessory title**. By this they mean a right to possession of a thing acquired by taking possession of that thing. This is contrasted with the usual way of acquiring title to things, by purchase or gift from the previous owner.

Obtaining Possession

As discussed above, possession requires both control and intention. It is obtained from the first moment that both those conditions exist simultaneously. Usually, intention precedes control, so that possession is acquired by some act of taking control. For example, you may see a coin on the pavement, form an intention to possess it, and then reach down and pick it up. It is conceivable that a person might obtain control of a thing before forming the intention to possess it. Using an earlier example, if someone unknowingly sat on and therefore had control of a $10 note on the seat of a train, he or she could obtain possession by becoming aware of the note and forming the intention to possess it. However, as discussed above, people can intend to possess things left, without their knowledge, in spaces they control. Therefore, it less likely that someone will obtain control of a thing before forming the intention to possess it.

Normally, possession of a thing is obtained with the consent of someone who previously possessed it. However, it can be obtained without such consent. These two situations are discussed separately.

Possession Acquired by Consent

Most of the things you possess were obtained with the consent of someone else who possessed it. They may have been purchased, received as gifts, leased, or borrowed. The transfer of possession of goods from one person to another is called **delivery**. For land, it is common to speak of granting or giving possession.

The transfer of possession may be permanent or temporary. For example, when you purchase a book, you buy the right to possess the book for as long as you choose. The bookshop parts with its right to the book forever. In contrast, when you borrow a book from the library, you acquire possession for a limited time only. At some point, the loan comes to an end and the library has the right to have the book returned.

A temporary transfer of possession is called a **bailment**. As Norman Palmer wrote, in *Bailment* (2nd ed, 1991) pp 1-2:

> "The essence of bailment is possession. The word derives from the French verb bailler, meaning 'to deliver'. The doctrine is confined to personal property and denotes a separation of the actual possession of goods from some ultimate or reversionary possessory right."

The person with actual possession is the **bailee** and the person with the right to possession in the future is the **bailor**.

Bailment is often regarded as the separation of ownership and possession. The library continues to own the book while you possess it and will have the right to possess it again when your right comes to an end. However, Palmer's definition of bailment does not mention ownership. Instead, he writes of a separation of possession and an "ultimate or reversionary possessory right." This is because it is possible to have a bailment between persons who are not owners of the thing bailed. For example, you might borrow a book from the library and let a friend use that book for an hour. You have temporarily transferred your possession to your friend and will soon have the right to possess it again, even though you do not own the book. In this example, the library loan to you is a bailment and your loan to your friend is a **sub-bailment**. The library is the bailor, your friend is the sub-bailee, and you wear two hats: bailee and sub-bailor.

Bailment without ownership does not always involve a sub-bailment. For example, you might find some jewellery and deliver it to the police in hopes of locating the true owner. Your delivery of possession to the police is a bailment, even though you do not own the jewellery. You have a right to recover possession if the true owner cannot be found.

Of course, the true owner of the jewellery might be found and you might never recover possession. The possibility that your loss of possession will be permanent does not prevent a bailment from arising. You still have a right to possession of the jewellery in the future if the owner cannot be found. This conditional right is a sufficient foundation for a bailment. This is because you did not transfer your entire right to possession to the police. They have possession, but subject to your right to have the jewellery returned if the true owner cannot be located.

Bailment differs from a sale or gift because the bailor retains some right to possession, but the seller or donor does not. This is true even if the bailor does not expect to ever recover possession. There is a common transaction, called a **conditional sale** or **hire-purchase**, in which the seller lets the buyer have possession of the thing before it is paid for. The buyer pays the purchase price in instalments and, when it is fully paid, ownership of the thing will be transferred from seller to buyer. If all goes well, the seller will never have possession of the thing again. This is still a bailment because the seller retains a right to possession of the thing in the event that the buyer fails to make the payments on time.

Automobiles are often sold under conditional sale or hire-purchase agreements. A similar method is a **chattel lease** coupled with an **option to purchase**. During the term of the lease, the **lessee** is a bailee with a right to possess the car (so long as the payments are made and the other terms of the lease are observed). At the end of the lease, the lessee has a right to buy the car. The **lessor** is a bailor who has the right to recover possession of the car only if the lessee breaches the terms of the lease or chooses not to exercise the option to purchase the car at the end.

Regardless of differences in terminology or form, these relationships are essentially the same. The conditional seller, hirer, or lessor is a bailor during the term of the contract. The bailment will most likely come to an end in one of two ways. Either the bailor will recover possession of the thing or ownership of the thing will pass to the bailee. There is also a possibility that the bailment will end because the thing is destroyed or is stolen by persons unknown, but that is another story.

Possession Acquired Without Consent

It is possible to obtain possession of a thing without anyone else's consent. This can happen in several different ways. First, you might take possession of something which has never been possessed before. This can occur when you catch a wild animal or pick up a sea shell washed up on a public beach. It can also happen when you create a new thing, such as a loaf of bread or a painting: see Chapter 26. Secondly, you might find something which someone else lost. Although the owner might not object to your possession, he or she is not aware of your possession and, therefore, has not consented to it. Thirdly, you might take something from another person without her or his consent. This happens when a person takes the wrong jacket home from a party, a thief steals, or squatters take over an empty house.

As discussed in the next chapter, possession acquired without consent is a property right which the law protects. It gives rise to a right to possession which is enforceable against everyone except those people with a better right to possession.

Chapter Seven

COMPETING CLAIMS TO POSSESSION

■■■

The nature and acquisition of possession were the subjects of the previous chapter. This chapter concerns the ways in which the law protects possession and deals with competing claims to possession.

Breach of Duty

Possession and the right to possession are property rights. As discussed in Chapter 2, this means that other members of society are under a general duty not to interfere with those rights. A breach of that duty is a legal wrong, called a **tort**: see Trindade & Cane, *The Law of Torts in Australia* (3rd ed, 1999). The most common torts of wrongly interfering with possession or a right to possession are **trespass, conversion,** and **detinue**.

Trespass

Trespass is the wrongful interference with other persons or with their possession of goods or land. To constitute trespass, the interference must be unauthorised, direct, and done voluntarily.

Trespass to goods or land is not committed unless there is a direct connection between the trespasser's actions and some physical interference with another's possession. For example, I would be guilty of trespass if, without your consent, I touched your goods, pushed you and caused you to drop an object, walked on your land, or threw something onto your land. Indirect interference is not trespass (although it may be some other type of wrong). For example, if you left your things in a library while you went for coffee and the library doors were locked when you returned, this would interfere with your possession of those things, but would not be sufficiently direct to be trespass.

Only a voluntary act can be trespass. So, for example, accidentally tripping and knocking over a vase would not be trespass. However, the tort does not require that the trespasser intended to commit a wrong. Taking the wrong coat home from a party is a voluntary act and a trespass, even though it was an honest mistake. So too is wandering by mistake onto the land of another while out bushwalking.

Conversion

Unlike trespass, the tort of conversion applies only to goods and not to land. It is the unauthorised interference with another's possession or right to possession of goods. Like trespass, a voluntary act causing such interference is conversion, even if the converter did not intend to do wrong. However, unlike trespass, indirect interference will suffice.

Conversion (which used to be called **trover**) is some dealing with goods which is repugnant to someone else's right to possess them. Using those goods for your own benefit or purporting to sell, give, or lend them to another would be conversion. These acts involve an intention to exercise dominion over the goods. Temporarily handling or detaining goods without that intention would not suffice. For example, it is not conversion to find a lost item and take possession of it with the intention of locating its owner.

A temporary interference with the right to possess a chattel can be conversion if that interference amounts to a repudiation of that right. In *Aitken Agencies Ltd v Richardson* [1967] NZLR 65, the defendant took the plaintiff's van for a joy ride and damaged it. He was guilty of conversion because, as McGregor J said (at 67), he "intended to exercise a temporary dominion over the van. He assumed possession of it for his own purpose, and such act was inconsistent with the rights of the owner." This can be compared with *Schemmell v Pomeroy* (1989) 50 SASR 450, in which a 14-year-old boy took his mother's car for a joy ride while she was at work. He intended to put the car back safely before she got home, but wrecked it in an accident. His intention to return the car meant that he was guilty of trespass, but not conversion (at least not before the accident).

Unlike trespass, which is interference with someone's possession of a thing, it is conversion to interfere with a right to possession. In other words, a person who does not possess, but has the right to possess goods, can sue for conversion of those goods. In *Motor Dealers Credit Corp Ltd v Overland (Sydney) Ltd* (1931) 31 SR (NSW) 516, the plaintiff had a right to possession of a car, which had been improperly seized by a car dealer. The dealer sold it to the defendant, who resold it without ever taking possession of the car. Even though neither the plaintiff nor the defendant had possession of the car at the relevant time, the defendant was guilty of conversion. As Street CJ said (at 519), "there may be a conversion of goods even though the defendant has never been in physical possession of them, if his act amounts to an absolute denial and repudiation of the plaintiff's right".

To sue for conversion, the plaintiff must have a right to immediate possession of the goods. A right to possession at some time in the future would not suffice. For example, if you borrowed a book from the library for four weeks and that book was taken from you the next day, you would be able to sue for conversion, but the library would not. The library's right to possession arises in 27 days and it could not sue for conversion until that time passed. This short wait is not much of a problem. However, what if you leased a car to someone for three years and it was stolen the next day? Having to wait three years before commencing action against the thief could cause considerable difficulty. This is why many leases of this kind contain a clause which gives the owner a right to immediate possession of the car if it is destroyed or stolen.

Detinue

Detinue, like conversion, is a tort which involves goods and not land. It is the wrongful detention of goods from a person with a right to immediate possession: see *Russell v Wilson* (1923) 33 CLR 538. A person who commits the tort of detinue will know of the plaintiff's claim to possession, since the essence of the tort is the failure to deliver the goods on demand. This sets it apart from trespass and conversion, which can be committed by people who have no idea that their actions are interfering with another's property rights. However, it is no defence to a claim of detinue that the defendant honestly believed that the plaintiff was not entitled to possession.

Overlap

The torts of trespass, conversion, and detinue are used to protect possession and the right to possession of goods. This similarity means that there are potential overlaps among them. All three torts might be committed by the same person in respect to the same goods. For example, if I took your lawn mower from your yard without your consent and then refused to return it, I would be guilty of trespass, conversion, and detinue, since I directly interfered with your possession of the mower, repudiated your right to possession, and failed to comply with your lawful demand for its return.

Despite the similarities, each tort is directed at a different type of wrong. The essence of trespass is the direct interference with actual possession. Brief interference, such as minor damage to goods, is trespass even though the plaintiff's possession otherwise remains intact. In contrast, the essence of conversion is the complete repudiation of the plaintiff's right to possession as a result of the defendant's use of, dealing with, or destruction of the goods: see *Penfold Wines Pty Ltd v Elliott* (1946) 74 CLR 204 at 229.

The essence of detinue is the failure to return the plaintiff's goods on demand. Although the defendant may have obtained possession wrongly, through trespass or conversion, this is not an element of the tort. Detinue is committed also by those who obtain possession of goods properly but refuse to return them when their rights to possession come to an end.

Other Wrongs

Trespass, conversion, and detinue are the main types of wrongful interference with possession or a right to possession. Four others are discussed here: permanent damage to goods, overholding by tenants, nuisance, and crime.

A person with a right to possession of goods in the future cannot sue for trespass, conversion, or detinue. Possession or a right to immediate possession is required. However, he or she can sue someone who causes permanent damage to the goods: *Dee Trading Co Pty Ltd v Baldwin* [1938] VLR 173. Normally, damage which can be repaired is insufficient, since it might be repaired before the time for possession arrives. However, if the goods have not been repaired when the owner or bailor does recover possession, he or she can sue for the "permanent" damage even though the damage can be repaired: see *Dee Trading*, above. There are so few cases involving this wrong that it does not have a name, but was called a "special action" by Dixon J in *Penfold Wines Pty Ltd v Elliott* (1946) 74 CLR 204 at 230. A person with a right to future possession of land has a right to sue for permanent damage to the land (called **waste** and discussed at page 102.

There are many cases in which someone obtained possession of land with permission of the owner, but refused to leave when that right came to an end. As discussed at page 95, that person is called an **overholding tenant**. This is not trespass to land, since the owner was not in possession of the land when the wrong was committed. However, it is wrongful interference with the owner's right to possession, similar to detinue. There is no specific tort of refusing to give up possession of land properly acquired. It is known simply as **adverse possession**, discussed in the next chapter.

Nuisance is the wrongful interference with someone's possession of land through actions which interfere with her or his use and enjoyment of that land. Those actions may cause physical damage to the land, such as a diversion of water which causes flooding or golf balls which break windows: see *Lester-Travers v City of Frankston* [1970] VR 2. However, physical interference is not necessary. Odour or noise can also be a nuisance: see *Oldham v Lawson* [1976] VR 654. Whether an activity constitutes a nuisance depends on the normal way in which land in that area is used. Noises and smells which are acceptable in an industrial section may be nuisances in a quiet residential suburb. Noise which is acceptable during the day, may be a nuisance if made in the middle of the night. Normally, nuisances are recurring or ongoing activities. People are expected to tolerate temporary annoyances, such as a renovation to a neighbour's house. However, in *Munro v Southern Dairies Ltd* [1955] VLR 332 at 335, Sholl J said "that the loss of even one night's sleep may amount to such a substantial interference with personal comfort as to constitute a nuisance."

The wrongful interference with possession or a right to possession may be a **crime** as well as a tort. For example, conversion of goods could also be theft and trespass to land might be breaking and entering, depending on the circumstances. The main difference between crime and tort is the intention of the actor. Crime requires both a criminal act (*actus reus*) and a criminal intention (*mens rea*), whereas a tort can be committed by someone who intends to act honestly. A secondary difference is the standard of proof required. Crime must be proved beyond a reasonable doubt, while torts need only be proved on the balance of probabilities. Therefore, someone acquitted of theft might be found liable for converting the goods alleged to have been stolen.

Responses to Breach of Duty

When someone wrongly interferes with another's possession or right to possession of a thing, the law will intervene to protect that right. There are a variety of possible legal responses, which can be organised into four main categories: direct enforcement of the right, compensation, restitution, and punishment. The particular response depends upon the nature of the wrongful interference and the consequences of that wrong.

Direct Enforcement

It is often assumed that the normal way to protect a plaintiff's right to possession is to enforce that right and restore possession to the plaintiff. This is generally true of land, but not of goods. As discussed below, the most common method of protecting a right to possession of goods is through compensation, not enforcement.

When a defendant refuses to give up possession of land to a plaintiff with a right to immediate possession, the plaintiff can obtain a court order for possession of the land. The action is called **ejectment** or simply an action to recover land. There are other cases in which the plaintiff has possession of the land and wishes to stop the defendant from trespassing on it. For example, in *Bendal Pty Ltd v Mirvac Project Pty Ltd* (1991) 23 NSWLR 464, the defendant erected scaffolding which protruded over the plaintiff's land. In such cases, the court might grant an **injunction** ordering the defendant to stop the continuing trespass.

The normal remedy for trespass to or conversion of goods is compensation (discussed below). It is possible to get an injunction to stop the trespass or conversion in cases where the wrongs are likely to continue and compensation is not a practical solution. For example, in *Model Dairy Pty Ltd v White* (1935) 41 Argus LR 432, the plaintiff and defendant ran competing dairies near Melbourne. The defendant made a practice of delivering milk to his customers using the plaintiff's milk bottles. It was impractical for the plaintiff to sue for a small amount of compensation each time the defendant converted the plaintiff's bottles in this manner, so the court granted an injunction to prevent further conversions.

Where a defendant commits detinue, the plaintiff can sometimes obtain an order for specific recovery of the goods. It used to be that the defendant had the option to return the goods or pay the plaintiff for their value. However, all states and territories now have statutes which allow the court to take away that option and order the defendant to return the goods being wrongly detained (see *Gollan v Nugent* (1988) 166 CLR 18 at 25-26). The court will do so in cases where the plaintiff would have difficulty replacing the goods. For example, in *Doulton Potteries Ltd v Bronotte* [1971] 1 NSWLR 591, the plaintiff was entitled to recover a machine part that it needed for its manufacturing business and that would have taken four months to replace.

People are also entitled to take reasonable steps to enforce their rights to possession without the assistance of the courts. A person with a right to immediate possession can simply take possession, if that can be done peacefully and without breaking the law. This is called **reaption** or **self help**.

Compensation

The most common method of protecting possession of goods is through compensation. It is also available to protect possession of land. A person who wrongly interferes with the property rights of another is liable to compensate her or him for any losses caused by that interference. As

Taylor and Owen JJ said of a claim for conversion in *Butler v Egg and Egg Pulp Marketing Board* (1966) 114 CLR 185 at 191:

> "the general principle upon which compensatory damages are assessed... is that the injured party should receive compensation in a sum which, so far as money can do so, will put him in the same position as he would have been in if... the tort had not been committed."

Depending on the nature of the interference, the award of damages might cover the cost of repair or replacement or it might make up for the loss of use of the thing.

The normal measure of compensation for conversion or detinue is the full market value of the thing converted. This allows the plaintiff to purchase a replacement for the thing lost as a result of the defendant's wrong. In some cases, the award of damages is reduced to avoid overcompensating the plaintiff. In *Aitken Agencies Ltd v Richardson* [1967] NZLR 65, the joyriding case discussed above, McGregor J said (at 67), "where goods have been restored to the owner after conversion, the owner must give credit for their value at the time when he received them". The plaintiff had recovered the van which the defendant had converted and damaged. Therefore, the plaintiff was entitled not to the full value of the van, but to the cost of repairing it and hiring a replacement while it was out of service.

Normally, the damages awarded for conversion or detinue are not reduced where the plaintiff has only a limited right to possession of the goods. For example, a bailee of goods can sue for the full value of the goods converted, even if the bailment is due to end in a short time. This can be difficult to reconcile with the general principle that compensatory damages are measured by the loss caused to the plaintiff. The market value of a right to possess goods for a finite period can be calculated and may well be less than the market value of the goods themselves. Why are damages for conversion and detinue not reduced to account for this difference?

There are several possible explanations, but none is entirely satisfactory. First, in many cases, the person with a right to future possession (the bailor) cannot sue for the wrongful interference. Therefore, if wrongdoers were liable only for the value of the bailee's limited right to the goods, and not the value of the goods themselves, they might avoid full responsibility for the consequences of their actions. However, the bailee can recover the full value of the goods even in cases where the interference causes permanent damage to the goods for which the bailor could sue.

Secondly, bailees might be liable to their bailors for damage to the goods or for their inability to return them when required. Therefore, bailees might be under-compensated if they could recover from wrongdoers only the value of their rights to the goods and not the value of the goods themselves. However, bailees can sue for the full value of the goods even when it is proven that they have no liability to their bailors for the damage to or loss of the goods.

Thirdly, persons who commit a tort are wrongdoers and not permitted to use the victim's dealings with others to be relieved of the consequences of their wrongful acts. In other words, the law does not allow the wrongdoer to raise the right of a third person (called **the jus tertii**, discussed below) as a defence. This has the advantage of limiting the complexity of legal actions for wrongful interference with possession or the right to possession. Otherwise, the court might be required to consider all potential rights to possession in what would otherwise be a simple case of damage to or destruction of goods. However, the rule can be harsh, especially in cases where well meaning, honest people unwittingly commit trespass or conversion. Should they be required to do more than compensate their victims for actual losses suffered? There are other legal responses available in cases where someone intentionally commits a tort or profits thereby (see restitution and punishment, below).

These issues were considered in *Winkfield* [1902] P 42. The defendants were at fault in a collision at sea which caused the loss of mail being carried on a ship that sank. The Postmaster-General, as bailee of the mail, was entitled to compensation for the full value of the letters and packages lost, even though he was under no liability to their owners. The English Court of Appeal relied on the third justification above for the bailee's right to sue for the full value of the goods. Collins MR said (at 55), "it is not open to the defendant, being a wrongdoer, to inquire into the nature or limitation of the possessor's right, and unless it is competent for him to do so the question of his relation to, or liability towards, the true owner cannot come into the discussion at all; and, therefore, as between those two parties full damages have to be paid without any further inquiry."

Restitution

The term restitution is sometimes used as a synonym for compensation. It is also used to refer to the direct enforcement of a right to possession. An order for the recovery of goods following a successful claim for detinue is often called **specific restitution**. These are not unnatural uses of the term. However, restitution has acquired a specialised legal meaning in recent years. It refers to those legal responses which require a person to give up some benefit received or its value in money: see Birks, *An Introduction to the Law of Restitution* (1985) p 13. In contrast to compensation, which is measured by the loss to the plaintiff, restitution is measured by the gain to the defendant.

When a defendant has wrongly interfered with a plaintiff's possession or right to possession, the plaintiff might seek restitution instead of compensation. He or she will want to do this when the gain the defendant received through that interference exceeds the loss caused to the plaintiff. This happened in *Yakamia Dairy Pty Ltd v Wood* [1976] WAR 57. The defendant intentionally and wrongly used the plaintiff's land to depasture cattle for more than four years. The plaintiff could not prove that this had caused any damage to its land. However, the plaintiff was, as Jackson CJ said (at 58), "entitled to recover damages based upon the agistment fees which would have been payable had there been an agreement to allow the cattle to pasture on the land." In other words, the damages were measured by the benefit to the defendant (who saved the normal expenses of depasturing cattle) rather than the loss to the plaintiff.

Restitution is not punishment (discussed below). By taking away the benefit of committing the tort, it leaves the defendant in a position no worse than if he or she had acted lawfully. However, in some cases, it can leave the plaintiff in a better financial position because of the defendant's wrong. For example, there was no proof that the plaintiff in the *Yakamia Dairy* case (above) would otherwise have been able to earn the fees which the defendant was required to pay. An important function of restitution is to deter people from doing wrong by taking away the benefits of wrongdoing.

Punishment

Punishment is the most common response to crime, but is seldom used as a response to torts. Courts sometimes award **exemplary** or **punitive damages** for the tort of trespass or conversion when they are committed intentionally with a blatant disregard for the plaintiff's legal rights. This is an order that the defendant pay to the plaintiff a sum of money as a means of punishing the defendant. Unlike most damage awards, it is intended not as compensation, but as a general deterrent to that type of conduct.

In *XL Petroleum (NSW) Pty Ltd v Caltex Oil (Australia) Pty Ltd* (1985) 155 CLR 448, the plaintiff acquired possession of land that had been used by the defendant as a service station two years earlier. On the day the plaintiff took possession, the defendant (a business competitor) "spiked" the underground petrol tanks, rendering them useless. The plaintiff was entitled to compensation for the trespass in the sum of $5,528 for the cost of replacing the tanks and the lost profits while they were being replaced. The plaintiff was also entitled to exemplary damages of $150,000. Brennan J said (at 471), "an award of exemplary damages is intended to punish the defendant for conduct showing a conscious and contumelious disregard for the plaintiff's rights and to deter him from committing like conduct again".

Punishment protects property rights indirectly by deterring people from interfering with those rights. The punishment itself does not help the victim recover or replace stolen items. However, the involvement of law enforcement agencies may help. Police have the power to seize stolen goods and, when they are no longer needed as evidence, have a duty to return them to the persons entitled to possess them: *Gollan v Nugent* (1988) 166 CLR 18 at 22. A criminal court might order the return of stolen goods or order the criminal to compensate the victim. Also, a criminal conviction for a property related offence is good evidence of a wrongful interference with property rights, which the victim can use in a civil action against the criminal.

Rights to Possession

As discussed above, the law protects not just possession, but the right to possession. There are two questions explored in this section. First, how is the right to possession acquired? Secondly, how does the law deal with competing rights to possess the same thing?

Obtaining the Right to Possession

Like possession, the right to possession is normally acquired by consent, through a sale, gift, or loan from someone who previously held that right. However, the right to possession can also be acquired simply by taking possession of a thing. *Armory v Delamirie* (1722) 1 Str 506, 93 ER 664, provides an early example. A chimney sweeper's boy found a jewel and took it to a goldsmith to have it appraised. The goldsmith offered to buy the jewel for three halfpence. When the boy refused, the goldsmith removed the gems from the jewel and returned the empty socket. The goldsmith was guilty of trover (conversion) and liable to compensate the boy for the full value of the gems converted.

The boy voluntarily gave possession of the jewel to the goldsmith. Therefore, the goldsmith was guilty of wrongly interfering not with the boy's possession of the jewel (trespass), but with his right to possess it. The only possible source of this right was his previous possession. His right to possession was better than the goldsmith's actual possession because he had possession before the goldsmith. In other words, the boy's superior claim to the jewel was simply, "I had it first!" Moreover, the damages were not discounted for the possibility that the jewel's owner might have recovered it from the boy some day. This means that the boy's claim against the goldsmith, based solely on his prior possession, was every bit as good as if it had been based on a purchase or gift.

Why does someone who takes and then loses possession of a thing have a continuing right to possession? That right is needed for two reasons: it protects both possession and the right to possession. First, possession without a right to possession would be a relatively fragile property right. It would exist only so long as the possessor could maintain control of the thing. All rights to a thing would be lost the moment possession was released and it would become freely available to next person able to seize control. You would have to think carefully before answering the question, "Can I take your coat?"

Secondly, the protection of all rights to possession would suffer if possession of a thing did not generate a right to possession. As the law now stands, plaintiffs suing for the wrongful interference with their rights to possession can prove the existence of those rights merely by proving their prior possession. The onus then shifts to the defendants to prove that they have better rights to possession. If plaintiffs could not rely on their prior possession for this purpose, the burden of proof could be difficult, if not impossible. For example, a simple claim for conversion of a coat could become a complex affair as the plaintiff attempted to prove that he or she acquired the manufacturer's right to possess the coat through a series of transactions involving shippers, importers, distributers, wholesalers, and retailers. The law avoids these problems with a simple rule that a person with possession of a thing also has a right to possession which is enforceable against everyone who cannot show a better right to possession.

Relativity of Property Rights

When a court deals with a claim for wrongful interference with possession or a right to possession, it must decide which of the parties before the court has the better right. It does not decide whether any of them has the best possible right to possession. Therefore, it is not a defence to a claim to show that some third person (not before the court) has a better right to possession than the plaintiff. Unless evidence of the third person's right (sometimes called a **jus tertii**) somehow establishes that the defendant has a better right to possession than the plaintiff, it is simply not relevant: *Oxford Meat Co Pty Ltd v McDonald* (1963) 63 SR (NSW) 423 at 427. Proof of a third person's right to possession will help the defendant if he or she acquired that right (for example, as bailee of the third person) or if it shows that the plaintiff has no right to possession at all (for example, because he or she sold that right to the third person). However, mere proof that the plaintiff does not have the best right is irrelevant. The defendant's interference with the plaintiff's better right to possession is still wrong, even if the plaintiff is liable to a third person with an even better right.

In *Wilson v Lombank Ltd* [1963] 1 All ER 740, the plaintiff purchased a car and took it to a garage for repairs. The defendant had also purchased the car and, seeing it at the garage, took it away. In fact, neither party owned the car, which belonged to a company not involved in these purported sales. The defendant returned the car to its owner, but was still liable to the plaintiff for wrongly interfering with his right to possession. The fact that the plaintiff was not the owner (and was also guilty of conversion) was not relevant since the plaintiff had possession before the defendant and therefore had a better right to possession.

This case illustrates a problem with the general rule that the rights of third persons should be ignored. Although the defendant had acted honestly throughout, it had been required to pay twice for a car it did not have: first, the purchase price to the person who pretended to sell it and, secondly, the damages for conversion to the plaintiff. In contrast, the plaintiff was helped by the defendant's tort, since the plaintiff was able to recover the price he had paid for the car and the cost of repairs from the defendant. Although the defendant would have a claim against the seller for damages for breach of contract, that person may have absconded or have insufficient assets to pay for the damages caused. In many property cases, two innocent persons have suffered from the actions of an absent rogue and the court must decide which of them should bear the loss.

Generally speaking, when two rights to possession are in competition, the earlier right is the better right. In *Asher v Whitlock* (1865) LR 1 QB 1, a man named Williamson took possession of land without the permission of its owner. He died and, in his will, left the land to his widow until she died or remarried and then to their daughter. The widow married the defendant, Whitlock, and then both she and the daughter died, leaving him in possession of the land. The plaintiff, Asher, was the daughter's heir and therefore able to obtain possession of the land from Whitlock through an action of ejectment. Asher had a better right to possession than Whitlock, not because she was the owner, but because she had inherited Williamson's right to possession, which had passed first to his widow, then to his daughter (when the widow remarried), and then to her (when the daughter died). That right first arose when Williamson took possession of the land, long before Whitlock's possession, and therefore it had priority.

Asher v Whitlock demonstrates the relativity of property rights. Whitlock had possession of the land, which was a property right enforceable against other members of society except someone with a better right. There were two people with earlier and better rights to possession: the owner of the land and Asher. That the owner had a better right to possession than Asher was not relevant to the dispute between Asher and Whitlock. It would have been relevant if Whitlock had obtained his right to possession from the owner. In that case, Whitlock would be claiming the owner's right, which was earlier and better than the right acquired by Williamson and passed to Asher.

Lost and Found

When someone finds and takes possession of a lost chattel, he or she acquires a right to possession which is good against the world except someone with a better right. Normally, the only person with a better right is the chattel's owner (or someone who has acquired the right to possession from the owner). However, as *Flack v National Crime Authority* (1998) 156 ALR 501 demonstrated (in the previous chapter), the person who occupies the land where the chattel is found can have a better right to possess the chattel than the person who found it. This happens where the occupier's possession of the land gives her or him possession of everything on that land. In other words, the occupier had possession of the chattel before the finder and, therefore, has a better right to possession.

In *Parker v British Airways Board* [1982] 1 QB 1004 (discussed in the previous chapter), the plaintiff found a gold bracelet in the defendant's airport lounge and delivered it to the defendant for the purpose of locating the true owner. The delivery to the defendant was not a gift, but a bailment, in which the defendant had possession and the plaintiff had a right to possession if the true owner could not be located. The defendant tried to establish a better right to possession than the plaintiff by showing that it had possession before the plaintiff found the bracelet. This it could not do since it neither controlled nor intended to possess the things left in the lounge by members of the public.

The general rule, that the earlier right is the better right, is not applied in cases where the defendant acquired possession by doing wrong to the plaintiff. If the defendant found something while trespassing on the plaintiff's land, he or she would not be permitted to assert a better right to possession against the plaintiff. This is true even if the plaintiff routinely invited members of the public onto the land and, therefore, did not have possession before the defendant. The commission of a tort does not itself disqualify a person from claiming a right to possession. There are many cases, like *Asher v Whitlock* and *Wilson v Lombank Ltd*, above, where possession was acquired by committing a tort of trespass or conversion against a third person. However, subject to the limitation of actions (discussed in the next chapter), one person cannot obtain a better right to possession than another by committing a tort against that other.

Master and Servant

Another notable exception to the usual priority accorded to earlier rights to possession is created by the master-servant relationship. Where an employee takes possession of a thing on behalf of her or his employer, that possession is treated as the employer's possession: *Willey v Synan* (1937) 57 CLR 200. The employee may have **custody** of the thing, but the employer has possession. This recognises the reality that many persons employ others as their instruments for controlling the things they possess. Corporations have no choice but to do so. So, when an employee takes control of a thing with an intention to possess it (for example, a sales clerk receiving money), her or his employer gets possession.

In many cases, it would not matter whether the employer had possession of the things in her or his employee's control or only a right to immediate possession. Both property rights are protected from conversion. However, it does matter in cases of trespass, since this is interference with possession. If, for example, an employer's goods were damaged (but not converted) while in the control of her or his employee, it would be impractical to say that the employee could sue for the tort, but not the employer. As the law recognises, it is the employer's rights which are affected by the trespass. Also, in large business enterprises, where the employer's things are controlled by a large number of employees, it could well be difficult to determine which employee controlled the thing at the time of the trespass. The law avoids these problems by treating the employer as having possession.

It can be difficult to tell whether employees take possession on behalf of their employers or for themselves. In *Byrne v Hoare* [1965] Qd R 135, a policeman found a gold ingot while on special duty at a drive-in theatre. The possession was his, and not his employer's, since the finding was not sufficiently connected to his duties as an employee. Gibbs J said (at 149):

> "He was not conducting a search when he found it, and he had not been allowed access to a private place for the purpose of performing his duties, but was walking where any member of the public coming from the theatre might have walked. The fact that he was on duty when he happened to see the gold was merely coincidental."

Chapter Eight

LIMITATION OF ACTIONS

▮▮▮

This chapter shows how possession and the right to possession can become ownership through the passage of time. As discussed in the previous chapter, if you take possession of my land without my consent, I can sue you for trespass and recover my land. By taking possession, you acquire a right to possession, which is enforceable against everyone else in society except me. My ownership gives me an earlier and superior right to possession. However, I cannot wait forever to sue. Each state and territory has a statute (called the *Limitation Act* or *Limitation of Actions Act*) which allows me a certain amount of time in which to commence my action for trespass. If I wait too long, my right is lost. Once I am out of the picture, your right to possession becomes ownership, since it is enforceable against everyone.

Limitation Statutes

The limitation statute in each jurisdiction applies not just to property rights, but to a wide variety of claims, such as actions for breach of contract or personal injury. It is a general principle that claims should not remain outstanding for too long: see *Marquis of Cholmondeley v Lord Clinton* (1820) 2 Jac&W 1, 37 ER 527 at 577. Evidence becomes unreliable as witnesses die or their memories fade. At some point, people need to be able to get on with their lives free of the threat of litigation.

Limitation statutes do not operate by declaring that the possessor of a thing becomes its owner after a certain length of time. They accomplish that result indirectly by eliminating better rights to possession from the queue. Assume that the priority of rights to possession are:

1).....owner;
2).....possessor; and
3).....world.

The best possible right to possession is equivalent to ownership: see Chapter 10.

If the owner loses her or his right, the possessor moves to the head of the queue. A person with a right to commence a legal action has a limited amount of time in which to do so. The time available is called the **limitation period**. In New South Wales, Queensland, Tasmania, and Western Australia, the limitation period to recover possession of land is

12 years. In South Australia and Victoria, it is 15 years. The Crown has a longer time in which to sue for possession of land (and no time limit in some states), presumably because governments are unable to maintain as much control over their lands as do private citizens.

The limitation period for the torts of conversion, detinue, and trespass to goods is six years, except in the Northern Territory, where it is three years. If the limitation period expires before the owner recovers possession of goods lost through conversion or detinue, her or his right to possession is extinguished in most jurisdictions (Australian Capital Territory, New South Wales, Northern Territory, Queensland, Tasmania, and Victoria). This stops the owner from later suing other people who deal with the goods. For example, suppose that I borrowed your painting and refused to return it and that you had six years to sue me for conversion or detinue. If I sold the painting after four years, the purchaser would also be guilty of conversion. However, since your right to possession of that painting will expire six years after my tort, you would have only two years in which to sue the purchaser. If I sold the painting seven years after my tort, the purchaser would not be guilty of conversion because you would no longer have a right to possession.

The limitation period is measured from the date on which the cause of action accrues (which is the day that the right to sue first arises). If, on that day (or, in New South Wales and South Australia, at any time during the limitation period), the plaintiff is under a disability (meaning minority or mental incapacity), then the limitation period is extended. It is also extended in cases where the facts giving rise to the plaintiff's claim are fraudulently concealed by the defendant.

Adverse Possession

The right to sue to recover possession of land arises when someone obtains **adverse possession**, which means possession of land without permission of the person with the right to immediate possession.

Adverse possession is a violation of another's right to possession. In most legal actions, defendants attempt to prove that they have not violated the plaintiffs' rights. In contrast, defendants invoking a limitation statute seek to prove that they violated the plaintiffs' rights so long ago that the limitation period has expired. Defendants wanting to prove adverse possession will need to show both that they had possession of the plaintiffs' land and that this possession was adverse (without permission). These elements can be difficult to establish.

Possession

As discussed in Chapter 6, possession is a legal concept, requiring both control and an intention to possess. In *Buckinghamshire County Council v Moran* [1990] Ch 623, the plaintiff acquired land for future use as part of a road to be constructed. The land was fenced on three sides, with a gate to the existing road, but was open to the defendant's land on the fourth side. The defendant changed the lock on the gate and used the land for a garden for more than 12 years. This amounted to adverse possession for the duration of the limitation period and the plaintiff's right to possession was thereby lost.

Changing the lock and using the land as a garden amounted to sufficient control. It also proved the defendant's intention to possess the land. The defendant was aware that the plaintiff planned to use the land for a road and that the defendant would probably be required to vacate the land at some point. However, there is no requirement that the adverse possessor intends to own the land in question or even to possess it for a long time. The intention to possess the land for the time being is sufficient to establish possession. Adverse possession for a long enough period destroys prior rights to possession and becomes ownership.

Adverse possession must be continuous for the duration of the limitation period or it will start over again. As discussed below, the adverse possession need not be held by the same persons throughout the limitation period. However, if the land ceases to be adversely possessed at any time before the limitation period expires, any subsequent adverse possession will begin with a new limitation period. This does not mean that the adverse possessor must remain on the land constantly. He or she continues to possess the land while absent temporarily, even if the absence is daily, to go to work, or for an extended period, while away on vacation. However, land will cease to be adversely possessed if the adverse possessor abandons it, leaving it unoccupied.

Adverse possession does not mean that everyone else in the world must be kept off the land. Like any other possession, it is not lost if the possessors choose to invite others to visit or make use of the land. As Murray J said in *Petkov v Lucerne Nominees Pty Ltd* (1992) 7 WAR 163 at 167, "If others are shown to be using the land, it must effectively be in a way which is not inconsistent with that exclusive possession. It must ostensibly be that the others are using the land by licence or permission of the adverse possessor, behaving as if he were the owner thereof." However, if someone with a better right to possession uses the land, that use is referable to her or his better right and is not dependent on the invitation of the adverse possessor. Such use would be evidence that there is no adverse possession of the land.

Permission

Possession is not adverse so long as it is held with permission of the person with the right to immediate possession (called the owner here for simplicity). That permission may be expressed (when the owner grants a lease to a tenant, as discussed in Chapter 12) or implied (when the circumstances indicate that owner consented to the arrangement). There is some controversy over what constitutes implied permission. If the owner's failure to object to another's possession was treated as implied permission, then possession would rarely be adverse. This would subvert limitation statutes by allowing plaintiffs to sit on their rights indefinitely. Conversely, if the law did not recognise implied consent, then many possessors, who had obtained the owner's permission informally, would be treated as wrongdoers.

Courts and commentators have expended a great deal of effort dealing with this problem. This suggestion may be controversial, but there is a relatively simple solution available. All possession of land is either with or without the permission of the person with the right to immediate possession. Without permission, it is adverse possession.

Possession with permission is called a **tenancy**: see Chapter 12. If there is no formal lease or payment of rent, it is called a **tenancy at will**. The limitation statutes treat tenancies at will as lasting for only one year, if they are not ended sooner. Thereafter, possession is adverse and the limitation period runs. Similarly, when a tenant stops paying rent, but continues to possess the land, the possession is deemed to be adverse, even if the owner takes no steps to remove the tenant or collect the rent.

The statutory solution promotes certainty by imposing an arbitrary limit on informal permission. However, it can create hardship for generous land owners who let others use their land without paying rent: see, eg, *Hayward v Chaloner* [1968] 1 QB 107. It also means that people who have no immediate use for their land, like the plaintiff in *Buckinghamshire County Council v Moran* (above), cannot let others use it for the time being without making formal arrangements. This promotes a "dog in the manger" attitude, since an owner who does not use her or his land will need to stop others from using it or risk losing it forever.

The provision regarding tenants at will, which is found in most limitation statutes, is not often used. This is probably because lawyers tend to think of a tenancy at will as an arrangement whereby the tenant obtained possession with the expressed permission of the owner. However, implied permission is genuine permission. The particular manner in which permission is manifested does not provide a basis for distinguishing one situation from the other. Also, if owners, who expressly permit others to have possession of their land, risk losing their land through adverse possession, why should owners, who have implied such permission, be preserved from that fate?

Successive Periods of Adverse Possession

The limitation period continues to run while the land is adversely possessed by somebody. It does not matter if the persons in possession change so long as there is no gap in adverse possession. In other words, successive periods of adverse possession by different possessors can be added together to bar a claim to recover land. For example, assume that you took adverse possession of the owner's land in 1984 and that I took adverse possession in 1995. If there was no gap between the end of your possession and the beginning of mine, and the limitation period was 15 years, the owner's right to possession was extinguished in 1999.

As far as the owner is concerned, it does not matter whether I took possession with or without your permission. If you sold or gave your right to possession to me, then you step out of the picture and I hold the right you acquired in 1984. If I leased the land from you or took possession adversely to you, then your right to possession survived and I acquired a right to possession which was good against everyone except you and the owner. The owner's claim was time barred in 1999, leaving me subject only to your right to possession (which will be lost if the land is adversely possessed continuously until 2010).

The ability to combine successive periods is somewhat odd. The owner in this example had separate claims against you and me for trespass. Why does the loss of the claim against you through the passage of time also bar the much newer claim against me? There are several justifications for this rule. First, the evidence proving the owner's right to possession dates from the time he or she first lost possession to you. It was not renewed or made more reliable when I took adverse possession. Secondly, the owner had 15 years to enforce her or his right to possession and yet chose not to act. There is no reason why the transfer of adverse possession from you to me should extend that limitation period. Thirdly, if successive periods of adverse possession could not be combined, very old rights to possession could survive to threaten the status quo. Land might be passed from adverse possessor to adverse possessor over many generations and still not become ownership if there was no one person in the line who maintained possession for 15 years. The right to possession acquired by the first adverse possessor, and relied on by her or his successors over the years, should not be disturbed by an older right to possession which lay dormant.

The Right to Possession Extinguished

Once the limitation period has run its course, the owner's right to possession is extinguished. He or she has no better right to the land than anyone else in society. If the former owner then manages to obtain possession again, the extinguished ownership does not revive. The possession reacquired has the priority of a new right and joins the queue behind the older and better rights of the adverse possessors who had previously dispossessed the owner: see *Kirk v Sutherland* [1949] VLR 33.

Part III
The Variety of Property Rights

Chapter Nine

VARIETY OF PROPERTY RIGHTS

III

Part III provides an introduction to the variety of property rights recognised in Australian law. It is a type of spotter's guide, designed to help you identify property rights, in much the same way a guide book might help you identify birds or trees in the bush.

This Part is concerned only with the nature and characteristics of property rights. For example, Chapter 14 answers the question, "What is a mortgage?", but does not deal with questions such as "How do I create a mortgage?" or "What happens if the same land is mortgaged twice?". The creation of property rights and their priority are examined separately in Parts IV and V. The separation of these inquiries helps the student of property law and makes it easier to see important connections and distinctions between different types of rights.

The property rights discussed here are arranged in a rough order, starting with the greatest (ownership, in the next chapter) and working down to licences (mere personal rights to use property) in Chapter 18. There are two exceptions. First, possession has already been examined in Part II (and is discussed further in Chapter 12 on estates). Secondly, native title is studied at the end of this Part in Chapter 19. This is because there are a wide variety of native title rights, ranging from ownership of land down to rights to make periodic use of land for activities like hunting and fishing. Although native title preceded the system of property law imported from England, it has been recognised as part of Australian property law only recently. An introduction to other property rights provides a helpful base of knowledge to which native title can be compared.

As discussed in Chapter 2, a property right is a right which both relates to a thing contingently connected to the right holder and corresponds to the general duty of other members of society not to interfere with that right. When courts decide whether particular rights are property rights, they rarely work from these first principles. Instead, they look to previously decided cases to see whether the right claimed has been recognised in Australian law as a property right. Does it share the essential characteristics of an existing property right?

Although, in theory, there could be an almost infinite variety of property rights relating to things, the law has developed well recognised categories of property rights and is reluctant to admit a new right which does not belong in an existing category. A claim to a property right which can be made to fit into an established pigeon hole is far more likely to succeed than one which requires the creation of a new hole. There are two very practical reasons for this. First, law is an applied science. The bewildering array of human affairs must be reduced to categories which allow like cases to be treated alike and enable people to plan their affairs with certainty. The limited number of recognised property rights helps us and our legal advisors to say with some degree of confidence whether a particular right is property.

Secondly, the limit on property rights helps promote the efficient use of resources. If every right to a thing was capable of being a property right, things could be encumbered in ways which reduced their utility and marketability, with little or no benefit to the right holder. For example, suppose you gave me the right to store my tennis gear in the boot of your car. This was convenient for me because you always parked next to my favourite tennis court. It is conceivable that I might have a personal right to use your car for that purpose, but the court would not recognise it as a property right. There is no benefit from enforcing the right against other members of society. If the car were sold, the new owners would be surprised to discover that I had a right to keep my gear in their boot. The right would be of little value to me if the car was kept in another location and yet the value of the car would be reduced if the boot was full or, worse yet, if the new owners were required to park the car near my tennis court.

Although Australian law recognises only a limited number of different property rights, this does not mean that the law of property is stagnant. It continues to develop and new categories are established from time to time. There are many property rights which evolved from personal rights, such as the beneficiary's right to trust assets (see Chapter 13), the equity of redemption in a mortgaged home (see Chapter 14), and the restrictive covenant (see Chapter 16).

Chapter Ten

OWNERSHIP

■■■

Most of us have a basic understanding of the concept of ownership. We have at least some idea of what it means to own a thing and would know how to respond to a visitor who asked, "Do you own this house?" In this chapter, the legal concept of ownership is explored in more detail.

To begin, it is important to note that ownership is not the same as property. There are many property rights which are not ownership, such as an easement to cross someone's land: see Chapter 16. The person who borrows a library book does not own that book, nor does the tenant own the flat he or she rents. We need to identify what distinguishes ownership from other property rights.

Ownership and Possession

The first task is to distinguish ownership from possession. Dictionaries provide little assistance, since most define ownership by reference to possession. It is clear that a person can possess a thing without owning it. However, it is not easy to identify the particular rights which make someone an owner and not just a possessor.

As discussed in Chapter 7, the law protects ownership and possession in precisely the same way. The remedies available to the owner are triggered by wrongful interference with her or his possession or right to possession, such as trespass, conversion, and detinue. When owners recover their things from others, it is not because they are owners, but because they have better rights to possession. Indeed, if an owner does not have a right to immediate possession, her or his interference with another's possession is a tort: *City Motors (1933) Pty Ltd v Southern Aerial Super Service Pty Ltd* (1961) 106 CLR 477. This leads to the question whether the right is not defined by the remedy. If the law protects ownership by enforcing the owner's possession or right to possession, how does ownership differ from the best possible right to possession?

One feature of ownership, which distinguishes it from possession, is its potential for permanence. While ownership normally includes the right to possess a thing indefinitely, possession without ownership is a temporary right. For example, while you have a library book properly on loan, no one is entitled to interfere with your possession. Still, it is clear that the library owns the book, because your right to possession is temporary and will revert to the library.

This does not mean that ownership will last forever or even for long. You can own an ice cream cone on a hot January day, even though it will be gone in minutes, one way or another. Owners are generally free to bring their ownership to an end by selling, giving, or destroying the thing owned. However, when we say that someone has possession, but not ownership, we mean that there is an owner with a greater right to possession which will revive when the possessor's right comes to an end. It is this **reversionary right** which characterises ownership.

The owner's right to possession in the future may be conditional upon the happening of certain events. Under a hire-purchase agreement (discussed at page 53), the hire-purchaser takes possession of the thing and becomes the owner when all the payments are made. This creates a bailment destined to become ownership if all goes well. Although the owner-bailor may never again have the right to possession, her or his ownership continues so long as that right remains possible.

People can own things even though their rights to possession are delayed for a very long time. For example, the owner of land might lease it for 100 years, in which case the tenant's right to possession will last over a lifetime and the owner's right to possession will not return until he or she is dead. Still, the owner has a reversionary right which will endure beyond the tenant's right. It is a property right which can be enjoyed by another when the time comes.

The difference between a sale or gift (which transfers ownership) and a lease or bailment (which transfers possession, but not ownership) is that the former disposes of all the owner's rights to the thing, while the latter leaves the owner with some residual right. This is true even if the residual right might be destroyed by certain events (such as the sale at the end of a hire-purchase) or will not be enjoyed for more than a lifetime.

Tony Honoré identified this "incident of residuarity" as a necessary element of ownership in an influential essay called "Ownership" in Guest, *Oxford Essays in Jurisprudence* (1961) 107 at 113. To distinguish ownership from possession, it is necessary to look at the rights a person has to use a thing in the future. An examination of the property rights which can be exercised at present is insufficient. For example, if you owned a house and leased it to me for five years, it might appear to a bystander that I own the house. As discussed in Chapter 12, the lease would entitle me to possession of your house, which means that I would get to use and enjoy it and exclude you from it. My payment of rent would provide a clue about your rights, but would not set me apart from an owner who makes mortgage payments or distinguish you from the bank which receives them. It is your right to possession at the end of the lease which identifies you as the owner.

Jeremy Waldron takes a similar approach, but looking back in time instead of forward. In *The Right to Private Property* (1986) p 56, he said that we cannot "tell who is and who is not an owner by concentrating on the rights, powers, and duties distributed around a society at a particular moment in time." However, unlike Honoré, who looks to the "incident of residuarity" to mark the owner of a thing, Waldron looks to the past to identify the person who decided how a particular thing would be used. He said (at p 47):

> "Ownership...expresses the abstract idea of an object being correlated with the name of some individual, in relation to a rule which says that society will uphold that individual's decision as final when there is any dispute about how the object should be used."

Turning to the previous example, in which you leased your house to me for five years, Waldron would identify you as the owner because you are the person who decided that I should enjoy possession of the house at present. One difficulty with this approach is that it does not distinguish between a sale and a lease. Suppose you buy a house and I lease the house next door. We each take possession and yet you are the owner and I am not. If we ask, "Who decided on this use of these homes?", we find that, in your case it was the vendor (previous owner) and in mine it was the landlord (current owner). The real distinction is that your vendor disposed of all her or his rights to the land, while my landlord retained the right to possession in the future.

Bundle of Rights

In "Ownership" (above), Honoré set out to describe the concept of ownership shared by most legal systems. He listed nine rights, one duty, and one liability as the elements which together constitute ownership. Six of those rights also belong to someone with a right to possession. These are the rights to **possess** the thing, to **use** it, to **manage** how it will be used, to **income** from it, to **security** from interference with the right to the thing, and to **transmit** that right to successors of choice. The duty and liability would also attach to the person with the right to possession. These are the duty to **prevent harm** and the liability to **execution** (which are discussed further below).

Honoré sets out three rights of ownership which do not belong to a non-owner with a right to possession. The right to **capital** entitles the owner to destroy or alienate the thing itself. Although the right to possession is a property right which usually can be sold or given away, the destruction of the thing, without the consent of the person with a right to future possession, would be an actionable wrong. The **absence of term**, meaning the potential to last indefinitely, and the incident of **residuarity**, discussed above, are also exclusive to ownership.

This provides a useful description of ownership. It should not, however, be confused with a description of property. There are property rights, such as the restrictive covenant (discussed in Chapter 16), which share very few of these characteristics. Perhaps more importantly, Honoré's description of ownership should not be used as a definition of property. Focussing on the ways in which people can use their things (sometimes called a **bundle of rights**) detracts from the essential characteristics which separate property from personal rights. As James Penner said in "The 'Bundle of Rights' Picture of Property" (1996) 43 *UCLA Law Review* 711 at 741:

> "The bundle of rights perspective on property is entirely innocuous if regarded merely as an elaboration of the scope of action that ownership provides. In that vein, the right to property does comprise

a bundle of rights — the right to use, consume, destroy, and transfer what one owns, and so forth. In the same way, the right to make contracts can be elaborated as the right to sell, the right to employ others, the right to take remunerative employment, the right to lend money at interest, and so on. There is nothing wrong with this. On the other hand, as any kind of *analysis* or substantial *thesis* about property, the bundle of rights can only be taken as meaning that property is a structural composite, *ie*, that its nature is that of an aggregate of fundamentally distinct norms. That is quite mistaken."

Alienability

Honoré said that the owner has the rights to sell the thing (the capital) and to let it for value (the income). Penner has challenged this idea, arguing that ownership includes the rights to give the thing away and to share it with others, but not necessarily to do so for value. He sees the right to exchange property rights for value as part of our freedom of contract and not part of the law of property.

Penner's argument is significant for at least two reasons. First, it explains why we can own things that we are not permitted to sell, such as human tissue and blood removed for donation: see Chapter 3. Secondly and more importantly, it identifies the separate interests protected by the law of property and the law of contract. Property protects our interests in using things, while contract protects our interests in dealing co-operatively with others. The rights to own things and make contracts go hand in hand in most societies. Many property rights are acquired through contract and many contracts concern the use of things. However, there is no necessary connection between property and contract. Each can exist independently of the other.

If Penner is correct to conclude that the right to make contracts is not part of the law of property, is he also correct when he says that ownership includes the rights to share and give? It is clear that ownership is a property right to something contingently connected to the owner and, therefore, the owner must be able to alienate the thing by severing that connection. Does the owner's right to alienate necessarily include the right to make a gift?

We are social creatures. As John Donne wrote in 1623 in his famous Meditation XVII, "No man is an island." Our enjoyment of life is enhanced when we share our experiences with others. Why else do we go with others to the cinema to sit quietly together in the dark? Since ownership is the greatest possible right to use and enjoy a thing, Penner argues that it must include the right to enjoy the thing socially, by giving to or sharing with others.

Responsibilities of Ownership

As discussed above, Honoré's description of ownership includes the duty to prevent harm and the liability to execution. The issue explored here is whether these are essential aspects of ownership, as Honoré suggests.

Duty to Prevent Harm

There are two types of harm to consider: the duty not to harm others with the thing owned and the duty not to harm the thing itself. First, it is uncontroversial that people must take care not to harm others with their things. The issue is whether this is a component of ownership or merely part of the general duty we all have not to interfere with the persons and things of others. If I throw a book and injure you, does it matter whether I own the book? As a book owner, do I have a duty to stop others from throwing it? In other words, does the benefit of ownership carry a burden which is distinct from the responsibilities we all bear as members of society? There are no easy answers.

Even if a duty to prevent harm is part of the law of property, it is not clear whether it attaches to ownership or to the right to possession. The essence of the wrong is allowing a thing to be used in a way which causes harm to another. The person with possession or the right to immediate possession of a thing has the power to control its use and, therefore, bears some responsibility for its misuse. The owner with a reversionary right to future possession does not necessarily have that power and is at least one step removed from the harm occasioned by the user. The law recognises this in some situations. For example, the liability for injuries caused by the dangerous condition of premises usually falls on the occupier of those premises, regardless of whether he or she is also the owner.

The second and perhaps more difficult question is whether the owner of a thing can have a duty not to harm the thing itself. It is clear that the possessor can be liable to the owner for damage to the thing (see, for example, the discussion of **waste** in Chapter 12). However, the sole owner of a thing, to which no one else has a property right, usually is free to destroy or damage that thing, provided this causes no harm to others. For example, you are free to throw your own wine glasses into your own fireplace, smash your own musical instruments on stage, or throw your own dinner in the bin. The law does not intervene, even though there are many people in the world who would love to have your glasses, instruments, or dinner.

There are situations in which the owner is not free to harm the thing owned. Usually, the owner of an animal is entitled to have it destroyed, so long as this is done humanely. However, the owner is not entitled to be cruel to the animal. As Napier J said in *Backhouse v Judd* [1925] SASR 16 at 21:

> "There is nothing novel in the idea that property is a responsibility as well as a privilege. The law which confers and protects the right of property in any animal may well throw the burden of the responsibility for its care upon the owner as a public duty incidental to the ownership."

It is interesting that Article 903 of the German Civil Code (the Bürgerliches Gestetzbuch or BGB), titled "Powers of the Owner", states: "The owner of a thing may, to the extent that it is not contrary to the law or the rights of third parties, deal with the thing as he pleases and exclude others from any interference; the owner of an animal must comply with the special legal provisions for the protection of animals when exercising his powers" (translated by Simon Goren, 1994).

The owners of animals of endangered species might have even greater duties to protect them from harm. Similarly, the owners of land with particular cultural or biological significance might have a duty to preserve that land. For example, the owner of a building listed as a special heritage site is not permitted to demolish or change it without special permission. Murray Raff has argued that the various duties to protect things from harm should include a general duty to preserve land from environmental harm. He said, in "Environmental Obligations and the Western Liberal Property Concept" (1998) 22 *Melbourne University Law Review* 657 at 691, that "an environmental responsibility should be presumed positively, even in the absence of positive legal regulation, as an aspect of property itself and at the deepest jurisprudential level".

Liability to Execution

For Honoré, ownership includes a liability to execution. This means that the rights of the owner may be expropriated by the government for the greater good and may be seized and sold to pay the owner's debts. Liability to expropriation is a generally accepted limit on ownership. Most of us agree that an owner's right to determine how her or his things are used must give way at times to society's need to interfere with that use for purposes such as public transportation, utilities, parks, and other essential services. Many jurisdictions have statutory mechanisms for regulating expropriation and determining the appropriate compensation for the rights expropriated.

When people are unable or unwilling to pay their debts, the generally accepted response is to force them to sell their property rights to raise money to pay those debts. If, for example, you obtain a judgment against me for the payment of money and I do not pay that sum, you are a **judgment creditor** and entitled to instruct the sheriff to seize and sell my things to pay the judgment. Similarly, if I am declared bankrupt (unable to pay my debts), my property rights are transferred to a person (called the **trustee in bankruptcy** or **receiver**) who sells those rights and distributes the proceeds among my creditors according to law.

It is not clear whether the liability to execution is an inherent limitation of ownership or merely part of everyone's obligation to pay her or his debts. There are four arguments in favour of the latter view. First, not all rights of ownership are subject to execution. For example, the *Bankruptcy Act* 1966 (Cth) and Regulations exempt many household items (including one television and one video recorder) from distribution among a bankrupt's creditors. Secondly, there are a wide variety of property rights, other than ownership, which are liable to execution. For example, possession of land or goods under a lease may have market value which can be realised to pay the possessor's debts. Thirdly, personal rights (such as a bank account or right to receive wages) can also be taken to pay a judgment debt. Finally, a society could choose to enforce judgment debts in other ways. For example, at one time in England, debts could be enforced by committing the debtor to prison: see Baker, *An Introduction to English Legal History* (3rd ed, 1990) pp 78-79 and, eg, *Dive v Maningham* (1550) 1 Plowden 96, 75 ER 96.

Chapter Eleven

TENURE

In the previous chapter, ownership was identified as the greatest of all possible property rights. This chapter concerns the ownership of land, which differs in some respects from the ownership of goods. The owner of goods is often the only person with any rights to those goods. For example, it is likely that you hold the only property rights which exist in relation to the shoes you are wearing. Your ownership is complete and unencumbered by other interests.

It is far less common for only one person to hold all the property rights to a parcel of land. Land is such a big investment that people often purchase it with the help of others. For example, a couple might pool their resources to become the co-owners of a house (see Chapter 15) which they have mortgaged to the bank (see Chapter 14). It is common for governments and utility companies to have easements over land for gas, electricity, water, and sewage lines and for governments and developers to restrict the use of land to conform to neighbourhood standards: see Chapter 16.

Even where only one person owns land to which no one else has any rights, that person is not the owner in the same way that he or she might be the owner of goods. The legal regime under which people own land in Australia is called **tenure**, which means that the Crown is (at least formally) the owner of all land in Australia and all private owners are tenants of the Crown. In substance, many of these tenants are the owners. However, to understand the formalities, it is necessary to look at the history of property law in England and Australia. Native title (discussed in Chapter 19) operates somewhat differently.

Feudalism

The history of tenure goes back at least as far as 1066, when William the Conqueror asserted sovereignty over England. Over the next dozen years, he gave land to faithful lords, or affirmed their existing land holdings, in exchange for fealty and promises of military and other services. The lords who received land directly from the Crown were called **tenants in chief**. They doled out portions of their land to lesser tenants in exchange for services, who in turn divided it among even lesser tenants. This process (which today might be called pyramid selling) was called **subinfeudation**. At the top was the Crown as lord of all and at the bottom were the tenants who lived on and worked the land (called

tenants in demesne). The people in between (called **mesne lords**) were both tenants to those higher up and lords to those lower down. Goods and services flowed up the chain in exchange for a lord's protection and permission to use the land.

This system is known today as **feudalism**. This word describes not just land ownership, but the range of social institutions under which people lived. The lords would exercise executive and judicial functions. In local manor courts, disputes would be resolved according to local laws (in contrast to the "common law" administered by the king's courts). Property rights to land were inextricably bound up with the feudal system of government. The relationship between landlord and tenant involved more than property.

Although we might say that the Crown "owned" the land and that the lords and others down the chain were merely tenants, this would not convey an accurate picture. As John Baker said in *An Introduction to English Legal History* (3rd ed, 1990) p 263, "no one thought of the lord king as being in any meaningful sense *owner* of all the land in England". Ownership was not a concept familiar to the medieval lawyer. The Latin word for ownership, *dominium,* also means "lordship".

Evolution from Tenure to Ownership

Ownership of land in Australia is not part of a feudal pyramid structure. People own land as tenants in chief, no services are due to the Crown in exchange, and the system of land ownership is separate from the system of government. This was achieved by evolution, not abolition. No drastic change brought the feudal system of tenure to an end. Aspects of that system were removed or withered bit by bit until it became the modern law of real property. Therefore, the formal system of tenure still survives and needs to be understood even if, in substance, it no longer functions in the same way.

The two main factors which contributed to the evolution of modern tenure are:

1) .....the abolition of subinfeudation; and
2) the gradual elimination of feudal services.

Abolition of Subinfeudation

At one time, tenants who wanted to transfer their land needed their lord's permission, which would be granted in exchange for the payment of a fine. This provided an incentive for tenants to subinfeudate instead. They would remain in the feudal chain, receiving services from their new tenants and remitting all or a portion of them to their lord. The extra links in the chain exacerbated a problem with subinfeudation. If a tenant in the chain failed to deliver the promised service to her or his lord, the land could be forfeit to the lord, even if the tenants further down the chain had faithfully performed their services.

Fines for transfers and most subinfeudation were abolished by the statute of **Quia Emptores** in 1290. Thereafter, tenants could transfer their land without the permission of their lords. Instead of adding to the feudal pyramid, tenants would be replaced. As tenancies came to an end, the number of layers in the feudal pyramid was reduced.

Quia Emptores 1290 was part of the law of property brought to Australia from England. That statute is still in force in Australia, except in New South Wales, Queensland, and Victoria, where it has been replaced by local versions. Section 18A of the *Property Law Act* 1958 (Vic) states:

"Land held of the Crown in fee simple may be assured in fee simple without fine and the person taking the assurance shall hold the land of the Crown in the same manner as the land was held before the assurance took effect."

As discussed in the next chapter, "fee simple" is equivalent to ownership of land. This statute says in effect that the tenant in chief can transfer her or his ownership without payment of a fine and the new owner becomes the new tenant in chief by substitution. Since Quia Emptores 1290 or an equivalent statutory provision has always applied in Australia, all land owners are tenants in chief (except the Crown).

It is important to note that the statute does not affect the way in which the Crown deals with its own land. So, when the Crown grants land to someone, the recipient does not replace the Crown, but acquires tenure as a tenant in chief.

It is also important to note that Quia Emptores 1290 and its equivalents do not apply to leases and life estates (discussed in the next chapter). In essence, a lease of land to a tenant is a form of subinfeudation (unless the lease is granted by the Crown). If, for example, you rent a house (from anyone other than the Crown), you become the tenant with a landlord between you and the Crown. It is also possible to add links to this chain, since you might be permitted to sublet the house and become a landlord to your sub-tenant.

Elimination of Feudal Services

There used to be a variety of services for which land was granted. For example, tenants might be required to provide knights for military service, say prayers for their lord, or provide grain: see Baker, *An Introduction to English Legal History* (3rd ed, 1990) pp 259-262. Tenures were classified according to the nature of service required in exchange. The most common form of tenure was socage (sometimes called "free and common socage"), in which the nature and amount of service required (normally agricultural) were fixed when the land was granted to the tenant.

Over time, most of these services were exchanged for fixed money payments. Inflation reduced the value of these payments to the point where they were not worth collecting. All but two of the tenures (frankalmoign and copyhold) were converted to socage by the *Tenures Abolition Act* 1660 (UK). Socage was the only form of tenure to come to Australia from England. Under the modern tenure relationship, land owners are still tenants of their lord, the Crown, but there are no services or fees due to the Crown and the land is freely alienable without permission of the Crown. These tenants of the Crown are now, in substance, owners of the land.

Nature of the Crown's Right to Land

The Crown is not the owner of all the land in Australia, but has the power, as sovereign, to grant land to others (thus creating the tenure relationship) or to take land for itself. In *Mabo v Queensland (No 2)* (1992) 175 CLR 1, the Crown's right to land was called **radical title**. Brennan J said (at 50), "radical title, without more, is merely a logical postulate required to support the doctrine of tenure (when the Crown has exercised its sovereign power to grant an interest in land) and to support the plenary title of the Crown (when the Crown has exercised its sovereign power to appropriate to itself ownership of parcels of land within the Crown's territory)." Where the Crown has taken possession of land for its own use, it cannot have a tenure relationship with itself, but has absolute ownership, called **allodial title** or **allodium** (meaning the entire property).

When the Crown acquired sovereignty over Australia, it acquired radical title, subject to the property rights of the indigenous inhabitants: see Chapter 19. The assertion of sovereignty, without more, did not entitle the Crown to prevent the holders of existing property rights from exercising those rights. Therefore, if land was already subject to property rights (even a right less than possession, such as native title to hunt and fish), the Crown had no right to possess that land unless it first exercised its sovereign power to claim that right and thereby extinguish existing rights. However, as Brennan J said (at 48), "If the land were desert and uninhabited, truly a terra nullius, the Crown would take an absolute beneficial title (an allodial title) to the land." The absence of any other rights to a parcel of land meant that the Crown had a right to immediate possession.

Some early Australian cases suggested that the Crown, as sovereign, had beneficial ownership of Australia and that tenure was created by the Crown's grant of a portion of that ownership to its subjects. For example, in *Attorney-General v Brown* (1847) 2 SCR (NSW) App 30 at 35, Stephen CJ said that, unless land was granted to a subject, it was possessed by the Crown as "universal occupant". This view was rejected by the High Court of Australia in *Mabo*, above.

The Crown's rights to land were not viewed this way in England. Many land holdings in existence before the Norman conquest were left undisturbed by William I. The tenure relationship with these landholders was created by the Crown's acquisition of sovereignty and not by its acquisition and transfer of a right to possession. For the peasant who lived on and worked the land, life continued more or less unchanged. As Brian Simpson said, in *A History of the Land Law* (2nd ed, 1986) pp 4-5, "In general the effect of the Norman Conquest was only to substitute a new, alien, lord for his Saxon predecessor; a new system of parasitism was substituted for the old."

The early Australian view of the Crown's right to land was a departure from the traditional English view of the law. The High Court of Australia's judgment in *Mabo* is a return to that earlier point of view. The divergence may have been a strategic device which facilitated or justified the expansion of the British empire. As Gummow J said, in *Wik Peoples v Queensland* (1996) 141 ALR 129 at 234:

> "The concept of *ownership* by the Crown of all land is a modern one, and its adoption in legal theory may have been related to Imperial expansion in the seventeenth and eighteenth centuries, well after the decline of feudalism."

Also see Edgeworth, "Tenure, Allodialism and Indigenous Rights at Common Law" (1994) 23 *Anglo-American Law Review* 397.

Chapter Twelve

ESTATES

▌▌▌

As discussed in the previous chapter, the concept of tenure means that people hold land not as absolute owners, but as tenants of the Crown. Coupled with this is the idea that people do not own the land itself, but have estates in land. An **estate** is the right to possess land as a tenant for a period of time.

Estates have four dimensions: width, depth, height, and time. An estate is the right to possess a volume of space, defined relative to the surface of the earth, for a period of time. It does not depend (much) on the physical state of the land itself. For example, if you bought a house and then removed the buildings, trees, grass, and soil, leaving behind only a large pit, you would still have exactly the same estate in land. It might be worth a lot less on the market, but your right to possess that space would not be changed by the destruction of the things within it.

Most estates are laid out on the surface of the earth and extend both down beneath the surface and up into the air. It is possible to have an estate which does not intersect the earth's surface. For example, an estate could exist as a volume of space on the 27th floor of a tall building.

If the vertical dimensions of an estate are not defined, it is not clear how high and low they extend. At one time it was suggested that the estate was an inverted pyramid, with the tip at the centre of the earth and the base out in space. However, the vertical dimensions of the estate are much shorter. Aeroplanes flying high overhead do not trespass, but cranes and scaffolding protruding over another's land (without permission) do: see *Graham v KD Morris & Sons Pty Ltd* [1974] Qd R 1; Chapter 7.

It is trespass to wrongly interfere with potentially usable space, above or below ground, whether that space is used by the estate holder or not. In *Edwards v Lee's Administrators* (1936) 96 SW2d 1028, the defendant discovered a cave in Kentucky which he developed into a popular tourist attraction. The entrance to the cave was on his land, but one third of it was under the plaintiff's land. The defendant's use of this space was a trespass, even though the plaintiff did not use it himself.

Most estates do not include the valuable minerals in the ground. At common law, an estate which included the land below the surface would also include the minerals found there, other than gold and silver, unless they were excepted from the grant: see *Wade v NSW Rutile Mining Co Pty Ltd* (1969) 121 CLR 177. Gold and silver did not form part of the estate, but belonged to the Crown as part of its royal prerogative. Today, every state and territory has legislation which reserves a wide variety of minerals for the Crown, such as clay, coal, gravel, limestone, metals, petroleum, sand, and shale.

Estates are classified according to how long they last. There are two main categories: **freehold** estates, which last for indefinite periods measured in lifetimes, and **leasehold** estates (or **leases**), which (in theory) last for definite periods, such as one week or five years. These categories are shared by most jurisdictions which inherited the English law of real property. There are several other estates created by statute in Australia which may fall outside the two English categories.

Freehold Estates

A person who has a freehold estate is said to be **seised** of that estate. Her or his right to possession is called **seisin**. At one time, seisin was merely a synonym for possession. However, it evolved into a term of art used only in connection with freehold estates to distinguish them from leasehold estates and rights to possess goods. The distinction between seisin and possession has lost much of its significance, now that freehold and leasehold estates are protected in the same way (as discussed in Chapters 5 and 7).

There are three kinds of freehold estates, which are also classified by their potential duration: **fee simple**, **fee tail**, and **life**.

Fee Simple

The fee simple estate is the greatest right to land recognised at common law. "Fee" means that the estate is inheritable and "simple" means that it is not qualified in any way. Although it is now equivalent to ownership, we still refer to the owner of land as the owner (or holder) of an estate in fee simple. This can be explained by tracing the development of this estate.

A fee simple estate is created by a grant of land to a tenant and her or his heirs. Originally, this would create an estate that would last as long as the tenant and any of her or his heirs survived. On the death of the last heir, the estate would come to an end and the land would **escheat**, meaning it would return to the Crown or lord from whom the tenant held tenure.

By the 13th century, it came to be understood that a grant to a tenant and her or his heirs did not give the heirs any right to the land. No one could know who the tenant's heirs would be until he or she died. Therefore, while the tenant lived, there were no heirs who could have property rights to the land. The estate in fee simple belonged wholly to the tenant and could be dealt with as he or she pleased.

For example, a grant of land to Steve and his heirs would give Steve a right to possess the land, which would pass to his heirs if he died (or would escheat if he died without heirs). However, Steve was free to transfer that estate before he died. If he sold the estate to Joan and her heirs, Joan would get the fee simple and Steve's heirs would get nothing. After the transfer, the estate would no longer depend on the survival of

Steve's heirs, but would continue for so long as Joan and her heirs were living. However, if Joan transferred the estate to Susan, it would then be measured by the lives of Susan and her heirs.

Another important change occurred when people gained the right to transfer their freehold estates by will (under the *Statute of Wills* 1540 and *Tenures Abolition Act* 1660). This meant that a fee simple estate would not come to an end when the tenant died without heirs, so long as it passed to a beneficiary of the tenant's will: see Chapter 22. The estate would only escheat if there were no heirs and no one entitled to receive the estate under the tenant's will.

A further change was the abolition of escheat in every state and territory but Western Australia: see, eg, *Administration and Probate Act* 1935 (Tas), s 45; *Escheat (Procedure) Act* 1940 (WA). If the tenant of a fee simple estate (outside Western Australia) dies without heirs and without disposing of the estate by will, it does not escheat, but is treated like all the tenant's other property rights and goes to the Crown as **bona vacantia** (ownerless goods). The right to possession of the land passes to the Crown, not because the estate has ceased to exist, but because it has become ownerless. On reaching the Crown, it should cease, because the Crown could not be both lord and tenant of the same land. This makes a fee simple estate barely distinguishable from the absolute ownership of goods.

Fee Tail

Many people wanted the power to keep land in the family. The fee simple estate could not accomplish this because the present tenant was free to deal with the land without regard for her or his heirs. To meet this need, the English Parliament made it possible for people to create an estate which came to be known as a **fee tail** (from feodum talliatum, meaning "cut-down fee").

If a person granted land to a tenant and the **heirs of her or his body**, it would be restricted to the tenant's lineal descendants. On the tenant's death, the estate would pass to the heir of her or his body (a child, grandchild, etc). If no lineal descendent survived the tenant, the estate would escheat, even if the tenant had other heirs. The fee tail was a permissible form of subinfeudation, not affected by **Quia Emptores** 1290 (as discussed in the previous chapter). Therefore, escheat of a fee tail would return the land to the person with the fee simple.

At one time, the courts treated this type of grant as a conditional fee simple estate. As soon as an heir apparent was born, it became a normal fee simple which could be freely alienated. Parliament intervened in 1285 with the statute **De Donis Conditionalibus** (of conditional gifts), which gave the heirs of the body an interest in the land. On the death of the tenant, the heir had a right to possession of the land, regardless of what had been done with the land during the tenant's life.

Today, the fee tail estate is almost, but not quite, of merely academic interest. For two reasons, they are now almost extinct in Australia. First, with the exception of South Australia and a part of Tasmania, it is no longer possible to create a new fee tail. A grant to a tenant and the heirs of her or his body now creates a fee simple estate. Secondly, most fee tails have been converted to fee simple estates.

In New South Wales, Queensland, and Western Australia, all fee tails were converted by statute. In other parts of Australia, the present tenant of the fee tail estate and her or his heir apparent can agree to **bar the entail**, which converts the estate to fee simple.

Life Estate

A life estate is a permissible form of subinfeudation for the duration of a person's life. For example, if you owned a fee simple estate and granted the land to me for life, I would have a freehold estate which endured for the remainder of my life. On my death, the right to possess the land would return to you or the person entitled to your fee simple estate.

The holder of the life estate (called the **life tenant**) may grant it to someone else, but the estate still comes to an end on the death of the original life tenant, by whom the estate is measured. For example, if I sold my life estate, the estate would end when I died. While I lived, the buyer would have a life estate **per autre vie** (for the life of another), except in the Australian Capital Territory, where the estate per autre vie was abolished by statute: *Law Reform (Abolitions and Repeals) Act* 1996 (ACT), s 3.

Leasehold Estates

The leasehold estate (also called a **lease** or **tenancy**) is a strange hybrid of estate and contract. It was not always an estate in land, but used to be (what would be regarded today as) a contract to use land. When it evolved into a property right, it was not an estate at first, since the tenant had no means of recovering possession of the land. Leasehold tenants gained that right through the action of ejectment (see Chapter 7) and the lease is now an estate in land. Nevertheless, the lease was never reclassified as real property. As discussed in Chapter 5, it is a **chattel real**.

The contractual aspects of leases have begun to reassert themselves. People who rent homes are consumers in need of consumer protection (provided by the Residential Tenancies Acts in most states). Also, leases of commercial space have become complex commercial transactions, often involving detailed contractual arrangements drafted by solicitors who specialise in commercial leasing. The protection of rights involved in a modern lease is no longer provided solely by the law of property. Nevertheless, a lease is an estate in land and its property aspects need to be understood.

Leases continue to differ from freehold estates in several respects. The first and most important is duration. As discussed above and below, freeholds are measured in lives, while leaseholds are measured in definite blocks of time. Secondly, a tenant of a freehold estate is said to be seised of that estate, while the tenant of a lease has possession. Although both have a right to possession to the land, the words "seised" and "seisin" are not used in connection with leases. Therefore, a statute or document which uses either term is generally understood to be referring only to freeholds. Thirdly, the creation of a lease is sometimes called a **demise**. This word is not used in connection with freehold estates, but might refer to the creation of other property rights to land: see *Wik Peoples v Queensland* (1996) 187 CLR 1, discussed below.

A lease is considered to be a lesser property right than a freehold estate, even if it lasts longer. For example, a life estate strangely is greater than a 150-year lease. This is a legacy of the age when leaseholds were not protected to the same extent as freeholds. One practical consequence of this hierarchy is that a life tenant can grant a lease, but a leasehold tenant cannot grant a life estate, even if the lease is set to last more than a lifetime. At common law, a lease granted by the life tenant comes to an end when he or she dies. This is because the lease is a right to possession carved out of the life estate. At the end of the life estate, the right to possession returns to the holder of the fee simple, even if the lease was set to run for many more years. However, by statute, a lease for a limited duration at a fair market rent can endure beyond the life estate. For example, section 44 of the *Settled Estates Act* 1880-1943 (SA) permits a life tenant to grant a lease for up to 21 years which will be binding on the fee simple estate if the life estate ends before the lease. In New South Wales, the limit is 10 years: *Conveyancing and Law of Property Act* 1898 (NSW), ss 68 and 69.

Relationship between Landlord and Tenant

The lease is held by the **tenant** (or **lessee**), who is entitled to possession of the land for the duration of the estate. The lease can be created by a grant from the Crown or by (what is essentially) subinfeudation. Therefore, every lease involves a **landlord** (or **lessor**), who is either the Crown or the person who holds a greater estate from which the lease is carved. Most landlords hold the fee simple estate, but it is possible to create a lease from a life estate (as discussed above) or from a greater leasehold estate.

Both landlord and tenant have property rights to the land (or **premises**). The tenant has the right to possess the land and the landlord has a right to possession when the lease comes to an end. The landlord has granted only a portion of her or his estate to the tenant. What remains is called the **reversion**.

The landlord and tenant also have obligations (or **covenants**) under the lease. Although these obligations vary from lease to lease, the landlord must not interfere with the tenant's right to possession (called the covenant for **quiet enjoyment**) and the tenant is obliged to pay the rent due under the lease, keep the premises in good repair, and permit the landlord to inspect the premises periodically. Leases often contain many other covenants, such as an allocation of responsibility for repairs between landlord and tenant, a restriction on the tenant's use of the land, and a promise that the tenant will not sublet or assign the lease (see below) without the landlord's consent.

The lease creates a property relationship between the landlord and tenant called **privity of estate**. Between the original landlord and tenant, who made a contract with each other to lease the land, there is also **privity of contract**. However, privity of contract is not necessary to create the landlord-tenant relationship. The landlord might sell her or his reversion (usually the fee simple estate). The buyer becomes the new landlord, even though he or she has no contract with the tenant. Similarly, the tenant might sell the leasehold estate and the buyer will become the new tenant. The new landlord and tenant have a relationship through privity of estate, even though they are not parties to the original contract of lease.

Instead of selling or giving away the entire leasehold estate (by an **assignment** of lease), the tenant might **sublet** (or **sublease**) a portion of that estate to a **subtenant**. So long as the tenant retains some portion of her or his leasehold estate (a reversion), he or she stands between the landlord and subtenant, both as tenant to the landlord and as landlord to the subtenant. The landlord and subtenant have neither privity of contract nor privity of estate. Since the sublease is carved out of a greater leasehold estate, it cannot survive the termination of that greater lease. This places the subtenant in a somewhat precarious position since the tenant's default (eg, a failure to pay rent) might give the landlord a right to immediate possession of the land, even though the subtenant has faithfully observed all the covenants of the sublease.

Duration

As mentioned above, all leases must have a definite duration, such as three years or one week. In *Lace v Chandler* [1944] KB 368, an attempt to create a lease which would last until the end of the war was invalid, because the duration was uncertain. The concept of "definite duration" can be misleading, because it does not always mean that the lease will end on a fixed date. As discussed below, there are leases which meet the test of definite duration even though they seem to last indefinitely.

Like freehold estates, leases are classified according to duration. There are three kinds: **fixed-term**, **periodic**, and **at will**.

Fixed Term

A lease has a fixed term if the end of the lease is known, or at least knowable, at the start. For example, leases for five years, until 28 December 2007, or until three days after the next Melbourne Cup would each have a fixed term. It does not matter whether the landlord and tenant know the precise date on which the lease will end, so long as it can be ascertained at the outset. A lease set to last until the Easter Sunday after next would be valid, even if neither party knows that date. The possibility that the lease might end early (for example, as a result of the tenant's default) does not detract from its status as a fixed-term lease. Conversely, the certainty that the end of a purported lease will later become fixed does not make it a valid lease if that date is not ascertainable at the outset.

A fixed-term lease need not run for consecutive days, but can consist of several discrete blocks of time. For example, the lease of a cottage for the next four school vacations would create a valid fixed-term lease, so long as those dates were ascertainable at the beginning of the lease.

Periodic

Many people are familiar with periodic tenancies. Homes are often rented by the week or month. These leases seem to last indefinitely, since most continue until ended by the landlord or tenant. However, the duration is definite. Each periodic tenancy is really a series of fixed-term leases, which are automatically renewed unless some event brings the tenancy to an end: see *Commonwealth Life (Amalgamated) Assurance Ltd v*

Anderson (1945) 46 SR (NSW) 47. The landlord or tenant can choose to end the lease, by giving the required notice (to quit or vacate the premises), or it might be terminated by a failure to perform the covenants of the lease.

It may seem odd to regard a periodic tenancy as definite, when no one can say for sure when it will end. However, it is important to remember that an estate is a right to possession of land and lasts only as long as the tenant has that right. Although a monthly tenancy (for example) might continue for another decade, the tenant has a right to possess the land only for the next month. The landlord is free to serve notice to quit and recover possession of the land at the end of the next period. At every moment during the tenancy, the end of the tenant's right to possession is known or knowable with certainty. Unknown is whether the tenancy will be renewed.

Strangely, it is possible for a periodic tenant to grant a sublease for a fixed term which is longer than the period of the main lease. For example, a monthly tenant might go overseas and sublet the premises for six months. Since the sublease must be carved out of a greater estate, this belies the characterisation of the periodic tenancy as a series of fixed-term leases. Nevertheless, the ability to sublet for terms longer than the period of a tenancy is desirable and practical. It is likely that the monthly tenancy will be renewed beyond the end of the six-month sublease and that the monthly tenant will have a reversion when the sublease comes to an end. Of course, if the landlord chooses to end the monthly tenancy before the six months has passed, the sublease will come to a premature end.

The period of the lease can be almost any length of time chosen by the landlord and tenant. The most common periodic tenancies are weekly and monthly, although annual leases of agricultural land are common (to give tenants sufficient time to plant and harvest crops). The period of the lease often matches the frequency of payment of rent. For example, the rent for most monthly tenancies is due at the beginning of each month. However, the rent and period need not match. An annual tenancy might, for example, have rent due each quarter.

If the period is not specified in the lease, it can be implied from the usual types of leases used in the community. In the absence of evidence to the contrary, agricultural leases are assumed to be annual and most other leases are assumed to have periods matching the frequency of rent: see *Dockrill v Cavanagh* (1944) 45 SR (NSW) 78.

At Will

A tenancy at will exists whenever the tenant obtains the right to possession of land on the (express or implied) understanding that it may be ended at any time by either landlord or tenant: see *Commonwealth Life (Amalgamated) Assurance Ltd v Anderson* (1945) 46 SR (NSW) 47. It can arise when the tenant remains in possession, with the landlord's permission, after the end of another type of lease. This is sometimes called a **tenancy at sufferance** and the tenant in this situation is sometimes called an **overholding tenant**. A tenancy at will can also arise when the tenant is let into possession before a contemplated formal lease or sale of the land to the tenant. Although there are variations in terminology, someone who has possession of land, with the permission of the person with the right to immediate possession, is a tenant at will.

The tenant does not become a trespasser the moment the landlord revokes her or his permission to possess the land. He or she is entitled to a reasonable amount of time to vacate the premises, which depends on circumstances such as the length of time the tenant has been in possession and the amount of work involved in removing the tenant's belongings and restoring the premises to its original condition.

Is the tenancy at will an estate? The landlord-tenant relationship exists, but seems to lack the definite duration required of leaseholds. Although the tenant has possession with permission, that right can be revoked by the landlord at any time. Therefore, the tenant's right to possession, which can be enforced against other members of society, is not really enforceable against the landlord. However, the requirement that the tenant be given a reasonable amount of time to vacate the premises makes the tenancy at will similar to a periodic tenancy with a very short period.

Combinations and Options

Combinations of leases are possible (and common). For example, the landlord and tenant might agree to a one-year fixed-term lease, which converts to a monthly periodic tenancy at the end of the year. Any time a tenant, with permission of the landlord, remains in possession at the end of the lease, he or she is, at the very least, a tenant at will. If the tenant pays (and the landlord accepts) rent, then the lease becomes a periodic tenancy, in the absence of evidence to the contrary.

A lease may contain an **option**, which grants the tenant the right either to renew the lease or to purchase the landlord's reversion. For example, the tenant might have a five-year, fixed-term lease with an option to renew the lease for a further five years. In some ways, a lease with an option to renew is similar to a periodic tenancy. There are, however, three important differences. First, the lease does not automatically renew at the end of the initial term. The tenant must elect to renew and give proper notice of that election to the landlord. Secondly, the option to renew belongs solely to the tenant. The landlord must accept the tenant's decision (provided the tenant has observed the covenants of the lease). Thirdly, most options for renewal give the tenant the right to renew the lease only a limited number of times: usually once, but sometimes more.

An option to renew or purchase an estate is a property right. It is not an estate, since it does not give the tenant a right to possession of the land after the current lease expires, unless it is properly exercised. However, as discussed at page 263, an option to acquire an estate is a lesser property right which will become an estate once it is exercised.

Other Estates

The freehold and leasehold estates described above are those which came to Australia as part of the English common law of real property. Of course, the Parliament of any jurisdiction can alter the common law and abolish or vary those estates or create new rights to land. The fee tail estate is an example of this process, having been created by statute in England and abolished by statute in most of the jurisdictions which received that estate as part of its common law.

As discussed in Chapter 11, the Crown can create estates (and tenure relationships) by granting rights to possess land. That power is defined in each jurisdiction by statute (usually called the Crown Lands Act or Land Act). The process of granting estates (discussed in Chapter 21) and the nature of the estates granted are both set by statute. As Isaacs J said in *Davies v Littlejohn* (1923) 34 CLR 174 at 187-188:

> "Whatever estates, interests or other rights are created by the Crown must owe their origin and existence to the provisions of the statute. In other words, they are statutory or legal estates, interests and rights."

Where a statute authorises the creation of a recognised estate, such as a fee simple, life estate, or lease, it is assumed that a property right created pursuant to that power is the estate defined by the common law. However, the statute may change the nature of the right that would have existed at common law. As Gaudron J said in *Wik Peoples v Queensland* (1996) 141 ALR 129 at 205:

> "Ordinarily, words which have an established meaning at common law are construed as having the same meaning in a statute unless there is something in the words or the subject matter of the statute to indicate otherwise."

The identification of a right to land granted by the Crown may require a detailed examination of the statute which authorised that grant. The first step is to determine if it is a right to possession. If so, it is an estate. If not, it is some lesser property or personal right. As the *Wik* case demonstrated, the use of the word "lease" is merely an indication of an estate and is not conclusive. A **pastoral lease** in Queensland is not an estate in land, but a lesser property right: see page 165.

If the Crown grant did create an estate, it need not be one of the freehold or leasehold estates recognised at common law. Again, the precise nature of that estate depends upon the particular statute which authorised its creation. One type of estate which fell outside the traditional categories was called a **perpetual lease** or **lease in perpetuity**. Although it entitled the tenant to possession of the land, it did not have the definite duration required for a valid lease at common law.

The perpetual lease is not a fee simple estate by another name. In *Fisher v Deputy Federal Commissioner of Land Tax (NSW)* (1915) 20 CLR 242 at 248, Isaacs and Gavan Duffy JJ said, "a perpetual lease is in its nature inherently distinct from a fee simple ... something less than the full estate of freehold is parted with". The Crown has a reversion which is slightly more substantial than the radical title it would hold in connection with a fee simple estate. As Dixon J said in *Hawkins v Minister for Lands (NSW)* (1949) 78 CLR 479 at 492:

"No doubt the reversionary interest in the Crown is slight and it may be said to be technical. But a rent is reserved, there are special conditions, the interest is capable of surrender and, for non-payment of survey fees, of forfeiture."

The perpetual lease is somewhat reminiscent of a fee simple estate under the feudal system, when feudal services and incidents were due to the Crown and the estate was subject to forfeiture and escheat. Perpetual leases were granted in Australia instead of fee simple estates in an effort to better control the settlement and development of land by European settlors. Conditions could be attached to the lease regarding such things as residence on the land, resale, fencing, pest control, and the cutting of timber. Of course, Parliament has the power to attach the same conditions to a grant of the fee simple, but those conditions are more palatable when attached to a lesser estate. It was easier politically to upgrade the leasehold estate than attempt to cut down the freehold.

Possession

The right to possession is what separates estates from all but two other property rights to land. The two exceptions are adverse possession and native title. First, an adverse possessor (discussed in Chapter 8) has a right to possession which is enforceable against everyone except persons with a right to immediate possession (either because of their estates or prior adverse possession). If all superior rights to possession are extinguished by the passage of time, adverse possession will become an estate. Secondly, native title (see Chapter 19) can (but need not) be a right to possession. Therefore, anyone with a right to possess land must have an estate, adverse possession, or native title.

It is not always easy to tell whether someone has the right to possession. When a person is granted a right to use land and that right is not defined clearly, he or she may have an estate, some other non-possessory property right (see Chapter 16), or a personal right to use land (often called a **licence**, discussed in Chapter 18). The language used by the parties is the most important clue to the right intended. People usually say what they mean. Words, such as estate, fee simple, lease, and licence, normally have legal effect according to their ordinary meanings. However, when interpreting the nature of a person's right to land, courts look at the substance and not just the form of the transaction. A person who has been granted the right to possession of the land has an estate, even if the language used by the parties indicates otherwise.

In *Radaich v Smith* (1959) 101 CLR 209, the plaintiff had a "licence to carry on the business of a milk bar" inside a larger building to which the public had access. Although the parties had called it a licence, the High Court held that the plaintiff had possession of the premises and, therefore, a leasehold estate. This entitled the plaintiff to apply to the Fair Rents Board to determine the fair rental for the premises. Conversely, in the *Wik* case, above, a right to use land called a "pastoral lease" was not a right to possess the land. Despite the language used, the pastoral tenants did not have leasehold estates and, therefore, did not have the right to exclude persons with native title.

In these cases, the nature of the right to use the land depends on the intentions of the persons creating that right. It is not conclusive that the parties thought they were creating a lease, a licence, or some other right. The central issue is what right was intended. If it was a right to possession of land for a term, it is, by definition, a lease, even if the parties did not recognise the legal consequence of their actions.

Lodgers and borders do not normally have a right to possession of the premises in which they reside. They may have exclusive control of a bedroom within a house, but the use and enjoyment of that room requires access to the rest of the house. It would be too great an interference with the landlord's right to possession of the house if he or she was forced to share the bathroom, kitchen, lounge, etc, with a lodger. Since the lodger's access to a bedroom inside the house depends upon the will of the landlord, it is usually regarded as a personal right (or licence).

Future Interests

Since an estate is a right to possession of a space on the earth for a period of time, it is possible to have a right to possession which arises in the future. For example, if Hemma has a fee simple estate and grants a life estate to Isaac, he will have the right to exclusive possession while he lives. Hemma does not have a right to possession during Isaac's life, but she does have a valuable property right. When Isaac dies, the right to possession will revert to Hemma.

While Isaac lives, Hemma has a right to possession which will arise in the future. Her right is called a **reversion** since the right to possession will come back to her. Hemma's right to future possession is not a new estate, but what remains after Ivan's life estate is carved out of her fee simple. Her fee simple estate began before Ivan's life estate and will continue afterwards. It does not matter that Hemma might die before Ivan. Her right to possession after Ivan's death is an existing property right which can be sold or given to another.

It is possible to create a new estate in which the right to possession will not arise for the first time until someday in the future. Suppose that Hemma had a fee simple estate and she granted a life estate to Isaac, with the remainder to Jana. Jana's new right to possession is called a **remainder** to distinguish it from a reversion (where the right to possession returns to grantor). Hemma has disposed of her entire estate and Jana gets everything which did not go to Ivan. In other words, Jana received a fee simple estate subject to a life estate.

Jana's right to possession does not begin until Ivan dies. However, Jana has an existing property right to possession in the future. Hemma's grant transferred the fee simple estate to Jana even though Jana's right to possession had been postponed until the termination of Ivan's life estate. Jana has a fee simple estate which is **vested in interest**. It will become **vested in possession** when Ivan dies. Ivan has a life estate which is vested in both interest and possession.

Contingent Remainders

All reversions are vested in interest, but this is not true of all remainders. If the identity of the person taking the remainder (called the **remainderman** or **remainder-person**) is not known at the date of the grant, a **contingent remainder** arises. For example, if Hemma has a fee simple estate, she might grant her estate to Ivan for life, with the remainder to her first grandchild to graduate from university. If none of Hemma's grandchildren have graduated from university at the date of the grant, then no one knows who will be entitled to possession when Ivan dies. When the first grandchild graduates, the identity of the remainder-person is known and the fee simple estate vests in interest. If no grandchildren ever graduate from university, the estate would revert to Hemma.

A remainder is vested in interest if the identity of the remainder-person is known and there is nothing postponing the right to possession except the natural termination of a prior estate. The identity of the remainder-person might be provided by the grant itself (such as "remainder to Jana") or by the circumstances. For example, a grant by Hemma "to Ivan for life, with remainder to my eldest child", could create a remainder which is either contingent or vested in interest. That depends on whether Hemma has a child at the date of the grant.

A remainder may be contingent even though the remainder-person is named in the grant. This occurs when there is some condition attached to the grant (other than the natural termination of a prior estate). For example, a grant to Ivan for life, with remainder to Jana provided she becomes a professional engineer, would create a remainder which is contingent until Jana attains that qualification. Even though Jana is named in the grant, if she is not an engineer, no one knows if she will take the remainder.

Rule Against Perpetuities

The common law does not like contingent remainders. A remainder which is vested in interest is a valuable property right which can be bought and sold. A contingent remainder is at best an expectancy. The holder of the future estate is unknown and therefore the estate is inalienable.

People like to create contingent remainders to control their things after death. A series of life estates could tie them up in perpetuity. The courts sought to limit this control from the grave with a device which became known as the **common law rule against perpetuities**. The rule invalidated any grant of a contingent remainder if the remainder could remain contingent for too long. Contingent remainders were permitted, but only so long as the contingency would be resolved one way or another within a period of time known as the **perpetuity period**.

At common law, a contingent remainder was void from the outset if it could possibly vest outside the perpetuity period. The remainder would be valid only if, at the date of the grant, it was clear that one of two things would happen within the perpetuity period:

1) .....the contingent remainder would vest in interest; or
2) .....it would become certain that the contingent remainder would never vest.

The law did not care whether the remainder vested in interest or not, so long as there was no possibility of it remaining contingent beyond the perpetuity period.

The common law rule can be difficult to understand and apply. The problem is the definition of the perpetuity period. Generally speaking, people were permitted to create contingent remainders which could remain contingent until their grandchildren became adults: see Lawson & Rudden, *The Law of Property* (2nd ed, 1982) p 185. Specifically, the contingent remainder must vest, if at all, within the lifetime of someone alive at the date of the grant (called a life in being) plus 21 years plus a gestation period. Of course, there are billions of people alive at the date of the grant. The trick is identifying a specific person who is a relevant life in being.

For example, a grant to Tom for life, with the remainder to his first child to attain 21 years is valid. If Tom has no children who are 21 or older at the date of the grant, the grant creates a contingent remainder since no one knows who (if anyone) will be Tom's first child to reach the age of 21 years. The remainder may never vest, since Tom might not have a child who reaches 21 years. However, if it does vest, it will do so during the perpetuity period. Tom is a life in being, since;

1) .....he is alive at the date of the grant; and
2) .....if any of his children attain 21 years, they will do so within 21 years of his death plus a gestation period (to take care of the possibility that he might die leaving someone pregnant with his child).

A grant to Lenore for life, with the remainder to her first child to attain 25 years would be invalid at common law if she had no children of that age or older at the date of the grant. There is a possibility that the contingent remainder could vest outside the perpetuity period. Lenore's first child to turn 25 may do so more than 21 years (plus gestation period) after Lenore dies. Lenore and everyone else alive at the date of the grant might die more than 21 years before the contingency is resolved. Therefore, there are no relevant lives in being which guarantee vesting within the perpetuity period.

The common law rule against perpetuities was concerned with logical, not realistic, possibilities. The remainder to Lenore's first child to attain 25 years would be invalid even if, at the date of the grant, Lenore was past childbearing age, happily married to a man with a vasectomy, and they had three children aged 24, 22, and 20. This is because all of Lenore's children might die before attaining age 25, Lenore might have another child after the date of the grant, and Lenore and everyone else alive at the date of the grant might die more than 21 years before that child's 25th birthday.

As these examples show, the common law rule against perpetuities is difficult. It was a trap for estate planners, since gifts in wills which seemed perfectly harmless could run afoul of the rule. Attempts to provide for grandchildren might be invalidated by unforeseen contingencies which, though logically possible, were realistically impossible. Legislatures came to the rescue with statutes designed to alleviate the problems created by the common law rule.

The common law rule against perpetuities was abolished in South Australia by section 61 of the *Law of Property Act* 1936 (SA). To prevent land in that state from being tied up for long periods by contingent remainders, the court can order the vesting of a remainder which has been, or is likely to be, contingent for 80 years or more.

Other states and territories have modified the common law rule. Remainders which would be void at common law are valid so long as there is a possibility of vesting within the perpetuity period. This is called the **wait and see** rule. For example, section 103 of the *Property Law Act* 1969 (WA) states: "A limitation shall not be declared or treated as invalid, as infringing the rule against perpetuities, unless and until it is certain that the interest that it creates cannot vest within the perpetuity period."

In New South Wales and the Australian Capital Territory, the perpetuity period is now 80 years. In other jurisdictions, the person creating the remainder can choose a perpetuity period defined by lives in being or as a specified number of years up to 80. There are a number of other statutory modifications of the common law rule. For example, several states have done away with unrealistic possibilities by presumptions that people under age 12 and females over age 55 are incapable of having children. The courts have powers to vary remainders to make them comply with rule.

The statutory modifications of the common law rule against perpetuities have not obviated the need to understand the common law. There may be remainders created before the relevant statute came into effect which are not be saved by the statute. More importantly, the application of the "wait and see" rule and the court's ability to modify contingent remainders both depend on knowing whether the remainder actually violates the common law rule. Legal advisors, who help people create contingent remainders in wills and trust deeds, still have at least three incentives to avoid violating the rule against perpetuities. First, legal professionals regard a remainder which needs to be fixed by statute as poorly drafted. Secondly, the statutory modification of the contingent remainder can change an estate plan in an unforeseen and potentially undesirable manner. Thirdly, a violation of the common law rule can create a long period of uncertainty as people "wait and see" whether the remainder will vest within the perpetuity period.

Waste

A person with a reversion or a remainder has a right to possession of land in the future, following the end of a prior estate. The value of that right can be adversely affected by the person in possession (the tenant for life or for years). For example, the life tenant might destroy the house or cut down the trees. Left unchecked, he or she could strip everything of value from the premises, leaving a worthless pit for the remainder-person.

The law limits what people in possession can do with their land, with a view to balancing their interests with the interests of those entitled to possession of that land in the future. If a tenant in possession deals with the land in a manner which adversely affects the interests of a person with a right to future possession, he or she may be liable for waste. The person with a right to future possession need not wait until her or his estate vests in possession, but can bring an action against the tenant in possession. This is somewhat similar to the "special action" for permanent damage to goods, discussed at page 57.

As with other breaches of duty (see Chapter 7), there are several legal responses to waste. A person with a future interest might seek:

1) .....an **injunction** to enforce the possessor's duty not to commit waste;
2) .....damages as **compensation** for losses caused by the waste; or
3) .....**restitution** of the possessor's profits from the waste (for example, from selling trees or gravel).

The common law recognised three types of waste. **Voluntary waste** is doing some act of damage to the premises which the possessor is not permitted to do. Cutting down large trees, destroying buildings, and starting a new mine have been identified as acts of voluntary waste. Both life and leasehold tenants may be liable for voluntary waste, unless exempted by the persons creating their estates. If the grant stated that the tenant was "unimpeachable for waste" (or conveyed that meaning in other language), then he or she was not accountable for waste at common law.

Permissive waste is the failure to take action to keep the premises in good repair. Failure to cultivate land or repair buildings are examples of permissive waste. A life tenant is liable for permissive waste only if the person creating that estate imposes an obligation to repair. The issue is not relevant to leasehold tenancies since both the common law and statutes in every state and territory impose covenants on leasehold tenants to maintain the property in good repair, which apply unless expressly negated by the lease.

Ameliorating waste is an act which does not harm the land, but fundamentally changes its character. Since it does not cause loss to the person with a right to future possession, the proper legal response to ameliorating waste is not compensation, but an injunction to stop the possessor from altering the premises (or perhaps to compel the possessor to restore the premises to their original condition). However, claims to stop ameliorating waste are rarely successful. The general principle, that tenants should leave land in the condition in which they receive it, is rarely used to prevent life tenants from improving the land.

In *Melms v Pabst Brewing Co* (1899) 79 NW 738, the Wisconsin Supreme Court held that the destruction of a large brick house by the life tenant (per autre vie) was not waste. This was because the house was the last residential dwelling in an area that had been converted to business use, complete with factories and rail lines. Since it was no longer desirable or valuable as a residence, the life tenant was permitted to change the character of the land and use it as a brewery.

A leasehold tenant's right to commit ameliorating waste may be restricted by statute. For example, section 64 of the *Residential Tenancies Act* 1997 (Vic) prohibits the tenant from altering the premises without the landlord's consent and, unless they agree otherwise, the tenant must restore the premises to their original condition at the end of the lease or pay the landlord for the cost of doing so.

The court of Chancery (see Chapters 5 and 13) would also intervene to prevent waste in some cases where the tenant in possession was "unimpeachable for waste" and therefore free at common law to deal with the land as he or she pleased. A court of equity would not permit the tenant to abuse this legal privilege and would restrain acts of wanton destruction, which became known as **equitable waste**. For example, pulling down a house or felling ornamental trees might be regarded as equitable waste, even though the possessor could not be held liable for waste at common law.

Chapter Thirteen

EQUITABLE RIGHTS

■■■

As discussed in Chapter 5, property rights are either legal or equitable. This dichotomy is the product of the English judicial system, which had separate courts of common law and equity until 1875. The body of law known as **equity** was developed by the court of **Chancery**. Although that court no longer exists, equity still survives and flourishes as part of the law administered by the courts of Australia.

There are three sources of property rights: statute, common law, and equity. The rights produced by equity are known as **equitable rights**. The rights produced by the common law are known as **legal rights**. The rights created by statute can be either legal or equitable, depending on whether those rights would, in days gone by, have been enforced in a court of common law or in Chancery. Though sometimes referred to as **statutory rights**, most rights created by statute are legal. However, there are statutes, such as the Trustee Acts in most states, which modify or create equitable rights.

There is a potential for confusion, because the word "legal" can be used in contrast to "equitable" or to describe all rights enforceable in a court of law, including those which are equitable. Also, the phrase "common law" has several meanings. Originally, it was used to distinguish the common law of England, administered by the royal courts based in Westminster, from the local laws and customs administered by manorial and other courts around the country: see Baker, *An Introduction to English Legal History* (3rd ed, 1990) Ch 2. Today, "common law" is used in three different ways. First, it is used (as above) to refer to the body of law created by the judges of the courts of common law, in contrast with Chancery's equity. Secondly, "common law" can be used to refer to all judge-made law (both common law and equity) to distinguish it from the statutes and regulations enacted by the legislative bodies of the Commonwealth, states, and territories. Thirdly, "common law" can mean the entire system of law in Australia and other jurisdictions which received law from England, in contrast with the "civil law" of jurisdictions (such as Italy, Mexico, and Quebec) with legal systems which depend less on judge-made law and more on statutory civil codes.

Development of Equitable Property Rights

The rights which today are regarded as equitable property rights were once regarded as personal rights. The transition from right *in personam* to right *in rem* was gradual and the debate over the nature of these rights continued into the early part of the 20th century. To understand this process, it is helpful to trace the history of Chancery.

The court of Chancery developed out of the office of the Lord Chancellor, who is a minister of the Crown responsible for the administration of justice in England. Litigants with complaints about the justice system would petition the Crown for special relief and the Lord Chancellor handled those petitions on the Crown's behalf. As the number of petitions increased, Vice-Chancellors, Chancellors, and a Master of the Rolls were appointed to assist the Lord Chancellor with this work. The nature of the Chancellor's intervention evolved from administrative to judicial and the basis of that intervention developed into the body of law known as equity.

The intervention of Chancery was originally reserved for procedural matters concerning the administration of justice in the common law courts, such as an allegation that the jurors had been bribed. However, it gradually moved to more substantive matters. For example, if a vendor of land refused to perform the contract of sale, the purchaser could go to a court of common law to seek an award of damages as compensation for loss. However, this would be of little use if the purchase price was the fair market value of the land and the purchaser had suffered no financial loss from the vendor's breach of contract. A purchaser dissatisfied with the common law result could go to Chancery for an order compelling the vendor to transfer the land as agreed.

An important feature of equity is that it works in conjunction with the common law and not by overruling it. Suppose, for example, that a court of common law declared that I was entitled to possession of land, but Chancery decided that you should have possession. Chancery did not give effect to its ruling by saying that the common law was wrong and that you had the legal right to possession. Instead, it acknowledged my right to possession at common law, but forced me to use that right for your benefit. Chancery did not take my common law right away from me, but would put me in gaol if I refused to let you enjoy the benefit of it.

At one time, your equitable right to possession of my land would have been regarded as a personal right. This is because it was a right enforceable against me personally. It was not enforced directly by an action of ejectment to recover possession of the land. Instead, it was enforced indirectly by compelling me (under threat of punishment) to let you use my right to possession. This is now regarded as a property right because a court will enforce your equitable right, not just against me, but against other members of society. If, for example, I gave that land to my son, you could force him to use his legal right to possession for your benefit.

The abolition of the court of Chancery did not substantially change the nature of equitable rights. The procedure changed. Litigants can go to one court to enforce both legal and equitable rights and gaol is seldom used as a means of enforcing equitable rights. However, the courts were reorganised in a way which preserved common law and equity as separate bodies of law. For example, section 29(1) of the *Supreme Court Act* 1986 (Vic) states that:

> "every court exercising jurisdiction in Victoria in any civil proceeding must continue to administer law and equity on the basis that, if there is a conflict or variance between the rules of equity and the rules of the common law concerning the same matter, the rules of equity prevail."

Judges continue to administer equity by recognising legal rights and then subjecting them, where necessary, to equitable rights.

Equity Today

Although equity is defined historically, by reference to a court which no longer exists, it is not stagnant. The rules of equity have continued to evolve since the abolition of the court of Chancery. Both common law and equity continue to be enlarged, developed, and refined by the courts charged with administering those bodies of law.

Equity first developed as a supplement to the common law and, therefore, many areas of law, such as contract and property, are a blend of common law, equity, and statute. The court of Chancery also had exclusive jurisdiction over several matters, such as trusts, partnerships, and corporations. Those areas of law were primarily equitable, but are now combinations of equity and statute.

Equity affects the law of property in many ways. For example, the modern mortgage (discussed in the next chapter) is a complex blend of common law, equitable, and statutory rules. There are three aspects of equity which are especially important to the modern law of property: the order for specific performance, the injunction, and the trust.

First, the normal common law response to a breach of contract is an award of damages (order to pay money) as compensation for losses caused by the breach. A court of equity can order the specific performance of the contractual obligations. This has had a profound effect on property. A person with a contractual right to obtain a property right can, in certain circumstances, count on obtaining that right and not just the payment of damages. As discussed at page 257, the right to acquire a property right through specific performance is itself a property right.

Secondly, a court of equity can issue an injunction to stop someone from interfering with the rights of another. This provides a powerful means of protecting property rights, which are usually enforced through personal rights to the payment of compensation: see Chapter 7. It also provided a means of developing new property rights. For example, the right to stop your neighbours from using their land in a certain way can be an equitable property right called a restrictive covenant: see page 156.

Thirdly, the **trust** is perhaps equity's greatest contribution to the law of property. Most trusts are combinations of personal and property rights. Therefore, most schools of common law teach the law of trusts as a separate subject or as part of a larger subject involving other areas of equity. Nevertheless, the law of property cannot be understood properly without dealing with the property aspects of the trust. This book deals with those aspects. There are a number of excellent books from Australia, Canada, England, and the United States, which provide a more complete picture of the personal rights and obligations involved in the trust relationship.

Trusts

A trust exists when a person has some right and is required by equity to use that right for the benefit of another person or for a particular purpose. The person with the right is called the **trustee**. The right is the **subject** of the trust. The person for whom (or purpose for which) the right must be used is the **object** of the trust. We say that the trustee holds the subject **in trust** for the object. Where the object of the trust is a person, he or she is called the **beneficiary** of the trust.

Trustees

Any person (individual or corporation) can be a trustee. The court has the power to replace a trustee who is an infant, mentally incapacitated, or otherwise unfit for the office. Each state has a *Trustee Companies Act*, which regulates the corporations that offer services to the public as professional trustees. It is common for two or more persons to be the trustees of a trust. They share the right which is the subject of the trust (see Chapter 15) and share the responsibility of ensuring that the right is used for the benefit of the trust objects.

Subjects

The subject of a trust can be any sort of right. It may be a property right (such as an estate in land or the ownership of a book) or a personal right (such as a bank account). The subject may be legal or equitable. For example, the beneficiary of a trust has an equitable property right which he or she could hold in another trust for others. There are two requirements of the subject matter which can interfere with attempts to create trusts:

1) .....the subject of a trust must belong to the trustee; and
2) .....it must be defined with certainty.

First, a trust cannot arise until the trustee obtains the right which is to be held in trust. When this happens, it is said that the subject is **vested in the trustee and that the trust is completely constituted**. Someone might intend to create a trust and do everything necessary for its creation, except transfer the intended subject to the intended trustee. For example, I might want you to hold my house in trust for my children, but fail to transfer the fee simple estate to you. The trust will not come into existence until that is done. This can be a significant problem if the person attempting to create the trust dies before it is constituted.

Secondly, all trusts require **certainty of subject matter**, which means that it must be possible to identify the subject of the trust. For example, my attempt to create a trust would fail if the subject was identified only as "my painting" (and I had more than one) or as "the bulk of my estate". The trustee would have no idea what particular things were supposed to be held in trust. An intended trust for two or more beneficiaries would fail if each beneficiary's share could not identified (for example, a trust of "most of my estate for Anna and the rest for Andy"). Although the trustee would know which things were held in trust, he or she would not know which things were supposed to belong to which beneficiary.

A trust can be valid if it provides a mechanism for allocating the property among the beneficiaries, such as the trustee's discretion. For example, a trust "to distribute my estate between Anna and Andy as my trustees see fit" would pass the test of certainty of subject matter. In *Boyce v Boyce* (1849) 16 Sim 476, 60 ER 959, a father died, leaving a will which gave his four houses to trustees to allow his daughter, Maria, to choose one of the houses and to give the remaining three houses to his daughter, Charlotte. Unfortunately, Maria died before her father and, with her, the mechanism for achieving certainty of subject matter was lost. Since the trustees and Charlotte were not given the right to allocate a house to Maria, the trust failed.

Objects

The objects of a trust can be persons (beneficiaries) or purposes. A trust can have many beneficiaries. For example, I might hold my house in trust for my spouse for life, with the remainder for my children and grandchildren, or a large pension fund might be held in trust for the employees of a company.

All trusts require **certainty of objects**, which means that it must be possible, at the time the trust comes into existence, to identify the persons or purposes entitled to the benefit of the trust. A trust for a person can fail if the intended beneficiary cannot be identified. For example, a trust for Joe, contained in a will made by someone who knew lots of people named "Joe", would fail if there was no evidence showing which Joe was intended to be the beneficiary. It is more common for an intended trust for persons to fail for lack of certainty of objects in cases where the trust is created for a class of persons, rather than for named individuals. For example, a trust for "all my friends" would fail if it was impossible to tell who belonged to that class: see *Re Gulbenkian's Settlement Trusts* [1970] AC 508.

The degree of certainty required for a trust in favour of a class of beneficiaries depends on the way in which the subject is to be distributed among the beneficiaries. If the trust requires distribution among all of the members of the class, then the trust is invalid unless all the members can be identified. Before the trustees can divide and distribute the subject matter, they need to know how many people are beneficiaries. If they are unable to make a complete list, the trust will fail for lack of certainty of objects.

A lesser degree of certainty is required if the trustees have a discretion to choose who among the class will receive assets from the trust. For example, a trust to award prizes to "the three most deserving pizza delivery persons in Australia as my trustees in their absolute discretion think fit" would be sufficiently certain. Although the trustees might not be able to list every possible beneficiary, they could tell who is or is not a potential object of the trust and could identify a sufficiently large pool of candidates from which to choose.

A trustee can also be a beneficiary of the trust, but the sole trustee cannot be the sole beneficiary. For example, Sophie could be the sole trustee for both Hanna and herself (or Sophie and Hanna could be trustees together for Sophie), but Sophie could not be a trustee for herself alone. This is because a trust will exist only if the trustee is under an enforceable equitable obligation to use the subject in a certain way. Since a person cannot enforce legal rights against herself or himself, a trust is not possible unless there is some difference between the interests of the trustees and the interests of the beneficiaries. This is discussed further in Chapter 15.

Normally, trusts for purposes are invalid unless the purposes are recognised by law as **charitable**, such as the relief of poverty or sickness, education, or the advancement of religion. Charitable trusts are possible because they are enforced by the Attorney-General on behalf of the Crown. However, with few exceptions, an attempt to create a trust for a non-charitable purpose will fail because there is nobody to enforce it: *Murdoch v Attorney-General (Tas)* (1992) 1 Tas R 117. There are several anomalous non-charitable purpose trusts (for example, to maintain a monument or a specific animal) which are permitted solely because they were allowed at one time and people have since relied on their validity. Also, there are statutes which authorise the creation of a trust for a purpose, such as section 41(2) of the *Land Act* 1994 (Qld) which states that "the Governor in Council may also grant, in fee simple in trust, unallocated State land for use for a community purpose." The statute provides the mechanism for enforcing the trust.

Where the object of the trust is a charitable purpose, it is likely that its subject will be used for the benefit of a particular group of people. For example, if a sum of money is held in trust to feed the homeless people of Sydney, it will be expended for the benefit of the people who meet that description. However, that trust is for a particular charitable purpose and not directly for the benefit of any particular persons and, therefore, they cannot enforce the trust.

Beneficial Ownership

Where the objects of the trust are persons (beneficiaries), they can enforce the trust in a court of equity. In other words, they have equitable rights to compel the trustee to use the subject of the trust for their benefit. As discussed above, these rights were originally regarded as rights *in personam*, corresponding only to the obligation of the trustees to perform the trust. In the 19th and 20th centuries, those rights came to be viewed as rights *in rem*, relating to the subject of the trust and corresponding to a general duty placed on members of society not to interfere with those rights.

The beneficiary of a trust has an equitable property right, sometimes referred to as a **beneficial interest**. The right to the benefit of a thing can be either legal or equitable. For example, the owner of a legal estate in fee simple is normally entitled to the beneficial use and enjoyment of that estate. However, if the owner holds the fee simple in trust for someone else (the trust beneficiary), then the beneficiary is entitled to that benefit. The term, **beneficial ownership**, can mean either legal or equitable ownership of a thing.

The beneficiaries of a **discretionary trust** have only limited equitable rights. A discretionary trust is one in which the trustees have the discretion to select beneficiaries from among a class or, in some cases, to decide whether to distribute the subject at all: see *Federal Commissioner of Taxation v Vegners* (1989) 90 ALR 547. The beneficiaries have the right to sue trustees who fail to observe the terms of the trust. However, since no beneficiary has an enforceable right to receive assets from the trust, they do not, as individuals, have the beneficial ownership of those assets. For example, in *Ontario v Henson* (1987) 28 ETR 121, the beneficiary of a trust worth $82,000 was a mentally incompetent adult. The trustees had complete discretion whether to use the trust assets for her benefit and anything left over on her death was to be paid to a local "Association for the Mentally Retarded". Since she had no enforceable right to receive any part of the subject of the trust, she was not the beneficial owner of those assets and was therefore entitled to receive benefits from the government, which were available only to people with less than $3,000 worth of assets.

Types of Trusts

Trusts are classified according to the manner of their creation. Some trusts are created by an expressed intention to create that trust. For example, the owner of a fee simple estate may want that estate to be held in trust for someone and, by following the proper procedures, he or she can create that trust. Trusts which are intentionally created are called **express trusts** and a person who creates an express trust is called a **settlor**.

Other trusts arise by operation of law. They come into existence not because someone intentionally created them, but because certain facts exist which prompt a court of equity to compel the holder of a right to use that right for the benefit of another. For example, de facto spouses might pool their assets and acquire a family home. If they split up and the home is owned by one of the spouses, he or she may be compelled to hold a portion of the fee simple estate in trust for the other. These trusts are called **resulting trusts** or **constructive trusts**.

Trusts can also be created by statute: see, eg, *Registrar of the Accident Compensation Tribunal v Federal Commissioner of Taxation* (1993) 178 CLR 145. They are sometimes called **statutory trusts**. Since trusts are classified according to the events which create them, these categories are explored in greater detail in the relevant chapters of Part IV (The Creation of Property Rights).

Development of the Trust

The modern trust developed from a device called the **use**, which was popular in the 15th and 16th centuries. The use was similar to the trust and allowed a person to hold an estate in land to the use of another. At that time, a transfer of land was called a **feoffment** (discussed at page 247), so the person who received land to the use of another was called the **feoffee que use** and the beneficiary of the use was called the **cestui que use**. (Today, the beneficiary of a trust is sometimes called a **cestui que trust**.)

The use became popular for two main reasons. First, fee simple estates could not be transferred by will. When the tenant died, the estate passed by law to her or his heir (usually the eldest son). The use allowed the tenant to provide for other family members, such as a widow, daughters, and younger sons. For example, a husband and father might transfer his fee simple estate to feoffees to hold to the use of himself for life, then his widow for life, then to be shared among his children.

The second reason for employing a use was the avoidance of **feudal incidents**. On the death of the tenant, the fee simple estate would pass to her or his heir, but not without considerable expense: see Simpson, *A History of the Land Law* (2nd ed, 1986) pp 15-20. The lord was entitled to the payment of **relief** (usually a year's rent) for recognising the heirs right to inherit the estate. If the deceased was a tenant in chief, the Crown was entitled to **primer seisin** (also a year's rent). If the heir was a minor, the lord had the right to **wardship** until he or she attained the age of majority. This gave the lord custody of the heir's land and the right to sell her or his hand in **marriage**. Additionally, if the tenant died without heirs, the estate would **escheat** to the lord: see Chapter 12.

A tenant could avoid these consequences by transferring the land to several feoffees to her or his own use. When the tenant died, the use would pass to the people chosen by the tenant, but the legal ownership of the estate (held by the feoffees) would not change. When a feoffee died, the estate would continue to be held by the surviving feoffees and not descend to an heir. Deceased feoffees could be replaced, thereby ensuring that the estate never descended to an heir and that feudal incidents were never paid.

The success and popularity of the use as a method of avoiding feudal incidents brought about its downfall. The substantial loss of revenue to the Crown (then King Henry VIII) resulted in the **Statute of Uses** 1536. This eliminated most uses of freehold estates by **executing the use**, which removed the estate from the feoffees que use and transferred it to the cestui que use. In other words, the beneficiary of a use became the legal owner of the fee simple estate and that use ceased to exist.

The *Statute of Uses* restored the Crown's revenues from feudal incidents, but also took away tenants' powers to choose the people to whom their estates would pass on death. This was remedied by the *Statute of Wills* 1540, which enabled tenants to devise their lands by will. The Crown's revenues were preserved because the recipient of an estate under a will was liable for the feudal incidents that would have been paid if the land had descended to an heir. Feudal incidents were finally ended by the *Tenures Abolition Act* 1660.

The modern trust arose from the ashes of the executed use. In the 17th century, Chancery began enforcing what was known as a **use upon a use**: see Simpson, above, at pp 199-207. If, for example, land was conveyed to Amanda to the use of Barbara to the use of Claire, the Statute of Uses would execute the first use, thereby giving the legal estate to Barbara. The second use for Claire would not be executed, but was considered repugnant to the first use and invalid at law. However, Chancery thought it wrong for Barbara to keep for her own benefit an estate intended for the use of Claire, so it began to enforce the second use.

The second (enforceable) use came to be called a trust, to distinguish it from the first (executed) use. So, a conveyance to Amanda to the use of Barbara in trust for Claire would create a valid trust for Claire, with Barbara holding the legal estate as trustee. The creation of the trust could be simplified by dropping Amanda from the transaction and conveying the land directly to Barbara to the use of Barbara in trust for Claire. This could be further shortened by a conveyance **unto and to the use of Barbara in trust for Claire**. The statute would execute the use for Barbara, but leave the trust for Claire intact.

The *Statute of Uses* was repealed in New South Wales, Queensland, and Victoria, but still applies in South Australia, Tasmania, and Western Australia. Where it does apply, express trusts continue to be created by transferring land unto and to the use of the trustee in trust for the beneficiaries.

Modern Uses of the Trust

The trust has endured because it proved to be a versatile and useful device for managing property rights over time. It allows people to make complicated estate plans, by creating equitable estates and remainders which are set up in ways not permitted at common law. The law did not tolerate a gap in seisin (any lapse of time between successive freehold estates), because the lord was entitled to know at all times who was responsible for the feudal services and incidents due from the freehold tenant. So, for example, a legal freehold estate could not be granted to arise in the future or as a remainder after a lease. The trust avoids this problem, since trustees can continue to hold the freehold estate, while the equitable beneficial ownership of that estate is allocated in a variety of different ways.

More importantly, the trust allows people to divide the equitable ownership of personal property over time in the same way that estates are used to divide rights to possession of land. The common law recognised temporary rights to possession of goods (bailments, discussed at page 52), but did not recognise life interests or remainders. Those rights to goods and personal rights can now be created in equity through the use of a trust. For example, funds in a bank or shares in a corporation could be held in trust for your spouse for life, with the remainder to your children. This is an important part of estate planning, since a great deal of personal wealth consists of rights other than interests in land.

The trust is a popular way to separate the management of property from its ownership (the corporation is another). People who are incapable of managing their own affairs, due to infancy or mental incapacity, can enjoy the beneficial ownership of property which is legally owned and managed for them by trustees. If parents are worried about making a large gift of property to a financially irresponsible son or daughter, they can create a **protective trust** (sometimes called a **spendthrift trust**) for that child, which protects the trust assets from the child's creditors.

Trusts are sometimes used by people who wish to be free of the responsibility of management. Their investments can be placed in trust and tended by trustees who specialise in that type of work. A politician might wish to avoid conflicts of interest by placing her or his wealth in a **blind trust**, which allows the trustees to invest that wealth without revealing the identity of the investments to the politician. The **trading trust** has long been used as an alternative to the corporate structure. The trustees use the trust assets to operate a business on behalf of the beneficiaries in much the same way that directors of a corporation manage its affairs on behalf of the shareholders. The choice of form may be dictated by income tax concerns.

The trust has proved to be a useful way for large groups of people to pool their wealth for investment purposes. Rather than venture into the share market by themselves, people might choose to invest in a large mutual, pension, or superannuation fund. A large investment trust might be called a **unit trust** if the beneficial ownership of the fund is divided into units which investors are invited to purchase. By concentrating the wealth of a large number of small investors, these large trust funds have the potential to wield significant power in corporate circles, both through their choice of investments and their voting as corporate shareholders: see Stapledon, *Institutional Shareholders and Corporate Governance* (1996).

Large **superannuation funds** are based on the traditional trust relationship (with trustees holding title to assets on behalf of large numbers of beneficiaries). However, they have evolved into more complex relationships shaped by equitable and statutory principles. The duties of the managers and the rights of the contributors to the fund are defined by contracts of employment, within a statutory framework. For example, in *Fouche v Superannuation Fund Board* (1952) 88 CLR 609, a member of the board of a superannuation fund was accused of misusing a portion of that fund for his own benefit. In a traditional trust, this would be a breach of duty to the beneficiaries, for which they could sue. The High Court held that the board member had breached his duty to the corporation which owned the fund and that the corporation was the proper plaintiff. They said (at 640):

> "We do not think...that the contributors *are* beneficiaries in the proper sense: they have, of course, an interest in the fund which would probably give them standing in a court of equity, but they have not such a beneficial interest in the trust fund as has an ordinary *cestui que trust*. The trust is not a trust for persons but for statutory purposes."

Trusts created by operation of law are also important in modern society. Although the express trust remains the most significant (whether measured by the number of trusts or the amount of wealth held in trust), constructive and resulting trusts have gained prominence in recent years. Equity's power to require people to use their legal rights for the benefit of others has proved to be a useful tool in a number of settings. The distribution of property between de facto spouses is just one of many important roles for these trusts. For example, courts can declare that wrongdoers hold the profits of their wrongs in trust for their victims and that people who receive property by mistake hold it in trust for its previous owners. These issues are explored in Part IV.

Nature of Equitable Property Rights

Like all property rights, an equitable property right relates to some thing and is enforceable generally against other members of society. It can have content similar to that of an equivalent legal right. For example, the tenant of a five-year leasehold estate has the same right to use and enjoy the land regardless of whether that estate is legal or equitable. However, legal and equitable property rights differ in some important respects. They are created in different ways (see Part IV) and are accorded different levels of priority in competition with other rights (see Part V). However, these are not the most important differences.

The essential difference between legal and equitable property rights concerns the things to which those rights relate. Legal property rights relate directly to things, such as land, goods, or intangibles. For example, a legal estate is a right to possess a space on the earth. The thing subject to that right is that space. In contrast, equitable property rights operate indirectly as parasites attached to other rights. The thing subject to an equitable estate is not the space on the earth, but another person's right to that space. The subject of a trust is the trustee's right to something and not the thing itself.

It is easy to overlook the true nature of equitable property rights. This is because a trust beneficiary has an indirect equitable right to a thing and can enjoy that thing in the same manner as someone with a direct legal right. For example, if a trustee holds a legal fee simple estate in trust, the beneficiary gets the use and enjoyment of the trustee's right to possession. In other words, for most practical purposes, it does not matter whether beneficial ownership is legal or equitable.

The parasitic nature of equitable property rights does have at least two important consequences. First, any sort of right can be subject to equitable property rights. This means that personal rights can be the things to which equitable property rights relate. For example (as discussed at page 11), a bank account is not property, but a personal right to be paid a sum of money by the bank. That right does not relate to any particular thing, but corresponds to the bank's obligation to pay its debt. However, that bank account can be held in trust. A trustee's personal right against her or his bank can be the subject of a trust and subject to the beneficiary's equitable property right. That property right is possible because it attaches to the trustee's right and not the underlying thing (if any) to which the trustee's right relates.

Secondly, equitable property rights are never carved out of legal property rights, but impressed upon them. The difference is subtle, but significant. If I have a legal fee simple estate and lease the land to you for 10 years, I have transferred a portion of my right to possession to you. In other words, I have carved out a portion of my estate, leaving behind a reversion. If instead I declare a trust of the estate for you for 10 years (that is, create an equitable lease), I still retain all my legal rights. My legal fee simple estate remains intact in my hands. However, I am required to use that estate for your benefit for 10 years.

In most cases (as in the preceding example), there will be few practical differences between a legal right carved out of a greater right and an equitable right impressed upon it. However, the distinction can be important. In *DKLR Holding Co (No 2) Pty Ltd v Commissioner of Stamp Duties* (1982) 149 CLR 431, one company transferred its fee simple estate to another company, which immediately created a trust of that estate for the benefit of the first company. They objected to the payment of stamp duty for the transaction, which had been assessed on the full market value of the land. The High Court of Australia rejected their argument that the beneficial ownership of the land had remained with the first company throughout and that the second company had received only a bare legal title without market value. The entire legal fee simple estate had been transferred and a new equitable fee simple had been created for the transferor. As Brennan J said (at 474):

> "A transferee does not become a trustee by failing to acquire an interest in the property transferred; a trustee holds on trust only such interest as he acquires. An equitable interest is not carved out of a legal estate but impressed upon it."

The equitable beneficial ownership created by a trust is just one type of equitable property right. There are a variety of lesser property rights, such as equitable mortgages, liens, and charges, discussed in the next chapter on security rights. There are also a number of equitable personal rights, such as the right to equitable compensation or an account of profits. Most legal rights have an equitable counterpart. In most cases, it will not matter whether a particular right is legal or equitable. However, the distinction should not be overlooked because there are a number of situations in which it is important.

Chapter Fourteen

SECURITY RIGHTS

▎▎▎

A security right (often called a **security interest**) is a property right which exists for the purpose of securing the performance of a personal obligation. For example, if I ask to borrow your petrol can, you might worry about whether I will keep my promise to return it. You might agree to lend it to me on the condition that I leave behind something of value, such as a set of keys, a wallet, or a credit card. If I leave something in your possession, say my keys, you would have a property right obtained for the purpose of making it more likely that I will fulfil my promise. When I return your petrol can, the reason for your property right to my keys ceases.

The most familiar security right is the mortgage. Most people who buy a home need to borrow money to pay the purchase price. The lender has the benefit of the borrower's promise to repay the loan, but usually insists on receiving a mortgage of the home as well. If the borrower fails to repay the loan, the lender can obtain or sell the home to satisfy the amount owing.

There are many other types of security rights, such as the pledge, lien, charge, and conditional sale. A security right may be legal or equitable and may be ownership, possession, or a lesser property right. Regardless of the form of the transaction, all security rights exist for the limited purpose of making it more likely that some personal obligation will be performed. They further that purpose in two ways. First, the existence of a security right creates an additional incentive to perform the obligation. In the example above, my desire to get my keys back motivates me to return your petrol can. Secondly, some security rights have a market value which can be used as a substitute for performance. For example, you might have insisted on receiving a credit card voucher, which could be used to pay for a replacement petrol can if necessary.

The usual type of personal obligation for which people take security rights to property is an obligation to pay money. As discussed in Chapter 2, this obligation is called a **debt**, the person who owes money is a **debtor**, and the person to whom money is owed is a **creditor**. A creditor who has taken a property right to secure payment of the debt is called a **secured creditor** (or **secured party**). A creditor without security is an **unsecured creditor**. Although security rights are often used for obligations other than debts, the person under the obligation is referred to below as the debtor for the sake of convenience.

Reasons for Taking Security Rights

Most obligations are unsecured, such as your promise to pay the balance owing on your credit card, your employer's promise to pay your salary at the end of the fortnight, or your travel agent's promise to deliver the airline tickets you reserved. Generally, we are happy to rely on the fact that most people keep their promises. We are willing to take a risk when the possibility and consequences of non-performance are relatively low.

There are two main disadvantages of unsecured obligations. The first is the expense, delay, and inconvenience of taking legal action to enforce the obligation in the event of non-performance. An unsecured creditor must obtain a court judgment for the debt (becoming a **judgment creditor**) and, if the judgment is not paid, must proceed to execution (as an **execution creditor**) by instructing the sheriff to seize the debtor's assets to pay the judgment. Having security can both reduce the risk of non-performance and provide a property right which can be used to satisfy the debt.

Secondly, unsecured creditors are vulnerable to the risk of their debtors' **insolvency** or **bankruptcy** (inability to pay their debts). If a debtor is declared bankrupt, her or his assets vest in the **trustee in bankruptcy,** who uses them to pay the bankrupt's creditors according to law. The process is designed to facilitate the orderly and fair payment of the bankrupt's debts. The unsecured creditors are then limited to a claim in the bankruptcy and can no longer take independent steps to obtain payment. If there is anything left after the secured creditors enforce their security rights and the **preferred creditors** (who have a statutory priority for certain debts, such as funeral expenses or wages) are paid, the ordinary creditors share what remains *pro rata* (for example, 10 cents for every dollar owed). After the assets are sold and distributed, the bankruptcy can be discharged and the bankrupt's debts are extinguished.

The risk of being adversely affected by a debtor's bankruptcy is reduced by taking security. This is because a bankruptcy affects personal rights against the debtor, but does not normally affect other people's property rights to the debtor's things. The theory of bankruptcy is that the debtor's property is used to pay her or his creditors. Bankruptcy does not allow other people's property to be used for that purpose. A security right (such as a mortgage of the debtor's home) is the property of the secured creditor and unavailable to the other creditors.

Types of Security Rights

There are three main types of property rights used as security: possession, ownership, and encumbrance.

Possession

Possession is the oldest form of security, in which the creditor is entitled to possession of something belonging to debtor until the debt is paid.

There are two main types of possessory security: the pledge and the legal or common law lien. These are legal security rights (the right to possession). The equitable lien is a different type of security: an encumbrance, discussed below.

Pledge

A **pledge** is the delivery of a chattel for the express purpose that possession of the chattel be held for security. For example, you might be asked to leave an identification card behind when you pick up a key to the tennis court. The card is pledged as security for your obligation to return the key. Any sort of chattel may be pledged, including goods and documents (such as a bill of lading for goods being shipped): see *ANZ Banking Group Ltd v Curlett, Cannon & Galbell Pty Ltd* [1992] 2 VR 647. A pledge is sometimes called a **pawn** and someone in the business of lending money in exchange for pledges is called a **pawnbroker**.

Although most pledges arise when the chattel is delivered to the secured party, he or she might already have possession when the owner agrees that it can be used as a pledge. The essence of a pledge is not an act of delivery, but the possession of a chattel to secure performance of an obligation. The secured party has a right to retain possession until the obligation is performed. If the debtor fails to perform the secured obligation, the creditor has the right to sell the thing pledged and use the proceeds to satisfy that obligation. Anything which remains after payment of the debt (and costs of sale) must be returned to the debtor.

Common Law Lien

A **lien** arises when a person has possession of a chattel for some other purpose and the law allows her or him to retain possession until a related obligation is performed. For example, an unpaid vendor has a lien on goods sold until the full purchase price is paid, a garage has a lien on goods repaired until its repair bill is paid, and accountants have a lien on their client's books until their fees are paid. The lien ends when either the debt is paid or possession of the goods is lost.

Unlike a pledge, a lien does not give the secured party a right to sell the chattel to satisfy the debt. There are some exceptions created by statute. For example, the Warehousemen's Lien Acts in most jurisdictions give the warehouse the right to sell the goods to pay the cost of storage charges. However, at common law, liens are passive security rights to do no more than retain possession until the relevant debt is paid. The lien arises because it is unfair to permit an owner of goods to enforce her or his right to possession without paying the bailee for services which have enhanced or preserved the value of those goods.

There is no right to a lien on a chattel unless the debt relates to that chattel in some way. For example, the debt might be the purchase price or the charges for storing, transporting, repairing, or improving that chattel. The connection required between debt and chattel varies according to the custom in each trade and profession. In some cases, a lien on a chattel will arise only for work done on that particular chattel. This is called a **particular lien**. For example, in *Dinmore Meatworks Pty Ltd v Kerr* (1962) 108 CLR 628, an abattoir butchered cattle for a customer who became insolvent and failed to pay for the work.

The abattoir still had some of the customer's meat and claimed a lien for the entire debt. The High Court held that the lien secured only those fees charged for preparing the meat in the abattoir's possession.

In some trades and professions, the secured party is entitled to a **general lien**. For example, a carrier of goods can claim a lien on part of a shipment for the shipping charges for the whole shipment. Also, solicitors have a lien on a client's file for all the fees owed by the client and not just the legal work done on that particular file.

The lien entitles a secured party to resist the debtor's claim to possession of the goods, but does not operate against other persons with a better right to immediate possession. For example, in *Anderson v Lockhart* [1991] 1 Qd R 501, a solicitor had a lien on his client's leasehold documents. A bank, which foreclosed on the property (foreclosure is discussed below), had a better right to possession of those documents than the client. The solicitor's lien did not entitle him to resist the bank's claim for possession of the documents. Also, there are cases where a bailee of goods delivered them to a shop for repairs (a sub-bailment, discussed in Chapter 6). The lien for the cost of repairs will not entitle the shop to resist the bailor's right to immediate possession, unless the bailee had the bailor's (express or implied) permission to get the goods repaired: see *Fisher v Automobile Finance Co of Australia Ltd* (1928) 41 CLR 167.

Ownership

In some cases, the secured party gets legal ownership of (or title to) some thing for the purposes of securing a personal obligation. On full performance of the secured obligation (usually payment of the debt), the creditor is required to transfer the ownership to the debtor. Normally, the debtor has possession of the thing unless he or she fails to perform the obligation as agreed, in which case the creditor becomes entitled to possession.

This is a desirable form of security for both creditor and debtor. Since the creditor is already the owner of the thing, it can be relatively easy to enforce her or his security rights in the event of default. Also, as discussed in Chapter 28, legal ownership is more durable than many other property rights and less likely to be adversely affected by competing claims. The debtor benefits from being entitled to the possession, use, and enjoyment of the thing while the obligation is being performed. This is especially important if performance of the secured obligation will continue over a long period of time (such as a mortgage payable over 25 years).

There are two main types of ownership security: the common law mortgage and the hire-purchase (or conditional sale). The Torrens mortgage is a type of encumbrance, discussed below.

Mortgage

Anything which can be owned (such as a car, an estate, or a violin) can be mortgaged. The common law **mortgage** of land has a long history and is discussed below in greater detail. A mortgage of goods is usually called a **chattel mortgage** or **bill of sale**. Most mortgages are used to help the debtor purchase the thing mortgaged. The debtor (as purchaser) asks the vendor to transfer ownership of the thing to the secured creditor, who lends money to the debtor to be used to pay the purchase price to the vendor. However, a mortgage can be used for any purpose. For example, you might borrow money to renovate your house or travel overseas and your bank might take a mortgage of your land as security for the loan.

Hire-Purchase and Conditional Sale

The **hire-purchase** and **conditional sale** are functionally similar to a mortgage: the secured creditor has ownership of the thing until the debt is paid. Unlike the mortgage, they are always used to secure the payment of a purchase price. The vendor is the secured creditor and the thing sold is subject to the security right. In other words, the vendor finances the purchase. He or she is the owner of the thing at the outset and retains ownership as a secured creditor until the full purchase price is paid. Both land and goods can be sold in this manner, but the term "hire-purchase" is not used in connection with land.

Encumbrance

As discussed above, possession and ownership can be held for security purposes. It is also possible to create a security right which is neither possession nor ownership. The secured creditor merely has the right to take and sell the thing if the debtor defaults. It is not some other type of property right (such as possession or ownership) which is used for security purposes. The security right is simply an encumbrance on the debtor's property right, which may, on default by the debtor, become a right to possession or ownership. The granting of this type of security is sometimes called **hypothecation**.

There are three types of encumbrances: the equitable charge, the equitable lien, and the statutory encumbrance.

Equitable Charge

The **equitable charge** is created by an agreement between the creditor and debtor. The debtor agrees that certain assets will be available to the creditor to satisfy the debt if payment is not made. The creditor gets neither possession nor ownership, but the equitable right to use the assets for the satisfaction of the debt in the event of default. The equitable charge is sometimes called an **equitable mortgage**, especially when it is a charge over land.

A debtor may grant an equitable charge or mortgage over a specific asset, such as an estate or piece of machinery, or may grant a charge over a pool of assets, such as the stock in trade of a business or all of a corporation's assets. A charge over a specific asset is sometimes called a **fixed charge** to distinguish it from a charge over a pool of assets, which is called a **floating charge**. The identity of the assets which constitute the pool subject to a floating charge can change. For example, a floating charge over all the assets of a corporation is a security interest over whatever assets the corporation has at any given time. Assets will be removed from and added to that pool as they are sold, consumed, created, or purchased. Floating charges are usually granted by corporations and are often created by a document called a **debenture**.

An equitable charge is comparable to a trust: see Chapter 13. The debtor (like the trustee) retains legal ownership. Equity compels the debtor to use her or his legal ownership for the purpose of securing the debt. The debtor's legal ownership is subject to the creditor's equitable property right (just as the trustee's legal ownership is subject to the beneficiary's equitable property right). Unlike the trust, the creditor does not get the full beneficial use and enjoyment of the assets, but merely a security interest. So, while debtor and trustee both have legal ownership, the debtor has beneficial ownership and the trustee has bare legal title. Conversely, the secured creditor and trust beneficiary both have equitable property rights, but the creditor has a limited security interest, while the beneficiary has full beneficial ownership.

There are two main advantages of an equitable charge. First, non-possessory and personal rights (such as a bank account) can be charged. Secondly, the debtor retains ownership (and possession) of the things charged and can deal with them subject to the charge. Floating charges permit debtors to deal with their assets in the ordinary course of business. This makes it possible for a debtor to give security to a creditor without sterilising assets needed by the debtor to carry on business (so long as the debt is being paid as required).

Equitable Lien

The **equitable lien** is equivalent to an equitable charge, but created by operation of law, rather than by an intention to create it. The distinction between the equitable charge and equitable lien can be compared to the distinction between the pledge and the common law lien or the distinction between the express and resulting trust: see Part IV. The equitable lien, like its common law counterpart, arises to secure payment of a debt related to the thing subject to the lien. Unlike the common law lien, the equitable lien is not possession, but an equitable property right attaching to the debtor's property or personal right.

There are a number of situations in which equitable liens are known to arise. The most familiar is the **unpaid vendor's lien** which arises on the sale of land. If an estate is transferred to the purchaser before the full purchase price is paid, the vendor has an equitable lien against the estate for the balance owing. This can be compared to the common law lien which the vendor of goods has to retain possession of those goods until the full purchase price is paid.

The purchaser of land can also have an equitable lien. If he or she pays any part of the purchase price before the land is transferred, a **purchaser's lien** arises to secure a refund in the event that the sale cannot be completed. The purchaser also has an equitable beneficial interest in the land so long as the sale can be performed. That interest and the vendor's and purchaser's liens are discussed in Chapter 21.

Equitable liens can also arise in favour of a person who has contributed to the improvement or preservation of land, goods, or some other right. In these cases, the lien attaches to that right to secure the right holder's obligation to pay for the value of the benefit. People are not normally required to pay for unrequested benefits. However, a lien can arise where the benefit was conferred by mistake or with the encouragement of the right holder. For example, in *Foskett v McKeown* [1997] 3 All ER 392, a trustee misused the trust fund to pay the premiums on his life insurance policy. He then committed suicide and the trust beneficiaries were entitled to an equitable lien on the death benefit to secure a refund of the trust monies used to maintain the policy. The lien in this situation is discussed further at page 335.

Statutory Encumbrance

There is no direct, common law equivalent to the equitable charge and lien. The law permitted people to use legal property rights (ownership and possession) for security purposes, but did not create a specific legal encumbrance. Legal encumbrances have been made possible by statute. The **statutory encumbrance** is like an equitable charge, except that the creditor obtains a legal security right.

The most important and familiar statutory encumbrance is the **Torrens mortgage**. Every jurisdiction in Australia has a Torrens system of land title registration, which is discussed in more detail in Chapter 32. A mortgage under that system is not a transfer of ownership to the creditor, but a legal encumbrance on the land. The debtor remains the owner of the land, but grants a registered charge over the land to the secured creditor. For example, section 74(2) of the *Transfer of Land Act 1958* (Vic) states that a Torrens mortgage "shall when registered have effect as a security and be an interest in land, but shall not operate as a transfer of the land thereby mortgaged or charged". This is a non-possessory legal security interest, which can become possession or ownership if the debtor fails to perform the obligation secured.

Although the Torrens mortgage is quite different from the common law mortgage, courts dealing with the Torrens mortgage have continued to use the principles and language developed in common law and equity in connection with the common law mortgage. Therefore, a proper understanding of the Torrens mortgage is not possible without some knowledge of the history and nature of the mortgage at common law.

There are many jurisdictions in North America that have statutes (patterned after the Uniform Commercial Code in the United States of America and commonly called Personal Property Security Acts in Canada) which allow for the creation of statutory legal encumbrances on chattels. Law reformers in Australia have on several occasions considered the reform of the law relating to security rights to personal property: see, eg, Australian Law Reform Commission, *Personal Property Securities* (Interim Report No 64, 1993). The use of statutory encumbrances may become the norm if the American approach is taken. At present, there are some statutes which permit the creation of a legal encumbrance on personal property. For example, section 5 of the *Chattel Securities Act 1987* (WA) states:

> "The parties to a security interest may agree that the security interest shall be a legal interest in the goods subject to the security interest and, if the parties so agree, the security interest is a legal interest in the goods."

Mortgages

Like many property rights, the modern mortgage is the product of centuries of development. The early mortgage was a lease of the land to the creditor with a condition that the creditor would become the owner of the reversion if the debt was not repaid when the lease came to an end. This was similar to a common law pledge of chattels, in that the creditor held possession of the land as security for the debt.

The pledge of land was called a **gage**. There were two kinds: the living pledge, where the income from the land was used to pay off the debt, and the dead pledge (**mort gage**), where the creditor kept the income. The mortgage was at one time regarded by the church as a sin, because the creditor's right to the income was equivalent to charging interest. The term "mortgage" has endured even though the form of the mortgage ceased to be a pledge and became a transfer of ownership, first with possession and later without possession unless the borrower defaulted on the loan. The debtor who grants a mortgage is called the **mortgagor** and the creditor who receives a mortgage is called the **mortgagee**.

Intervention of Equity

The mortgage evolved from a lease (with a transfer of the reversion on default) into a conveyance of the fee simple (coupled with a promise by the mortgagee to reconvey the title if the debt was repaid within a fixed time). It became common to charge interest on the debt. The court of Chancery thought it was wrong that the mortgagee should receive both the payment of interest and the income from the mortgaged land. It began to require the mortgagee to account for any profits earned over and above the interest and principal due on the loan. As a result, there was no longer any advantage for mortgagees to possess the land. Therefore, they would take ownership of the estate, but leave their mortgagors in possession. This is the modern form of common law mortgage.

Chancery's intervention on behalf of mortgagors contributed to the development of the modern concept of the security interest. Although the mortgagee had ownership of the land at common law, this was only for the purpose of securing a debt. Her or his interest in the property extended no further than necessary for the fulfilment of that purpose. Once the debt had been paid, the mortgagee's interest in the land was completely satisfied. The debtor was the true beneficial owner of the land and Chancery would intervene to prevent mortgagees from using their legal ownership unfairly to deprive debtors of the benefit of the land.

Chancery began to intervene routinely in cases where mortgagors had defaulted on payment of the debt and had therefore lost their legal rights to have the legal estate reconveyed by the mortgagee. At common law, a mortgagor who missed a payment could lose all rights to the land, even though the debt secured by the mortgage was a small fraction of the value of the land. Chancery would not permit this unjust enrichment of the mortgagee and would allow the mortgagor to redeem the land, even if the time for payment had passed. This was called the **equity of redemption**. Since the mortgagee held the land for security purposes only, he or she could not complain about losing the land if the mortgagor paid the entire debt, including interest and costs.

There had to be some limit on the mortgagor's right to redeem the land. It could not last forever. So long as the mortgagor had an equity of redemption, the mortgagee was not free to deal with land or sell it, because the mortgagor could show up at any time with the necessary funds and redeem the land. Left unchecked, this negated much of the mortgage's usefulness as a security device. To deal with this problem, Chancery came up with the decree of **foreclosure**. This is a court order which puts an end to (forecloses) the equity of redemption and converts the mortgagee into the beneficial owner of the land. If the mortgagor has any hope of raising the money needed to redeem the land, the decree of foreclosure will give the mortgagor a fixed period of time in which to do so.

Chancery also thought it unfair that a mortgagor might lose land worth more than the debt due to the mortgagee. Rather than let the mortgagee keep the land on the mortgagor's default, the court would order the sale of the land. The sale proceeds would be used to pay the debt due to the mortgagee (and the costs of the sale) and the remainder would belong to the mortgagor. This right, to the value of the land over the amount needed to pay the mortgagee, came to be seen as part of the mortgagor's equity of redemption.

Today, the term "equity of redemption" is no longer just the equitable right to redeem the land, but refers to the totality of the mortgagor's equitable beneficial ownership of that land. It has an economic value which can be calculated by subtracting the debt secured by the mortgage from the market value of the land. This value is often called the mortgagor's **equity** in the land (short for equity of redemption). It is possible to have **negative equity** if the value of the land drops below the debt due to the mortgagee.

These equitable principles and terms are still used in connection with the Torrens mortgage, even though the mortgagor retains the legal estate and grants only a legal charge to the mortgagee. The courts have recognised that the substantial rights of the parties are the same regardless of the form of mortgage. The Torrens mortgagor's right to discharge the legal encumbrance is equivalent to the common law mortgagor's right to obtain reconveyance of the legal ownership. Both mortgagors have an equity of redemption: see Re Forrest Trust [1953] VLR 246.

Mortgages and Trusts

The common law mortgage bears striking similarities to the trust. The mortgagee (like a trustee) has the legal estate, subject to the mortgagor's equitable property rights. The equity of redemption is equitable beneficial ownership as is the beneficiary's interest in a trust. However, the courts have held that a mortgage is not a trust. Normally, trustees have only the bare legal title and are not permitted to use that property right for their own benefit. In contrast, mortgagees have a security right designed to protect their own interests. This is not full beneficial ownership, but it is a valuable property right and a much greater interest than a trustee's bare legal title.

An important difference between the trust and the mortgage lies in the different duties owed by trustees and mortgagees. Trustees are expected to act selflessly on behalf of the trust beneficiaries. They owe what are called **fiduciary** duties to act in the best interests of the beneficiaries. In contrast, mortgagees are entitled to act selfishly in their own best interests. They owe duties of **good faith** toward the mortgagor. For example, mortgagees must make reasonable efforts to get a fair market price when the land is being sold to pay the mortgage debt. It would be a breach of that duty to sell land worth $100,000 for only $50,000 because that was all that was due under the mortgage. However, mortgagees need not place their mortgagors' interests ahead of their own in the same way that trustees must favour the interests of their trust beneficiaries.

For more information on the development of the mortgage, see Baker, *An Introduction to English Legal History* (3rd ed, 1990) pp 353-356, or Megarry & Wade, *The Law of Real Property* (5th ed, 1984) pp 913-979. For more about the modern law of mortgages in Australia, see Bradbrook, MacCallum, and Moore, *Australian Real Property Law* (2nd ed, 1997) Ch 14, or Duncan and Willmot, *Mortgages Law in Australia* (2nd ed, 1996).

Substance over Form

As discussed above, there is a wide variety of security rights. Regardless of the form of the transaction, all security rights are limited property rights designed to secure the performance of a personal obligation. Even if the creditor has legal ownership of something for security purposes, the debtor is the true beneficial owner of that thing. The debtor is entitled to the benefit of any increase in its value and must bear the burden of a decrease in value. In contrast, the creditor's security right is measured by the value of the personal obligation secured. The fulfilment of that obligation brings to an end the creditor's interest in the thing used as security.

A person's property right can change from beneficial ownership to a security right and back again, even though that right has not changed in form. For example, a conditional sales contract will convert a vendor from beneficial owner of the thing sold into a secured creditor, even though her or his legal ownership will continue until the entire purchase price is paid. Conversely, a mortgagee who has legal ownership for security purposes only can become the beneficial owner through foreclosure. At each stage, a court can see through the form to identify the essential interests of the parties.

As new forms of security evolved, the courts continued to intervene in an effort to achieve a proper balance between the interests of creditors and debtors. Although debtors might be willing to grant extensive property rights in exchange for credit, the courts would recognise that the rights had been given as security and limit the creditors' rights accordingly: see Nyuk Nahan (née Chin), "Relieving Against Forfeiture: Windfalls and Conscience" (1995) 25 *UWA Law Review* 110. Today, the rights of creditors and debtors are closely regulated by statute. For example, most jurisdictions in Australia have a Consumer Credit Code, which controls many forms of transactions in which credit is extended to individuals for personal, domestic, or household purposes.

The following table provides a quick comparison between the rights which debtors and creditors have under the various forms of security rights recognised in Australian law. Regardless of form, the debtor is the beneficial owner of the thing or right used as security and the creditor has a property right which is limited to its purpose of securing performance of a personal obligation.

Table of Security Rights

Security Right	Debtor's Interest	Creditor's Interest
Pledge	Legal ownership or right to possession of goods	Legal possession, with power to sell on default
Common law Lien	Legal ownership or right to possession of goods	Legal possession, with no power to sell unless provided by statute
Common law Mortgage Bill of Sale Conditional Sale Hire Purchase	Equitable beneficial ownership, normally with right to possession	Legal ownership, with power to sell or obtain possession or beneficial ownership on default
Equitable Charge Equitable Mortgage Equitable Lien	Any personal or property right	Equitable right to use debtor's right for payment of debt
Torrens Mortgage	Legal estate	Legal right to sell or obtain possession or beneficial ownership on default
Statutory Encumbrance	Any personal or property right	Legal right to use debtor's right for payment of debt

Chapter Fifteen

SHARED RIGHTS

As discussed in previous chapters, several people can have property rights to the same thing at the same time. For example, you might own a house which is mortgaged to the bank and leased to me. It is also possible for a right to be shared. It is common for two people to share the fee simple estate in a family home or to have a joint bank account (which is the shared ownership of their personal claim against the bank).

There are two ways in which the ownership of a right can be shared: **joint ownership** and **co-ownership**. These are also called **joint tenancies** and **tenancies in common**, respectively. Although people often talk of joint or common "ownership", they mean ownership of a particular right. It need not be the full ownership discussed in Chapter 10, but can be any sort of personal or property right. Similarly, a joint or co-tenant need not be a "tenant" in the normal sense of someone possessed of an estate in land. Those terms are often used in connection with shared ownership of other rights.

There are two main differences between joint and common ownership. First, joint tenancies must be identical in every respect, while tenancies in common need not be. If two or more joint tenants share a right, each joint tenant must have the same interest as every other joint tenant. Tenants in common can share rights unequally. The second difference is **survivorship** (sometimes called the *jus accrescendi*). When a joint tenant dies, her or his interest in the shared right ceases and the surviving joint tenants keep the right for themselves. When a tenant in common dies, her or his interest continues after death and can be transferred to another person by will.

Although joint tenants have separate rights, it is said that, in relation to everyone else in society, they are treated as a single owner. They share the joint tenancy so completely that they cannot deal with their individual rights separately, unless they convert their joint tenancy into a tenancy in common (as discussed below). In contrast, tenants in common have distinct (though undivided) shares and are entitled to deal with them separately. They can be sold or given away without destroying the tenancy in common.

Four Unities

A joint tenancy cannot exist unless all joint tenants have exactly the same rights. This is sometimes identified as the requirement of "four unities", which means that the rights of the joint tenants must be identical in four respects: possession, interest, title, and time. Each of these "unities" is discussed further in this part. Tenants in common might also have rights which are identical in these four respects. However, they need not be. The only unity which tenants in common must share is possession.

Unity of Possession

All joint tenants and tenants in common are entitled to shared possession of the thing subject to their property right (assuming that the right being shared is or includes a right to possession). One tenant is not entitled to exclude another tenant from any part of the shared land or goods, except by agreement. This is why tenants in common are said to have **undivided shares**.

The division of an estate according to space or time would not produce joint or co-ownership, since there would be no unity of possession. For example, if a block of land was divided in two so that one tenant received the western half and the other received the eastern half, this would produce two separate estates and not co-ownership of the whole block. Similarly, if the block of land was given to one tenant for life and the remainder to another, this would produce two separate estates: see Chapter 12.

Agreements Regarding the Use of Shared Rights

Joint or co-tenants can agree that some of them are entitled to possession of certain parts. For example, we could lease a house together as joint tenants and agree that you would have possession of one bedroom and I would have possession of another. However, as joint tenants of the leasehold estate we both have the right to possession of the entire house. Our agreement regarding the use of the bedrooms is either a sublease or licence, which we, as joint tenants, granted to each of us as individuals. It would be no different if we took in a lodger and gave her or him the exclusive use of a third bedroom.

Sharing Non-Possessory Rights

When the right being shared is non-possessory (such as an easement, discussed in Chapter 16), it makes no sense to talk about unity of possession. However, in this context, the phrase is used to mean that all joint tenants and tenants in common are entitled to make use of the right. One tenant cannot exclude another from that use. The exercise of a shared right *in personam* may depend on the contract creating that right. For example, if you and I are joint owners of a bank account, our right to withdraw money from that account will depend on our contract with the bank. Normally, we are each entitled to make use of the entire balance of the account without the assistance of the other. However, our contract with the bank might require that both of us sign any withdrawals or cheques drawn on the account.

Unity of Interest

All joint tenants must have the same interest in the right they share. For example, where there are two joint owners of a fee simple estate, both tenants share that estate with no distinction between their rights. Neither tenant has any lesser or greater rights than the other.

Tenants in common need not have the same rights. It is possible for them to own a property right in unequal shares. For example, one tenant might have 60% of a fee simple estate, while the other has 40%, or three tenants might share a lease in the following proportions: 5/12, 4/12, and 3/12. Unequal sharing by tenants in common does not affect their unity of possession. However, it will (absent an agreement to the contrary) determine the distribution of the sale proceeds at the end of the tenancy in common and the proportions of required contributions to the costs of ownership.

Unity of Title

Normally, all joint tenants must derive their shared right from the same source, such as a conveyance, registration, or will. In other words, they share the same title. If shared ownership arises from different sources, it must be a tenancy in common.

There is an important exception to this rule. All the states and territories have legislation which permits new trustees to be appointed as joint owners, along with the existing trustees, of the rights held in trust: see, eg, *Trustee Act* 1893 (NT), ss 13 and 57. Although the new trustee will derive her or his title from a deed of appointment and the existing trustees will obtain theirs from previous deeds, they are permitted to be joint tenants of a shared right.

Unity of Time

The general rule is that the rights of joint tenants must arise at the same time. For example, a gift of an estate to Mitchell for life, with the remainder to his children, could not produce a joint tenancy for the children, unless they were all alive at the date of the gift (or perhaps were all born later at the same time as twins, triplets, etc). Otherwise, each child will acquire an estate which is vested in interest (as discussed at page 99) at birth and their rights will arise at different times.

There are several exceptions to this rule. The statutory exception for new trustees (discussed above) is one. Also, joint ownership can be created by a trust (see Chapter 13) or a will (see Chapter 22) even though the beneficiaries of that trust or will take their shares at different times. Since most gifts like the remainder for Mitchell's children will be created by trust or will, the exceptions do not leave much room for the general rule. In other words, there will not be many cases in which the absence of unity of time is the only bar to joint ownership.

Sharing the Benefits and Burdens of Ownership

The right of each joint or co-owner to make use of the whole property affects the manner in which the benefits and burdens of ownership are shared among them. What happens when tenants take more than their fair shares of the benefit or fail to pay for their fair shares of the costs of maintenance? Can they be compelled to pay their fellow tenants for the extra benefit or for a portion of the costs?

Normally, this problem is dealt with by agreement among the tenants. Just as they can agree that one of their number will have the exclusive use of all or a portion of the shared thing, so can they agree on who will be responsible for repairs, taxes, or other costs. For example, if we were the joint owners of a boat, we would be free to make any sort of agreement concerning a schedule for using the boat and the payment of mooring fees, repairs, fuel, insurance, etc.

Problems arise when joint or co-owners cannot agree on how their right should be shared. In certain situations, tenants can be made to pay the other tenants to ensure that they enjoy the benefits and bear the burdens of their shared right in proportion to their interests in that right. The basis of that liability requires some explanation. As discussed in Chapters 5 and 20, legal rights and obligations can be created by consent, wrongdoing, unjust enrichment, or other events. If the tenants cannot agree, then any adjustments among tenants must depend on one of the other three categories of events.

Wrongdoing

If one tenant wrongly excludes another from possession (and is thereby guilty of trespass or conversion), he or she can be compelled to pay for the use of the property which has been wrongly kept from the other tenant. However, in most cases, where one tenant takes a greater proportion of the benefits of a shared right, he or she does no wrong. This is because each tenant is entitled to the possession or use of the entire shared right.

For example, in *Luke v Luke* (1936) 36 SR (NSW) 310, two sisters, Ada and Laura, were tenants in common of land in equal shares and lived there together for many years. After Laura died, Ada continued to live on the land alone for 16 years. The administrator of Laura's estate then claimed that Ada should pay rent for half the value of the land for those 16 years in which she had the entire property to herself. The claim was dismissed because Ada had done nothing to exclude Laura or those entitled to her estate from the land. Therefore, Ada had not interfered with her co-tenant's right to possession and had merely been exercising her own right to possession of the entire estate.

Wrongdoing also fails to provide a justification for one tenant's claim that the other tenants should contribute to the costs of maintaining or improving the shared property. This is because tenants are not normally under any duty to maintain or improve their own property (unless perhaps it is listed as a special heritage site or has become a danger to the public). Therefore, a tenant does no wrong if he or she refuses to contribute to the cost of improvements or maintenance.

Unjust Enrichment

A tenant can be compelled to share the benefits and burdens of joint or common ownership on the basis of unjust enrichment, but only in limited circumstances. There are two difficulties with such a claim, which explain why it is not generally available to people who share rights. First, I cannot compel others to pay for benefits that I decide to confer on myself. Secondly, I cannot compel others to pay for benefits they do not want.

Suppose, for example, that I plant a beautiful, ornamental garden in my front yard. My neighbours are free to enjoy the view and any increase it brings to the market values of their own homes. By planting the garden, I have acted in my own best interests and cannot claim that my neighbours are unjustly enriched by any incidental benefits my garden provides to them. My neighbours did not choose to receive that benefit and cannot be required to help pay for it.

The same logic applies to shared ownership. If we are joint tenants and you do not wish to pay for the cost of a new garden, I cannot compel you to do so. Since I am entitled to use and enjoy the whole property, the garden can be regarded as an expenditure for my own benefit. The incidental benefit to you (for which you did not agree to pay) does not normally amount to an unjust enrichment. I cannot force you to accept the benefit by planting it without your consent and then billing you for half the cost. As Bowen LJ said in *Falke v Scottish Imperial Insurance Co* (1886) 34 Ch D 234 at 248, "Liabilities are not to be forced upon people behind their backs any more than you can confer a benefit on a man against his will."

There are two main situations in which these two difficulties are overcome and it is possible to require a joint or co-tenant to pay for an unjust enrichment at another tenant's expense. The first is where one tenant is required to discharge the liability of another tenant. Suppose, for example, that we are joint owners of land and the local government orders us to control the pests on our land. If you pay to control those pests, you can compel me to pay my share of the cost. Since you were compelled to act, this overcomes the first objection that you merely chose to spend money on the land for your own benefit. Since we were jointly liable for the costs of pest control and you have discharged my share of that liability, this overcomes the second objection that I did not want the benefit and should not have to pay for it.

Secondly, the benefits and burdens of shared ownership can be taken into account when that ownership comes to an end and the shared property is sold. Suppose, for example, that my garden raised the market value of our jointly owned house by $10,000. When the house is sold, we would normally divide the sale proceeds equally. However, your share has been increased by $5,000 at my expense. The law may allow me to deduct this amount from your share of the proceeds: see *Brickwood v Young* (1905) 2 CLR 387.

Although I cannot make you pay for the garden while our joint ownership continues, the sale of the land and division of the proceeds overcomes the two objections to that liability. First, if we divided the sale proceeds equally, you would be enjoying half of the value of my garden separately from me. You could no longer argue that the garden was solely for my own benefit. Secondly, you could no longer complain about being forced to pay for a garden you did not want, since you are only being asked to give up the money which you obtained from the sale of my garden. You are left no worse off than you would have been if I had never created the garden.

When a shared right is sold and a tenant seeks to deduct the costs of maintenance or improvements from another tenant's share, the law requires that he or she also account for any extra benefits derived from the shared ownership. In other words, a claim for bearing a greater share of the burden of ownership will be reduced if the tenant also received a greater share of the benefit of that ownership. For example, in *Forgeard v Shanahan* (1994) 35 NSWLR 206, a man and woman were joint owners of, and lived together in, a house near Sydney. In 1981, he moved out and she remained in the house until it was sold 10 years later. She paid the mortgage payments and rates during that time and wanted to be reimbursed for those costs from his share of the sale proceeds. She was required to deduct from those costs half the value of the market rent for that period. She had not wrongly excluded him from the property and, therefore, he did not have an independent claim for the benefit she had derived from her sole occupation of their house. However, she could not require him to pay for half the costs of maintenance and improvement without accounting for that extra benefit: see Brereton, "The Rights Between Co-Owners of Land" (1995) 69 *Australian Law Journal* 316.

Statute

As discussed above, joint and co-tenants can sometimes be required to share the benefits and burdens of ownership on the basis of wrongdoing or unjust enrichment. In every jurisdiction except New South Wales and the Australian Capital Territory, there is also a statute which requires them to account to their fellow tenants for income received from the shared right. These are rights and obligations created by "other events". The requirement to account for rents is found in the *Statute of Anne* 1705 (UK), which was received by every state and territory when English law was adopted in Australia. That statute has been replaced in Queensland and Victoria (see the *Property Law Act* 1974 (Qld), s 43, and *Property Law Act* 1958 (Vic), s 28A) and simply repealed in New South Wales and the Australian Capital Territory (see *Forgeard v Shanahan* (1994) 35 NSWLR 206).

Survivorship

The most important distinction between joint and co-ownership is survivorship. When tenants in common die, their interests continue to exist. Those interests become part of their estates and can be given away by will. On the death of a joint tenant, the other joint tenants take her or his interest. The interest of the deceased tenant ceases to exist and the interests of the other tenants expand. For example, if a fee simple estate is owned by three joint tenants and one dies, the two surviving joint tenants continue to own the entire estate. When the second joint tenant dies, the last surviving joint tenant becomes the sole owner of the estate and the joint tenancy comes to an end.

This expansion of a surviving joint tenant's interest is called "survivorship". This happens automatically upon the death of a joint tenant. It is not regarded as a transfer from the deceased joint tenant to the surviving tenants. The deceased tenant's interest simply ceases to exist and there is nothing which that tenant could have given away by will. The right of survivorship is the possibility that a joint tenant will outlive the other joint tenants and acquire a greater interest in the joint tenancy or sole ownership. It is an integral part of the joint tenancy and exists from the outset, when the tenancy is created. It is not a new property right created by the death of a fellow joint tenant.

Corporations

At common law, a corporation could not be a joint tenant. This is because a corporation has the potential to exist perpetually, thereby effectively destroying the right of survivorship of its human joint tenants. However, most corporations do not last forever. Many are dissolved after a relatively short life. Although there are well-known corporations which have existed for many years, the average life expectancy of a new business corporation is probably less than that of a human.

This common law rule has been changed in most jurisdictions by statute. For example, section 28 of the *Property Law Act* 1958 (Vic) states that, "A body corporate shall be capable of acquiring and holding any real or personal property in joint tenancy in the same manner as if it were an individual", and that, "Where a body corporate is joint tenant of any property then on its dissolution the property shall devolve on the other joint tenant." This enables trust corporations to become joint trustees with humans.

Order of Death

Difficulties can arise when joint tenants die at the same time. For example, suppose that a husband and wife own their home and many other assets as joint tenants. If they die together in a car accident, it may be impossible to tell if one spouse outlived the other and thereby became entitled to those assets by virtue of the right of survivorship. The order of death will affect the distribution of their estates unless they both made wills in favour of the same persons: see page 287. Should their joint property pass to the heirs of the husband or the heirs of the wife?

In most jurisdictions, there is a statutory presumption that the oldest joint tenant died first: for example, section 65 of the *Succession Act* 1981 (Qld), states that:

> "where 2 or more persons have died in circumstances rendering it uncertain which of them survived the other or others, such deaths shall (subject to any order of the court), for all purposes affecting the title to property, be presumed to have occurred in order of seniority, and accordingly the younger shall be deemed to have survived the elder for a period of 1 day."

This type of presumption applies only where the order of death is unknown. It would not apply if the order of death was proved, for example, by a rescuer at the scene of the accident or by autopsies.

This presumption does not exist in South Australia or Western Australia. If the order of death of joint tenants is uncertain in Western Australia, the joint tenancy is treated as a tenancy in common and there is no survivorship: *Property Law Act* 1969 (WA), s 120(d). In South Australia, there is no statute dealing with this problem and, therefore, the solution must be found in common law and equity. In *Bradshaw v Toulmin* (1784) Dickens 633, 21 ER 417, Lord Thurlow C said, "if two persons being joint tenants, perish by one blow, the estate will remain in joint tenancy, in their respective heirs". It is not clear what would happen if the deceased joint tenants had more than one heir each. Using our example above, if the wife had one heir and the husband had two, would their joint property rights pass to all three heirs as joint tenants or would the joint tenancy become a tenancy in common, with the wife's heir taking a half share of the property and the husband's heirs each taking a quarter share? The latter solution is consistent with the treatment of joint tenancies in other situations. As discussed below, a transfer of a joint tenant's interest to another converts the joint tenancy into a tenancy in common.

No Survivorship

When joint tenants own land which is registered in a Torrens system (see Chapter 32), it is possible in most jurisdictions to have the words "no survivorship" noted on the title: see, eg, *Transfer of Land Act* 1893 (WA), s 61. This does not remove the right to survivorship, but prevents the surviving joint owners from dealing with the land without the approval of the court. Without that notation on the title, the survivors would be entitled to receive a new title simply by proving to the Registrar of the appropriate land titles office that their former joint tenant was dead. The restriction created by the words "no survivorship" was intended primarily to protect the beneficiaries of trusts of Torrens land from improper dealings with that land by the sole surviving trustee.

Creation of Shared Ownership

The creation of property rights is the subject of Part IV. Although this brief discussion of the creation of shared ownership might have been delayed until that part of the book, it is taken here for the purpose of further distinguishing between joint and common ownership. For the most part, the answer to the question, "Is this a joint tenancy or a tenancy in common?", depends upon how the right was divided when it was first created. We are not yet concerned with methods of creating rights. For example, the sale of goods and transfer of estates are discussed in Chapter 21. This section deals only with the division of those rights among joint or co-owners.

To begin, if there is no unity of possession, there can be no shared ownership. If unity of possession exists, but one of the other three unities is missing, then the shared ownership is normally a tenancy in common. Even if people think they are creating a joint tenancy, the absence of a unity will mean that their expectation is not fulfilled and a tenancy in common comes into being. However, if all four unities are present, that does not necessarily mean that the shared ownership is a joint tenancy. It might be either joint or common ownership. The central issue is what type of sharing was intended.

Normally, the intention to divide a right is found in the instrument creating that right, such as a transfer, deed, will, or contract. It is easiest when the creator specifies how the right is divided. For example, the instrument might say "to Hanako and Charles as joint tenants" or "to Kate and Ben in equal shares as tenants in common". In many cases, the method of sharing is not made clear. For example, an estate might be given simply "to Geoff and Andrea". In such a case, the law had to find ways to decide whether this created a joint tenancy or tenancy in common. Rules to determine the creator's intention were developed by courts of common law and enacted by statute. In addition, there are rules in equity designed to avoid the unjust enrichment of one tenant at the expense of another.

Common Law

At common law, joint tenancy is the preferred method of sharing property rights to land. This is because survivorship leads to greater certainty of title. As each joint tenant dies, there is no need to identify all the heirs of that tenant, since her or his interest disappears and the shared right belongs to the surviving joint tenants. This makes conveyancing simpler and, at one time, made it easier to collect feudal dues. In contrast, when tenants in common die, their shares continue to exist and are transferred to others. Identifying the owners of a shared estate becomes more complicated with the death of each co-tenant, rather than simpler. As Holt CJ said in *Fisher v Wigg* (1700) 1 Salk 391 at 392, 91 ER 339 at 340, "joint-tenancies were favoured, for the law loves not fractions of estates, nor to divide and multiply tenures".

If land is conveyed to two or more people, a joint tenancy would be created at common law unless one of the four unities was missing or an intention to create a tenancy in common could be discovered. That intention might be revealed by the language used by the person creating the shared right or by the surrounding circumstances.

Words which indicated that each tenant was to have a distinct share in the property are called **words of severance** and taken as an indication that a tenancy in common is intended. A variety of words and phrases are regarded as words of severance, such as a transfer to tenants "in equal shares" or "to share and share alike". In many cases, the common law presumption in favour of joint tenancy was rebutted by a very slight indication to the contrary. This may be a reflection of increasing judicial unhappiness with the common law rule after the feudal conditions which gave rise to that rule were left behind.

In some cases, the document creating the shared right combined words of severance with words indicating a joint tenancy. For example, a gift might be made to people "as joint tenants in common in equal shares". When faced with contradictory expressions such as these, the courts try to discover the creator's intention from the entire document and the circumstances surrounding the creation of the shared right. For example, in *Re Barbour* [1967] Qd R 10, a man died, leaving 102 acres of grazing land to his sister and two brothers "to share and share alike as joint tenants". The judge decided that the man must have intended to create a joint tenancy, because a tenancy in common would have produced great inconvenience. One of the brothers had died four years earlier and, if he was entitled to a share as a tenant in common, it would be shared by his eight children. The small parcel of grazing land would not be usable if it was divided among so many owners.

Statute

In New South Wales and Queensland, the common law presumption in favour of joint tenancies has been reversed by statute: see *Conveyancing Act* 1919 (NSW), s 26(1); *Property Law Act* 1974 (Qld), s 35. Unless the intention to create a joint tenancy is clearly expressed, the shared right will be a tenancy in common. This reversal of the common law does not apply to transfers to trustees, executors, administrators, and mortgagees. In Queensland, transfers to partnerships are also exempt.

The preservation of the common law presumption makes sense when a right is to be shared by trustees, executors, or administrators. They have been chosen to hold the land in a representative capacity for the benefit of others. There is no reason why that right should pass to their heirs when they die. It is better that the surviving trustees, executors, or administrators take the whole right and appoint a replacement, if necessary. Therefore, they will hold the shared right as joint tenants unless it is clear that a tenancy in common was intended.

The exemptions for mortgagees and partners can be explained by the need for business efficiency. Tenancies in common can create difficulties in these situations and are not created unless clearly intended. If a mortgagee's right passed on death to her or his heirs, the mortgagors might have difficulty knowing who is entitled to payment of the debt secured by the mortgage. Similarly, the death of a partner might create problems if her or his heirs became entitled to a share of the partnership assets. This does not mean that joint mortgagees and partners lose all rights on death. As discussed below, equity will intervene to ensure that their investments in the jointly owned assets can be enjoyed by their heirs.

The Torrens statutes in some jurisdictions contain provisions like that found in section 74 of the *Real Property Act* 1886 (SA), which states that, "Two or more persons registered as joint proprietors of an estate or interest in land shall be deemed to be entitled to the same as joint tenants". This does not affect the common law and statutory presumptions in favour of joint or common ownership. "Proprietor" is the term used by most Torrens statutes to describe a "person seised or possessed of or entitled to any estate or interest in land": *Transfer of Land Act* 1958 (Vic), s 4(1). The provisions concerning **joint proprietors** make it clear that the term means joint ownership: see *Hircock v Windsor Homes (Development No 3) Pty Ltd* [1979] 1 NSWLR 501 at 506. That term is not used in Queensland or the Australian Capital Territory, where the holders of shared rights to Torrens land are described as joint tenants or tenants in common.

The problem created by the failure to specify the nature of a shared right to Torrens land is avoided by Registrars who insist that documents lodged for registration of a shared right must specify whether the right is to be held as a joint tenancy or a tenancy in common: see Bradbrook, MacCallum, and Moore, *Australian Real Property Law* (2nd ed, 1997) s 10.26. In Tasmania, the common law presumption in favour of joint tenancy is preserved with respect to Torrens land. Section 44 of the *Land Titles Act* 1980 (Tas) states that, "Two or more persons who are named in a dealing as transferees or proprietors of an estate or interest shall, in the absence of words of severance, be entitled as joint tenants, and every such dealing, when registered, takes effect accordingly."

Equity

It is said that "Equity leans against joint tenants and favours tenancies in common": see Megarry and Wade, *The Law of Real Property* (5th ed, 1984) p 427. This means that, in some cases, equity will intervene to compel joint tenants to hold their shared right in trust for themselves as tenants in common. In other words, the tenants continue to share the legal right as joint tenants, but share the beneficial use and enjoyment of that right as equitable tenants in common.

As discussed at page 110, a person cannot be a trustee for herself or himself. Since people cannot enforce legal or equitable rights against themselves, a trust cannot exist if one person is both trustee and beneficiary. The same is true when two or more people share a right. They cannot compel themselves to use their shared right for their own benefit. However, so long as there is some difference between their sharing of the legal ownership as trustees and their sharing of the equitable ownership as beneficiaries, a trust is possible. The difference between joint and common ownership is slight, but enough to a support a trust.

For example, you and I could own a legal fee simple estate as joint tenants and hold that estate in trust for ourselves as tenants in common. If our shares of the equitable tenancy in common were unequal, the trust would compel us to distribute the proceeds of a sale of that estate unequally in proportion to our shares. Even if our shares in the equitable tenancy in common were equal, the trust would prevent us from enjoying the benefit of survivorship. If I died, you would become the sole owner at law, but would continue to hold that right in trust for yourself and my heirs as tenants in common.

Unlike the common law and statutory rules discussed above, which help determine the intention of the person creating the shared right, the rules of equity operate in a different manner in this context. They are not direct responses to the intention to create either a trust or a tenancy in common. The trust is imposed by operation of law to prevent the unjust enrichment of one joint tenant at the expense of another. So, for example, where two people purchase a house as joint tenants, and they contribute unequally to the payment of the purchase price, they will hold their joint tenancy in trust for themselves as tenants in common, in proportion to their contributions, unless it is proved that the person making the greater contribution intended to make a gift to the other: see *Calverley v Green* (1984) 155 CLR 242. The trust prevents one joint owner from enjoying an unintended benefit obtained at the expense of the other.

A trust is also imposed when partners acquire partnership assets as joint tenants or when lenders become joint mortgagees. It is assumed that people who make business investments do not want to lose their investments when they die. A trust is imposed to compel the surviving joint tenants to hold the share of the deceased tenant in trust for her or his estate. The creation of these trusts is discussed in more detail in Chapter 24 (Unjust Enrichment).

Equity will also intervene in cases where one joint tenant unlawfully kills another. The killer will hold the shared right in trust for the victim and herself or himself as tenants in common: see *Rasmanis v Jurewitsch* (1969) 70 SR (NSW) 407. This trust is also imposed by law, but for a different reason: to prevent the killer from profiting from her or his crime. It is discussed further in Chapter 25 (Wrongdoing).

Severance and Partition

The creation of shared rights was discussed above briefly. The destruction of those rights is the subject of this short section. A joint tenancy can be severed and thereby converted into a tenancy in common in equal shares. A tenancy in common can be destroyed by a partition of the estate into separate parts or a sale of the shared right and distribution of the proceeds among the tenants.

Severance of a Joint Tenancy

There are three main ways in which a joint tenancy can be severed and converted into a tenancy in common: destruction of the four unities, agreement among the tenants, and (in some jurisdictions) unilateral declaration. It is not always easy to tell whether a joint tenancy has been severed. The issue usually arises after one of the joint tenants has died. Her or his heirs will be arguing that the joint tenancy was severed before the death and that they are entitled to her or his interest in the tenancy in common. The surviving tenants will be claiming that the joint tenancy was left intact and that they are entitled to their rights of survivorship.

Destruction of the Four Unities

As discussed above, the interests of joint tenants (normally) must be identical in every respect. Therefore, any event which alters the interest of a tenant will convert the shared right into a tenancy in common. For example, if we were joint tenants and I sold or gave my interest to a friend, you and the friend would become tenants in common in equal shares. Although you both share unity of possession and interest, you do not have unity of title or time. Similarly, if I became bankrupt, my interest in the shared right vests in my trustee in bankruptcy, who would hold that right as a tenant in common with you: see *Sistrom v Urh* (1992) 117 ALR 528.

The unities are also destroyed when a joint tenant transfers her or his interest in the shared right to herself or himself. Although a transfer to oneself was not possible at common law, it is permitted by statute in each jurisdiction. For example, section 40(3) of the *Law of Property Act*

1936 (SA) states that, "A person may convey land or any other property to himself or to himself and others." Upon completion of the transfer, the tenants no longer derive title from the same source and it becomes a tenancy in common.

In Queensland, the power to transfer land to oneself is found in the Torrens statute, section 59(1) of the *Land Title Act* 1994 (Qld), which states that, "A registered owner of a lot subject to a joint tenancy may unilaterally sever the joint tenancy by registration of a transfer executed by the registered owner." However, registration of the transfer is permitted "only if a registered owner satisfies the registrar that a copy of the instrument has been given to all other joint tenants": s 59(2). This is a sensible restriction. Otherwise, the other tenants might be unaware that the joint tenancy has been severed and they have thereby lost their rights of survivorship.

If a right is shared by three or more joint tenants, and the unities are destroyed with respect to one tenant's interest, this will sever only that tenant's share and not the whole joint tenancy. For example, suppose that Joshua, Ben, and David were joint tenants of an estate in fee simple and that Joshua transferred his interest to Jesse. Jesse would acquire one-third of the estate as a tenant in common with Ben and David, who hold two-thirds of the estate. However, Ben and David would hold their two-thirds share between themselves as joint tenants. In other words, the property right which they own jointly is no longer the fee simple estate, but their two-thirds interest in that estate as tenants in common with Jesse.

Agreement

Without destroying the four unities, all the joint tenants can sever the tenancy by agreement. If the shared right is a property right to land, then (normally) this agreement must be made in writing: see *Lyons v Lyons* [1967] VR 169 and Chapter 21. However, it is possible to achieve this less formally. If all the joint tenants have been dealing with the shared right in a manner which proves that they are all treating it as a tenancy in common, then the agreement can be inferred from their conduct and the joint tenancy will be severed.

In *Abela v Public Trustee* [1983] 1 NSWLR 308, a husband and wife owned a matrimonial home as joint tenants. After they separated, they negotiated a separation agreement, under which the house was sold and the sale proceeds held in trust by solicitors. The husband died and the wife argued that the joint tenancy had not been severed. This was rejected by the court. The separation agreement was a sufficient agreement to sever the joint tenancy and, in any event, it was a course of conduct which proved that they were both treating the tenancy as having been severed into undivided shares.

Unilateral Declaration

In Tasmania, it is possible for a joint tenant of Torrens land to sever the tenancy by registration of a declaration of severance at the land titles office: *Land Titles Act* 1980 (Tas), s 63(1). This is a logical progression from the statutes which enable people to transfer property rights to themselves. A transfer to oneself serves no purpose except to achieve a formal destruction of the unity of title. There is no reason to preserve this artificial hurdle, so long as the unilateral decision to sever the joint tenancy is effected by some formal act which leaves the question of severance beyond doubt. Since a dispute about severance is most likely to occur after the death of a joint tenant, the method of severance serves an important evidentiary role.

The New South Wales Law Reform Commission recommended that people should be permitted to sever joint tenancies of Torrens land by registration of a declaration of severance: *Unilateral Severance of a Joint Tenancy* (LRC 73, 1994). The Western Australian Law Reform Commission recommended that severance should be made possible by written notice to other tenants: *Report on Joint Tenancy and Tenancy in Common* (No 78, 1994). If the notice was ineffective to change the legal title, it would be effective in equity. For example, a transfer of a legal right to Torrens land normally requires registration of the appropriate document: see page 249 below. In that situation, the written notice proposed in Western Australia would cause the joint tenants to hold their legal right to land in trust for themselves as tenants in common.

Partition of a Tenancy in Common

Co-tenants are free to bring their tenancy in common to an end by an agreement. If the thing subject to their shared right can be divided into portions, they can simply allocate portions among themselves. For example, if you and I were equal tenants in common of a flock of 100 sheep, we could each take 50 sheep. If we were co-owners of 100 shares in a corporation, we could each take 50 shares and, if we were co-owners of 100 hectares of land, we might each take 50 hectares.

It might not be possible to divide the thing between ourselves. For example, our local government might not permit us to subdivide our 100 hectares into smaller parcels of land or we might be tenants in common of a race horse, which is much more valuable in one piece. In this situation, we could either sell the right and distribute the sale proceeds between ourselves or one of us could purchase the other's share. There is no problem, so long as we can reach an agreement.

Problems arise when co-tenants cannot agree on whether or how to end their co-tenancy. Most jurisdictions have statutes designed to deal with the problems. For example, section 187 of the *Property Law Act* 1958 (Vic) states: "Where any chattels belong to persons in undivided shares, the persons interested in a moiety or upwards may apply to the Court for an order for division of the chattels or any of them, according to a valuation or otherwise, and the Court may make such order and give any consequential directions as it thinks fit." This gives a tenant in common with a half or greater share in personal property the right to bring the tenancy to an end without the consent of the other tenants. The court might order a division of the chattels among the tenants (if possible) or a sale of the chattels and distribution of the proceeds.

There are separate statutory provisions which deal with the partition and sale of shared rights to land. They usually permit tenants to apply to the court to end the co-tenancy, regardless of the size of their shares. The court then considers the wishes and interests of the other tenants and may grant the request. Tenants with a half or greater share normally have the right to an order for the partition or sale of the land, unless the court "sees good reason to the contrary": *Property Law Act 1969* (WA), s 126(1). That statute enabled an equal co-tenant, in *Nullagine Investments Pty Ltd v Western Australian Club Inc* (1993) 177 CLR 635, to obtain an order for the sale of a fee simple estate, even though the two co-tenants had previously agreed not to sell their shares without first offering them to each other. That case contains a useful discussion of the partition and sale of co-tenancies for those wishing to learn more about this subject.

Chapter Sixteen

NON-POSSESSORY PROPERTY RIGHTS TO LAND

This chapter concerns a variety of property rights that do not include a right to possession. It might have been called "Non-Possessory Property Rights to Tangible Things", to distinguish it from the next chapter on property rights to intangible things. However, the only rights discussed here are rights to land which is possessed by another (or by no one). There are no comparable rights with respect to goods. The common law did not recognise non-possessory rights to goods. As discussed in Chapters 6 and 7, legal rights to goods are either possession or a right to possession. This may be because it is difficult to use a chattel without possessing it or because the common law failed to develop adequate remedies to protect non-possessory rights to goods. The court of Chancery did create a few non-possessory rights to chattels, such as the trust and the equitable charge and lien. However, these have already been discussed in Chapters 13 and 14.

The rights discussed here are divided into five categories:

1) .....**profits à prendre**, which are rights to take things from another person's land;
2) .....**easements**, which are rights to make limited use of a neighbour's land;
3) .....**restrictive covenants**, which are rights to prevent neighbours from using their own land in certain ways;
4) .....**pastoral rights**, which are rights to use land for agricultural purposes; and
5) .....**mineral rights**, which are rights to explore for or remove minerals from another person's land.

This chapter provides an introduction to the main categories of non-possessory property rights to land recognised in Australian law. It is not intended to be a comprehensive list of such rights. There are others recognised in common law or equity and the legislature is always free to create more. For example, in *Harper v Minister for Sea Fisheries* (1989) 168 CLR 314, the High Court of Australia considered the nature of a commercial licence to fish for abalone, granted under the *Fisheries Act* 1959 (Tas). Mason CJ, Deane and Gaudron JJ said (at 325), "This privilege can be compared to a profit à prendre. In truth, however, it is an entitlement of a new kind created as part of a system for preserving a limited public natural resource".

Profits à Prendre

A profit à prendre (using the law French which means "to take") is a right to take something, such as sand, timber, or wild rabbits, from land belonging to another person: see *Permanent Trustee Australia Ltd v Shand* (1992) 27 NSWLR 426 at 431. It is not a right to the things that may be taken, but a property right to the land from which they may be taken. A profit holder does not obtain a property right to the things taken until he or she obtains possession of them. Someone who wrongly interferes with the profit holder's right is guilty not of trespass to or conversion of chattels, but of nuisance for interfering with a right to land: see Chapter 7.

Profits à prendre may be granted by the Crown or a holder of an estate. As discussed in Chapter 12, an estate is the right to possession of land. Normally, estate holders have the rights to exclude others from their land and to make use of things found on or in their land. A profit à prendre is a right carved out of an estate and transferred to another. The estate subject to the profit is called the **servient tenement**. The profit holder has the right to enter that land and take away certain things. In other words, the property rights that are normally part of an estate are diminished by the creation of the profit.

A profit à prendre can be an exclusive right. For example, the holder of a profit to take timber from a parcel of land might be the only person with that right. In that case, the estate holder would not be entitled to take timber nor could he or she grant the same profit to anyone else. A profit à prendre can also be a shared right. For example, the holders of an estate might grant a right to fish and yet maintain that right for themselves and grant additional fishing rights to others.

What Things?

Profits à prendre are restricted to the taking of things that are the natural produce of the land:

1) .....soil and minerals;
2) .....natural vegetation (such as nuts, berries, and wood); and
3) .....wild animals found on the land.

This limitation is consistent with the nature of the profit à prendre as a right to land and not to the things which may be taken. The value of the profit is derived from the land itself.

Water is not on this list, probably because the common law did not regard the owner of land as the owner of the water flowing through the land. Since water is not part of the estate, the owner did not have the power to grant a property right to take water. This theory does make it difficult to explain why a right to fish or take other wild animals can be a valid profit à prendre. Land owners have the right to use the water on their estate and can grant an easement (discussed below) to their neighbours to allow them to use that water. The inability to grant a profit à prendre over water might be better explained as a recognition of the importance of fresh water and the undesirability of separating the property right to water from the use of the land. Unlike profits à prendre, easements are normally restricted to benefit neighbouring lands.

Profits à prendre cannot be granted with respect to the fruits of industry, such as farm crops, garden vegetables, or domestic animals. These things are regarded as the product of human labour and not of the land itself. There is a right to harvest crops called an **emblement**, which differs from a profit à prendre. It is the right of a former tenant to harvest an annual crop which he or she planted during the tenancy. This is a one-off right designed to protect agricultural tenants in cases where their tenancies end unexpectedly.

It is possible to have a profit à prendre to harvest trees that were planted by humans (or their machines). The labour involved in planting trees is considered to be only a small part of their production, when compared to the benefits obtained from the land through slow growth over many years. Legal problems were created by modern tree farming techniques, which accelerated tree growth and required more active care between planting and harvest. This problem was resolved in New South Wales and Tasmania by the creation of a statutory **forestry right**, which is "deemed to be a profit à prendre": *Conveyancing Act* 1919 (NSW), s 88AB(1); *Forestry Rights Registration Act* 1990 (Tas), s 5(1).

A right to take minerals can be a profit à prendre: see *Emerald Quarry Industries Pty Ltd v Commissioner of Highways* (1976) 14 SASR 486. However, mining rights are often granted by mineral leases, which confer a collection of rights on the leaseholder. In such cases, the right to take the mineral is not a separate profit à prendre, but merely part of the larger collection of rights under the lease: see *Commissioner of Stamp Duties (NSW) v Henry* (1964) 114 CLR 322. Mineral rights are discussed separately below.

Profit à Prendre or Sale of Goods?

When estate holders sell rights to take things from their land, there can be some confusion about whether the contract is for the sale of the thing taken or the grant of a profit à prendre. For example, if you paid the owner of land for the right to pick up a load of soil for your garden or for the right to pick wild berries one afternoon, no one would suppose that you had just purchased an interest in that land. You have paid for the temporary right to enter the land (a licence, discussed in Chapter 18) and for the soil or berries you take with you (a sale of goods, discussed at page 243). What distinguishes this contract from a contract to grant a profit à prendre?

The answer to this question depends on the intentions of the parties to the contract. In many cases, their intentions are clearly expressed. They might produce a formal deed which states that a profit à prendre is granted or they might sign a written contract which defines the right as a licence and sale of goods. However, people often leave legal details such as these unspoken and a court may be called upon later to determine the rights of the parties. The nature of the right intended has to be gleaned from the circumstances in which it was granted.

When people create rights to land, they tend to use more formalities than they would for the creation of a personal right. Therefore, when people intend to create a profit à prendre, it might be expected that they would do so with a deed or transfer of land: see Chapter 21. However, this is not always so. People do make oral contracts to grant profits à prendre: see *Mason v Clarke* [1955] AC 778.

In *Corporate Affairs Commission v ASC Timber Pty Ltd* (1989) 18 NSWLR 577, a company made contracts with investors concerning seedling pine trees, which would be managed by the company and harvested for the investors when mature. The company became insolvent and the court was asked to decide whether the contracts were for the sale of mature trees or for the grant of a profit à prendre. The contracts did not state expressly which right was intended. Powell J decided that an intention to grant a profit à prendre could be inferred from the circumstances. He said (at 590) that:

> "[T]he distinction is to be found to lie in the intention of the parties: is it the intention of the parties that the trees may be, or are to be, felled and removed within a reasonably short time — in which case the arrangement is one of sale — or is it intended that the trees shall be retained for a considerable period of time while they grow to maturity — in which case the arrangement is one involving the grant of a profit à prendre."

This case illustrates the importance of the distinction between a sale of goods and a profit à prendre. As discussed at page 244, the property rights to goods cannot pass to the buyer before the goods come into existence. Therefore, the buyers of standing trees as goods cannot obtain a property right to those trees until they are cut down. Until that happens, the trees are considered to be part of the land: see page 364. Therefore, if the seller refuses to perform the contract or sells the land to someone else, the buyer's only remedy is to sue the seller for damages for breach of contract. This personal right will not be of much value if the seller is insolvent, as in the case of *ASC Timber*. However, if the seller granted a profit à prendre, then the buyer has a property right to the land which can be enforced against others and gives the buyer priority over the seller's creditors.

Duration

The duration of a profit à prendre depends upon the intention of the person creating it. It could be perpetual, for life, or for a term of years or months. A profit à prendre might also be made on the same basis as a periodic tenancy, automatically renewing until one party decides to bring it to an end. The only limitation is the duration of the estate of the person creating the profit à prendre. Since the profit is carved out of that estate, it cannot exceed it, in much the same way that a sublease cannot normally exceed the greater estate from which it is carved: see page 94.

It seems that a profit à prendre does not require the same certainty of term needed to make a valid lease. In *Corporate Affairs Commission v ASC Timber Pty Ltd* (1989) 18 NSWLR 577 at 591, Powell J decided that the profit à prendre had been granted for the time needed to harvest the trees when mature. This term would not be sufficiently certain to create a valid lease, but this difficulty was not addressed in his judgment. Powell J assumed that a profit à prendre for an uncertain term would be valid. There are profits à prendre which come to an end when the thing to be taken is consumed. For example, a profit to remove all the gravel from a parcel of land will exist for a limited, but indefinite, period of time.

Easements

An easement is a right to use a neighbour's land without possessing it. The best known example of an easement is a right of way to travel across a neighbour's land. Of course, not all rights to use land are easements. A right to possession is usually an estate of some kind, but may be adverse possession or native title. There are other non-possessory property rights to use land, such as profits à prendre, pastoral leases, and native title. It is also possible to have merely personal rights to use land, such as the permission to retrieve a ball knocked into a neighbour's yard by mistake. A personal right to use land is called a **licence**, discussed in Chapter 18.

A feature of easements, which distinguishes them from many other property rights, is that (normally) they must provide some benefit to nearby land. The two main questions explored in this part are:

1) .....what counts as a benefit to nearby land; and
2) .....what rights can be easements.

This is followed by brief discussions of:
3) .....the creation of easements; and
4) .....the manner in which changes in the use of land can affect easements.

Benefit to Nearby Land

Land subject to an easement (like land subject to a profit à prendre) is called the **servient tenement**. Land benefited by an easement is called the **dominant tenement**. The benefit to the dominant tenement is called **accommodation**. It is said that the servient tenement must accommodate the dominant tenement. Like a profit à prendre, an easement is carved out of the estate which constitutes the servient tenement. However, that right cannot be given to any member of society. The easement attaches to, and becomes part of, the estate which constitutes the dominant tenement. In other words, the easement is removed from one estate and grafted onto another, neighbouring estate. Normally, it cannot exist separately from the dominant tenement.

Proximity of the Dominant Tenement

The dominant tenement need not be adjacent to the servient tenement. However, it must be nearby. For example, a right of way might exist in favour of land at the other end of the street if it benefits that land in some way (for example, by providing a shortcut to the main road). A decision that land is too far away to be a dominant tenement may simply be another way of saying that the easement does not really benefit that land.

Benefit to the Land

The benefit to the dominant tenement must be connected to the normal use and enjoyment of that land. A benefit to the owners or occupiers of land, which is unconnected to the land, would not be a valid easement. For example, suppose that someone living in a house near the Melbourne Cricket Ground (MCG) received an annual pass to all the events held there. This is a valuable right which is useful to the occupier of the house. It may even increase the value of that house if sold together with it. However, that does not make it an easement. There is an insufficient connection between the use and enjoyment of the house and the right to attend events at the MCG.

A purported easement might fail to accommodate a dominant tenement if the exercise of the right is not limited to purposes which benefit the dominant tenement. For example, in *Clapman v Edwards* [1938] 2 All ER 507, the defendant leased a petrol station and the right to use the wall of an adjoining block of flats "for advertising purposes". This did not create an easement since the right to advertise was not limited to purposes connected with the use of the land leased by the defendant. Therefore, the defendant had acquired a personal right to use the wall for advertising and he was free to assign that right to a bill posting company. If the right had been an easement, it would have attached to the dominant tenement and could not have been assigned separately from the lease.

Easements in Gross

At common law, an easement cannot exist without a dominant tenement. However, there are statutes which make this possible. For example, section 88A of the *Conveyancing Act* 1919 (NSW) authorises the creation of an "easement without a dominant tenement" in favour of the Crown, local governments, or utility companies for the purpose of providing utility services. An easement without a dominant tenement is called an easement in gross.

Statutory easements for utilities services, such as electricity, gas, water, and sewage, overcame two problems which prevented them from being recognised as easements at common law. The first is the lack of a dominant tenement. A utility easement is a benefit to the service provider's business and not to any particular parcel of land. Even if the facilities which produce electricity or gas or treat water or sewage could be regarded as dominant tenements, they are probably too far away from the lands they service to qualify as such.

The second difficulty overcome by statute relates to the nature of the use of the servient tenement. A permanent installation of pipes or cables on the servient tenement might be regarded as possession of part of the estate, since they occupy space in the air or underground. As discussed below, possession of even part of an estate cannot be an easement at common law.

Ownership of the Dominant and Servient Tenements

Normally, an easement cannot exist unless the servient and dominant tenements are possessed by different people. For example, suppose that you and I are neighbours and that I grant a right of way to you to cross my land to get from your land to the main road. If you buy my land, then (normally) the easement will cease to exist since you own both the servient and the dominant tenement.

The end of your easement in this manner can be explained in two ways. First, it is an application of the normal principle that people cannot have enforceable legal rights against themselves. Just as you could not be a sole trustee for yourself or a sole mortgagee of your own land, you cannot have an easement over your own land. Secondly, the end of your easement can be explained as its **merger** into your new estate. Your easement was a specific right to use my land. When you acquired my estate, the easement lost its separate identity as part of your greater right to possess that land. In other words, the specific right which was your easement is merely one of the rights which can be exercised as part of your new estate.

An easement is possible so long as the estates which constitute the servient and dominant tenements are not owned by the same people. The joint owners of an estate could have an easement over a neighbouring estate owned by one of them, and vice versa. Also, even if two fee simple estates were owned by the same person, an easement would be possible if another person had a lesser estate over one of the parcels. For example, if you owned two adjoining parcels of land in fee simple and leased one parcel to me, you could have an easement over my leasehold estate in favour of your fee simple estate next door and I could have an easement over that fee simple in favour of my lease. In each case, the easement is carved out of one person's right to possession and grafted onto another's.

There are some statutes which permit the creation and continuation of easements even though the dominant and servient tenements are owned by the same person; see, eg, *Land Title Act* 1994 (Qld), ss 86-88; *Real Property Act* 1900 (NSW), s 47(7). Also, essential easements can survive the common ownership of both tenements. As Needham J said in *Margil Pty Ltd v Stegul Pastoral Pty Ltd* [1984] 2 NSWLR 1 at 10, "unity of ownership or possession does not cause to disappear a right of way (or other easement) where that way or other easement is necessary to the use of the land which previously had the benefit of the easement". A necessary easement is, perhaps, suspended until the possession of the dominant and servient tenements is separated again.

Rights which can be Easements

Easements can be divided into two categories: positive and negative. Whether positive or negative, a right cannot be an easement unless it is less than possession, is clearly defined, and does not require the owner to spend time or money to maintain the easement.

Positive Easements

A positive easement allows a neighbour to do things which would otherwise be a trespass or nuisance. For example, a right of way allows a neighbour to cross the servient tenement. Without that easement (or the owner's permission), crossing that land would be a wrongful interference with the owner's right to possession and, therefore, a trespass. The law has recognised a variety of positive easements, including the right to enter the servient tenement to maintain a wall on the dominant tenement and the right to use a neighbour's outdoor lavatory: see *Hedley v Roberts* [1977] VR 282. A right to make excessive noises heard by the neighbours can be a positive easement, as can a right to discharge surplus water onto neighbouring land: see *Waterloo v Hinchcliffe* (1866) 5 SCR (NSW) 273 at 286. These activities would otherwise be a wrongful interference with the neighbour's enjoyment of her or his land and, therefore, a nuisance: see page 58.

Negative Easements

A negative easement prevents the occupier of the servient tenement from doing certain things, which would otherwise be permitted as part of the normal use and enjoyment of her or his estate. For example, an easement for light would prevent the occupier from obstructing the flow of light into windows on the neighbour's land: see *Commonwealth v Registrar of Titles (Vic)* (1918) 24 CLR 348. An easement for support would prevent the occupier from removing a structure which supports a neighbouring wall and a right to a windbreak can be an easement which prevents an occupier from removing a stand of trees.

There are two rights which look like negative easements, but are part of the normal rights and duties between neighbours and exist without the need to create an easement. One is the right to the natural support provided by the neighbour's land. It is wrong to excavate in a manner which causes a neighbour's land to collapse. The other is a right to the natural flow of water from one parcel of land to the next. Although landowners are entitled to use the water flowing through their land, it is wrong to impede the flow excessively.

Less than Possession

A right cannot be an easement if it amounts to possession of any part of the servient tenement. A right to possession must be an estate, adverse possession, or native title. For example, in *Copeland v Greenhalf* [1952] Ch 488, the owner of a garage claimed an easement to store vehicles on his neighbour's land. Since the storage of vehicles prevented the neighbour from making use of that part of his land, the court held that the right claimed was adverse possession.

It is sometimes said that an easement must not be too wide. This means that it cannot interfere with the use and enjoyment of the servient tenement to the extent that it would nullify the rights associated with that estate. If a right claimed is that wide, it amounts to possession of the servient tenement and cannot be an easement. This issue was confronted by the English Court of Appeal in *Re Ellenborough Park* [1956] Ch 131. People who purchased houses surrounding Ellenborough Park were granted "the full enjoyment...at all times hereafter in common with the other persons to whom such easements may be granted of the pleasure ground...called Ellenborough Park".

The court decided that this was an easement, which could be enforced against subsequent owners of the park. This decision requires some explanation, because it appears to violate two basic requirements for a valid easement: it must accommodate the dominant tenement and cannot amount to possession of the servient tenement. These two requirements were met in this case because the use of the servient and dominant tenements was limited by two restrictive covenants. (Restrictive covenants are discussed below.)

First, the houses could only be used for residential purposes. The only commercial uses allowed were lodging houses, private schools, and seminaries. Therefore, the right to wander around and have picnics at Ellenborough Park was an extension of the normal use of a residential dwelling for recreation. It enhanced the value of those houses as residences and, therefore, accommodated the dominant tenements. If the right to use the houses had not been restricted in this manner, the required connection between the easement and the use and enjoyment of the dominant tenement might have been absent. Would the right to enjoy the park accommodate a factory, shop, or office building? It could be argued that factory and office workers need places to relax during lunch and after work, but that might not provide a sufficient connection for a valid easement.

Secondly, the owner of Ellenborough Park had promised to maintain it as an "ornamental pleasure ground" and not to build, "except any grotto bower summerhouse flower-stand fountain music-stand or other ornamental erection". This was a valid restrictive covenant, which meant that the land could only be used as an ornamental garden. Given that restriction, it was not too great an interference with the owner's use of the park if the occupiers of certain houses near the garden had the right to use it for recreation. As Evershed MR said (at 176):

> "We see nothing repugnant to a man's proprietorship or possession of a piece of land that he should decide to make of it and maintain it as an ornamental garden, and should grant rights to a limited number of other persons to come into it for the enjoyment of its amenities."

The result would have been different without this restrictive covenant in place. Otherwise, the right to "full enjoyment" of the park would have prevented the owner from using that land as he or she wished. It would have been impossible to use it for residential or commercial purposes with neighbours wandering all over it. The words, "full enjoyment", took their meaning from the nature of the thing to be enjoyed: land which could only be used as an ornamental garden. In this context, the words did not grant possession of the land, but merely a right to use it for recreational purposes.

Clearly Defined

It is often said that an easement must not be too vague or that it must be capable of forming the subject matter of a grant of land. These are ways of saying that an easement must be clearly defined. A right would be too vague to be a valid easement if someone proposing to deal with the servient tenement would not know what is required to observe the easement. As discussed above, the right to "full enjoyment" of Ellenborough Park satisfied this requirement because it could be defined by reference to the restrictive covenant over the park. The easement was a right equivalent to the right which the public had to use a public garden. They could wander on those parts of the land intended for that purpose and enjoy the surroundings without destroying flowerbeds, etc. However, they could not take possession of any part of the park.

Cost of Maintaining the Easement

Normally, easements cannot impose positive duties on the owner of a servient tenement. They operate to restrict the rights the owner would otherwise have to exclude the easement holder from the property, sue for trespass or nuisance, or alter the servient tenement as he or she wished. A right which requires the owner to spend money or labour is not normally regarded as an easement. The duty to maintain an easement, such as the repair of a road or path used as a right of way, falls on the holder of that right: see *Byrne v Steele* [1932] VLR 143.

An obligation to maintain a fence created a problem for the common law, because it imposed a positive duty on the owner to spend money or effort to build it and keep it in good repair. In *Jones v Price* [1965] 2 QB 618 at 631, Willmer LJ called it a "quasi-easement", meaning a property right which is similar to, but not, an easement. He said (at 631):

> "It is not a true easement, for, properly speaking, an easement requires no more than sufferance on the part of the occupier of the servient tenement, whereas an obligation to maintain a hedge involves the performance of positive acts."

In Australia, the obligation to maintain fences is created and regulated by statute: see, eg, *Fences Act* 1975 (SA).

Creation of Easements

The creation of property rights is the subject of Part IV. Like other property rights, most easements are created by intention: see Chapter 21. Also like other property rights, they are sometimes created by other events. Two of the other ways to create easements should be noted here: necessity and prescription.

Easement of Necessity

When a parcel of land becomes isolated from public roads, a right of way may arise by operation of law to connect that parcel to the road. This can happen when land is subdivided into two parcels and one parcel is cut off from the road. Suppose, for example, that I owned a block of land with access to the road at the north end of the block. If I sold or leased the north half of that block to you without reserving a right of way for myself, a right of way might arise over the usual route from the south half to the road. This easement is created to save me from my own folly. It might be regarded as a response to my mistake of transferring more property to you than I intended: the right to exclusive possession of the north half without keeping an easement for myself.

Easement by Prescription

Another way to create an easement is by prescription. If a person makes unauthorised use of her or his neighbour's land for a long period of time

(20 years or more, depending on the jurisdiction), the neighbour may lose the right to prevent that use. The person thereby acquires a property right to continue to make use of the neighbour's land. In other words, an easement is born. Not every use of land will give rise to an easement by prescription. It must be something which can be the subject of a valid easement, such as a right of way, right of support from an adjacent building, or a right to discharge water onto the neighbour's land.

The creation of an easement by prescription is similar to the acquisition of an estate by adverse possession: see Chapter 8. In both situations, the failure to take action to stop the trespass or nuisance causes the land owner to lose the right to do so. It is different from adverse possession in two ways. First, the acquisition of a right by prescription does not depend on the operation of the limitation of action statutes. It is a separate body of common law and statute: see, eg, *Delohery v Permanent Trust Co of New South Wales* (1904) 1 CLR 283; *Prescription Act* 1832 (WA). Secondly, a person making unauthorised use of a neighbour's land (without taking possession) does not thereby acquire a property right. The easement comes into existence only after the neighbour's land has been used for a sufficient period of time. In contrast, a person taking adverse possession acquires a property right from the outset: possession of the land, which is enforceable against everyone else in society except someone with a better right to possession. When the limitation period expires, the owner's better right to possession is lost.

The creation of negative easements by prescription is a problem. For example, if I enjoy the unobstructed flow of light through my windows overlooking your land for 20 years, should I thereby acquire an easement which prevents you from obstructing that flow? It would be odd if your decision not to make the fullest possible use of your estate caused you to lose that right. This is why courts are reluctant to allow the creation of new types of negative easements. Otherwise, development might become difficult or impossible as neighbouring land owners acquired the rights to insist that they each maintain the status quo.

This problem was recognised in *Phipps v Pears* [1965] 1 QB 76. In that case, the defendant demolished a building which had been standing close to the plaintiff's house and protecting one wall of that house from the weather. The court rejected the plaintiff's claim that he had acquired a negative easement by prescription for protection from the weather. Lord Denning MR said (at 83) that "if we were to stop a man pulling down his house, we would put a brake on desirable improvement".

Australian courts have authorised a broader range of negative easements than have the English courts. For example, the High Court of Australia decided, in *Commonwealth v Registrar of Titles (Vic)* (1918) 24 CLR 348 at 349, that a "full and free right ... to the uninterrupted access and enjoyment of light and air" over a "strip of land 10 feet wide" on the servient tenement was a valid negative easement. The English courts restrict such easements to the flow of light through defined openings in buildings on the dominant tenement. The Australian legislatures reacted to this court decision by abolishing the creation of easements of light by prescription: see, eg, *Law of Property Act* 1936 (SA), s 22. Queensland has also abolished the creation of rights of way by prescription: see *Property Law Act* 1974 (Qld), s 198A.

Changes in Use

Suppose that you granted a right of way to your neighbours to pass over your land to get to theirs, at a time when your neighbours were a single family with a small car, two bicycles and a dog. They later sold their land and your new neighbour wanted to build a popular fast-food restaurant and use the right of way for access to the "drive through" service window. Would you then be required to let 2,000 hamburger seekers drive over your land every day?

You might have avoided the problem if you had limited the right of way you granted to the neighbours. It might have been restricted to provide access to the land only so long as the dominant tenement was used for residential purposes. However, you did not foresee the danger you now face and did what many people have done: granted a right of access to your neighbour's land without limitation.

The courts have provided a solution to this problem. Even though the increased use of an easement falls within the express terms of the right granted to the owner of the dominant tenement, the courts will not permit the easement to be used in that manner if it goes significantly beyond that which was contemplated by the parties when the easement was created. For example, in *Jelbert v Davis* [1968] 1 All ER 1182, a small farm was converted into a recreational caravan park with a capacity for 200 units per day. Although the farmer had a right of way over his neighbour's narrow driveway "for all purposes", it could not be used by the customers of the caravan park.

Restrictive Covenants

A **covenant** is a promise made in a document under seal. If land owners make a covenant to their neighbours to restrict the use of their land, this may give the neighbours a property right to that land which entitles them to enforce that restriction. If it does create a property right, it is called a restrictive covenant. As discussed above, there were two restrictive covenants in *Re Ellenborough Park* [1956] Ch 131. The owners of the park had promised their neighbours not to build on the park and the neighbours had promised not to use their land for commercial purposes.

Compared to Other Property Rights

Estates

Restrictive covenants are not estates because they are always rights less than possession. They can, however, bear some resemblance to rights associated with leasehold estates. As discussed at page 93, leases often contain covenants which restrict the use of land. For example, it is common for residential tenants to covenant that they will not use the land for commercial purposes and for business tenants to covenant that they will not use the land for residential purposes. These are not restrictive covenants. They are called **leasehold covenants** and are enforceable because of the **privity of estate** between the landlord and tenant. Privity of estate is a property relationship which arises when a lesser estate is carved out of a greater estate. Leasehold covenants affect only the single parcel of land subject to those two estates. In contrast, restrictive covenants are called **freehold covenants**. They exist without privity of estate between the owners of neighbouring parcels of land.

Profits à Prendre and Positive Easements

Restrictive covenants differ from profits à prendre and positive easements because they do not give neighbours the right to enter or use the land subject to the covenant. Restrictive covenants merely prevent the possessors of land from doing things that would otherwise be permissible. They never allow the neighbours to make positive use of the land subject to the covenant. In other words, a restrictive covenant is never a restriction on the possessor's right to exclude others from her or his land.

Negative Easements

Restrictive covenants are similar to negative easements. Both operate to restrict the use of land for the benefit of neighbouring land. Anything which can be the subject of a negative easement can also be the subject of a restrictive covenant. However, the converse is not true. Not everything which can be a restrictive covenant can be a negative easement. For example, the restrictions on the use of land, which were valid restrictive covenants in *Re Ellenborough Park*, would not have been valid negative easements.

Why does the law bother to say that a right cannot be a negative easement, if it can take effect as a restrictive covenant? There are three explanations for this. First, the negative easement is the creation of courts of common law, while the restrictive covenant was invented by the court of Chancery. Since those two property rights evolved separately in different courts, they are subject to different rules. The merger of those courts (discussed in Chapters 5 and 13) means that two similar, but distinct property rights are now enforced in one court.

Secondly, easements can be created without the consent of the land owner (by prescription), but restrictive covenants are created only by consent. Therefore, the reason for limiting the variety of possible negative easements, discussed above, does not apply to restrictive covenants. A restrictive covenant is always created by a land owner's conscious decision to limit her or his freedom to use that land. Lord Denning MR had this in mind when he said, in *Phipps v Pears* [1965] 1 QB 76 at 83-84:

> "There is no such easement known to the law as an easement to be protected from the weather. The only way for an owner to protect himself is by getting a covenant from his neighbour that he will not pull down his house or cut down his trees."

A third reason to permit a broader range of restrictive covenants than negative easements relates to the priority of those rights: see Part V. People might purchase land and later discover that the land is subject to an easement. They are bound to observe that easement even though they had no idea it existed when they made the decision to buy the land. In contrast, a restrictive covenant will affect purchasers of land only if they had notice that the land is subject to the covenant. The same is true of land registered under a Torrens system: see Part VI. Easements can bind purchasers without notice, but a restrictive covenant will affect purchasers only if the covenant is recorded on the title. Therefore, the risk of being unpleasantly surprised by restrictions on the use of land is greatly reduced if those restrictions are created by restrictive covenants and not as negative easements.

Privity of Contract

People who are familiar with the law of contract are sometimes surprised to discover that restrictive covenants are property rights. A basic principle of contract law is **privity of contract**, which means that (normally) a contract is enforceable only between the parties to the contract. It does not create rights and obligations for others. The restrictive covenant is an exception to that basic principle, made possible by the judgment in *Tulk v Moxhay* (1848) 2 Ph 774, 41 ER 1143. It is helpful to trace the problem created by privity of contract and the development of the restrictive covenant as the judicial solution to this problem.

Consider the following example and assume that it takes place before the development of the restrictive covenant. Sylvia owns a fee simple estate in a large block of land and wants to sell part of that land to Donna. However, she does not want Donna to use that land for commercial purposes or to build higher than two stories. So, Sylvia obtains Donna's written promise not to do those things and the purchase price for the land is set accordingly. Everything is fine until Donna sells the land to Claire. The normal rules of privity of contract mean that Sylvia cannot enforce Donna's promise against Claire, who is now free to build a large office tower on the land. Sylvia would not have sold the land to Donna if she had known that the restriction on its use would not be effective or at least she would have sold it for a higher price.

If, instead of selling her fee simple estate, Sylvia had retained it and granted a leasehold estate to Donna, the promise would have been enforceable against Donna's successors. If Claire purchased Donna's lease, she would be bound to observe the covenants in that lease by reason of privity of estate. Privity of contract is not required. Moreover, if Francesca purchased Sylvia's fee simple estate, she would be entitled to enforce those leasehold covenants against Claire, even though Francesca and Claire are not parties to the original contract: see page 93.

The law of restrictive covenants allows neighbours to create enforceable restrictions on the use of their land, which do not depend on either privity of contract or privity of estate. It solves two problems related to the absence of privity. First, it allows subsequent owners of the dominant tenement to enforce the promise and, secondly, it requires subsequent owners of the servient tenement to keep the promise. In other words, both the benefit and the burden of the covenant can be transferred to others, along with the land.

Benefit of the Covenant

Transferring the benefit of a restrictive covenant was never a difficult problem. People who have rights arising under a contract are normally free to assign those rights to others. This is a routine exception to the requirement of privity of contract. For example, if we made a contract in which I promised to pay you a sum of money, you would be free to transfer your right to be paid to another person (such as a debt collector). Not every right can be assigned. For example, contracts of service are not normally assigned. Unless you are a professional athlete, you do not have to worry that you will go into work tomorrow and discover that your employer has traded you to another company in another city. It is a bit too much like slavery if you are not free to choose the people entitled to the benefit of your labour.

There is no public policy which prevents the transfer of rights under contracts restricting the use of land. The only concern is that the benefit of a restrictive covenant remains associated with the land benefited by that covenant. The right to restrict the neighbours' use of their land is a benefit only because they are neighbours. That right loses its value if it becomes separated from the land. Returning to the example above, if Sylvia sells her land to Francesca and moves to another city, there is no reason why she should retain the right to restrict the use of Donna's land. That right is of no benefit to Sylvia. She has no interest in enforcing the covenant and would suffer no loss if Donna failed to observe it. However, the covenant is valuable to Francesca as Donna's new neighbour. It should be transferred to her along with the land.

It has long been recognised that personal rights, which benefit a person only because he or she is the owner of a particular parcel of land, can become attached to, and pass with, the ownership of that land. If this occurs, it is said that the benefit of the covenant runs with the land.

Obligation to Perform the Covenant

Normally, the burden of a covenant cannot run with the land at common law. So, if the owner of land promised to use it in a certain way, that promise could not be enforced against subsequent owners of that land. This is a standard application of the common law rule that the obligation to perform an obligation cannot be assigned. The person with the right corresponding to the obligation has a right to look to the obligated party for performance of that obligation. People make contracts after carefully considering whether the other party will perform the contract well and be pleasant to deal with. There would be little point to this if the other party was free to shift the burden of performing that contract to someone else. The benefits of most contracts can be assigned, but not the burden, unless the parties agree to cancel the existing contract and create a new contract with new parties (a process called **novation**).

The restrictive covenant is an exception to the normal rule. Thanks to *Tulk v Moxhay* (1848) 2 Ph 774, 41 ER 1143, the burden of performing the covenant can be shifted to subsequent owners of the land subject to the covenant. In that case, the plaintiff owned a garden in Leicester Square and the houses surrounding it. He sold the garden in 1808 and the purchaser covenanted to keep the garden in its present state as a garden and not to build on it. The garden was sold to the defendant in

1848, who did not make a covenant to the plaintiff, but had notice of the original covenant. The court of Chancery decided that it would enforce the restrictive covenant against a purchaser who acquired the land with notice of the covenant. Since the covenant reduced the market value of the land, it would be unfair if a purchaser could buy the land at a reduced price and then sell it the next day at an increased price to someone who was not required to observe the covenant.

Although the restrictive covenant was first regarded as a personal right, which could be enforced against subsequent owners of the land, it came to be regarded as an equitable property right. The intervention of the court of Chancery was responsible for this development. The normal response to a breach of contract in a court of common law is an order that the defendant pay a sum of money to the plaintiff as compensation for the loss caused by the breach: see Chapter 7. In some situations, the plaintiff could go to the court of Chancery and obtain an order that the defendant must perform her or his obligations under the contract. Chancery would compel the performance of a restrictive covenant by granting an **injunction** prohibiting the defendant from using the land in a manner contrary to the covenant. This gave the plaintiff the power to restrict the use of the defendant's land.

When the court of Chancery decided, in *Tulk v Moxhay*, to enforce the restrictive covenant by granting an injunction against a subsequent owner of the land, it began to look like a property right. There were doubts about whether it really was property, because it could not be enforced against people who purchased the land without notice of it. An essential characteristic of property (discussed in Chapter 2) seemed to be missing: the restrictive covenant was not enforceable against members of society generally, but only against the covenantor and people who later received a property right in the land either as a gift or with notice of the covenant. However, these doubts were resolved and the restrictive covenant is now regarded as a property right which is enforceable against all members of society, except those who acquire legal property rights to the land in good faith, for value, and without notice of the covenant. In other words, the class of persons affected by the covenant is indefinite and excepted from that class are those people entitled to the defence of **bona fide purchase**: see page 405. The potential destruction of a restrictive covenant by a bona fide purchaser is now understood to be a question of priorities between competing property rights and not an indication that the restrictive covenant is not property.

Rights which can be Restrictive Covenants

Not every contract regarding the use of land can be a restrictive covenant. The right and corresponding obligation created by that contract must be negative. It may impose a restriction on the owner's use of the land, but never a positive obligation to actively use the land in some manner. For example, a covenant to erect and maintain a building would not be enforceable against subsequent owners of the land, even if they acquired the land with notice of the covenant: see, eg, *Haywood v Brunswick Permanent Benefit Building Society* (1881) 8 QBD 403.

There are two explanations for this requirement that restrictive covenants be restrictive and not compulsive. First, the restrictive covenant is a limited exception to the normal rule of privity of contract. This exception is tolerable if it merely prevents people from acting, but would be too wide if it could be used to compel people to actively perform the obligations in contracts made by others. Secondly, the restrictive covenant is possible because a court of equity will grant an injunction to restrain a breach of the covenant. That court is far more willing to grant an injunction which prohibits action than an order which compels action: see *Doherty v Allman* (1878) 3 App Cas 709 at 719-720. Courts will compel the performance of some positive obligations. For example, it is possible to get an order for **specific performance** of a contract of sale: see page 258. It is also possible to compel positive action with **mandatory injunctions**, but these are seldom granted.

In some cases, an obligation which appears to be positive may be construed to be negative. For example, a covenant to use land for residential purposes can be enforced as a restrictive covenant not to use it for any other purpose: see *German v Chapman* (1877) 7 Ch D 271. This type of interpretation is not possible if the performance of the covenant requires the outlay of expense and effort. The essential test for the validity of a restrictive covenant is whether it can be enforced effectively by a prohibitive injunction.

The creation and enforcement of positive obligations regarding the use of land can be achieved by statute. For example, a restrictive covenant would be insufficient to protect a building of historical significance. It could be used to prevent the land owners from destroying or modifying the building, but could not compel them to repair and maintain it. The owners could rid themselves of the building merely by doing nothing and waiting for it to fall down. A statute can be used in this situation to designate the building as a heritage site in need of preservation and impose positive obligations on the owners to preserve it. For example, under section 60 of the *Historical Cultural Heritage Act 1995* (Tas), the "Heritage Council may serve a notice on the owner of a registered place who by any intentional act or omission is likely to affect the historic cultural heritage significance of the place" and thereby require the owner "to take specified action to repair any damage" or "to commence or complete any specified works".

Not every restriction on the use of land will be enforceable as a restrictive covenant. Like easements, restrictive covenants must benefit neighbouring lands: *Clem Smith Nominees Pty Ltd v Farrelly* (1978) 20 SASR 227 at 235. A restriction will not be enforced if it is being used to further an illegal or immoral purpose or is otherwise contrary to public policy. For example, covenants restricting the sale of houses to people of certain races used to be enforced by courts in the United States of America until the United States Supreme Court decided that was unconstitutional. In *Shelley v Kraemer* (1948) 334 US 1 at 20, Vinson J said "that in granting judicial enforcement of the restrictive agreements in these cases, the states have denied petitioners the equal protection of the law and that, therefore, the action of the state courts cannot stand".

A restrictive covenant might not be enforced if it caused the land to become useless. This can happen when it conflicts with local government planning regulations. For example, if land was subject to a restrictive covenant that it not be used for commercial purposes and was zoned for commercial use only, it would not be possible to use the land without breaking the covenant or the law. In most jurisdictions, the courts have the statutory authority to deal with this problem by modifying or discharging the restrictive covenant: see, eg, *Property Law Act* 1958 (Vic), s 84.

The court is not required to discharge or modify a restrictive covenant just because it conflicts with zoning regulations. Otherwise, people with influence over local governments could obtain the zoning regulations needed to rid themselves of the burden of a restrictive covenant. This was attempted in *Perth Construction Pty Ltd v Mount Lawley Pty Ltd* (1955) 57 WALR 41. A company purchased a lot subject to a restrictive covenant that it be used only as a residential dwelling. Over the next few months, it obtained a permit to build three shops on the lot and had the lot rezoned for commercial use only. It then applied to the court to discharge the restrictive covenant, with the neighbours objecting. Virtue J said (at 48):

> "It would be difficult to imagine a more unmeritorious application ... than this one by an applicant which entered into a binding legal obligation without the slightest intention of abiding by it, which appears to have used public authorities vested with powers in such matters for its own ends in order to manoeuvre itself into a position where it might have some shadow of pretext for making the application."

Attaching Covenants to Land

The Burden of the Covenant

If a covenant restricts the use of land, it is clear that the burden of that covenant can run with the land. However, that does not necessarily mean that it will do so. This depends on whether it was intended to bind all future owners of the land or merely the person making the promise. Usually, that intention is expressed in the document creating the restrictive covenant: the owners of the land will promise on behalf of their successors and assignees to restrict the use of that land. Some jurisdictions have statutes which help resolve this issue if it is left in doubt. For example, section 79 of the *Property Law Act* 1958 (Vic) states that, "A covenant relating to any land of a covenantor ... shall, unless a contrary intention is expressed, be deemed to be made by the covenantor on behalf of himself, his successors in title."

The Benefit of the Covenant

The same question arises in connection with the benefit of the covenant: was it intended to benefit only the party to the covenant or all future owners of the neighbouring land? Again, there may be statutory help available. For example, section 78 of the *Property Law Act* 1958 (Vic) states that, "A covenant relating to any land of the covenantee shall be deemed to be made with the covenantee and his successors in title."

It can be difficult to identify the land to which the benefit of a restrictive covenant relates. This is because the covenant does not affect the use of the land benefited, but merely restricts the use of the land burdened. If the covenant is made to someone who owns several parcels of land in the neighbourhood, was it intended to benefit them all? If he or she owns a very large parcel of land which is later subdivided and sold to a number of purchasers, was it intended to benefit every smaller parcel? Normally, the answer to these questions is found in the document creating the restrictive covenant. In most cases, the lands burdened and benefited by the covenant are clearly described.

If the land benefited by the covenant is not clearly described by the parties creating the covenant, a court may be called upon to decide the matter. English courts have taken a generous approach to this problem and allowed the benefit to run with all of the covenantee's lands which can benefit from that covenant: see *Federated Homes Ltd v Mill Lodge Properties Ltd* [1980] 1 All ER 371. There does not appear to be a uniform Australian approach to the resolution of this issue. In *Re Arcade Hotel Pty Ltd* [1962] VR 274, the Full Court of the Supreme Court of Victoria decided that the benefit of a restrictive covenant did not pass to subsequent owners of smaller portions of a larger parcel benefited by that covenant. The Victorian legislature reacted to this decision with section 79A of the *Property Law Act* 1958 (Vic), which states that the benefit of a restrictive covenant is "annexed to the whole and to each and every part of such other land capable of benefiting from such restriction" unless the covenant states that this was not intended.

Development Schemes

A problem can arise when a large parcel of land is being subdivided and developed into a new residential neighbourhood. The developer may wish to create a restrictive covenant which is intended to benefit and burden every lot in the new neighbourhood. However, as lots are sold one by one, it can be very difficult to ensure that each purchaser receives the benefit of all the covenants made by other purchasers and that her or his covenant will benefit all of them. Getting the web of mutual restrictive covenants in place can be an expensive and time consuming task and, if just one lot is inadvertently omitted from that web, the plan of development for the entire neighbourhood could be adversely affected.

There are at least two possible solutions to this problem. The first is to permit the developer to create the restrictive covenants when the land is subdivided, even though the land benefited and burdened by the covenant is owned by the same person. There are several statutes which permit this: see *Real Property Act* 1900 (NSW), s 88B; *Transfer of Land Act* 1893 (WA), s 136H. Each lot in the subdivision will be subject to the restrictive covenant in favour of every other lot, without having to obtain separate covenants from any of the purchasers.

The other solution was devised by the court of Chancery: see *Elliston v Reacher* [1908] 2 Ch 374; *Re Louis and the Conveyancing Act* [1971] 1 NSWLR 164. It relaxes the strict requirements for creating a restrictive covenant, when that covenant is part of what is called a **development scheme** or **building scheme**. All of the purchasers will acquire the benefit and burden of the restrictive covenant over all of the lots in a development if:

1) .....the purchasers acquired their lots from a common vendor or from vendors working co-operatively on the development;
2) .....before selling any of the lots, the vendor(s) created a scheme for development which would be furthered by a restrictive covenant over every lot; and
3) .....the restrictive covenant over each lot was intended to benefit every other lot in the development.

This is a practical solution to the problem, which takes the restrictive covenant one step further. It allows a purchaser to acquire the benefit of a covenant between two other people, even though he or she is not a successor in title to either of them. This may seem to be a remarkable inroad on the doctrine of privity of contract, but it helped facilitate the orderly development of new residential neighbourhoods.

Today, much of the work which used to be performed by restrictive covenants and development schemes is now handled by planning legislation which regulates the use of land. For example, some lots in a neighbourhood might be restricted to be used for single-family dwellings, while others are zoned for multi-family use or retail businesses. Restrictive covenants still play an important role in the regulation of land use. Many older covenants have survived the advent of planning legislation. A restrictive covenant can also be used to help create a unique character for a new neighbourhood. It enables the developer to create restrictions on land use which are more detailed than the broad zoning requirements established by local governments.

Pastoral Rights

The term "pastoral rights" has no technical meaning and is being used here as a generic label for a variety of statutory rights to use land for agricultural purposes, such as **pastoral leases**, **grazing licences**, and **occupation licences**. The rights discussed here were not recognised at common law or in equity. They are created by statute and entitle the holder to make use of land, often without having possession of that land.

As discussed in Chapter 9, not every right to use a thing can be a property right. A court faced with a novel claim to use a thing would compare the right claimed to the variety of property rights recognised in Australian law to see if it falls within one of the established categories. If it does not, the court is likely to decide that it is a personal right and not property. The list of property rights is not closed. The courts have developed new property rights from time to time, such as the restrictive covenant, created in England in the 19th century, and the recognition of native title in Australia at the end of the 20th century. However, courts are constrained by precedent and, therefore, tend to develop new rights incrementally and slowly.

Parliament is not under the same constraint and is free to create new rights. When a statute uses a word which has a technical meaning at common law, it is assumed that Parliament intended the word to have its technical meaning. In other words, when a statute describes a right, using a label borrowed from common law or equity (such as lease, easement, or licence), it is assumed that Parliament was not inventing a new right, but merely authorising the grant of the common law or equitable right. However, this is only an assumption, which can be disproved by references to other passages in the statute.

For example, a common law or equitable lease is a right to possession of land for a definite duration. Parliament sometimes refers to rights as leases, even though they lack one or both of these characteristics. The **perpetual lease**, discussed at page 97, is a right to possess land for an indefinite period of time. In other words, it is a new estate created by statute. In *Wik Peoples v Queensland* (1996) 187 CLR 1, the High Court of Australia said that a pastoral lease in Queensland did not give the leaseholder a right to possession. In other words, it was not an estate, but a new non-possessory right created by statute.

There are two questions discussed briefly below. First, what determines whether a statutory right to use land is possessory or not? Secondly, if a right is non-possessory, what determines whether it is personal or property?

Possession

The main issue before the court in the *Wik* case was whether a pastoral lease necessarily extinguished native title. This depended on whether the lease gave the pastoralist a right to possession of the land. If it did, the pastoralist would be entitled to exclude other people from the land, including aboriginal people seeking to exercise their native title to that land. As discussed at page 395, the right to possession would have had priority over native title.

The pastoral leases in *Wik* were granted pursuant to the *Land Act* 1910 (Qld) and *Land Act* 1962 (Qld). Those statutes used technical terms, such as "lease", "estate", and "demise for a term of years", which indicated that the right granted was a leasehold estate. However, they also authorised many other people to make use of the land subject to the pastoral lease. The government could issue licences to people to enter the land to remove timber, gravel, clay and the like. People were also entitled to drive stock through the land, so long as they kept off enclosed cultivated areas and at least one mile away from the principal homestead or head station.

The statutory rights which other people had to use land subject to a pastoral lease could be interpreted in two ways. First, they could be used to support the view that the pastoral lease conferred a right to possess the land, since other people required specific statutory authority to enter the land without the permission of the pastoralist. This was the view of the minority of the High Court of Australia. Brennan CJ said (dissenting at 74):

> "If, as a matter of construction, it is right to hold that the right to exclusive possession was conferred on a pastoral lessee, the statutory provisions that authorised entry onto leased land for a variety of purposes were qualifications of that right but they did not destroy it. They merely limited the enjoyment of that right to the extent that the particular statute described."

The second view, which prevailed in the High Court of Australia, was that the rights granted to others detracted from the rights of a pastoralist to such an extent that what remained was not possession of the land. There were three other factors which supported this view. First, the statute provided a mechanism for removing a person in unlawful occupation of Crown land and gave the pastoralist the right to make a complaint to the Crown to bring proceedings against that person (see 187 CLR 146). This indicated that the pastoralist did not have an independent right to exclude people from the land, but had to rely on the Crown's right to do so.

Secondly, the pastoral leases covered large areas of land (sometimes more than 1,000 square miles) which could support relatively few cattle (for example, one animal for every 60 acres). The pastoralist did not need exclusive possession of the land to achieve the purpose for which the lease was granted.

The third and most important factor was the potential effect of the lease on the rights of aboriginal people to use the land. As Gaudron J said (at 146-147), "general words in a statute are not to be construed as extinguishing native title rights unless that intention is manifest, as evidenced by the use of clear and unambiguous words to that effect". In other words, the doubt concerning the nature of a pastoral lease had to be resolved in favour of the view that the lease is not a right to possession.

Just as a non-possessory right to use land can be called a lease, so can a right to possession be called a **licence**: see *Radaich v Smith* (1959) 101 CLR 209. Normally, that word is used to describe a personal right to use land (discussed in Chapter 18), which is enforceable only against the person who granted it. However, as Gummow J said in the *Wik* case (at 197), "there is nothing remarkable in the use of a term such as 'lease' or 'licence' to identify new institutions not fully to be identified with either term as understood at common law".

O'Keefe v Malone [1903] AC 365 and *O'Keefe v Williams* (1910) 11 CLR 171 concerned an occupation licence granted under the *Crown Lands Act* 1884 (NSW). The Crown granted that licence to the plaintiff and then, by mistake, granted another occupation licence over the same land to the defendant. The defendant entered the land and was thereby guilty of trespass and required to pay damages to the plaintiff: see Chapter 7. In other words, the plaintiff had possession of the land and could exclude other members of society from that land.

In *O'Keefe v Malone* [1903] AC 365, the Privy Council advised that the occupation licence was indistinguishable from a lease and conferred a right to possession (that is, an estate). In *O'Keefe v Williams* (1910) 11 CLR 171 at 193, the High Court of Australia decided that the licence carried with it the Crown's promise that it "will not disturb or authorize the disturbance of the lessee in his occupation". This is the **covenant of quiet enjoyment**, which is one of the leasehold covenants usually made by landlords to their tenants: see page 93.

What distinguished this occupation licence, which was granted "for grazing purposes", from the pastoral leases considered in the *Wik* case? First, they were created by different statutes. Whether a statutory right is possession or not depends upon a careful reading of the statute which creates that right. Secondly, the occupation licence in the *O'Keefe* cases covered a much smaller area than the pastoral leases in the *Wik* case: three square miles compared to more than a 1,000 square miles. It is likely that the occupier required possession of the whole parcel of land to fulfil the purpose of the occupation licence. Thirdly, consideration of the native title rights of aboriginal people did not influence the interpretation of the occupation licence in the *O'Keefe* cases.

Property

A right to possession is always a property right. It relates to some thing contingently connected to the right holder (land or goods) and is enforceable generally against other members of society, who can be excluded from access to that thing. In contrast, a non-possessory right need not be property. It need not relate to any particular thing, but might correspond solely to another person's obligation to fulfil that right (for example, a bank account). If it does relate to some thing, it need not be enforceable generally against other members of society, but might be enforceable only against a specific person. For example, a non-possessory right to use land might be a licence enforceable only against the person who granted that right.

Since a pastoral lease is a non-possessory right to use land, it need not be property. It is conceivable that a pastoral lease could be a personal right enforceable only against the Crown who granted that lease. This would depend on how the right is defined in the statute which authorised its creation. If a pastoral lease is a property right, it would be similar to (but greater than) an easement or profit à prendre: the right holder cannot prevent others from using the land, but can enforce that right against other members of society and not just against the person who granted it.

The pastoral leases considered in the *Wik* case were property rights because they were capable of displacing native title rights to the land leased. In other words, they were enforceable generally against others and not just against the Crown. As Kirby J said (at 242-243):

> "Pastoral leases give rise to statutory interests in land which are sui generis. ... Such an interest could, in law, be exercised and enjoyed to the full without necessarily extinguishing native title interests. The extent to which the two interests could operate together is a matter for further evidence and legal analysis. Only if there is inconsistency between the legal interests of the lessee (as defined by the instrument of lease and the legislation under which it is granted) and the native title (as established by evidence), will such native title, to the extent of the inconsistency, be extinguished."

Not every pastoral right is property. For example, *The Queen v Toohey* (1982) 158 CLR 327 concerned grazing licences granted under the *Crown Lands Act* 1931 (NT). The court was asked to decide whether the land subject to those licences could be placed in a land trust under the *Aboriginal Land Rights (Northern Territory) Act* 1976 (Cth). That land could be placed in trust only if it was "unalienated Crown land", which section 3(1) of the latter statute defined as "Crown land in which no person (other than the Crown) has an estate or interest".

The High Court of Australia decided (at 342) that the grazing licence was not a property right and, therefore, the holders of those licences did not "have an 'estate or interest' in that land". Although the licence was similar to a profit à prendre, it was a personal right enforceable only against the Crown who granted it. In other words, the term "licence" accurately described the right granted.

Mineral Rights

Lord Macnaghten provided a legal definition of "minerals" in *Lord Provost and Magistrates of Glasgow v Farie* (1888) 13 App Cas 657 at 689: "In its widest signification it probably means every inorganic substance forming part of the crust of the earth other than the layer of soil which sustains vegetable life." He also said (at 690) that "the word 'minerals' when used in a legal document, or in an Act of Parliament, must be understood in its widest signification, unless there be something in the context or in the nature of the case to control its meaning".

Today, minerals are defined by statute in every state and territory. These statutory definitions add to, or subtract from, the meaning of minerals at common law. For example, section 4 of the *Mineral Resources Development Act* 1990 (Vic) defines minerals to include fine clay and peat, while section 8 of the *Mining Act* 1978 (WA) excludes limestone, rock, gravel, sand, and clay located on private land.

Most statutory definitions of minerals exclude petroleum, which is commonly defined as "any naturally occurring hydrocarbon (whether in a gaseous, liquid or solid state)", except coal and oil shale: see, eg, *Petroleum Act* 1998 (Vic), s 6. Although petroleum is a valuable mineral, most jurisdictions regulate petroleum rights separately from other mineral rights. Each jurisdiction (except Tasmania and the Australian Capital Territory) has a *Petroleum Act*, which deals with onshore petroleum rights, and every state has a *Petroleum (Submerged Lands) Act* 1982, which helps regulate offshore petroleum in cooperation with the Commonwealth government. Most other mineral rights are governed in each state and territory (except the Australian Capital Territory) by a statute called the *Mining Act*, *Mineral Resources Act*, or *Mineral Resources Development Act*. In the Australian Capital Territory, they are dealt with under section 219 of the *Land (Planning and Environment) Act* 1991.

Rights to the minerals in land can be, and commonly are, separated from the right to possession of the land itself. Most minerals in Australia are owned by the state or territory in which they are located. When the Crown grants an estate in land, it usually keeps the minerals for itself and can then transfer or licence mineral rights to others in exchange for the payment of royalties.

If the owner of an estate does have a right to the minerals found there, it is not a separate property right, but merely part of the estate. As discussed in Chapter 12, an estate is the right to possession of a volume of space measured relative to the face of the earth. It normally extends down into the earth and entitles the owner to use any minerals there, unless that right is excepted from that estate.

Where a right to minerals is separated from the estate, it exists as a non-possessory right. It may be a profit à prendre (discussed above), but is usually a right created by statute. Three types of mineral rights are discussed briefly here:

1) .....the Crown's right to minerals;
2) .....rights to explore for minerals; and
3) .....rights to take minerals.

The Crown's Right to Minerals

Australia adopted the rule of English common law that a grant of an estate by the Crown did not include gold and silver unless it was stated otherwise: see *Wade v NSW Rutile Mining Co Pty Ltd* (1969) 121 CLR 177. The existence and nature of the Crown's right to gold and silver was debated at length in the *Case of Mines* (1567) 1 Plowden 310 at 336, 75 ER 472 at 510, where the court declared "that by the law all mines of gold and silver within the realm, whether they be in the hands of the Queen, or of subjects, belong to the Queen by prerogative, with liberty to dig and carry away the ores thereof, and with other such incidents thereto as are necessary to be used for the getting of the ore". This rule means that no grant of Crown land will include a right to gold or silver unless the grant specifically stated that the gold or silver was intended to pass to the recipient.

At one time, a grant of land from the Crown would include all the minerals except gold and silver, unless the grant reserved other minerals to the Crown. It was fairly common for the Crown to keep other minerals or at least those minerals which were regarded as valuable at the time. However, there were many instances in which people received estates from the Crown which included valuable mineral rights.

Today, a grant of land by the Crown does not include the mineral rights, unless they are specifically included as part of the estate. This is accomplished in each jurisdiction by a statutory reservation of minerals to the Crown. For example, section 9 of the *Mining Act* 1978 (WA), reserves "all gold, silver, and any other precious metal" to the Crown and states that "all other minerals existing in their natural condition on or below the surface of any land in the State that was not alienated in fee simple from the Crown before 1 January 1899 are the property of the Crown".

There are not many estates in Australia which include mineral rights that were not expressly included in the Crown grant. These are the older estates which were granted before the statutory reservation of minerals took effect. In South Australia and Victoria, even these older estates do not include the mineral rights, since those two states have since taken the mineral rights for themselves: see *Mining Act* 1971 (SA), s 16; *Mineral Resources Development Act* 1990 (Vic), s 11. Also, the Crown has a statutory right to petroleum in the ground in every jurisdiction except Tasmania. For example, section 9 of the *Petroleum Act* 1923 (Qld) states "that petroleum on or below the surface of all land in Queensland ... is and always has been the property of the Crown".

The Crown retains mineral rights for at least two important reasons. The first, of course, is the economic value of those rights to the states and territories. Secondly, it enables the government to have greater control over the development of mineral resources. This can be used to encourage that development and to regulate it to protect the environment, heritage sites, and the interests of other members of society. These objectives can be achieved, at least partially, even without Crown ownership of the mineral rights. For example, section 9 of the *Mineral Resources Act* 1989 (Qld) prohibits people from making arrangements "authorising the prospecting or exploring for mineral or the mining of any mineral ... notwithstanding that the mineral is not the property of the Crown". This allows the Queensland government to control the development of privately owned minerals in that state and raise money by charging fees for licences and permits.

The Crown's right to minerals in the earth is a property right. This is true even where the Crown has granted a fee simple estate, reserving only the mineral rights to itself. The Crown would not be free to enter that estate to explore for or take those minerals without providing compensation to the owners of the fee simple for interfering with their right to possession of the land. Therefore, its right to minerals is not a right to possession of those minerals. Nevertheless, it is a property right which can be transferred to, and enforced against, other members of society.

There are a variety of mineral and petroleum rights which may be granted by the Crown under the mining and petroleum statutes in force across Australia. There are many different names for these rights, such as a "miner's right", "prospecting permit", "exploration licence", and "mineral lease". The nature of the right depends upon the particular statute under which it is granted. Despite important differences from state to state, there are similarities among the various mineral rights which may granted in Australia. They fall into two broad classes: rights to explore for minerals and rights to take minerals from land.

When the Crown grants a mineral right to someone, the ownership of the mineral does not pass immediately to that person. The Crown retains ownership of the mineral until the miner removes it from the soil and pays the royalty due to the Crown: see, eg, *Mineral Resources Act* 1989 (Qld), s 310; *Mining Act* 1971 (SA), s 18. If the estate where the minerals are found belongs to people other than the Crown and the miner, the property right to the minerals will pass directly from the Crown to the miner when they are taken and paid for. Although the estate holders do not own the minerals, they will receive compensation from the miner for any interference with their rights to possession of the land.

Right to Explore for Minerals

The wide variety of statutory rights to explore for minerals are of two basic types. The first (which are often called **miner's rights**) are personal rights to look for minerals on Crown land, without disturbing the land to any great extent. The second (which are often called **exploration licences**) are much greater rights to actively dig for minerals in specific locations.

Miner's Rights

These rights are called **miner's rights** in the Northern Territory, South Australia, and Victoria, **prospecting permits** in Queensland, and **prospecting licences** in Tasmania. Western Australia also issues prospecting licences, but these are more extensive rights, which have more in common with exploration licences, discussed below. In South Australia, it is also possible to obtain a **precious stones prospecting permit** under section 7 of the *Opal Mining Act* 1995 (SA).

A miner's right (or its equivalent) is a permit to look for minerals on Crown land. It does not entitle the miner to enter private land or interfere with other property rights to Crown land (such as native title and other mineral rights granted by the Crown). It is clear that a miner's right is a personal right, because it is enforceable only against a specific person: the Crown. When searching for minerals, the miner must use only hand tools and small devices (such as a hand held metal detector) and must take care to disturb the land as little as possible.

Many states allow people to **fossick** (rummage about for minerals) in designated fossicking areas, without a special permit. Fossicking is normally a recreational activity for collectors and tourists and is allowed so long as it does not interfere with other property rights and is done relatively unobtrusively. For example, in Tasmania, fossickers are allowed "to search for minerals for a purpose other than for commercial gain to a depth of 2 metres by (a) digging by hand; or (b) using hand held instruments": *Mineral Resources Development Act* 1995 (Tas), s 3. A **fossicker's permit** is required in the Northern Territory, which may be issued to individuals or commercial tour operators. Victoria requires a **tourist fossicking authority** and, in Queensland, **fossicking licences** are issued under the *Fossicking Act* 1994 (Qld).

Exploration Licences

An exploration licence is one type of right to look for minerals in a specific location. There are many other rights in this category, which are more or less extensive. For example, the *Mining Act* 1971 (SA) authorises three rights of this type: a **mineral claim**, which can cover up to 240 hectares and last for up to 12 months, an **exploration licence**, which can cover up to 2,500 square kilometres and last for up to five years, and a **retention lease**, which allows the miner to remove and retain samples of minerals for testing purposes. These types of rights may have different names in different states. For example, a retention licence in South Australia is similar to an **assessment lease** in New South Wales and a **mineral development permit** in Queensland.

Some states have special licences to explore for specific minerals. For example, it is possible to obtain a **special prospecting licence** in Western Australia to look for gold in a specific location: *Mining Act* 1978 (WA), s 70. In New South Wales, a person can obtain an **opal prospecting licence**, which confers the exclusive right to prospect for opals in a designated area (called an **opal prospecting block**): *Mining Act* 1992 (NSW), s 232. Rights to explore for petroleum are granted under the Petroleum Acts in each jurisdiction. For example, an **exploration permit** granted under the *Petroleum Act* 1998 (Vic) confers an exclusive right to explore for petroleum for five years in a specified area up to 12,500 square kilometres.

Exploration licences and other rights of this type confer exclusive rights to look for specified minerals in a certain location. The right lasts for a specified term and is subject to the fulfilment of a number of conditions designed for the protection and restoration of the land and to encourage the economic development of the minerals. The licence holder is expected to actively explore for minerals and must report to the government regularly on minerals discovered. Another common feature of these licences is that they shrink over time. For example, half the area covered by an exploration licence, granted under the *Mining Act* 1978 (WA), must be surrendered after three years: s 65. This encourages licence holders to use their rights efficiently.

Unlike miner's rights (discussed above), exploration licences (and similar mineral and petroleum rights) are property rights; see, eg, *Commonwealth v WMC Resources Ltd* (1998) 152 ALR 1. They relate to things (parcels of land) and are enforceable generally against other members of society. Some statutes expressly identify them as property rights to land. For example, section 70 of the *Mineral Resources Development Act* 1990 (Vic) states that "A licence, on registration, confers on the licensee a proprietary interest in the land covered by the licence and attaches to the licensee all rights and obligations under the licence."

In contrast, section 10 of the *Mineral Resources Act* 1989 (Qld) states that a "grant of a prospecting permit, mining claim, exploration permit, mineral development licence or mining lease under this Act does not create an estate or interest in land". This does not mean that these rights are not property, but indicates that they are **personal property** rights rather than **real property** (see Chapter 5) in Queensland. This classification can affect the manner in which rights are created and transferred (see Chapter 21). In *Adamson v Hayes* (1973) 130 CLR 276, a majority of the High Court of Australia decided that a mining claim, under the *Mining Act* 1904-1971 (WA), was an interest in land, even though section 273 of that statute said that it "shall be deemed and taken in law to be a chattel interest" (that is, personal property). However, section 10 of the Queensland Act is a much stronger assertion that this type of right is not an "interest in land".

Right to Take Minerals

Discussed here are rights to enter land, mine or drill for minerals, and take them away. They can arise in three different ways. First, if the owners of an estate own any of the minerals found there, they could (if permitted by law) grant profits à prendre to take those minerals. Secondly, the Crown could grant a statutory right to take a specific mineral under the relevant mining or petroleum statute. This is the most common method of granting rights to take minerals, because the Crown owns most of the minerals in Australia. Thirdly, the government might make an agreement to grant mining rights to a mining company and then validate that agreement with a new statute. This happened in *Wik Peoples v Queensland* (1996) 187 CLR 1, where the *Commonwealth Aluminium Corporation Pty Limited Agreement Act* 1957 (Qld) was enacted to authorise the grant of a bauxite mining lease for a term of 84 years. The second of these three methods is discussed here.

A statutory right to take minerals from a specific parcel of land is usually called a **mining lease** or **mining licence**. The right to take petroleum is usually called a **petroleum lease** or **production licence**. There are also other statutory rights to take specific minerals, such as a **precious stones claim** or an **opal development lease** granted under the *Opal Mining Act* 1995 (SA).

These rights entitle the miner to use the land solely for mining purposes and to take away and sell the minerals recovered during the term of the lease. They are usually granted for a fixed term, with a right to renew the lease or licence if the miner has met the statutory requirements. In *Wade v NSW Rutile Mining Co Pty Ltd* (1969) 121 CLR 177 at 192, Windeyer J said that a "mining lease of this kind is really a sale by the Crown of minerals reserved to the Crown to be taken by the lessee at a price payable over a period of years as royalties". The ownership of the minerals passes to the miner when they are recovered and the royalties are paid. In other words, statutory mineral leases are similar to profits à prendre.

A miner might also acquire the right to exclusive possession of the parcel of land during the term of the lease. This might be necessary for certain kinds of mining operations. Under section 86 of the *Mining Act* 1978 (WA), a miner can obtain a **general purpose lease**, which confers a right to exclusive possession of the land. In other cases, the miner might obtain a lease of the surface rights from the persons entitled to possession. In either situation, the miner has an estate, which includes the right to take minerals or exists in addition to that right.

Chapter Seventeen

PROPERTY RIGHTS TO INTANGIBLE THINGS

■■■

The rights discussed here, like those in the previous chapter, do not include a right to possession. However, these rights are non-possessory for a different reason: they relate to things which are intangible and cannot be possessed (such as ideas, expressions, and corporations). This chapter is not a comprehensive list, but deals with the main rights of this type. They are divided into two main categories:

1)......**intellectual property**; and
2)......**corporate shares**.

Intellectual property is a generic term describing a variety of rights to control or profit from ideas and information, such as copyrights, patents, and trade marks. Like corporate shares, most of these rights are created or heavily regulated by statute and are regarded as property because they are enforceable generally against other members of society. There are doubts about the nature of the right to **confidential information**, which is discussed at the end of the section on intellectual property. Unlike most other forms of intellectual property, this right is created and enforced apart from statute by courts of equity and it might be a personal right enforceable only against specific persons. There are also doubts about the nature of a corporate share. It is commonly regarded as a property right to the corporation, but might be a personal right enforceable against the corporation.

Intellectual Property

This discussion is divided into four main parts:

1)......**Forms of Expression** is concerned with rights to prevent others from copying the forms in which ideas are expressed. These rights are protected by the *Copyright Act* 1968 (Cth), *Designs Act* 1906 (Cth), or *Circuit Layouts Act* 1989 (Cth).
2)......**Scientific Advances** is about rights to exploit inventions, protected by the *Patents Act* 1990 (Cth), and new varieties of plants, protected by the *Plant Breeders Rights Act* 1994 (Cth).

3) .....**Reputation** discusses rights to preserve and exploit the value of commercial and professional reputations, which can be protected from the tort of passing off or by the *Trade Marks Act* 1995 (Cth).
4) .....**Confidential Information** concerns the right to prevent the publication or misuse of government, personal, or trade secrets. This right can be protected in a court of equity by an action for breach of confidence.

With the possible exception of confidential information, these are property rights. Intellectual property relates to some alienable (but intangible) thing and can be enforced generally against other members of society. Someone who wrongly interferes with an intellectual property right commits a breach of duty. The legal responses to that breach are regulated by statute and are similar to the responses to a wrongful interference with possession, described in Chapter 7. A common response to a wrongful interference with intellectual property is the direct enforcement of the plaintiff's right by means of an **injunction** to stop the defendant from further interference. Other possible responses include an award of **damages**, as compensation for the loss caused to the plaintiff, and an **account of profits**, as restitution of the value of the gain made by the defendant. In many cases, the right to compensation or restitution is not available if the defendant's breach of duty was unintentional: see, eg, *Designs Act* 1906 (Cth), s 32B(2); *Patents Act* 1990 (Cth), s 123.

As discussed at page 25, the recognition and protection of intellectual property rights attempts to reconcile the public's right to freedom of information with the right to exploit commercially valuable information for private gain. This section provides only an introduction to the concept and main forms of intellectual property. It deals briefly with the nature of these rights and the things which are subject to these rights. There are a number of excellent books available which can provide the reader with comprehensive information about the varieties of intellectual property recognised in Australia.

Forms of Expression

Copyrights

A copyright is an exclusive right to reproduce an original form of expression, such as a new book, drawing, or song. It does not protect the ideas or information conveyed, but the form in which they are expressed. The forms of expression protected by copyright are set out in the *Copyright Act* 1968 (Cth). They include four categories of **works** (artistic, dramatic, literary, and musical) and a few forms which fall outside the definition of a work, such as a film, television or radio broadcast, or new edition of a work.

Artistic works are paintings, sculptures, engravings, photographs, buildings, models of buildings, and works of artistic craftsmanship (such as pottery, embroidery, and wood carvings). With the exception of works of artistic craftsmanship, the work need not have any artistic merit. Therefore, it is possible to have copyrights to designs for things like machine parts. For example, in *Wham-O MFG Co v Lincoln Industries Ltd* [1984] 1 NZLR 641, the models, moulds, and dies used to manufacture frisbees (plastic toys) were held to be sculptures and engravings protected by copyright.

Dramatic works include scripts, screenplays, and choreographed shows. A cinematograph film (movie) or television broadcast made from a screenplay does not fall within the definition of a dramatic work. Copyrights to movies and broadcasts are protected separately, as discussed below.

Literary works can be most anything reduced to writing, so long as the form of expression is original. It is not limited to the popular concept of literature, but can include mundane things such as written tables, business forms, or examination papers. As Peterson J said in *University of London Press Ltd v University Tutorial Press Ltd* [1916] 2 Ch 601 at 608:

> "In my view the words 'literary work' cover work which is expressed in print or writing, irrespective of the question whether the quality or style is high. The word 'literary' seems to be used in a sense somewhat similar to the use of the word 'literature' in political or electioneering literature and refers to written or printed matter."

In *Computer Edge Pty Ltd v Apple Computer Inc* (1986) 161 CLR 171, the High Court of Australia decided that computer software contained in the ROM (read-only memory) of a computer was not a literary work, because it was not reduced to print and not intended to convey meaning to humans, but designed to operate the computer. Parliament responded to this decision by amending the definition of literary work, in the *Copyright Act* 1968, to include computer programs.

Musical works are not defined in the statute. In keeping with the manner in which other works are understood, a musical work need only be original and not necessarily pleasing to the listener. It may be a composition which cannot be represented by standard musical notation or played on traditional musical instruments. Copyrights to sound recordings are dealt with separately, as discussed below.

The wide definitions of the four different works mean that they will overlap to some extent. For example, a screenplay can be a dramatic as well as a literary work and a map can be an artistic and literary work. The copyright to a song may be divided between the right to the music as a musical work and the lyrics as a literary work.

The *Copyright Act* 1968 also protects certain forms of expression which do not qualify as works. These are sound recordings, cinematographic films, sound or television broadcasts, and published editions of works. The copyright to these forms of expression exists independently of the copyright to the underlying works on which they are based. This recognises the originality and expertise which goes into the making of a film or record, over and above the writing of the original screenplay or song. The same can be said about a television or radio broadcast and a new edition of a previously published work. The copyright to a broadcast is particularly important where the content of the broadcast is a sporting or other event which is not a work and, therefore, not subject to copyright.

In Australia, copyright does not depend on registration of that right. It arises when an original work (or sound recording, etc) is reduced to **material form**. Publication of that form is not necessary, but it must be reduced to some form which would allow it to be reproduced (such as a file on a computer). Merely working out the idea for a new book or song would not be sufficient.

The requirement of originality does not refer to the ideas or information expressed, but the manner in which they are expressed. The work must not be copied and must be the product of some degree of skill or judgement. For example, the skill and judgement required to prepare a map means that it can be an original work, even though there is nothing new about the information conveyed: see *Sands & McDougall Pty Ltd v Robinson* (1917) 23 CLR 49.

Generally speaking, the holder of a copyright has the exclusive right to reproduce, publish, perform, broadcast, or adapt the work. There are a few exceptions. For example, people are permitted to record television broadcasts for home use, make back-up copies of computer software, and copy small portions of literary works for research or study purposes. People can make two-dimensional reproductions of buildings and public statues and, therefore, can photograph, draw, or paint them without breaching copyright.

Copyright can be transferred to others. It may be sold, given away, or licensed and may be divided up among several people. For example, one person might have the copyright to a sound recording in Australia, while others have the copyright to that same recording in other parts of the world. One person might have the exclusive right to publish copies of a book in hard cover, while another has the right to publish copies in soft cover.

Some countries recognise the author's **moral rights** to the work. This is the idea that the author is entitled to be identified with the work and to prevent it from being distorted, even though the copyright has been transferred to someone else. Moral rights are not a feature of Australian copyright law, but Part IX of the *Copyright Act* 1968 provides some limited protection of the author's right to be identified with the work. It creates a duty not to falsely attribute the authorship of a work to someone other than the author and entitles the author to sue to stop the false attribution or receive the payment of damages for it.

In some European countries, the author's moral rights cannot be transferred, but remain with the author regardless of what becomes of the copyright. This does not mean that moral rights are not property. They are enforceable generally against other members of society and relate to an alienable thing (the original form of expression). As discussed at page 10, most property rights can be transferred to others, but this is not an essential characteristic of property.

Copyright relates primarily to the form of expression and not to the physical thing in which that form is reproduced. The distinction between the two was discussed in *Pacific Film Laboratories Pty Ltd v Federal Commissioner of Taxation* (1970) 121 CLR 154. The plaintiff processed photographs and argued that it should not have to pay sales tax on the prints it made for its customers. Since the customers owned the copyright to the photographs, the plaintiff did not own them and could not sell them, but was merely providing a film developing service. The High Court of Australia rejected this argument. Although the plaintiff had only a limited right to copy the photographs, with the permission of its customers, the physical pieces of photographic paper belonged to the plaintiff and were sold to customers when the photographs were developed.

In many cases, the copyright holder is not the owner of the physical copies of the work subject to her or his copyright. For example, the author of a book has the copyright to that book (unless it has been assigned), but the publisher will own the books printed, which will be sold to distributors, bookshops and consumers. Although the author never owned those copies of her or his books, the copyright does give the author a limited right to control the use of them, similar to a restrictive covenant: see Chapter 16. The owner of a book is entitled to do almost anything with it, but is not permitted to make copies of it. Similarly, the owner of books purchased abroad might not be permitted to import those books into Australia if that would violate the Australian copyright to the book: *Interstate Parcel Express Co Pty Ltd v Time-Life International (Nederlands) BV* (1977) 138 CLR 534.

Section 116 of the *Copyright Act* 1968 also gives the holder of copyright the right to "bring an action for conversion or detention in relation to: (a) an infringing copy; or (b) a device used or intended to be used for making infringing copies". This statutory right is not as strong as the common law right to sue for conversion or detinue (discussed in Chapter 7), since section 116 gives the court the discretion to refuse relief (if the defendant had no reason to suspect that the copy or device infringed copyright) or to grant an alternative remedy (such as an injunction or account of profits).

In *Autodesk Inc v Yee* (1996) 139 ALR 735 at 740, Burchett J referred to the right created by section 116 as "fictional ownership":

> "The Act does not say that the copyright owner *is* the owner of the copy; but only that certain rights are conferred as if that were so. These rights are rights and remedies by way of an action for conversion or detention. In effect, a fictional ownership is imposed, so as to give rise to the rights in conversion or detention which that ownership would bring."

Although the copyright holder is not the owner of infringing copies or devices, he or she has a right to possession of them in certain circumstances and, therefore, does have a property right to those goods.

Most copyrights last for 50 years from either the creator's death or the first publication of the work, whichever occurs last. Copyrights to photographs, films, recordings, and broadcasts last for 50 years from the first publication or broadcast and the copyright to a published edition of a work lasts for 25 years from the first publication of that edition.

Designs

A design is defined by section 4 of the *Designs Act* 1906 (Cth) as "features of shape, configuration, pattern or ornamentation applicable to an article, being features that, in the finished article, can be judged by the eye, but does not include a method or principle of construction". A building is not an "article", so these designs always relate to the external appearance of goods (although those goods might be things, such as plumbing fixtures, which are intended to become part of a building). Designs may be two-dimensional, such as an image printed on a T-shirt, or three-dimensional, such as the shape of a computer.

The owner of an original design can register it at the Design Office and thereby obtain an exclusive right to manufacture articles of that design. The initial registration lasts for one year, but it can be renewed for three more terms of five years each (for a total of 16 years). The Registrar of Designs decides whether the design is registerable. To qualify, the design must be original and relate to the form and not merely the function of the article to be manufactured. Designs can be given away, sold, or licensed to others.

There are problems created by the overlap between copyrights and designs. The copyright to the plans for manufacturing an article includes the exclusive right to use that design to manufacture that article (that is, make three-dimensional copies of a two-dimensional artistic work): *Copyright Act* 1968 (Cth), s 21(3)(a). The long term of protection provided by copyright (50 years from the author's death) conflicts with the scheme of the *Designs Act* 1906, which provides a much shorter period of monopoly. The *Copyright Act* 1968 attempts to deal with this conflict by removing the copyright protection when the design is registered or the article is manufactured with consent of the copyright holder. If either event occurs, the designer must use the *Designs Act* 1906 to enforce her or his rights to the design. The copyright is not affected if the design is a two-dimensional image applied to a manufactured article (for example, a printed T-shirt).

Circuit Layouts

The *Circuit Layouts Act* 1989 (Cth) allowed Australia to join the *Treaty on Intellectual Property in Respect of Integrated Circuits*. It provides for the registration and protection of original designs for the layouts of integrated circuits (silicon chips) used in computers. Registration confers the exclusive rights (called **eligible layout rights** or **EL rights**), for 10 years, to "(a) to copy the layout, directly or indirectly, in a material form; (b) to make an integrated circuit in accordance with the layout or a copy of the layout; (c) to exploit the layout commercially in Australia": *Circuit Layouts Act* 1989, s 17.

There are several important exceptions to the registrant's right to the design. Copying for private use, research, or teaching is permitted. So is reverse engineering (that is, taking a circuit layout apart to see how it functions). The free exchange of information concerning circuit layouts is thereby encouraged. People cannot use reverse engineering simply to produce their own copies of the layout. However, they can use it to help them create new layouts. Also, a person is free to purchase computer chips lawfully manufactured overseas and import them into Australia. Unlike copyright, the Australian right to a circuit layout in Australia does not give the holder an exclusive right to distribute chips of that design in this country.

Under section 20 of the *Circuit Layouts Act* 1989, people do not infringe EL rights if they "could not reasonably be expected to have known" that their use of a circuit layout was unauthorised. Once they become aware of the problem, they can continue to use the layout if they pay to the holder of the EL rights "such equitable remuneration" as they can agree upon or as the Federal Court of Australia determines.

Scientific Advances

Patents

A patent is the exclusive right to exploit an invention. According to section 18 of the *Patents Act* 1990 (Cth), a **patentable invention** is a "manner of manufacture" which is new, inventive, and useful. The invention might be a manufactured product or a process of manufacturing. The right is created by registration of the patent and lasts for up to 20 years, depending on the type of patent.

The word "patent" comes from the **letters patent** which were used by the Crown in England to grant trading monopolies to its subjects. These monopolies covered all kinds of business activities and became unpopular, since they inhibited otherwise legitimate business pursuits and depended on having favour with the Crown. The *Statute of Monopolies* 1624 prohibited the Crown from granting such monopolies, but made an exception for certain types of inventions. Monopolies to exploit new inventions were granted by letters patent until modern patent legislation was enacted. Section 18 of the *Patents Act* 1990 (Cth) still refers to "a manner of manufacture within the meaning of section 6 of the *Statute of Monopolies*".

Before granting a patent, the Commissioner of Patents must be satisfied that the invention is both new and inventive. This decision is made by comparing the invention to the **prior art base**, which is the information publicly available in that field. A new idea will not be inventive if it "would have been obvious to a person skilled in the relevant art in the light of the common general knowledge as it existed in the patent area": *Patents Act* 1990 (Cth), s 7(2). The invention must also be useful, meaning that it can be exploited as a product or process of manufacturing. Ideas that advance scientific knowledge are not patentable unless they have a practical application which can be exploited in this manner.

A scientific discovery (for example, of some previously unknown organism or substance) cannot be patented, because it does not require an inventive step. It is possible to patent genetically engineered organisms, because they are invented and not merely discovered. However, section 18(2) of the *Patents Act* 1990 states that "Human beings, and the biological processes for their generation, are not patentable inventions." Genetic modifications of human tissue that are new and inventive could otherwise qualify as patentable inventions. This prohibition helps maintain the important legal and moral distinction between people and things, discussed in Chapter 3.

Implicit in the *Patents Act* 1990 is the principle that inventiveness will be encouraged if inventors are granted monopolies to exploit their inventions. However, the statute also recognises that the public has a legitimate interest in freedom of information and in the use of scientific advances which will enhance the quality of human life. It safeguards the public interest in three ways:

1) .....the monopoly lasts for a limited period of time (20 years for a standard patent);
2) .....the monopoly is conditional upon making full public disclosure of the invention; and
3) .....the inventor must permit the exploitation of the invention.

Full disclosure of inventions is promoted in two ways. First, a person applying for a patent is required to provide a **specification** for the invention, which must "describe the invention fully, including the best method known to the applicant of performing the invention": s 40(2)(a). The specification is made available to the public, except in cases where public disclosure of the invention should be prohibited "in the interests of the defence of the Commonwealth": s 173(1).

Secondly, an invention cannot be patented if it has been secretly used with permission of the inventor: ss 9, 18(1)(d). This encourages the earliest possible disclosure of the invention by presenting inventors with a choice. They can either apply for patents (and thereby disclose their inventions to the public) or keep their inventions secret (and exploit them as valuable confidential information, discussed below). However, an inventor cannot secretly use the invention for a while and then later apply for a patent. If an invention is kept secret, the inventor faces the risks that the information might be leaked to the public or that someone else will independently make the same invention, apply for a patent, and thereby obtain the exclusive right to exploit it.

If the holder of a patent (the "patentee") fails to exploit it, a person can apply to the court for a **compulsory licence** of the patent. A compulsory licence is not exclusive and will be granted to the applicant on payment of an appropriate fee to the patentee. It will not be granted unless the court is satisfied that the applicant made reasonable efforts to obtain a licence from the patentee and "that: (a) the reasonable requirements of the public with respect to the patented invention have not been satisfied; and (b) the patentee has given no satisfactory reason for failing to exploit the patent": s 133. Two years after the grant of a compulsory licence, a person can apply to the court "for an order revoking the patent": s 134. These provisions recognise that the patentee's monopoly is not justified if it prevents the public from having access to the benefit of the invention.

There are two types of patents: a **standard patent** (which lasts for 20 years) and a **petty patent** (which lasts for one year, but can be extended to a total of six years): ss 67, 68. The process of obtaining a standard patent can be long and expensive, since it requires a determination that the invention is new and inventive in relation to the prior art base that exists internationally. The process of obtaining a petty patent is designed to be quicker and cheaper and to protect small inventions which can be exploited locally for a relatively short time. It requires only a comparison with the prior art base in Australia.

Chapter 8 of the *Patents Act* 1990 allows inventors to apply for patents in other countries in accordance with the *Patent Cooperation Treaty* 1970 (called the **PCT**). If an international application for a patent under the PCT specifies Australia as a designated state, it is taken to be an application for a standard or petty patent in Australia.

Plant Breeder's Rights

The *Plant Breeder's Rights Act* 1994 (Cth) replaced the *Plant Variety Rights Act* 1987 (Cth). Both statutes were enacted to allow Australia to fulfil its obligations as a member of the *International Convention for the Protection of New Varieties of Plants*. Plant breeders can use the statutory registration scheme to register new plant varieties and thereby obtain the right to profit from the use of those varieties.

The right created by registration of a new variety of plant is called a **plant breeder's right** (or **PBR**). It is somewhat similar to a patent. A person who simply discovers a new variety of plant is not entitled to a PBR. To qualify, the variety must be the product of selective breeding. However, the creation of a new variety of plant does not require the degree of inventiveness required for a patent. It might involve established methods of selective breeding and chance genetic mutation, rather than any new inventive process.

A **registrable plant variety** must be **distinct**, **uniform**, and **stable**. These requirements are defined in the *Plant Breeder's Rights Act* 1994 (Cth). Section 43(2) states that "a plant variety is distinct if it is clearly distinguishable from any other variety whose existence is a matter of common knowledge". It is uniform if the relevant characteristics of the variety are the same in each plant which is propagated, "subject to the variation that may be expected from the particular features of its propagation": s 43(3). A "plant variety is stable if its relevant characteristics remain unchanged after repeated propagation": s 43(4).

The grant of a PBR gives the breeder the exclusive right to sell, or prepare for sale, propagating material for the registered plant variety. **Propagating material** is any part of the plant used to propagate new plants, such as seeds, bulbs, cuttings, roots and spores. A PBR lasts for 25 years for trees and vines and 20 years for other plants. People who lawfully acquire the plants or propagating material are free to deal with their plants as they wish, except to use them to produce new propagating material. There are several exceptions to the plant breeder's exclusive rights. For example, people are allowed to produce new propagating material for private or experimental use or to breed new varieties. Seed saved from harvesting can be used to plant a new crop and propagating material can be sold for food (for example, sprouts for salads). As with patents and circuit layouts, the statute is designed to encourage new research and to use existing varieties to generate new varieties.

Section 19(1) of the *Plant Breeder's Rights Act* 1994 states that "the grantee of PBR in a plant variety must take all reasonable steps to ensure reasonable public access to that plant variety". This requires her or him to ensure that "propagating material of reasonable quality is available to the public at reasonable prices, or as gifts to the public, in sufficient quantities to meet demand": s 19(2). If this is not done within two years of the grant of the PBR, people are entitled to apply to the Secretary of the Department of Primary Industries and Energy for a licence of the PBR. The licence can be granted by the Secretary on "the provision of reasonable remuneration to the grantee": s 19(3). This is similar to the compulsory licence of a patent, discussed above.

Another important right protected as part of a PBR is the use of the name of the new plant variety. The selection and registration of the name of a new variety is similar to the registration of a trade mark, discussed below. The name can include real and invented words and the names of people. It cannot "be likely to deceive or cause confusion, including confusion with the name of another plant variety of the same plant class" nor can it be, or include, a trade mark that is registered with respect to a plant: s 27(5). A PBR is infringed by anyone who uses the registered name of the variety to describe other varieties of the same plant class: s 53(1)(c). This is similar to the tort of passing off or the infringement of a trade mark, discussed below.

Reputation

The law protects reputations. Someone who says false things about another person, and thereby damages her or his reputation, is guilty of the tort of **defamation** and liable to compensate the victim for that harm. Defamation is sometimes called **libel**, if done in writing, or **slander**, if done orally. This protection recognises the value of a good reputation.

Reputations can also have commercial value. Famous people, such as actors and athletes, can earn a great deal of money by endorsing or advertising products for sale. For example, a professional tennis player might be paid to use a certain brand of tennis rackets or wear advertisements on her or his clothing. Businesses, goods, and services can also have commercially valuable reputations. Many people make decisions to buy things, such as soft drinks, tins of fruit, and clothing, based primarily on their brand names. The same is true of decisions to use the services of restaurants, financial institutions, shops and other businesses.

The law protects the commercial value of reputations. It is wrong to misappropriate someone else's reputation. For example, it is wrong to mislead the public to believe that a famous person has endorsed a product or that some goods are made by a well-known manufacturer. Two types of misappropriation are discussed here:

1) .....the tort of **passing off**; and
2) .....infringement of a registered **trade mark**.

Also discussed briefly are the statutes which provide for the registration of **business names**.

The protection of reputations from misappropriation means that they can be property rights. The right to a reputation can be enforced generally against other members of society and, where that reputation relates to a business, goods, or services, the right can be alienated. When a business is sold, its reputation will normally be transferred to the purchaser along with the other assets of the business. The reputation is often called the **good will** of the business. The purchase price may be apportioned among the various assets of that business, including the good will.

In contrast, an individual's professional reputation is not a property right. Although it may have great commercial value and can be enforced generally against other members of society, it cannot be alienated. The reputation is an intrinsic part of the individual and therefore not a separate thing subject to property rights. The protection of an individual's reputation from defamation or passing off is similar to the protection of the person from other torts, such as assault, battery and negligent personal injury. These rights protect persons and not things.

It is possible for an individual to sell or give away her or his business reputation. For example, Doreen may have established a valuable local reputation by operating Doreen's Diner for many years. She may choose to retire from the business and sell it to Grant, who will want to carry on business in the same location under the same name. He will purchase the goodwill of the business from Doreen and get her to promise that she will not start another cafe or restaurant in the vicinity for several years. Although Doreen was personally responsible for creating the reputation now associated with her name, it is the reputation of a business which is being sold and not her personal or professional reputation. The reputation of Doreen's Diner is a property right which is separate from Doreen's personal reputation.

Passing Off

At common law, it is wrong for people to deceive the public by passing off their business, goods, or services as those of another person. If the deception causes harm to that other person, he or she can sue for the tort of passing off. The essence of this tort is a wrongful misappropriation of the plaintiff's reputation. This might cause harm to the plaintiff in two different ways. First, it might decrease sales of the plaintiff's own goods or services as consumers use the defendant's goods or services, believing them to be provided by, or associated with, the plaintiff. Secondly, it might devalue the plaintiff's reputation, by diminishing the special significance of that reputation or by its public association with inferior goods or services.

Even if people do not provide goods or services themselves, their reputations can be commercially valuable if they can earn fees by endorsing the goods or services of others. A misappropriation of someone's reputation might cause harm to that person if it devalues that reputation and decreases the profits he or she might earn from future endorsements. Therefore, it is wrong to make unauthorised use of a person's image or name. For example, in *Henderson v Radio Corp Pty Ltd* (1960) 60 SR (NSW) 576, the plaintiffs were professional ballroom dancers. The defendant placed their picture on the cover of a record of dance music and thereby committed the tort of passing off. The damage to the plaintiffs was identified as the impairment of their right to exploit their reputations for profit.

Trade Marks

Trade marks are words, logos, or symbols that are associated with goods or services offered to the public. For example, "Coke" and "Coca-Cola" are trademarks associated with a famous soft drink. The stylised shape of an apple and the phrase "Think different" are trademarks associated with Apple computers. Trade marks can be protected in two different ways: by registration and through an action for the tort of passing off, discussed above. Registration of a trade mark protects only words and symbols associated with goods or services. The common law can protect a wider range of business and professional reputations, such as the image or name of a famous athlete or the name of a retail shop (for example, Myers or David Jones) which is not associated with any particular goods or services.

Unlike other forms of intellectual property, the value of a trade mark is not so much the intrinsic value of the information, but its use in connection with certain goods and services. The value is generated by the sale of goods or services which the public perceives as more desirable because they are associated with that mark. However, trade marks have become valuable commodities apart from the goods or services they represent. For example, many people purchase shoes or clothing bearing Nike's famous symbol primarily because they want to wear that symbol. To make a profit, Nike does not have to manufacture any shoes or clothing itself, but can licence the right to the use its trade mark to others. Similarly, young children like to have things, such as clothing, lunch boxes, and school supplies, which bear the marks of popular cartoon characters primarily because they bear those marks. In a triumph of form over substance, trade marks can be more valuable to consumers than the goods with which they are associated.

Trade marks can be registered under the *Trade Marks Act* 1995 (Cth). Registration lasts 10 years and can be renewed for further 10 year terms without any limit on the number of renewals. Unlike a patent (discussed above), registration does not create the right, but makes it easier for the owner of a trade mark to prevent others from using that mark or deceptively similar marks. A trade mark cannot be registered if it might be confused with a trade mark which is already registered. Once registered, a trade mark is presumed to be valid. However it is possible for others to prove that it is not valid, because, for example, it is not distinctive or is not used by the registrant. Registration confers a procedural advantage on the registrant since anyone disputing the validity of the trade mark bears the onus of establishing its invalidity. As time passes, it becomes increasingly difficult to challenge the validity of a registered trade mark.

Registration of a trade mark does not create an exclusive right to use it, but is merely evidence of that right. Therefore, a defendant sued for infringing a registered trade mark can defend the action by showing that he or she used the mark before it was registered: *Trade Marks Act* 1995 (Cth), s 124. Also, people are entitled to use their own names or places of business in association with their goods and services, even if they are substantially similar to a registered trade mark.

If goods are imported to Australia which infringe a registered trade mark, the registered owner or authorised user of that mark can give a written notice to the Chief Executive Officer of Customs (the "Customs CEO") objecting to the importation of those goods. The Customs CEO can seize those goods and, depending on the resolution of the dispute, the seized goods might be forfeited to the Commonwealth.

Business Names

As discussed above, the name of a business can have commercial value, even if it is not a trade mark (for example, because it is an ordinary name or is not associated with any particular goods or services). The right to use a business name can be protected by the common law, since a use of that name by others might be a tort of passing off.

Each state and territory maintains a register of business names. People and corporations are free to carry on business using their own names, but if they carry on business in a jurisdiction using any other name, they must register that other name. This is designed to protect members of the public who might deal with a business by giving them access to the names of persons operating that business.

The registers of business names are not intended to protect the right to use a particular name. That protection is provided by the common law or by registration of a trade mark. In most states, people are permitted to register business names which other people are using and have registered. Section 7A of the *Business Names Act* 1962 (NSW) states that the registrar will give notice of the registration of a new business name to others who have already registered the same or a similar business name. This will help existing users of that name become aware of potential infringements of trade marks and passing off.

South Australia takes a slightly different approach. Section 8(4) of the *Business Names Act* 1996 (SA) states that the registrar will not register a business name likely to be confused with another business name which is already registered. Priority for the right to register similar names depends on the order in which applications are submitted for registration: s 9. This provides additional protection of the right to use a particular name.

Confidential Information

A right to confidential information can be protected by an action for **breach of confidence**. That action can be used to protect a wide variety of confidential information, including business or trade secrets (such as secret recipes or manufacturing processes), personal secrets (told to friends or relatives in confidence), and government secrets (such as information concerning the defence of the Commonwealth). A breach of confidence occurs when someone receives confidential information, has a duty to use that information only in certain ways (sometimes called a **duty of confidence**), and misuses that information in breach of that duty.

Five questions are discussed briefly here:

1) .....What is confidential information?
2) .....What creates a duty of confidence?
3) .....What constitutes a breach of confidence?
4) .....How does the law respond to a breach of confidence?
5) .....Do people have property rights to confidential information?

What is Confidential Information?

Generally speaking, information is confidential if it is not public knowledge. It may be a closely guarded secret, shared only by two people, or it might be known to a relatively large group, such as the employees of a large, multinational corporation. In either case, the information can be regarded as confidential so long as it is not available to the public. Information can be public knowledge even if it is not widely known. For these purposes, the public consists of those people who might be interested in the information. Therefore, if information is available to most members of a particular trade or profession, it will not be confidential even though other members of society might have difficulty accessing it.

Information can be confidential even though components of that information are not. For example, the list of the customers of a business can be confidential information, even though the names and contact details of those customers are available to the public via telephone books and the internet. However, their inclusion in a particular customer list conveys additional information which is not publicly available: that those customers purchase certain products or services regularly and pay their bills. It might also contain additional information which facilitates sales, such as the contact details of individuals within customer organisations and the particular needs and desires of each customer. A customer list can have significant commercial value and may be the product of years of development.

If information is disclosed to the public, it ceases to be confidential. This is true even though the disclosure was a breach of confidence. Although the person breaching the confidence will be liable for the consequences of that breach (as discussed below), there can be no further duty of confidence in relation to that information once it becomes public knowledge. If there has been a limited disclosure of the information, it may retain its confidential nature until it becomes more widely known.

Creation of a Duty of Confidence

People are free to use or publish confidential information unless they are under a duty not to do so. That duty is often created by contract. For example, it is a common feature of many contracts of employment that the employee will not disclose or misuse the employer's trade secrets. However, the duty of confidence can arise even in the absence of a contract. For example, physicians and solicitors have duties not to misuse confidential information received from their patients and clients. Those duties are part of their professional responsibilities to the public they serve and would exist even in the absence of a contractual relationship. The same is true of a priest's duty regarding information heard in the confessional.

Duties of confidence can also arise in purely personal relationships between friends, relatives, lovers, or spouses. For example, in *Argyll v Argyll* [1967] 1 Ch 302, a husband was not permitted to disclose personal information shared by his wife during their marriage. Although there is no contract or professional responsibility in these situations, the duty of confidence arises for a similar reason: the person receiving the information undertakes a duty to maintain the confidence. In the vast majority of cases, it is this undertaking (whether contractual, professional, or merely personal) which creates the duty of confidence. The undertaking may be expressly given (for example, "I promise not to tell") or it may be implied from the circumstances in which the information is communicated (for example, a secret told behind closed doors).

A duty of confidence can arise without an undertaking. If a person receives information and knows, or ought to know, that the information is confidential, he or she will come under a duty not to misuse that information. This can happen when information is received by mistake, such as a fax sent to the wrong telephone number. It can also happen when someone obtains confidential information wrongly (for example, by theft, trespass, or electronic surveillance). For example, in *Franklin v Giddings* [1978] Qd R 72, the plaintiff had produced a new variety of nectarine trees, which could be reproduced only by grafting bud wood onto an existing tree. One of the two defendants heard about the trees and their location, entered the plaintiff's orchard at night, and stole four twigs of bud wood. From these twigs, he and the other defendant established their own orchard of that variety. Dunn J decided that the "genetic structure" of the new variety was confidential information and that the defendants were guilty of breach of confidence.

A person who receives information, with no reason to suspect that it is confidential, can later come under a duty of confidence when he or she discovers that fact. This happened in *Franklin v Giddings*, when the second defendant learned that the first defendant had stolen twigs from the plaintiff nine years earlier. It also happened in *Talbot v General Television Corp Pty Ltd* [1980] VR 224 where the plaintiff presented a confidential idea for a new television programme to several television producers, which was used to make the programme for the defendant. The defendant first learned about a possible breach of confidence when the plaintiff contacted it to complain about the breach. Harris J said (at 239-240) that "once the defendant had been put on notice that the programme had been made by an unauthorised use of confidential information, then an obligation attached to the defendant not to make any use of it".

Breach of Confidence

As Megarry V-C said, in *Coco v AN Clark (Engineers) Ltd* [1969] RPC 41 at 47, a breach of confidence occurs when someone makes "an unauthorised use of [confidential] information to the detriment of the party communicating it". Whether a use is unauthorised depends upon the nature of the duty created. If the duty is to keep the information secret, then any disclosure of that information will be a breach of confidence. If the duty is to use the information only for a specific purpose, then any other use of that information will be a breach of confidence.

For example, in *Castrol Australia Pty Ltd v Emtech Associates Pty Ltd* (1980) 33 ALR 31, the plaintiff disclosed a confidential report of motor oil tests to the Trade Practices Commission. The purpose of the disclosure was to enable the Commission to determine whether a proposed television advertisement of that oil might be misleading and therefore contrary to the *Trade Practices Act* 1974 (Cth). The Commission then decided to use the information to prosecute the plaintiff for a potentially misleading magazine advertisement. The court held that this was an unauthorised use of the information and, therefore, a breach of confidence. The confidential report had been disclosed solely for the purpose of evaluating the legality of the proposed television advertisement and not, as Rath J said (at 47), "for the purpose of investigating possible breaches of the *Trade Practices Act* by the plaintiff".

It is sometimes said that a misuse of confidential information is not a breach of confidence unless that misuse causes a detriment to the plaintiff. This requirement is not an obstacle for most plaintiffs. The misuse of a trade secret, or other commercially valuable information, will cause financial loss by interfering with the plaintiff's ability to exploit that information. A disclosure of personal information is detrimental if it might embarrass the plaintiff. However, a government might have difficulty proving a detriment from misuse of information, unless the information is commercially valuable or its disclosure might harm the security of the state.

In *Commonwealth of Australia v John Fairfax & Sons Ltd* (1980) 147 CLR 39, the government was unable to establish that a publication of its confidential documents would be detrimental. Mason J said (at 52):

> "It may be a sufficient detriment to the citizen that disclosure of information relating to his affairs will expose his actions to public discussion and criticism. But it can scarcely be a relevant detriment to the government that publication of material concerning its actions will merely expose it to public discussion and criticism. It is unacceptable in our democratic society that there should be a restraint on the publication of information relating to government when the only vice of that information is that it enables the public to discuss, review and criticize government action."

Sometimes, public duty can override the duty of confidence to particular persons. For example, if people receive confidential information concerning the commission of a crime or a danger to public health or safety, they may have a legal or moral duty to report that crime or danger. Reporting confidential information in the public interest is not a breach of confidence. However, there are limits to this defence. In the *Castrol v Emtech* case (discussed above), the Trade Practices Commission argued that its use of the plaintiff's confidential report was justified for the protection of the public from misleading advertising. The court rejected this plea, since the public interest might be better served if people are able to disclose confidential information to the commission without fear of its misuse. The risk of misleading advertising was not sufficiently serious to override the duty of confidence.

Responses to Breach of Confidence

A breach of confidence can have the same legal consequences as a breach of another intellectual property right. The three main responses to breach of confidence (mentioned above and discussed in more detail in Chapter 7) are:

1) .....direct enforcement of the duty of confidence by an **injunction** restraining the defendant from misusing the information;
2) .....the payment of **compensation** for the loss and harm caused to the plaintiff by the breach of confidence; and
3) .....**restitution** of the profits earned by the defendant through the breach of confidence.

The court can also order a defendant to **deliver** to the plaintiff goods which contain the confidential information, such as documents, computer files, and tools made using that information. In *Franklin v Giddings*, above, the defendants were required to destroy the trees derived from the twigs stolen from the plaintiff.

It can be difficult determining the appropriate response to a breach of confidence where that breach has caused the information to cease to be confidential. Should the defendant be prevented from using that information when everyone else in the world is free to do so? Courts have said that the defendant should not be allowed to use a breach of confidence as a "spring board" to develop products or other business interests in advance of other members of the public. To prevent this, a court might issue a temporary injunction preventing the defendant from taking advantage of its wrongly acquired lead or order the defendant to give up to the plaintiff the profits earned from that advantage.

Is the Right to Confidential Information Property?

There is considerable controversy over whether the right to confidential information is a property right. Some judges treat it as property, while others reject that notion. For example, in *Deta Nominees Pty Ltd v Viscount Plastic Products Pty Ltd* [1979] VR 167, the defendants misused the plaintiff's confidential idea about a manufacturing process. Fullagar J said (at 194) that "the defendants were clearly obliged in equity not to use this property of the plaintiff (this information) for any purpose other than that for which it was conveyed". In contrast, Deane J said of the duty of confidence, in *Moorgate Tobacco Co Ltd v Philip Morris Ltd* (1984) 156 CLR 414 at 438:

> "Like most heads of exclusive equitable jurisdiction, its rational basis does not lie in proprietary right. It lies in the notion of an obligation of conscience arising from the circumstances in or through which the information was communicated or obtained."

It is easy to understand the reluctance to treat confidential information as property. As discussed in Chapter 3, freedom of information is necessary to maintain a free and democratic society. There are a limited number of exceptions to the general rule gathered together under the label "intellectual property". Most of these are carefully designed by statute to limit the right to freedom of information only to the extent necessary to promote the creation of valuable information. The maintenance of confidences is also a desirable goal and worthy of legal protection. However, if unchecked, the protection of confidential information could easily overrun many of the carefully defined limits of intellectual property.

Although these are legitimate concerns, there is no need to continue to debate whether people *should* have property rights to confidential information. If the right to confidential information is compared to the definition of property in Chapter 2, it becomes clear that it *is* property. It shares the two essential characteristics of property:

1) .....confidential information is a thing which can be subject to property rights; and
2) .....the right to confidential information is enforceable generally against other members of society.

First, there is no doubt that information can be a thing subject to property rights. This is proved by the existence of intellectual property rights, such as copyright and patent. However, it is also true that some forms of information should not be subject to property rights. As discussed in Chapter 3, the right to freedom of expression means that most information (such as the news of public events and the components of ordinary speech) is excluded from the law of property on moral grounds. The fact that the law permits people to control confidential information, through the action for breach of confidence, means that the maintenance of confidences can be more important than freedom of information. As discussed above, the law tries to balance these competing moral claims by permitting the disclosure of confidential information in the public interest.

It has been suggested that information is different from other things because it cannot be alienated. For example, Dawson and Toohey JJ said, in *Breen v Williams* (1995) 186 CLR 71 at 90, that "there can be no proprietorship in information as information, because once imparted by one person to another, it belongs equally to them both". There are two answers to this contention. First, the ability to transfer a thing to another is not an essential characteristic of property. As discussed in Chapter 2, there are non-transferable property rights, such as a non-assignable lease or native title. The important question is whether the thing is an intrinsic part of a person or merely contingently connected to her or him. Information falls in the latter category. People can forget, destroy, or abandon information or simply choose not to use it.

The second answer is that rights to confidential information are transferable. For example, a person might sell a business, including the customer lists and trade secrets associated with it. The buyer will acquire the exclusive right to use that information and the seller will give up that right. Although the seller may still remember some or all of that information, he or she is no longer entitled to use it. This can be compared with the assignment of other intellectual property rights, such as a copyright, patent, or trade mark. The originator of the information does not forget it, but gives up certain rights to make use of that information.

Part of the difficulty with this issue is caused by the failure to distinguish between full ownership and lesser property rights. As discussed in Chapter 10, ownership is generally understood as the greatest possible property right in a society. Normally, it includes the rights to exclude others from the thing owned and to destroy it. Intellectual property rights are much more limited than this. For example, a copyright gives the holder the exclusive right, for a limited time, to make copies of the form in which the information is expressed. Subject to that right, other members of society are free to deal with the information as they please. Similarly, a right to confidential information gives the holder a right to control the use of the information so long as the information remains confidential. It does not confer rights equivalent to full ownership.

The right to confidential information also bears the second characteristic of property, because it is enforceable generally against other members of society. The duty of confidence is placed not just on specific persons, but on anyone who knows, or ought to know, that the information is confidential. It can apply even to people who innocently acquire information for value and later receive notice that it is confidential: see *Wheatley v Bell* [1982] 2 NSWLR 544.

Some doubt about the enforceability of the right to confidential information is raised by comments, like the quotation from the *Moorgate* case (above), in which Deane J said that the right corresponds to "an obligation of conscience" placed on the recipient of the information. This implies that it is a personal right which is enforceable only against specific persons. However, since that obligation can be imposed upon people who innocently receive confidential information, it is merely an extension of the obligation placed on every member of society to respect the property rights of others. The nature of the right is not changed because it is called "an obligation of conscience" or of justice, fairness, or decency.

There is no doubt that the right to confidential information was at one time a personal right enforceable only against specific persons who undertook the duty of confidence. However, it has evolved into a property right which can be enforced against anyone with notice of the confidential nature of the information. The same can be said of the trust (discussed in Chapter 13), the equity of redemption (in Chapter 14), and the restrictive covenant (in Chapter 16). In each case, a personal right was transformed into a property right when courts of equity began to enforce that right against anyone with notice of the right.

There is little to be gained by continuing to debate whether the right to confidential information is property. The recognition that people can have limited property rights to control the use of confidential information will enable judges, lawyers, and legislators to focus on the essential issue: what are the proper limits of those rights? In other words, how do we achieve (or maintain) a proper balance between two important, but competing, values: the maintenance of confidences and freedom of information?

Corporate Shares

There is some controversy over whether shares in a corporation are property rights: see, eg, Bird, "A Critique of the Proprietary Nature of Share Rights in Australian Publicly Listed Corporations" (1998) 22 *Melbourne University Law Review* 131; Spender, "Guns and Greenmail: Fear and Loathing After *Gambotto*" (1998) 22 *Melbourne University Law Review* 96. They look like property rights and are often thought of as such. They can be valuable assets, are traded on stock exchanges, and represent a large portion of Australia's wealth. However, there is an argument that they are not property rights, because they do not relate to any particular thing, but correspond only to the obligations of a specific person: the corporation that issued the shares.

What is a Corporation?

Corporations are legal persons: Corporations Law, s 124. They can own property, make contracts, and have most of the rights and obligations of human beings (who are called individuals or **natural persons** to distinguish them from corporations). Corporation do not have all the rights of natural persons. For example, they cannot vote for (or be) candidates in parliamentary elections nor can they be directors of other corporations: Corporations Law, s 221. Nevertheless, they are persons holding legal rights and can be contrasted with animals, which are not persons, but things subject to legal rights: see Chapter 3.

There are different types of corporations, such as municipal or charitable corporations, but we are concerned here with the most common variety: the business corporation. It exists for the purpose of making a profit. There are other ways for people to carry on business, such as a partnership or business trust (discussed briefly in Chapter 13). The most important feature which distinguishes the corporation from these other business organisations is its separate legal personality. The corporation owns the assets of the business, makes contracts with its employees, customers, suppliers, etc, and can be personally liable for the harm caused by its activities. In other types of business organisations, these legal rights and obligations attach directly to the humans involved in the business, such as the partners or trustees.

The modern business corporation is a democratic institution. It issues shares to its shareholders, which entitle them to vote for the directors who are responsible for the management of the corporation. The directors make the larger policy decisions concerning the affairs of the corporation and appoint its officers (such as a managing director or president, vice presidents, and other managers) to implement those policies. The duties, powers, and rights of everyone involved in the corporation are defined by statute, common law, and the corporation's constitution.

What is a Share?

Corporations issue shares to people who thereby become shareholders. The shares represent legal rights, which are defined by the corporate constitution. Although shares vary, most confer three rights on the shareholder:

1).....to vote at meetings of the shareholders;
2).....to receive any dividends declared by the corporation; and
3).....to share any assets of the corporation which remain after it is dissolved.

Not every share must bear all three of these rights. A corporation may have different classes of shares and could, for example, issue non-voting shares. However, all three rights must be distributed somehow among the corporation's shareholders.

Shares are sometimes called **stock** (which is why they are traded at stock exchanges). A share is just one right that can be issued by a corporation. Other rights include **bonds**, **debentures**, and **options** to purchase shares, bonds or debentures. These rights, including shares, are referred to generically as **securities** (which is why they are regulated by bodies called securities commissions or securities exchange commissions). Securities should not be confused with security rights, discussed in Chapter 14. In this context, the word "securities" is used to describe a variety of personal and property rights which are sold by corporations to raise capital. The right sold may be a security right, but need not be. For example, a debenture might include a floating charge over the assets of the corporation to secure the corporation's promise to pay: see Chapter 14.

Shares are issued by corporations for valuable consideration. The consideration is usually the payment of money, but may take other forms, such as a transfer of other assets or the performance of services. The issue of shares is just one way in which corporations raise capital with which to carry on business. They can also borrow money or use business profits for this purpose. Once issued, shares can be traded. The shares of many corporations are publicly traded on stock exchanges, while other corporations (usually called **proprietary companies**) issue shares which can be traded only privately with the approval of the corporation's directors. The sale of shares by a shareholder does not produce any new value for the corporation. The net proceeds of the sale go to the selling shareholder. However, if a corporation's shares have value and can be traded, it is easier for the corporation to raise capital in the future by the issue of more shares.

The value of each share is not determined by the value of the consideration given in exchange for the issue of that share. There are several ways to calculate its value. If the share is traded on a stock exchange, it has a market value which is easily determined. If the share is not publicly traded, a valuation can be much more difficult. One measure is the present value of the right to receive dividends in the future. This requires a prediction about the dividends that the corporation is likely to pay. Another measure is the value of the corporation, divided by the number of shares it has issued. The difficulty with this approach is determining the value of the corporation. It might be the value of the corporation as a going concern, the value obtained by breaking up the corporation and selling its assets, or something in between.

Is a Share Property?

The difficult question discussed here is whether shares are property. There is no doubt that they can be valuable assets, but this does not answer the question. As discussed in Chapter 2, personal rights also have value. For many people, their most valuable assets are not property, but personal rights, such as a bank account or the right to receive a salary. The only way to determine whether a share is property is to examine the nature of the rights conferred by the issue of a share. Are they rights to use a thing, which are enforceable generally against other members of society, or rights which are enforceable only against specific persons and correspond only to the obligations of those persons?

Shares can be represented by paper certificates which identify the shareholder, the number and type of shares held, and the corporation which issued them. It is clear that people can have property rights to a share certificate, since it is a tangible thing which can be possessed. However, unlike money, possession of a share certificate is not the same as the rights conferred by those shares. It is merely a property right to that certificate and evidence that the possessor is the holder of the shares identified by that certificate: see Corporations Law, s 1087. A person can be a shareholder without possession of a share certificate and those rights are not lost if the certificate is destroyed: see Corporations Law, s 1089. In contrast, there is no difference between possession of a current $20 note and the value which that note represents. That value is transferred by delivering possession to another and is lost if the note is destroyed.

Share certificates can have value independently of the shares they represent. Certificates issued by now defunct companies are valued today for their rarity and beauty. For example, the *National Post* (Saturday, 13 November 1999, page C5) reported that a share certificate issued by Houdini Motion Pictures in 1923, and signed by Harry Houdini, was worth $4,200 (US). Like a rare stamp, coin, or note, the value of such a share certificate is no longer linked to the value it represents, but is the value placed on the physical piece of paper by collectors: see, eg, the internet site of the International Bond & Share Society at http://www.scripophily.org.

Section 1085 of the Corporations Law states that a share "is personal property". This, however, does not decide the issue. As discussed in Chapter 16, parliament is free to borrow terms from the common law (such as lease and licence) and give them new meanings. If the rights conferred by a share are not property, the nature of those rights is not changed by calling them property. Section 1085 classifies shares for the purpose of determining the laws which apply to them. It states that "the laws applicable to ownership of and dealing with personal property apply to a share or other interest of a member in a company as they apply to other property". This helps answer questions such as: how are shares transferred, how are they taxed, what happens when a shareholder dies, and which jurisdiction's laws apply to the shares? The share is a **chose in action**: see *Archibald Home Pty Ltd v Commissioner of Stamp Duties (NSW)* (1948) 77 CLR 143 at 157. However, as discussed in Chapter 5, that term describes both property rights to intangible things and personal rights.

The High Court of Australia referred to the "valuable proprietary rights attaching to shares", in *Gambotto v WCP Ltd* (1995) 182 CLR 432 at 453-454. In that case, the majority shareholders voted to amend the corporation's constitution to enable them to purchase the shares of the minority shareholders without their consent. The court compared this to an expropriation of private property and limited the situations in which it would be permitted. The shares were treated as property rights for the purpose of enhancing their value, thus strengthening the minority's claim to retain that value. This appeals to the common misperception that property rights are more important than personal rights. However, as discussed in Chapter 3, the most important rights in society are personal, such as the rights to be free from false imprisonment, personal injury and defamation.

The issue in the *Gambotto* case was not whether shares were property rights, but whether the majority could use its voting power to unfairly oppress the minority. This can be a problem in any democracy, including society as a whole, and the courts have an important role controlling that sort of abuse. It should not matter whether the right taken or trampled by the majority is personal or property. Would it have made any difference in *Gambotto* if the corporation owed money to the minority shareholders and the majority voted to cancel that debt? If the majority in a society voted to confiscate the bank accounts of members of a minority group, or to take their liberty or their children, would this be any less oppressive because the rights taken were personal and not property? The basis for intervention is the oppression and not the legal nature of the particular right at risk.

The question whether a share is property depends on the nature of the rights conferred by that share. Does a shareholder have a right to a thing which is enforceable generally against other members of society? It is commonly accepted that the shareholders own the corporation (meaning that the corporation is the thing subject to the shareholder's rights). For example, we might speak of the foreign ownership of a corporation, if some of its shareholders are foreigners, or we might refer to a corporation as a wholly-owned subsidiary of another corporation, if all of its shares are owned by that other corporation. A corporation can take its identity from its shareholders. For example, it might be called a Crown corporation if a majority of its shares are owned by the Crown.

Like many other areas of law, the common perception of the rights of a shareholder differs somewhat from the actual legal nature of those rights. This mismatch is created by the separate legal personality of the corporation. Since the corporation is a person, the rights to that corporation will differ significantly from rights to all other things which are not persons. This makes it difficult to identify which of the shareholder's rights are personal rights enforceable against the corporation as a person and which are property rights to the corporation as a thing. Of the shareholder's three main rights (to vote, receive dividends, and share any corporate assets which remain after the corporation is dissolved), the right to vote seems most like a property right and will be discussed at the end.

Right to Dividends

In *Peters American Delicacy Co Ltd v Heath* (1939) 61 CLR 457 at 503-504, Dixon J said that, "Primarily a share in a company is a piece of property conferring rights in relation to distributions of income and of capital." This suggests that shareholders have property rights to dividends and to share any assets of the corporation remaining after its dissolution. However, like the *Gambotto* case, the issue before the court was not whether shares were property, but whether the majority could vote to amend the corporate constitution and thereby alter the rights of the minority shareholders. The court did not ask whether those rights had the two essential characteristics of property rights: do they relate to some thing and are they enforceable generally against other members of society?

The directors decide whether and when the corporation will pay dividends to the shareholders, how much it will pay, and the manner in which they will be paid: Corporations Law, s 254U. Dividends may consist of a payment of money, the issue of securities, or a combination of the two. The corporation is not required to pay dividends and is not permitted to pay dividends unless the corporation makes a profit: Corporations Law, s 254T. A shareholder's right to receive dividends is merely a right to receive any dividends which the corporation chooses to pay. When a dividend is declared, it becomes a debt due to the shareholders on the date set for payment or, if the corporate constitution provides, on the date it is declared: Corporations Law, s 254V.

It is clear that the right to receive dividends is a personal right which is enforceable only against the corporation. That right affects the value of the shares, but only because the corporation is likely to pay dividends. In the same way, a bank account is a valuable personal right because the bank is likely to pay its debts. A right to receive dividends is less certain than a debt, because a shareholder normally cannot compel a corporation to declare a dividend. At most, the shareholder has a mere expectancy that a dividend will be declared.

Right to Assets on Dissolution

Shareholders do not have any property rights to the assets of the corporation while it is a going concern. The corporation, as a separate legal person, owns those assets and can enforce its property rights against its own shareholders. For example, if I owned shares in Telstra, this would not entitle me to drive off in one of Telstra's vehicles. I would be guilty of theft and conversion if I did.

If the corporation is dissolved, the shareholders are entitled to any assets which remain after all of its debts are paid: Corporations Law, s 501. Normally, the remaining assets are sold and the proceeds are distributed among the shareholders *pro rata* according to the number of shares they own. However, it is possible for the shareholders to agree to distribute those assets among themselves. It is also possible to create different classes of shares, with some having a preferred right to the remaining assets and others having no right to them at all.

While the corporation continues to exist, a shareholder's right to share the remaining assets after its dissolution is not a property right. It is not certain whether the corporation will be dissolved, whether that shareholder will still be a shareholder when the corporation is dissolved, and whether there will be anything left once the corporation has paid its debts. Therefore, like the right to receive dividends, a right to share the remaining assets of the corporation is at best a mere expectancy.

This right can be compared to the right of a beneficiary named in a will: see page 278. Suppose, for example, that you have a great uncle who has named you as a beneficiary in his will. If he dies and the will is valid and his estate has sufficient assets, you will receive the gift made in his will. While he lives, you do not have any right to that gift, but a mere expectancy. He might change or revoke his will, you might pass away before him, or there might be nothing left in his estate after all his debts are paid. You cannot have a property right to your great uncle's gift before it becomes certain that you will receive it. The shareholders of a corporation are in a similar position. They cannot have a property right to the corporation's assets until the corporation is dead and its debts are paid.

Right to Vote

The corporation must hold a meeting of its shareholders every year and the shareholders (with voting shares) are entitled to vote at that meeting and at any other special meetings of the shareholders. Shareholders with at least 5% of the voting shares issued by the corporation can compel the directors to call a shareholders' meeting: see Corporations Law, s 249D. A shareholder can vote in person at meetings and, for larger corporations, can vote by appointing a **proxy** to vote on her or his behalf: see Corporations Law, s 250A. The corporation is required to provide sufficient information to its shareholders to enable them to vote properly.

The primary voting right is the election of the directors of the corporation. However, shareholders can also vote on other questions concerning the affairs of the corporation. They can pass resolutions on matters such as the amendment of the corporate constitution, policies to be pursued by the corporation, and the approval of actions already taken by the directors. Shareholders can also vote to wind up the corporation.

In *Peters American Delicacy Co Ltd v Heath* (1939) 61 CLR 457 at 504, Dixon J said that "the right to vote is attached to the share itself as an incident of property to be enjoyed and exercised for the owner's personal advantage". This is the right which most resembles property, because it entitles the shareholders to control the corporation. However, several conceptual difficulties are encountered when the nature of the right to vote is examined:

1) .....it seems to be a right enforceable against the corporation as a person;
2) .....it may in fact give the shareholder very little control over the corporation; and
3) .....the control it does give to shareholders is indirect.

Enforcement of the Right

First, the right to vote looks like a personal right because it is enforceable against a specific person: the corporation. When that right is infringed, the shareholder can apply to the court to compel the corporation to conduct itself in a manner which enables the shareholders to exercise their right to vote: see, eg, *Papaioannoy v Greek Orthodox Community of Melbourne* (1978) 3 ACLR 801. Although the problem will be caused by other humans (the directors, officers, or other shareholders of the corporation), the complaint is that the corporation has not fulfilled its obligations to the shareholder.

Similarly, a shareholder can apply under section 246AA of the Corporations Law for what is commonly called an **oppression remedy** if the corporation's treatment of the shareholders is oppressive, unfairly prejudicial, or unfairly discriminatory. Although, in substance, it is triggered by some humans treating other humans unfairly, it is a complaint about the actions of the corporation or the manner in which its affairs are being conducted. The complaint is, at least formally, directed against the corporation.

This creates a conceptual difficulty. How can the right to vote be a property right to the corporation as a thing when it is enforced against the corporation as a person? As discussed in Chapter 3, the law maintains a distinction between persons (who hold rights) and things (which are subject to rights). There have been societies which have tolerated slavery and allowed humans to be classified as either persons or things. It may have been possible for people in those societies to shift from one category to another, by being sold into or released from slavery. However, the distinction between person and thing was maintained, since people were not both persons and things at the same time. The modern business corporation appears to straddle that line.

Can the right to vote accommodate the dual nature of the corporation as a person with rights and a thing subject to rights? Formally, it is a personal right enforceable against the corporation as a person. However, a court order that the corporation shall do or not do something is, in essence, a command to the directors and officers of the corporation. Therefore, it might be said that the shareholder's right to vote is, in substance, a right to control a thing (the corporation) which is enforceable against the other humans involved in that corporation. The difficulty with this view of the right to vote is that the same might be said about every right which is enforceable against a corporation. Since a corporation depends upon humans to act on its behalf, it can perform its obligations only if its directors, officers, and employees do what is required to achieve that performance. This does not change the nature of the personal rights which others, such as banks, suppliers and employees, can enforce against the corporation.

Lack of Control

The second conceptual difficulty is less troublesome. Although the right to vote is supposed to give the shareholder a right to control the corporation, that right may in fact give the shareholder little or no control. For example, if you own a few shares in a large corporation which has issued millions of shares worldwide, your right to vote those shares will not influence the outcome of any decision made by the shareholders. The directors might be constrained by a fear that the shareholders will collectively vote them out of office if enough of them become unhappy with their decisions. However, you will not have even that level of influence over the corporation if one shareholder or a group of shareholders controls a majority of the issued shares. In that situation, the directors need not worry about pleasing the minority.

Do shareholders, with no real control over the affairs of the corporation, have property rights to the corporation by virtue of their rights to vote? Peta Spender argued that they do, in "Guns and Greenmail: Fear and Loathing After *Gambotto*" (1998) 22 *Melbourne University Law Review* 96 at 117:

> "[S]hares always carry some form of control in so far as shareholders vote for the board of directors. The question of whether ordinary shareholders are capable of controlling the general meeting, and therefore the composition of the board, is a question of quantum."

If a shareholder, who owns all the shares issued by a corporation, is the owner of that corporation, then a shareholder with only a portion of those shares must also have a property right. If all the shares were issued to two or three shareholders, each would be regarded as a part owner of the corporation. What happens when the shares are distributed among thousands of shareholders? Is the ownership of one part per million still ownership in any meaningful sense? If not, that does not mean that the right cannot be property. As discussed in Chapters 3 and 10, it is a mistake to confuse property and ownership. There are many property rights that are much less extensive than ownership. Therefore, if a corporation is a thing capable of being subject to property rights and a majority shareholder's right to vote is a property right to control that corporation, then every shareholder's right to vote should at least be some lesser property right.

If a share is a property right to the corporation because the shareholder has a right to vote, what is the nature of a non-voting share? The other rights which can be attached to non-voting shares (to receive dividends and share any remaining assets if the corporation is dissolved) are not property rights. A share which does not give its holder any possibility of controlling or influencing the conduct of the corporation appears to be nothing more than a personal right enforceable against the corporation.

However, shareholders with non-voting shares do get a right to vote in certain circumstances. For example, a proposal to amend the corporation's constitution, to vary or cancel the rights attached to a class of non-voting shares, would normally require the approval of the shareholders of that class: see Corporations Law, s 246B. If a voting share is a property right because the shareholder has some control over the affairs of the corporation, regardless of the amount of control, then a non-voting share can also be a property right. The holder of non-voting shares will have a right to vote in certain exceptional circumstances and, therefore, has some small amount of control over the corporation.

Indirect Control

The third and final conceptual difficulty is created by the nature of the shareholders' control of the corporation. The right to vote does not entitle the shareholders to manage the corporation directly, but allows them to select the directors who will manage the corporation. Although shareholders might be able to use their voting power to elect themselves to the board of directors, their control of the corporation, as shareholders, is only indirect.

The directors are not agents of the shareholders, but have an independent duty to serve the best interests of the corporation. They are free to make decisions which would be contrary to the wishes of the majority of shareholders, so long as they are acting honestly and in the corporation's best interests: see, eg, *Teck Corp v Millar* (1972) 33 DLR (3d) 288. The shareholders' remedy in that situation is to call a meeting and elect new directors.

Since the directors serve the best interests of the corporation and not the shareholders which elect them, this casts doubt on the argument that the shareholders' right to vote is a property right to control the corporation. Of course, it is nonsense to speak of a corporation as having interests of its own, separate and apart from the humans involved in that corporation. As JE Parkinson said, in *Corporate Power and Responsibility* (1995) pp 76-77:

> "A requirement to benefit an artificial entity, *as an end in itself*, would be irrational and futile, since a non-real entity is incapable of experiencing well-being. Indeed, it is doubtful that an inanimate entity can meaningfully be said to have interests, or if it could, what they would be.... [T]he enterprise's purpose can be understood only in terms of serving human interests or objectives."

If the interests of a corporation are identified completely with those of its shareholders, then the orientation of the directors' duties toward the corporation does not diminish the extent of the shareholder's control. At one time the interests of the corporation and those of its shareholders were identical. The corporation was viewed merely as the personification of its shareholders as a group. However, that has changed. The corporation is now a separate legal person and its creditors are regarded as also having an interest in its welfare. For example, the creditors have standing to apply to the court to have the corporation wound up: Corporations Law, s 462. The directors cannot disregard their interests when serving the best interests of the corporation. As Mason J said in *Walker v Wimborne* (1976) 137 CLR 1 at 7:

> "[T]he directors of a company in discharging their duty to the company must take account of the interest of its shareholders and its creditors. Any failure by the directors to take into account the interests of creditors will have adverse consequences for the company as well as for them."

Some countries recognise that a corporation's employees also have legitimate interests which the directors are entitled to consider when managing the corporation. For example, section 309(1) of the *Companies Act* 1985 (UK) states that, "The matters to which the directors of the company are to have regard in the performance of their functions include the interests of the company's employees in general, as well as the interests of its members." As the corporation's interests become identified with additional groups of people, whose lives are affected by the corporation, the shareholders look less like "owners" of the corporation and more like "investors" in the corporation. They choose the directors of the corporation, but those directors are required to serve interests in addition to their own. Just as some personal rights have evolved to become property rights (for example, the restrictive covenant), so may shareholder's rights be evolving from property to personal.

The shareholder of a large business corporation can be compared to an Australian citizen with a right to vote. The government of Australia is (at present) personified by the Crown (a corporation). The actions of the Crown are dictated by the government elected by the voters. However, we do not regard voters as owners of the Crown. The government must also consider the interests of many persons who do not vote, such as children, those who are mentally incompetent, corporations, and foreign residents. It also considers the protection of things, such as land, water, and endangered species of plants and animals. This is done for the benefit not just of voters, but for all present and future Australians and as part of the nation's international responsibilities.

The Power of Life and Death

Despite the conceptual difficulties created by the separate legal personality of corporations and the manner in which shareholders control them, there is one strong argument in favour of the view that a corporation is a thing owned by its shareholders: they have the power of life and death over it. The shareholders are free to vote to wind up an otherwise healthy corporation. Although this rarely happens, the power to destroy the corporation indicates that a shareholder's right to vote is indeed a property right and that the corporation is both a legal person and a thing.

Chapter Eighteen

LICENCES

■■■

A licence is a right to do something. Some licences are property rights. For example, an **exploration licence** is a property right to search for minerals in a particular location and a **grazing licence** can be an estate: see Chapter 16. A licence of intellectual property is a property right, comparable to a lease of land or bailment of goods: see Chapter 17. However, most licences are personal rights. It may be a personal right which is unrelated to any particular thing. For example, a **driver's licence** is a permit to drive a motor vehicle on public roads. It does not confer the right to use any particular vehicle, but merely allows the licence holder to engage in an activity which would be unlawful without that licence. A licence can also be a personal right to use a thing. This is the type of licence which is the subject of this chapter.

As discussed in previous chapters, rights to use things can be either personal or property. With the exception of native title, all the main property rights to things have already been discussed. They range from complete ownership (in Chapter 10) down to the right to limit how other people use their land (a restrictive covenant, in Chapter 16). In this chapter, we have not only reached the bottom of the long, sliding scale of property rights, but have dropped off the end. Although most of the rights discussed here are personal (and may seem out of place in a book on the law of property), it is very helpful to be able to distinguish between personal rights to use things and property rights. Also, personal rights can evolve into property rights (such as the trust, equity of redemption, and restrictive covenant). This may be happening with some licences.

There are three main issues discussed here:

1) .....When the owner of a thing grants permission to use it, how do we know whether the right granted is personal or property?
2) .....When (and how) will a licence be enforced against the grantor?
3) .....When will a licence be enforced against other members of society?

Before the discussion of these issues begins, it is helpful to look at the categories into which judges and lawyers have organised licences.

Categories of Licences

It is often said that there are three kinds of licences to use things:

1) .....a bare licence;
2) .....a contractual licence; and
3) .....a licence coupled with an interest.

Bare Licence

A bare licence (sometimes called a **mere licence**) is the permission to use something. It is never a property right and, strictly speaking, is not a right at all. All legal rights correspond to obligations placed on specific persons or on members of society generally. A bare licence does not correspond to any obligation, but merely permits the licensee to do something which would otherwise be unlawful. As Wilson J said of a mere licence to use land, in *The Queen v Toohey* (1982) 158 CLR 327 at 352, "It is a personal privilege conferring no interest in the land.... It is generally revocable and merely excuses a trespass until it is revoked."

For example, if you invite me to your home for dinner, I have a licence to do what would otherwise be a trespass (and perhaps a crime). In a general sense, your invitation gives me a right to be there. However, I do not have a legal right to be there. All I have is your permission. You are under no legal obligation to let me stay (even if I gave you a bottle of wine when I arrived). You would be free to revoke your permission and ask me to leave at any time. The only thing constraining you is a moral obligation imposed by good manners or the bonds of friendship.

The terms "bare licence" and "mere licence" are usually used to describe the permission to use another person's land. However, people can also have similar licences to use chattels. For example, you might give me a ride in your car or let me make a copy of a photograph you took (which is subject to your copyright, as discussed in Chapter 17). Again, I have your permission to do something which would otherwise be a wrongful interference with your property right, but you are under no legal obligation to give that permission.

In most cases, the permission to use another person's goods creates not a licence, but a property right. This is because most goods cannot be used unless the person using them has possession. For example, if you lend a book to me, I will possess it. Although you were under no obligation to lend the book, the loan creates a bailment and not a licence: see page 52. You are free to revoke the bailment at any time and, therefore, I cannot enforce my right to possession against you. Nevertheless, I have a property right because I can enforce that right against everyone else in the world.

Contractual Licence

A contractual licence is, like a bare licence, the permission to use something. However, that permission is granted under a contract and this creates an important difference. The contract creates a legal right to use that thing, which corresponds to the owner's legal obligation to permit that use. For example, if you hire a taxi or pay for admission to a movie cinema, you have more than permission to be in the taxi or cinema. You have a contractual right to be there, which corresponds to someone's contractual obligation to let you stay.

The term "contractual licence" is slightly misleading. The important difference between bare and contractual licences is not the contract, but the existence of a legal right and corresponding obligation regarding the use of something. It is true that most rights to use things are created by contract. However, as discussed in Part IV, rights are also created by other events. For example, a licence might be created by a process called "estoppel", which can occur when someone is misled into believing something and relies on that belief to her or his detriment: see Chapter 23. If a personal right to use a thing is created by estoppel, it is not a bare licence. The right created is the same as a contractual licence, despite the absence of a contract.

A contractual licence is simply the most common right of its type. It must not be forgotten that the same right can be created in other ways. Also, it should be noted that the label says nothing about the method of enforcing the right. There are two important questions concerning the enforcement of contractual licences (and other legal rights to use things). First, can the owner of the thing be compelled to let the licensee use it or merely to pay compensation for not permitting its use? Secondly, can the licence be enforced against other members of society or only against the person who granted it? These issues are discussed below.

Licence Coupled with an Interest

While the term "contractual licence" is slightly misleading, the phrase "licence coupled with an interest" (sometimes called a **licence coupled with a grant**) is downright confusing. It suggests that there are two rights in existence: a personal right to use a thing combined somehow with a property right to that thing. However, there is really just a property right.

For example, if I gave you a profit à prendre (discussed in Chapter 16) to gather firewood on my land, you would have a right to enter my land and take away firewood. Some people would say that you have a licence (to enter my land) coupled with an interest (to take firewood). In reality, you have one property right (a profit à prendre), which includes the rights to enter my land and take something away. The two components of that right cannot be separated from each other and both can be enforced generally against other members of society. There is nothing gained by referring to part of that right as a licence.

The phrase "licence coupled with an interest" has two similar, but distinct, meanings. First, it can be used, as above, to describe a right to enter land which is a component of a recognised property right (such as a profit à prendre or an easement). Secondly, it can be used to describe a property right which does not have a clearly established place in Australian property law. For example, in *Smith v Tamworth City Council* (1997) 41 NSWLR 680 at 695, Young J said that a **right of burial** is "more than a contractual licence, it is really a licence coupled with a grant". He was trying to describe the nature of the executor's right to the grave in which the deceased is buried. It is a property right, since it can be enforced against other members of society, but it is difficult to describe. It is not an estate, since there is no right to exclusive possession. Family members and others are free to place flowers and gifts on the grave. Also, the duration of the right is uncertain. In *Beard v Baulkham Hills SC* (1986) 7 NSWLR 273 at 278, Young J said that "there was an irrevocable licence, so far as that body was concerned, for it to remain, at least until the natural process of dissolution".

By calling the right to an occupied grave "a licence coupled with a grant", Young J did not mean that it involved two different rights (personal and property). He meant simply that it did not have a place in the list of familiar property rights, but was nevertheless a property right. It was called a licence in default of a better label and "coupled with a grant" was added to warn the reader that the right was not personal, but property. Although the description suggests two rights, there was only one and it was property.

Personal Right or Property?

It is not always easy to tell whether a right to use a thing is personal or property. Since the right relates to some thing which can be subject to property rights, the issue is whether that right is enforceable generally against other members of society or only against specific persons. This may depend on one or more of the following factors:

1) .....Is the right recognised as a property right in Australian law?
2) .....Did the grantor of the right take the steps necessary to create a property right?
3) .....Did the grantor intend to create a property right?

If the answer to any of these three questions is "no", then the right is most likely a personal right to use something (in other words, a licence enforceable only against the grantor).

Is the Right Recognised as Property?

Some rights to use things are simply not recognised as property. For example, the right to occupy a seat in a taxi, aeroplane, or cinema is not property. Although it relates to a particular thing, the right will be enforced not against everyone else in society, but only against the person who granted it. Therefore, the right is necessarily personal.

Steps Needed to Create Property

As discussed in Chapter 21, property rights are created when a person intends to create that right and takes all the steps necessary to give effect to that intention. The intention and the action combine to bring the property right into existence. It often happens that the owner of a thing intends to grant a property right to it, but fails to do what the law requires for the successful creation of the intended right. Suppose, for example, that you agree to lease my house for five years. If we fail to take the steps necessary to create that lease (register the lease or execute a deed of lease), what right do you have? There are three possibilities: you might have a different property right, a personal right (licence), or no right at all.

First, a failed attempt to create one property right sometimes leads to the creation of another. If our agreement regarding the lease of my house is a specifically enforceable contract, then you may have an equitable lease. If you take possession of the house and begin paying rent, you may have a periodic tenancy: see page 94. These methods of creating property rights are discussed in Chapter 21.

Secondly, if our agreement fails to produce any property right, it may be effective to create a licence. You might have a contractual right to use my house, which is enforceable only against me. This is not a common response to promises to grant property rights to land. If the promise is a valid contract, then it will probably be specifically enforceable and produce an equitable property right. However, contracts to grant property rights to goods are usually not specifically enforceable. Therefore, it is more likely that a valid contract to use goods will produce a licence if the contract is not performed. For example, suppose that I promise to lease my car to you for three years, but do not let you have possession of it. Your property right will not arise until you obtain possession (a bailment, discussed at page 52, but you cannot compel me to deliver the car to you. Our contract gives you a personal right to use the car, which is enforceable only against me. If I deliver the car to someone else, you cannot enforce your right against that person, but can sue me for damages caused by my breach of contract.

The third alternative is that a failed attempt to produce a property right will generate no rights whatsoever. For example, suppose that I promise to give my house to you. If I do not complete the gift, what right do you have? Unless you are able to complete the gift without my help (see page 273) or have relied on my promise to your detriment (see Chapter 23), it is unlikely that you have any right to the house. This is true even though I think I have completed the gift and believe the house is yours. If you have possession of the house, you would be a tenant at will (see page 95). Without possession, you would have at most a bare licence (my permission to the use the house, but no legal right to do so).

Intention to Create Property

If a person does what is necessary to create a recognised property right, this will not necessarily bring that property right into existence. Generally speaking, the intention to create that right is an essential condition for its creation. It must not be forgotten that property rights can be created by events other than intention. As discussed in Part IV, they can be created by unjust enrichment, wrongdoing, and other events. However, when dealing with a right created by intention, a central issue will be the intention of the person creating the right.

There are a number of rights which may be personal or property. For example, if you give your neighbour permission to cross your land, you may be doing a personal favour for your neighbour or may be granting an easement. Similarly, your permission to dig for worms could be a profit à prendre or merely lead to a gift or sale of the worms removed. Whether the right granted is personal or property depends primarily on your intention.

For example, in *King v David Allen & Sons Billposting Ltd* [1916] 2 AC 54, the defendant granted a licence to the plaintiff to post bills on the wall of a theatre to be built on the defendant's land. The defendant leased that land to a company and the theatre was built. The defendant was a director of the company and had assumed that it would honour his contract with the plaintiff. However, the company refused to let the plaintiff post bills on the wall. The company could not be compelled to allow this, since it had a property right to possess the land and the plaintiff had only a personal right to post bills. Therefore, the plaintiff's only remedy was to sue the defendant for damages for breach of contract.

There are two reasons why the plaintiff's right to post bills was merely personal. First, the right was not recognised as a property right at common law. Although it was similar to an easement, it did not benefit nearby land and, therefore, could not be property: see Chapter 16. Secondly, even if the right was capable of being property, it was clear from the wording of the billposting contract that the defendant had intended to grant a personal right to the plaintiff. The use of the word "licence" was one indication of this. As Lord Buckmaster C said (at 61), nothing "beyond personal rights was ever contemplated by the parties".

Enforcing the Licence

If you do have a personal right to use something of mine (created by contract, estoppel, or some other event), there are two important questions concerning your ability to enforce that right. First, can I be compelled to let you use that thing or merely to pay damages for failing to do so? Secondly, can you enforce that right against other members of society or only against me?

Enforcing the Licence Against the Grantor

As discussed in Chapter 7, there are several different ways in which the law might respond to the breach of a plaintiff's legal right. The most common response is to compel the wrongdoer to pay compensation for the loss caused by her or his breach. Less commonly, the law may compel the wrongdoer to fulfil the plaintiff's right. This can be accomplished in one of two ways. First, the court might order the wrongdoer to stop interfering with the right (a **prohibitive injunction**). Secondly, the court might order the wrongdoer to perform the obligation which corresponds to the plaintiff's right (either an order for **specific performance** or a **mandatory injunction**).

Where the right breached is a licence, the normal legal response is an order to pay compensation for any loss caused by the breach. In other words, someone with a personal right to use a thing usually cannot compel the owner of that thing to permit that use. For example, if you pay for a seat on an aeroplane or train or at a cricket ground, the owners may refuse to admit you or ask you to leave. They may have to pay compensation for your loss, hurt feelings, embarrassment, etc, but are otherwise free to say "get out" or "stay out". In other words, the promise to grant a licence is not specifically enforceable. This is true of most promises.

In *Cowell v Rosehill Racecourse Co Ltd* (1937) 56 CLR 605, the plaintiff paid for a ticket to attend a race meeting. The defendant's servants asked him to leave and, when he refused, they used force to evict him. The plaintiff sued the defendant for damages for assault. The defendant contended that it had merely used reasonable force to evict a trespasser, which a person in possession of land is entitled to do. The resolution of this dispute depended on whether the plaintiff was a trespasser at the time, which in turn depended on whether his contractual licence to attend the meeting had been revoked.

The majority of the High Court of Australia held that the defendant could not be compelled to grant a licence to attend the meeting, nor could it be restrained from revoking it. Even if the defendant had acted in breach of contract by refusing to admit the plaintiff or demanding that he leave, the plaintiff's only remedy was to sue for damages caused by the breach of contract. Therefore, the plaintiff was a trespasser when he refused to leave the racecourse, even if the defendant was wrong to ask him to leave.

A minority of the court disagreed. Evatt J thought that a court of equity would grant an injunction to prevent the defendant from revoking the licence in breach of contract. Therefore, the defendant would not be allowed to plead its own breach of contract as a defence to the plaintiff's claim for assault. This view has been taken by courts in England. For example, in *Hounslow London Borough Council v Twickenham Garden Developments Ltd* [1971] Ch 233, the council wanted a court order to remove a building contractor from its land. The contractor was on the land performing construction work under its contract with the council. The council claimed that the contractor was in breach of contract and that the council had properly terminated the contract and revoked the contractor's licence to be on the land. Megarry J refused to grant an injunction against the contractor without first deciding that the licence was properly revoked. Therefore, the contractor was entitled to remain on the land pending a trial (which could take several years).

Megarry J said (at 254) that, "even if a contractual licence is not specifically enforceable, the court will not grant equitable remedies in order to procure or aid a breach of the licence". This creates an undesirable asymmetry: the holders of a licence to enter land cannot compel the land owner to admit them but, once on the land, the land owner cannot compel them to leave. The legal response ought to be the same, regardless of whether the licence holders are inside or outside the gates. Otherwise, people have an incentive to take the law into their own hands. Licence holders will attempt to gain entry to the land because, if they can do so without violence, the court will not order them to leave. Conversely, land owners will try to remove the licence holders and their things from the land, because the court will refuse to readmit them. It is important that the law provides a legal mechanism to achieve the status which the law would subsequently sanction.

Megarry J's solution allows the availability of a particular remedy to obscure the more important question: should a person who promises to grant a licence be compelled to keep that promise? Most promises are not specifically enforceable. Even where the promise breaker has acted despicably, he or she is not compelled to keep the promise (but might be ordered to pay punitive or exemplary damages as punishment): see Chapter 7. Is there anything about a promise to grant a licence which justifies a departure from the normal rule?

As discussed at page 258, most contracts to transfer property rights to land are specifically enforceable. The courts have long recognised that no two parcels of land are exactly the same. The disappointed purchaser will have difficulty finding a suitable replacement for the promised land and, therefore, an order to pay damages for breach of contract will not be an adequate substitute for performance of the contract. To solve this problem, a court of equity will grant an order for specific performance of the contract, which will compel the vendor to keep her or his promise. It may be that some contracts to grant licences to use land should also be specifically enforceable. Although the licence is not a property right, the disappointed licensee will have difficulty obtaining a similar licence from someone else. Therefore, an award of damages would not provide adequate compensation for the breach of contract.

However, there is an important difference between most licences to use land and most property rights to land. Since licence holders do not have possession of the land, they will share the use of it with the owner (or other people entitled to possession). As Goddard LJ said, in *Thompson v Park* [1944] KB 408 at 409, "the court cannot specifically enforce an agreement for two people to live peaceably under the same roof". Therefore, even though an award of damages for breach of a contract to grant of licence may be inadequate, specific performance of the contract might not be a viable alternative. In contrast, the specific performance of a contract to grant a property right will not require the same degree of continued co-operation between the parties. If the property right is an estate, the land owner will be compelled to give up possession. If it is a lesser property right (such as a mortgage, easement, or restrictive covenant), the parties will be able to exercise their rights without a great deal of personal interaction.

Although most contracts are not specifically enforceable, an exception should be made for a contract to grant a licence to use land, if the licence is similar to a property right in two respects:

1) .....another licence would be difficult to obtain and, therefore, damages would not be an adequate substitute for performance of the contract; and
2) .....the exercise of the licence would not require a great deal of co-operation between the parties to the contract.

These two conditions were satisfied in two English cases in which a contract to grant a licence was specifically enforced: *Winter Garden Theatre (London) Ltd v Millennium Productions Ltd* [1948] AC 173; *Verrall v Great Yarmouth Borough Council* [1981] QB 202. The former concerned a licence to use a theatre to present a series of plays and the latter concerned a licence to use a meeting hall to hold a political convention. It would have been difficult, if not impossible, for the licence holders to find alternative facilities and the licences granted were very similar to leases. Although the licence holders were not entitled to possession of the premises (since the owners had retained control), they were entitled to occupy them almost exclusively. Both licences were similar to leases and required little more co-operation between the parties than expected of landlords and tenants. Therefore, there was no impediment to an order of specific performance.

Enforcing the Licence Against Others

Most licences are personal rights. In other words, they are enforceable only against specific persons and not against other members of society. Some licences to use things can be enforced against others and are therefore property rights. This can be a source of confusion because, in this context, the word "licence" is often used to indicate that the right in question is not property. A reader, who encounters the word in a statute, judgment, contract, or other legal material, needs to be aware that the right described may be property.

When attempting to identify the nature of a particular licence, attention must be paid to the context in which the word is used. As discussed at page 165, words used in a statute do not always bear their ordinary meanings. It is assumed that a word, with a specific legal meaning at common law, has the same meaning in the statute. However, Parliament is free to depart from that definition and give it another. For example, a pastoral lease granted under the *Land Act* 1962 (Qld) is not a lease, but a non-possessory property right to use land: *Wik Peoples v Queensland* (1996) 187 CLR 1. There are many statutory licences which are property rights, such as the licences for mineral exploration or petroleum production discussed at pages 171-173. The essential question is whether the statutory right relates to some thing and is enforceable generally against other members of society. If the right lacks one or both of these attributes, it is personal.

Similar things can be said about a licence created by contract. The use of the word "licence" is a strong indication that a personal right was intended, but the whole contract must be examined to determine the exact nature of the right granted. For example, in *Radaich v Smith* (1959) 101 CLR 209, a contractual "licence to carry on the business of a milk bar" was really a grant of possession of land for a term and, therefore, a lease.

When a judge refers to a non-statutory right as a licence, this usually means that the right is personal. As discussed above, the words "coupled with an interest" might be added as an indication that the licence in question is really a property right. Using the word "licence" to describe a property right is not particularly helpful. It might mislead the reader into thinking that the right is personal. Also, it does not tell the reader anything about the property right. However, a suitable alternative might not be available. If a property right has emerged only recently or has been neglected by property lawyers (such as the right of burial, discussed above), it may have no place in the accepted taxonomy of property law. It is then labelled a licence by default.

Sometimes, a property right is called a licence because it has not been properly identified. The judge or lawyer may have overlooked the similarity between that licence and an established property right. *Errington v Errington* [1952] 1 KB 290 might be an example of this.

A father purchased a house as a residence for his son and daughter-in-law. One third of the purchase price was paid by the father as a down payment and he raised the balance through a mortgage on the house. The father said that the down payment was a gift and, if the couple made the mortgage payments, they could reside in the house and become its owners when the mortgage was paid. They made those payments for many years until the father died and the son moved in with his widowed mother, leaving the daughter-in-law in possession of the house. The mother became the owner of the house and commenced a legal action to evict her.

This case remains controversial because Denning LJ said (at 298-299) that the couple's right to the house was "a mere personal privilege to remain there" and that this licence could be enforced against other members of society, "except a purchaser for value without notice". This is a clear contradiction. A right to a thing which can be enforced generally against others is, by definition, a property right. It has been suggested that the court was wrong to enforce that right against others. However, the couple did have a property right and the mistake seems to be the court's characterisation of that right. Unfortunately, the label used by the court, "contractual licence", tells us nothing about the right except that it was created by contract. It is necessary to resort to a few basic propositions to identify the right created.

To begin, Denning LJ said (at 298) that "the couple had exclusive possession of the house". This must be correct. Otherwise, the couple would have no right to prevent strangers from entering their home. This tells us two things about the right. First, possession is a property right and, secondly, possession with permission of the owner is an estate. At a minimum, it is a tenancy at will. However, the couple had a greater right to possession since they could also enforce it against the owner.

A difficulty was created by the informal nature of the arrangement between the father and the couple. If they paid all the mortgage payments, they would be entitled to receive the legal title to the house. However, they were not obligated to make those payments. They were free to stop paying the mortgage and abandon their interest in the house. This was stumbling block for the court: the mortgage payments could not be treated as rent if the couple was not required to make them. However, the estate could be characterised as a periodic tenancy, which was renewed each time the couple paid the mortgage. A failure to pay the mortgage would convert the leasehold estate into a tenancy at will.

The couple's right to possess the house, so long as they paid the mortgage, meant that, at a minimum, they had a periodic tenancy. However, they had a greater right, since they were entitled to obtain the legal fee simple estate once the mortgage was paid off. As the court recognised, this was similar to a recognised equitable property right: the right of a purchaser under a conditional sale contract. As discussed at page 121, a conditional sale is a transaction in which the purchaser obtains possession of the land, but the vendor retains title until the purchase price is paid in full. Although the vendor is the legal owner of the land, that ownership is held as security for the purchaser's obligation to pay for the land. The purchaser has the equitable beneficial ownership of the land and has a right to obtain title when the purchase price is paid in full.

The only impediment to this analysis of the couple's right is that they were not obligated to pay the mortgage. Therefore, the father's legal right could not be security for their obligation to pay the purchase price. However, the contract (though unusual) did give the couple a legal right to purchase the home. This gave them an equitable fee simple estate, subject to the father's right to possession if the couple stopped paying the mortgage: see Chapters 14 and 21. If the court had identified their rights as such, the judgment would be unremarkable. However, since the court referred to the right as a personal licence, the reader is surprised and confused to discover that it was enforced against other members of society. A closer analysis reveals that the right was property, leaving the reader with the difficult task of identifying the nature of the right to determine whether it is a recognised property right or something new.

A great deal of confusion could be avoided if the term "licence" was used only to describe personal rights. However, it is too late for that. As discussed above, there are many statutory licences which are property rights and there are other common law and equitable rights which are called licences in default of a better name. A property right should not be called a licence if a better description is available, but, if it must be called a licence, care should be taken to identify the true nature of that right.

Chapter Nineteen

NATIVE TITLE

This is the final chapter of Part III and the last instalment in this brief survey of the variety of property rights recognised in Australia. Two basic issues are discussed here: first, what is native title and, secondly, how is it incorporated into the Australian legal system? There is another important issue left for Part V: how does native title relate to other property rights in that system? In other words, how does the law resolve conflicts between native title and other property rights to the same land? This third issue is discussed in Chapter 28, which deals with the priority of conflicting legal property rights.

What is Native Title?

Native title is a generic label for a variety of property rights to land which are held by Aboriginal Australians and Torres Strait Islanders. They range from rights to use land for specific purposes (such as fishing or visiting sacred sites) up to rights to permanent possession. For example, in *Yanner v Eaton* (1999) 166 ALR 258, the Gungaletta tribe had native title to hunt crocodiles near the Gulf of Carpentaria. In *Mabo v Queensland (No 2)* (1992) 175 CLR 1, the Meriam people had native title to permanent possession of most of the island of Mer.

In *Mabo (No 2)* at 57, Brennan J defined native title as follows:

"The term 'native title' conveniently describes the interests and rights of indigenous inhabitants in land, whether communal, group or individual, possessed under the traditional laws acknowledged by and the traditional customs observed by the indigenous inhabitants."

That definition provided the basis for the definition of native title found in section 223 of the *Native Title Act* 1993 (Cth):

"The expression native title or native title rights and interests means the communal, group or individual rights and interests of Aboriginal peoples or Torres Strait Islanders in relation to land or waters, where:

(a) the rights and interests are possessed under the traditional laws acknowledged, and the traditional customs observed, by the Aboriginal peoples or Torres Strait Islanders; and

(b) the Aboriginal peoples or Torres Strait Islanders, by those laws and customs, have a connection with the land or waters; and
(c) the rights and interests are recognised by the common law of Australia."

It is helpful to consider the essential elements of these definitions.

Rights to Land

We begin with two basic points. First, native title is always a right to land and never a right to chattels or intangible things. For example, the native title in *Yanner v Eaton*, above, was a right to use certain lands to hunt crocodiles and not an independent right to the crocodiles (before they were killed). In other words, it was similar to a profit à prendre and not ownership of goods: see page 147.

Secondly, native title is a property right. It shares the two essential characteristics of property, since it relates to some thing (land) and is enforceable generally against other members of society. In *Mabo (No 2)*, Deane J and Gaudron J cast doubt on this basic proposition. They said (at 110) that the "rights of an Aboriginal tribe or clan entitled to the benefit of a common law native title are personal only" and that the "personal rights conferred by common law native title do not constitute an estate or interest in the land itself".

However, the majority of the court made it clear that native title was property. Brennan J said (at 75) that "their native title is effective as against the state of Queensland and as against the whole world". The court declared (at 76 and 217) "that the Meriam people are entitled as against the whole world to possession, occupation, use and enjoyment of the island of Mer".

Although the Meriam people had permanent possession of the land, rather than a lesser right to use the land for limited purposes, this was not the factor that made it property. The same general principles apply to all native title in Australia: see *Mabo (No 2)* at 26 and 179. Just as the common law recognises a wide range of property rights to land, from ownership to easements, so can a wide range of native title be recognised as property. For example, native title, which consists solely of a right to fish or hunt, is property because it relates to the land and is enforceable against other members of society.

Recognised by Australian Common Law

The third basic point is that native title is a common law (or legal) property right to land (and not an equitable or statutory right). It is recognised by Australian common law and many of its characteristics (such as its enforceability against others) are defined by the common law (although some have been modified by statute).

When Britain acquired sovereignty over Australia, English common law (modified by equity and statutes) became the dominant legal system in Australia. However, the imposition of a new system of property law did not destroy the property rights which existed under old systems. The existing property rights of the indigenous inhabitants of Australia, which had been created and protected by their traditional laws and customs, were preserved and protected by the new common law. This process is discussed further below.

Traditional Laws and Customs

Since native title is created under the traditional laws and customs of Aboriginal Australians or Torres Strait Islanders, its exact nature depends on the those laws and customs. The wide variety of traditional laws and customs across Australia has produced a wide variety of property rights that can be called native title. As Gummow J said, in *Yanner v Eaton* (1999) 166 ALR 258 at 278:

> "Native title is not treated by the common law as a unitary concept. The heterogeneous laws and customs of Australia's indigenous peoples, the Aboriginals and Torres Strait Islanders, provide its content."

Native title is merely a generic label for a variety of property rights to land. What ties them together is the manner in which they became part of the common law. Those rights existed when Australia became a British colony and were recognised and protected by the common law imported from England.

If you want to describe the native title held by a particular group of people, you need to answer two questions. First, what rights to land are held under the traditional laws and customs of that group? Secondly, to what extent and how are those rights protected by common law and statute? The property rights we call native title are created by "an intersection of traditional laws and customs with the common law": *Fejo v Northern Territory* (1998) 195 CLR 96 at 128.

The nature of native title is (to use a phrase familiar to lawyers) a question of mixed fact and law. The particular rights which constitute any particular form of native title depend primarily on the traditional laws and customs under which it was created. That is not a legal question to be determined by a judge (as a legal expert), but a question of fact to be decided on the basis of evidence placed before a judge (as a trier of fact).

Issues, that would be regarded as legal questions under the traditional laws and customs of Aboriginal Australians or Torres Strait Islanders, become questions of fact when transferred to the common law. This is the normal way in which one legal system deals with the laws of another legal system. Suppose, for example, that a bank in Melbourne received a payment by mistake from a bank in London, via banks in New York and Sydney. If the case came before a judge of the Supreme Court of Victoria, he or she could apply the laws of Australia and Victoria as a legal expert. However, if the resolution of the dispute depended on the laws of England, New York, or New South Wales, those laws would need to be proved as facts by expert witnesses.

This same problem arises in connection with all native title. The rights to land, which exist according to traditional laws and customs, must be proved as facts before the proper court (or other tribunal). The court then determines whether those rights are enforceable under Australian law.

In contrast, the nature of other property rights in Australia is primarily a question of law. For example, if you have a fee simple estate, the rights you hold will be defined by common law, equity, and statute. Of course, whether you acquired that estate (by inheritance, sale, or gift) and continue to own it are questions involving both facts and law. However, while you have that estate, the nature of the rights you hold is a question of law.

Indigenous Inhabitants of Australia

Another feature of native title, which distinguishes it from other property rights, relates to the identity of the people who hold it. As discussed in Chapters 2 and 3, all property rights (like all legal rights) are held by persons and enforced against other persons. So far, we have focused on the nature of the rights and have not bothered to consider the identity of the persons who hold them.

Generally speaking, every person with legal capacity (whether human being or corporation) is able to hold property rights and enforce them against others. The capacity to own property can be reduced or eliminated by several different factors, such as infancy, mental incapacity, or bankruptcy. At one time, married women had only a limited capacity to own property, but that rule has long been abolished. Normally, the capacity to hold property rights is unaffected by personal characteristics, such as sex, race, place of birth, or marital status.

Native title is excepted from this general principle. Generally speaking, Aboriginal Australians or Torres Strait Islanders are the only people with capacity to hold native title. This can be explained in three different ways. First, it can be regarded as a limit imposed by the common law, which does not permit anyone other than indigenous persons to acquire native title: see *Mabo (No 2)* at 88. This prohibition does not apply to the government. As Brennan J also said (at 60), "the Crown's sovereignty over all land in the territory carries the capacity to accept a surrender of native title".

Secondly, the nature of native title is defined primarily by traditional laws and customs. This includes the rules for transferring native title (by gift, inheritance, sale, or otherwise). It cannot be transferred to strangers if that is not permitted by those laws and customs: see *Mabo (No 2)* at 59.

Thirdly, since native title consists of rights enforced by traditional laws and customs, people can hold native title only if they observe those laws and customs. As Brennan J said, in *Mabo (No 2)* at 60, "native title cannot be acquired from an indigenous people by one who, not being a member of the indigenous people, does not acknowledge their laws and observe their customs".

Communal, Group, or Individual Rights

As discussed in Chapter 4, property rights can be owned privately, collectively, or communally. Private property may be held by one person or shared by two or more persons as joint tenants or tenants in common: see Chapter 15. Collective property is held by governments or other public institutions on behalf of the public. Communal or common property is available to every member of the public (or some large cross-section of the public). Apart from native title, most property in Australia is owned privately or collectively.

Native title can be owned in any of these three ways. This depends primarily on the traditional laws and customs which define the native title in question. Do those laws and customs allocate property rights to individuals, groups, the whole community, or representatives of the community?

If native title is recognised as the common property of a particular aboriginal community, then individuals or groups within that community might have personal rights to make use of that common property (or a portion of it) for their own benefit. In other words, the whole community might have a property right to land, which is enforceable generally against other members of Australian society, but individuals and groups in that community have personal rights to use the land, which are enforceable only against other members of that community. Brennan J raised this possibility in *Mabo (No 2)* at 51-52:

> "The fact that individual members of the community ... enjoy only usufructuary rights that are not proprietary in nature is no impediment to the recognition of a proprietary community title. ... That being so, there is no impediment to the recognition of individual non-proprietary rights that are derived from the community's laws and customs and are dependent on the community title."

The *Native Title Act* 1993 (Cth) provides a mechanism by which native title can be owned collectively. Under section 56, the holders of native title can transfer it to a "registered native title body corporate" to be held in trust for them. The corporation becomes the legal owner of the native title and is required to use that property right for the benefit of the indigenous community as a whole or for individuals and groups within that community. (Trusts are discussed in Chapter 13.)

Native Title in Australian Law

This part of the chapter takes a closer look at the manner in which native title is incorporated into Australian law. That process has been difficult for two reasons. First, as discussed above, it involves many different legal systems. Various forms of native title are created and defined by a variety of traditional laws and customs of Aboriginal Australians and Torres Strait Islanders. Each form of native title needs to be preserved and protected by Australian laws derived from English land law.

Secondly, in *Mabo v Queensland (No 2)* (1992) 175 CLR 1, the High Court of Australia declared that native title has been a part of the common law since it was first introduced to Australia in 1788. However, that declaration was not made until 1992. Therefore, much of the development of Australian land law proceeded on the basis that native title did not exist. This required a change in the way in which governments dealt with land under their control. It also made it difficult to prove the continued existence of native title, since that requires a reconstruction of land use and dealings over the past two centuries.

Three aspects of the incorporation of native title into Australian law are discussed here:

1) .....the survival of native title upon a change in sovereignty;
2) .....the place of native title in Australian land law and, particularly, its relation to the doctrine of tenure; and
3) .....proof of the existence of native title.

Native Title and Sovereignty

Acquisition of Sovereignty

There are three main ways in which a government can acquire sovereignty over land:

1) .....conquest (such as the Norman conquest of England in 1066);
2) .....cession (which is the voluntary surrender of land by its inhabitants); or
3) .....occupation (of *terra nullius*, which means land belonging to no one).

It had long been assumed that Australia was *terra nullius* when it became a British colony. It was said that the land did not belong to anyone, either because there were no settled inhabitants or because the inhabitants did not have a legal system under which ownership of the land could be allocated to anyone. In *Mabo (No 2)*, the High Court rejected that view. This created a contradiction. Britain had acquired sovereignty over Australia by occupation, because it was *terra nullius*. As the High Court of Australia said in *Mabo (No 2)*, it does not have jurisdiction to determine the sovereignty of Australia and, therefore, its rejection of *terra nullius* does not affect that issue. However, it did affect the ownership of land within Australia.

If the land had been *terra nullius*, there would be no possibility of native title, because there would be no existing property rights which the common law could recognise and protect. The rejection of that notion means that, when Britain acquired sovereignty over Australia, property rights were already in existence, according to the traditional laws and customs of its inhabitants. This raises the question whether those rights will be preserved and protected by the common law.

Recognition of Existing Property Rights

When Britain acquired sovereignty over Australia, English law became the law of Australia (modified as necessary to adapt to local conditions). The indigenous inhabitants continued to observe their traditional laws and customs, including those laws and customs which allocated and enforced property rights to land. However, the new Anglo-Australian law had become the dominant legal system and property rights created under that system took precedence over property rights enjoyed under old systems. If the new legal system did not recognise the existing property rights of Aboriginal Australians and Torres Strait Islanders, they would be unable to enforce those rights against arriving immigrants and their new governments. As Brennan J said in *Mabo (No 2)* at 55, "pre-existing rights and interests in land must be established, if at all, under the new legal system introduced on an acquisition of sovereignty".

When English common law is applied to a new territory, it does not automatically destroy existing property rights. Although the new sovereign has the power to reallocate property rights, the introduction of

English common law does not, itself, cause that to happen. As Deane J and Gaudron J said in *Mabo (No 2)* at 82:

> "The strong assumption of the common law was that interests in property which existed under native law or customs were not obliterated by the act of State establishing a new British Colony but were preserved and protected by the domestic law of the Colony after its establishment."

This principle is well established in relation to territories acquired by conquest or cession. An issue facing the High Court in *Mabo (No 2)* was whether it also applied to territories acquired by occupation. There is no reason why the same legal principle should not apply, but there is an apparent contradiction: the acquisition of sovereignty by occupation presupposes that the territory was *terra nullius*. By definition, the land belonged to no one and there were no existing property rights which could be recognised by the newly introduced common law. However, once it is accepted that the land did belong to people, the method of acquiring sovereignty should not affect the common law's ability to recognise those property rights.

The common law's recognition of existing property rights does not mean that those rights are directly enforceable under the common law. They were created and exist under the traditional laws and customs of the indigenous people of Australia. Those laws and customs are not enforceable in common law courts (in the absence of special legislation creating that jurisdiction: see *Mabo (No 2)* at 62). They cannot be enforced against people who do not observe them and a common law court would not enforce them even among the people who do observe them.

Native title cannot be enforced by the common law unless it is imported into the common law system and becomes a common law right. This process does not affect the rights held under traditional laws and customs. The people who continue to observe those laws and customs can continue to enforce those rights against others who observe the same laws and customs. However, in addition to those rights, they acquire common law rights to enforce their native title against all members of Australian society. The additional common law right is essential to the survival of native title. Since the traditional laws and customs are no longer the dominant legal system, native title could not otherwise be enforced against an ever increasing number of people who do not observe the same laws and customs.

The translation of existing property rights of indigenous people to common law native title alters the nature of those rights. The obvious benefit of this change is the ability to enforce native title against all Australians. However, it can also limit native title in three different ways. First and most importantly, those property rights may be less durable under the common law than they were under traditional laws and customs. As Brennan J said in *Mabo (No 2)* at 63:

> "Sovereignty carries the power to create and to extinguish private rights and interests in land with the Sovereign's territory. It follows

that, on a change of sovereignty, rights and interests in land that may have been indefeasible under the old regime become liable to extinction by exercise of the new sovereign power."

Secondly, as discussed above, the common law limits the transferability of native title. It cannot be transferred to people other than the indigenous inhabitants (and the Commonwealth, state, and territorial governments), even if the traditional laws and customs would have permitted such a transfer.

Thirdly, the rights enforceable under traditional laws and customs would not be enforced by the common law if that would be contrary to public policy. This is a general limitation on all property rights. For example, courts have refused to enforce covenants restricting the sale of houses to people of certain races, because those covenants are contrary to public policy: see page 161. Although no particular aspects of native title have been identified as contrary to public policy, Brennan J noted, in *Mabo (No 2)* at 61, that native title is not exempt from that limitation:

> "The incidents of a particular native title ... are matters to be determined by the laws and customs of the indigenous inhabitants, provided those laws and customs are not so repugnant to natural justice, equity and good conscience that judicial sanctions under the new regime must be withheld."

This does not mean that native title must be similar to other forms of property recognised by the common law. As discussed in Chapter 9, there is a limit on the variety of property rights that the common law will recognise. This limit is justified because it promotes the utility and marketability of resources and the manageability and consistency of the common law. Although these might be regarded as public policies which constrain the law of property, they do not inhibit the recognition of native title. As Brennan J said in *Mabo (No 2)* at 59:

> "The general principle that the common law will recognize a customary title only if it be consistent with the common law is subject to an exception in favour of traditional native title."

Radical Title

When Britain acquired sovereignty over Australia, the British Crown acquired title over all the land in Australia. This happened in stages, beginning with the Colony of New South Wales in 1788. The western boundary of that colony was extended from the 135th to the 129th degree of east longitude in 1824. The Colony of Western Australia was established in 1829 and its eastern boundary was set at the 129th degree of east longitude in 1831. Sovereignty over the Torres Strait Islands was acquired in 1879.

The nature of the Crown's title to Australia depended on the existence of native title. If native title did not exist over a parcel of land, the Crown became the beneficial owner of that land, with a right to immediate possession. If native title did exist, the Crown acquired only **radical title** to the land. This gave the Crown the power to do two things: take the land for its own use or grant property rights to others. As Brennan CJ said, in *Wik Peoples v Queensland* (1996) 187 CLR 1 at 94, "radical title ... is essentially a power of alienation controlled by statute". It does not give the Crown a right to possession of land, unless it first exercises its sovereign power to acquire that land for its own use.

In *Mabo (No 2)* at 48, Brennan J said, "If the land were desert and uninhabited, truly a *terra nullius*, the Crown would take an absolute beneficial title (an allodial title) to the land [because] there would be no *other* proprietor." In other words, the Crown's title would expand from radical title to full beneficial ownership to fill a void. However, this was possible only in the complete absence of native title. The Crown obtained only radical title, even where native title was not a right to possession of land, but a right to use it for limited purposes. In such cases, no one has a right to possess the land (unless the Crown exercises its sovereign power to take possession or grant possession to others).

Native Title and Tenure

As discussed in Chapter 11, when the Crown grants an estate to someone, it creates a tenure relationship between itself and the recipient of that estate. This relationship has long ceased to have any practical significance for the owners of freehold estates. It still matters for leasehold estates, because of the leasehold covenants which bind the landlord to the tenant (now called **privity of estate**): see page 93. However, the tenure relationship between landlord and leasehold tenant is not peculiar to Crown grants, but applies to all modern leases. In other words, when the Crown does grant a leasehold estate, the last vestiges of tenure are relevant because of the landlord–tenant relationship and not because the Crown holds radical title to the land: see Megarry and Wade, *The Law of Real Property* (5th ed, 1984) p 37.

Native title is not a form of tenure. It is not an estate and is not granted by the Crown or by anyone who holds an estate. It became a common law right (by operation of law) as soon as the Crown acquired radical title to the land. These basic principles are important, because they help explain the process by which native title was incorporated into the common law. However, they tell us little about the nature of native title or its place within the common law.

It is significant that native title is not a form of tenure granted by the Crown, but only because this enables the Crown to grant inconsistent property rights (as discussed below). For all other purposes, it is irrelevant. This is not surprising, because tenure has ceased to have any meaningful significance (outside the law relating to landlords and tenants).

Consider the difference between a fee simple estate and native title to permanent possession of land. In both cases, the Crown has radical title to the land, the owners have a right to possess the land indefinitely, and that right is enforceable against everyone else in society, including the Crown. Of course, there are significant differences between the two rights. As discussed above, native title is less durable, less transferable, and more likely to be owned communally than other common law property rights. However, durability is the only difference that relates to the Crown's radical title and the concept of tenure.

After the Crown grants a fee simple estate, it cannot grant an inconsistent property right to the same land, unless that right is excepted from the grant of fee simple (such as a reservation of mineral rights) or the Crown expropriates at least part of that estate. Once the Crown, as holder of radical title, exercises its power to grant a particular property right, that power is spent and cannot be exercised again, unless the Crown recalls that right through expropriation.

In contrast, native title exists without a Crown grant and, therefore, the Crown has not used its power (as holder of radical title) to grant property rights to that land. Therefore, even though the holders of native title have a common law right to permanent possession of the land, the Crown retains a sovereign power to grant inconsistent property rights to the same land.

It is worth noting that this difference, between a fee simple estate and the equivalent native title, is not due to the presence or absence of a tenure relationship. The difference exists because the Crown cannot use its radical title repeatedly to create inconsistent property rights. The same principle would apply if the Crown granted a profit à prendre. The grant would not create a tenure relationship and yet the Crown would not be permitted to grant an inconsistent right without expropriation. The existence of the equivalent native title (such as a right to hunt crocodiles) would not disable the Crown from using its radical title to grant inconsistent property rights.

This fundamental difference, between native title and other property rights to land, existed until the *Racial Discrimination Act* 1975 (Cth) came into effect. That statute obligated the Commonwealth, state, and territorial governments to treat native title in the same manner as other, equivalent property rights. In essence, the Crown could no longer use its radical title to grant inconsistent rights without first expropriating the native title. Therefore, this difference between native title and other property rights is relevant only for land dealings which took place before 31 October 1975. This issue is discussed further at page 395.

Proof of Native Title

Most property rights are easy to prove. For example, your claim that you own something might depend on proof that you obtained possession of it, purchased it under a contract of sale, or registered the appropriate transfer document: see Chapter 21. In contrast, native title tends to be difficult to prove. There are a number of reasons for this, relating to the nature of native title, the manner in which it is incorporated into Australian law, and the late recognition of its existence by Australian courts. This part considers some of the major hurdles faced by native title claimants.

To begin, native title cannot exist today unless it existed when Britain acquired sovereignty over the land to which it relates. Otherwise, the land would have been *terra nullius* and the Crown would have acquired full beneficial ownership of it. Native title could not arise later, because the Crown would already have a right to exclusive possession of the land and not merely radical title. Therefore, people claiming native title (called the plaintiffs here for convenience) must prove that:

1) .....they hold those property rights today, according to their traditional laws and customs;
2) .....indigenous people held those property rights when Britain acquired sovereignty over the land; and
3) .....they acquired those rights from those indigenous people.

Native Title Today

The first step is the easiest of the three and, yet, it is still more difficult than proving the existence of other property rights. As with all property rights, it is necessary to identify both the property rights and the thing subject to those rights. Therefore, the plaintiffs must identify the land and the nature of their rights to that land. As discussed above, they must also prove the existence of the legal system under which they hold those rights. In other words, the plaintiffs must show that they observe traditional laws and customs which recognise the property rights claimed.

Native Title When Britain Acquired Sovereignty

The second step can be very difficult and, if strict proof was required, would be impossible for most plaintiffs. In *Mabo (No 2)* the plaintiffs were able to show that, in 1879, the island of Mer was possessed by the Meriam people, according to their traditional laws and customs. Records of relevant events were kept by the London Missionary Society (which maintained an office on the island), representatives of the government of the Colony of Queensland, and others who visited the island.

For most Aboriginal Australians, the task is much more difficult. British sovereignty began much earlier (between 1788 and 1831, as discussed above) and records of land use by indigenous peoples at that time are scarcer and less detailed. That land use differed markedly from the forms of land use most familiar to British settlers. The property rights that existed did not resemble the common law of property (based on estates) and was often disregarded as non-existent.

Transfer of Native Title

The same difficulties can be encountered at the third step. Strictly speaking, the plaintiffs are trying to show that rights to land, which were held by indigenous people at the start of British sovereignty, have been transferred from generation to generation, according to the traditional laws and customs which regulate the transfer of property (and the additional rules imposed by the common law), and are now held by them.

For most other property rights, this process would be accomplished by producing a chain of title documents (such as transfers, mortgages, and wills) showing the right passing from one person to another. In contrast, most native title is communal and is transferred without using documents. Therefore, it is necessary to show, on the basis of available evidence, that the plaintiffs (as a group) hold native title that used to belong to a group of indigenous people at the time of British settlement.

The plaintiffs were able to accomplish this in *Mabo (No 2)*. Although, as Deane J and Gaudron said (at 115), "it is impossible to identify any precise system of title, any precise rules of inheritance or any precise methods of alienation ... there was undoubtedly a local native system" which allocated occupation of the land among individuals and family groups. The Meriam people, as a group, had possession of the island in 1879 and had possessed the land continuously ever since. There was no doubt that the plaintiffs had acquired the native title that existed in 1879.

For many Aboriginal Australians, it will be impossible to establish the transfer of native title, from past to present holders, with the same degree of certainty. Where native title is not a permanent possession, but the right to use land periodically for specific purposes, continuity of ownership is not readily apparent to an outside observer. While the Meriam people were left to enjoy their property rights with relatively little disturbance by other Australians, many Aboriginal people were trying to maintain their use of the land through periods of violent conflict. It is not surprising that the descent of native title cannot be tracked with precision through turbulent times in the absence of direct documentary evidence.

Level of Proof

Proof of native title is difficult because it is not sufficient to show that the plaintiffs currently hold property rights under their traditional laws and customs. They must also prove the continuous existence of those rights over a very long period of time. If the level of proof is set too high, this task would become impossible for most Aboriginal Australians who currently hold native title and that title would thereby be eliminated. Although their common law rights would exist in the abstract, they would have no substantial existence if they could not be enforced.

With this in mind, courts have been willing to draw inferences on the basis of circumstantial evidence. If the plaintiffs can meet the first step (of proving that they currently hold rights to land under their traditional laws and customs), courts will assume the necessary continuity of native title if the plaintiffs can also show that:

1) .....indigenous people were using the land in a similar fashion at some time before it became a British colony; and
2) .....the plaintiffs are the biological descendants of those indigenous people.

The fact that the plaintiffs currently hold certain rights under their traditional laws and customs, together with the fact that their ancestors used the land in a similar manner, is evidence that their ancestors held similar rights when Britain acquired sovereignty over the land. The similarity of use, biological connection, and continued existence of traditional laws and customs is evidence that those property rights have been passed from generation to generation to the plaintiffs.

In *Yarmirr v Northern Territory* (1998) 156 ALR 370, the plaintiffs established their claim to native title on the basis of their oral history and traditions, an anthropologists' report, and other historical records. From that evidence, Olney J was able (at 406) to "draw the inference" that the plaintiffs' ancestors were indigenous inhabitants of the land "prior to the acquisition of sovereignty in 1824 and that those ancestors and their descendants have inhabited the [land] continuously ever since".

In *Western Australia v Ward* (2000) 170 ALR 159, the court relied on oral histories, other historical records, and evidence given by anthropologists, an archeologist, and a linguist. It concluded (at 217) that the plaintiffs were:

> "a descendent community identifiable with the Aboriginal people in occupation of the [land] at sovereignty, and that the community has substantially maintained connection with the land by observing, as far as practicable, the traditional laws and customs of its predecessors as presently acknowledged and observed."

The requirement of biological descendent was not interpreted strictly to mean patrilineal descent. The plaintiffs' traditional laws and customs permitted membership in the community based on "a broad spread of links with ancestors" and this was, as Beaumont J and von Doussa J said (at 219), "sufficient proof of 'biological' connection between the present community and the community in occupation at the time of sovereignty".

The court also took a broad approach to the requirement that the Aboriginal people have maintained their connection with the land over that time. Physical presence on the land might be limited by factors beyond their control, such as the activities of European settlers. Beaumont J and von Doussa J said (at 222):

> "In circumstances where it is impracticable for the descendent community to continue a physical presence, it may nevertheless maintain its spiritual and cultural connection with the land in other ways."

Loss of Native Title

There are at least three ways in which native title might be lost. First, the Aboriginal people may have lost their connection with the land. Willingly or not, if they abandon their use of the land, it becomes *terra nullius* and the property of the Crown.

Secondly, the Aboriginal people might no longer observe the traditional laws and customs under which the native title existed. They cannot hold rights under a legal system which has ceased to exist for them and, if those rights do not exist, there is nothing that can be recognised by the common law. This does not mean that those laws and customs must remain constant. Like the common law, they will evolve over time and the nature of their rights to the land may be modified accordingly.

Thirdly, native title may have been extinguished or reduced if the Crown used its radical title to allocate the land to itself or others. If the government lawfully exercised its statutory authority to acquire beneficial ownership of the land or to grant a property right to another person, the new right will take priority over the native title. If there is any inconsistency between those rights, the native title will be reduced or eliminated accordingly. This is discussed further at page 395.

The Native Title Act

According to section 3 of the *Native Title Act* 1993 (Cth), one of its main objects is "to establish a mechanism for determining claims to native title". The preamble of the Act states that:

> "A special procedure needs to be available for the just and proper ascertainment of native title rights and interests which will ensure that, if possible, this is done by conciliation and, if not, in a manner that has due regard to their unique character."

The act provides rules for making applications to the Federal Court for a determination of whether native title exists in relation to certain land. These are intended to facilitate the processing of identifying existing native title in Australia. As the High Court noted, in *North Ganalanja Aboriginal Corp v Queensland* (1996) 185 CLR 595 at 614, this should benefit Aboriginal Australians, since "the task of tracing the tenure history of any parcel of land during the previous 200 years was likely to be beyond the resources of many would-be claimants". It should also meet the "perceived commercial need for despatch in the settlement of claims for native title and in the administrative disposition of applications by miners and others seeking access to unalienated land".

The *Native Title Act* 1993 (Cth) fulfils other important functions, including the protection of native title and the creation of mechanisms for validating previous government activity that was contrary to the *Racial Discrimination Act* 1975 (Cth) and for facilitating the future use of lands subject to native title. Some of these functions are discussed at page 399.

Part IV
Creation of Property Rights

Chapter Twenty

CREATING RIGHTS

III

The focus so far has been on the nature of property rights. Here begins a study of the ways in which those rights are created. The creation of several different property rights has already been discussed. As explained in Chapter 6, possession is acquired by taking control of a tangible thing with the intention to possess it. The creation of other rights (such as shared ownership, easements, and licences) is discussed in Part III whenever it helps explain the nature of those rights.

Property rights, like personal rights, are legal responses to particular events. Things happen which trigger those responses. In other words, the existence of certain facts will produce certain legal consequences. It is helpful to look at the creation of rights generally, before we consider the creation of property rights. This is followed by a brief introduction to the creation of trusts.

Creation of Rights

As discussed at the end of Chapter 5, the events which create rights can be organised into four categories: wrongs, consent, unjust enrichment, and others. Wrongs and consent are the most common sources of legal rights and obligations. Most law students begin their studies with events found in those categories: torts and contracts. Other sources of rights and obligations tend to be dispersed among many different subjects and studied piecemeal over several years. This makes it difficult to see and understand the structure of the common law.

Wrongs

Crime and torts are the wrongs most often in the news. Proof of crime gives the state the right to punish the criminal and can lead to the creation of rights for other persons by a court order that the criminal must compensate or return property to the victim. However, torts are the wrongs which most commonly create rights and obligations between private persons. For example, if I drive my car carelessly and injure you, I may have an obligation to compensate you for the loss I have caused. The negligent breach of my duty of care is a tort which creates your personal right to be paid a sum of money as damages.

There are many other torts (such as trespass and conversion, discussed in Chapter 7) and there are many wrongs which are not torts. For example, breach of confidence (discussed in Chapter 17) is an equitable wrong which can create a right to compensation or restitution. There are other equitable wrongs (such as breach of fiduciary duty) and statutory wrongs (such as unfair trade practices).

Consent

Contracts are the most common way to create rights by consent. We make them daily without much thought, whenever we buy something, such as a newspaper, train ticket, or cup of coffee. The law of contract concerns the creation and enforcement of binding promises. For example, if I agree to buy a book from you, our exchange of promises with the intention to create legal relations gives rise to a contract. This is an event in the second category (consent) which creates your personal right to be paid the agreed price. It also creates my personal right to receive a copy of the book and may, as discussed in the next chapter, create my property right to that book.

Rights and obligations can also be created by other forms of consent, such as gifts, declarations of trust, and wills.

Unjust Enrichment

At one time, the rights created by events other than wrongdoing or consent seemed to be little more than a jumble of common law and equitable doctrines. An important advance has been the recognition of unjust enrichment as a distinct category, which can be separated from the miscellany. It is now recognised that many different legal rights, such as the rights to recover money paid under duress or to rescind a contract obtained by misrepresentation, can be explained as restitution of unjust enrichment. For example, if you pay money to me by mistake, I may come under an obligation to repay that sum. You have a personal right to be paid which is generated neither by my wrongdoing nor by my consent to repay. The event creating your right is my unjust enrichment at your expense.

Other Events

There are also many rights created by events which belong in none of the first three categories. For example, the receipt of income by an Australian resident may give rise to an obligation to pay income tax according to the relevant taxation statute. The Australian Tax Office has a personal right to receive payment of the tax due, which cannot be explained as a response to wrongdoing, consent, or unjust enrichment. It flows from the exercise of Parliament's power to require residents to pay for the cost of government and belongs in the category of other events.

A large category of other events may seem unhelpful. However, any method of organising rights would require a residual category to catch things which do not belong elsewhere. This is true regardless of the number of categories used.

Importance of Taxonomy

Wrongs and consent are still, by far, the most common causes of legal rights. For many years, the dominance of those two categories caused lawyers and judges to overlook many other sources of legal rights. For example, it was once believed that the obligation to repay a mistaken payment was based on an implied promise to repay. Since reasonable people would repay money received by mistake, it was not unreasonable to imply a promise to do so.

That sort of reasoning leads to error and confusion. First, it can produce incorrect results in some cases. For example, a promise to repay cannot be implied if the money was received by a person who lacks the legal capacity to make such a promise. The recognition that this liability flows not from promises, but directly from unjust enrichment, corrects this error. Secondly, basing rights on fictional promises hides the real reasons for legal intervention. Taken to extremes, it could obscure almost any area of law, since reasonable people would agree to compensate others for the harm they have caused, to pay their taxes, to support their children, etc. Those rights do not depend on implied promises and it merely impedes legal analysis to pretend that they do.

There is a similar temptation to expand the category of wrongs to explain legal rights and obligations which do not fit in the two main categories. It is wrong not to keep a promise or not to refund money received by mistake. It is unconscionable not to let a de facto spouse share the value of the house which both worked to acquire. However, the failure to do something is wrong only if there is a duty to act. The wrong cannot be the source of that duty. If legal analysis reveals only the wrong, the real bases of those rights and obligations remain hidden.

It is generally agreed that a just system of law will treat like cases alike. Two different people, in similar situations, ought to receive similar legal treatment, unless there is some essential distinction between those situations which justifies different treatment. However, it is impossible to compare those situations intelligently if we do not know the bases for comparison. If we cannot identify, with precision, the events which create legal rights and obligations, irrelevant similarities can obscure essential differences and irrelevant differences can obscure essential similarities.

When presented with a long, complicated story, we need to be able to identify the relevant facts which attract legal intervention. In other words, what are the particular events which create legal rights? The answers to this question are the basic building blocks of the law. If those answers are not clear, the law lacks certainty and predictability and those bound to observe the law suffer. At the very least, this uncertainty will increase the cost and likelihood of litigation. At its worst, like cases are not treated alike and the law ceases to be just.

Creation of Property Rights

Unlike most personal rights, which spring from two main categories of events (wrongs and consent), most property rights are created by consent. Think of all the property rights you have (to a home, car, bicycle, clothes, dishes, books, etc). Almost all of them were obtained with the consent of other persons, by means of sales, gifts, leases, or bailments. A few may have been obtained in other ways. You may have possession of something you found, such as a coin on the ground or a shell on the beach. You may also have property rights to things you created, such as the copyright to a photograph or possession of a home baked desert.

The dominance of consent as the source of property rights means that they are rarely organised into the categories of wrongs, consent, unjust enrichment, and other events. Instead they are usually divided into two categories: those created by intention and those created by operation of law. In this context, "operation of law" means simply "events other than intention". Therefore, this dichotomy is a complete taxonomy of the events which create property rights. However, it does not help explain why property rights arise by operation of law. We need to know which events, other than intention, produce property rights.

Part IV makes use of the system of classifying personal rights into wrongs, consent, unjust enrichment, and other events. This has two great advantages. First, it begins the process of identifying and organising the sources of property rights which arise by operation of law. In other words, the events other than intention are subdivided to produce two new categories (wrongs and unjust enrichment) and a smaller miscellany. Secondly, the use of a taxonomy, which is familiar to lawyers working in other areas of law, enhances communication among various branches of law and makes it easier to compare property creating events with events which create personal rights and obligations.

Since (unlike personal rights) very few property rights are created by wrongdoing, the category of other events remains fairly large and needs to be explored further to see if any other categories of events can be recognised within that miscellany. Two further categories are identified and discussed in Part IV: detrimental reliance on expectations and physical changes to things. There is no separate chapter dealing with miscellaneous other events. However, the removal of four categories should leave behind a much smaller and more manageable category of other property rights arising by operation of law.

The chapters in Part IV reflect this taxonomy. Consent is the most important category of property creating events and is studied next in Chapter 21, "Intentional Transfers". Detrimental reliance, unjust enrichment, wrongdoing, and physical changes to things are studied in Chapters 23–26. Chapter 22, "Succession on Death", deals with the transfer of property rights in a particular situation: the death of the owner of those rights. As discussed in that chapter, the passing of property on death is governed both by the intention of the deceased person and a number of rules of law applicable to that situation.

Creation of Trusts

The traditional classification of trusts is based on the events which create them. The main categories are express, implied, resulting, constructive, and statutory. Unfortunately, this does not match the taxonomy used in the common law of obligations nor that which is applied to property rights generally. This may be because the trust is the creation of the court of chancery with no real counterpart at common law. There have been few attempts to align them with other personal or property rights, possibly because trusts involve a unique combination of both.

Rather than perpetuate the isolation of trusts, this book integrates them into the law of property as much as possible. Therefore, the creation of trusts is discussed in several chapters along with the events which create other property rights. Since **express trusts** are created by intention, they are discussed with other intentional transfers in Chapter 21. **Resulting trusts** are found in Chapter 24, which deals with unjust enrichment.

Constructive trusts are created by several different types of events and, therefore, are dispersed among several different chapters. The two main categories are detrimental reliance (discussed in Chapter 23) and profit from wrongdoing (in Chapter 25). Constructive trusts are also discussed in Chapters 21 (intentional transfers) and 22 (succession on death) for reasons of convenience. Since constructive trusts commonly arise when land is sold, it is best to discuss them in that context. Similarly, constructive trusts can affect the distribution of property on death and are also discussed in that context.

Statutory trusts and implied trusts are not discussed in this book. The former are created by statute to fulfil particular objectives of Parliament (such as priority in bankruptcy or the protection of consumers) and do not form a coherent subject of study on their own.

Implied trusts are excluded because that category has fallen into disuse. The term means different things to different people, so it was always necessary to provide further clarification whenever it was used. Some people used the term to describe trusts created by intention, where that intention was not clearly expressed, but could be implied from the circumstances. Other people used it to mean a trust implied by law and still others used it as a synonym for a resulting trust. Since every implied trust can be reclassified without difficulty as an express, constructive, or resulting trust, it is far better to avoid the term and the confusion it creates.

Chapter Twenty-One

INTENTIONAL TRANSFERS

III

Most property rights are created by consent. The main way in which someone acquires a property right is by receiving a transfer of that right from someone else. For example, your right to this book, whether borrowed or owned, was obtained with the consent of the person who loaned, sold, or gave it to you. Your property right arose because the person who previously had that right intended to transfer it to you and took the steps necessary to give effect to that intention.

There is an important difference between wanting to transfer a property right and actually transferring that right. The intention is necessary, but not sufficient to cause that right to pass. Something else must occur to give effect to that intention. Suppose that I want to give you a book for your birthday. Wanting to give a book to you will not get you a property right. Neither will buying the book, gift wrapping it, putting a card on it, and telling you I got the book for you. As discussed below, the gift is completed by delivery of possession coupled with an intention to give.

The method which must be used to transfer a property right depends primarily upon two factors: the nature of the right involved and the nature of the thing subject to that right. It also depends on whether the transfer is between living persons (***inter vivos***) or is intended to take effect on the transferor's death (**testamentary**). *Inter vivos* transactions are discussed in this chapter and testamentary dispositions are the subject of the next.

This chapter is divided into five main sections:

1).....intentional transfers of legal property rights;
2).....intentional transfers of equitable property rights;
3).....specific performance of contracts to transfer property rights;
4).....vendors' and purchasers' liens; and
5).....incomplete gifts.

The first two sections deal with the steps needed to give effect to an intention to transfer a property right. The remaining three sections concern equitable property rights which may arise by operation of law during the course of a transaction involving an intentional transfer of legal property rights. For example, there is often a long delay between the sale of a house and the date on which legal title to the house will pass from vendor to purchaser. As discussed below, the purchaser usually acquires an equitable property right to the house when the contract is made and the vendor may have an equitable property right after the title passes. Although these rights are not created directly by intention and could be dealt with in other chapters, they are so closely connected to intentional transfers of legal property rights that it seemed better to discuss them here.

Legal Property Rights

This section concerns the creation of legal property rights only and, therefore, paints an incomplete picture of intentional transfers of property. As discussed below, many of these transactions involve the creation of equitable property rights. Also, it sometimes happens that a failed attempt to transfer a legal property right will create an equitable property right or personal right. Still, it is helpful to begin by focussing separately on the creation of legal property rights. The important distinctions between legal and equitable rights, and between personal and property rights, make it essential that we know which events create which sort of rights.

Formalities

The common law tends (more than equity) to insist that all necessary formalities are observed before a property right can be created. A great number of cases are concerned with attempts to create legal property rights which failed because the parties did not jump through all the hoops necessary to create the intended right. In contrast, most personal rights can be created relatively informally. For example, a contract to perform services or to pay a very large sum of money can be created over the telephone.

The common law's insistence on formalities is justified by the nature of property rights. While personal rights correspond only to obligations placed on specific individuals, property rights generate general duties of non-interference imposed on all members of society. Since property rights can affect many more people than those who entered into the transaction in question, they ought to be generated by events which are easily proven and observable.

Methods of Transferring Legal Property Rights

As mentioned above, the method of transferring a property right depends on the nature of the right and the nature of the thing subject to that right. There are four main ways in which legal property rights are transferred:

1) .....**delivery** of the thing;
2) .....a **document** transferring the right;
3) .....a **contract** for the sale of the thing; and
4) .....**registration** of a document transferring the right.

Not all methods can be used with all rights or all things. The appropriate method for transferring a legal property right varies with the nature of the thing being transferred. Therefore, the discussion of these methods is divided into four parts, according to the four main categories of things:

1) .....goods;
2) .....money;
3) .....intangible personal property; and
4) .....land.

Goods

As discussed in Chapter 5, goods are those things which can be possessed, other than land and money. The three main ways to transfer legal property rights to goods are delivery, document, and contract.

Delivery

The most common way to transfer a property right to goods is by delivery of possession, coupled with the intention to transfer that right. The transferor's intention defines the right and the transfer of possession gives effect to that intention. Suppose, for example, that I give you a book for your birthday and, on that same day, you borrow a book from the library. Possession of both books was delivered to you and yet your property rights to those books are not the same. You have ownership of the birthday gift and only a temporary right to possession (a bailment) of the library book. The act of delivery was the same in both cases, but the intentions of the transferors were different: I intended a gift and the library intended a loan.

For the intended property right to pass, delivery of possession and the intention to transfer the property right must coincide. If either is missing, the intended right will not pass. This does not mean that the intention to transfer the property right must exist at the moment of delivery. All that is required is that the intended recipient has possession of the goods at a time when the transferor has the intention to transfer. It does not matter whether delivery occurs before or after the intention to transfer the property right is formed.

For example, in *Re Stoneham* [1919] 1 Ch 149, the plaintiff had possession of his grandfather's furniture for two years before his grandfather said he could keep it. The gift was effective, without a separate act of delivery, because the donee's possession coincided with the donor's intention to give. As Lawrence J said (at 154), the gift would be complete "where chattels have been delivered to the donee before the gift as bailee or in any other capacity, so long as they are actually in his possession at the time of the gift to the knowledge of the donor".

The events occurred in reverse order in *Thomas v Times Book Co* [1966] 2 All ER 241. Dylan Thomas lost his original manuscript of *Under Milk Wood* and told a BBC producer that he could have it if he could find it. The gift was complete when the producer later found the manuscript in a pub. Since Thomas was still alive and had not revoked the gift, his intention to give continued until the producer obtained possession.

When an attempt to transfer legal property rights to goods fails, it is often because there is a problem with delivery. In other words, the disputed issue is whether the recipient obtained possession of the goods in question. As discussed in Chapter 6, possession requires both control of the thing and an intention to possess it. If the transferor intends to transfer and the recipient intends to receive, then the issue boils down to whether the recipient obtained control. This depends on whether the intended recipient was able to exclude others, including the transferor, from the thing. This, in turn, depends on the nature of the thing and how it is controlled.

For example, suppose you visit my house and, as we are sitting in the lounge, I point to a book across the room and say "You can have that book". Since I have possession of the house, I also have possession of its contents: see Chapter 6. Possession (and ownership) of the book will not pass until you take control of it and my possession will continue until that happens. This example becomes slightly more complicated if we also assume that you and I live together in the house. Since we both have possession of the house, we both control access to, and have possession of, many things inside the house. Is your shared control of the book sufficient to cause legal ownership to pass to you?

This issue was addressed in *Re Cole* [1964] Ch 175. In 1945, a husband leased a mansion and spent £20,000 furnishing it. He took his wife to the mansion, showed her around the rooms, and told her it was all hers. They lived together in the mansion until 1961, when the husband became bankrupt. The furnishings still belonged to the husband (and could be sold to pay his creditors) because he never ceased to have possession. It was not enough that the wife also had possession. In order to complete the gift, she had to have possession which excluded her husband. The result should have been different if the husband had ceased to reside in the home at a time when he still intended to give the furnishings to his wife.

This rule (that delivery is not complete until the donor relinquishes possession) reduces the risk of people fraudulently hiding assets from their creditors. Such fraud would be easy if a bankrupt could say that goods he or she purchased and still possessed had been given away. The transfer of possession provides some evidence of the intention to give. It can also help prove when the gift was made. The date when legal title passes can be relevant for a number of reasons, including insurance, taxation, and the limitation of actions: see Chapter 8. It is also important if the donor becomes bankrupt, because a gift made shortly before the bankruptcy can be recovered by the trustee in bankruptcy.

Document

There are times when delivery is not a suitable method of transferring legal property rights to goods. Another method might be dictated by statute. For example, a ship registered under the *Shipping Registration Act 1981* (Cth) "shall be transferred by a bill of sale made in accordance with the regulations": s 36. Usually, delivery is unsuitable because the transferor wants to transfer legal ownership but not possession (as in *Re Cole*, above). Also, if the goods are exceptionally valuable, the recipient may wish for better evidence of ownership than a transfer of possession. In these situations, it is advisable or necessary to use a document to cause legal title to pass. There are two main types: a **deed** and a **bill of sale**.

Deeds are most commonly used in connection with transfers of land or the creation of trusts (both discussed below). However, it is possible to make an effective gift of goods by deed. This may be advisable where delivery is awkward, the goods are valuable, or other circumstances (like hungry relatives) indicate that the gift might be contested. Not every document is a deed and, therefore, merely writing a letter announcing the intention to give will not cause legal title to pass. A deed must be signed and sealed by the donor and delivered to the donee. Since deeds are seldom used in connection with goods, these formal requirements are discussed below in relation to transfers of land.

A bill of sale is a way to sell goods and, as discussed at page 120, can be used to create a security right to goods (which might be called a **chattel mortgage**). The execution of the document causes legal ownership to pass to the buyer or creditor. When used to create a security right, legal ownership of the goods is held as security for the performance of a personal obligation (usually the payment of a debt). Normally, the debtor retains possession of the goods and, therefore, delivery is not a useful method of transferring title to the creditor. The debtor continues to be the beneficial owner of the goods and is entitled to recover legal title when the secured debt is paid.

Most jurisdictions require that bills of sale, chattel mortgages, and other security rights to personal property be registered. Registration is designed to reduce the potential for fraud by debtors who have possession and apparent ownership of chattels they do not own. Creditors have a strong incentive to register, since unregistered bills of sale (and similar documents) are unenforceable against others who later acquire property rights to the goods: see, eg, *Bills of Sale Act* 1898 (NSW), s 4.

Contract of Sale

Like most common law jurisdictions, every state and territory in Australia has a *Goods Act* or *Sale of Goods Act*, which is patterned after the English *Sale of Goods Act* 1893. That statute was more or less a codification of the existing common law on the subject (sometimes called the **law merchant**). These statutes deal with a number of issues, such as the time for payment and the warranties provided by the seller. We are concerned here only with the passing of property rights to goods and not with these other aspects of contracts of sale.

Most intentional transfers of property happen pursuant to contract. Therefore, it is easy to forget that there is an important distinction between a contract to transfer property and the transfer itself. In many transactions, the contract creates an enforceable promise to transfer a property right and the transfer is a separate act done in fulfilment of that promise. This is true of most contracts to sell land and many contracts to sell goods.

There are many other transactions in which the making of the contract is the event which causes legal title to pass to the buyer. For example, when I go to the milk bar to buy milk, the ownership of the milk will pass to me when I take it to the shopkeeper and our contract of sale is made. The contract creates my legal property right. A separate act, such as delivery or the execution of a document, is not required to give effect to the shopkeeper's intention to transfer her or his property right to me.

In each state or territory, the *Goods Act* or *Sale of Goods Act* provides rules for the passing of property on a sale of goods. It states that no formalities (such as writing or witnesses) are required to make a contract for the sale of goods. The passing of property from seller to buyer depends primarily on whether the goods are **ascertained** or **unascertained**. In other words, do the parties know precisely which goods are being sold? For example, if you make a contract to buy six tins of paint from a shop which owns many more tins of that same type of paint, it is impossible to say which tins are to be sold unless they are identified in some way. Until that occurs (when they are separated from the bulk or labelled) the contract relates to **unascertained goods** and property rights to the paint cannot pass to you.

Goods might be unascertained because they do not exist yet or because the seller does not yet own them. For example, the paint shop might have to mix the paint and fill the tins or it might have to order the paint from a supplier. In these situations, the contract is for the sale of **future goods**. They are unascertained and property cannot pass until they are acquired by the seller and ascertained.

If the goods are **specific goods** (which are identified when the contract is made) or **ascertained goods** (which are identified later), the property passes from buyer to seller when the parties intend. That intention is gleaned from "the terms of the contract, conduct of the parties, and the circumstances of the case": *Sale of Goods Act* 1895 (SA), s 17.

The statutes provide several rules for ascertaining the parties' intentions in the absence of evidence to the contrary. First, if there is an unconditional contract for the sale of specific goods in a deliverable state, property passes when the contract is made, even if payment or delivery is postponed.

Secondly, if the seller has to do something to put the goods in a deliverable state, property passes when that is done and notice is given to the buyer. Notice can be given in advance. For example, the seller might say, "It will be ready on Thursday".

Thirdly, when goods are unconditionally appropriated to the contract, with the consent of the both parties, the property passes. For example, suppose you go to a lumber yard, pay for some wood, and go into the yard where a worker fills order. The goods are unascertained when the contract is made and ownership of the wood does not pass to you until you and the worker (as the seller's agent) select particular pieces of wood and thereby appropriate them to the contract.

These statutory rules, regulating the transfer of ownership on a sale of goods, apply only if the parties have not come to some other agreement. The contract governs and the statute merely fills in matters left unspecified by the parties.

Money

What is Money?

Money is unique in the law of property. It is the medium of exchange and the measure of value. The rules relating to the transfer of property rights to money are special to allow it to fulfil its function as **currency**.

Normally, there is nothing intrinsically valuable about the paper notes or metal coins themselves. Actually, money may lose its utility as a form of currency if the value of the thing (such as the silver in a coin) exceeds the value it represents. Money differs from other paper forms of value (such as share certificates, bills of exchange, or cheques) because money is not a chose in action: see Chapter 5. In other words, its value as a currency is not because it represents other personal or property rights.

People often fail to differentiate between money (as currency) and money in the bank. As discussed in Chapter 2, a bank account in credit is merely a personal claim against a bank to be paid a sum of money (in other words, the bank's debt to its customer). When you write a cheque, you are instructing your bank to act as your agent to pay a sum of money to another. The distinction between these forms of value and actual money (notes and coins) is important.

Notes and coins cease to be currency when they are no longer accepted as **legal tender** for the payment of debts. They might be replaced by new designs or simply discontinued (like the Australian penny) and cease to be a form of currency. Money which is not used as currency becomes goods for the purposes of the law of property. Notes and coins which become collectibles can be sold, traded, or given away like other goods. It is possible for money to be currency or goods, depending on how it is traded. For example, you might purchase a commemorative set of new coins. Although each coin in the set is legal tender and could be used as currency, it is more valuable if it is kept in mint condition as part of the set. If you choose to sell the coins, it is likely that you will sell the set as goods to another collector, rather than break it up and spend the coins at the milk bar as currency.

Transfer of Money

When used as currency, the ownership of money passes on delivery. Although most notes and coins are delivered as payment due under a contract, it is not the contract which causes ownership of the money to pass, but the transfer of possession.

It is possible for possession of money to pass without a transfer of ownership. For example, if I ask you to hold my wallet while I go swimming, I am still the owner of the wallet and the few notes it may contain, even though you have possession of the wallet and those notes. Although I delivered the notes to you, I did not intend to make a gift. Similarly, if a thief steals my wallet, he or she obtains possession of the wallet and its contents, but not ownership. I am still the legal owner of the money and could assert my property rights if ever the money could be found and identified. I did not intend to transfer ownership to the thief and it does not pass.

In neither of these examples was the money used as currency. As with goods, delivery did not cause ownership to pass because the owner did not intend to give. However, unlike goods, the ownership of money passes very easily when it is used as currency and can pass even without the owner's knowledge or consent. The thief who stole my wallet does not own my money. However, if he or she spends it at a shop, my ownership will pass directly to the shopkeeper, even though I know nothing of the transaction and do not want it to happen. If the thief used one of my $20 notes to purchase a loaf of bread for $2, the shopkeeper is the owner of that note and the thief is the owner of the bread and the $18 in change (since the $18 worth of notes and coins belonged to the shopkeeper, who intended to transfer ownership to the thief).

Although this result may seem hard on the victims of theft, it is essential if money is to fulfil its function as currency. People would be unwilling to accept cash payments if they had to investigate whether the person making payment actually owned the notes and coins tendered. Recipients need not worry about obtaining ownership of the money, so long as they are **bona fide purchasers for value without notice**. In other words, so long as they do not know or suspect that the money is stolen, and give value in return for the payment, ownership will pass on delivery regardless of the payer's right to spend it. This issue is discussed further in Chapter 28, concerning the priority of legal property rights.

Intangible Personal Property

Intangibles (by definition) cannot be possessed and, therefore, cannot be transferred by delivery. Documents are used to deal with, and provide evidence of, property rights to intangible things. There are two ways in which intangible personal property rights are transferred:

1).....by a document assigning the right; or
2).....by registration of such a document.

Document

The usual way to transfer an intangible property right is by **assignment**. This is simply the express transfer of the right to another. Normally, it is accomplished by execution of a document. The formalities required depend on the nature of the right being transferred. For example, an "assignment of a patent must be in writing signed by or on behalf of the assignor and assignee": *Patents Act* 1990 (Cth), s 14.

As discussed at page 41, a chose in action may be either a property right to an intangible thing or a personal right. Both types can be assigned to others. Since personal rights correspond to obligations of specific persons, the assignment of such a right requires that notice of the assignment be given to the person with the corresponding obligation. There are many cases involving competing assignments of the same personal rights and the question of who gave notice first.

Some forms of intangible property rights are initially created by documents issued by government officials. This is true of both patents and plant breeder's rights: see Chapter 17. For example, section 44(10) of the *Plant Breeder's Rights Act* 1994 states that a "PBR is granted to a person by the issue to that person by the Secretary of a certificate in an approved form, signed by the Secretary or the Registrar, containing such particulars of the plant variety concerned as the Secretary considers appropriate".

Registration

There is an important distinction between transfer by registration and transfer by another act (such as an assignment) which is protected by registration. The latter is far more common. In most cases, legal title passes when the assignment or other document is executed and the new owner then registers that document to protect the priority of her or his new right. In some cases, registration is the event which causes legal title to pass.

The normal way to transfer legal title to corporate shares is by registration of the transfer in the corporation's register of shareholders. Of course, this may be awkward if the shares are actively traded through a stock exchange. In Australia, corporations can apply to have the Securities Clearing House look after the transfer and registration of their shares through the Clearing House Electronic Subregister System (CHESS). This is governed by the Listing Rules of the Australian Stock Exchange.

Land

There are two main ways in which legal property rights to land are transferred: by deed and by registration. It is also possible for some legal property rights to be created merely by a transfer of possession. It is helpful to consider the historical development of methods of transferring land, which evolved from simple transfers of possession, to the use of deeds, and then to registration.

Livery of Seisin

Freehold estates used to be transferred by **livery of seisin**. Roughly translated into modern English, this means delivery of possession. As discussed in Chapter 12, a person with an estate (whether freehold or leasehold) has a right to possession of land. However, where that estate is a freehold, we say that he or she is seised of the estate or has seisin.

Livery of seisin used to be a public ceremony on the land, in which there was a symbolic delivery of possession by handing over a branch or a clod of earth in the presence of witnesses. This served an evidentiary purpose. If a dispute concerning ownership of the land arose, it could be settled with the help of neighbours who were familiar with the events. A transfer of a freehold estate by livery of seisin was called a **feoffment**. The transferor was the **feoffor** and the recipient was the **feoffee**, who was **enfeoffed** following the ceremony.

There were three main drawbacks to livery of seisin as a method of transferring land. First, it was inconvenient. If two people in London wanted to deal in land in Manchester, it meant that they both had to go there to close the deal. The feoffor could not simply say, "I'll have my people send a clump of dirt to your office in the morning". Secondly, it did not provide reliable proof of title. A person's property rights might depend on a feoffment that took place many long years ago. It could be a problem having to rely on the memories of witnesses to the event, who grew old and died. Thirdly, since livery of seisin was a public ceremony, people could not keep their land dealings confidential.

To deal with these problems, the law slowly developed other forms of conveyancing. The first change was the introduction of documents. In the 17th century, the law required documentary evidence of livery of seisin, called a **charter of feoffment**. This did not replace livery of seisin, but was an extra requirement designed to provide more reliable proof of title.

This change did not solve the problems of inconvenience and publicity, so lawyers devised ways to get around the requirement of livery of seisin. The most popular method was called a **lease and release**. The seller could lease the land to the buyer and then execute a deed which released the landlord's reversion to the tenant. In this way the buyer would end up with the fee simple estate without a public ceremony on the land. The buyer had to take possession of the land to begin the lease, but lawyers soon found a way around this requirement. After the *Statute of Uses* 1536 (discussed at page 112), a **bargain and sale** of a leasehold estate would produce a legal leasehold estate without the tenant having to take possession of the land. On execution of a contract for the sale of a lease, the seller would hold that estate to the use of the buyer. The *Statute of Uses* would execute the use, thereby giving the buyer the legal lease. Combining a bargain and sale with a lease and release enabled lawyers to quietly transfer freehold estates using only documents.

Deed

In England, all the old forms of transferring legal property rights to land were replaced by one method: a grant of land by deed. This change is found in the English *Property Law Act* 1925 and has been copied in most common law jurisdictions. For example, section 51 of the *Property Law Act* 1958 (Vic) states:

> "All lands and all interests therein shall lie in grant and shall be incapable of being conveyed by livery or livery and seisin, or by feoffment, or by bargain and sale; and a conveyance of an interest in land may operate to pass the possession or right to possession thereof without actual entry, but subject to all prior rights thereto."

Although this suggests that a deed is the only method of creating legal property rights to land, this is not true. It is not even the primary method. Most privately owned land in Australia is registered in a Torrens system, in which most legal property rights are created by registration. For land not in that system, legal property rights are created by deed. It is also possible to create legal property rights, without deed or registration, simply by taking possession of land. Registration and possession are discussed below.

Not every document is a deed. At common law, a deed must be made in writing on paper (or vellum or parchment), signed and sealed by the grantor and delivered to the grantee. Deeds usually contain the words, "signed, sealed, and delivered by", just above the signature of the grantor. This is written evidence that the deed was properly signed, sealed, and delivered, which the grantor is not normally permitted to contradict. People rarely, if ever, use wax seals any more. These have been replaced by self-adhesive legal seals which the grantor will place next to her or his signature. Even these are no longer required in most jurisdictions. It is enough that the deed states that it is sealed: see, eg, *Property Law Act* 1974 (Qld), s 45. Most corporations continue to execute formal documents by embossing the corporate seal next to the signature of the appropriate signing officer.

Requirement of Writing

A major development in property law was the enactment of the English *Statute of Frauds* in 1677. It required that dealings with land be made in or evidenced by writing (and, as discussed in the next chapter, that wills be made with certain formalities). That statute is in force or has been copied in common law jurisdictions around the world. A typical example is section 34 of the *Property Law Act* 1969 (WA), which states that "no interest in land is capable of being created or disposed of except by writing signed by the person creating or conveying the interest, or by his agent".

At first glance, it may appear that this requirement of writing is redundant in a legal system which also requires that legal property rights be granted by deed or registration of a document. However, the writing requirement inherited from the *Statute of Frauds* applies to all intentionally created property rights to land, including equitable property rights. Deeds or registration are only needed for the creation of legal property rights.

There are several important exceptions to the requirement that property rights to land be created by writing, including informal leases, adverse possession, the doctrine of "part performance", and trusts arising by operation of law. These exceptions are discussed below in this and subsequent chapters.

Registration

There are two main types of land registration systems operating in Australia: the deeds registration system and the Torrens system. These are discussed in more detail in Part VI. They operate in fundamentally different ways. In a deeds system, legal property rights are created by deeds and the priorities of those rights are protected by registration of those deeds. In a Torrens system, legal property rights are, with few exceptions, created by the registration of documents. This difference is important: it is not the execution of documents, but their registration, which creates legal property rights to Torrens land.

In every Torrens statute, there is a statement to the effect that documents "shall not be effectual to pass any estate or interest in registered land" until they are registered: *Land Titles Act* 1980 (Tas), s 49. This has been interpreted by the courts to refer only to legal property rights. Therefore, equitable property rights to Torrens land are created in the same manner as they were before the introduction of the Torrens system. They arise and exist without the need for registration. It is also possible for short leases (up to three years) and easements to exist as unregistered legal property rights.

The Torrens statutes prescribe the forms of the documents which can be registered. The main forms are a transfer of land, a lease, and a mortgage. Most statutes do not prescribe special forms for creating other registered property rights, such as easements and profits à prendre. Therefore, the form of transfer of land is used to create freehold estates and other legal property rights except leases and mortgages.

Short leases cannot be registered in many Torrens systems. This is a practical limitation which prevents land titles registers from being overwhelmed by requests to register the massive number of short term and periodic residential and commercial tenancies created daily across Australia. The Torrens statutes do not provide a method for creating short leases of Torrens land, so the methods used outside the Torrens system still apply. Short legal leases can be created by deed or informally and, as discussed below, equitable leases can be created by contract.

Possession

As discussed in Part II, a person who takes possession of land thereby acquires a property right. Her or his right to possession is enforceable against everyone except someone with a better right to possession. No formalities are required. Possession without the consent of those who have a right to immediate possession is **adverse possession**: discussed in Chapter 8. Where possession is obtained by consent, it is a legal estate. At a minimum, the possessor will be a **tenant at will**. However, he or she may have a greater estate.

Legal freehold estates and leasehold estates longer than three years can only be created by registration or deed. Legal leases of three years or less can be created by deed, but can also be created without writing. The common law allowed for the informal creation of short leases to reflect the reality that many people take possession of land under informal arrangements.

An informal lease for a fixed term up to three years is possible if the rent is set at full market value. Otherwise (or in the absence of proof of that fact), the tenant will have at best a periodic tenancy, with the period depending in part on the usual practices in the area. In the absence of evidence to the contrary, agricultural leases are assumed to be annual and other leases are assumed to match the frequency of payment of rent: see *Dockrill v Cavanagh* (1944) 45 SR (NSW) 78.

Equitable Property Rights

The intentional creation of equitable property rights involves the same two basic questions discussed above in relation to legal rights: did the transferor intend to create that right and did he or she take the steps necessary to give effect to that intention. As with legal property rights, the steps needed to transfer an equitable property right depend upon the nature of the right and the nature of the thing subject to that right.

The previous discussion, of the creation of legal property rights, was organised according to the nature of the thing. This section is organised according to the nature of the right. It begins with the formalities required for the intentional creation of all types of equitable property rights and then focuses on each of the three main types: trusts, equitable charges, and restrictive covenants.

Formalities

As a general rule, the creation of an equitable property right requires less formality than does the creation of the equivalent legal right. This increases the risk that people dealing with things will be unaware of property rights affecting those things and may seem to run counter to the policy of the common law. However, the lower level of formality is acceptable because equitable rights are less durable than legal rights. As discussed in Part V, they are less likely to affect people who buy things for value without notice of those rights. One advantage of this difference between common law and equity is that people who deal informally with others, and fail to acquire any legal property rights, may thus obtain a less durable equitable property right (which is better than nothing at all).

Writing is usually required for the intentional creation of equitable property rights in three situations:

1) .....testamentary dispositions (discussed in the next chapter);
2) .....property rights to land; and
3) .....the transfer of existing equitable property rights.

In most other situations, no special formalities need be observed.

Deeds are often used to create equitable property rights, but are not necessary. For example, express trusts are often created by deed, whether writing is required or not. Even where writing is required to create an enforceable equitable property right (such as an express trust of land or a restrictive covenant), it does not have to be a deed. There need only be written evidence of its creation, signed by its creator. A typical example of this requirement is section 29 of the *Law of Property Act* 1936 (SA), which states that "a declaration of trust respecting any land or any interest therein must be manifested and proved by some writing signed by some person who is able to declare such trust".

Strictly speaking, an express trust is created not by the execution of a document, but by the settlor's declaration of trust (which may be, and usually is, made in writing). Where a document is required, it is merely a written manifestation of the declaration. Therefore, a trust of land could be declared orally, but it would be unenforceable until that declaration was confirmed in writing. This differs from the creation of legal property rights to land, where the execution of a deed or registration of a document is the property creating event.

The requirement that trusts of land be manifest in writing is not surprising. People expect a certain level of formality when dealing with land. They can be surprised, however, by the requirement that a transfer of any existing equitable property right be made in writing, whether or not it relates to land. Section 11 of the *Property Law Act* 1974 (Qld) states that "a disposition of an equitable interest or trust subsisting at the time of the disposition, must be manifested and proved by some writing signed by the person disposing of the same, or by his agent". Other jurisdictions require that the disposition itself be made in writing.

This requirement can have unexpected results because it is not limited to equitable property rights to land: see *Adamson v Hayes* (1973) 130 CLR 276. For example, I can create a trust of a book for you without formality, simply by manifesting an intention to create that trust. However, if you want to transfer your new equitable property right to your sister, you must do so in writing. This mismatch, between informal creation and formal transfer, is odd. I could create the trust by telling you casually that I hold the book in trust for you, but you should not be equally casual when you ask me to hold it in trust for your sister.

Why does the law require that a transfer of an existing equitable property right be manifest in writing, if that right can be created without it? This may be designed for the protection of trustees. The duties of express trustees are onerous and they can be strictly liable to compensate their beneficiaries if they transfer trust assets to the wrong persons. Therefore, to alleviate the problem of competing claims by supposed beneficiaries, the law requires that a transfer of an existing equitable property right be manifest in writing and signed by the transferor: see *Vandervell v Inland Revenue Commissioners* [1967] 2 AC 291.

This rule also applies to the assignment of equitable charges. Although debtors are not subject to the same duties as express trustees, they do want to be sure they are paying the right creditors. The writing requirement helps debtors to avoid or resolve dispute among competing claimants to the same charge.

Express Trusts

All express trusts are created by declaration of the settlor. The settlor is the person who owns or controls the assets which will become the **subject** of the trust, decides to create the trust, and chooses the **objects** of the trust, which can be people (beneficiaries) or purposes. The creation of an express trust is often called a **trust settlement**. It is done in one of two ways:

1)......the settlor can declare herself or himself to be the trustee of assets for the intended beneficiary of the trust; or
2)......the settlor can transfer assets to the intended trustee to hold in trust for the intended beneficiary.

As discussed at page 109, all trusts require certainty of both subject and object. In other words, a trust cannot exist unless it is known exactly what assets are held in trust and for whom (or for what purposes). There are three other requirements for the creation of an express trust:

1)......the settlor intended to create a trust (certainty of intention);
2)......the settlor expressed that intention properly (the formal requirements discussed above); and
3)......the trustee obtained title to the trust assets (constitution of the trust).

The language used to discuss the creation of express trusts differs from that used in other areas of property law. People often talk of the **three certainties** (of intention, subject, and object) and properly constituted trusts. However, this special terminology can be boiled down to the two essential questions which should be asked of any attempt to create a property right: did the settlor really intend to create a trust and did he or she do everything necessary to give effect to that intention?

Certainty of Intention

There is no magic in the word "trust". People can create trusts without using that word and can use it without creating a trust. People can even create trusts without realising that a trust is being created. The important issue is whether the settlor intended to create the relationship which equity recognises as a trust.

This flexibility can make it difficult to tell whether a trust has been created, especially where the assets are personal rights or personal property and writing is not required. This is compounded by the fact that "trust" is both a legal term of art and a word commonly used in ordinary conversations. For example, if I die and leave $5,000 to you in my will, "trusting that you will support the home for lost dogs and cats", have I created a trust? In other words, did I intend to impose a binding obligation on you regarding the use of the money? Probably not, but my poor choice of words has placed the matter in doubt and it may be necessary for a court to look over my entire will for clues to my intention.

The creation of an express trust brings new property rights into being and places the trustees under onerous duties of care and loyalty. Therefore, courts of equity are reluctant to say that a trust has been created unless they are certain that the settlor did in fact intend to create it. This is the requirement of certainty of intention, which is sometimes referred to as **certainty of words**. The latter expression is misleading since a trust can be created without any words if it is clear from the circumstances that it was intended.

The creation of the trust depends on the intention of the settlor and not on the intentions of the trustees or beneficiaries. An express trust can be created even though the trustees and beneficiaries are unaware of its existence. The intended trustees are free to decline that office and will not have any duties to perform until they accept it. The beneficiaries are also free to disclaim their interests in the trust. However, their knowledge and acceptance are not needed to bring the trust into being.

Constitution of Trusts

All trusts must be properly constituted, which means that the trustees must have title to the subject matter of the trust. For example, if I want Ian to be a trustee of a book for Lisa and manifest that intention properly, the trust cannot come into existence until Ian gets title to the book. The trust exists because Ian has a right which a court of equity says must be used for Lisa's benefit. Unless Ian has the right which will be the subject of the trust (ownership or at least possession of the book), he cannot be compelled to do anything for Lisa. An intended trust is said to be **incompletely constituted** until the trustee gets title to the trust property.

There are two situations in which the constitution of the trust is never a problem. The first is where the settlor declares herself or himself to be a trustee for another. For example, if I declare that I hold my car in trust for you, the trust will be constituted when I make the declaration, since I already own the car. I am both settlor and trustee and will change hats when the declaration is made.

Secondly, constitution is not a problem for testamentary trusts, discussed in the next chapter. The settlor will create the trust and appoint the trustees in her or his will. On the settlor's death, the ownership of the trust assets will pass to her or his personal representatives, who will have a duty to transfer them to the trustees when the estate is distributed. This ensures that the assets will be transferred from settlor to trustees when the time comes.

Constitution is a potential problem only where a trust is to be created *inter vivos* by a transfer of assets from settlor to trustee. Normally, the settlor will transfer the assets to the trustee when the declaration of trust is made. However, the transfer might not take place as intended if the settlor fails to take the steps needed to cause legal title to pass. For example, in *Corin v Patton* (1990) 169 CLR 540, a dying woman wanted to create a trust of Torrens land, with her brother as trustee. The transfer document and trust deed were executed and handed to her solicitor. Unfortunately, the transfer could not be registered before she died, because the bank had possession of the duplicate certificate of title: see page 449. Therefore, the brother never received legal title to the land and the trust was never constituted.

In some cases, a failure to constitute a trust can be cured by a court of equity. If the settlor made a contractual promise to create the trust and that contract is specifically enforceable, then a mechanism exists to constitute the trust. The specific performance of the contract (discussed below) will cause ownership of the trust assets to be transferred from settlor to trustee. However, most trusts are created as gifts for the beneficiaries and, therefore, this solution is not normally available.

Where a promise to create the trust is not specifically enforceable, it may be possible to achieve the same result with a constructive trust. If the intended beneficiaries had a reasonable expectation that they would receive an interest in the trust assets, and relied on that expectation to their detriment, then a trust might be raised by operation of law to fulfil that expectation. This is discussed in Chapter 23.

Equitable Charges

The creation of equitable charges involves the same issues as the creation of express trusts. This is not surprising since both are equitable property rights created by intention. The primary difference between them is that a charge is a security right (discussed in Chapter 14), while a trust is beneficial ownership. A secondary difference is that most trusts are created as gifts, while most charges are created pursuant to contract (to secure performance of an obligation to pay a debt). A third and important difference is that most charges need to be registered to preserve their priority over competing property rights.

The creation of equitable charges is discussed separately from express trusts because the language used is different. People never talk of the three certainties in relation to equitable charges and yet the same issues are taken before the courts: did the debtor intend to create a charge, what assets are subject to the charge, and for whose benefit was the charge created? No one talks of the constitution of a charge even though the same issue arises when a charge is granted in relation to assets yet to be received by the debtor.

Intention to Create a Charge

All equitable charges (like express trusts) are created by the intention of the person who holds the personal or property right which will be subject to that charge. This distinguishes charges from liens, which (like resulting and constructive trusts) are created by operation of law. As with express trusts, there is no special formula for the creation of a charge.

All that is required is that the holder of a right intends to use it as security for the performance of a personal obligation.

Giving Effect to that Intention

The intention to create a charge can be manifested in a variety of ways. Although it is usually set out in a document, writing is only required to charge land or testamentary gifts or to transfer an existing equitable charge (as discussed above). It is also possible to charge land without writing by a pledge of the title documents to that land. This is discussed below.

Since most charges are created by contract, the intention to create that charge will be found in the contract between the debtor and creditor (which is usually contained in a written document). It is also possible to create a charge by deed. When a corporation creates a charge by deed, it is usually called a **debenture**.

A charge can be created by a pledge of documents. For example, suppose that I borrow money from you and deliver my corporate share certificates to you in return. Your possession of the certificates is itself a legal security right called a **pledge**: see page 119. However, it does not give you legal title to the shares represented by those certificates. This requires registration of a transfer in the corporation's register of shareholders. Nevertheless, the pledge of the certificates is a good indication that I want you to hold those shares as security for the loan. That intention is sufficient to create an equitable charge over those shares.

Land can also be charged by a pledge of title documents. When the land is registered in a Torrens system, the debtor hands the duplicate certificate of title (see page 449) to the creditor. For land outside the system, the title deeds are pledged. Normally, an intention to create a property right to land must be expressed in writing. Therefore, a deposit of title documents is usually accompanied by a written contract in which the debtor agrees to repay the loan and charges the land as security for that obligation. However, the deposit of title documents operates as **part performance** of the contract and (as discussed below) this permits the parties to dispense with the writing requirement.

Charges can also be created as gifts, but these are uncommon and usually found in wills. For example, I might make a will giving my land to my brother, subject to his payment of $10,000 to each of our two sisters. If my brother accepts the land, he will be required to pay the bequests to our sisters. Unfortunately, I did not state clearly whether our sisters have property rights to the land in addition to their personal rights. There is no trust, since my brother is not required to use the land for their benefit, but is free to obtain the money from other sources. However, our sisters may have charges on the land as security for my brother's debts to them. I should have chosen my words better to make this plain.

Legal or Equitable?

As discussed in Chapter 14, the common law did not recognise charges, which are either equitable or statutory. All common law security rights are either possession or ownership. Therefore, unless authorised by statute (like a registered mortgage of Torrens land), a charge is necessarily equitable.

When people create a security right, they might not know whether that right is legal or equitable. They simply intended to use a particular asset as security for the performance of a particular obligation. Whether that security right is legal or equitable depends on whether it would have been recognised by a court of common law (or pursuant to statute) or only by a court of equity. If the creditor obtains possession, legal ownership, or a statutory charge, the security right is legal. In other cases it is equitable.

Sometimes, the parties intend to create a legal security right, but fail to take the steps necessary to create that right. In such cases, an equitable charge may arise (although it is often called an **equitable mortgage** in this situation). For example, you might agree to lend money to me in exchange for a mortgage of my house. Since it is Torrens land, I will give you a registerable mortgage (in the prescribed form) in exchange for the loan. Once you register that mortgage, you will have a legal charge over my house. However, until it is registered, you have an equitable charge created by our contract and the mortgage document.

In some cases, the security right is equitable because a legal property right is not possible in the circumstances. This happens in two situations. The first is where the asset used as security is an equitable right. For example, I cannot create a legal security right to my beneficial interest in a trust, since that interest is not recognised by the common law.

Secondly, a security right is necessarily equitable where the asset is **future property** which the debtor has not yet acquired. For example, suppose that I execute a bill of sale to you of all the present and after acquired stock in my book shop. This will create a legal security right to the books in the shop when the bill is executed, since it will cause legal ownership of those books to pass to you. However, it cannot affect the property rights to any books I might acquire in the future. Those books belong to someone else or may not exist yet. There is nothing to which your property right to "after acquired stock" might relate.

What happens when I receive a new shipment of books a few days later? The bill of sale has done its work at common law and does not affect the legal ownership of the new books. However, I have promised you a security right to those new books and equity will compel me to keep my promise. As Lord Westbury C said in *Holroyd v Marshall* (1862) 10 HLC 191 at 211, 11 ER 999 at 1007:

> "[I]f a vendor or mortgagor agrees to sell or mortgage property, real or personal, of which he is not possessed at the time, and he receives the consideration for the contract, and afterwards becomes possessed of property answering the description in the contract, there is no doubt that a Court of Equity would compel him to perform the contract, and that the contract would, in equity, transfer the beneficial interest to the mortgagee or purchaser immediately on the property being acquired."

The equitable charge in this case arises because the debtor can be compelled, by a court of equity, to grant the security right to the creditor as promised. The court treats the promise as having been fulfilled as soon as that becomes possible. Therefore, the equitable security right passes to the creditor when the debtor acquires the new assets. This principle is explored further below in the section on specific performance.

Restrictive Covenants

As discussed in Chapter 16, a restrictive covenant is an equitable property right, which entitles a land owner to stop her or his neighbours from using their lands in some way. For example, they might not be allowed to build higher than two stories or to use their lands for commercial purposes.

With one exception, restrictive covenants are created by a contract between neighbouring land owners. Since the contract creates rights to land, it must be made in writing. Typically, restrictive covenants are made with sealed documents, in the form of a deed.

The exception applies to Torrens land in some jurisdictions. Section 88B of the *Real Property Act* 1900 (NSW) and section 136H of the *Transfer of Land Act* 1893 (WA) permit a developer to subdivide land and register restrictive covenants over the entire subdivision, even though each parcel of land is still owned by the developer. Since a person cannot make a contract with herself or himself, the event creating the restrictive covenants is registration. This is the only equitable property right which can be created by registration. In other situations, the registration of an equitable property right (such as a charge) does not create that right, but preserves its priority over competing rights.

The creation of restrictive covenants involves many of the same issues which arise in connection with trusts. However, different language is used. Much of the discussion of restrictive covenants in Chapter 16 would be called the "three certainties" if it concerned the law of trusts. Three similar requirements must be satisfied in order to create a restrictive covenant. First, the parties must intend to create a property right, which will bind and benefit subsequent owners of the lands, and not merely a personal right between themselves (certainty of intention). Secondly, the land burdened by the restrictive covenant must be identifiable (certainty of subject) and, thirdly, the lands benefited by the covenant must also be identifiable (certainty of objects).

A restrictive covenant creates equitable property rights because it depends upon the intervention of a court of equity. A covenantee can obtain an injunction from the court restraining the covenantor from using her or his land in breach of the covenant. This right arises when the covenant is made and will bind subsequent owners of that land (except a bona fide purchaser for value without notice, as discussed in Chapter 29). The contract creates a restrictive covenant in much the same way that a specifically enforceable contract of sale gives rise to a constructive trust.

Specific Performance

As discussed above, a contract to sell specific goods (in a deliverable state) will cause ownership of those goods to pass immediately to the buyer, if that is what the parties intend. For other contracts of sale, the contract is not the event which transfers ownership. It is simply the seller's binding promise to take steps to transfer ownership in the future. In other words, the contract creates personal rights, not property rights. One of the rights created is the buyer's personal right to receive a transfer in the future, which corresponds to the seller's obligation to do what is necessary to effect that transfer. However, if the buyer can compel the specific performance of the seller's obligation, then the buyer also has an equitable property right to the thing being sold.

Responses to Breach of Contract

Of major importance for the law of property are the legal responses to the seller's failure to perform her or his obligation to transfer ownership. As discussed in Chapter 7, there are four main types of possible responses to a breach of duty:

1) .....direct enforcement of the duty;
2) .....compensation;
3) .....restitution; and
4) .....punishment.

People are rarely, if ever, punished for breach of contract. Compensation is, by far, the most common response (discussed below). Restitution might also be available. For example, a seller in breach might be required to refund the purchase price to the buyer. Direct enforcement of a contractual promise is also possible by means of an injunction or an order for specific performance of the contract.

At common law, a buyer cannot compel a seller to keep her or his promise and is entitled only to the payment of money (**damages**), either as compensation for the loss caused by the breach of contract or as restitution of the purchase price. The payment of compensation is a substitute for performance of the contract and is intended to put the buyer in the financial position he or she would be in if the contract had been performed. The buyer can then use that money to buy the same thing from someone else.

As discussed at page 210, some contracts of sale can be specifically enforced under the rules of equity. In such cases, the buyer has an equitable personal right to specific performance of the obligation to transfer ownership, in addition to a legal personal right to be paid compensation if the seller fails to keep that promise. Most contracts to transfer property rights to land are specifically enforceable and most contracts to transfer other property rights are not. This is because the right to specific performance arises only when the right to compensation is regarded by equity as an inadequate substitute for performance of the contract.

The payment of money allows the disappointed buyer to go into the market and obtain the desired property rights from another seller. Since it is impossible to obtain the same parcel of land from someone else, damages are inadequate and specific performance of contracts to sell land is the norm. Most other property rights are readily available in the market and, therefore, contracts for the sale of personal property rights are specifically enforceable only where those rights are difficult to obtain.

A contract for the sale of personal property might be specifically enforced where the thing is rare or unique, such as an original oil painting or one of the few surviving first editions of an old book. In some cases, the thing might be fairly common, but difficult to obtain in the market. For example, shares in a proprietary company are not publicly traded and, even though thousands of identical shares may have been issued by the company, the disappointed buyer might be unable to obtain them from someone else. In *Dougan v Ley* (1946) 71 CLR 142, the buyer was entitled to specific performance of an oral contract for the sale of a taxicab and licence. Although there were some licensed cabs on the market (and the buyer was able to purchase another cab before the trial), they were hard to find because only a limited number of cab licences had been issued.

Most contracts to grant security rights are specifically enforceable, even though similar rights are easily obtained in the market. The underlying reason for equity's intervention is the same: damages do not provide an adequate substitute for performance of the contract. However, they are inadequate for a different reason. As discussed in Chapter 14, a security right is a property right granted to secure the performance of personal obligation (usually the payment of a debt). If the debtor fails to pay, the creditor can use the property right to obtain satisfaction of the debt and thus avoid the risk of the debtor's bankruptcy. If the debtor fails to grant the security right as promised, the creditor's personal right to compensation is no substitute for performance of that promise. It is exactly the same as not having the promised security right. Therefore, such promises have long been specifically enforceable: see *Holroyd v Marshall* (1862) 10 HLC 191, 11 ER 999.

Effect of Specific Performance

The specific performance of contracts is very important for the law of property. A buyer's right to compel a seller to transfer a property right is itself significant. However, of greater significance is the proprietary effect of a specifically enforceable contract of sale. On making the contract, the equitable ownership of the thing being sold passes to the buyer, even though the parties intend to transfer legal title at some future date. In other words, the seller holds that property right in trust for the buyer between the contract and the transfer: see *Bunny Industries Ltd v FSW Enterprises Pty Ltd* [1982] Qd R 712.

This rule was an established feature of English property law when it was imported to Australia. As Jessel MR said in *Lysaght v Edwards* (1876) 2 Ch D 499 at 506:

> "It appears to me that the effect of a contract for sale has been settled for more than two centuries ... [T]he moment you have a valid contract for sale the vendor becomes in equity a trustee for the purchaser of the estate sold, and the beneficial ownership passes to the purchaser".

As Lord Westbury C said in *Holroyd v Marshall* (1862) 10 HLC 191 at 209, "this is true, not only of contracts relating to real estate, but also of contracts relating to personal property, provided that the latter are such as a Court of Equity would direct to be specifically performed".

Why Does the Trust Arise?

The rule is relatively easy to describe and apply. The difficulty is understanding why a specifically enforceable contract of sale has an immediate proprietary effect when the parties intend that the property right will be transferred at a future date. For example, suppose we make a contract to sell my house to you, with the closing set to take place in three months. We have agreed that I will continue to own and possess the house for the next three months and that I will transfer those rights to you on the closing date. Since my promise is specifically enforceable, you are, according to the rules of equity, the beneficial owner of the house from the date the promise is made. This seems to run contrary to our intentions.

This trust is often explained as an application of the equitable maxim, "equity considers as done that which ought to be done". Since I ought to transfer the house to you (and can be compelled to do so), equity treats that as having already occurred. However, this does not explain why equity jumps the gun. I ought to transfer my house to you on the closing date and could not be compelled to transfer it before that day arrives. The maxim does not seem to fit very well and, even if it did, it would merely be describing what equity does and not why.

James Penner suggested that an owner's relation to an asset changes when he or she makes a binding promise to sell it. In *The Idea of Property in Law* (1997), p 91, he said, "The owner shifts from treating the property as something to be used to enhance his interests to treating it as something to be traded". Before making the contract of sale, the seller had the full beneficial ownership of the asset. The contract reduced her or his interest in the asset to a right to possess it until the transfer and a right to receive the purchase price. The rest of the benefit of the seller's beneficial ownership passed to the buyer and is recognised in equity as a constructive trust.

We can see the changing relationships to the asset when a home is sold. The sellers need a place to live until they move and need to use the capital value of their present home to pay for the next. The decision to sell and move has shifted their attentions to their next home (and matters such as decoration, renovations, the garden, and new neighbours). The buyers have likewise committed themselves to their new home and are deeply concerned about its preservation. The reality (which equity recognises) is that the beneficial ownership moved when the contract was signed.

When the sellers made the specifically enforceable promise to transfer their home, they thereby chose to dispose of their options to deal with that asset. Previously, they were free (within the limits of the law) to renovate, destroy, lease, sell, or give away their home. Their rights as legal owners, to make full beneficial use and enjoyment of their home, were curtailed by their promise to sell. As Lord O'Hagan stated in *Shaw v Foster* (1872) LR 5 HL 321 at 349, "By the contract of sale the vendor in the view of a Court of Equity disposes of his right over the estate, and on the execution of the contract he becomes constructively a trustee for the vendee".

The Role of Intention

A specifically enforceable contract of sale is an event which creates a trust. The seller's intention to transfer legal ownership to the buyer is necessary but not sufficient to bring the trust into being. The trust arises when that intention is combined with two other factors (which entitle the buyer to specific performance of the contract): first, valuable consideration is given in exchange for the seller's promise and, secondly, compensation is not an adequate substitute for the promised property right.

This is not an express trust, since it is not created by an intention to create a trust. It is a constructive trust, which arises by operation of law in response to another event (a contract of sale). People are sometimes confused by this classification. It is often said and commonly believed that constructive trusts "are imposed, without regard to the intentions of the parties": Glass JA, in *Allen v Snyder* [1977] 2 NSWLR 685 at 690. Yet the trust in this situation arises in response to the intentions of the parties as revealed in their contract of sale.

This apparent mismatch is resolved by a proper understanding of the role of intention in the creation of rights. As Peter Birks said, in *An Introduction to the Law of Restitution* (1989) p 65:

> "There is a fine but important distinction between intent conceived as creative of rights, as in an express trust or a contract, and intent conceived as a fact which, along with others, calls for the creation of rights by operation of law."

In most cases, intention operates to create rights directly. Someone intends to create a right and that intention (when combined with the steps necessary to give effect to it) produces the intended right. For example, a contract to sell specific goods can cause legal ownership to pass to the buyer as intended, a declaration of trust can bring an express trust into existence as intended, and the registration of a transfer of land can transfer a legal estate as intended.

In many other cases, intention creates rights indirectly. The right arises not because someone intended to create it, but because the intention is one component of an event which creates that right by operation of law. Often, the relevant intention is a promise or desire to transfer a property right to another. The intention is not effective to create the intended right, but is a fact which is central to the creation of another right. A specifically enforceable contract of sale falls in this category, as an event which gives rise to a constructive trust. Other examples of the constructive trust operating in this fashion are found in the next two chapters.

Nature of the Trust

The trust created by a specifically enforceable contract of sale differs from most express trusts in two respects. First, the seller is not subject to all of the duties which express trustees usually owe to their beneficiaries. The seller is not under a fiduciary duty of loyalty to the buyer nor does he or she have any active duties to perform, other than to preserve the asset and perform the contract of sale. Secondly, the seller has a beneficial interest in the asset, being entitled to both possession and its value through payment of the purchase price. In contrast, most express trustees have no beneficial interest in the trust assets, but only bare legal title.

The buyer also has a beneficial interest in the asset sold. It is not merely a security right, but the partial beneficial ownership of the asset under a trust. The beneficial ownership of the asset is shared by the seller and buyer between the contract of sale and the transfer of legal ownership to the buyer. This is not joint or co-ownership of the asset (see Chapter 15), since the parties have different property rights to the asset. The seller still has the beneficial legal ownership of the asset, but holds some of those rights in trust for the buyer.

Sale of Goods

As discussed above, most contracts for the sale of goods are not specifically enforceable. Unless the goods are rare or unique, the normal remedy for breach of contract (compensation at common law) is sufficient, because the disappointed buyer can use the money to buy other goods from another seller.

If a contract for the sale of goods is specifically enforceable, does the seller become a constructive trustee of the goods for the buyer when the contract is made? The equitable maxim, "equity considers as done that which ought to be done", should apply to this situation just as it applies to a sale of land. However, Aitken LJ suggested, in *Re Wait* [1927] 1 Ch 606 at 635-636, that this principle was excluded by the *Sale of Goods Act*:

> "It would have been futile in a code intended for commercial men to have created an elaborate structure of rules dealing with rights at law, if at the same time it was intended to leave, subsisting with the legal rights, equitable rights inconsistent with, more extensive, and coming into existence earlier than the rights so carefully set out in the various sections of the Code."

That suggestion raised doubts about the creation of equitable property rights during a sale of goods. Those doubts remain unresolved because the courts have not yet had sufficient opportunity to consider this issue. There are two reasons for this. First, the vast majority of sales are not specifically enforceable. Secondly, a contract of sale can pass the legal ownership of goods to the buyer without further action. Therefore, in those cases where the goods are rare or unique (and specific performance could be available), there might be little or no delay between making the contract and the transfer of ownership. Since a constructive trust can only exist in the interval between contract and transfer, very few trusts will arise and those that do will be short lived.

This uncertainty will get resolved one day and, hopefully, the resolution will lead to the consistent application of equitable principles to both land and goods. A constructive trust should be created by a specifically enforceable contract for the sale of goods, if there is a gap between the contract and the transfer of legal ownership. The *Sale of Goods Act* does provide a complete code for the transfer of legal ownership, but says nothing about the creation of equitable ownership. This is similar to the sale of land. The comprehensive statutory codes for the transfer of legal title to land do not prevent the creation of equitable property rights when land is sold. As discussed above, the Torrens statutes emphatically declare that documents cannot create property rights until they are registered and yet specifically enforceable contracts of sale continue to give rise to constructive trusts of Torrens land. Why should a *Sale of Goods Act*, which is silent on this issue, displace the normal rules of equity?

Other Property Rights

A specifically enforceable contract of sale creates a constructive trust for the buyer. The seller has promised to transfer legal ownership to the buyer and, therefore, the buyer obtains equitable ownership when the contract is made. This principle applies not just to contracts of sale, but also to contracts to transfer other property rights. So long as the contract is specifically enforceable, the promised right will pass in equity when the contract is made.

Most contracts to grant leases of land are specifically enforceable. Therefore, when the landlord and tenant make their contract, the tenant obtains an equitable leasehold estate: see *Walsh v Lonsdale* (1882) 21 Ch D 9. In essence, the landlord holds the promised property right on constructive trust for the tenant and we could say that the landlord is a constructive trustee of a leasehold estate. However, we say instead that the tenant has an **equitable lease**. This principle is so well established that many tenants are happy with an equitable lease and never bother to obtain the promised legal lease. The parties will sign a contract of lease, but never create a legal leasehold estate by executing a deed of lease or registering a Torrens form of lease.

Contracts to grant mortgages are also specifically enforceable. On making the contract, the mortgagee will obtain an **equitable mortgage** or **charge**. This is the very same principle which produces a constructive trust on a contract of sale. However, it would be misleading to say that the mortgagor becomes a constructive trustee of a mortgage. This is because the word "trust" is not used to describe equitable security rights. The latter are called equitable mortgages, charges, and liens to distinguish them from the wide range of beneficial interests which can be held in trust.

Options to Purchase

A possibility of specific performance can have a proprietary effect even before a contract of sale is made. If the contract would be specifically enforceable when made, then a right to obtain that contract will give the potential buyer an equitable property right: see *O'Neill v O'Connell* (1946) 72 CLR 101 at 129.

A buyer's right to obtain a contract of sale is called an **option to purchase**. He or she decides whether or not to buy and the seller is bound by that decision. This is equivalent to an offer to sell, which is irrevocable for a certain period of time. Normally, the option agreement will specify a time limit for exercising the option, the manner in which it can be exercised, and the terms of the contract of sale which will arise if it is exercised. For example, I might grant you an option to purchase my house for $150,000 anytime within the next two years, which you can exercise by providing me with written notice and a down payment of $15,000.

Options to purchase can be valuable rights. For example, you might be willing to pay a few thousand dollars for an option to purchase my house if you believe that its market price will rise and the option or the house could be sold at a profit. A large company might reward its senior managers with options to buy shares in the company. If the business does well, the market price of the shares will rise and the managers can profit by buying shares at the option price and reselling them.

Options to purchase are frequently attached to leases. For example, I might lease your car for three years with an option to purchase it at the end of the lease. An option can be a right to acquire a property right less than full ownership. For example, you might lease office space for five years with an option to lease it for an additional five years. The option to purchase the additional leasehold estate is called an **option to renew**.

If the exercise of an option will produce a specifically enforceable contract of sale or lease, that option is itself an equitable property right. This is because the option holder has the power to obtain that property right. As Martland J said in *Canadian Long Island Petroleums Ltd v Irving Industries Ltd* (1975) 50 DLR (3d) 265 at 277, "forthwith upon the granting of the option, the optionee upon the occurrence of certain events solely within his control can compel a conveyance of the property to him". The option holder's right is not beneficial ownership under a constructive trust, nor is it merely a security right. It is an equitable property right which limits the owner's freedom to deal with the asset.

There is a similar right, called a **pre-emptive right** or **right of first refusal**, which is not a property right. The holder of such a right cannot compel the owner to sell. However, if the owner chooses to sell, then he or she must offer the asset to the right holder before selling to anyone else.

Although a pre-emptive right restricts the owner's ability to deal with the asset, courts have decided that this degree of control is too slight to be property. It does become an equitable property right when the owner decides to sell and the right holder has the power to obtain legal title: see *Mackay v Wilson* (1947) 47 SR (NSW) 315 at 325; *Pata Nominees Pty Ltd v Durnsford Pty Ltd* [1988] WAR 365 at 372.

Part Performance

Contracts to transfer property rights to land are supposed to be made in writing: see, eg, *Conveyancing Act* 1919 (NSW), s 54A. If such a contract is made orally, it is not enforceable at law and the buyer will not be entitled to compensation if the seller chooses not to perform the contract. Normally, the oral contract is also unenforceable in equity. However, a court of equity might enforce the contract if there has been sufficient part performance of it by either or both of the parties.

Part performance is an equitable doctrine which allows a court of equity to dispense with the statutory requirement of writing in certain circumstances and specifically enforce a contract to transfer a property right to land. It has been preserved as an exception to the writing requirement in each jurisdiction: see, eg, *Property Law Act* 1958 (Vic), s 55(d).

How Does Part Performance Work?

In some cases, the parties to an oral contract have performed obligations or exercised rights under it. A court of equity may regard those actions as sufficient evidence of the existence of the contract. The evidential value of the part performance is a safeguard, which allows the court to say that the policy behind the statute (avoiding fraud) is fulfilled and that writing is not required.

For example, in *Mason v Clarke* [1955] AC 778, the owner of land granted a lease to Clarke, but reserved the right to hunt on that land. The owner then made an oral contract with Mason to grant him a right to hunt rabbits on the land, but did not execute the deed needed to create a legal profit à prendre. Mason paid £100 to the owner and set snares on the land but, when he returned to collect the rabbits, Clarke stopped him from entering the land. The court was asked to decide whether the contract created only a personal right, which Mason could enforce only against the owner, or also created a property right, which he could enforce against Clarke.

The court decided that Mason's actions (paying the owner, setting snares, and attempting to collect rabbits) were referable to the existence of the oral contract between the owner and Mason. This meant that Mason was entitled to specific performance of the contract and had an equitable profit à prendre. Since the oral contract would not be specifically enforceable until sufficient acts of part performance had taken place, the profit à prendre would arise not when the contract was made, but only later when it was partly performed.

The payment of money to the owner was not itself sufficient part performance of the contract, since there are many reasons why one person might pay money to another. The setting of snares provides an indication of the nature of Mason's right, but did not itself indicate that he had a contract with the owner. It is the combination of the two which provides sufficient confirmation of the existence of the contract.

Part performance works because it provides evidence of the oral contract. It does not depend on losses suffered by one party or detrimental reliance on expectations. Despite the name of this doctrine, the actions which constitute part performance need not be the performance of a party's obligations under the contract. As in *Mason v Clarke*, the exercise of rights under the contract can be used as proof of the contract.

The court will not specifically enforce the oral contract unless it believes that it exists. However, belief in the existence of the contract is not sufficient without acts of part performance. A court might have no doubt that an oral contract was made and still be unable to enforce it. Part performance is a limited exception to the statutory requirement that contracts dealing with land be in writing. Unless the actions of the parties count as part performance according to the rules of equity, the contract cannot be enforced.

This was the problem Ms Ryan faced in *Ogilvie v Ryan* [1976] 2 NSWLR 504. She and Mr Ogilvie made an oral contract that she would reside with him and care for him for the rest of his life (he was 82 at the time) and, in return, she could live in his house for the rest of her life. Ryan fully performed the contract, but when Ogilvie died two years later, his executor attempted to evict her from the house. Holland J believed her evidence about the contract, but could not enforce it because it was not made in writing. Her actions were not sufficient acts of part performance because they were not unequivocally referable to the existence of the contract. They could also be explained by love and affection or her expectation of receiving a gift under his will. However, Ryan was entitled to the promised life estate on another basis: her detrimental reliance on her reasonable expectation of receiving it. This is discussed at page 304.

In England, the courts reduced the requirements of part performance, so that it was no longer necessary to prove actions which were unequivocally referable to the existence of the oral contract. It was sufficient if those actions indicated the existence of some contract between the parties and were consistent with the oral contract: see *Steadman v Steadman* [1976] AC 536. However, this relaxation of the traditional requirements has not found favour in Australia and the doctrine of part performance has since been abolished in England by statute.

The limits of part performance need to be understood. Part performance will not make a contract where none exists, nor will it cure impediments to specific performance other than a lack of writing. It is merely a way to get around the writing requirement and cannot lead to anything more than specific performance of the oral contract. For this purpose only, the parties are in the same position as if their contract had been made in writing. Specific performance is only possible if the contract is otherwise specifically enforceable under the normal rules of equity.

Oral Mortgages

Part performance is often relied on in cases where a mortgage of land is made informally. Suppose, for example, that I borrowed money from you and we orally agreed that my land would be used as security for the loan. If our contract had been put in writing, you would have no problem obtaining specific performance of my promise to transfer a security right to my land. Our specifically enforceable contract would create an equitable mortgage for you.

We have a valid contract of loan and I am indebted to you as agreed. However, your payment of money to me is not sufficient part performance of the contract to grant a mortgage, since it could be referable to almost anything. If I also pledge my title documents to you in exchange for the loan, these two actions will constitute part performance. The lack of writing is no longer an impediment to specific performance and you will obtain an equitable mortgage.

The delivery of documents does not create the equitable mortgage. It does two things. First, it creates a legal security right to the documents (a pledge) and, secondly, it is part performance of the contract. The specifically enforceable contract creates the equitable mortgage and, therefore, a pledge of documents is unnecessary where the contract is made in writing. Lenders prefer the additional security provided by the pledge, since it is difficult for the owner to deal with the land without the title documents.

Vendors' and Purchasers' Liens

As discussed in Chapter 14, liens are security rights created by operation of law. There are two different types: **common law liens**, which entitle a creditor to retain possession of goods until a related debt is paid, and **equitable liens**, which entitle a creditor to have the proceeds from the sale of an asset used to pay a related debt.

Liens arise for various reasons but, in every case, there is some connection between the assets subject to the lien and the debt secured by it. For example, a mechanic who repairs a car has a lien on it for the repair bill and a person who improves land may have a lien on it for the value of the improvement. In this part, we are concerned with liens which arise during a sale to secure the payment or refund of the purchase price.

A **vendor's lien** (also called an **unpaid vendor's lien** or **unpaid seller's lien**) can arise at common law or in equity. If a buyer obtains ownership of the asset sold before the purchase price is paid in full, the seller may have a lien on that asset to secure payment of that debt.

A **purchaser's lien** is always equitable. If a buyer pays all or part of the purchase price before receiving ownership of the asset sold, he or she may have a lien on that asset to secure payment of a refund in the event that the sale cannot be completed.

Common Law

Vendors' Liens

Since common law liens arise only in connection with tangible personal property, this kind of vendor's lien always relates to a sale of goods. It is a passive security right which entitles the seller to retain possession of the goods until the purchase price is paid, even though ownership of those goods has already passed to the buyer.

This lien is regulated by sale of goods legislation in every jurisdiction. For example, section 40 of the *Sale of Goods Act* 1895 (SA) states:

> "Subject to the provisions of this Act, the unpaid seller of goods who is in possession of them is entitled to retain possession of them until payment or tender of the price in the following cases, namely:—
> (a) Where the goods have been sold without any stipulation as to credit; (b) Where the goods have been sold on credit, but the term of credit has expired; (c) Where the buyer becomes insolvent."

This is just one part of a code, which regulates when these liens arise and how they are enforced. A lien is just one of several statutory remedies available to the seller if a buyer breaches a contract of sale.

Purchasers' Liens

There is no purchaser's lien at common law. It is helpful to consider why not. If the buyer has received possession of the goods and paid for them, the contract of sale will be performed and the buyer will be the owner of those goods. Even if the seller is required to refund a portion of the purchase price, the buyer cannot have a lien on her or his own goods.

There are two situations in which a buyer might have possession, but not ownership, of goods and be entitled to a refund of the purchase price paid to the seller. In neither case is a common law lien of any use.

The first is where the buyer is entitled to reject defective goods delivered by the seller. Ownership of the goods will revert to the seller if they are rejected, but a common law lien cannot be used to secure payment of a refund. This is because a buyer's refusal to give up possession of defective goods would be treated as acceptance of those goods and a waiver of the right to reject them.

Secondly, a buyer might fail to obtain ownership of goods delivered by the seller because the seller does not own them. Again, a lien is of no use. Although the seller's right to possession will have passed to the buyer, the true owner has a better right to possession and could sue both seller and buyer for conversion: see page 56.

Equity

Equitable liens can arise in relation to any asset. However, it is not clear whether vendors' and purchasers' liens can apply to the sale of any asset. It is well established that they arise when land is sold, but it is commonly believed that they cannot apply to a sale of goods. This issue is avoided for the moment as vendors' and purchasers' liens are discussed in connection with sales of land. After this introduction, the possibility of liens arising when other things are sold is discussed. This part ends with a summary of the way in which equitable liens affect property rights during a sale.

Vendors' Liens

If legal title is transferred to the buyer before the purchase price is paid in full, the seller has an equitable lien on the land to secure payment of the amount still owing. This can be seen as the natural continuation of the seller's diminishing interest in the land sold. As discussed above, a specifically enforceable contract of sale reduces the seller's interest from full beneficial ownership to the rights to possession and payment of the purchase price. This resembles a lease combined with a security right. When legal ownership passes to the buyer, the vendor's lien arises to secure payment of the purchase price. All that remains of the seller's interest is that security right.

The vendor's lien can also be seen as the *quid pro quo* for the buyer's constructive trust. Since the buyer has the equitable right to compel the seller to transfer title as promised, it seems only fair that the seller should have a corresponding equitable right to secure performance of the buyer's promise to pay for the land once title has passed. The seller can sue for this debt, if necessary, but that personal right may be meaningless if the buyer becomes insolvent before the debt is paid. Without a vendor's lien, the land could be sold and the money used to pay the buyer's creditors *pro rata*. The lien ensures that the other creditors will not receive the benefit of that land without paying for it.

Purchasers' Liens

If any portion of the purchase price is paid before title is transferred, the buyer has an equitable lien on the land to secure performance of the seller's obligation to pay a refund to the buyer if the sale cannot be completed. Normally, this equitable security right is subsumed in the greater equitable beneficial interest under the constructive trust. It becomes important only when it is not possible to complete the sale. The lien is security for the seller's obligation to make restitution of all or part of the purchase price. When performance of the sale contract becomes impossible, the buyer's interest diminishes from beneficial ownership to a security right.

It is easy to confuse the purchaser's lien with her or his interest under the constructive trust. It is sometimes said that the interest under the trust is commensurate with the value of the purchase price paid, but this is not true. The buyer does not have full beneficial ownership (since the seller also has a beneficial interest), but has more than a security right.

An example may help. Suppose you agreed to buy my house for $100,000, paid a $10,000 deposit, and the market value of the house increased to $120,000 before completion of the sale. Your purchaser's lien is worth up to $10,000, since I might be obliged to refund all or part of that sum if the sale cannot be completed. However, your interest under the constructive trust is worth more than $10,000. You are the beneficial owner of the house (subject to my right to possess it and receive the balance of the purchase price still owing) and, therefore, the increase in market value benefits you, not me. The value of your constructive trust interest has risen to $30,000 ($120,000 less the $90,000 still owed to me).

If the market value of the house declined, the value of your trust interest would be reduced accordingly. With beneficial ownership comes the risk of gain or loss. Your lien is unaffected by fluctuations in the value of the house, since it is merely a security right linked to my obligation to pay a refund. Similarly, my interest as legal owner of the house looks more like a security right, since it is tied to your obligation to pay the balance of the purchase price and not the market value of the house.

What Things?

In *Hewett v Court* (1983) 149 CLR 639, the High Court confirmed that vendors' and purchasers' equitable liens can arise in relation to things other than land. The Hewetts had agreed to buy a house from a company which would build, transport, and attach it to their land. They paid more than $20,000 to the company, which became insolvent before the house was completed. A majority of the Court decided that the Hewetts had an equitable lien on the partially completed house even though it was not attached to land.

The Court deliberately avoided the question whether equitable liens can arise on a sale of goods. Although the house was goods when the purchasers' lien arose, their contract was not a sale of goods. It was a contract to perform services (build a house and attach it to land) and, therefore, the *Sale of Goods Act* did not apply.

There is a good argument that the *Sale of Goods* legislation provides a complete code of sellers' and buyers' remedies and leaves no room for equitable liens. On the other hand, the legislation does not expressly exclude them. In exceptional cases, where goods are rare and the contract of sale is specifically enforceable, perhaps the seller should hold the goods on constructive trust for the buyer (as discussed above) and the parties should have liens securing payment or refund of the purchase price.

If this controversy over the effect of the *Sale of Goods Acts* is ignored, there are still doubts about the availability of vendors' and purchasers' liens. It had long been assumed that these liens could arise only if a contract of sale was specifically enforceable (or would have been but for a defect in the vendor's title). However, the High Court said in *Hewett v Court* that this assumption was false, so it is necessary to identify other factors which might lead to the creation of these liens.

The link to specific performance provided a useful way to control and explain vendors' and purchasers' liens. The vendor's lien seemed to follow naturally as a consequence of a specifically enforceable contract of sale. Beneficial ownership shifts to the buyer when the contract is made, but the seller still has an interest which includes the right to be paid the balance of the purchase price. That right continues, after legal ownership passes to the buyer, as an equitable lien. In other words, property passes differently in equity than at common law and the vendor's lien is part of that difference.

Specific performance also provided a justification for the purchaser's lien. The seller is under an equitable obligation to transfer an asset to the buyer because damages are not an adequate substitute for performance of the contract. A court of equity imposes a lien on the asset to ensure that the seller cannot keep both the asset and the purchase price. However, if damages are an acceptable substitute, then the contract is not specifically enforceable and equity is not involved. Since the buyer has only a personal right to receive a transfer, there is little or no justification for using any particular asset as security for the seller's obligation to refund the purchase price.

If a contract of sale is not specifically enforceable and there are no other equitable rights involved, what justifies the creation of vendors' and purchasers' liens? Although the contract in *Hewett v Court* was not specifically enforceable (because it was a contract to perform services), two of the judges emphasised that the company had an obligation to transfer that particular house to the Hewetts. It was not free to sell the house to someone else and start building another house for them. Perhaps a lien is justified whenever a seller is contractually bound to transfer a particular asset to the buyer, regardless of whether that contract could be specifically enforced.

How Liens Affect a Sale

A typical sale of land is more complicated than a typical sale of goods. Normally, there is a significant gap between a contract to sell land and the actual transfer of legal title. As the sale unfolds, equitable property rights are created and extinguished by operation of law. In other words, the ownership of land does not shift from seller to buyer in one swift movement. Instead, there is a flow of property rights over the course of the transaction. This is also true when other things are sold, if constructive trusts and equitable liens are involved.

It may be helpful to outline the stages in which property passes between seller and buyer. In this example, I sell my house to you:

1) .....Before our contract of sale is made, I am the beneficial owner of the land and you have no rights to it (unless you have an option to purchase). Other people may have property rights to the land (such as a mortgage to the bank or an easement for utilities). Some of those rights (like the easement) may continue after the land is sold and others (the mortgage) may be discharged at the time of sale.
2) .....If our contract of sale is specifically enforceable, you will acquire beneficial ownership of the land when the contract is made. I hold the land on constructive trust for you, but am not a bare trustee. I still have beneficial interests of my own: the rights to retain possession until an agreed date and to be paid the purchase price. However, I am no longer free to deal with the land as I please.
3) .....You will probably pay a portion of the purchase price when the contract is made (or sometime before the sale is complete). This creates your purchaser's lien on the land. Normally, this equitable security right remains submerged in the greater equitable beneficial ownership created by the contract of sale. However, if the sale cannot be completed and you become entitled to a refund of any portion of the price, the lien will secure performance of my obligation to make that refund.
4) .....When legal title is transferred, your constructive trust and purchaser's lien come to an end (since you cannot have rights enforceable against yourself). Your new legal ownership entitles you to the full beneficial use and enjoyment of the land.
5) .....The purchase price might be paid in full when legal title passes to you. If so, I cease to have any property rights to the land when you become the legal owner. If any portion of the purchase price remains unpaid, I will have a vendor's lien on the land to secure performance of your obligation to pay that debt. This lien cannot exist before legal title passes to you (since I cannot have rights enforceable against myself). Before the transfer, my right to the purchase price is part of my legal ownership.

Incomplete Gifts

When something is purchased, the buyer has a contractual right to receive legal ownership of that thing. Therefore, if the seller fails to transfer title as promised, the buyer has a legal remedy: a right to compensation for loss of the bargain and, in some cases, specific performance of the promise. A promise to make a gift is quite different. If the donor fails to make the gift as promised, there is no breach of contract. The hopeful donee is disappointed, but no poorer than before.

Normally, courts will not intervene to help a disappointed donee. This is sometimes expressed as the maxim, "equity will not assist a volunteer". Therefore, intentions or attempts to make gifts rarely have a proprietary effect before legal ownership passes to the donee and the gift is complete. There are two important exceptions. First, if a hopeful donee relies on the expectation of receiving a gift and thereby suffers a detriment, the court might intervene to fulfil that expectation. This is discussed in Chapter 23. Secondly, if a donor has done everything he or she needed to do to make a gift, a court of equity will treat the gift as complete, even though legal ownership has not yet passed to the intended donee. This second exception is the subject of this part.

Completion of Gifts

A gift is complete when legal ownership passes from donor to donee. As discussed above, this requires an intention to give, combined with an act to give effect to that intention. The method chosen depends on the nature of the thing given. If the donor chooses the wrong method or fails to do it properly, legal title does not move.

If a donor's attempt to make a gift does fail, legal title might pass to the donee later in an unexpected way. If it does and the donor still intends to give, the gift will be complete. This possibility was considered in *Re Stoneham* [1919] 1 Ch 149 (discussed above, p 241), in which a grandfather gave furniture to his grandson and then died. Since, the grandson already had possession of the furniture, the gift was complete without a further act of delivery. However, the court also said that, if the gift had not been completed during the grandfather's life, it would have been complete on his death. This is because the grandson was the executor of his grandfather's estate and (as discussed in the next chapter) legal ownership to that estate passed to the grandson by operation of law.

This exceptional method of making a gift is sometimes referred to as the rule in *Strong v Bird*, after the case which made it famous: (1874) LR 18 Eq 315. So long as the donor does not change her or his mind about the gift, the donee's acquisition of title (as executor or administrator of the donor's estate) completes the gift. This rule seems a bit odd. The donee does not obtain legal title until the donor is dead, at which time the donor no longer intends to give. Therefore, the intention to give and passing of title do not coexist. However, the rule does not operate to cause a transfer of legal ownership. That occurs by operation of law. The rule merely determines whether the donee must include the gift in the donor's estate (to be distributed according to law) or is permitted to keep it for herself or himself.

Incomplete Gifts and Express Trusts

When a donor attempts to make a gift and fails, there is a temptation to construe that attempt as a declaration of trust for the intended donee. There are two arguments in favour of this construction. First, the donor wants the donee to have the benefit of the asset, but retained legal title. This resembles the relationship that would have been produced if the donor had declared herself or himself to be a trustee for the donee. Secondly, the equitable beneficial ownership created by a declaration of trust is not far removed from the legal ownership which the donee was intended to have. It may seem better to let the donee have a similar property right than nothing at all.

These arguments have not found favour with the courts. An intention to give legal ownership is not the same as an intention to create a trust and one should not be confused with the other. As Professor Maitland said in *Equity* (revised ed, 1936), p 72:

> "The two intentions are very different — the giver means to get rid of his rights, the man who is intending to make himself a trustee intends to retain his rights but to come under an onerous obligation. The latter intention is far rarer than the former."

An express trustee has many onerous duties to perform, including preservation of the trust assets and loyal service of the beneficiary's best interests. If those duties are breached, the trustee may be liable to compensate the beneficiary. A failed attempt to give should not have such serious legal consequences. Also, it should not remove the donor's freedom to change her or his mind and keep the asset or give it to another.

Incomplete Gifts and Constructive Trusts

A constructive trust arises when a donor has done everything he or she needed to do to make the gift and has placed the donee in a position to complete the gift without further help from the donor: see *Corin v Patton* (1990) 169 CLR 540. This occurs when registration is needed to transfer legal ownership and the donee has obtained the documents needed for registration. At that point, a court of equity treats the gift as complete. This is not a true exception to the rule that equity will not assist a volunteer, because the donee does not need the court's help.

For example, suppose that I want to give Torrens land to you. The gift will not be complete until the transfer of land is registered. However, if I give you the necessary transfer documents, you have the power to complete the gift without my help. You then become the equitable owner of the land and I hold the land in trust for you.

This trust can be compared to that which arises when a specifically enforceable contract of sale is made. Since the buyer can compel the seller to keep her or his promise, the buyer has an equitable interest in the land. Although a donee cannot compel the donor to complete a promised gift, he or she does not need to: the donor has already done everything necessary. Like the buyer, the donee has the power to obtain legal ownership of the asset and is therefore regarded as its equitable owner.

Once the donee has the power to complete the gift, it is too late for the donor to change her or his mind. The choice to give becomes binding on the donor. This is somewhat surprising since the usual reasons for equitable intervention are missing. There is no contract, detrimental reliance, wrongdoing, or unjust enrichment. However, the power to complete the gift exists because the donor gave the donee the documents needed for registration. A donor who changes her or his mind would need the court's help to recover those documents and restrain the donee from registering them. The gift of the documents is complete and irrevocable and the court will not interfere with the donee's legal ownership of them: see *Mascall v Mascall* (1984) 50 P&CR 119 at 128.

The trust in this situation is not created by an intention to create a trust and, therefore, is not an express trust. It arises by operation of law in response to the donor's intention to make a gift of legal title, coupled with actions which empower the donee to complete the gift. This is a constructive trust designed to perfect the donor's intention to give: see Elias, *Explaining Constructive Trusts* (1990), pp 48-49.

Chapter Twenty-Two

SUCCESSION ON DEATH

❚❚❚

When we die, we cease to be legal persons capable of holding property rights. However, that does not mean that our property rights will cease to exist. Life estates and joint tenancies come to an end (see Chapters 12 and 15), but most of our rights will survive us and be transferred to others, either in accordance with our instructions or by operation of law. Legal rules allocating the rights formerly held by deceased persons are essential. As Leroy Certoma said, in *The Law of Succession in New South Wales* (3rd ed, 1997) p 3, "If death were to extinguish rights, the transmission of property would merely depend upon possession and thus be arbitrary and result in unjust enrichment".

The law concerning the transfer of rights and obligations on death is often called the law of **succession**. It governs a variety of issues, including the validity of wills, the duties of executors, and (as discussed in Chapter 3) the disposition of dead bodies. We are concerned here only with the ways in which property rights are transferred on death. This chapter is divided into three main parts. The first, called "testamentary dispositions", is an introduction to the ways in which the assets of deceased persons are disposed of. The second part concerns intentional dispositions (wills, codicils, and *donationes mortis causa*) and the third concerns dispositions by operation of law (secret trusts, mutual wills, intestacy, *bona vacantia*, and family relief legislation).

Testamentary Dispositions

Testamentary and Inter Vivos

As mentioned in the previous chapter, all transfers of property can be divided into two categories: transfers *inter vivos*, which take place between living persons, and testamentary transfers, which take effect on death. Testamentary transfers are usually called "testamentary dispositions", because they are not normally achieved by simple transfers from the deceased directly to the intended recipients. The process can take a very long time, as all the financial affairs of the deceased person are wound up, and the property rights may pass through the hands of several people *en route* to their final destinations.

The distinction between *inter vivos* and testamentary dispositions is important, primarily because different rules govern the intentional transfer of rights in each category. As discussed below, people are usually expected to observe more formalities (with writing and witnesses) when making testamentary dispositions of their property. The distinction can also be important for taxation purposes, especially in jurisdictions which impose estate duties on testamentary dispositions.

There are some transactions which appear to be testamentary, but are really *inter vivos*. Suppose that I created a trust of my house for myself for life, with the remainder to you. Your right to possession will arise on my death, when my equitable life estate comes to an end, and appears to be a transfer which takes effect on my death. However, the transfer is *inter vivos*. Your equitable fee simple estate arose when I created the trust. As discussed at page 99, it was **vested in interest** during my life, even though your right to possession was postponed until the termination of my life estate.

When property is jointly owned and one joint tenant dies, the surviving joint tenants acquire a greater ownership of the property by operation of law. This is not a testamentary disposition, but a normal incident of joint ownership. The right of survivorship arises when the joint tenancy is created *inter vivos*.

Wills and Codicils

Strictly speaking, a testamentary disposition is a transfer made by **will**. Testament (from the Latin *testamentum*) means will, which is a document containing instructions for dealing with a deceased person's estate. However, the adjective **testamentary** is being used here in a broader sense to refer to any disposition which takes effect on death. Most testamentary dispositions are made by will, but it is possible to make them in other ways, as discussed below.

A person who dies leaving a valid will is called a **testator** and is said to have died **testate**. A female testator is sometimes called a **testatrix**, but she can also be called a testator. A person who dies without leaving a valid will has died **intestate**. A **partial intestacy** occurs when a valid will fails to dispose of all of the testator's assets.

When we speak of a person's last will (or last will and testament), we are really speaking of the sum of the instructions which will have legal effect after her or his death. Normally, these are all contained in one document (the will), but may be found in several documents, since a person could make more than one will, relating to different parts of her or his estate, and could amend those wills many times. A document which amends or adds to an existing will, without revoking it, is called a **codicil**.

A will normally contains two main instructions. First, it appoints one or more **executors**, who will be responsible for administering the testator's estate. Secondly, it tells the executors how to dispose of that estate. A will might also give instructions for the funeral and disposal of the body and for the appointment of guardians of the testator's minor children. A valid will or codicil might perform one or more of these functions.

Executors and Administrators

The executors are responsible for dealing with the testator's body, gathering together all the assets which belonged to the testator, paying all of her or his debts, and distributing what remains in accordance with the instructions contained in the will. One of their first tasks is to prove (or **probate**) the will, by obtaining the court's confirmation of the documents which comprise the testator's last will. The court will issue a grant of probate to the executors, which confirms their authority to deal with the testator's estate.

If a deceased person does not have an executor, the court will appoint one or more **administrators** to fulfil that function. This is necessary when a person dies intestate, but may also happen when the will does not appoint an executor or the people appointed could not or would not accept that office. The administrators derive their authority from the court's grant of administration, which fulfils the same function as a grant of probate. Administrators and executors are often referred to as the **personal representatives** of the deceased person's estate.

Transfer to Personal Representatives

When a grant of probate or administration is made, the rights of the deceased pass automatically to the executors or administrators to whom the grant is made. How that happens varies slightly from one jurisdiction to another. The applicable rules have been copied from English law and modified by statute in each jurisdiction: see *Succession Act* (Qld); *Wills, Probate and Administration Act* (NSW); *Administration Act* (WA); and *Administration and Probate Act* in other jurisdictions.

The gap between the death and the grant creates a problem, since the estate cannot be left without an owner during that time. There are two different solutions to this problem. The first is to backdate the transfer of property to the date of death. The second is to have the estate vest in the **public trustee** between the date of death and date of the grant.

Backdating the Transfer

An example of the first strategy is found in section 8 of the *Administration Act* 1903 (WA):

> "Upon grant of probate or administration, all real and personal estate which a deceased person dies seised, possessed of, or entitled to in Western Australia shall, as from the death of such person, pass to and become vested in the executor to whom probate has been granted, or administrator for all the estate and interest of the deceased therein."

This enables the personal representative to take action over any wrongful interference with the estate between the death and the grant. Suppose, for example, that Malcolm died and Cole wrongly removed a number of valuables from his home the next day. He should be guilty of conversion (see page 56), but there was no one with a better right to possession on that day. When Anna later obtains probate as Malcolm's executrix, she becomes the owner of his estate from the date of Malcolm's death and, therefore, is treated as if she had a right to immediate possession of the valuables when Cole took them.

The Public Trustee

In the Australian Capital Territory and New South Wales, the transfer of property to the personal representatives is not backdated from the grant to the death. Instead, the estate belongs to the public trustee during that gap. Public trustees are government officials who take care of the estates of deceased persons when there are no relatives or friends able or willing to act as personal representatives. They are also available to deal with matters arising before personal representatives are appointed.

Combinations of the Two

The Northern Territory uses both strategies to bridge the gap between death and grant. The estate passes on death to the public trustee and then on to the personal representative "as from the death": *Administration and Probate Act* (NT), s 52. Although this might seem redundant, it enables the public trustee to deal with problems that arise before a grant and ends her or his involvement when it is made. After the grant, the estate is treated as if it had never been vested in the Public Trustee.

In South Australia, the assets of a deceased person pass to the Public Trustee only if they are not given away by will (in other words, when there is a complete or partial intestacy). Where they are given away by will, there is likely to be an executor, who can respond quickly to preserve the estate, and at least one beneficiary interested in its preservation. The law is similar in Tasmania and Victoria, except the assets of an intestate pass to the Chief Justice in Tasmania and to the State Trustee in Victoria.

In Queensland, the estate passes to the executors on death but, if there are no executors named or willing to act, then to the Public Trustee. If the grant of probate or administration is made to other people, the estate then passes to them.

Transfer to the Beneficiaries

When an estate passes to executors or administrators, they become the legal owners of the property, subject to the duties to gather in the estate (including the collection of debts due to the deceased), pay all taxes and creditors, and distribute the estate according to law. Those duties can be enforced by the creditors and beneficiaries of the estate.

The **beneficiaries** of an estate are those people who are entitled to receive some or all of it as a gift, either because they are named in a will or otherwise by operation of law. They do not have property rights to the gifts they are entitled to receive, but only a personal right to receive them. Like many personal rights, a beneficiary's right can look like property because it is valuable and transferable: see *Official Receiver in Bankruptcy v Schultz* (1990) 170 CLR 306. However, the personal representatives do not hold the estate in trust. They are its only owners between death and distribution.

Executors and administrators do look remarkably like trustees. Even though no one else has any property rights to the estate, they are not free to deal with it as they please. They must distribute it according to law and will be liable to compensate the beneficiaries if they distribute it improperly. Also, if an executor or administrator becomes bankrupt, the estate cannot be used to pay her or his personal debts. It seems that the personal representatives have only bare legal title and that the beneficial ownership of the estate must belong to someone else. However, it does not.

There are two reasons why the estate is not held in trust pending distribution. The first is historical. While the court of chancery created trusts, it acquired jurisdiction over the estates of deceased persons only later. Much of the law of succession is the creation of ecclesiastic courts. Two different courts produced different rules to deal with remarkably similar relationships.

Secondly, a gift to a beneficiary might be needed to pay taxes and other creditors. Therefore, a beneficiary's right to a gift is conditional upon there being sufficient assets in the estate to meet all of its legal obligations. This conditional right is perhaps too uncertain to be property. Since the beneficiary cannot say for sure which assets he or she will be receiving, there may be insufficient certainty of subject matter for a trust.

Intentional Testamentary Dispositions

Estate planning is the process of thinking ahead about the distribution of assets on death and making the necessary arrangements. People want to reduce the payment of taxes, provide for loved ones, and possibly give something to friends and charities. Although most estate plans use a will, they also make use of *inter vivos* dispositions. For example, most people own their homes and other assets jointly with spouses or lovers. On death, those assets do not form part of the estate, but pass automatically to the survivor. Also, people may make *inter vivos* trust settlements, which retain a life estate and give the remainder away to a spouse, children, and grandchildren.

This part concerns the two ways to make intentional testamentary dispositions: formally, through a will or codicil, and informally, through a **donatio mortis causa** (a gift made in contemplation of death). Some judges and lawyers would also place **secret trusts** in this category. They are discussed below as transfers by operation of law.

Wills and Codicils

Wills take effect only on the death of the testator and, therefore, can be revoked at any time (although some people make contracts not to revoke their wills, as discussed below under the heading, mutual wills). This means that a beneficiary named in a will does not thereby acquire any rights. All he or she has is a hope of receiving a gift when the testator dies. If that will is valid, then the beneficiary will acquire a personal right when the testator dies and, if there are sufficient assets in the estate, a property right when the estate is distributed.

If all or part of a testamentary gift must be used to pay creditors of the estate, then the gift **abates** and the beneficiary might receive less or nothing at all. The law of succession provides rules for the order in which estate assets should be used to pay creditors. Sometimes, a will makes gifts of specific assets which are not part of the estate. For example, I might leave my saxophone to my aunt Selma and not have a saxophone when I die. In this situation, the gift **adeems**.

If a beneficiary under a will dies before the testator, the gift **lapses**. This is because the will becomes operative only on the testator's death and it was not possible for the beneficiary to acquire a right to the potential gift before her or his death. Most wills make alternative gifts (often to the beneficiary's children, siblings, or spouse) to deal with this problem.

Real and Personal Property

At one time, real property and personal property were treated differently by the law of succession. Before the *Statute of Wills* 1540, real property could not be given away by will, but passed to the heir (and not the personal representative). If the owner died without leaving an heir, the estate would **escheat** to the Crown (or lord) from whom the owner held tenure: see page 90. The distinction between freehold and leasehold estates had greater significance back then, because leases were **chattels real** and could be given away by will: see page 39.

Today, all assets are treated the same. They can be given away by will and pass to the personal representatives on or soon after death. However, some of the old language survives to remind us of former differences. A gift of personal property in a will or codicil is called a **bequest** or **legacy**, while a gift of real property is called a **devise**. Testators **bequeath** personalty and **devise** realty and the recipients can be called **legatees** and **devisees**.

Residuary Estate

Wills usually make a number of specific gifts and the entire estate could be given away in this fashion. However, a good will contains a clause distributing everything not specifically given away. The collection of assets which will remain after the creditors are paid and the specific gifts are made is called the **residuary estate**, **residuum**, or **residue**, and the persons entitled to it are called **residuary beneficiaries**.

Formalities

Normally, wills must be made in writing and signed by the testator in the presence of two witnesses, who will not derive a benefit from the will. If the will does make a gift to a witness or her or his spouse, the will is still valid. However, in most jurisdictions, that gift is invalid. Witnesses and their spouses are "not disqualified from taking a benefit under the will" in Victoria: *Wills Act* 1997 (Vic), s 11. In Tasmania they can ask the court to validate the gift: *Wills Act* 1992 (Tas), s 45.

South Australia started a trend towards relaxing the formalities needed to make a valid will. Section 12 of the *Wills Act* 1936 (SA) states, "Subject to this Act, if the Court is satisfied that a document that has not been executed with the formalities required by this Act expresses testamentary intentions of a deceased person, the document will be admitted to probate as a will of the deceased person." The courts in other Australian jurisdictions now have similar powers.

Testamentary Trusts

Wills are often used to create trusts. Since the testator will not be around to respond to the changing needs of her or his spouse, children, and grandchildren, many wills place most of the estate in a trust designed to deal with a variety of contingencies. There is no difficulty constituting the trust, since the personal representatives will obtain title to the estate by operation of law and have a duty to transfer the trust assets to the trustees when the estate is distributed.

In many cases, testators choose the same people to be both executors and trustees. When the administration of the estate is complete and it is ready for distribution, the executors simply become the trustees. This can lead to some uncertainty over the date on which the trust is created. It is not always easy to identify the moment when the personal rights of beneficiaries named in the will are exchanged for the property rights of beneficiaries under the testamentary trust.

Donationes Mortis Causa

A *donatio mortis causa* is a gift made in contemplation of the donor's impending death. The donee receives control (sometimes called **dominion**) over the thing during the donor's life, but the gift is not complete until the donor dies. While the donor lives, he or she is free to revoke the gift.

Conditional Gift

Donationes mortis causa are conditional gifts. The donor's intention to give is conditional upon her or his death. This need not be the only condition. A *donatio mortis causa* can be conditional on the donor's death and some other event. It can also be used to create a trust. For example, in *Hills v Hills* (1841) 8 M&W 401, 151 ER 1095, a dying woman gave her brother a purse containing £80, wanting him to have everything she had and to bury her comfortably. This was a valid *donatio mortis causa*, subject to a trust to pay for the burial and keep the rest for himself.

It is not always easy to tell whether a gift is conditional on the donor's death or made absolutely. Courts assume that gifts made in the shadow of impending death are conditional on that event, unless there is some evidence to the contrary. This assumption is made even though the donor has no hope of recovery and will die in the near future: see *Wilkes v Allington* [1931] 2 Ch 104. The *donatio mortis causa* is conditional even in that situation, because there is a possibility that the donee will die before the donor.

Inter Vivos or Testamentary

It is not clear whether *donationes mortis causa* are *inter vivos* or testamentary. They can be viewed as conditional gifts *inter vivos*, where the condition for giving just happens to be the donor's death rather than some other event (such as the donee's marriage or graduation from university). They can also be viewed, as they are here, as testamentary gifts.

It is sometimes assumed that *donationes mortis causa* are *inter vivos*, because they can be made without observing the formalities needed to make a valid will. All that is required is that they be made in contemplation of the donor's impending death and that the donee receive control of the subject matter of the gift before the donor dies.

The transfer of control before death distinguishes *donationes mortis causa* from other testamentary gifts and supports the view that they are gifts *inter vivos*. However, the distinction is not that significant. Since the donor is free to revoke the gift and recover control before death, a *donatio mortis causa* (like all testamentary gifts) remains ambulatory during the donor's life and is only perfected by her or his death. Also, if there are not enough assets in the rest of the donor's estate to pay its debts, a *donatio mortis causa* can be recalled and used for that purpose.

Before Death

The donee must receive control over the *donatio mortis causa* before the donor dies. What suffices for this purpose depends on the nature of the thing being given. For goods, the donee usually obtains control by delivery of possession, although delivery of a key providing access to the goods may do. For other things, control can be achieved through delivery of the indicia of ownership (such as a bank deposit book or title deed). The donee might even receive legal ownership of the thing, as in *Re Craven's Estate* [1937] Ch 423, where he received title to shares and money before the donor died.

While the donor lives, the distribution of property rights between the donor and donee will depend on the nature of the control given to the donee. Where a donee receives possession of goods or indicia of ownership, he or she will be a bailee of those things. In other words, the donor has ownership and the donee has only possession of the goods or documents prior to the donor's death. A donee who receives legal ownership of the *donatio mortis causa* is not free to use it in a manner inconsistent with the donor's right to recall the gift and recover ownership. In other words, the donee holds the *donatio mortis causa* in trust for the donor, who continues to be its beneficial owner.

After Death

The death of the donor satisfies the condition on which the *donatio mortis causa* is made (provided the donee survives and the donor did not revoke the gift). At that point, the donee's possession of goods or documents becomes legal ownership. The property rights to those things do not pass to the donor's personal representatives (unless they are needed to pay estate debts).

If the donee has only indicia of ownership, death might not complete the gift. For example, if the subject of a *donatio mortis causa* is an interest in Torrens land, it will not pass to the donee until registration of a transfer of that interest. If the donee does not have the documents needed to complete the transfer, he or she will require the assistance of the donor's personal representatives to complete the gift. Surprisingly, a court of equity will compel them to do so. As Cotton LJ stated in *Re Dillon* (1890) 44 Ch D 76 at 82, "This would not be so in the case of an incomplete gift *inter vivos* — the Court would not interfere to compel either the donor or his executors to perfect it; the doctrine is an anomalous one peculiar to the case of a *donatio mortis causa.*"

Since the donor's personal representatives can be compelled to transfer the *donatio mortis causa* to the donee, they hold it in trust for the donee. This is a constructive trust created to perfect the donor's intention to give. As Lord Eldon said in *Duffield v Elwes* (1827) 1 Bli NS 497 at 543, 4 ER 976 (where a father made a *donatio mortis causa* of a mortgage by delivery of the mortgage deed to his daughter), "this is a good *donatio mortis causa*, raising by operation of law a trust; a trust which being raised by operation of law, is not within the statute of frauds, but a trust which a Court of Equity will execute".

What Things?

It had long been assumed that only some things could be transferred by *donatio mortis causa*. For example, mortgages could be transferred, but not beneficial ownership of land, and there were doubts about corporate shares. This incoherent patchwork of rules is difficult to justify, but could perhaps be explained by judicial dissatisfaction with this exception to the usual formalities needed to make a valid testamentary gift and a desire to limit it as much as possible.

In *Bayliss v Public Trustee* (1988) 12 NSWLR 540, Needham J decided that freehold estates could not be *donationes mortis causa*. He could not find a reason for this rule other than precedent set by old English cases. Fortunately, in *Sen v Headley* [1991] Ch 425, the English Court of Appeal declared that the traditional assumptions were false and that a *donatio mortis causa* of a freehold estate could be made by delivery of the title deeds. Nourse LJ said (at 440):

> "Let it be agreed that the doctrine is anomalous. Anomalies do not justify anomalous exceptions. If due account is taken of the present state of the law in regard to mortgages and choses in action, it is apparent that to make a distinction in the case of land would be to make just such an exception. A *donatio mortis causa* of land is neither more nor less anomalous than any other. Every such gift is a circumvention of the *Wills Act* 1837. Why should the additional statutory formalities for the creation and transmission of interests in land be regarded as some larger obstacle?"

Delivery of the indicia of ownership does not normally transfer legal title to the donee, but produces a *donatio mortis causa* by way of a trust for the donee arising on the death of the donor. There is no reason why it cannot have the same effect for all property rights to land, corporate shares, and other assets. The essential question is this: does possession of the indicia of ownership give the donee some degree of control over the thing in question? If a transfer of ownership would normally involve delivery of those documents to the new owner, then a person should be able to make a *donatio mortis causa* by delivering them to the donee.

Cheques can be the subject of *donationes mortis causa*, so long as they are not written by the donor. A third party cheque is an asset in the donor's hands and delivery to the donee would give her or him control over it. The donor's own cheque is different. It is merely an instruction to her or his bank to pay the donee (which ceases to be effective when the donor dies). Possession of the cheque does not give the donee control over the donor's bank account or any other assets.

Transfers on Death by Operation of Law

This part concerns transfers of property rights by operation of law. One such transfer has already been discussed: the transfer of the estate from a deceased person to her or his personal representatives. Discussed here are situations in which the law intervenes to cause the transfer of property rights from those representatives to others.

In some cases, the law intervenes to perfect an intention or promise to make a testamentary gift. These are discussed below under the headings, **secret trusts** and **mutual wills**. In other cases, deceased persons fail to express any intention to give or the law is unable to give effect to their intentions. Their property rights are distributed according to the law of **intestacy** or as **bona vacantia**. In yet other cases, the law overrides the choices of deceased persons to benefit surviving family members who ought to have received a portion of the estate. This is made possible by **family provision legislation**.

Secret Trusts

A secret trust can arise when someone receives an asset from a deceased person's estate, having previously agreed to use it for the benefit of another. The recipient can be compelled by a court of equity to fulfil that undertaking and, therefore, holds that asset in trust for that other person.

This is called a secret trust because it is not set out in a will (which gets admitted to probate and becomes a public document). The settlor is hoping to keep the existence of the trust secret by making the arrangement informally with a friend who agrees to act as the secret trustee. The settlor then arranges his affairs so that, after her or his death, the friend will receive the trust assets when the estate is distributed. At one time secret trusts were used by wealthy men who wanted to provide for lovers and illegitimate children, without disclosing those relationships to the public.

Sometimes the trust appears in the will but its objects are missing. For example, I might die leaving a will which gives you $10,000 "to be used only for the purposes that I have communicated" to you. It is clear that you are not intended to keep this money for your own benefit, but the entire trust is not disclosed in the will. This is called a **half secret trust** and is valid provided I have previously communicated the objects of the trust to you and you agreed to carry it out.

Secret trusts are valid even though they are made informally, without writing, signature, and two witnesses as required by the *Wills Act*. The creation of a secret trust requires just three steps: communication to the intended trustee, acceptance by that trustee, and constitution of the trust: see *Voges v Monaghan* (1954) 94 CLR 231.

Communication

The terms of a secret trust must be communicated to the trustee before the settlor dies. This was not done in *Re Boyes* (1884) 26 Ch D 531 and, therefore, the trust failed. Boyes made a will leaving his entire estate to his friend and solicitor, Carritt, and told him to hold the estate on trust, with instructions to follow by letter. Those instructions were contained in a letter found after Boyes' death among his personal papers. Carritt wanted to carry out the secret trust, but this was not permitted. Instead, he held the estate on resulting trust for Boyes' next of kin: see page 328.

The deadline for communicating the terms of a secret trust may exist for the same reason as the formalities required by the *Wills Act*: the prevention of fraud. Deceased persons are not available to contradict false claims of entitlement to their estates. The formalities required by the *Wills Act* reduce the risk that forged documents will be admitted to probate. If secret trusts could be created or varied by unsigned or unwitnessed papers found among a deceased person's things, that risk would be greatly increased. Communication during the settlor's life provides some safeguard. At least the secret trustee can verify instructions if there is any doubt about their validity.

In England, Canada, and New Zealand, the deadline for communication of a half secret trust is the execution of the will. This rule is difficult to justify. An informal communication of trust objects, which follows an incomplete declaration of trust in a will, might be objectionable because it looks like an informal codicil. However, a similar criticism can be made of fully secret trusts. Also, it is strange that the execution of a will should have any immediate significance. For all other purposes, wills are effective only on the death of the testator.

In *Ledgerwood v Perpetual Trustee Co Ltd* (1997) 41 NSWLR 532, Young J noted criticisms of the rule abroad and the absence of authority on it in Australia. He chose to follow the rule in Ireland and most of the United States, where half and fully secret trusts are both valid so long as there is communication and acceptance before the death of the settlor. It is not clear how the law will develop outside New South Wales, but it is likely that this departure from a much criticised rule will be welcome across Australia.

Acceptance

The second step in the creation of a secret trust is acceptance of that trust by the intended trustee. Acquiescence is sufficient. If the terms of the trust are communicated and the trustee does not decline the trust, the settlor can assume that the arrangement is acceptable.

Of course, people cannot be forced to accept the onerous responsibilities of trusteeship. If a secret trustee does not want to carry out the trust, replacement trustees can be appointed. However, the trust will not fail unless the settlor knew about the intended trustee's decision and had time to make alternate arrangements.

Constitution

The last step needed to create a secret trust is its constitution by a transfer of the subject of the trust to the trustee: see page 253. This happens when the estate is distributed and the trustee receives the assets which he or she agreed to hold in trust. In most cases, those assets are given to the secret trustee as a specific or residuary gift in the settlor's will. However, a secret trust can be created without a will, if the intended trustee is the settlor's heir and will receive the trust assets according to the rules of intestacy, discussed below.

Inter Vivos or Testamentary

It is sometimes suggested that secret trusts are *inter vivos*. This is because they require communication and acceptance during the settlor's life and because they can be created informally without complying with the *Wills Act*. However, a secret trust cannot come into existence before the settlor dies, the debts of the estate are paid, and the trust assets are transferred to the secret trustee. There is no certainty of subject matter or constitution of the trust until then. After communication and acceptance, the settlor remains free to change or revoke the instructions or not give those assets to the secret trustee.

Express or Constructive

There is also some debate about whether secret trusts are express or constructive. It is true that the settlor intends to create the secret trust and that the law gives effect to that intention if the minimal requirements for a secret trust are met. However, that intention does not create the trust directly as a declaration of express trust. This is because it has not been manifest properly as required by the *Wills Act*. The trust arises by operation of law to perfect that intention because the settlor died relying on the trustee's undertaking to perform the trust.

Secret trusts are frequently criticised. Why should equity intervene to cure the settlor's failure to observe the formalities required for testamentary dispositions? At least three different answers to this question have been proposed: unjust enrichment, fraud, and detrimental reliance.

First, it is true that secret trustees would be unjustly enriched if they were allowed to keep the trust assets, because the settlor did not intend to make a gift to the secret trustee. However, the normal response to unjust enrichment is restitution: see Chapter 24. If the trust is created by unjust enrichment, it should carry the asset back to the settlor's estate (as happened in *Re Boyes*, above, where the secret trust failed). Since the unjust enrichment is not at the intended beneficiary's expense, it does not explain why the secret trust carries the enrichment forward to that beneficiary.

Secondly, it is often suggested that secret trusts arise to prevent fraud. It would be wrong for the secret trustee to keep the asset and not fulfil the trust, but this cannot explain why there is a trust in the first place. Also, most secret trustees are honest friends (like the solicitor in *Re Boyes*) who want to carry out the trust. There is no hint of fraud or other wrongdoing. Even if a secret trustee was guilty of fraud, it would not explain why the beneficiary becomes entitled to the trust assets.

The third explanation is best: a secret trust responds to the settlor's detrimental reliance on the trustee's undertaking. The settlor died with the expectation that the trust would be performed and could have made other arrangements if he or she had reason to suspect otherwise. It is now too late for that, so equity fulfils that expectation with a secret trust (so long as the minimal requirements for a secret trust have been met).

Mutual Wills

Spouses (married or de facto) sometimes make agreements about the distribution of their estates when they die. For example, my wife and I might agree that the last to die will leave everything to our children. So, we make mutual wills in which everything goes to the surviving spouse and is otherwise divided equally among our children.

One spouse cannot prevent the other from making a new will. However, if one of us dies (say me) with the agreed will in place, a court of equity will intervene to ensure that our agreement is performed. If the survivor (my wife) changes or revokes her will and disposes of her estate differently than agreed, her personal representatives will hold her estate in trust for the agreed beneficiaries (our children). This is a constructive trust which perfects the survivor's promise to dispose of her estate in a particular way.

When does the Trust Arise?

Normally, the survivor has agreed to leave her or his estate (whatever it might be) to certain beneficiaries. The assets available for distribution will not be identified until the survivor dies and the estate debts are paid. This is when the constructive trust arises: see *Birmingham v Renfrew* (1937) 57 CLR 666 at 689-691. Since the agreement did not relate to any particular thing, it does not affect the survivor's freedom to deal with her or his assets during life.

In some cases, the spouses agreed that a specific asset (such as a house) would be given to certain beneficiaries once they were both dead. The promise affects the survivor's use of that asset. He or she is not free to deal with it, but must preserve it and give it to the beneficiaries as agreed. Therefore, the constructive trust arises when the first spouse dies. The survivor holds the asset in trust for herself or himself for life, with the remainder belonging to the agreed beneficiaries: see *Fisher v Mansfield* [1997] 2 NZLR 230.

Why does the Trust Arise?

As with secret trusts, various theories have been proposed to explain mutual wills. As before, unjust enrichment and fraud are inadequate for this purpose. If the survivor is unjustly enriched, it is not at the expense of the constructive trust beneficiaries. He or she may have received assets from the estate of the first spouse to die, but that is not required. The trust can attach to the survivor's own assets to perfect her or his promise to make the agreed testamentary disposition: see *University of Manitoba v Sanderson Estate* (1998) 155 DLR (4th) 40 at 57.

The failure to make the agreed testamentary disposition might be a breach of contract, but is not necessarily fraud. The survivor might have made the promise honestly intending to keep it, but later changed her or his mind. Also, the survivor might break the agreement unintentionally by remarrying. Marriage automatically revokes a person's will and, therefore, the survivor could die intestate without realising that the mutual will was no longer valid. The constructive trust will arise to perfect the agreement even in the absence of fraud.

Mutual wills and secret trusts are enforced for similar reasons. The first spouse to die expected the survivor to make the agreed testamentary disposition and could have made other arrangements in the absence of that agreement. That detrimental reliance on the survivor's promise justifies equitable intervention (by way of constructive trust) to perfect that promise.

Intestacy

As stated above, intestacy occurs when a person dies without completely disposing of her or his estate by will (or by *donatio mortis causa*). Usually, this is because there is no valid will and the deceased is wholly intestate. However, a valid will might fail to dispose of everything (for example, where the residuary beneficiary dies before the testator), resulting in a partial intestacy.

In each jurisdiction, the distribution of an intestate's estate is governed by statute, which determines who is entitled to that estate and in what proportions. The rules vary from one jurisdiction to another, but they follow the same general pattern. The relatives of the deceased person are divided into three groups: spouse (married or de facto), issue (meaning children, grandchildren, etc), and others. If the deceased is survived by a spouse or issue, they get everything in most jurisdictions. Otherwise, the estate goes to the closest surviving relatives.

Where both spouse and issue survive, the estate is divided among them according to a formula. For example, section 51 of the *Administration and Probate Act* 1958 (Vic) allocates to the surviving spouse the "personal chattels" of the deceased, $100,000 worth of residuary estate, and one third of the balance. Anything left over is divided among the issue. Each jurisdiction uses a different formula. Western Australia also requires a surviving spouse to share with other relatives when there is no surviving issue: *Administration Act* 1903 (WA), s 14.

Where the deceased person is not survived by spouse or issue, the estate goes to the next closest relatives. In many jurisdictions, surviving parents take everything. If the parents are dead, then everything might go to the next closest relatives, as ranked by statute. For example, section 61B of the *Wills, Probate and Administration Act* 1898 (NSW) sets the priority of claims on the estate as follows: spouse and issue, parents, brothers and sisters, grandparents, and (last of all) aunts and uncles. Alternatively, all of the relatives might share the estate if there is no surviving spouse or issue: see, eg, *Administration and Probate Act* 1919 (SA), s 72G.

Bona Vacantia

The group of relatives who have a claim against the estate of an intestate is defined by statute in each jurisdiction. Most definitions are broad enough to include first cousins, but may be wider or narrower. If there are no surviving relatives, the estate belongs to the Crown.

The Crown's right to these estates is now statutory, but it can be traced back to two sources. First, if land owners died without heirs, their estates would **escheat** to the Crown as the landlord from whom they held tenure: see page 90. Secondly, the Crown had a prerogative right to all *bona vacantia* (ownerless goods). In most jurisdictions, escheat has been abolished and all otherwise ownerless property, whether real or personal, belongs to the Crown as *bona vacantia*: see *Administration and Probate Act* 1935 (Tas), s 45. In Western Australia, "the whole of the intestate property passes to the Crown by way of escheat": *Administration Act* 1903 (WA), s 14. South Australia avoids these historical contradictions and declares simply that "the intestate estate shall vest in the Crown": *Administration and Probate Act* 1919 (SA), s 72G.

Family Provision

In each state and territory, dependants and former dependants of a deceased person can apply to the court to vary the way in which the estate would be distributed under the will or on intestacy. If the deceased person failed to make adequate provision for people who previously depended on her or him for financial or similar support, the court can redistribute the estate to make that provision: see *Singer v Berghouse* (1994) 181 CLR 201.

The list of people entitled to apply varies from one jurisdiction to another, but includes spouses and children and might also include parents, grandchildren, and others who resided with the deceased and depended on her or him for support: see, eg, *Family Provision Act* 1969 (ACT), s 7; *Testator's Family Maintenance Act* 1912 (Tas), s 3A. Spouses can be married or de facto and, in some places, a person who was divorced from the deceased person can apply: see *Inheritance (Family and Dependants Provision) Act* 1972 (WA), s 7.

If the court believes that the applicant deserved a greater share of the estate, it can vary the distribution of the estate to include payments or transfers of assets to the applicant. This means that the rights of other beneficiaries of the estate will be reduced to make provision for the applicant. The court can specify how that burden will be allocated among the estate assets. The court order takes effect as if it was a will or codicil.

In New South Wales, the court has the power to increase the size of the estate for the purpose of making provision for an applicant. It can do this by setting aside *inter vivos* dispositions of assets by the deceased person during the last year of her or his life, if the deceased had a greater moral duty to provide for the applicant, and during the last three years, if the transaction was intended to defeat the applicant's claim for provision: *Family Provision Act* 1982 (NSW), s 23. The assets then become part of the "notional estate" available for distribution to the applicant and other rights to those assets can be extinguished: s 29.

Chapter Twenty-Three

DETRIMENTAL RELIANCE

■■■

Normally, a promise to create a property right will have legal consequences only if the promise is contractual or the promisor has done everything necessary to give effect to it. In most other cases, the promise is wholly ineffective, since "equity will not assist a volunteer" (see the discussion of incomplete gifts at page 271). There are several important exceptions to this maxim. Almost all of them depend on detrimental reliance: the promise is enforced because someone relied on it and thereby suffered a detriment.

Detrimental reliance on promises can create property rights in several situations. Two were discussed in Chapter 22: secret trusts and mutual wills. In both situations, someone wanted to make a testamentary gift and died relying on another's promise to complete the gift. The detriment suffered by the donor was the lost opportunity to make alternate arrangements. A court of equity will intervene to compel the promisor (or her or his personal representatives) to make the gift as promised.

Discussed in this chapter are two more situations in which detrimental reliance can lead to the creation of equitable property rights. The first is a principle called estoppel. The second is a particular context: the breakdown of a marriage or similar relationship. In these cases, someone has relied (to her or his detriment) on an expectation of receiving a property right and a court of equity intervened to fulfil that expectation in whole or in part. This differs from cases of secret trusts and mutual wills, where the court intervened because the donor had relied on another's promise to complete a gift.

Estoppel

Estoppel is an odd word likely to be encountered only in legal circles. It comes from the Old French word for bung or stopper: see Birks, Equity in the Modern Law (1996) 26 *UWA Law Review* 1 at 21-22. Traditionally, estoppel occurred when someone was not permitted to deny in court the truth of a representation he or she had made earlier. That person was **estopped** from giving evidence which contradicted the earlier representation. However, the concept has been enlarged and is now used to enforce promises and create property rights.

Varieties of Estoppel

There are a variety of reasons why a person might be estopped and a variety of legal consequences of estoppel. This chapter is concerned with estoppel as a source of property rights. Those cases (like most cases of estoppel) are based on detrimental reliance. Someone has been led to believe that he or she will acquire a property right, has arranged her or his affairs accordingly, and will suffer a serious detriment if that expectation is disappointed. A court of equity can intervene to fulfil that expectation.

There are now two main types of estoppel: **common law estoppel** and **equitable estoppel**. Although both are based on detrimental reliance, they operate differently and produce different legal consequences. Equitable estoppel is the only kind which creates property rights.

There are other types of estoppel which do not depend on detrimental reliance. For example, a person who executes a deed is not normally permitted to contradict its contents in litigation involving that deed. This is called **estoppel by deed**. Its underlying rationale is that people should be entitled to rely on representations made in the form of a deed. However, it does not depend on proof of reliance or detriment.

Common Law Estoppel

Estoppel began, and still has a valuable role to play, as a rule of evidence. If I lead you to believe that a certain fact is true and you rely on my representation to your detriment, then, in litigation between us, I am not permitted to prove that the fact is false. For example, suppose that I overpay you by mistake. You suspect an error and call me to verify the amount. I assure you that it was calculated correctly. Relying on your belief that you are entitled to the whole amount, you take a trip that you could not otherwise afford. When you return, I call to say that I was mistaken after all and ask you to refund the overpayment. My right to restitution of the overpayment (see Chapter 24) is destroyed by estoppel, since I am not permitted to deny my prior representation that I was not mistaken.

This form of estoppel affects only the conduct of the litigation. However, that can affect our legal rights and obligations by preventing me from proving the facts needed to establish the existence of those rights and obligations.

This type of estoppel is often called common law estoppel, because it is used by courts of common law. However, the name is misleading since this estoppel is not restricted to those courts, but is a general rule of evidence available to litigants in any court. There are two main limits to common law estoppel. These are:

1) .....it is a defence and not a cause of action; and
2) .....the representation must relate to existing facts and not future conduct.

Dissatisfaction with both these limits led courts of equity to expand its operation.

Equitable Estoppel

Courts of equity began to use estoppel in cases where representations related not to existing facts, but to future conduct. Although this may seem like a small step, it is a major change. It means that non-contractual promises can be enforced on the basis of detrimental reliance. Estoppel is no longer just a defence, but can be a source of new rights, including property rights.

This form of estoppel is called equitable estoppel to distinguish it from common law estoppel and to indicate that the principles involved are equitable. The label is not very helpful, since it suggests that someone is stopped from doing something, whereas the actual outcome is the creation of new rights. However, it does convey two important ideas. First, rights created by equitable estoppel, whether personal or property, are equitable. Secondly, someone familiar with common law estoppel will suspect that detrimental reliance is involved in the creation of those rights.

What is now known in Australia as equitable estoppel evolved from two similar types of estoppel, which developed in England: **proprietary estoppel** and **promissory estoppel**. Proprietary estoppel occurs when someone improves land, believing that he or she has, or will get, a right to use that land. If the owner is responsible for creating or encouraging that belief, the improver might acquire the right as believed. Promissory estoppel occurs when one party to a contract is led to believe that the other party will not enforce her or his rights under the contract. If the first party acts in reliance on that belief, the other party might be prevented from enforcing those rights.

In *Walton Stores (Interstate) Ltd v Maher* (1988) 164 CLR 387, the High Court of Australia recognised that proprietary and promissory estoppel were applications of the same general principle. Mason CJ and Wilson J said (at 404), "One may discern in the cases a common thread which links them together, namely, the principle that equity will come to the relief of a plaintiff who has acted to his [or her] detriment on the basis of a basic assumption" for which the defendant is responsible.

Creation of Estoppel

Estoppels based on detrimental reliance depend on two things. First, one person has made a representation which induces another person to believe something to be true. Secondly, the other person relies on that belief to her or his detriment. It is the combination of those two factors which produces legal consequences.

Representation

A representation is any conduct which induces another to believe something to be true. It might be a promise which is clearly expressed, as in *Giumelli v Giumelli* (1999) 196 CLR 101, where parents told their son that, if he continued to work in their orchard and built a house on their land, he could have that house and the land on which it stood.

The representation can be a failure to act, as in *Walton Stores (Interstate) Ltd v Maher* (1988) 164 CLR 387, where Maher was negotiating to lease commercial space to Walton Stores. The negotiations proceeded to the stage where Maher's solicitor had sent the lease to Walton's solicitor for execution. Believing that the legal formalities would soon be completed, Maher began demolishing its existing building to make way for a new building to be constructed to Walton's specifications. Walton was aware of the demolition work and yet chose not to tell Maher that he was having second thoughts about the lease and looking for another location. Walton's failure to speak up and correct Maher's mistaken belief amounted to a representation that Walton would execute the lease.

Detrimental Reliance

Detrimental reliance occurs when people believe a representation and arrange their affairs accordingly. The falsification of that belief leaves them worse off than if the representation had never been made. Detrimental reliance may consist of positive acts, such as the demolition work in *Walton Stores v Maher* or construction work in *Giumelli v Giumelli*. It can also be a failure to act, such as Robert Giumelli's decision to continue working in his parents' orchard and not pursue an alternative career.

The reliance on the representation must be reasonable in the circumstances. In most cases, it will not be reasonable to rely on a gratuitous promise, since the promisor is under no legal obligation to fulfil it. As Robert Goff LJ said, in *Amalgamated Property Co v Texas Bank* [1982] QB 84 at 107, the "promise will not generally give rise to an estoppel, even if acted on by the promisee, for the promisee may reasonably be expected to appreciate that, to render it binding, it must be incorporated in a binding contract or contractual variation, and that he cannot therefore safely rely on it as a legally binding promise without first taking the necessary contractual steps".

It is more reasonable to rely on non-contractual promises when they are made by family members, as in the *Giumelli* case. Most intra-family arrangements are informal. In the absence of a binding legal obligation, love and affection provide some assurance that the promise will be kept. Outside the family, people are expected to take greater care to look after their own interests. It will not be reasonable to rely heavily on a gratuitous promise in a commercial setting, unless something unusual occurs, as in *Walton Stores v Maher*.

The use of estoppel to give legal effect to non-contractual promises involves a fairly high level of uncertainty. When is it reasonable to rely on such a promise and what amount of detriment will cause it have legal effect? At what point did the representation become binding in *Walton Stores v Maher*? When demolition was completed? When it began? When the demolition crew was hired? In contrast, it is fairly easy to tell when a contractual promise is binding. The parties know they have a contract and can identify with precision when it was made.

This uncertainty is unsettling. However, equitable estoppel is a relatively rare event and most dealings between people are unaffected by it. Also, equitable estoppel is a relatively new concept and has not yet had the attention needed to produce a mature body of law (like the law of contracts). A greater level of certainty will emerge as courts have more opportunities to consider and refine its principles.

Consequences of Estoppel

The consequence of common law estoppel is indicated by its name. The person who represented a fact to be true is "estopped" from denying it in subsequent litigation. In contrast, equitable estoppel fails to describe the outcome. The person "estopped" is not prevented from doing something, but is compelled to fulfil another's expectation, in whole or in part, or provide compensation for failing to do so.

Possible Responses to Equitable Estoppel

As with contracts, equitable estoppels usually create personal rights, but sometimes give rise to property rights. If the estoppel concerns an expectation of receiving a property right, it might produce one of three different equitable rights:

1) .....the equitable version of the expected property right;
2) .....a similar property right; or
3) .....a personal right to compensation.

Crabb v Arun District Council [1976] 1 Ch 197 provides an example of the first outcome. The council led Crabb to believe that he would be granted a right of way over its road. When it erected a fence between Crabb's land and the road, it left a gap at the proposed access point. Crabb then subdivided his land (with the council's approval) and sold the portion with the only other access to the road. The council then refused to grant the right of way unless Crabb paid £3,000. He refused to pay that much and the council closed the right of way, leaving him without access to his land for five years. Crabb was entitled to the promised right of way in equity. In other words, he had an equitable easement.

The second outcome is exemplified by *Silovi Pty Ltd v Barbaro* (1988) 3 NSWLR 466. The owners of a plant nursery made a contract to obtain a 10 year lease of a portion of their neighbour's land and spent over $100,000 installing an irrigation system and planting trees on that land. The contract could not be performed because a lease of more than five years would be an illegal subdivision of the land. Equitable estoppel could not create the promised, illegal lease, but did give rise to the next best thing: an equitable profit à prendre.

Giumelli v Giumelli (1999) 196 CLR 101 demonstrates the third outcome. A son was promised a portion of his parents' land on which he constructed a house. A subdivision of that land was not suitable, since the relations between the son and his parents were strained and his younger brother was now living in the house with his family. The son did not get the promised property right, but a personal right to payment of the value of that property right (secured by a lien on the land).

Choosing the Appropriate Response

The three cases above demonstrate three possible outcomes of equitable estoppel. A property right is not possible unless the claimant detrimentally relied on an expectation of receiving a property right. However, the estoppel might not produce the expected right, but create a lesser property right or a personal right. What determines the appropriate outcome? This question is not easy to answer. However, a comparison with contractual promises to grant property rights is helpful.

As discussed at page 258, most contracts to grant property rights are not specifically enforceable. The normal response to a breach of contract is compensation. Specific performance is possible only when compensation is not an adequate substitute for performance of the contract.

Equitable estoppel operates in a similar fashion. The court compels the owner to fulfil the expectation only when there is no other satisfactory way to correct the detriment resulting from reliance on that expectation. If the payment of compensation will correct the problem, it is the preferred choice. The middle ground, chosen in *Silovi Pty Ltd v Barbaro*, above, is used when compensation is inadequate, but the expected property right is unavailable. The court can then select a similar available property right.

There is (in theory) an important difference between contracts to grant property rights and equitable estoppel. The courts are worried about using estoppel to circumvent the requirements for making valid contracts to create property rights. Why have a well developed law of contracts if detrimental reliance can produce the same results? In response to this concern, the High Court was very careful to say that equitable estoppel was used not to enforce non-contractual promises, but to alleviate the detriment involved. As Brennan J said in *Walton Stores (Interstate) Ltd v Maher* (1988) 164 CLR 387 at 423-424:

> "The object of the equity is not to compel the party bound to fulfil the assumption or expectation; it is to avoid the detriment which, if the assumption or expectation goes unfulfilled, will be suffered by the party who has been induced to act or to abstain from acting thereon. If this object is kept steadily in mind, the concern that a general application of the principle of equitable estoppel would make non-contractual promises enforceable as contractual promises can be allayed."

The application of this principle should mean that estoppels are rarely used to fulfil expectations. However, this does not seem to be true. Although there are relatively few cases of estoppel arising from an expectation of receiving a property right, the expected property right is created in a large portion of those cases.

Also, the different objects of estoppel and contract should mean that compensation is calculated differently for estoppel and breach of contract. As discussed at page 258, damages for breach of contract are designed to put the plaintiff in the position he or she would have been in had the contract been performed. They are measured by the value of the promised property right.

In contrast, a right to compensation created by estoppel should be measured by the detriment suffered by the plaintiff. However, this does not seem to be the case. In *Giumelli v Giumelli* (1999) 196 CLR 101 at 128, the High Court declared that the son was "entitled to payment by [his parents] of a sum representing the present value of the promised lot". This is the same measure that would have been used if the promise had been contractual and not the value of the detriment suffered by the son in reliance on that promise.

The difference between theory and practice means that responses to equitable estoppel are somewhat unpredictable. In contract law, there are well settled rules dictating when specific performance is available and how damages are calculated when it is not. That level of certainty does not yet exist in relation to equitable estoppel: see Gardner, "The Remedial Discretion in Proprietary Estoppel" (1999) 115 *Law Quarterly Review* 438.

Family Property

Most Australians share their homes with others, such as a spouse, de facto spouse, same-sex partner, children, parents, other relatives, or friends. People who live together and love each other are likely to pool their wealth or work cooperatively to acquire things and pay expenses. In most relationships, the legal ownership of things acquired co-operatively will be shared. Most couples rent or own their homes as joint tenants, keep joint bank accounts, and own many other assets jointly. Other things are owned separately because it is agreed that they belong to individual members of the family and not to the couple or family as a whole.

Sometimes, legal ownership of things acquired by family members does not reflect accurately their agreements concerning ownership or their contributions to the relationship. For example, one person might be the sole owner of the house, even though her or his partner contributed to its acquisition or expected to receive a share of that house. The partner without legal title shares the use and enjoyment of the house while the relationship continues. However, without a legal right to possession, the partner is relying on the love or affection of the owner to protect her or his interest in the house.

Ownership of Assets at the End of a Relationship

Problems can arise when a family relationship comes to an end through death, divorce, or separation. If the legal ownership accurately reflects the agreement between the parties concerning the sharing of their family assets, the division of those assets can be made according to the rules which govern the enforcement and division of legal property rights. Each party will retain legal ownership of any interests held as a sole owner, tenant in common, or joint tenant. If they cannot agree on the division of their shared property rights, they can apply to a court for a partition of those rights, as discussed at page 142. If the relationship ends through death, the surviving party will acquire sole legal ownership of any jointly-owned assets and the remainder of the deceased party's assets will be distributed according to the rules discussed in Chapter 22.

If the legal ownership of family assets does not match the parties' understanding regarding their rights to those assets or their contributions to the acquisition of those assets, the end of the relationship can create substantial hardship for the party who lacks legal title. The legal owner has a right to exclude others from using those assets, including the other party to that relationship. The party without title may have contributed to the relationship for many years and made many sacrifices in reliance on her or his expectation of owning a share of the family assets. For example, it is not uncommon for a woman to forego educational and career opportunities to raise children and maintain the household, while her spouse or de facto spouse pursues his career and acquires wealth. The end of the relationship can leave him with the bulk of the family's wealth and her with very little to show for her contributions and sacrifices over many years.

Courts can intervene in these cases to prevent the legal owner of the family assets from using her or his legal property rights to exclude her or his spouse, de facto spouse, or partner from using and enjoying a share of those assets. In essence, the court has the power to redistribute the legal ownership of the family assets in certain situations. There are two sources of that power: statutes and equity.

Statutes

The Commonwealth has the constitutional authority to legislate concerning the redistribution of family assets on the breakdown of a marriage. That power is conferred on the courts by the *Family Law Act* 1975 (Cth). Most of the states and territories have statutes which deal with the division of assets between de facto spouses. Some of those statutes also provide for people in other relationships.

This method of creating property rights has nothing to do with detrimental reliance. It is not based on consent, wrongdoing, or unjust enrichment, but is an event which belongs in the category of miscellaneous other events: a statutory discretion to vary property rights at the end of a marriage or similar relationship.

Marriage

Section 79 of the *Family Law Act* 1975 (Cth) states that:

> "In proceedings with respect to the property of the parties to a marriage or either of them, the court may make such order as it considers appropriate altering the interests of the parties in the property."

This confers a power on the court to exercise its discretion to vary property rights on the breakdown of a marriage, whenever it appears to be "just and equitable" to do so.

The court's discretion is controlled by a list of factors which must be taken into account. Some of them relate to past events, such as the financial and other contributions of the parties "to the acquisition, conservation or improvement of" their property and their contributions "to the welfare of the family". Other factors relate to future needs of the parties, including their income, financial resources, age, health, and child care responsibilities. This enables the court to take into account sacrifices and lost opportunities which do not add to the family's wealth.

Several judgments of the Family Court suggested that an equal division of family assets was an appropriate starting point on the breakdown of a long marriage. However, the High Court of Australia rejected that approach in *Mallet v Mallet* (1984) 156 CLR 605 at 610, where Gibbs J said:

> "Even to say that in some circumstances equality should be the normal starting point is to require the courts to act on a presumption which is unauthorized by the legislation. The respective values of the contributions made by the parties must depend entirely on the facts of the case and the nature of the final order made by the court must result from a proper exercise of the wide discretionary power whose nature I have discussed, unfettered by the application of supposed rules for which the *Family Law Act* provides no warrant."

The wide statutory discretion causes some concern, since it can make it difficult for parties to predict the outcome of court proceedings and settle their differences without litigation. Also, as Brennan J said in *Norbis v Norbis* (1986) 161 CLR 513 at 536, "[t]he anguish and emotion generated by litigation of this kind are exacerbated by orders which are made without the sanction of known principles and which are seen to be framed according to idiosyncratic notions of an individual judge". Guidelines for the exercise of this discretion continue to be developed and refined by the courts, but that form of law making is expensive for the parties concerned.

Other Relationships

There are statutes in the Australian Capital Territory, New South Wales, the Northern Territory, South Australia, and Victoria which authorise courts to redistribute the property rights of de facto spouses at the end of their relationship. In the Australian Capital Territory and New South Wales, those statutes apply to other relationships as well. Two questions are discussed briefly here: first, to what relationships do the statutes apply and, secondly, what factors are taken into account when redistributing property rights?

What Relationships?

The family property statutes in the Northern Territory, South Australia, and Victoria deal only with de facto spouses. For example, section 3 of the *De Facto Relationships Act* 1996 (SA) defines "de facto relationship" as "the relationship between a man and a woman, who although not legally married to each other, live together on a genuine domestic basis as husband and wife". This excludes gay and lesbian couples and couples who live in nonsexual relationships.

The statutes in the Australian Capital Territory and New South Wales apply to a broader range of relationships. Under section 15 of the *Domestic Relationships Act* 1994 (ACT), "a court may make an order adjusting the interests in the property of" parties to a "domestic relationship", which is defined (in section 3) as "a personal relationship (other than a legal marriage) between 2 adults in which 1 provides personal or financial commitment and support of a domestic nature for the material benefit of the other, and includes a de facto marriage".

The definitions in sections 4 and 5 of the *Property (Relationships) Act 1984* (NSW) are at least as broad. A "de facto relationship" does not depend on the sex of the parties, but means "a relationship between two adult persons who live together as a couple, and who are not married to one another or related by family". The court can redistribute the property rights of a couple in a "domestic relationship", which is defined as either a de facto relationship or "a close personal relationship (other than a marriage or a de facto relationship) between two adult persons, whether or not related by family, who are living together, one or each of whom provides the other with domestic support and personal care".

The court does not have the power to redistribute property rights of people in de facto or domestic relationships unless the relationship lasted for at least two years, the parties have a child, or one party as made substantial contributions for which he or she "would otherwise not be adequately compensated if the order were not made": see *De Facto Relationships Act* 1996 (NT), s 16. In South Australia, the power to redistribute property rights arises only where "the de facto relationship existed for at least three years or there is a child of the de facto partners": *De Facto Relationships Act* 1996 (SA), s 9.

What Factors?

In most states and territories, the factors which guide the court's redistribution of property rights between de facto spouses (and other couples) are narrower than those which apply to married couples, under the *Family Law Act* 1975 (Cth). Section 285 of the *Property Law Act* 1958 (Vic) is typical. It lists only past events, such as "the acquisition, conservation or improvement of" their property or financial resources, the contributions as a "homemaker or parent ... to the welfare of the family", and "any written agreement entered into by the de facto partners". It does not refer to the future needs of the parties.

The *Domestic Relationships Act* 1994 (ACT) does include the future needs of the parties in the list of factors which can affect the redistribution of their property rights. It includes their "income, property and financial resources", "physical and mental capacity ... for appropriate gainful employment", and "financial needs and obligations": s 19.

The differences among factors listed in the various statutes dealing with the property of married couples, de facto spouses, and others, may not be that important. In *Dwyer v Kaljo* (1992) 15 Fam LR 645, the New South Wales Court of Appeal considered the factors now located in section 20 of the *Property (Relationships) Act* 1984 (NSW). Like most states and territories, these are limited to the contributions of the parties to the assets or welfare of the family. The majority of the court decided that it was not bound by that list, but could use its statutory power to fulfil the reasonable expectations of the parties. Unfortunately, this makes it even harder for couples to predict the outcome of litigation.

Equity

The statutes for redistributing family assets do not displace the rules of equity. They also leave gaps which must be filled by those rules. A traditional role of courts of equity is to compel legal owners to use their property rights for the benefit of others. When equity intervenes to redistribute family assets, the party lacking legal title becomes entitled to the equitable beneficial ownership of a share of those assets. This is, by definition, a trust. We are concerned in this chapter (and others) with the events which create that trust.

The trust might be an express trust (created directly by intention), a resulting trust (created by unjust enrichment), or a constructive trust (created by other events). Although express and resulting trusts can have a role in the division of family assets on the breakdown of a marriage or similar relationship, equity's most significant contribution in this situation is the constructive trust. There are three ways in which a constructive trust might be created: a specifically enforceable contract, detrimental reliance, or unconscionability. The last two are the most important methods of creating a trust of family assets, but it is helpful to consider all of the ways in which a trust might be created.

A trust of family assets is created not by the end of the relationship, but by events which took place during the relationship. This means that the trust will exist before the relationship comes to an end. The statutes which authorise the redistribution of family property recognise this. Section 78 of the *Family Law Act* 1975 (Cth) states:

> "In proceedings between the parties to a marriage with respect to existing title or rights in respect of property, the court may declare the title or rights, if any, that a party has in respect of the property."

The court could declare that some or all of the family assets are held in trust and then proceed to redistribute them, if necessary, under section 79, as discussed above.

The same is true of the state and territorial legislation. For example, section 8 of the *Property (Relationships) Act* 1984 (NSW) confirms the court's power to declare existing property rights, in terms similar to section 78 of the *Family Law Act* 1975 (Cth). In addition, section 7 of the New South Wales statute states:

> "Nothing in this Act derogates from or affects any right of a party to a domestic relationship to apply for any remedy or relief under any other Act or any other law."

This confirms that the creation of trusts of family assets is not inhibited by the court's statutory power to redistribute those assets.

Intention to Create a Trust

If the parties agree that their assets will be shared in proportions which do not match the legal ownership of those assets, this could well be an express trust. For example, if I own a car and tell my wife that it belongs to both of us, this is a declaration of express trust. Even if I knew nothing about trusts or how they were created, I could still create a trust in this fashion.

As discussed at page 252, there are two essential questions concerning the creation of an express trust. First, did I manifest an intention to create the relationship which equity recognises as a trust? Secondly, did I manifest that intention in the appropriate manner?

These two requirements mean that express trusts are unlikely to be created in this situation.

First, many families acquire assets without addressing their minds to issues of beneficial ownership. Unless the legal owner of an asset manifests a clear intention that the asset will be shared with other family members, there is no certainty of intention to create a trust. Vague notions about sharing may not be enough.

Secondly, a declaration of express trust of land must be manifest in writing. If the legal owner of the family home does manifest a clear intention to share the ownership of that home, that will not create an enforceable express trust unless it is put in writing and signed by the owner. Most families do not observe these sorts of formalities.

Contract

As discussed at page 259, if a contract of sale is specifically enforceable, the seller will hold the asset sold on constructive trust for the buyer. Therefore, if the legal owner of the family home makes a contract to transfer an interest in that home to a family member, it is conceivable that he or she will hold that interest on constructive trust for that person.

However, agreements between family members are unlikely to be specifically enforceable contracts. Those arrangements tend to be informal. The rights and obligations of the parties are unlikely to be defined with sufficient certainty to constitute a binding contract. Also, like an express trust of land, a contract to transfer an interest in land is not enforceable unless made in writing. It is unlikely that the family members will observe that formality. Part performance can be used to get around the problem created by lack of writing. However, it is unlikely that the actions taken by the parties will provide the necessary proof of the existence of the contract: see *Ogilvie v Ryan* [1976] 2 NSWLR 504, discussed in Chapter 21 and below.

Unjust Enrichment

A trust can arise when someone pays all or part of the purchase price for an asset, but does not obtain a corresponding share of the legal ownership. Unless a gift was intended, the legal owner will hold it on resulting trust for the purchasers in proportion to their contributions. This is a way to redistribute family assets among those family members who contributed directly to the purchase of those assets. However, there are many situations in which it will be of little or no assistance.

In many families, one person earns most of the family income, while other members contribute primarily in other ways. For example, one parent might stay at home with the children, while the other parent earns employment income, or someone might accept a lower salary in another city to be near a partner with better career prospects. In these situations, the payment of the purchase price for the family home and other assets will not reflect the overall contributions and sacrifices made by the parties. Therefore, a resulting trust, based solely on payment of the purchase price, will not produce the desired outcome.

Detrimental Reliance

A constructive trust of family assets can arise when the parties to the relationship have a common intention regarding the beneficial ownership of those assets and the party without legal title relies on that intention to her or his detriment. This is often called a **common intention constructive trust**. However, as many courts and commentators have recognised, it seems to be an application of the principle of equitable estoppel: see *Austin v Keele* (1987) 61 ALJR 605; *Gillies v Keogh* [1989] 2 NZLR 327; and *Lloyds Bank plc v Rosset* [1991] 1 AC 107. As Browne-Wilkinson VC said in *Grant v Edwards* [1986] 1 Ch 638 at 656, "[t]he two principles have been developed separately without cross-fertilisation between them: but they rest on the same foundation and have on all other matters reached the same conclusions".

There are four questions discussed here. First, what is the difference between detrimental reliance on a common intention and equitable estoppel? Secondly, what, if anything, does fraud have to do with the creation of a trust in this situation? Thirdly, what is the appropriate response to detrimental reliance on a common intention? Fourthly, is this an effective way to achieve a proper division of family assets at the end of a marriage or similar relationship?

Similarity to Equitable Estoppel

The most obvious (and perhaps only) difference between the common intention constructive trust and equitable estoppel is the intention required. Several cases suggest that the former cannot arise unless the parties have an agreement or at least a shared understanding regarding the beneficial ownership of the family assets. As discussed above, equitable estoppel can be created when one party has a reasonable expectation, which the other party induced but did not share: see *Walton Stores (Interstate) Ltd v Maher* (1988) 164 CLR 387.

It is not clear why a constructive trust of the family home should require an agreement between the parties. The agreement has no direct effect as a contract or declaration of trust, since it is not made in writing. It is relevant because it caused the party without title to expect to receive an interest in the home and he or she relied on that expectation to her or his detriment: see *Gissing v Gissing* [1971] AC 886 at 905. If the legal owner induced the same reasonable expectation in some other way, it should lead to the same result.

For example, in *Grant v Edwards* [1986] 1 Ch 638, the defendant told his de facto spouse (the plaintiff) that she could not share legal title to their family home until she was divorced from her husband. However, he never intended to share legal ownership with her when the divorce was concluded. Nourse LJ said (at 649) that this raised:

> "a clear inference that there was an understanding between the plaintiff and the defendant, or a common intention, that the plaintiff was to have some sort of proprietary interest in the house; otherwise no excuse for not putting her name onto the title would have been needed."

This finding of a common intention seems strained and unnecessary: see Gardner, "Rethinking Family Property" (1993) 109 *Law Quarterly Review* 263 at 265. The defendant had induced the plaintiff's belief that she would obtain an interest in the home, regardless of whether he shared that belief or not. Her expectation was reasonable and she relied on it to her detriment. The ingredients needed to create a constructive trust of the home were present without a common intention.

Fraud

Some cases suggest that fraud is an element in the creation of a trust of a family home through detrimental reliance. For example, in *Ogilvie v Ryan* [1976] 2 NSWLR 504, Holland J said that the trust was based on three factors: a common intention regarding the beneficial ownership of the home, detrimental reliance on that intention, and the owner's fraudulent use of her or his legal title to defeat that intention.

In *Ogilvie v Ryan*, Mr Ogilvie bought a house when he was 84 years old and asked Mrs Ryan to live with him and look after him for the rest of his life. In return, she could reside in the house for rest of her life. She lived with and cared for him until he died two years later. He did not make any provision for her in his will and his executor sued her to recover possession of the house. The executor was unsuccessful because he held the house on constructive trust for her for life.

It is clear that Mr Ogilvie and Mrs Ryan had an agreement concerning her interest in the house and that she had relied on that agreement to her detriment. This was sufficient to give rise to a constructive trust. The additional requirement of fraud was unhelpful and wholly unnecessary. It could not be fraudulent for the executor to deny Mrs Ryan's interest in the house unless she had an interest. Otherwise, he did nothing wrong when he attempted to enforce his legal right to possession as the owner of the fee simple estate. Mrs Ryan's interest could not be created by denying its existence.

What would the court have done if the executor had not tried to enforce his legal rights, but merely asked the court for directions about possession of the house? Surely the outcome would have been the same: a declaration that the house was held in trust for Mrs Ryan for life. The requirement of fraud is superfluous and distracts from the real reasons for equitable intervention.

Responses to Detrimental Reliance

If detrimental reliance on a common intention regarding ownership of family assets is a form of equitable estoppel, then both events should produce the same equitable response. As Edward Nugee QC said in *Re Basham* (decd) [1986] 1 WLR 1498 at 1504:

> "A common theme can be discerned in each of these classes of case; and although different situations may give rise to differences of detail in the manner in which the court will give effect to the equity which arises in favour of the [plaintiff], one would expect the general principles applicable in the different situations to be the same unless there is a sound reason to the contrary."

As discussed above, equitable estoppel is (in theory) directed at alleviating the detriment suffered in reliance on a reasonable expectation. If this same approach is applied to cases involving the division of family assets, then the same three responses should be possible: a trust which gives effect to the common intention of the parties, some other property right, or a personal right to compensation. However, a trust of some portion of the family assets seems to be the most common response to detrimental reliance on a common intention concerning the ownership of those assets. As John Mee said, in *The Property Rights of Cohabitees* (1999) p 147, "the 'flexibility' envisaged in the common intention context appears to be limited to varying the fraction of the beneficial interest to be awarded to the claimant".

In many cases, such as *Ogilvie v Ryan*, the claimant obtains the beneficial interest which he or she expected to get. The courts find it easiest to give effect the parties' common intention, if possible, since this avoids the difficulty of trying to quantify the detriment suffered in reliance on that intention. In *Green v Green* (1989) 17 NSWLR 343 at 358, Gleeson CJ said:

> "[I]n my opinion the proper approach to the resolution of this issue is to seek a result which will most closely give effect to the common intention of the parties bearing in mind, first, that they did not themselves specifically address the matter of the legal form which would be conducted to give effect to their intention, and secondly, that this is an area in which equity is at its most flexible."

There are many other cases where the parties intended to share the beneficial ownership of the family home, but did not specify the proportions in which it would be shared. In these cases, the court is more likely to divide the beneficial ownership between the parties in proportion to the values of their contributions to the relationship. There are two possible justifications for this approach. First, it might be assumed that the parties intended to share the home in proportion to their contributions. Secondly, shares measured by the relative contributions of the parties might be the minimum response needed to eliminate the detriment suffered by the claimant.

The longer the relationship, the more likely it is that the family home will be divided equally between the parties. This is true even in cases where the parties did not specify how the home would be shared. This could be explained on the basis of either intention or detriment. It might be assumed that parties in long relationships intend to share their home equally or it might be impossible to cure the detriment suffered over a long period of time with anything less than an equal share of the family home.

Effectiveness

There are family relationships in which the parties do not share a common intention regarding the beneficial ownership of their assets. Although they live together and have acquired wealth as a family, they never discussed the sharing of that wealth. If the relationship ends, leaving one party with the bulk of the family assets and the other party with little to show for years of contributions and sacrifices, a redistribution of those assets is needed. However, the lack of a common intention makes it difficult both to justify the imposition of a trust and to quantify the shares held in trust.

There are at least three different ways to deal with this problem. The first is by statute. As discussed above, parliament can decide that a redistribution of family assets will be available at the end of certain relationships (such as domestic relationships lasting more than two years) and give the courts the power to perform that task. These statutes are very important, but do not obviate the need to develop the law of trusts to cope with these situations. The statutory redistribution schemes vary from state to state and do not apply to every relationship where they might be needed. Also, if a fair result can be achieved through the law of trusts, the sharing of beneficial ownership is possible without a court order redistributing the family assets.

The second solution is to relax the requirement of common intention to allow for the creation of trusts of family assets in response to detrimental reliance on reasonable expectations. This would produce a more coherent body of law by integrating the common intention constructive trust and equitable estoppel. It would also help the law keep pace with the changing nature of the family, since the reasonable expectations of family members continue to evolve. As Richardson J said, in *Gillies v Keogh* [1989] 2 NZLR 327 at 347:

> "Whatever the position in other countries, it seems to me that social attitudes in New Zealand readily lead to expectations, by those within apparently stable and enduring de facto relationships, that family assets are ordinarily shared, not the exclusive property of one or the other, unless it is agreed otherwise or made plain."

A similar view was expressed by the Supreme Court of Canada. In *Peter v Beblow* (1993) 101 DLR (4th) 621 Cory J said (at 633):

> "In today's society it is unreasonable to assume that the presence of love automatically implies a gift of one party's services to another. Nor is it unreasonable for the party providing the domestic labour required to create a home to expect to share in the property of the parties when the relationship is terminated."

A third solution is to find another method of dividing family assets at the end of a relationship. This was the path taken by the High Court of Australia. A constructive trust can arise, in the absence of detrimental reliance on a common intention, to redistribute family assets according to the relative contributions made by the parties to their relationship. The trust is imposed in this situation to prevent the unconscionable use of legal title to family assets.

Unconscionability

In most relationships, the parties arrange their affairs so that legal ownership of their assets matches their agreement concerning beneficial ownership. In cases where legal ownership does not match their agreement, a trust based on detrimental reliance can be imposed to give effect to their common intention. In the absence of a common intention, a trust can be imposed to allocate the beneficial ownership of their assets in proportion to their contributions to that relationship. This provides a safety net: in cases where it is not possible to give effect to the parties' intentions, directly or indirectly, courts can ensure that contributions to their relationship do not go unrewarded. They justify the imposition of this trust by saying that it would be unconscionable for the legal owner of those assets to deny the other party's claim to them.

Muschinski v Dodds

This alternative method of dividing family property was first introduced in *Muschinski v Dodds* (1985) 160 CLR 583. Ms Muschinski and Mr Dodds purchased land, as joint tenants, planning to use it both as an arts and crafts centre and as their personal residence. They intended to share the beneficial ownership of the land and to contribute equally to its purchase and improvement. However, the end of their personal relationship brought the project to an end before all the intended improvements had been made. Since Ms Muschinski had contributed 10 times more than Mr Dodds to the acquisition and improvement of the land, the court declared that they held their joint legal ownership in trust for themselves as tenants in common in proportion to their contributions.

The solution in this case was a form of restitution of unjust enrichment (discussed in the next chapter). Mr Dodds was supposed to enjoy the benefit of Ms Muschinski's contributions, but only for a particular purpose: their joint business and residence. When that purpose became impossible to fulfil, he was left with a substantial, unintended benefit, obtained at her expense. In the law of restitution, this is called a failure of consideration. *Muschinski v Dodds* could have been discussed in the next chapter as an example of restitution of unjust enrichment. However, further development of this principle showed that the trust is not created by unjust enrichment.

Baumgartner v Baumgartner

In *Baumgartner v Baumgartner* (1988) 164 CLR 137, the High Court applied and extended the principle set out in *Muschinski v Dodds*. The parties, Frances and Leo Baumgartner, lived together as de facto spouses for six years, had a child together, pooled their incomes, and acquired a house and furniture. Leo contributed $13,000 from the sale of his old house and his income of $51,000, while Frances contributed her income of $38,000. When the relationship ended, Leo had title to the house, worth $68,000, while Frances had the furniture worth $7,000 to $10,000. The court declared that Frances was the beneficial owner of 45% of the house under a constructive trust, subject to a lien to secure repayment to Leo of the sale proceeds from his old house and the value of the furniture (which Frances was allowed to keep for herself).

The house had been acquired at the expense of both Leo and Frances for a particular purpose (accommodation for themselves and their child) and not for Leo's sole use. When the relationship ended, he was not permitted to keep what could be described as a windfall obtained at her expense. Although this looks somewhat like restitution of unjust enrichment, two aspects of the court's method of apportioning the beneficial ownership of the house shows that it is based on something else.

First, unlike *Muschinski v Dodds*, the ownership of the house was not divided according to the contributions which the parties had made to the acquisition and improvement of the house, but according to their contributions to their overall relationship. Therefore, the trust did not restore to Frances an unjust enrichment obtained by Leo at her expense. It was used to reward Frances for the value of contributions she had made to the relationship, whether or not those contributions survived as family assets.

Secondly, the division of the house was calculated by giving Frances a $3,000 "credit" for the income she had lost while giving birth to and caring for their child. This important contribution to their family had no possible connection to the value of the assets surviving at the end of their relationship. The trust of the house was designed, at least in part, to compensate Frances for sacrifices and lost opportunities and not to effect restitution of unjust enrichment.

The advantage of this form of equitable intervention is that it fills gaps in the law of property to achieve what most people would regard as a fair outcome. When two people join forces and pursue life together as a family, one person should not be allowed to keep a disproportionate share of the family assets if the relationship comes to an end. In the absence of a trust based on detrimental reliance (discussed above) or unjust enrichment (discussed in the next chapter), a trust based on unconscionable conduct provides a fall-back position.

There are, however, two major limitations of a trust based on unconscionability. First, it will not provide a fair solution in every family situation. Secondly, it involves a high level of uncertainty because the basis for equitable intervention has not yet been clearly identified.

Limited Utility

The reallocation of family assets in proportion to the value of each party's contributions to the relationship will not produce the desired outcome in a large number of relationships. One party (often the female partner) may have made significant sacrifices (by not pursuing educational, career, and other opportunities) to raise children and maintain the family home. If the other party is free to pursue a career and earn a high income, there may be a large disparity between the market values of their contributions to the relationship. A redistribution of family assets based on those values will fail to account properly for sacrifices made for the sake of the family.

It is important to recognise this limitation. A trust based on unconscionability cannot do the work of a trust based on detrimental reliance and must not be allowed to replace it. This is demonstrated by *Green v Green* (1989) 17 NSWLR 343, in which the plaintiff left her home in Thailand at the age of 14 to become the de facto spouse of an Australian man. Over the next 15 years, she bore and raised their children and remained in Australia in reliance on his promise that she would own the house he had purchased for her. The majority of the New South Wales

Court of Appeal gave effect to their common intention and declared that the house was held on constructive trust for both of them, as joint tenants, and that she had become the sole owner when he died.

Mahoney JA dissented from the opinion of the majority and said (at 369) that a constructive trust should not be imposed because the plaintiff "made no claim of contributions to the house, pooling of resources, or anything other than a de facto relationship". In his view, *Baumgartner v Baumgartner* brought about "an important change in the law: at least, it provides a significant change in the circumstances hitherto seen as warranting the imposition of a constructive trust": at 369. If allowed to prevail, this view would lead to significant injustice in many cases. Trusts based on detrimental reliance will always be needed and ought to prevail over trusts based on unconscionability if they lead to different results. It is better to give effect to the parties' intentions where possible.

Uncertainty

The second limitation of the principle established in *Baumgartner v Baumgartner* is the uncertainty it creates. The language of unconscionability does not identify the events which give rise to the trust of family assets. The constructive trust was imposed in *Baumgartner* because Leo's assertion of sole beneficial ownership of the house amounted "to unconscionable conduct". However, it could not be wrong for Leo to enforce his legal rights as sole owner of the fee simple estate unless Frances had a property right to that estate. His denial of her right to the house was unconscionable because he held a share of that house in trust for her. His denial of her right cannot possibly be the source of that right.

This leaves us with the difficult task of trying to identify the event which created the constructive trust for Frances. Her share of the house was based on her contributions to the relationship and not on her contributions to the acquisition and improvement of the house. What is the connection between her contributions and the house? Despite suggestions that a constructive trust based on unconscionability has nothing to do with intention, the link seems to be the parties' expectations. As Mason CJ, Wilson J, and Deane J said in *Baumgartner v Baumgartner* (1988) 164 CLR 137 at 149, they had "pooled their earnings for the purposes of their joint relationship, one of the purposes of that relationship being to secure accommodation for themselves and their child". Frances contributed to the relationship expecting to receive an interest in the house. She never intended to make a gift of her contributions to Leo to be used and enjoyed without her. Leo cannot retain for his own benefit an asset which was intended to be used for the family.

If Frances's property right to the house was based in part on her expectation of sharing that house, this raises an important question: why was her share of the house limited to the value of her contributions to the relationship? Why not give effect to her expectations? This would avoid the problem of trying to assign values to contributions which produce neither income nor valuable assets. Parenting and other work inside the home tends to be undervalued in these calculations.

For example, why should the value of the birth and care of a child be measured (as it was in *Baumgartner*) by the mother's earning potential outside the home? Surely the value is the same regardless of her station in life.

The parties' expectations concerning the beneficial ownership of their assets might be a more sensitive measure of the relative values of their contributions to, and sacrifices for, the relationship. They will choose to pursue the activities they value most in light of those expectations. Expectations of sharing family assets provide some indication of the subjective values placed on their contributions to the family, because it indicates the terms on which the parties are willing to make and accept those contributions. It is, perhaps, the measure which best approximates market value in this setting.

The uncertainty created by *Baumgartner v Baumgartner* has left lower courts with the difficult task of trying to determine when it is unconscionable not to share the ownership of assets at the end of a marriage or similar relationship. *Parij v Parij* (1997) 72 SASR 153 provides an example of how difficult this task can be. The parties lived together as de facto spouses for 17 years, had two children together, and acquired a house, a car, and furniture together as joint tenants. In addition, the defendant acquired an accounting business, two other houses, a car, and a boat in his own name.

The court held that there was no reason to interfere with the legal ownership of the jointly-owned assets or the defendant's own car and boat. However, it was unconscionable for him to retain sole beneficial ownership of his business and the two additional houses. The majority of the court decided that the plaintiff deserved 20% of those assets, while the minority thought that she deserved one third of each of them.

While the result seems fair enough, it is almost impossible to understand how unconscionability led to that conclusion. Why did two judges believe it was unconscionable for the defendant to retain more than 80% of his business, while another judge believed it was unconscionable for him to retain more than two thirds? There did not seem to be any attempt to assign values to the relative contributions made by the parties. The difference seems to reflect only that the judges had different ideas of what might be fair in the circumstances.

Why was it not unconscionable to share the second car or the boat? What connected her contributions to one asset, but not another? Cox J said (at 154) that,

> "The plaintiff's maintenance of the home and her care for the defendant and their children over a period of many years helped to make it possible for the defendant to earn a substantial income and thereby acquire the assets that are the subject of this dispute."

If this is true of the business, it must also be true of the car and boat.

It is very difficult to predict the outcome of a claim that a trust is needed to prevent unconscionability. There is a worry that the redistribution of family assets depends more on individual notions of fairness than on articulated principles of law. If like cases are not treated alike, the public will lose confidence in the legal system and have difficulty resolving their disputes without resort to litigation. The reallocation of wealth at the end of a marriage or similar relationship is a notoriously difficult task that has troubled courts around the world. However, this does not excuse the lack of certainty, which is needed and must be sought in every area of law.

Chapter Twenty-Four

UNJUST ENRICHMENT

■ ■ ■

As discussed at page 234, the term "unjust enrichment" describes a category of events which give rise to legal rights and obligations. According to Deane J, in *Pavey & Matthews Pty Ltd v Paul* (1987) 162 CLR 221 at 256-257:

> "[U]njust enrichment ... constitutes a unifying legal concept which explains why the law recognizes, in a variety of distinct categories of case, an obligation on the part of a defendant to make fair and just restitution for a benefit derived at the expense of a plaintiff and which assists in the determination, by the ordinary processes of legal reasoning, of the question whether the law should, in justice, recognize such an obligation in a new or developing category of case."

The category of unjust enrichment includes a variety of different events, such as payments made by mistake, gifts induced by undue influence, and contracts which have become frustrated. What ties them together is a common reason for legal intervention. In each situation, one person has been enriched at the expense of another and that enrichment is regarded as unjust. They can be grouped together as instances of unjust enrichment, in the same way that other legally significant events can be organised into general categories. For example, contracts, wills, and gifts can be grouped together as events which create rights by consent, while torts, breach of contract, and breach of confidence can be classified as wrongs.

The only possible legal response to unjust enrichment is **restitution**. The person who has been enriched must give up the enrichment or pay for it. No other obligation is justifiable. Suppose, for example, that I deposit $1,000 in your bank account by mistake. You did nothing wrong, made no promises to me, and induced no reasonable expectations. There is no reason to punish you or make you compensate me for my loss. There are no promises or expectations to fulfil. The only coherent legal response to your enrichment is an obligation to give up that enrichment (or what survives of it when the mistake is discovered).

The normal method of restitution is to require the person enriched (called the defendant here for convenience) to pay the value of the enrichment to the person at whose expense it was obtained (the plaintiff). In other words, the unjust enrichment creates a debt. Sometimes, the plaintiff is entitled to recover the enrichment itself and, therefore, has a property right to that enrichment. These are the situations in which we are interested. When does unjust enrichment create property rights? We begin by looking briefly at the different types of unjust enrichment and the different ways in which the law effects restitution of unjust enrichment. We then look more closely at the main situations in which unjust enrichment gives rise to property rights.

Types of Unjust Enrichment

Unjust enrichment occurs in many different situations and takes many different forms. This variety makes it difficult to see the common thread which ties these cases together. Indeed, in common law jurisdictions, the formal recognition of unjust enrichment occurred only in the 20th century. The ground-breaking work took place in the United States and led to the publication by the American Law Institute of the *Restatement of the Law of Restitution* (1937). This had a remarkable influence (directly or indirectly) on the development of the law in Australia, Canada, England, and New Zealand.

It is helpful to begin with two basic questions which underlie the law of unjust enrichment: what is an enrichment and what makes it unjust?

Enrichment

An enrichment can be anything of value. There are three basic types:

1) ..... **personal or property rights received** by the defendant (such as a bank account deposit, possession of goods, or an interest in land);
2) ..... **services performed** for the defendant (such as automobile repairs, house renovations, or medical treatment); and
3) ..... **expenses saved** by the defendant, through the transfer of rights to, or performance of services for, others (such as the payment of the defendant's mortgage or taxes).

Whether any particular benefit counts as an enrichment depends upon the circumstances in which it was conferred. The law on this issue has been shaped by a respect for freedom of choice. People should not be forced to pay for things they do not want. Therefore, the fact that a benefit has a market value does not necessarily make it an enrichment to the defendant.

There is no difficulty where the plaintiff seeks the return of the enrichment itself. For example, if you order 27 cases of wine and I ship 28 cases by mistake, enrichment is not an issue if you are able to return the extra case. Its value on the market or to you personally is irrelevant. The situation changes if the case cannot be returned and you are asked to pay for it. Your liability to pay for the wine should leave you no worse off than you would have been if I had not made my mistake. That will be true if you consumed or sold it and would have paid for another case in any event. It might not be true if the wine was stolen from you or destroyed. The law has had to develop rules to deal with problems like these.

Where the defendant is unable to return the enrichment received at the plaintiff's expense, it becomes necessary to determine its value to the defendant. That is easy to do where the defendant was enriched by the receipt of money. Since money is the very measure of value, the enrichment is undeniable and easily quantified. That is not true of other forms of enrichment. For example, if I cut your lawn and trim your trees by mistake (having misread the address on the work order), it is not at all clear that you are enriched, even if we agree on the market value of the service I performed. You might not have wanted the work done or had better uses for your money and, therefore, should not be forced to pay for the work unless it is clear that you were enriched.

The law developed two alternative methods of proving enrichment in situations like this. First, it asks whether the enrichment is an **incontrovertible benefit**. In other words, would everyone agree that the defendant was enriched? This will be true when he or she has been saved a necessary expense or has sold the enrichment (and converted it to money). Either way, it is clear that the defendant is financially better off because of the enrichment. Secondly, the law asks whether the defendant has **freely accepted** the enrichment. A defendant who accepts an enrichment, knowing that it was not offered as a gift, cannot argue that the enrichment is of no value personally and should be required to pay its market value.

It sometimes happens that a defendant was enriched by the receipt of a benefit, but is no longer enriched when the unjust enrichment is discovered and he or she is called upon to pay for it. Suppose that I paid $1,000 to you by mistake, you invested the money in the stock market, and the shares you bought declined in value to $600 before the mistake was discovered. Unless you would have purchased those shares in any event, you are no longer enriched by $1,000. If you have to make restitution of the full amount, you will be $400 worse off than when you started.

The law deals with problems like this by allowing the defendant to plead the defence of **change of position**. If the enrichment is diminished without benefit to the defendant before the unjust enrichment is discovered, the liability to make restitution will be reduced by that amount. The fact that the enrichment has been spent or consumed is not itself a change of position. If, for example, you used the $1,000 to buy your normal groceries you are still $1,000 better off because of my mistake. A relevant change of position is an extraordinary expenditure or destruction of the enrichment which reduces the defendant's overall wealth.

Unjust Factors

Of course, people enrich each other all the time. Very few enrichments are unjust. The majority are conferred as intended, either as gifts or in exchange for value. Unjust enrichment occurs only where there is some problem with a particular transaction, which indicates that the enrichment should be given back or paid for. It is important to note that the adjective "unjust" does not connote any wrongdoing or impropriety on the part of the defendant. It indicates only that the enrichment ought to be given back or paid for. Indeed, a defendant may be entirely innocent or even unaware of an unjust enrichment, which occurred as a result of the plaintiff's own carelessness.

Non-Voluntary Transfer

There are a wide variety of reasons why an enrichment might be unjust and therefore reversible. In most cases, the reason for restitution (sometimes called the "unjust factor") is that the plaintiff did not truly intend to benefit the defendant in the circumstances. This might be due to some defect in the plaintiff's decision to confer the benefit. For example, the plaintiff might have been operating under a mistaken belief, duress, or undue influence or the defendant might have exploited the plaintiff's weakness (such as her or his drunkenness, inexperience, or limited language ability) to obtain the desired transfer of wealth.

In some cases, the plaintiff had no intention to benefit the defendant whatsoever. The defendant might be a stowaway on the plaintiff's ship, a thief who stole valuables from the plaintiff's home, or a neighbour who depastured cattle on the plaintiff's land without permission. In many of these cases, the defendant will be a wrongdoer who could be punished or made to pay compensation. However, unjust enrichment is also present, regardless of the wrong done, since the defendant obtained a benefit at the plaintiff's expense, without consent.

In other cases, the plaintiff's intention to benefit the defendant was conditional upon the happening of a specified event. For example, the plaintiff might have made a large gift in contemplation of marriage or paid a deposit under a contract of sale. If the anticipated event does not occur, the condition for enrichment is not met and the defendant's continued retention of the benefit becomes unjust. In this situation, there is a **failure of consideration** and the defendant may be required to make restitution.

In the situations introduced above, the plaintiff can prove a lack of intention to benefit the defendant by showing that the decision to confer the enrichment was defective, wholly absent, or conditional on events which failed to take place. There are other cases in which the plaintiff's lack of intention to benefit the defendant is presumed. Where the plaintiff makes an unexpected apparent gift to the defendant, it is presumed that the plaintiff did not intend to benefit the defendant. Unless the defendant can show that a gift was intended, he or she will hold the assets on **resulting trust** for the plaintiff. This is discussed further below.

Most cases of unjust enrichment can be explained as instances of what Peter Birks called "non-voluntary transfer", in *An Introduction to the Law of Restitution* (1989) p 100:

> "Where there is a 'non-voluntary transfer', so that the circumstance calling for restitution is 'a factor negativing voluntariness', the explanation of the response is always reducible in the simplest terms to the statement that the plaintiff did not mean the defendant to have the money in question or the other enrichment, whatever it might be."

However, as Birks warned, whether an enrichment is unjust due to non-voluntariness is not a simple matter to be resolved on the basis of first impressions. He said (p 100) that "you have to go down to the cases to see if it was non-voluntary in the way in which the law counts as calling for restitution".

Public Policy

There are a few other reasons why an enrichment might be unjust. There may be overriding public policies calling for restitution, without regard to the plaintiff's intention to confer the enrichment. For example, if a government collects taxes to which it is not entitled, a court might compel it to make restitution to preserve the common law principle that there should be no taxation without the authority of Parliament: see *Commissioner of Stamp Revenue (Vic) v Royal Insurance Australia Ltd* (1994) 182 CLR 51 at 69.

A person who helps another in need is sometimes entitled to restitution of the value of the benefit provided. That right may be derived from a public policy which encourages people to help others. Although there is no general right to restitution for being a good Samaritan, the law has allowed recovery in certain situations where intervention was necessary, such as the provision of medical treatment or other essentials to an incapacitated person, the payment of funeral expenses when executors and relatives could not be found, and the preservation of property when the owner could not be contacted.

Restitution of Unjust Enrichment

The law responds to unjust enrichment in a number of ways, all of which require the defendant to make restitution of the enrichment or its value. It is usually the latter. In other words, unjust enrichment normally creates only a personal right to payment, but sometimes leads to a property right to the enrichment itself, either instead of or in addition to that personal right.

All property rights created by unjust enrichment arise for the same purpose: to effect restitution of that enrichment. However, the nature of the right varies from case to case. It may be legal or equitable and may be beneficial ownership, a security right, or an even lesser right. The nature of the right depends on the nature of the unjust enrichment, as discussed below.

In some cases, the defendant has sold the enrichment received from the plaintiff and used the proceeds to purchase other assets. The plaintiff might have a property right to the new assets if he or she can prove that the value of the original enrichment was used to acquire those assets. The process of identifying value surviving in substitute assets is called **tracing** and is discussed briefly at the end of this chapter. Most of this chapter deals with the four main ways in which people become entitled to property rights to restitution of unjust enrichment: rescission, rectification, resulting trusts, and equitable liens.

Rescission

A person who makes a contract or other transfer of value (such as a gift or trust settlement) by mistake or as a result of duress, undue influence, or exploitation of weakness, is sometimes entitled to **rescind** that transaction. Once rescinded, the transaction is treated, as far as possible, as if it never occurred. This differs from the frustration or termination of a contract, which has no retrospective effect, but relieves the parties from further performance of their primary obligations under the contract. It also differs from cases where the transaction is completely void from the outset and never had any legal effect. A transaction which can be rescinded is not void, but **voidable**.

Upon rescission of a transaction, each party is normally entitled to recover any benefits that were transferred to the other party as part of that transaction. The goal is to reverse the transaction and restore the parties to their pre-transaction positions. This process is called **restitutio in integrum**.

Rescission is often a necessary first step in the process of obtaining restitution of unjust enrichment. Suppose, for example, that I sell a jacket to you for an exorbitant price by telling you (falsely) that it used to belong to Elvis. I have been enriched at your expense and that enrichment was the product of your mistake (induced by my fraudulent misrepresentation). However, as long as the contract exists, I am entitled to keep the purchase price and you cannot get restitution. Once you rescind the contract, my right to the payment disappears and you are entitled to restitution of the unjust enrichment (provided you can return the jacket).

The Act of Rescission

Rescission is a simple process that may be accomplished without formalities or the assistance of a court. The party entitled to rescind a transaction need only make an unequivocal election to rescind and communicate that decision to the other party. Communication is not necessary if the other party has made it impossible (for example, by fraudulently absconding with the enrichment). The rescinding party may need to take the matter before a court if the other party contests the right to rescind. The court will then decide whether the transaction has been rescinded or continues to be effective. If rescinded, the court may make orders which help undo the transaction and restore the parties to their pre-transaction positions.

The right to rescind can be lost in several different ways. First, *restitutio in integrum* may become impossible, because property which must be returned has been destroyed or sold to a *bona fide* purchaser. Secondly, the party entitled to rescind may affirm the transaction. If he or she becomes aware of the right to rescind and chooses not to do so, that right will be lost. Thirdly, the right can be lost through the passage of time. A party must elect whether to affirm or rescind a transaction before too many years have passed. The delay is called **laches** in a court of equity and leads to a loss of equitable rights in much the same way that delay can lead to the loss of legal rights under the limitation of actions statutes: see Chapter 8.

Rescission at Common Law and in Equity

Rescission was recognised by courts of common law and equity. However, the right to rescind is much more restricted at common law than in equity. With few exceptions, rescission at common law is permitted on two grounds: fraud and duress. In other words, only some mistakes (those induced by dishonest misrepresentations) and some pressures (those which the law regarded as illegitimate) entitle a party to rescind a transaction at common law. Other factors affecting a decision to enter a transaction do not count.

The main exceptions to the common law limits on rescission are contracts of insurance. The parties to an insurance contract are required to disclose all facts which might affect the premiums charged or the decision to make the contract. A failure to disclose a material fact is a ground for rescission.

The Court of Chancery took a broader approach and permitted rescission for a wider variety of mistakes and influences. Equitable rescission is possible when a party enters a transaction by a mistake induced by a negligent or innocent misrepresentation. It is also possible where the mistake is not induced, but the other party shared the mistake (sometimes called **mutual mistake**) or was at least aware of the mistake. In some cases, nondisclosure can give rise to a right to rescind. Fiduciaries (such as agents, solicitors, and trustees), who deal with the people they are bound to serve loyally, are required to disclose all relevant information to them. If the fiduciary fails to make full disclosure, the other party will have a right to rescind the transaction. Equitable rescission is also available for undue influence and exploitation of disadvantage: see *Commercial Bank of Australia Ltd v Amadio* (1983) 151 CLR 447.

The common law also restricted rescission to cases where it is possible to make full and precise *restitutio in integrum*. If all the benefits conferred under the transaction cannot be returned, rescission is no longer possible at common law. The Court of Chancery was more lenient and permitted rescission so long as the parties could be restored to positions which were substantially equivalent to the state of affairs before the transaction. As the High Court of Australia said in *Alati v Kruger* (1955) 94 CLR 216 at 223-224:

> "[E]quity has always regarded as valid the disaffirmance of a contract induced by fraud even though precise *restitutio in integrum* is not possible, if the situation is such that, by the exercise of its powers, including the power to take accounts of profits and to direct inquiries as to allowances proper to be made for deterioration, it can do what is practically just between the parties, and by so doing restore them substantially to the *status quo*."

In most cases, it will not matter whether rescission is recognised at common law or only in equity. The end result will be the same in both cases: the transaction will be set aside and the benefits which flowed between the parties under that transaction will be returned or paid for. However, the difference between law and equity can affect the nature of the plaintiff's rights before rescission is complete. This is discussed below.

Statutory Rights to Rescind

There are a number of statutes which create or regulate rights to rescind contracts and other transactions. For example, the right to rescind a contract of insurance is regulated by Part IV of the *Insurance Contracts Act* 1984 (Cth). Many of these statutes create or regulate rights to rescind transfers of property. Three types are introduced here:

1) .....legislation designed to protect creditors;
2) .....the sale of goods legislation; and
3) .....fair trading legislation.

Protection of Creditors

If a debtor is unable to pay her or his creditors, they (or someone acting on their behalf) may be able to recover assets which were sold or given away by the debtor. This is not rescission based on unjust enrichment, but it has a similar effect: transactions can be set aside, thereby restoring assets to the debtor.

The *Bankruptcy Act* 1966 (Cth) enables a trustee in bankruptcy to recover assets which were transferred previously by the bankrupt in three main situations:

1) .....the assets were given away or sold at an undervalue up to five years before the bankruptcy (s 120);
2) .....the main purpose of the transfer was to keep the assets from being used to pay the bankrupt's creditors (s 121); or
3) .....the transfer was made when the bankrupt was insolvent and had the effect of preferring one creditor over another (s 122).

Every state has a statute which can be used to set aside transfers made for the purpose of defrauding creditors. Section 86 of the *Law of Property Act* 1936 (SA) is typical. It states that "[e]very conveyance of property made with intent to defraud creditors shall be voidable at the instance of the party prejudiced thereby".

There are a number of similar statutory provisions, which apply to specific debtors or specific legal obligations. For example, section 565 of the *Corporations Law* allows the liquidator of a company to recover assets transferred by the company before it went into liquidation. Under section 85 of the *Family Law Act* 1975 (Cth), the court can set aside transfers "made to defeat an existing or anticipated order" under that statute. Courts have similar powers with respect to transactions made to defeat the redistribution of property rights at the end of a de facto relationship: see *De Facto Relationships Act* 1996 (SA), s 14; and Chapter 23. As discussed at the end of Chapter 22, the *Family Provision Act* 1982 (NSW) enables the court to increase the size of a deceased person's estate by setting aside transactions made up to three years before death.

Sale of Goods

In *Watt v Westhoven* [1933] VLR 458, the Supreme Court of Victoria decided that the *Goods Act* 1928 (Vic) removed the equitable right to rescind a sale of goods on the basis of an innocent misrepresentation.

Like all sale of goods legislation copied from England, it said that the "rules of the common law ... relating to ... the effect of misrepresentation ... continue to apply to contracts for the sale of goods". The Court concluded that the reference to the common law was intended to exclude the rules of equity.

That decision was not followed in South Australia or New South Wales: see *Graham v Freer* (1980) 35 SASR 424; *Leason Pty Ltd v Princes Farm Pty Ltd* [1983] 2 NSWLR 381. In the former case (at 424), King CJ said:

> "In my opinion the words 'the rules of the common law' in s 59(2) of the *Sale of Goods Act*, 1895, as amended, include the rules of equity ... [T]he section does not take contracts for the sale of goods outside the general rule that contracts obtained by innocent misrepresentation are voidable in equity."

In the Australian Capital Territory and Victoria, the problem was corrected by amending the *Sale of Goods* legislation. Section 62(1A) of the *Sale of Goods Act* 1954 (ACT) states that the "remedy in equity of the buyer or the seller in respect of a misrepresentation" is not affected by that statute. Section 100 of the *Goods Act* 1958 (Vic) states:

> "Where a buyer enters into a sale of goods after a misrepresentation that is not fraudulent is made to him and, if the misrepresentation had been fraudulent, the buyer would have been entitled to rescind the sale by reason of the misrepresentation, the buyer may rescind the sale by notice given to the seller before, or within a reasonable period after, acceptance of the goods."

Fair Trading

There are several statutes which regulate the supply of consumer goods and services. The *Trade Practices Act* 1974 (Cth) applies to corporate suppliers, while the states and territories have similar statutes dealing with many types of consumer contracts. These statutes prohibit sellers from misleading consumers or treating them unfairly. A breach of the statute may give the consumer a right to rescind a contract for the sale of goods: see, eg, *Trade Practices Act* 1974 (Cth), s 75A; *Fair Trading Act* 1987 (WA), s 41.

Some statutes confer the power to rescind contracts on a court or tribunal. For example, section 7 of the *Contracts Review Act* 1980 (NSW) gives the court the power to "make an order declaring the contract void, in whole or in part" if the contract was "unjust in the circumstances relating to the contract at the time it was made". A power to rescind a contract of sale is conferred on the Victorian Civil and Administrative Tribunal by section 108 of the *Fair Trading Act* 1999 (Vic).

The Effect of Rescission

The rescission of a contract or other transaction may produce personal rights, property rights, or both. This depends upon the nature of the enrichment which the plaintiff is entitled to recover when that transaction is rescinded.

In many cases, the benefit to the defendant is the plaintiff's contractual promise to pay money, transfer property, or perform services. Rescission of the contract will free the plaintiff from the obligation to perform and cause the defendant to give up the benefit of the plaintiff's promise: see *Vadasz v Pioneer Concrete (SA) Pty Ltd* (1995) 184 CLR 102. This does not create property rights, but affects only personal rights and obligations.

In some cases, the plaintiff transferred assets to the defendant under the transaction before it was rescinded. If rescission entitles the plaintiff to recover those assets, then it will create property rights. The act of rescission will cause the legal or equitable ownership of those assets to be returned to the plaintiff: see *Hunter BNZ Finance Ltd v CG Maloney Pty Ltd* (1988) 18 NSWLR 420 at 431-433.

Rescission will often entitle the plaintiff to recover money paid to the defendant. *Restitutio in integrum* does not require the return of the same money, but only repayment of the same sum of money. Therefore, rescission will create a personal right (a debt due from the defendant). However, if the value from that money can be traced into some asset, the plaintiff might also have a property right to that asset: see *El Ajou v Dollar Land Holdings plc* [1994] 2 All ER 685.

Property Rights Created by Rescission

Property rights created by rescission may be legal or equitable. This depends primarily on whether rescission was effective at law or only in equity. It can also depend on whether any additional steps are needed to restore title to the plaintiff. The plaintiff does not choose whether to rescind at law or in equity, but merely elects to rescind. The effect of that election depends upon the ground for rescission and the possibility of *restitutio in integrum*.

Rescission at Common Law

The plaintiff will be entitled to rescind at common law if the transaction was induced by fraud or duress and it is possible to make full *restitutio in integrum*. In these situations, the plaintiff's rescission will mean that the transaction will cease to have any legal effect and that any property rights created directly by that transaction will cease to exist.

In *Car and Universal Finance Co Ltd v Caldwell* [1965] 1 QB 525, the plaintiff was induced by fraud to sell his car. He discovered the fraud the next day and rescinded the contract of sale. This caused legal ownership of the car to revert from the purchaser to the plaintiff (and meant that the poor defendant, who later bought the car in good faith, was guilty of conversion). Since the contract of sale had caused ownership of the car to pass to the purchaser (see page 243), the rescission of that contract caused it to jump back automatically to the plaintiff. The event which had created the purchaser's ownership of the car (the contract) no longer existed and the purchaser became a bailee.

If the plaintiff is entitled to rescind a deed at common law, the act of rescission will invalidate the deed and cause any legal rights conveyed by that deed to revest in the plaintiff. In *Barton v Armstrong* [1976] AC 104, the plaintiff executed a deed after the defendant threatened to kill him. Although the Privy Council said the deed was void, it is generally agreed that it was voidable pending the plaintiff's election to rescind and only void once that election had been made.

Rescission at common law will not cause legal title to revert to the plaintiff in cases where legal title passed to the defendant by registration. Since the contract between the parties did not cause legal title to pass, rescission of that contract will have no immediate effect on the legal title. The defendant will continue to be the registered owner, but will hold that right in trust for the plaintiff and can be compelled to restore legal title to the plaintiff. This trust is discussed below. If necessary, the court could order the person in charge of the land titles or corporate register to restore title.

Statutory Rescission

Rescission pursuant to a statute affects property rights in the same manner as it does at common law. The transaction will cease to have legal effect when the plaintiff elects to rescind. That may be enough to restore legal title to the plaintiff, but additional steps might be required, as discussed above.

The statute which creates the right to rescind might also regulate the effect of rescission. For example, section 101(e) of the *Goods Act* 1958 (Vic) states, "Where the property in the goods passed to the buyer before the discharge or the rescission, the property re-vests in the seller" when the seller rescinds. Section 75A of the *Trade Practices Act* 1974 (Cth) states:

> "[I]f the property in the goods had passed to the consumer before the notice of rescission was served on, or the goods were returned to, the corporation — the property in the goods re-vests in the corporation upon the service of the notice or the return of the goods."

Some of the statutes designed to protect creditors (such as the *Bankruptcy Act* 1966 (Cth), discussed above) say that certain transactions are "void". However, the High Court of Australia has interpreted that to mean "voidable". In *Brady v Stapleton* (1952) 88 CLR 322 at 333, Dixon CJ and Fullagar J said, "although the statute uses, and most emphatically uses, the word 'void', the courts have always treated a fraudulent assignment as effective unless and until a creditor or creditors intervene by levying execution or taking legal proceedings".

Rescission in Equity

Rescission will be equitable where the ground for rescission (like undue influence) is not recognised at common law or by statute or where *restitutio in integrum* depends upon the application of the rules of equity. Also, where the transaction created equitable rights (such as a trust settlement), rescission will be equitable, since the matter falls within the jurisdiction of a court of equity.

Equitable rescission produces equitable rights. They may be personal rights (to be paid a sum of money or to be relieved of contractual obligations) or property rights (if rescission entitles the plaintiff to recover assets transferred to the defendant under the rescinded transaction). Since equitable rescission does not destroy the legal effect of a transaction, it cannot cause legal title to revert automatically to the plaintiff. However, it can cause the beneficial ownership of assets to be returned to the plaintiff in equity. In other words, the defendant will hold those assets in trust for the plaintiff once the plaintiff elects to rescind.

There is some debate about the proper classification of this trust. It is clear that it is not an express trust, since it is not created by intention, but arises by operation of law when the plaintiff rescinds the transaction. It is also clear that the trust arises to effect restitution of unjust enrichment. However, it is not clear whether it is constructive or resulting. This is discussed below at the end of the section on resulting trusts.

It is helpful to compare the trust in this situation to the trust which arises when a specifically enforceable contract of sale is made. As discussed in Chapter 21, if a buyer can compel the seller to transfer the asset sold (with an order of specific performance), then the seller holds that asset in trust for the buyer from the moment the contract is made. Equity considers as done that which ought to be done. This maxim can also be applied to a case of rescission. If the plaintiff elects to rescind a transaction and can compel the defendant to return an asset, then the defendant holds that asset in trust for the plaintiff. An election to rescind has an immediate proprietary effect so long as it entitles the plaintiff to recover an asset from the defendant.

Property Rights Before Rescission

If an election to rescind will create property rights to recoverable assets, then the right to make that election also creates property rights to those assets. However, before the election, the rights are weaker and less durable. The plaintiff does not have the full beneficial ownership of the recoverable assets, but has what is best described as a **power** to obtain beneficial ownership. This power is not a personal right, but a property right, since it relates to some thing (the recoverable asset) and can be enforced against other members of society.

The right to rescind and recover assets does not have a name, but might be called an **option to rescind** because it is similar to an option to purchase. As discussed at page 263, an option to purchase is a property right if the exercise of that option will create a specifically enforceable contract of sale. Since the option confers the power to compel a transfer of property (through a constructive trust), the option is itself a lesser equitable property right. An option to rescind can be legal or equitable, depending on whether the election to rescind will cause legal title to revert to the plaintiff or create a trust for the plaintiff.

The power created by an option to rescind, whether legal or equitable, is less durable than most other property rights. As discussed in Chapter 28, legal property rights are not normally defeated by the defence of *bona fide* purchase for value without notice of those rights. There are several exceptions to this rule. The most important is the *bona fide* purchase of money used as currency: see page 246. A legal option to rescind is another exception. If legal title will be restored when the plaintiff elects to rescind a transaction, then he or she has a legal power over that asset, which can be defeated by a *bona fide* purchaser.

The power will be lost if the defendant sells the asset to someone else, who buys it without notice of the plaintiff's right to rescind: see *Hunter BNZ Finance Ltd v CG Maloney Pty Ltd* (1988) 18 NSWLR 420.

Equitable options to rescind are similarly fragile. As discussed in Chapter 29, the normal priority of competing equitable property rights depends on the order in which they are created: earlier rights usually prevail over later rights. However, an equitable option to rescind can be defeated by a subsequent equitable property right acquired for value without notice of the option. Since it is less durable than most equitable property rights, equitable options to rescind are sometimes called **mere equities**: see *Latec Investments Ltd v Hotel Terrigal Pty Ltd* (1965) 113 CLR 265, discussed further at page 240.

Rectification

Rectification is the process of correcting errors in legal documents. The document might be a written contract, which differs from the actual agreement between the parties, or it may be some other document (such as a deed, transfer, or will), which does not do what the signatory intended. In this situation, a court of equity can order that the document be rectified to make it accord with the parties' intentions.

The legal issues concerning rectification are similar to, but simpler than, those already discussed in connection with rescission. Rectification is simpler than rescission for two reasons. First, there is only one ground for rectification: a mistake made translating the parties' intentions into print. There is no need to assess the quality of their intentions to enter the transaction to determine if they were affected by mistake, duress, undue influence, or exploitation. Secondly, rectification is available only in equity. Therefore, the right to rectify is equitable as are any property rights which flow from that right.

The Effect of Rectification

In most cases, rectification affects only personal rights and obligations. For example, suppose that you agree to lease a flat for $130 per week and, by mistake, the lease sets the rent at $180 per week. Rectification of the lease will reduce your obligation to pay rent.

Rectification can sometimes have proprietary consequences. Suppose that you agree to lease a house from me for five years and, by mistake, the lease sets the term at six years. Rectification will enable me to recover a portion of the legal estate which was transferred to you when the deed was executed or the lease was registered. This is restitution of unjust enrichment. You received a greater estate than I intended and I am able to recover the portion that you were not intended to receive.

Rectification is not always restitutionary. It is often used to carry out promises. If our written lease was incorrectly set for a term of only four years, you would be entitled to rectify it to match our agreement. This would not be restitution, but the performance of my promise to grant a lease for five years. I would not recover an interest in land, but would be compelled to grant a greater interest as promised.

The right to obtain an asset through rectification can create a trust in the same manner as a contract of sale or election to rescind. If the plaintiff has an equitable right to receive a transfer of that asset from the defendant, then (since equity considers as done that which ought to be done) the defendant holds that asset in trust for the plaintiff.

The trust created by a right to rectification modifies the transaction to make it conform (in equity) to the contract between the parties. However, it must be remembered that the trust may be perfectionary or restitutionary, depending on which way the equitable property right is carried. If too little property is transferred, the trust perfects the contractual promise to transfer the property mistakenly left behind. If too much property is transferred, the trust effects restitution of unjust enrichment by returning the extra property transferred by mistake.

Perfectionary Trust

USA v Motor Trucks Ltd [1924] AC 196 provides an example of a perfectionary trust arising in this context. The plaintiff agreed to buy a manufacturing plant from the defendant. By mistake, some of the land was omitted from the written contract. However, the defendant held that land in trust for the plaintiff, because the court could order both rectification of the contract to include the land and specific performance of the rectified contract.

In this situation, the trust is created not by rectification, but by a specifically enforceable contract of sale. Rectification merely cures an impediment to specific performance, in much the same way that part performance of a contract can cure the impediment created by the absence of writing: see Chapter 21. This leads to three conclusions about this trust. First, it is a constructive trust created to perfect the defendant's contractual promise to transfer an asset to the plaintiff. Secondly, it arises when the contract of sale is made. Thirdly, it will not arise unless that contract is otherwise specifically enforceable. There is no reason why the need to rectify a contract or ensuing transaction should give the contract a proprietary effect it would not otherwise have.

Restitutionary Trust

Where rectification allows a seller to recover property mistakenly conveyed to the buyer, the trust is restitutionary. It is created not by contract, but by the unjust enrichment of the buyer at the seller's expense. The true contract between the parties is relevant, of course, but only in a negative sense. It proves that the seller did not intend to transfer the extra property to the buyer.

Taitapu Gold Estates Ltd v Prouse [1916] NZLR 825 provides an example of a restitutionary trust. The plaintiffs agreed to sell land to the defendants, not including the mineral rights. By mistake, the minerals were not excepted from the transfer of land. When that transfer was registered, legal title to the whole estate, including the minerals, passed to the defendants. Hosking J declared that the defendants held the mineral rights in trust for the plaintiffs.

When Does the Trust Arise?

If the plaintiff can rectify a transaction and thereby recover an asset from the defendant, that asset will be held in trust for the plaintiff. However, it is not entirely clear when the trust arises. Unlike rescission, there is no election to rectify nor independent act of rectification which brings the trust into being. The right to rectify arises when the document containing the error is executed (and legal title to the asset is transferred by mistake to the defendant). If the parties cannot agree to correct the error, rectification is made by court order (and legal title is returned to the plaintiff). There is nothing between those two events which might mark a change in the nature of the plaintiff's equitable property right to the recoverable asset.

This indicates that the trust of the recoverable asset is created at the outset when the error is made and the right to rectification arises. Several cases are consistent with this view. For example, in *Blacklocks v JB Developments (Godalming) Ltd* [1982] Ch 183, a misdescription in a transfer document caused the plaintiff to transfer a larger parcel of land than intended to a purchaser. Before the error was discovered, the purchaser sold all the land to the defendant. The court declared that the defendant held the extra land in trust for the plaintiff, but did not say when that trust arose. However, it was clear that the plaintiff had an equitable property right to the recoverable land from the outset, even though no one was aware of the mistake. There was nothing to indicate that the property right was something other than a trust or that it might have been changed by an intervening event.

The difficulty with this view is that the right to rectification is often called a mere equity, like the option to rescind. However, there is an important difference between the two rights. The plaintiff with an option to rescind can choose whether to rescind or not and, as Lord Millett said, in "Restitution and Constructive Trusts" (1998) 114 *Law Quarterly Review* 399 at 416, the defendant "cannot anticipate his decision". Before the plaintiff elects to rescind, the transaction is effective and binding on the defendant.

In contrast, a plaintiff with a right to rectification does not have the power to affirm the transaction unilaterally. The defendant would also be entitled to rectify it (even if that is unlikely because the mistake worked in her or his favour). Both parties could affirm it (and thereby amend their contract) or one party could waive her or his right to seek rectification or lose it through delay. The right to rectify the document, and thereby recover an asset, is not contingent on an election to do so. Therefore, there is no event which might convert the plaintiff's property right to the recoverable asset from a power to a trust.

Resulting Trusts

Like constructive trusts, resulting trusts are created by operation of law. In other words, they are not created directly by an intention to create a trust. However, as with constructive trusts, intention is important for the creation of resulting trusts. In one sense, resulting trusts are simply a species of constructive trust arising in certain situations. Unlike constructive trusts, which are created for several different reasons (such as perfection of intention or restitution of profits from wrongdoing), all resulting trusts arise for one purpose: to effect restitution of unjust enrichment.

All resulting trusts follow a similar pattern. In each case, the defendant received an asset at the expense of the plaintiff and is required to hold that asset in trust for the plaintiff. The label "resulting" comes from the Latin, *resalire*, meaning "to spring back". It tells us that the subject of the trust is being returned to the person who provided it, but not why. When we look closer at the situations in which resulting trusts arise, we see another common feature: in each case, the plaintiff did not intend that the defendant should keep the asset for her or his own benefit.

Situations in Which Resulting Trusts Arise

There are two main situations in which resulting trusts arise: when an express trust fails and when someone receives an apparent gift. In the first situation, the plaintiff transferred assets to the defendant, intending to create a trust, but that trust failed to dispose of those assets fully. If the defendant was not supposed to keep the surplus for her or his own benefit, then it is held on resulting trust for the plaintiff. In the second situation, there is no attempt to create a trust, but an apparent gift of assets from the plaintiff to the defendant. If the plaintiff did not intend to make a gift, then the defendant will hold those assets on resulting trust for the plaintiff.

These are the two traditional categories of resulting trust. A trust which follows either fact pattern is clearly recognised as resulting. Resulting trusts can also arise in other situations. However, the law becomes much more controversial outside the traditional categories. There is no agreement on the further extent to which trusts can respond to unjust enrichment nor whether they should be called resulting or constructive. This is discussed below.

Trusts Which Fail

When an express trust fails, it is easy to see why a resulting trust arises. The plaintiff (as settlor) transferred assets to the defendant (as trustee) with the intention of creating a trust. For some reason, the intended trust did not dispose of all of those assets. For example, suppose that Andy transferred a house to Blythe in trust for Chris for life. Blythe received the legal fee simple estate, subject to Chris's equitable life estate. However, Andy did not indicate what she was to do with the remainder. In the absence of evidence of Andy's intention to give the surplus to Blythe, it is assumed that a gift was not intended. Blythe would be unjustly enriched if she kept it for her own benefit and, therefore, equity compels her to return it to Andy (or to his estate if he is dead). In other words, Blythe will hold the remainder on resulting trust for Andy.

There are many reasons why an express trust might fail in part or entirely. A failure to deal with remainders is one reason. A failure to comply with formalities is another. For example, suppose that I transfer a house to you (by deed or registration) and tell you that I want you to hold it in trust for my son. My attempt to create an express trust of land will fail because it is not manifest in writing: see Chapter 21. However, it shows that I did not intend to make a gift of the house to you and, therefore, you will hold it on resulting trust for me.

It has been suggested in England that the failure of an express trust leads automatically to a resulting trust, regardless of the settlor's intention: *Re Vandervell's Trusts (No 2)* [1974] Ch 269. However, this idea has not found favour in other common law countries, nor does it take into account a number of English cases which make the resulting trust in this situation dependent on the settlor's intention. For example, in *Cook v Hutchinson* (1836) 1 Keen 42, 48 ER 222, a father transferred property by deed to his son in trust for himself for life and then for his wife and others. The trust did not dispose of all the property and the court was asked to decide whether the surplus belonged to the son beneficially or was held on resulting trust for the father. Lord Langdale MR looked at the deed, considered the relationship between the parties, and concluded (at Keen 51, ER 225) "that the father intended to part with all beneficial interest in the property, and that he meant his son to have the benefit of that part of the property of which the trusts are not expressly declared".

When an express trust fails, a resulting trust arises because the settlor did not intend to give the surplus to the trustee, who would therefore be unjustly enriched if he or she was permitted to keep it. Normally, trustees are not supposed to take any personal benefit from the trusts they perform. Therefore, a transfer of assets to someone in trust is a good indication that a gift was not intended. However, if it is proved that the settlor intended to give the surplus to the trustee, there is no unjust enrichment and a resulting trust will not arise.

Apparent Gifts

Resulting trusts can also arise in cases where no express trust was intended or created. When someone makes an unexplained apparent gift to another, there may be a presumption that a gift was not intended. If this presumption is not rebutted, the recipient will hold the asset on resulting trust for the apparent donor. As Aickin J said in *Napier v Public Trustee (WA)* (1980) 32 ALR 153 at 158:

> "The law with respect to resulting trusts is not in doubt. Where property is transferred by one person into the name of another without consideration, and where a purchaser pays the vendor and directs him to transfer the property into the name of another person without consideration passing from that person, there is a presumption that the transferee holds the property upon trust for the transferor or the purchaser as the case may be."

Presumption of Resulting Trust

The presumption of resulting trust can be traced back five centuries to the presumption of resulting use. As discussed in Chapter 13, the use was popular before the *Statute of Uses* 1536, because it allowed people to control the disposition of their land after death and avoid feudal incidents. Land owners often created uses of their lands for themselves for life, with the remainder for people to be named later. This transaction became so common that courts began to assume that an apparent gift of land was intended to be held for the use of the apparent donor. This developed into the rule of law known as the **resulting use**.

When the modern trust began to develop more than a century later, the courts began to apply the presumption of resulting trust, by analogy to the resulting use: see *Dyer v Dyer* (1788) 2 Cox Equity 92, 30 ER 42. However, the conditions which had given rise to the resulting use had ceased to exist. Land could be given away by will and most feudal incidents had been abolished. There was no longer any reason for a court to assume that the apparent donor had intended to create a trust for herself or himself.

There was, perhaps, a new reason for the presumption of resulting trust: equity's suspicion of gifts. When confronted with a large, unexpected gift, the Court of Chancery assumed that something was wrong or at least wanted to double check to make sure that everything was right. It asked the donee to prove that a gift had been intended and, if that proof was not forthcoming, declared that he or she held the apparent gift on resulting trust for its donor.

Presumption of Advancement

In some situations, equity is not suspicious and assumes that an apparent gift was intended as such. This occurs when the donor is the donee's parent or guardian or stands *in loco parentis* (in the place of a parent) to the donee. It also occurs when the donor is the donee's husband. This assumption that a gift was intended is called the **presumption of advancement** because, at one time, fathers were under a moral duty to advance their children in life. Therefore, it was assumed that a gift from father to child was intended to be for the child's benefit in fulfilment of that duty. Applied at first only to fathers, it was later modified to apply to gifts from other parental figures, with mothers added to that list only towards the end of the 20th century.

The application of the presumption of advancement to gifts from husbands to wives may have started for a similar reason. Since husbands were under a legal duty to support their wives, a large gift from husband to wife could be explained as performance of that duty. In *Pettitt v Pettitt* [1970] AC 777 at 793, Lord Reid suggested the possibility "that wives' economic dependence on their husbands made it necessary as a matter of public policy to give them this advantage". Whatever the reason, it is anomalous, since it does not apply to gifts from wives to their husbands or between de facto spouses.

The unequal treatment of men and women is not defensible, but courts seem unsure of how to proceed. Applying the same presumption, of either resulting trust or advancement, to both husbands and wives would remove a legal advantage currently enjoyed by married women: see Sarmas, "A Step in the Wrong Direction: The Emergence of Gender 'Neutrality' in the Equitable Presumption of Advancement" (1994) 19 *Melbourne University Law Review* 758. Also, the courts have few opportunities to review the presumptions in this context, since most questions concerning the allocation of assets in a marriage are decided on the breakdown of the marriage and are governed by the *Family Law Act* 1975 (Cth).

The Presumptions Today

The presumptions of resulting trust and advancement seem a bit odd today. Why does the presumption of resulting trust exist at all? Why not assume that people intend the consequences of their actions and leave apparent gifts alone? If courts are willing to assume that a gift was intended in certain relationships, why only when the donor is the donee's parent or husband? Why not apply the presumption of advancement to all relationships in which love and affection provide motives for giving?

Although the presumptions do seem somewhat out of date, they continue to be useful. The presumption of resulting trust survives as a general rule which applies to every apparent gift, except for those made by parents and husbands. It serves as a general safeguard against the unintended loss of assets. There are many reasons why someone might transfer an asset to, or buy an asset for, another person. The presumption is equity's way of confirming that an apparent gift really was intended as such.

The presumption of advancement is a limited exception to the general rule, which is applied in situations where the protection of the presumption of resulting trust is not required. Economically more powerful parents and husbands did not need to be protected from unintended transfers of wealth to their children and wives. However, if this is the reason for preserving the presumption of advancement, then two adjustments might be needed. First, as the balance of power within marriage is achieved, husbands should become entitled to the same protection of the presumption of resulting trust which everyone enjoys (except parents). Secondly, perhaps the presumption of advancement should cease to apply to apparent gifts from parents once their children have achieved full economic independence. A presumption of resulting trust might be a better starting point in cases where elderly parents are making large gifts to adult children on whom they have become dependent.

The presumptions of resulting trust and advancement are merely inferences of fact drawn from the proof of other facts. An apparent gift leads to an assumption about the donor's state of mind, depending on the relationship between the parties. Where the donor's intention is proved, there is no room for the presumptions. The presumption of resulting trust is easily rebutted by circumstantial evidence of an intention to give. Conversely, the presumption of advancement can be rebutted by proof of a lack of intention to give. Equity's response to the lack of intention to benefit the donee is the resulting trust. It effects restitution to the apparent donor of what would otherwise be the unjust enrichment of the donee.

Contributions to the Purchase Price

In some cases, two (or more) people have contributed to the purchase of an asset, but legal title is not shared in proportion to their contributions. A resulting trust can arise in this situation to ensure that one person is not unjustly enriched at the expense of another.

For example, in *Calverley v Green* (1984) 155 CLR 242, the parties purchased a house together, taking title as joint owners. Mr Calverley paid one third of the purchase price up front, raised the remaining two thirds by mortgaging the house, and made all the mortgage payments for several years. When the relationship ended, Ms Green claimed one half of the house as the joint owner and Calverley claimed the house for himself. The court declared that their joint legal ownership was held in resulting trust for themselves as tenants in common, with two thirds of the beneficial ownership belonging to him and one third to her.

The resulting trust arose because both parties had contributed to the purchase price and neither party intended to make a gift to the other. Even though he had paid the down payment and all the mortgage payments, she had contributed as a joint mortgagor. Since they were both jointly liable to pay the mortgage, she had provided half of the mortgage proceeds, which amounted to one third of the purchase price for the home. Her joint legal ownership was greater than her contribution to the purchase price and she was unjustly enriched by the difference.

She was also unjustly enriched by his payment of her share of the mortgage debt. However, this did not affect the resulting trust, which arose when the house was purchased by the couple. Instead, he was entitled to be reimbursed for paying her share of the mortgage and had an equitable lien on her share of the house for that amount. This is discussed below.

The Donor's Intention

In England, it has been suggested that the resulting trust of an apparent gift is created by the donor's presumed intention to create that trust: see William Swadling, "A New Role for Resulting Trusts?" (1996) 16 *Legal Studies* 110. However, this has not found favour in other countries, nor can it explain every case of resulting trust. There are a number of cases in which the donor could not or would not have intended to create a trust for herself or himself. Also, there is no reason to exempt a resulting trust of land from the requirement of writing if it is based on a presumed intention to create it.

All resulting trusts arise because the donor did not intend to benefit the donee. In some cases, the donor may have intended to create a trust for herself or himself. However, if the intended trust fails to take effect as an express trust, a resulting trust is created, not to give effect to that intention, but to remove the unjust enrichment from the donee. The intention to create a trust is relevant because it proves that the donor did not intend to make a gift. A resulting trust for the donor would arise even if the intended trust was for the benefit of others.

Brown v Brown (1993) 31 NSWLR 582 demonstrates the negative role of intention in the creation of a resulting trust. In 1958, Mrs Brown's house was sold and the proceeds used to purchase a larger house in the name of her two adult sons. She lived in the house with her sons until she moved into a nursing home in 1987. She then claimed a resulting trust of the house based on her contribution to the purchase price.

Mrs Brown's claim was successful because she was able to rebut the presumption of advancement which operated in favour of her sons. The trial judge determined that, in 1958, there was no agreement between Mrs Brown and her sons about ownership of the new house and that she had no positive intention to make a loan or gift. The proof that she failed to form any intention regarding the ownership of the house displaced the assumption that she had intended to make a gift. Equity responded to the proven lack of intention to give by raising a resulting trust in her favour.

Unjust Enrichment in Other Situations

Trusts can arise in response to unjust enrichment in situations which do not fall within the traditional categories of resulting trust. As discussed above, a trust can be created by an election to rescind a transaction (or a right to rectify it), even though there is no apparent gift or intention to create a trust. However, there is a great deal of uncertainty over the connection between unjust enrichment and trusts. The courts have not yet established a set of principles which will determine when unjust enrichment will give rise to a trust or to some other right to restitution. Also, it is not clear whether a trust created by unjust enrichment is resulting or constructive. A comprehensive discussion of these issues would require a book of its own. A brief introduction is the most that can be provided here.

When is a Trust Appropriate?

Like other property rights, a trust can exist only where there is some specific thing subject to the trust. Therefore, a trust cannot arise to effect restitution of unjust enrichment unless that enrichment is an existing asset. If the enrichment is a service performed (such as medical treatment or education) or goods consumed (such as food or petrol), the only possible method of restitution is payment of the value of that enrichment.

If the unjust enrichment is an existing asset, then a trust is possible in theory. Whether a trust is created depends, in part, on the nature of that asset (money is treated differently than other things) and whether the plaintiff's right to restitution is conditional upon rescission of a transaction with the defendant.

As discussed above, the parties to a transaction have to make *restitutio in integrum* when that transaction is rescinded. Normally, they will have to return any specific assets (other than money) which they received in that transaction. If the act of rescission does not cause legal ownership of those assets to revert to the plaintiff, the defendant will hold them in trust for the plaintiff. This does not apply to money paid in the transaction, since *restitutio in integrum* can be achieved by payment of the same sum of money.

In many cases, the unjust enrichment of the defendant was not part of a contract or other transaction and, therefore, rescission is not involved. For example, the defendant might have stolen money or forged a cheque or the plaintiff might have lost money or paid it to the defendant by mistake. These situations do not create the same legal problems when they involve assets other than money. For example, if the plaintiff's bicycle is lost or stolen, he or she will continue to be its legal owner and can enforce that right against anyone who interferes with it: see Chapter 7. Unjust enrichment is not involved.

The theft or finding of the plaintiff's money does not destroy her or his legal ownership. However, as discussed at page 245, the legal ownership of money passes very easily and will be lost if the defendant deposits it in the bank or pays it to any other *bona fide* purchaser. The plaintiff will then have a personal right to repayment of the sum stolen, lost, or paid by mistake, but might also have a property right (under a trust) to any assets purchased with the plaintiff's money. This depends on the reason why the enrichment was unjust.

The consensus of opinion seems to be that a trust will arise where legal ownership of money is obtained by theft, fraud, or breach of fiduciary duty. For example, in *Black v S Freedman & Co* (1910) 12 CLR 105, a man stole money from his employer and paid it into his wife's bank account. O'Connor J said (at 110), "Where money has been stolen, it is trust money in the hands of the thief." Since Mrs Black was not a *bona fide* purchaser of the money, she held her bank account in trust for Mr Black's employer. The defendant's wrongdoing may be a factor in cases like this. A trust helps to ensure that no one will benefit from that breach of duty. This is discussed further in the next chapter.

Where the receipt of money is unjust for some other reason (such as mistake, duress, undue influence, or exploitation of disadvantage), it is not clear whether a trust will arise. *Ilich v The Queen* (1987) 162 CLR 110 concerned money paid by mistake. The High Court of Australia suggested (at 129 and 143) that the defendant might hold it in trust for the plaintiff, but did not resolve the issue. It is difficult to predict what the court will do in the future, especially since the law has developed in different directions in North America and England.

In North America, the defendant will hold the mistaken payment in trust for the plaintiff. In *Re Berry* (1906) 147 F 208, the plaintiffs and defendants were stock brokers in New York. As a result of a bookkeeping error, the plaintiffs paid a sum due to the defendants twice by mistake. The defendants became bankrupt two weeks later. The court declared that the defendants held the second payment in trust for the plaintiffs. A Canadian court would reach the same conclusion.

An English court was presented with the same problem in *Chase Manhattan Bank NA v Israel-British Bank (London) Ltd* [1981] Ch 105. The plaintiff made a clerical error and paid two million dollars twice by mistake to the defendant shortly before the defendant became insolvent. Goulding J decided that the defendant held the second payment in trust for the plaintiff. However, in *Westdeutsche Landesbank Girozentrale v Islington LBC* [1996] AC 669, the House of Lords doubted whether that decision was the correct. It now seems likely that they will overrule that case when the opportunity arises.

Classification of the Trust

Despite the many uncertainties encountered in this area of law, we do know that trusts arise to effect restitution of unjust enrichment and that they are called resulting trusts in two situations: where an express trust fails to dispose of all the trust assets and where someone receives an apparent gift not intended as such. In other situations, it is not always clear when a trust will arise or whether to call it constructive or resulting.

In North America, the trusts responding to unjust enrichment (outside the traditional categories of resulting trust) are labelled as constructive. This has long been the law in the United States. Canada chose to follow the American convention in a series of family property cases, beginning with *Pettkus v Becker* (1980) 117 DLR (3d) 257. Earlier Canadian cases labelled the trust as resulting: see *Sharp v McNeil* (1913) 15 DLR 73 and *Re Kolari* (1981) 36 OR (2d) 473.

In England and Australia, the proper classification remains a subject of debate. In *Westdeutsche Landesbank Girozentrale v Islington LBC* [1996] AC 669, Lord Browne-Wilkinson suggested that English courts should adopt the North American approach. However, in "Restitution and Constructive Trusts" (1998) 114 *Law Quarterly Review* 399 at 410, Lord Millett said that "the development of a coherent doctrine of proprietary restitution for subtractive unjust enrichment is impossible unless it is based on the resulting trust as traditionally understood".

It would simplify matters if all the trusts responding to unjust enrichment were labelled as resulting. However, this debate is not just about nomenclature, but about the principles which will determine when unjust enrichment will create a trust. As other chapters in Part IV have revealed, there is a great deal of uncertainty over the creation of constructive trusts. They arise for a variety of different reasons and, in many cases, those reasons are not fully articulated. In contrast, resulting trusts respond to unjust enrichment in accordance with well established principles. Those principles are much more likely to provide a clear answer to the vexing question of when a trust is an appropriate method of restitution of unjust enrichment.

Equitable Liens

As discussed at page 122, equitable liens arise by operation of law to secure the payment of a debt related to the asset subject to the lien. In some cases, that debt is created by unjust enrichment. When a defendant is required to make restitution by payment of the value of the unjust enrichment, that obligation might be secured by an equitable lien over some of her or his assets.

When does an equitable lien arise in response to unjust enrichment? This question can be divided into two parts. First, what connects the debt to an asset sufficiently to justify an equitable lien over that asset? Secondly, why is the plaintiff entitled to a security right (a lien) in some cases and full beneficial ownership (a trust) in others?

Connection to the Asset

Equitable liens arise for a number of different reasons. In every case, there is some connection between the debt secured by the lien and the asset subject to that lien. For example, a vendor's lien can arise when land is sold to secure the buyer's obligation to pay the purchase price: see page 267. The debt is created by the contract of sale and the lien attaches to the asset sold.

Where a debt is created by unjust enrichment, a lien might arise if there is a sufficient connection between that unjust enrichment and the asset subject to the lien. In most cases, that connection is the improvement or preservation of the value of that asset through unjust enrichment. A portion of that value represents the surviving enrichment of the defendant.

The improvement or preservation of the value of an asset can occur in a number of ways. It might be caused by the repair, renovation, or maintenance of the asset or by the payment of expenses related to the asset, such as a mortgage or taxes. In each case, the value of the defendant's right to that asset would be lower if the plaintiff had not provided the unjust enrichment.

For example, if we own a house as joint tenants and you pay my share of the mortgage payments for a year, I am unjustly enriched at your expense. You have a personal right to be paid the value of the enrichment and will also have an equitable lien on the house to secure the performance of my obligation. The lien is justified because the unjust enrichment has both preserved the value of my interest in the house (by preventing foreclosure) and enhanced it (by increasing the value of my equity of redemption): see page 122.

A lien to secure the payment of restitution will (like all security rights) become important if the defendant is unable to pay that debt. On bankruptcy, the defendant's assets would be sold to pay her or his creditors. Without a lien, those creditors would share the entire value of the asset, including the portion that was preserved or enhanced by unjust enrichment at the plaintiff's expense. The lien gives the plaintiff a right to that value in priority to the defendant's unsecured creditors.

In most cases, the unrequested improvement of an asset is not an unjust enrichment and, therefore, cannot create a lien. For example, in *Brand v Chris Building Society Pty Ltd* [1957] VR 625, a builder constructed a weatherboard house on Mr Brand's land by mistake. Brand's neighbour had hired the builder to construct the house, but had pointed to the wrong block when giving instructions. Since Brand had not freely accepted the improvement of his land, he was not unjustly enriched and was not required to pay for it.

The improvement or preservation of the defendant's asset can be an unjust enrichment if it was freely accepted or an incontrovertible benefit. There is no doubt that the defendant is enriched if he or she was saved a necessary expense or sold the asset for more money because of the improvement or preservation. See Chapter 15 for a discussion of this issue in relation to joint and common ownership.

Trust or Lien?

There are important similarities between trusts and equitable liens in this context. They are both equitable property rights created by operation of law to effect restitution of unjust enrichment. However, there is also an important difference between the two rights. A trust is beneficial ownership of an asset and a lien is a security right. The trust arises to effect restitution of the unjust enrichment itself, while the lien secures performance of the obligation to make restitution by payment of the value of the enrichment.

A trust is justified when the unjust enrichment is an asset received by the defendant at the plaintiff's expense. It causes the defendant to give up that asset and restores the parties to their pre-enrichment positions. Since the asset is the enrichment and the law regards the defendant's receipt or retention of that asset as unjust, a trust of that asset is an acceptable level of interference with the defendant's property rights. In contrast, if the enrichment is the improvement or preservation of an asset which the defendant already owns, then a trust is not justifiable. There is no reason why the defendant should be required to transfer that asset to the plaintiff.

An equitable lien over an improved or preserved asset leaves the defendant free to use other resources to meet the obligation to pay restitution. If the defendant cannot or will not pay that debt, the lien gives the plaintiff the right to have the asset sold to pay it. The lien interferes with the defendant's freedom of choice to a lesser extent than does a trust. This difference is important. As Professor Birks said in "Proprietary Rights as Remedies" in Birks, *The Frontiers of Liability*, Vol 2 (1994) 214 at 218:

> "A judgment for the surrender of items of property inflicts loss, as does a money judgment, but, unlike a money judgment, also entangles itself in the complexities both of unwanted consequences for third parties and of individual economic priorities. The latter point is important and often neglected. Taking money from people makes them worse off and narrows their options, taking specific things is a more erratic instrument of justice, because of their subjective value: the same 'adjustment' will cause vastly different degrees of pain, depending on the sentiments and tastes of the loser."

Another important difference between a trust and a lien is the potential value of each property right. Since a trust is the beneficial ownership of all or a portion of an asset, the value of that trust depends on the value of the asset (which fluctuates in response to market conditions and damages or improvements to the asset). Where the unjust enrichment is an asset received by the defendant, the trust is an appropriate method of restitution because it causes the defendant to give up that asset, whatever its value.

In contrast, the value of the lien is measured by the debt secured by the lien. That debt can be affected by defences, such as change of position (discussed above) or the limitation of actions (see Chapter 8), but is not affected directly by the fluctuating value of the asset subject to the lien. Where the unjust enrichment is the improvement or preservation of the defendant's asset, there is no reason why the plaintiff should share any increase in the value of that asset which is caused by factors other than that unjust enrichment.

Calverley v Green (1984) 155 CLR 242, discussed above, demonstrates the difference between the acquisition of an asset and its preservation. Mr Calverley's contribution to the purchase of Ms Green's joint interest in the house gave rise to a resulting trust, while his payment of her share of the mortgage gave rise to an equitable lien. Both property rights were created by unjust enrichment. The trust required her to give up the portion of her joint interest that was acquired at his expense. The lien secured her obligation to pay for his preservation of that interest.

Tracing

What is Tracing?

Tracing is a process of identifying the location of value. It is used to determine, for certain legal purposes, that the value of one asset was used to acquire another asset. In some cases, a person who had a property right to the first asset can trace the value of that asset into the second asset and assert a similar property right to the second asset.

For example, suppose that I stole $500 from you and used it to buy a television set. The theft of your cash did not destroy your legal ownership of those notes. However, as discussed in Chapters 21 and 28, that ownership was lost when the notes were used as currency (and the shop became their new legal owner as a *bona fide* purchaser for value). You have a personal claim against me for the value of the money stolen. Do you also have a property right to my new TV?

According to *Black v S Freedman & Co* (1910) 12 CLR 105, discussed above, I would hold the TV in trust for you. This is not a continuation of your original ownership of the money (which was lost when it was paid to the shop), but a new property right created when I purchased the TV. It is not an express trust (since no one intended to create it), but a constructive or resulting trust which arose because I used your assets without your consent to buy the TV. In other words, I am unjustly enriched at your expense and the TV is the surviving enrichment. The trust is restitutionary since it causes me to give up that TV to you.

Your property right to the TV depends upon proof that I used your value to buy the TV. Tracing is the process which provides that proof. In this example, tracing is easy. The simple exchange of cash for a TV shows that the enrichment I received at your expense continues to survive in that TV. However, tracing can be much more difficult if value from several different sources is mixed together. Most of the rules of tracing (discussed below) are designed to deal with this problem.

The law of tracing used to be more difficult and controversial. However, many problems in this area have been alleviated by Lionel Smith's book, *The Law of Tracing* (1997). He usefully distinguished tracing from two other concepts with which it was often confused. First, people do not trace property, they trace value. When you trace from your stolen money to my new TV, it is not because your legal ownership of your money survived. Your claim to the TV is based on my use of the value of your money. Through tracing, you show that your value survived.

Secondly, tracing is distinct from any claim that might be made against any assets into which value might be traced. As Millett LJ stated in *Boscawen v Bajwa* [1996] 1 WLR 328 at 334:

> "Equity lawyers habitually use the expressions 'the tracing claim' and 'the tracing remedy' to describe the proprietary claim and the proprietary remedy which equity makes available to the beneficial owner who seeks to recover his property in specie from those into whose hands it has come. Tracing properly so-called, however, is neither a claim nor a remedy but a process."

The fact that you can trace your value to my TV does not mean that you have any particular property right to that TV. A trust arises because the TV is an unjust enrichment that I acquired at your expense. If I had used your money to pay the mortgage on my house, you would have been entitled to an equitable lien, as discussed above. Tracing and claiming are separate activities. A right which depends on tracing might be legal or equitable and might be personal or proprietary.

Tracing Through Mixtures

Suppose that I stole $500 from you, deposited the money in my bank account (which already had a balance of $700), and then paid for a television set with a $500 cheque drawn on that account. Did I pay for the TV with your value, my value, or both? No one can say for sure which part of the $1,200 in my account was used to buy the TV.

The law of tracing provides rules to deal with problems like this. When value from different sources gets mixed together, so that separate identification is no longer possible, artificial rules are used to identify the location of surviving value. The three main rules are:

1).....presumptions against wrongdoers;
2).....pro rata sharing among innocent parties; and
3).....the rule in *Clayton's Case*.

Presumptions Against Wrongdoers

Tracing problems are often created by the defendant's breach of duty. In the example above, I wrongly converted your cash and deposited it in my bank account. My wrongdoing created your inability to locate your value, which may be in my bank account, my new TV, or both. Its location might be important if the rest of the money in the bank was spent or the TV was destroyed.

In cases like this, where the evidence points to two or more possible locations of the plaintiff's value, the plaintiff is entitled to choose its location. The defendant, who wrongly mixed that value with her or his own, does not get a say. As Lionel Smith said, in *The Law of Tracing* (1997) p 195, "the interests of a wrongdoer are subordinated in resolving the evidential impossibility as to which part of the account is the plaintiff's". This rule is an application of what he called (p 77) "a well-established principle of law and equity that a person whose unlawful act brings about an evidential difficulty will have that difficulty resolved against him".

The presumption against wrongdoers is not meant to be a form of punishment. It is merely a way of resolving an evidential difficulty created by the defendant's wrongful act and does not displace actual evidence of the location of the plaintiff's value: see *Indian Oil Corp Ltd v Greenstone Shipping Co SA* [1988] QB 345 at 369. The principle is used to trace the plaintiff's value only to the extent that its location is unknown.

In *Lofts v MacDonald* (1974) 3 ALR 404, a trustee deposited $1,600 of trust funds in a bank account. The balance of that account was then reduced to $8.42 and later restored to $2,824.50. The beneficiaries of the trust could trace only $8.42 of their value. Although they could not identify the precise location of their value, the evidence proved that no more than $8.42 had remained in the account. The presumption against wrongdoers cannot be used to contradict a proven fact. This particular limit on the presumption is sometimes called the **lowest intermediate balance** rule.

Sharing Pro Rata

In some cases, competing claimants to a mixed fund are innocent parties and, therefore, a presumption against wrongdoers is of no assistance. For example, in *Keefe v Law Society of NSW* (1998) 44 NSWLR 451, a solicitor mixed money belonging to 14 different clients in his trust account. In breach of trust and his duties as a solicitor, more than half of the money was spent improperly. It was impossible to say whose money had been misappropriated. All the claimants to the remaining trust funds were innocent of any wrongdoing in the matter and there was no reason to subordinate one claim to another.

In cases like this, the mixture of value in the bank account is treated like a mixture of coins in a box: see Chapter 26. So long as there is enough in the mixture to satisfy everybody's claim, each contributor is permitted to withdraw an amount equal to her or his contribution. However, if some of the mixture is lost, the loss is shared by the contributors in proportion to their contributions to the mixed fund.

Clayton's Rule

Courts in England have used a different rule to identify the location of value in cases where funds belonging to innocent contributors have been mixed in a bank account. Rather than treat the account like a physical mixture of coins, an English court might match deposits and withdrawals on the basis of first in, first out (or FIFO for short): see *Re Diplock* [1948] Ch 465 at 550. The rule is often called Clayton's rule because it was derived from *Clayton's Case* (1817) 1 Mer 572, 35 ER 781.

The rule treats a bank account as a series of debts owed by the bank to its customer, rather than as a mixture of value. A deposit in the account increases the sum of the bank's debts to its customer and a withdrawal is a reduction of that sum. According to Clayton's rule, each withdrawal is matched against the earliest deposit, unless the bank and customer have agreed otherwise.

In *Clayton's Case*, the court applied a general rule concerning the payment of debts to a bank account. Suppose that I borrow $10 from you on Monday, another $10 on Tuesday, and another $10 on Wednesday. On Friday, I repay $10. Which debt did I repay? According to the general rule, I (the debtor) can choose which debt to repay and, if I do not, then you (the creditor) get to choose. If neither of us allocate the money to a particular debt, then it is assumed that I intended to pay the most onerous debt (for example, the one with the highest rate of interest). If all the debts are the same, then it is assumed that I intended to pay the earliest debt. Change the facts, so that I am a bank and your loans to me are deposits in your bank account, and you have Clayton's rule.

Clayton's rule is useful for resolving disputes between the bank and its customers (which was how it was used in *Clayton's Case*) and it does add an element of certainty when applied to mixed funds. However, it can produce undesirable results in disputes among innocent contributors to a mixed bank account. As Smith said, in *The Law of Tracing* (1997) p 194, "The main objection to using *Clayton's Case* among multiple claimants ... is its arbitrariness as between people in substantially identical situations."

Smith argues (at 194) that there is no need to use Clayton's rule in this situation: "It only requires a decision that, except as between banker and customer, a bank account is not made up of a series of debts, but is a uniform mixture of value." Fortunately, this is the law in Canada and the United States of America and has recently been followed in Australia. In *Keefe v Law Society of NSW* (1998) 44 NSWLR 451 at 460, the New South Wales Court of Appeal rejected the "first in, first out basis" and decided that the innocent contributors to the mixed fund were "rateably entitled to the available funds". There are indications that English courts are moving in the same direction: see *Barlow Clowes International Ltd v Vaughan* [1992] 4 All ER 22 at 44.

Chapter Twenty-Five

WRONGDOING

■■■

In most cases, the law responds to wrongdoing by creating personal rights and obligations. For example, the wrongdoer might be fined or imprisoned or be required to compensate the victim for loss. However, the law also responds to wrongdoing by creating property rights. This can happen in two different ways. First, the government might confiscate the assets of a wrongdoer as a form of punishment. Secondly, a wrongdoer might be compelled to give up assets acquired through wrongdoing to the government, to the victim of the wrong, or (if the victim is dead) to other persons.

This chapter concerns the ways in which wrongdoing leads to the creation of property rights. It begins by considering briefly what constitutes wrongdoing and the range of possible responses to it. This is followed by a discussion of each of the three different groups that might acquire property rights to the wrongdoer's assets: governments, victims, and others.

What is Wrongdoing?

This question is not part of a grand philosophical or theological quest for the meaning of good and evil, but (like most things legal) is a mundane inquiry. Since this chapter concerns property rights created by wrongdoing, it is helpful to state clearly what is meant by that term. A legal wrong is a breach of legal duty. The defendant has done something which is prohibited by statute, common law, or equity or has failed to perform an obligation imposed by one of those sources.

Wrongdoing does not necessarily involve moral turpitude. Honest people can breach their legal duties unintentionally. For example, I might trespass on my neighbour's land by mistake or buy a bicycle without realising that it was stolen: see Chapter 7. A person in financial difficulties might be unable to pay her or his debts. Trustees might unwittingly breach the strict rules which prohibit them from having conflicting financial interests.

Similarly, the word "victim" is used here to describe the person to whom the legal duty is owed. It is not meant to connote any sense of suffering, powerlessness, or harm beyond the infringement of the victim's legal right. A person can be a victim of a legal wrong (such as trespass) even though it causes no loss whatsoever.

Responses to Wrongdoing

As discussed in Chapter 7, there are four main types of responses to wrongdoing:

1) .....direct enforcement;
2) .....compensation;
3) .....restitution; and
4) .....punishment.

Direct Enforcement

The direct enforcement of duties is fairly uncommon. In some cases, the victim of a wrong can obtain an injunction prohibiting the wrongdoer from further interference with the victim's rights or an order compelling the wrongdoer to perform a contract or other duty.

The right to an injunction or order for specific performance can be a property right if it relates to a particular thing. As discussed in Chapter 16, a restrictive covenant became a property right because a court of equity would grant an injunction preventing a breach of that covenant. Similarly, a contract of sale creates property rights if the purchaser is entitled to an order for specific performance of the contract: see page 259. However, these property rights are created by contract and not by the wrong of breach of contract. They arise when the contract of sale or restrictive covenant is made, regardless of whether it is properly performed or not.

Compensation

The most common response to torts (such as trespass or negligence), breach of contract, and equitable wrongs (such as breach of confidence or fiduciary duty) is to compel the wrongdoer to compensate the victim for any losses caused by the wrong. These are sometimes called **civil wrongs** to distinguish them from crimes and breaches of statutory duties. Courts can also order criminals to compensate the victims of their crimes: see, eg, *Penalties and Sentences Act* 1992 (Qld), s 35. The right to compensation is always a personal right to payment of the value of the loss caused by the wrong.

Restitution

There is a general legal principle that people should not be allowed to profit from their own wrongs. As Lord Goff said, in *Attorney-General v Guardian Newspapers (No 2)* [1990] 1 AC 109 at 286, this principle is stated "in very general terms, and does not of itself provide any sure guidance to the solution of a problem in a particular case". However, it is the reason why the law intervenes in many different situations to require a person to give up the profit of wrongdoing. This is usually called restitution, but is also called **disgorgement**.

A right to restitution of the benefit of wrongdoing is usually a personal right (to payment of the value of that benefit), but can also be a property right (to the benefit itself). It is similar to restitution of unjust enrichment, discussed in the previous chapter. In both situations, it can be difficult to tell whether restitution is available and whether the right to restitution should be personal or proprietary. However, there are two important differences between these two situations. First, restitution is the only possible legal response to unjust enrichment. In contrast, it is just one possible response to wrongdoing and is used far less often than either compensation or punishment.

Secondly, unjust enrichment and profit from wrongdoing are two different events. Unjust enrichment does not depend on wrongdoing. An innocent defendant can be required to make restitution of an enrichment received from the plaintiff (such as a mistaken payment). Conversely, profit from wrongdoing does not depend on unjust enrichment. A defendant can be required to make restitution of the profit of wrongdoing even though it was not obtained at the plaintiff's expense.

In many cases, a benefit is both an unjust enrichment and the profit from wrongdoing. For example, stolen money is an unjust enrichment (because value has flowed from the victim to the thief without the victim's consent) and the profit from a crime. However, it is important to remember that these are independent reasons for restitution: unjust enrichment does not require fault, and profit from wrongdoing does not require an expense to the plaintiff.

Punishment

Punishment is the most common response to crime and breach of a statutory duty. On rare occasions, a court might punish a tortfeasor with an award of punitive or exemplary damages: see page 62. Most punishments take the form of personal rights and obligations: the government will have the right to receive payment of a fine from the wrongdoer or to deprive the wrongdoer of her or his liberty. In some cases, the government will obtain a property right to the wrongdoer's assets. This is called forfeiture or confiscation.

Forfeiture to the Government

At common law, when people were sentenced to death or outlawed for felony or treason, they were attainted and their assets would be forfeited to the Crown or escheat to the lords from whom they held tenure: see Megarry and Wade, *The Law of Real Property* (5th ed, 1984) pp 17, 1026. This was abolished by statute in England and Australia: see *Re Director of Public Prosecutions; Ex parte Lawler* (1994) 179 CLR 270 at 289; eg, *Criminal Code Act* 1924 (Tas), s 11.

There are now a large number of statutes which authorise the government to take things away from people who commit crimes or breach statutory duties. They serve two main purposes. First, they provide for restitution to the government of the benefits of wrongdoing. Secondly, they provide additional punishment of wrongdoers by allowing the government to take away things used to break the law.

Recovery of the Benefits of Wrongdoing

There are two ways to take away the benefits of wrongdoing: a personal right to payment of the value of those benefits or a property right to the benefits themselves. The statutes, which entitle the government to take the benefits of wrongdoing, use both methods. For example, the *Proceeds of Crime Act* 1987 (Cth) enables the court to make "forfeiture orders" (which transfer property rights to the proceeds of crime to the Commonwealth) and "pecuniary penalty orders" (which require criminals to pay to the Commonwealth the value of benefits derived from the commission of crimes). Each state and territory has a similar statute: see, eg, *Crimes (Forfeiture of Proceeds) Act* (NT).

In addition to the statutes concerned with the proceeds of crime, there are many other statutes which allow governments to take away the benefits of other wrongs. For example, the *Trade Marks Act* 1995 (Cth) provides for the forfeiture of imported goods which infringe registered trade marks: see page 186. Section 229 of the *Customs Act* 1901 (Cth) provides a long list of illegally imported goods which "shall be forfeited to the Crown" and section 229A provides for the forfeiture of cheques, money, and goods obtained through the sale of imported narcotics. Section 243B provides for the payment to the Commonwealth of the value of benefits derived from "prescribed narcotics dealings".

Things Used by Wrongdoers

The government's right to take property from wrongdoers is not limited to restitution. It can also take property which was used to commit a crime or breach a statute. For example, section 228 of the *Customs Act* 1901 (Cth) provides for the forfeiture of a "ship or aircraft used in smuggling, or knowingly used in the lawful importation, exportation, or conveyance of any prohibited imports or prohibited exports". Section 106 of the *Fisheries Management Act* 1991 (Cth) provides for the forfeiture of boats and fishing equipment used to commit an offence under that act.

Things which are used to break the law may have been acquired honestly. The forfeiture of those things to the government is not restitution of the profits of wrongdoing, but a form of punishment. Also, the government can take things from honest people, who did not know they were being used to break the law. This extraordinary interference with property rights is a form of deterrence. If people are going to let others have possession of their things, they bear the risk that those things might be used to break the law and be forfeited to the government.

In *Re Director of Public Prosecutions; Ex parte Lawler* (1994) 179 CLR 270, the owners of a boat leased it to a company under a hire-purchase arrangement: see page 53. The company used it to fish illegally and it was forfeited to the Commonwealth government under the *Fisheries Management Act* 1991 (Cth). The High Court decided that this was not a form of expropriation, which required the payment of just compensation, but a right which was incidental to the Commonwealth's right to protect Australian resources.

Transfer of Property Rights

Statutes which allow for the forfeiture of things to the government usually specify the manner in which the property rights to those things will pass to the government. For example, section 205G of the *Customs Act* 1901 (Cth) states:

> "When goods are, or are taken to be, condemned as forfeited to the Crown, the title to the goods immediately vests in the Commonwealth to the exclusion of all other interests in the goods, and the title cannot be called into question."

According to section 20 of the *Proceeds of Crime Act* 1987 (Cth), "where a court makes a forfeiture order against property, the property vests absolutely in the Commonwealth". That section also provides for the forfeiture of "registrable property". It states that "the Commonwealth is entitled to be registered as owner of the property". However, "the property vests in equity in the Commonwealth but does not vest in the Commonwealth at law until the applicable registration requirements have been complied with". This ensures that the forfeiture provisions do not undermine the certainty of title provided by registration: see Part VI. Some of the state and territorial forfeiture statutes contain similar protection for registered property rights: see, eg, *Crimes (Confiscation of Profits) Act* 1988 (WA), s 11.

Restraining Orders

If property might be subject to forfeiture to the government, the court may be able to grant an order restraining any dealing with that property until the issue is resolved. For example, section 15 of the *Criminal Assets Confiscation Act* 1996 (SA) states:

> "If a court is satisfied, on application by the Director of Public Prosecutions, that there are reasonable grounds to suspect that property may be liable to forfeiture, the court may make a restraining order prohibiting, subject to the exceptions (if any) stated in the order, any dealing with the property."

The "restraining order may be varied or revoked at any time" and will lapse if the accused person is acquitted, the "forfeiture order is decided", or "there are no relevant proceedings before a court" within two months following the order.

In some jurisdictions, restraining orders can have a greater proprietary effect. For example, section 35 of the *Confiscation Act* 1997 (Vic) provides for the "automatic forfeiture of restrained property on conviction of certain offences", such as trafficking in narcotics or fraud involving more than $100,000. If all the conditions are met, the property will be transferred to the government automatically following the defendant's conviction.

Restitution to the Victim

The victim of a wrong has a right to compensation for loss. However, there are times when the profit to the wrongdoer exceeds that loss. If the wrongdoer is responsible only for the victim's loss, there is a financial incentive to commit the wrong, pay compensation, and pocket the difference. Restitution can be used in these cases to take the profit away from the wrongdoer and remove that incentive.

For example, in *Edwards v Lee's Administrator* (1936) 96 SW2d 1028 (discussed in Chapter 12), Lee turned a cave into a tourist attraction and made a substantial profit. However, one third of that cave was under land belonging to his neighbour, Edwards, and Lee's use of it was an intentional trespass. Even though this caused no loss whatsoever to Edwards, Lee was required to pay one third of his net profit to him. Stites J justified this result (at 1032) on the basis that "a wrongdoer shall not be permitted to make a profit from his own wrong".

If a wrong causes both loss to the victim and gain to the wrongdoer, the victim may be entitled to receive compensation or restitution. However, as Windeyer J said in *Colbeam Palmer Ltd v Stock Affiliates Pty Ltd* (1968) 122 CLR 25 at 32, the victim "cannot have both. They are alternative remedies." He or she must choose one or the other.

It is sometimes suggested that restitution of the profits of wrongdoing is economically inefficient: if the gain to the wrongdoer exceeds the loss to the victim, the law should not discourage that activity by requiring the wrongdoer to give up that gain. However, the wrongdoer could obtain the desired result by negotiating with the victim beforehand to acquire the right to engage in that activity. According to Richard Posner, the victim's right to restitution encourages people to acquire rights consensually. In *Economic Analysis of Law* (5th ed, 1998) p 227, he said:

> "[B]ecause we want to channel resource allocation through the market as much as possible, we want to make sure that I am not allowed to be indifferent between stealing and buying my neighbor's car. ... [T]he restitutionary measure of damages ... is used in intentional tort cases to try to make the tort worthless to the tortfeasor and thereby channel resource allocation through the market."

It is not easy putting theory into practice in this area of law. The general rule, that people should not profit from their own wrongs, is not a universal rule. The victim is not entitled to restitution in every case. There are two controversial issues. First, why is restitution available for some wrongs but not others? Secondly, when restitution is available, why does the victim have a property right to the profit in some cases, but only a personal right in others?

Which Wrongs?

There are two types of wrongs for which restitution is available:

1) .....interference with property rights, such as trespass, conversion, detinue, and infringement of intellectual property rights; and
2) .....equitable wrongs, such as breach of fiduciary duty and breach of confidence.

Other Wrongs

As a general rule, restitution is not available for other torts (such as defamation or negligence) or for breach of contract. In *Halifax Building Society v Thomas* [1996] Ch 217, Mr Thomas borrowed 100% of the purchase price of a flat by making a fraudulent mortgage application.

He defaulted on the mortgage, the flat was sold, and the mortgage was repaid in full, leaving a large surplus. The building society claimed restitution of the surplus as the victim of the tort of deceit, but lost because there was no interference with its property rights nor was there any breach of fiduciary duty. Gibson LJ said (at 226) that "there is no English authority to support the proposition that a wrongdoing defendant will be required to account for a profit which is not based on the use of the property of the wronged plaintiff".

In *Hospital Products Ltd v United States Surgical Corp* (1984) 156 CLR 41, the defendant was the exclusive distributor of the plaintiff's medical products in Australia. Through intentional breach of contract and fraud, it set up a competing business. However, the plaintiff was not entitled to restitution of the defendant's profits, because there was no breach of fiduciary duty.

The restriction of restitution to certain wrongs is not entirely satisfactory. It is not clear why it is permissible to profit from some wrongs but not others. A recent judgment of the House of Lords indicates that the law may be changing. *Attorney-General v Blake* (27 July 2000) concerned a British spy, who betrayed his country and was sent to prison in 1961. Blake escaped to Moscow in 1966 and wrote his autobiography in 1989. The British government wanted restitution of the royalties owed to Blake by his publisher in the United Kingdom.

The publication of the book was not a breach of fiduciary duty (since Blake was no longer an employee) and not a breach of confidence (since the information had become public knowledge). However, it was a breach of his contract "not to divulge any official information ... after employment has ceased". The government was entitled to restitution of Blake's profits as the victim of that breach of contract. Lord Nicholls said:

> "Property rights are superior to contractual rights in that, unlike contractual rights, property rights may survive against an indefinite class of persons. However, it is not easy to see why, as between the parties to a contract, a violation of a party's contractual rights should attract a lesser degree of remedy than a violation of his property rights."

It is not yet known whether courts in Australia will be influenced by this decision. However, if restitution does become available for breach of contract on this basis, then it should also be available for torts which involve interference with personal rights.

Intention

It is often suggested that a wrongdoer should be required to make restitution only if he or she committed the wrong intentionally. This is the law in the United States of America. It is also the law in Australia with respect to intellectual property rights. In *Colbeam Palmer Ltd v Stock Affiliates Pty Ltd* (1968) 122 CLR 25, the defendant imported "Craftmaster" paint-by-number sets into Australia which violated the plaintiff's trade mark. The defendant was required to account for its profits to the plaintiff, but only for those profits earned after it became aware of the plaintiff's trade mark.

Some lawyers believe that the right to restitution should not depend on whether the wrong was committed intentionally. They argue that no one should profit from wrongdoing, regardless of motive. Others say that restitution is only needed to remove the incentive to do wrong and will have no effect on wrongs committed unintentionally. Therefore, anything more than full compensation of the victim is an unnecessary windfall in cases where the wrongdoer is honest.

This debate concerns only torts and breach of contract. It is well settled that restitution is available for equitable wrongs, whether committed intentionally or not. For example, in *Keech v Sandford* (1726) 25 ER 223, a trustee held a lease in trust. When the lease came to an end, the landlord refused to renew it for the benefit of the beneficiary. So, the trustee renewed it for his own benefit. This conflict of interest was a breach of trust and the trustee was required to make restitution of that lease to the beneficiary. Even though the trustee had acted honestly, the court believed that it was necessary to take away the benefit to remove any possible temptation to disregard the trustee's duty to the beneficiary.

Property or Personal Right?

Most rights to restitution of the profit of wrongdoing are personal rights to payment of the value of the profit. This personal right can take several different forms. If the wrongdoer received money by committing a tort (for example, by selling the victim's chattel or charging rent or admission to trespass on the victim's land), the victim could sue for **money had and received**. In many cases, the court awards damages to the victim which are measured according to the wrongdoer's gain rather than the victim's loss. These are sometimes called **restitutionary damages** or **disgorgement damages**. The victim could also seek an **account of profits** in a court of equity. This compels the wrongdoer both to account for the profit from the wrong and to pay that sum to the victim.

There are two wrongs for which the victim can also have a property right to restitution: a breach of trust and a breach of fiduciary duty. If a trustee or other fiduciary acquires an asset in breach of trust or fiduciary duty, he or she will hold it in trust for the victim. Both duties were breached in *Chan v Zacharia* (1984) 154 CLR 178. The parties had formed a partnership to practice medicine and leased office space in a desirable location. When they dissolved their partnership, Dr Chan refused to cooperate with Dr Zacharia to obtain a renewal of the lease, but took a new lease of the space for himself. This was both a breach of trust (since the partners owned their partnership assets, including the lease, in trust for the partnership) and a breach of fiduciary duty (since partners are in fiduciary relationships with their fellow partners). Deane J said (at 205):

> "Dr Chan abused his fiduciary position as a trustee and former partner to seek an advantage for himself and in which he subjected the performance of his fiduciary obligations to the pursuit of his personal interests. He holds and will hold any fruits of that abuse of fiduciary position and pursuit of personal interest upon constructive trust for those entitled to the property of the dissolved partnership."

The trust in this case is constructive, since it arises by operation of law to strip the trustee or other fiduciary of the profit of wrongdoing. This method of creating trusts is uncontroversial and well established. It dates back at least as far as *Keech v Sandford* (1726) 25 ER 223, discussed above. What remains difficult to understand is why the victim of a breach of trust or fiduciary duty has a property right to any assets acquired by the wrongdoer as a result of that breach, but the victims of other wrongs have only personal rights to the value of those assets (or perhaps no right to restitution at all). What justifies the creation of a property right in the former situation and not in the latter?

In *Attorney-General for Hong Kong v Reid* [1994] 1 AC 324, the Director of Public Prosecutions for Hong Kong accepted bribes and used that money to purchase land in New Zealand. The Privy Council advised that he held the bribe money on constructive trust for the Hong Kong government and, since that money could be traced to the land in New Zealand, that land was also held in trust. Lord Templeman said (at 331):

> "As soon as the bribe was received it should have been paid or transferred instanter to the person who suffered from the breach of duty. Equity considers as done that which ought to have been done. As soon as the bribe was received, whether in cash or in kind, the false fiduciary held the bribe on a constructive trust for the person injured."

The maxim, "equity considers as done that which ought to have been done", has been used to justify the creation of trusts in other situations, such as a specifically enforceable contract of sale: see Chapter 21. This may be the first time it was applied to a right to restitution of the profit of wrongdoing. The difficulty is understanding why it would not apply to every wrong and convert every personal right to restitution into a property right. There is no satisfactory answer to that question. As a matter of precedent, we know that the acquisition of assets in breach of trust or fiduciary duty will create a constructive trust of those assets for the victim. For other wrongs, the right to restitution (if any) is only a personal right to be paid the value of the wrongdoer's gain.

Restitution to Others

In most cases, the only people entitled to restitution of the profits of wrongdoing are the government or the victim of the wrong. However, if the wrongdoer has obtained a benefit by unlawfully killing the victim, restitution to the victim is not possible. As a result of the wrong, the victim has ceased to be a legal person and is no longer capable of holding a right to restitution (or any other legal right). In this situation, the wrongdoer might be compelled to make restitution to other people entitled to receive the victim's assets.

There are a number of ways in which the death of a human being will produce financial benefits for others. People will be entitled to the deceased person's estate under her or his will or according to the rules of intestacy: see Chapter 22. A person may be a beneficiary of an insurance policy on the deceased person's life or have been joint tenants with the deceased (and take sole ownership of their jointly held assets by way of survivorship, as discussed at page 134).

There are two ways to ensure that a killer does not benefit from her or his wrong. First, the law can refuse to enforce the rights the killer would have received if the victim had died in normal circumstances. Secondly, the killer can be compelled to hold those rights on constructive trust for other people entitled to the victim's estate. Before those two methods are discussed, it is helpful to consider what is meant by unlawful killing. This section ends with a brief note about the statutes which allow the killer to apply for relief from forfeiture.

Unlawful Killing

A killer will be deprived of any financial benefits acquired as a result of the victim's death if the killing was a crime. This is true even if the killing was not intentional. For example, one person might assault and kill another, without meaning to cause death and without any thought of possible financial gain. If the killer is guilty of manslaughter, he or she will be required to give up any benefits derived from the victim's death. This rule is designed not just to remove the financial incentive to kill, but to ensure that killers receive no benefits from their crimes. Therefore, the motive of the killer is irrelevant: see *Troja v Troja* (1994) 33 NSWLR 269.

The killer will not be deprived of those benefits if the killing is not a crime. For example, it might be justified as self-defence or the killer might lack criminal responsibility by reason of insanity. Also, there are cases where no crime is committed, but the killer bears civil responsibility for the death. For example, the victim's death may have been caused by negligent driving. Although the driver is a wrongdoer, guilty of a tort, and liable to pay compensation, he or she will not be stripped of any financial benefits flowing from the victim's death.

Loss of Rights

One way to ensure that killers do not benefit from their crimes is to refuse to enforce any rights which they acquired as a result of the victim's death. For example, in *Troja v Troja* (1994) 33 NSWLR 269, a wife deliberately shot and killed her husband and was convicted of manslaughter. In his will, he gave his whole estate to his wife, if she survived him, and otherwise to his mother. Since the wife was precluded from taking any benefit under her husband's will, his estate passed to his mother.

This rule (sometimes called the **forfeiture rule**) meant that property rights, which would have been transferred to the wife if the husband had died in normal circumstances, were transferred to someone else. However, the rule did not have a direct proprietary effect. The wife's claim to her husband's estate was only a personal right: see page 278. She lost that right when she committed the crime of killing him.

Although the wife was imprisoned and lost her right as a beneficiary of her husband's estate, she did not lose other rights, which did not depend on her husband's death. She had contributed to their relationship over seven years of marriage and helped her husband acquire a family home and business. As discussed in Chapter 23, she had an equitable property right to a share of those assets based on the value of her contributions to the relationship. That right was unaffected by her crime.

Constructive Trust

The rule, that a killer cannot enforce rights arising on the victim's death, will prevent most killers from profiting from their crimes. However, there are a few situations in which a killer can acquire enforceable legal rights upon the victim's death. In those cases, a court of equity will intervene to remove the benefit of those rights from the killer: he or she will hold them on constructive trust for other people entitled to the victim's assets.

Suppose, for example, that a husband murdered his wife and was the sole beneficiary of her estate, but the evidence suggested that someone else was responsible for the crime. He would not have been permitted to enforce his claim to receive her estate if his crime had been revealed. However, the wife's executors fulfilled what they perceived to be their legal duty and transferred the estate to him. If his crime is discovered and he is convicted of her murder, legal ownership of those assets will not revert to the wife's executors. However, the husband will hold them (or what remains of them) in trust for the people entitled to his wife's estate (with himself excluded).

A constructive trust will also arise if one joint tenant unlawfully kills another. The trust is needed because the courts do not want to adversely affect certainty of legal title by preventing the killer from enforcing her or his right of survivorship. That right is not a new right acquired on the death of the victim, but is a normal feature of joint ownership, which was acquired along with the joint ownership before the crime was committed: see page 135. The legal property rights are unaffected by the crime, but a court of equity will intervene to ensure that the killer does not profit from her or his crime.

If there are only two joint tenants (the killer and the victim), the killer will become the sole legal owner of the asset and will hold it in trust for herself (or himself) and the victim's estate (with the killer excluded) as tenants in common in equal shares. The trust is not intended as punishment. Therefore, the killer does not lose her or his entire beneficial interest in the asset, but only the benefit brought about by the victim's death. The end result will be the same as if the joint tenancy had been severed and converted to a tenancy in common before the victim died.

The application of the rule is slightly more complicated if there are three or more joint tenants and one joint tenant unlawfully kills another. This occurred in *Rasmanis v Jurewitsch* (1969) 70 SR (NSW) 407. A husband killed his wife and was convicted of manslaughter. They and Anatole Jurewitsch were joint owners of land. The husband and Anatole continued to be joint owners of the land, but held it in trust for themselves as tenants in common, with the husband entitled to one-third and Anatole entitled to two-thirds of the beneficial ownership.

The wife's estate did not have any right to the land because Anatole was innocent of any wrongdoing and there was no reason for equity to interfere with his right of survivorship. Since the husband was not permitted to enjoy the benefits of his legal right of survivorship, the wife's one-third interest in the land belonged in equity to Anatole as a surviving joint tenant.

Although the husband and Anatole were joint owners of the legal estate, they had become tenants in common in equity. There were two reasons for this. First, since they had unequal shares of the equitable ownership, they lacked the unity of interest required for a joint tenancy: see Chapter 15. Secondly, an equitable tenancy in common would ensure that the husband would not acquire any part of his wife's interest if Anatole died. The husband would then become the sole legal owner of the land, but would hold two-thirds of it in trust for Anatole's estate. Since Anatole's share of the land included an interest obtained through the wife's death, the husband was precluded from taking that share.

Relief from Forfeiture

In the Australian Capital Territory and New South Wales, the court has a statutory power to modify the rules which prevent a killer from obtaining a benefit from the death of the victim: *Forfeiture Act* 1991 (ACT); *Forfeiture Act* 1995 (NSW). The power does not apply to murder, but can be used to allow killers convicted of lesser crimes to obtain benefits from the victim's estate, as a surviving joint tenant, or otherwise. A court might use this power in cases where the loss of benefits would be an overly harsh consequence of the particular crime.

Chapter Twenty-Six

PHYSICAL CHANGES TO THINGS

■■■

Since property rights relate to things, they can be affected by physical changes to those things. The market value of a property right is dependent on the status of the thing subject to that right. For example, what someone will pay for the ownership of your car depends on its age, previous use, state of repair, etc. However, those factors do not affect the nature and existence of your property right to your car. Your ownership entitles you to possess and use it (as discussed in Chapter 10), regardless of its market value.

This chapter concerns physical changes to things that cause property rights to be created, destroyed, or altered. For example, when a house is painted, the paint ceases to exist as a separate thing and becomes part of the house, which is part of the land beneath it. There are no longer any property rights to the paint which are distinct from the property rights to the land. The physical change to the paint (from liquid in a can to solid on a wall) destroyed the ownership of the paint as goods.

This chapter is divided into three main sections. The first concerns changes to property rights brought about by the creation and destruction of things. The second deals with the problems which arise when goods belonging to one person get attached to, or mixed with, something belonging to another, as accessories. The third section concerns mixtures of indistinguishable goods (such as oil or grain) belonging to more than one person.

Creation and Destruction of Things

The creation and destruction of things is a normal part of daily life. Agricultural products are turned into food and consumed, goods are manufactured, used and discarded, etc. The creation of a new thing brings about the possibility of new property rights. Those rights may arise automatically when the thing comes into existence. For example, if your dog had puppies, you would be the owner of the puppies from the moment of their birth. This is just one of many rules which allocate the ownership of new things among members of society.

Conversely, the destruction of a thing will necessarily bring to an end any property rights to it. Sometimes, its destruction will give rise to a personal right to compensation or restitution (as discussed in Chapter 7) or a property right to some other thing, but property rights to the destroyed item are no longer possible.

It is helpful to discuss goods and land separately. Goods are created and destroyed all the time, but this is a relatively rare occurrence with land. Also, the nature of property rights to land means that those rights are unlikely to be affected by physical changes to the land or the things attached to it.

Goods

The creation of new goods is called **specification** (from *specificatio* in Roman law, which is the making of a new thing or *nova species*). This can happen naturally, such as a plant growing from a seed or producing fruit or an animal giving birth, laying eggs, or making milk. It also occurs when something is manufactured, such as a car, dress, or loaf of bread.

There are two potentially difficult issues. First, when does specification occur? How do we know (for legal purposes) whether we have a new thing or merely a modification of an existing thing? For example, if I mix an egg with flour, sugar, chocolate, and bake a cake, the egg is gone and a new cake has come into existence. What if I mix the egg with a few vegetables and turn it into an omelette? What if I simply boil or fry the egg?

Secondly, when specification does occur, how do we allocate property rights to the new thing? In most cases, this is not a problem. If I make a cake in my kitchen using my ingredients, I will own the cake. What if I make it in your kitchen with your ingredients? What if only some of the ingredients belonged to you?

Since new goods do not spring into existence out of thin air (divine intervention and science fiction aside), the creation of goods requires the destruction or use of other goods or the use of land. This can pose a legal problem if the creation of new goods involves things and creative effort supplied by more than one person. The law must provide a mechanism for allocating the property rights to the new goods in a fair, peaceful, and efficient manner.

Making New Things

There is no set rule for deciding when a new thing is created. Judges tend to rely on their common sense. For example, in *Associated Alloys Pty Ltd v Metropolitan Engineering & Fabrications Pty Ltd* (1996) 20 ACSR 205, steel belonging to the plaintiff had been made into pressure vessels and heat exchangers by the defendant. Bryson J decided that the manufactured steel products were new things and, therefore, the plaintiff's steel no longer existed. He said (at 209):

> "The question whether goods which have been used in some manufacturing process still exist in the goods produced by that process, or have gone out of existence on being incorporated in the derived product is, in my opinion, a question of fact and degree not susceptible of much exposition. When wheat is ground into flour it is

reasonably open to debate whether the wheat continues to exist; when flour is baked into bread there could be little doubt that the flour does not. Many examples might be encountered or imagined, and each must be addressed separately."

Very little has changed over the centuries. Debates over this issue can be found in Roman law and the solution seemed to depend on common sense. As Barry Nicholas said, in *An Introduction to Roman Law* (1962) p 138:

"In short the question 'is there a *nova species*?' can be restated in the form 'would the ordinary man give the thing as it is a name different from that of the thing as it was?'"

Although new goods are being manufactured all the time, there are very few cases dealing with this issue and many of them are fairly old. The reason is simple. Most people use their own materials when making things and it does not matter whether the materials continue to exist in modified form or have been turned into something new. Either way, the maker will be the owner of the product.

The issue has gained prominence in recent years, because of the popularity of contractual terms called **Romalpa clauses** (named after *Aluminium Industrie Vaassen BV v Romalpa Aluminium Ltd* [1976] 1 WLR 676). They are used by suppliers of raw materials to reserve legal ownership of those materials after they have been delivered to manufacturers. One was used in the *Associated Alloys* case, discussed above. It stated (at 207) that "the title of the subject goods/product shall not pass to the purchaser until payment in full of the purchase price". This meant that the defendant did not own the steel it had used to manufacture steel products, but possessed it as a bailee. This is why Bryson J had to decide whether the products were merely modified forms of the plaintiff's steel or new steel products owned by the defendant.

A manufactured product is not a new thing if it can be reconverted easily to its original form. For example, in *The Law of Tracing* (1997) pp 111-112, Lionel Smith refers to a case in which the plaintiff's clay had been made into bricks by the defendant: *Lampton's Executors v Preston's Executors* (1829) 24 Ky 455. Some of the bricks that had not yet been fired and, since they could be returned to their original (lack of) form, they were still clay and not new bricks.

As Bryson J noted in the *Associated Alloys* case (at 209-210), this issue is not resolved by asking whether it is possible to restore the manufactured article to its original form, but whether it is practical to do so:

"[W]hether goods are reducible to the original materials is not simply a matter of physics. Other perspectives have to be considered, including the economic perspective. The scraps of leather produced by cutting up a manufactured shoe could not in reality be regarded as the original leather from which the shoe was manufactured. The steel which would be produced by cutting up a pressure vessel and flattening out the cylindrical parts would not be the steel which Associated Alloys delivered under the sale; it would be scrap steel."

Allocating Property Rights

Most things are subject to property rights from the moment they come into existence. The exceptions include animals born in the wild. If no one owns the mother, then no one owns the offspring: see *Yanner v Eaton* (1999) 73 ALJR 1518. A newborn domestic animal belongs to its mother's owner and a plant belongs to the owner of the land on which it grows. In "Dialogue on Private Property" (1954) 9 *Rutgers Law Review* 357 at 366-369, Felix Cohen justified these rules on the grounds of fairness, certainty, and economic productivity.

When goods are manufactured, the materials used to create those goods cease to exist (in law) and so do any property rights to those materials. Therefore, any property rights to the new goods are new rights, which need to be allocated to somebody. In most cases, the new goods will belong to their creator. As Goff LJ said, in *Clough Mill Ltd v Martin* [1985] 1 WLR 111 at 119:

> "Now it is no doubt true that, where A's material is lawfully used by B to create new goods, whether or not B incorporates other material of his own, the property in the new goods will generally vest in B, at least where the goods are not reducible to the original materials."

There are two situations in which new goods might belong to the supplier of the materials, rather than their creator. The first is where the supplier and creator agree that it will. For example, you might deliver some cloth to a tailor or dressmaker on the understanding that you will own the garment made from that cloth. Your agreement displaces the normal rule and causes ownership of the garment to pass to you when it comes into existence.

Secondly, the ownership of a new thing may belong to the supplier of the materials if the creator used those materials without the supplier's consent. For example, in *Silsbury v McCoon* (1850) 3 NY 379, corn was stolen from the plaintiff and made into whiskey. The court decided that the plaintiff was the owner of the whiskey because his ownership of the corn was not lost when it was wrongly transformed into whiskey. This reasoning is criticised by Lionel Smith, in *The Law of Tracing* (1997) pp 113-114. The plaintiff's property right to the corn could not survive the destruction of that corn. The ownership of the whiskey was a new property right which was allocated to the plaintiff, as former owner of the stolen corn.

The wrongdoing of the creator of a thing can explain why he or she might be disentitled from owning it. However, this can be very hard on the creator (or someone who buys it from the creator) and may produce a large windfall for the supplier of the materials. For example, suppose an artist used stolen paints and canvas worth $100 to produce an oil painting worth $1,000. Should the painting belong to the owner of the art supplies or the artist? The artist is guilty of conversion of the art supplies and liable to compensate the supplier for their full value. Is there any reason why the artist should also be required to give up the painting? It is not the profit of wrongdoing nor was it used to commit a wrong. Therefore, restitution or forfeiture of the painting is not justified (as discussed in the previous chapter).

It has been suggested that the supplier of materials should own the new goods if the creator knew that he or she was not entitled to use those materials. However, this would add an element of uncertainty, because the ownership of a new thing would depend on the creator's knowledge at the time of conversion. Lionel Smith suggests (at p 114) that it would be better to allocate ownership of new goods to their creator in all cases (unless the parties agree otherwise). If the creator's use of the raw materials is unauthorised, he or she will be liable to compensate the supplier for conversion. If the use is a crime, then punishment is also available.

Land

As with goods, the market value of land is affected by its physical condition (such as the number and quality of buildings and other improvements). Unlike goods, physical changes to land rarely affect property rights to it. This is because of the nature of those rights.

As discussed in Chapter 12, an estate is a right to possess a volume of space, measured relative to the surface of the earth, for a period of time. These four dimensions (three spatial and one temporal) are not affected by most changes to the physical condition of the land or the things attached to it. For example, if I own a house in fee simple, and it is destroyed by fire, my estate will continue unchanged (but with a reduced market value). I still have the right to possession of the same space on the earth, even though the contents of that space have changed. In contrast, if my books, furniture, and other belongings are destroyed in the fire, my property rights to those goods are gone.

Since estates are almost immune to physical changes to land, so too are most other property rights to land. This is because other rights, such as mortgages, easements, and restrictive covenants, are attached to estates and not directly to the land subject to those estates. They depend on the continued existence of an estate and not on its physical contents. There are a few rights which are not attached to estates, such as native title (discussed in Chapter 18) and non-possessory rights to Crown land (discussed in Chapter 16). However, these also tend to exist independently of the physical condition of the land.

A physical change to land can affect an estate only if it alters one of its four dimensions. This can happen in two different ways. The first is by accretion to or erosion from a shore line. The second is by total destruction of the premises to which the estate relates.

Accretion and Erosion

Sometimes, the horizontal dimensions of an estate are defined by reference to the shore of a river, lake, ocean, or other body of water. If a shoreline forms part of the boundary of an estate and that line moves, the dimensions of the estate will change. An increase in the size of the estate, through the addition of land to the shore, is called **accretion** and a decrease in the size of an estate, through the removal of land from the shore, is **erosion**.

A change to the shoreline will not affect an estate unless the boundary of the estate is defined as the shoreline. Also, the change must be gradual and not brought about intentionally by the estate holder.

Definition of the Boundary

In *Southern Centre of Theosophy Inc v South Australia* [1982] AC 706, the plaintiff held a perpetual lease of Crown land to the west of Lake George in South Australia. The lease described the land (at 714) as "containing by admeasurement 500 acres or thereabouts being ... delineated in the public maps deposited in the Land Office in the City of Adelaide". The eastern boundary of the land shown on the map was the high-water mark of the lake as surveyed in 1879. The shoreline had changed significantly over the years, creating about 20 acres of new land. However, it was still possible to determine the original boundary of the estate by reference to the surveyed map.

The state argued that the description of the land in the lease, by reference to the map and not the shoreline, meant that the boundary was fixed and unaffected by movement of the shoreline. The Privy Council rejected that argument. There was nothing on the map which suggested that the boundary of the estate was intended to be anything other than the shoreline. Lord Wilberforce said (at 716):

> "[W]here land is granted with a water boundary, the title of the grantee extends to that land as added to or detracted from by accretion, or diluvion, and ... this is so whether or not the grant is accompanied by a map showing the boundary, or contains a parcels clause stating the area of the land, and whether or not the original boundary can be identified."

Lord Wilberforce described this rule (at 716) as "manifestly convenient" and "fair". The potential for loss through erosion was balanced by the possibility of gain by accretion. Water-front property would not become landlocked over time because of accretion nor would the boundary wind up out in the water because of erosion. Therefore, it is assumed that a water boundary will move with the shoreline unless the grant of the estate clearly states otherwise.

This rule can also be excluded by statute. For example, according to section 172 of the *Crown Lands Act* 1989 (NSW), "The doctrine of accretion does not apply, and never has applied to a non-tidal lake." Instead, the boundary is fixed as "the bank of the lake at the time of the Crown survey for the purposes of alienation".

Gradual Change

The doctrine of accretion and erosion applies only if the shoreline changes gradually. Therefore, even if the boundary of an estate is defined by reference to the shoreline, that boundary will not move if a major change to the shoreline occurs rather suddenly. It is not clear why this is so. As Lord Wilberforce said, *in Southern Centre of Theosophy Inc v South Australia* [1982] AC 706 at 721, "One naturally searches for a reason or rationale for the requirement that the process be gradual and imperceptible, but this proves elusive."

Also unclear is the distinction between gradual and sudden change. Lord Wilberforce said (at 721) that "there is a logical, and practical, gap or 'grey area' between what is imperceptible and what is to be considered as 'avulsion'" and, therefore, the issue is a question of fact for the jury to decide. In the *Theosophy* case, the lake was receding by almost 10 metres per year and this was a gradual change to which the doctrine of accretion applied.

Intervention by the Estate Holders

Gradual changes to a shoreline count as accretion or erosion, whether caused naturally or by human intervention. The one exception is accretion caused deliberately by estate holders wanting to increase the size of their estate. There is nothing wrong with preventing erosion, but if they intentionally cause accretion, it will not affect the boundary of their estate. Land created intentionally by reclamation belongs to the Crown at common law and, in Queensland, by statute: see *Land Act* 1994 (Qld), s 10.

Total Destruction of the Premises

As stated above, estates are not normally affected by physical changes to the land or the things attached to it. However, the total destruction of the premises might bring an estate to an end. In *National Carriers Ltd v Panalpina (Northern) Ltd* [1981] AC 675 at 709, Lord Russell suggested that "the total disappearance of the site ... into the sea" would cause both freehold and leasehold estates to cease to exist. Although its location might still be identified, the estate holders would not have a right to possess that part of the ocean. If the land disappeared gradually, it might be regarded as the elimination of the estate by erosion. However, a sudden loss of the land would produce the same result.

Lord Russell also suggested that the destruction of a building would destroy a lease of an upper-floor flat. The vacant air space would be of no use to the tenants and there would be no reason to continue their rights to possess it. If a new building was constructed on that site, it would be highly unlikely that it would be identical to the old building and occupy precisely the same space. It would be bizarre if tenants of the old building had rights to possess spaces that intersected floors and walls of the new building.

The boundaries of a leasehold estate of an upper-floor flat are defined, not directly in relation to the surface of the earth, but by the walls, floors, and ceilings of the building. If a 42-storey building sways in the wind, the leasehold estates on each floor sway with it. The destruction of the building destroys the boundaries which defined those estates. As Megarry and Wade said, in *The Law of Real Property* (5th ed, 1984) p 692, "there would no longer be any physical entity which the tenant could hold of his landlord for any term, and there can hardly be tenure without a tenement".

In contrast, if a tenant leased an entire building and that building was destroyed, the lease would continue to exist (unless the parties had agreed that it would be terminated for that reason). The boundaries of that estate would continue to exist and the tenant's right to possess that space could be valuable and useful.

Accessories

If goods are attached to or mixed with other goods or attached to land, they might lose their separate identity and cease to exist (in law). For example, if you install a new window in your car or house, the window no longer exists as a separate thing. The same is true of sugar added to a cup of coffee. The accessory becomes part of the principal object and the property rights to the accessory are destroyed. The existing property rights to the principal object attach to the whole thing, including the accessory.

This is similar to the fate of raw materials used to manufacture new goods (specification, discussed above). Accessories, like consumed materials, cease to exist as separate things. There is an important difference between the two situations. Newly manufactured items are subject to new property rights. Those rights are allocated to the manufacturer in most cases, but can be allocated to the owner of the destroyed materials. In contrast, if something loses its identity as an accessory to another thing, no new thing is created. The other thing continues to exist, subject to pre-existing property rights. In most cases, those rights are unaffected by the addition of the accessory.

Like specification, things are added to other things all the time and yet this rarely causes legal problems. In most cases, the same person owns both accessory and principal and is free to join them together or take them apart. A problem arises when the two things are subject to different property rights and everyone involved did not consent to their combination and cannot agree on the consequences. This might happen if one of the things is stolen or otherwise converted or is subject to a security right: see Chapter 14. The physical act of joining those things together can destroy the separate property rights to the accessory.

People who lose property rights to accessories may acquire new personal and property rights. For example, suppose that I used your bricks without consent to add a new room to my house. I would be guilty of conversion and you would have a personal right to compensation for your loss or, possibly, restitution of my gain: see Chapter 7. You might also have a property right to my land based on tracing and unjust enrichment. As discussed at page 336, if my use of the value of your bricks increased the value of my land, you might be entitled to an equitable lien on my land to secure my obligation to pay for that unjust enrichment. If a lien arises, it is not a continuation of your previous ownership of your bricks, but a new property right based on my unauthorised use of your value.

The addition of goods to other goods is called **accession**. Goods which are attached to land are called **fixtures**. The law of accession differs from the law of fixtures and, therefore, it is helpful to discuss them separately.

Accession

If goods are joined together, accession will occur if it is impractical to separate them again and one thing is regarded as an accessory to the other. Accession differs from specification, where the operation creates a new thing. For example, thread and cloth can be joined together to make a new garment (specification) or to embroider a design on an existing garment (accession). It also differs from mixtures of indistinguishable things (discussed below), where nothing new is created and there is no principal and accessory. For example, combining ground pepper from two sources produces a mixture. Adding pepper to a stew is accession.

There are two questions which can be difficult to answer:

1) .....when is it practical to separate two items joined together; and
2) .....which is the accessory and which is the principal?

Is Separation Practical?

If it is practical to separate things which have been joined together, they will not lose their separate identity and property rights will not be affected by their combination. Separation will not be practical if it will injure or destroy one of the items or costs more than the accessory is worth.

In *Rendell v Associated Finance Pty Ltd* [1957] VR 604, the plaintiff sold an engine under a hire-purchase agreement to a man named Pell, who installed it in a utility truck he had bought from the defendant under another hire-purchase agreement. Pell had not paid fully for the engine or the truck and, therefore, merely had possession of both things. The defendant seized the truck and refused to return the engine to the plaintiff.

Pell's agreement with the defendant said that any accessories attached to the truck would become part of the truck. However, that contract could not cause ownership of the plaintiff's engine to pass to the defendant. So, the defendant claimed that the engine had ceased to exist as a separate thing when it was installed in the truck. The court rejected that argument, because the engine could be removed without damage to engine or truck. O'Bryan J said (at 610):

> "Prima facie the property in the accessory does not pass to the owner of the vehicle if the owner of the accessory did not intend it to pass. It is for the defendant by proper evidence to show that the necessity of the case requires the application of principles whereby the property is deemed to pass by operation of law. The accessories continue to belong to their original owner unless it is shown that as a matter of practicability they cannot be identified, or, if identified, they have been incorporated to such an extent that they cannot be detached from the vehicle."

Accessory or Principal?

When two things are joined together, usually it is easy to tell which is the principal item (that continues to exist) and which is the accessory (that does not). For example, when milk is added to a cup of tea, there is no doubt that the combination is still a cup of tea. However, there are cases where the choice is not so easy. The resolution of this issue does not depend on the relative sizes or values of the components. For example, embroidery on a shirt may be far more valuable than the shirt and yet the shirt continues to exist as the principal item.

In *McKeown v Cavalier Yachts Pty Ltd* (1988) 13 NSWLR 303, the defendant constructed a yacht (worth $24,409) in a hull (worth $1,777), not knowing that the hull belonged to the plaintiff. The defendant argued (at 311) "that the accretions accordingly are the major chattel, and the laminated hull the minor chattel, so that the doctrine of accession operates that the property in the laminated hull has now acceded to the later accretions rather than the other way around". Young J rejected that argument, because the work had been done gradually. As each piece was installed in the hull, it was clear that it acceded to the hull and belonged to the plaintiff. Therefore, the plaintiff was entitled to possession of the entire yacht, on the condition that he pay the defendant for the unjust enrichment caused by the mistaken improvement of that hull.

When two things of equal status are joined together, it is impossible to say which is the principal and which is the accessory. For example, two boards might be glued together to make a thicker board or two quilts might be stitched together to make a larger quilt. Lionel Smith suggested that the product should be regarded as a new thing and allocated to its creator: *The Law of Tracing* (1997) pp 106-107. However, Peter Birks treated it as a mixture (discussed below) that should belong to the contributors as tenants in common in proportion to their contributions: "Mixtures", in Palmer and McKendrick, *Interests in Goods* (2nd ed, 1998) 227 at 238.

Fixtures

Fixtures are goods which get joined to land and thereby become part of an estate. This is a form of accession. However, there is no difficulty discerning which is the accessory and which is the principal. Goods become part of the land to which they are joined, regardless of value. For example, an office tower worth millions of dollars, constructed on land worth thousands of dollars, becomes part of that land.

The difficulty in this area of law is determining when goods have become fixtures. Something which is not attached to land, but merely resting on it (such as a statue in the garden), can be a fixture. Even though it could be removed easily, without damage to it or the land, a fixture will cease to be a separate thing subject to separate property rights.

This treatment of fixtures is possible because the owner of an estate has a right to possess a volume of space. The law can then determine which things within that space form part of the estate and which things continue to exist separately as goods. The decision to treat unattached objects as part of an estate was made at a time when personal property could be given away by will, but real property passed to the owner's heir: see page 280. The rules were designed to ensure that the assets of deceased persons were properly divided among their heirs and the beneficiaries of their wills. In contrast, the law of accession to goods was designed to ensure that people would not lose their property rights without consent, except as a practical necessity.

There are two factors which are used to determine whether goods have become fixtures:

1) .....the **degree of annexation** (extent of attachment to the land); and
2) .....the **object of annexation** (apparent purpose of attachment).

These factors are discussed below, followed by a discussion of two situations in which people are entitled to remove fixtures from land belonging to others:

3) .....fixtures installed by tenants; and
4) .....fixtures that were subject to security rights before they were joined to the land.

Degree of Annexation

There is no legal uncertainty when goods are joined to land and cannot be removed again, without injury to the land or goods. For example, paint applied to a wall cannot be removed without destroying the paint and a tree planted in the yard cannot be removed without destroying the tree or digging a big hole in the yard. It is clear that these things ceased to be goods and became part of the real estate when they were joined to the land.

A legal question arises when goods are joined to land in a way which permits their removal. The assumption is that goods merely resting on land continue to be goods and that any degree of attachment (by bolts, nails, cement, etc) turns them into fixtures. As Kaye J said, in *Belgrave Nominees Pty Ltd v Barlin-Scott Airconditioning (Aust) Pty Ltd* [1984] VR 947 at 953:

> "Even slight fixing to the land is sufficient to raise the presumption that a chattel is a fixture. In those circumstances, the onus of proving otherwise rests upon the party so contending."

The greater the degree of annexation, the more likely it is that goods have become fixtures. However, unattached goods can be fixtures and attached goods need not be.

Object of Annexation

If it is practical to remove a possible fixture from the land, then its status is determined by the object of annexation. The essential question is this: was it joined to the land for its better use as a chattel or for the improvement of the land? In *Leigh v Taylor* [1902] AC 157, valuable tapestries were tacked to canvasses, which were nailed to strips of wood, which were nailed to the walls of a mansion house. The circumstances revealed an intention that the tapestries would remain goods. They could be removed easily without damage to them or the land. Although their attachment improved the enjoyment of land, that was the only practical way to enjoy tapestries.

In *Belgrave Nominees Pty Ltd v Barlin-Scott Airconditioning (Aust) Pty Ltd* [1984] VR 947, an airconditioning plant was installed on the roof of a building. It was resting on pads on the roof and connected with nuts and bolts to water pipes and electrical cables in the building. It could be removed easily without damage to the plant or building. The purpose of installing the airconditioning plant was clearly not for the better enjoyment of the plant, but for the permanent improvement of the land. Although the company that installed the plant did not own the land, it had been hired to make that improvement on the owner's behalf.

The object of annexation does not depend on what anyone was actually thinking when the thing was joined to the land. It is the apparent purpose for joining something to land, as revealed by observable circumstances. What would a bystander, with knowledge of the relevant facts, assume was intended?

The use of apparent (objective) intention, rather than actual (subjective) intention, helps create greater legal certainty. A judicial decision that something is or is not a fixture in certain circumstances can guide others dealing with similar circumstances. If the status of each thing on land depended on the actual intention of the person who put it there, it could be very difficult to determine what things formed part of an estate.

The physical connection of something to the land is just one of the facts which reveal the object of annexation. Therefore, two things can be joined to land in the same way and yet one will be a fixture and the other will not. Blackburn J used this example in *Holland v Hodgson* (1872) LR 7 CP 328 at 335:

> "[I]f the intention is apparent to make the articles part of the land, they do become part of the land ... Thus blocks of stone placed one on the top of another without any mortar or cement for the purpose of forming a dry stone wall would become part of the land, though the same stones, if deposited in a builder's yard and for convenience sake stacked on the top of each other in the form of a wall, would remain chattels."

Tenant's Fixtures

At common law, tenants of life or leasehold estates are entitled to remove fixtures that they installed for domestic, trade, or ornamental purposes and not for the permanent improvement of the land. These are called **tenant's fixtures** to distinguish them from permanent fixtures which tenants are not entitled to remove. A tenant's removal of a permanent fixture, without consent, is not trespass (since the tenant has possession of the land), but waste: see page 102. It might also be a breach of a leasehold covenant.

Tenant's Fixture or Permanent Fixture?

It is not always easy to tell tenant's fixtures from permanent fixtures. This is because tenant's fixtures, like all fixtures, are no longer goods, but part of the land. The only question is whether the tenant is permitted to remove them and turn them back into goods. As Romer LJ said in *Spyer v Phillipson* [1931] 2 Ch 183 at 209-210:

> "So long as the article can be removed without doing irreparable damage to the demised premises I do not think that either the method

of annexation or the degree of annexation, or the quantum of damage that would be done to the article itself or to the demised premises by its removal, has really any bearing upon the question of the tenant's right to remove, except in so far as they throw light upon the question of the intention with which the chattel was affixed by him to the demised premises."

In that case, the tenant leased a flat for 21 years and, half way through the term, installed valuable antique wood panelling and period fireplaces and chimneys. He died and his executors were entitled to remove them, even though that would cause some damage to the flat. Tenants are liable to repair the damage caused by removing fixtures, but this does not affect their right to remove them.

The question whether something is a tenant's fixture or permanent fixture (like the question whether it is a chattel or a fixture) depends a little on the degree of annexation and a lot on the object of annexation. If its removal would cause serious damage to the land or destroy the fixture, then it is permanent. Otherwise, its character depends on the object of annexation: was it attached so the tenant could better enjoy the leasehold estate or as a permanent improvement to the land? There is another way to phrase the question: was the fixture attached to the leasehold estate or to the freehold (which is leased to the tenant)?

There is an assumption that tenants are not intending to make valuable gifts to others when they attach things to the land. As Barton J said of a life estate in *Registrar of Titles v Spencer* (1909) 9 CLR 641 at 651, the tenant "should be able to improve the estate for his own enjoyment without being thereby compelled to make a present to the remainderman". The same assumption was used in *Leigh v Taylor* [1902] AC 157, discussed above, to decide that tapestries, attached to walls by the life tenant, were goods and not fixtures. If they had been fixtures, they would have been tenant's fixtures.

Generally speaking, structural additions or repairs to buildings are normally regarded as permanent improvements to the land, while other fixtures installed by the tenant are tenant's fixtures. However, the common law treats agricultural fixtures, such as pens and sheds, as permanent improvements to the land.

Statutory Changes

The law of fixtures has been modified by statute in several states. For example, section 155 of the *Property Law Act* 1974 (Qld) permits tenants to remove buildings, engines, machinery, fences, and other fixtures they installed, so long as they perform their obligations under the lease and give the landlord a month's notice in writing of their intention to remove them. This removes the distinction between agricultural and other fixtures and probably means that tenants are allowed to remove any fixtures they install, unless it would cause permanent damage to the land. Section 28 of *the Landlord and Tenant Act* 1958 (Vic) is similar. Section 26 of the *Landlord and Tenant Act* 1935 (Tas) deals with the removal of agricultural and trade fixtures and section 14 of the *Agricultural Tenancies Act* 1990 (NSW) only with agricultural fixtures.

Some jurisdictions also have statutes which modify the rules relating to short-term residential tenancies. For example, section 27 of the *Residential Tenancies Act* 1987 (NSW) states that "the tenant shall not, except with the landlord's written consent or unless the agreement otherwise provides, remove any fixture that the tenant has affixed to the residential premises". In contrast, section 64 of the *Residential Tenancies Act* 1997 (Vic) requires tenants to remove their fixtures and "restore the premises to the condition they were in immediately before the installation", unless the parties agree otherwise.

Removal of Tenant's Fixtures

At common law, tenants are entitled to remove their fixtures at any time during the lease or while they continue in possession thereafter. In *McMahon's (Transport) Pty Ltd v Ebbage* [1999] 1 Qd R 185, the court decided that tenants could also remove their fixtures within a reasonable time after they gave up possession. Pincus JA said (at 198):

> "There is authority in favour of the view that once the tenant gives up physical possession ... the right to remove fixtures is gone ... But the better view, and certainly one more in accordance with practical justice, is that the right to remove continues for a reasonable time after a lease has been terminated."

The time for removing fixtures is set by statute in some states. For example, section 155 of the *Property Law Act* 1974 (Qld) allows tenants to remove fixtures up to two months after the tenancy ends. According to section 28 of the *Landlord and Tenant Act* 1958 (Vic), fixtures may be removed by a tenant "during his tenancy or during such period of possession by him as he holds the premises but not afterwards".

Most cases and statutes about tenant's fixtures are concerned with the tenant's right to remove those fixtures. As discussed above, section 64 of the *Residential Tenancies Act* 1997 (Vic) creates a duty to remove those fixtures when the lease comes to an end. However, that applies only to short-term residential tenancies in Victoria.

In *Wincant Pty Ltd v South Australia* (1997) 69 SASR 126, the court decided that tenants may be required to remove fixtures at the end of the lease, if they would interfere with the landlord's use of the premises. The government leased seven floors of an office tower in Adelaide for 25 years and left its fixtures behind at the end of the lease. The premises could not be leased again without removing them at a cost of $58,550. The government was required to pay this cost, because the failure to remove them was a breach of its covenant to leave the "premises in good and substantial repair". It might also be regarded as waste.

If tenants do not remove their fixtures within the allotted time, they are abandoned by the tenant and belong to the landlord. In one sense, the abandonment does not affect the landlord's property rights, since the fixtures became part of the estate when they were attached to the land. However, tenant's fixtures are attached when the tenant has possession of the land and the landlord does not. Whether they will still be part of the land when the lease ends and possession reverts to the landlord is contingent on the tenant's decision to leave them behind.

Security Rights

In most cases, people do not attach things to their land unless they own them. There is one common exception. People buy goods under hire-purchase contracts and attach them to land before the purchase price is paid in full. This happened in *Kay's Leasing Corp Pty Ltd v CSR Provident Fund Nominees Pty Ltd* [1962] VR 429. A company hired manufacturing machinery from the plaintiff and attached it to its land, which was mortgaged to the defendant. The company defaulted on both the hire-purchase contract and the mortgage and the court had to decide whether the plaintiff or the defendant was entitled to the machinery.

The hire-purchase contract entitled the plaintiff to enter the company's land and seize the machinery if the company breached the contract. However, the machinery had become fixtures and ceased to exist as goods. It was part of the land and the defendant was entitled to possession of the land, including the fixtures, when the company defaulted on the mortgage.

Since the machinery was part of the land, the plaintiff no longer owned it. However, it still had a right to enter the company's land, remove the machinery, and take it away. As Adam J said (at 436):

> "In law, no doubt, fixtures become part of the freehold while they remain annexed thereto and the legal title to them belongs to him who owns the freehold. But the contractual right, which the owner has against the hirer, to repossess on default confers on him a species of equitable interest which entitles him, as against the hirer, to enter upon the premises and sever and remove the chattels which have become fixtures."

The plaintiff's right to enter the company's land and remove the machinery was an equitable property right to that land (which had priority over the defendant's legal property right): see Chapter 29. As AL Smith LJ said, in *Hobson v Gorringe* [1897] 1 Ch 182 at 192, "this right was not an easement created by deed, nor was it conferred by a covenant running with the land". It was created both by the contract and by the attachment of the machinery to the land as fixtures.

This property right is produced not just by hire-purchase contracts, but by any security agreement, such as a chattel mortgage or bill of sale (see Chapter 14), which entitles the secured creditor to enter the debtor's land and seize goods that have become fixtures. It could also be created by a chattel lease or other contract of bailment (see Chapter 6) which gives the bailor the same right.

Without a right to enter land and remove goods, the owner of goods fixed to another person's land will not have an equitable property right to that land. For example, the victim of conversion does not have a right to enter the wrongdoer's land. Also, he or she would probably not have a right to recover the converted goods even if they had not become fixtures. As discussed in Chapter 7, the normal response to conversion is to compel the wrongdoer to pay the victim for the value of the goods (as compensation or restitution).

In Queensland, Tasmania, Victoria, and Western Australia, the *Hire Purchase Act* 1959 alters the law of fixtures for goods obtained under a hire-purchase contract. It states that the goods "shall not ... be treated as fixtures" so long as the contract is in force. Therefore, the seller would continue to have legal ownership of the goods, rather than an equitable property right to the land. Victoria and Western Australia also have a *Chattel Securities Act* 1987, which treats goods, that are subject to a security interest or obtained under a lease or hire-purchase contract, in a similar fashion.

Mixtures

This final part of the chapter concerns the property rights created when similar goods belonging to two or more people get mixed together and it is impractical to identify each person's goods in the mixture. For example, 10 litres of your petrol might be poured into a tank which contained my petrol or 10 boxes of your paper might be stacked together with 10 boxes of my paper. The mixture does not create a new thing (specification) nor does one contribution cease to exist and become part of the other (accession).

There is no difficulty dividing the mixture into portions, but it is no longer possible (or at least not practical) to identify each person's contribution. If we take a drop of petrol from the tank or a box of paper from the stack, no one can say for sure whether it was yours or mine. The drop of petrol is probably a mixture of both. If we divide the mixture again, and you take 10 litres of petrol or 10 boxes of paper, you will have some of the petrol or paper that used to belong to me and I will have some of yours. (The chance of you randomly selecting all 10 boxes of your own paper is 1 in 184,756.)

Your reaction to this might be "Who cares?" So long as you recover the same quantity and quality of goods with which you started, it does not matter whether it used to belong to you or me. This is also true if all the goods get destroyed. If all the petrol in the tank is consumed, we know that both contributions to the mixture are gone. A problem arises when some of the goods are damaged, destroyed, or stolen. If seven boxes of paper are ruined by flooding, who suffered the loss: you, me, or us? If, instead of small quantities of petrol or paper, the mixture consists of gold ingots or tonnes of oil, people become very concerned about its ownership.

Possible Property Rights

If our goods are mixed indistinguishably, it is impossible to restore the status quo. We can deal with the mixture in several different ways, but cannot ensure that we will end up with the same things we had before the mixture. There are five possible ways to allocate the property rights to the mixture:

1) .....We both lose our property rights to our goods and the mixture becomes *bona vacantia* (ownerless goods) available to the next possessor or the Crown.
2) .....The whole mixture belongs to you or me.
3) .....We share the mixture equally as joint tenants or tenants in common.

4) .....We share the mixture as tenants in common in proportion to our contributions to it.
5) .....We continue to own the goods we contributed to the mixture, even though we cannot identify them.

The first possibility is not imposed by the common law. There is no reason why the mixing of our goods should produce losses for us and a potential windfall for others. The mixture will belong to you, me, or us, according to one of the four remaining possibilities. This depends primarily on whether we both consented to the mixture and, if not, whether one of us was responsible for the mixture. It might also depend on the nature of the goods that were mixed. These factors are discussed below.

The second possibility is that one of us owns the whole mixture. The property rights to the owner's contribution continue unchanged, while the other's contribution is transferred to the owner. In other words, the property rights to only some of the goods in the mixture are affected by their combination.

The third and fourth possibilities are joint or common ownership of the whole mixture. The property rights to all the goods in the mixture are changed. Everything used to have one owner (you or me) and now has two owners (you and me). We have both exchanged sole ownership of our separate contributions for an undivided share of the whole.

The fifth possibility is continuing ownership of our contributions to the mixture. Our property rights are unaffected by the mixture, but we no longer know which goods belong to you and which belong to me. Our property rights will be changed if we divide the mixture again. At that point, some of the goods which used to belong to you will be transferred to me and vice versa.

Mixture by Consent

If we agree to mix our goods, then the property rights to the mixture will be determined by our agreement. We might choose any of the possibilities discussed above (including abandonment of the mixture). If we do not specify the rights we intend to create, the law assumes that we want to own the mixture as tenants in common, in proportion to our contributions to it.

Mixture Without Consent

If we do not agree to mix our goods, any alteration of our property rights occurs not by intention, but by operation of law. In other words, the mixing together of similar goods is an event which can create and destroy property rights.

Generally speaking, we are each entitled to take from the mixture an amount of goods equal to our contribution to it. If some of the goods are consumed, damaged, destroyed, lost, or stolen, we bear the loss proportionately to our contributions and our right to take goods from the mixture is reduced accordingly. However, these rights can be affected by wrongdoing. If I mixed our goods without your consent, I am guilty of wrongly interfering with your goods and my rights to the mixture will be subordinated to yours as a result. This is discussed below.

If we do not know how much we contributed to the mixture, then we share it equally. This is subject to any evidence that might define the limits of our contributions. For example, suppose that I have an unknown quantity of petrol in a 25 litre container. If it is poured into a tank which holds an unknown quantity of your petrol, we know that the most I could have contributed to the mixture is 25 litres. Therefore, we would share the mixture equally, unless it contained more than 50 litres, in which case I would have a right to take only 25 litres. These rights are also affected by wrongdoing, as discussed below.

Wrongful Mixture

Our rights to the mixture of our goods can depend on whether one of us was at fault for mixing the goods without the other's consent. If so, the wrongdoer's interests will be subordinated to those of the other contributor, if necessary. For example, if I mixed our goods by mistake, I am guilty of wrongly interfering with your goods. Although I did not commit the wrong intentionally, I breached my duty not to interfere with your things (without consent) and made it impossible for you to identify your own goods. Therefore any uncertainty will be resolved in your favour. This is the same presumption against wrongdoers which is used when tracing value through mixtures, as discussed in Chapter 24.

The presumption against wrongdoers can help resolve uncertainties relating to two different issues: how much each person contributed to the mixture and what happened to each person's contribution after they were mixed. First, if it is impossible to tell how much each person contributed to the mixture, the person who wrongly caused it will have no right to any of it. The other contributors will be entitled to the whole mixture. Using a previous example, if I had an unknown quantity of petrol in a 25 litre container and I poured it into a tank containing an unknown quantity of your petrol, we could not ascertain how much each of us had contributed to the mixture. Since I wrongly caused the problem, the law assumes that you contributed all the petrol and own the whole mixture.

Change the facts again and assume that your petrol was in the 25 litre container and mine in the tank. If I pour your petrol into my tank by mistake, the law will resolve any uncertainty in your favour. We do not know how much we each contributed, but do know that you did not contribute more than 25 litres. Therefore, you are entitled to all the petrol in the tank up to that amount.

Secondly, the presumption against wrongdoers is used to help determine the fate of the goods after they are mixed. For example, if I stole 42 bales of your hay and added it to my haystack, you would be entitled to recover 42 bales from that stack. If some of the bales are damaged or destroyed, the law assumes that my bales were harmed and not yours. The loss does not affect your property rights until the number of good bales in the stack drops below 42.

The presumption against wrongdoers is not used to punish or deter wrongdoing, but merely to resolve uncertainties created by the wrongdoer. The wrongful mixing of goods is a breach of duty which can destroy evidence of ownership. The uncertainty created by that lack of evidence is resolved adversely to the person who caused the problem.

The presumption is used no more than necessary and does not displace actual evidence regarding contributions to or losses from a mixture: see *Indian Oil Corp Ltd v Greenstone Shipping Co SA* [1988] QB 345.

Nature of Property Rights to a Mixture

Where goods are mixed without consent, each contributor is entitled to take from the mixture an amount of goods equal to her or his contribution, subject to two exceptions. First, if goods in the mixture are damaged or destroyed, the contributors bear the loss in proportion to their contributions. Secondly, if a contributor wrongly caused the mixture, he or she is subordinated to the other contributors and cannot take goods from the mixture until the others have received their full shares.

What remains uncertain is the nature of the property rights to the mixture before it is divided among the contributors. There are two possibilities:

1) .....the contributors own the mixture together as tenants in common (**common ownership**); or
2) .....the contributors continue to own the goods they contributed to the mixture, even though those goods cannot be identified (**continuing ownership**).

In Roman law, the choice between common and continuing ownership depended on the nature of the goods that were mixed. A mixture of fluids, such as oil or molten silver, was called **confusio** and produced common ownership. A mixture of solid things, such as rice or lumber, was called **commixtio** and produced continuing ownership. Although Roman law has influenced the development of common law, it is not clear whether this distinction is part of the common law and, if not, whether a mixture of goods produces common or continuing ownership.

Fluids and Solids

It is easy to understand why Roman law would apply different rules to mixtures of fluids and mixtures of solids (usually called **granular mixtures**). If our petrol gets mixed together it is likely that every drop contains petrol from both sources. If our rice gets mixed together, you can pick up a grain and know that it used to belong to just one of us. However, as Peter Birks said in "Mixtures", in Palmer and McKendrick, *Interests in Goods* (2nd ed, 1998) 227 at 234:

> "With the advance of science we know that there is no absolute line to draw between the two kinds of mixture. At the atomic level the particles retain their integrity in every case, though the higher the physics the less certain it is which model should prevail. At a more humdrum domestic level even a substance such as talcum powder clouds the distinction between units which do and units which do not retain their integrity."

The problem is not that mixed goods have lost their integrity or identity. Whether liquid or solid, they are easily divided into smaller portions without changing their quality or nature. The difficulty, to which the law responds, is the inability to identify the owners of those goods. This is equally true of molecules of petrol and grains of rice. There is no reason to treat fluid and granular mixtures differently.

Common or Continuing Ownership

Since fluid and granular mixtures create the same problems and should be dealt with in the same manner, they should both produce either common or continuing ownership. It is generally accepted that a fluid mixture creates common ownership and there are cases which suggest that a granular mixture should do the same.

For example, in *Spence v Union Marine Insurance Co Ltd* (1868) LR 3 CP 427, a ship carrying bales of cotton was wrecked near Florida. Although most of the bales were recovered, the majority had lost the marks that indicated who owned which bales. Bovill CJ applied the rules that governed fluid mixtures to the mixture of indistinguishable cotton bales (at 437):

> "[W]hen goods of different owners become by accident so mixed together as to be indistinguishable, the owners of the goods so mixed become tenants in common of the whole, in the proportions which they have severally contributed to it."

Lionel Smith agreed that there is no meaningful distinction between fluid and granular mixtures. However, he argued, in *The Law of Tracing* (OUP, 1997) pp 74-75, that the correct response to all mixtures (without consent) is not common ownership, but continuing ownership. This is because the rights of the contributors differ from those of an ordinary co-tenant. As discussed at the end of Chapter 15, tenants in common are not normally entitled to take a portion of the shared goods without the consent of the other tenants or authorisation of a court. However, an involuntary contributor to a mixture has that right.

Peter Birks said that this problem could be solved by adjusting the law relating to common ownership to allow the contributors to end their co-tenancy without agreement. Common ownership could then become the normal response to all mixtures of goods without consent. He said in "Mixtures", in Palmer and McKendrick, *Interests in Goods* (2nd ed, 1998) 227 at 248-249:

> "The position that the law will ultimately take is reasonably predictable. Involuntary co-ownership will be the consequence of all mixtures without regard to the nature of the substance mixed, provided only that the units have ceased to be identifiable: the penal rule will only be invoked where and to the extent that it is necessary to break an evidential deadlock brought about by the wrongdoer; and special rules for unilateral partition will be worked out for all cases of involuntary co-ownership."

Part V
Priority of Property Rights

Chapter Twenty-Seven

COMPETING PROPERTY RIGHTS

▌▌▌

It is common for more than one person to have property rights to the same thing (such as the owner and bailee of a library book, the joint owners of a home, or mortgagors and their mortgagee). Most of those rights coexist without conflict. However, people sometimes claim property rights which are incompatible with each other. Every system of law needs rules that provide clear solutions to disputes between rival claimants to things. These rules help prevent breaches of the peace and help people resolve their differences and manage their affairs without expensive and time consuming litigation. They are often called **priority rules** because they determine the priority of competing claims to things.

Not every dispute over a thing is a question of priority (as property lawyers understand that issue). Many disputes are really about the creation of property rights. For example, suppose that I am the sole legal owner of a house and deny my de facto spouse's claim to a beneficial share of it. Although we have competing claims to the same thing, the problem is not whether her property right is better than mine, but whether she has a property right at all. Our dispute concerns the creation of property rights. Did a trust arise in her favour, based on her contributions or expectation of getting that interest (as discussed in Chapters 23 and 24)?

A true priority dispute occurs when two or more people claim independent property rights that cannot coexist. The rival claimants can point to separate property creating events, which do not depend on their dealings with each other. The priority rules determine which right takes precedence in the event of a conflict. For example, suppose that I hold my house on constructive trust for my de facto spouse and then mortgage it to the bank. She claims an equitable beneficial interest in the house and the bank claims a legal security interest. If there is not enough house to satisfy both claims, who wins: my spouse or my bank?

While Part IV concerns the creation of property rights, this Part is really about the destruction of property rights. When one property right has priority over another, the latter right is extinguished or diminished to the extent of any inconsistency between them. The inconsistency causes the partial or total destruction of the property right with the lower priority.

As discussed in this Part, the priority rules are fairly straight forward. The priority of competing property rights depends primarily on two factors: the nature of those rights and the order of their creation. Generally speaking, legal rights take priority over equitable rights and earlier rights take priority over later rights. This order can be changed by other factors, such as the defence of *bona fide* purchase and the registration or lack of registration of the rights involved. Chapter 28 concerns the priorities of legal property rights and Chapter 29 concerns the priorities of equitable property rights. The effect of registration on priorities is discussed in Part VI.

Chapter Twenty-Eight

PRIORITY OF LEGAL PROPERTY RIGHTS

Nemo Dat

The starting point, when dealing with a priority dispute involving legal property rights, is the principle that *nemo dat quod non habet* (no one can give what he or she does not have). Often called *nemo dat* for short, it means that (normally) people continue to hold onto their legal property rights until they choose to dispose of them. Subject to many important exceptions discussed below, other people cannot take those rights away without consent.

For example, if a thief steals my bicycle and sells it you, you do not acquire legal ownership of the bicycle, even though you paid fair market value and had no reason to suspect that it was stolen. The thief did not obtain ownership and cannot give you more than he or she had: possession. Despite the apparent ownership creating event (the sale) and your firm belief that you obtained ownership of the bicycle, all you acquired was possession, which is enforceable against everyone except someone with a better right to possession (me). As discussed in Chapter 7, you and the thief are both guilty of conversion and liable to compensate me for my loss.

Innocent Purchasers

The example above is typical of many priority disputes. Two innocent people have suffered at the hands of a rogue and the law must decide who should bear the loss. The loser will have a right to be compensated by the rogue: the owner for conversion or the buyer for breach of contract. However, that claim may not worth pursuing, since the rogue may be hard to find or have insufficient assets to pay the claim.

The common law favoured the protection of owners, from the misappropriation of their property, over the protection of buyers, who parted with their money in good faith in reliance on the rogue's apparent ownership. Justice does not compel this choice, and the balance could well have been set in favour of innocent buyers. As discussed in the next chapter, equity does favour buyers with the defence of *bona fide purchase*. This is also true of the Torrens system, which provides buyers with the protection of indefeasible title: see Chapter 32.

The rule, *nemo dat quod non habet*, might be justified by asking who is better able to avoid the loss. Buyers have an opportunity to assess a seller's character and her or his title to the asset sold. They part with their money deliberately after weighing the risks involved. Victims of theft do not have the same opportunity. Possession is lost without knowledge or consent. Owners can take precautions to increase their physical control of things and thereby minimise the risk of losing possession, but cannot prevent it entirely. It is notable that some of the exceptions to *nemo dat* (discussed below) occur where owners do have a better opportunity to prevent the loss in question.

Regardless of how the priority rules are set, the choice between competing claims will cause many innocent people, deserving of our sympathy, to lose their property rights through no fault of their own. This cannot be helped. However, the priority rules can at least provide a simple and certain mechanism for resolving these disputes. The thief, who stole my bicycle and sold it to you, harmed us both. One of us must bear the loss. That choice is perhaps less important than the fact that we are able to resolve this dispute without resort to litigation.

Careless Owners

An owner will not be deprived of legal ownership merely because he or she did not take adequate precautions to prevent theft. We might have less sympathy for owners who fail to lock their cars and bicycles, but do not, for that reason alone, allow innocent buyers to obtain priority.

In *Northern Counties of England Fire Insurance Co v Whipp* (1884) 26 Ch D 482, the manager of the plaintiff company mortgaged his land to that company. The title documents to the land, including the mortgage, were kept in the company safe, to which the manager had access. He removed those documents, except the mortgage, and used them to mortgage the land to the defendant, Ms Whipp. Although Whipp thought she was getting a legal mortgage, legal title had already passed to the company and the manager could give no more than he had: an equity of redemption: see page 124. Therefore, Whipp obtained only an equitable mortgage of the manager's equitable ownership.

After the manager's deception came to light, the company brought an action for foreclosure against the manager and Whipp. This would destroy the manager's equity of redemption and Whipp's mortgage of it. Whipp claimed that her equitable mortgage had priority over the company's legal mortgage. She argued that the company's carelessness, in letting the manager have access to the title documents, was a reason for postponing its legal property right to her equitable property right. Fry LJ rejected this argument, saying (at 493):

> "The decisions on negligence at common law have been pressed on us in the present case, but it appears to us enough to observe, that the action at law for negligence imports the existence of a duty on the part of the defendant to the plaintiff, and a loss suffered as a direct consequence of the breach of such duty; and that in the present case it is impossible to find any duty undertaken by the Plaintiff company to the Defendant, Mrs Whipp. The case was argued as if the legal owner of land owed a duty to all other of Her Majesty's subjects to

keep his title deeds secure; as if title deeds were in the eye of the law analogous to fierce dogs or destructive elements, where from the nature of the thing the Courts have implied a general duty of safe custody on the part of the person having their possession or control."

While carelessness is not a reason for depriving a person of legal property rights, it can affect equitable property rights. As discussed in the next chapter, a failure to protect equitable property rights can lead to a loss of priority.

Exceptions to Nemo Dat

There are many exceptions to the principle that *nemo dat quod non habet*. They have evolved over the years to alleviate the harshness of that principle. As Denning LJ said, in *Bishopsgate Motor Finance Corp Ltd v Transport Brakes Ltd* 1 KB 322 at 336-337:

"In the development of our law, two principles have striven for mastery. The first is for the protection of property: no one can give a better title than he himself possesses. The second is for the protection of commercial transactions: the person who takes in good faith and for value without notice should get a good title. The first principle has held sway for a long time, but it has been modified by the common law itself and by statute so as to meet the needs of our own times."

There are a variety of ways in which people can lose legal property rights without consent. Many of them are discussed in previous chapters. Chapter 26 explains how physical changes to things can destroy legal ownership. For example, if I steal your bricks and give them to my sister, you will continue to own those bricks, since *nemo dat quod non habet*. However, if she builds a new fence with them, they cease to exist as goods and become part of her land. You will have a personal right to be compensated for our conversion of your bricks (and might even have an equitable lien on my sister's land), but your property rights to the bricks are gone.

There are many statutes that enable people to acquire legal property rights without the owner's consent. For example, the limitation statutes extinguish rights to possession that are not enforced within the prescribed time periods. Adverse possession for a sufficient length of time becomes legal ownership: see Chapter 8. Property rights can be expropriated by the government or seized to pay judgment creditors. The property rights of a bankrupt person are transferred to the trustee in bankruptcy to be distributed according to law. As discussed at page 298, the *Family Law Act* 1975 (Cth) gives judges the power to redistribute property rights between husbands and wives.

Although legal property rights are the most durable form of property, they are not absolute. They can be used to satisfy the owner's responsibilities to others or for the common good (see Chapter 10) and cannot survive the destruction of the things to which they relate. However, those methods of destroying legal ownership are usually regarded, not as exceptions to the *nemo dat* principal, but as general limitations applicable to all property rights.

The "true" exceptions to *nemo dat* are discussed below. They are situations in which people obtain legal property rights, without the owner's consent, because they bought those rights in good faith. In other words, there are circumstances in which people can sell legal property rights they do not own and cause those rights to pass from their true owners to the buyers. They are grouped into two general categories. In the first group, the exception is linked to the circumstances of the transaction. In the second, the exception is linked to the nature of the property right.

Exceptional Transactions

As discussed above, buyers are not excepted from the *nemo dat* principle merely because they acted honestly. However, there are situations in which an honest buyer can obtain good title, even though the seller had no right to sell. Four of these situations are discussed below:

1) **estoppel** (where the owner led the buyer to believe that the seller had authority to sell and is therefore estopped from denying the seller's authority);
2) **apparent agency** (where the owner helped create the buyer's belief that the seller is the owner's agent);
3) **buyer in possession** (where the owner of goods let a buyer have possession before they were sold) or **seller in possession** (where the owner bought the goods but let the seller keep possession of them); and
4) **market overt** (where goods were sold in an open market).

In each situation, the transaction involves an additional factor that justifies the exception to *nemo dat*. Except for a sale in market overt, the true owner bears some responsibility for creating the seller's apparent authority to sell. Although the owner is not guilty of wrongdoing, her or his involvement is enough to tip the scale in favour of the innocent buyer who relied on that apparent authority.

Most exceptions to *nemo dat*, like the principle itself, were created by the common law and later codified or modified by statute. Although some exceptions can apply to a wide variety of legal property rights, most of the cases and statutes deal with the sale of goods. This is because ownership of goods is commonly transferred by delivery: see page 241. Buyers often rely on a seller's possession of goods and representation of ownership as proof of her or his right to sell. In contrast, most other property rights are transferred by document or registration. Buyers tend to investigate the quality of the seller's title, with the aid of legal advice, and place less reliance on the seller's representations of ownership.

It is important to remember that these exceptions to *nemo dat* are available only to honest buyers. They will not assist either a buyer with notice of the seller's lack of authority or the recipient of a gift. A buyer cannot possibly obtain priority over the true owner unless he or she obtained a property right for value in good faith without notice of the seller's lack of authority to sell it.

Notice

Many cases turn on the issue of notice. Generally speaking, a person has notice of something if he or she knows or ought to know about it. What a person ought to know can be a difficult question. In this context, it depends on the nature of the property right being sold. When someone buys a right to land, they are expected to take steps to investigate the quality of the seller's title. Therefore, a buyer will have notice of rights that would be discovered by reasonable buyers who carried out the appropriate investigations.

In contrast, most people do not bother to investigate the seller's title when they buy consumer goods. It is reasonable to assume that a retail shop has authority to sell and, therefore, buyers will not have notice of rights that might have been discovered by investigation. This is not true of all goods. A reasonable buyer will take greater care when buying very expensive things, such as an aircraft, ship, or rare violin. What a buyer ought to know will be measured by the conduct of a reasonable buyer in that situation.

The concept of notice is discussed in more detail in the next chapter, in connection with the defence of *bona fide* purchase for value without notice.

Estoppel

The principle of estoppel is discussed in Chapter 23. At common law, if you represent a fact to be true, and someone suffers a detriment in reliance on that representation, you may be estopped from denying it in subsequent litigation. This principle can apply to a sale of property rights. If the owner of those rights leads a buyer to believe that a seller is the owner or otherwise has authority to sell them, and the buyer buys them from the seller in reliance on that belief, the owner will not be allowed to deny the seller's right to sell. The buyer obtains priority over the owner, because the owner is unable to establish the priority of her or his rights.

The principle that *nemo dat quod non habet*, and the estoppel exception, are found in the sale of goods legislation in each jurisdiction. For example, section 26 of the *Sale of Goods Act* 1954 (ACT) states:

> "Subject to this Act, where goods are sold by a person who is not the owner of them and does not sell them under the authority or with the consent of the owner, the buyer does not acquire a better title to the goods than the seller had unless the owner of the goods is, by his conduct, precluded from denying the seller's authority to sell."

This does not change the common law, but merely preserves it with respect to the sale of goods. Like the *nemo dat* principle, the estoppel exception is not limited to that context, but can apply to a wide variety of transactions, property rights, and things.

Representations of Authority

What conduct counts as a representation that someone has authority to sell a property right? Owners will not be estopped from asserting their property rights merely because they let someone else have possession of their goods or the title documents to them. Although an honest buyer might rely on a seller's possession as proof of ownership, the owner's consent to that possession is not a representation that the seller has authority to sell. Something more is needed. Otherwise, every bailment would place ownership at risk. Every time you loaned a book to someone or took your car to the shop for repairs, you would be creating a situation in which your ownership could be destroyed.

In *Big Rock Pty Ltd v Esanda Finance Corp Ltd* (1992) 10 WAR 259, the plaintiff finance company obtained and registered a legal mortgage of a car to secure a loan of $12,484. Two months later, the plaintiff wrote a letter to the borrower saying that the loan was paid out and that the plaintiff had "no further interest in the" car. This was a mistake caused by an error in the plaintiff's computer records. The borrower then sold the car to the defendant car dealer. When asked about the registered mortgage to the plaintiff, the borrower produced the letter to support his fraudulent claim that the mortgage had been discharged. The plaintiff sued the defendant for conversion and lost because it was estopped by its representation that it had no interest in the car.

The *Big Rock* case was fairly straightforward (even though the judges in that case disagreed about whether the plaintiff should be estopped). The plaintiff made a clear representation that it was not the owner of the car and the defendant relied on that representation to its detriment. There are cases in which honest buyers claimed they were misled, not by an owner's statements, but by her or his actions. These claims rarely succeed. As McHugh JA said, in *Thomas Australia Wholesale Vehicle Trading Co Pty Ltd v Marac Finance Australia Ltd* (1985) 3 NSWLR 452 at 469, the owner will not be estopped unless his conduct, "expressly or impliedly, constitutes an unambiguous representation to the buyer that the seller has his authority to make the sale".

Failure to Protect Ownership

In the *Thomas* case, above, the owner had leased a car to Kerr, who sold it while fraudulently pretending to be the owner. The buyer claimed that the owner was estopped from denying Kerr's right to sell the car. This claim was based not on anything the owner had said or done, but on the fact that the owner had failed to take steps to protect its ownership. It did not stick labels on the car nor did it stop Kerr from registering the car in his own name. These failures misled the buyer to believe that Kerr was the true owner. The court rejected that argument. As McHugh JA said (at 469), "inaction, silence, or even gross carelessness in the protection of property is not of itself enough to preclude an owner from asserting his title".

Estoppel cannot be based on an owner's failure to speak or act unless that inactivity amounts to a clear representation to the buyer about the owner's rights. For example, suppose you want to buy some farm machinery that is mortgaged to me. You ask me how much money is needed to discharge the mortgage. I tell you, but fail to mention that I also have a second mortgage of that machinery to secure another loan to the seller. You buy the machinery, pay me the amount needed to discharge the first mortgage, and pay the balance of the purchase price to the seller. I may be estopped from claiming ownership of the machinery under the second mortgage.

This is sometimes called **estoppel by negligence**, which means that owners may be estopped if they fail to perform their duties to inform others of their property rights. However, this is misleading. There is no duty to inform others about our property rights. If I fail to assert my property rights in a situation in which reasonable people would do so, there is no duty breached. No wrong is committed. If that failure is a clear representation that I do not have those property rights, then I risk losing them if an honest buyer relies on that representation to her or his detriment. However, I am not a wrongdoer and not liable to pay compensation.

Apparent Agency

Agency is a relationship in which one person (the agent) has the power to affect the legal rights of another person (the principal) in dealings with others. For example, the clerk at a shop has the authority to make contracts of sale on behalf of the business, even though he or she does not own the business or the goods being sold. When you buy something from a shop clerk, you know that he or she does not own the thing purchased and that you did not make a contract with the clerk. You made the contract with, and obtained ownership from, the person who owns the shop. The clerk, as agent, helped make the contract of sale, but is not a party to it.

We deal with agents all the time. Most manufacturers, wholesalers, and retailers are corporations. Although they are legal persons (as discussed at pages 193-194) and can have property rights and make contracts, corporations cannot act without the help of human agents, such as directors, officers, and employees. Whenever we buy something from a corporation, the contract of sale is made with the help of an agent.

The use of agents rarely causes problems, because they have **actual authority** to make contracts on behalf of their principals. The sale by an agent is not an exception to *nemo dat*, because the principal is a willing party to the contract and thereby consents to the transfer of her or his property rights. This is true even though the principal is unaware of the particular sale transaction. The agent's authority is given in advance and continues until revoked (or the principal dies).

Problems can arise when agents exceed their authority or people pretend to be agents even though they have no authority to act on behalf of a principal. Normally, the principal is unaffected by the unauthorised actions of the agent. Although buyers believe they are dealing with an authorised agent, they will not obtain ownership because the agent does not have authority to make those contracts and cannot give what he or she does not have. (They can, however, sue the agent for breach of warranty of authority.)

Apparent Authority

An exception to *nemo dat* occurs when a principal gives an agent **apparent authority** to act on her or his behalf. If the principal is responsible for creating the impression that the agent does have authority to make a sale, then he or she will be bound by that contract. This is a form of estoppel, discussed above. The principal is estopped from denying the agent's authority, because he or she represented that the agent had authority to make the contract of sale and the buyer relied on that representation to her or his detriment.

In *Farquharson Brothers & Co v C King & Co* AC 325, the plaintiffs were a company that owned timber stored in a dock warehouse. They instructed the dock company to let the plaintiffs' employee, Capon, deal with timber. Capon told the dock company to deliver the timber to a man named Brown. However, Brown did not exist. Capon, pretending to be Brown, sold the timber to the defendants and instructed the dock company to deliver the timber to them. After Capon's fraud was discovered and he was convicted of forgery, the plaintiffs sued the defendants for return of the timber or payment of its value.

Capon was not authorised to sell the timber to himself. Although the plaintiffs had represented that Capon was their authorised agent, the defendants did not rely on that representation. They thought they were dealing with a man named Brown and knew nothing about Capon's relationship with the plaintiffs. In the absence of reliance by the defendants, the plaintiffs' representations about Capon's authority were irrelevant. The case would be the same if Capon had been a thief who stole the plaintiffs' timber and purported to sell it to the defendants. Therefore, the defendants were guilty of conversion.

Mercantile Agents

A mercantile agent (sometimes called a **factor**) is a person who carries on business buying or selling goods for others. For example, a dealer in second-hand cars might sell them on **consignment**. He or she does not buy them from the owner, but takes possession (as bailee) and sells them for a fee. On completion of the sale, ownership will pass directly from the owner to the buyer.

If the mercantile agent exceeds her or his authority when selling or otherwise dealing with goods, the owner may be bound by that transaction. By giving the agent possession of the goods or documents of title, the owner represents to the public that the agent has authority to deal with them. Therefore, an honest buyer will obtain priority over the owner, so long as the buyer deals with the agent in the normal course of business without notice of the agent's lack of authority.

In these cases, there is no direct communication between owner and buyer. The buyer relies on the mercantile agent's possession of goods or documents as proof of her or his authority to sell. However, reliance alone does not excuse the buyer from the *nemo dat* principle. The exception is justified because the owner created the apparent authority by giving possession of those goods or documents to the agent. The owner chose the agent and should bear the risk that he or she will exceed her or his authority. If a thief stole goods and gave them to a mercantile agent to sell, the buyer would not obtain priority over the true owner. Although the buyer relied on the agent's possession of the stolen goods, the owner was not responsible for creating that situation.

In each jurisdiction, the common law has been modified by statute to make it clear that this exception to *nemo dat* applies not just to sales, but also to pledges and other dealings with goods. For example, section 3 of the *Factors Act* 1892 (Qld) states:

> "When a mercantile agent is, with the consent of the owner, in possession of goods or of the documents of title to goods, any sale, pledge, or other disposition of the goods, made by the agent when acting in the ordinary course of business of a mercantile agent, shall, subject to the provisions of this Act, be as valid as if the agent were expressly authorised by the owner of the goods to make the same: Provided that the person taking under the disposition acts in good faith, and has not at the time of the disposition notice that the person making the disposition has no authority to make the same."

Buyers and Sellers in Possession

The legislation regulating mercantile agents and sales of goods creates exceptions both for buyers in possession of goods belonging to the seller and for sellers in possession of goods belonging to the buyer. A buyer or seller, who obtains possession of the goods or documents of title, can transfer ownership to another buyer: see, eg, the *Goods Act* 1958 (Vic), ss 30, 31.

Seller in Possession

Suppose that I sell a book to you and you arrange to pick it up next Tuesday. Before you get your book, Annette offers me a higher price and I sell it to her. Even though I no longer owned the book (since my ownership was transferred to you when we made our contract of sale), Annette gets priority because I was a seller in possession. This is similar to the exception for mercantile agents, discussed above. The difference is that Annette was not dealing with an agent, but thought she was dealing with the true owner of the book.

Why does Annette's belief in my apparent ownership affect your right to the book? She did not communicate with you, but simply relied on my possession of the book as proof of ownership. You did not give me any authority to deal with it. Although you consented to my possession, normally that does not justify an exception to *nemo dat*. You would not lose your ownership if instead you had loaned the book to me before I sold it to Annette.

The exception might be justified by the context of a contract of sale. You relied on my promise to deliver possession of the book to you next Tuesday. This is true whether ownership of the book passed to you when the contract was made or was supposed to pass to you on delivery. If we had agreed that ownership would pass to you on delivery, then my sale to Annette would not be an exception to *nemo dat*. My ownership of the book would pass to her and I would have to obtain another book for you by Tuesday or compensate you for my breach of contract.

The exception for sellers in possession does two things. First, it means that Annette's right to the book is unaffected by the terms of my contract with you. The outcome is the same whether or not ownership passed to you before delivery. Secondly, I am the only person who is liable for wrongful interference with your new ownership of the book. This exception ensures that innocent buyers do not become involved in what is, essentially, a dispute over a contract of sale.

Buyer in Possession

Similar considerations apply when a buyer obtains possession of goods before ownership is transferred. The primary reason for postponing the transfer of ownership is to ensure that the buyer will pay for the goods. The seller is relying on the buyer's promise to pay and retains ownership as security for the performance of that promise. There is a risk that the buyer will breach the contract and fail to pay for the goods. There is also a risk that the buyer will deal with the goods before the purchase price is paid in full. The exception for buyers in possession ensures that innocent people, dealing with the buyer, do not become embroiled in the contractual dispute between the seller and buyer.

What is the point of the seller retaining ownership of goods until the purchase price is paid in full? If the buyer in possession can sell the goods to an honest buyer, the seller's title is not very secure. However, the seller will retain priority over anyone who receives the goods as a gift or with notice of the seller's rights. More importantly, the seller's ownership will continue if the buyer becomes bankrupt. The buyer's assets will be transferred to the trustee in bankruptcy and used to pay the buyer's debts, but this will not affect the seller's ownership. The trustee will have to pay the balance of the purchase price owed to the seller, return the goods to the seller, or compensate the seller for detinue or conversion: see Chapter 7.

Hire-Purchase

Suppose that you want to sell a car to me and are willing to let me take three years to pay for it. We agree that you will keep ownership of the car until I have paid the purchase price in full. This is often called a **conditional sale**. It provides you with security for the performance of my debt to you. However, I am a buyer in possession and have the power to destroy your ownership by selling the car to an honest buyer.

You can avoid this exception to *nemo dat* by using a slightly different contract. Instead of a conditional sale, you lease the car to me for three years, combined with an option to purchase at the end of the lease. This is often called a **hire-purchase contract** (although the terms "conditional sale" and "hire-purchase" are sometimes used interchangeably). As discussed at page 263, an **option to purchase** gives the holder the right to buy the thing without an obligation to do so. Although I have possession of the car, I am not a buyer in possession until I exercise the option at the end of the lease.

The only difference between the conditional sale and the hire-purchase is that I am not obligated to buy the car under the latter contract. However, if the option price is less than the market value of the car at the end of the lease, I will probably exercise the option. The two transactions are essentially the same and it is odd that one should attract an exception to *nemo dat*, but not the other. For other purposes, such as consumer protection legislation, they are treated in the same manner: see, for example, the definitions of "hire-purchase agreement" in the *Hire Purchase Act* 1959, in Queensland, Tasmania, Victoria, and Western Australia.

Market Overt

There used to be a rule in England that a sale of goods in an open market (called **market overt**) transferred ownership to the buyer, so long as the buyer acted in good faith without notice of the seller's lack of ownership. The rule was justified on the basis that victims of theft could go to the market and search for their goods. Thieves and dealers would not risk exposing those goods in the market and buyers could assume that goods on public display were not stolen: see *Bishopsgate Motor Finance Corp Ltd v Transport Brakes Ltd* 1 KB 322. However, this justification does not make sense in a jurisdiction with a large and easily mobile population. Goods stolen in Melbourne could be offered for sale the next day at a market in Adelaide, with little risk.

However, the main criticism of this exception to *nemo dat* is that the owner has no involvement with the seller's apparent authority to sell the goods. The other exceptions exist because the owner has represented to the buyer that the seller has that authority or has at least consented to the seller's possession of the goods or title documents. Although an honest buyer in market overt is relying on the seller's possession as proof of authority, that possession was obtained without the owner's consent or knowledge.

The rule was abolished in England in 1995 and earlier in every Australian jurisdiction, except South Australia, Tasmania, and Western Australia. Section 4 of the *Sale of Goods Act* 1923 (NSW) states that "there shall not be deemed to be or to have been any market overt in New South Wales". In other jurisdictions, the exception for market overt is abolished by necessary implication. As discussed above, every state and territory has a statutory rule equivalent to section 26 of the *Sale of Goods Act* 1954 (ACT):

> "Subject to this Act, where goods are sold by a person who is not the owner of them and does not sell them under the authority or with the consent of the owner, the buyer does not acquire a better title to the goods than the seller had ..."

Therefore, the common law exception for market overt is abolished, unless the legislation expressly preserves it. Only South Australia, Tasmania, and Western Australia have statutory exceptions for market overt. For example, section 22 of the *Sale of Goods Act* 1895 (SA) states:

> "Where goods are sold in market overt, according to the usage of the market, the buyer acquires a good title to the goods, provided he buys them in good faith, and without notice of any defect or want of title on the part of the seller."

There are exceptions to the exception for market overt. In Tasmania, the exception for market overt does not "affect the law relating to the sale of cattle": *Sale of Goods Act* 1896 (Tas), s 27. In all three states, if a person is convicted of theft, ownership of the stolen goods is restored to the owner even if the goods have been sold in market overt: see *Sale of Goods Act* 1895 (WA), s 24.

This last exception to the exception is difficult to understand. The thief's criminal conviction has no connection to a previous sale in market overt. It affects neither the honest buyer's reliance on the seller's authority nor the owner's involvement in the sale. Why should the buyer's rights be lost if the police are fortunate enough to solve the crime, catch the thief, and secure a conviction, but not in other cases where it is proven that the goods were stolen? Perhaps the exception exists to give owners an incentive to come forward and give evidence in the criminal trial.

Less Durable Rights

Some legal property rights are less durable than most. They can be extinguished by transactions that would not affect the priority of an ordinary legal property right. Three such rights are discussed here: money, options to rescind, and native title. These exceptions to *nemo dat* are linked, not to the type of transaction (such as a sale in market overt or by a seller in possession), but to the nature of the property right.

Money

The most important exception to *nemo dat* concerns money. If it is used as currency, ownership will pass to an honest recipient who gives value in return. As Wilson J and Dawson J said in *Ilich v The Queen* (1987) 162 CLR 110 at 128:

> "Money is, of course, capable of being stolen and if it is stolen, property in the notes or coins does not pass to the thief. But if the thief passes the money into currency, which he may do by making payment with it, ownership will pass with possession notwithstanding the thief's lack of title providing the transaction was bona fide and for valuable consideration."

The owner's rights are not lost if stolen money is given away or is paid to a person who suspects that it is stolen. However, a *bona fide* purchaser of money need not worry about competing claims to it. He or she will obtain ownership of the money by accepting it honestly as payment of a debt. This allows money to function as a medium of exchange and a measure of value. Both functions would be impaired if the *nemo dat* principle applied to money with full force. If people were not sure of getting ownership of the money paid to them, they would be less willing to exchange goods and services for money and the market value of money would be affected.

For example, you are happy to accept a $20 note as payment for goods or services of that value. There is a slight risk of forgery, but that is minimised by the hard work of the people who designed the note. If there was also a risk that you would not get ownership of the $20 because of *nemo dat*, you might have to charge more to account for that risk or to pay for the expense of investigating the title to the money you receive. The market value of money would be less than its face value, making it difficult to measure the value of goods and services accurately in monetary terms.

Of course, not all debts are paid in cash. We buy many things using credit or debit cards and pay our monthly bills with cheques or at automated banking machines. Like cash, these methods of payment are accepted because they are excepted, partially or completely, from the *nemo dat* principle.

Credit Cards and Electronic Funds Transfers

A payment by credit card is not affected by the *nemo dat* principle because it does not involve a transfer of money directly from customer to merchant. Both parties have separate contracts with the credit card company. By accepting payment by credit card, the merchant obtains a contractual right to receive payment from the credit card company (less an agreed service charge) and the customer accepts a contractual obligation to pay that amount to the credit card company (plus an agreed interest charge).

What happens when payment is made using a stolen credit card? The thief has no right to use the card and commits fraud when he or she offers it to the merchant as payment. If the merchant obtains authorisation from the credit card company before accepting payment, he or she will have a contractual right to be paid the agreed amount by that company, regardless of the theft and fraud. Normally, the owner of the card will not be liable to pay for charges incurred by the thief, but that depends on the contract between the owner and the credit card company. In most cases, the loss is borne by the credit card company as a business expense.

The same principles apply to payments made with a debit card or other form of electronic funds transfer. It looks like a transfer of property from customer to merchant: when payment is made, the customer's bank account is reduced by that amount and the merchant's bank account is increased by that amount (less an agreed service charge). However, there is no direct transfer of money from customer to merchant. When the customer's bank authorises payment, it agrees to pay the merchant's bank and reduces the balance of the customer's bank account.

The customer's bank account is simply the measure of the bank's debt to the customer. This depends on the contract between them. The terms of that contract will determine whether the unauthorised use of a stolen debit card will reduce the bank's debt to its customer. If the customer is not responsible for the unauthorised use of the debit card (for example, because he or she previously reported the theft to the bank) and unauthorised deductions are made from the customer's account, he or she can insist that the bank account be corrected.

Cheques

A cheque is a written order to a bank (or similar financial institution) telling it to pay a certain sum of money on demand: *Cheques Act* 1986 (Cth), s 10. It is a type of **bill of exchange**. Bills of exchange, like bank drafts, bearer bonds, and promissory notes, are **negotiable instruments**. The common feature of all these documents is their negotiability: the rights associated with the document can be transferred to another person by delivery of the document.

Negotiable instruments are excepted from the *nemo dat* principle to some extent. Normally, a person who obtains possession of a negotiable instrument, for value and in good faith, can exercise the rights associated with it, even though possession was obtained without the consent of the person entitled to possess it. This allows negotiable instruments to fulfil important roles as forms of payment and forms of security.

To keep this section from becoming too long and cumbersome, only cheques are discussed here. They are governed by the *Cheques Act* 1986 (Cth) (which used to be called the *Cheques and Payment Orders Act* 1986 (Cth)). Other bills of exchange are governed by the *Bills of Exchange Act* 1909 (Cth). The same basic principle of negotiability applies to both.

If I write a cheque to you for $50 and give it to you, you have my written instruction to my bank to pay $50 to you. This enables you to present the cheque to my bank and obtain payment of $50 (assuming my bank will pay). Rather than go to my bank to get the money, you can take the cheque to your own bank for deposit in your account. By doing so, you authorise your bank to present the cheque to my bank, collect the money, and increase the balance of your account.

The cheque itself does not transfer any money to you, nor does it assign to you any portion of my bank account (which is my bank's debt to me): *Cheques Act* 1986 (Cth), s 88. Whether my bank will pay $50 to you (or your bank) depends primarily on my contract with my bank. There is a very small risk that my bank will become insolvent and cannot pay, but the essential question is whether the terms of my contract with my bank requires it to pay $50 to you. It can refuse to pay (**dishonour** the cheque) for a variety of reasons. For example, the balance of my account might be less than $50 and the bank has not agreed to let me have an overdraft, I may have instructed the bank to stop payment on that cheque, the cheque might be stale (more than 15 months old), or I may have died or become mentally incompetent: see *Cheques Act* 1986 (Cth), ss 89, 90.

Unlike $50 in cash, the value of my $50 cheque depends on whether my bank will pay $50 when it is presented or dishonour it, which in turn depends on my dealings with my bank. Unlike payment by credit or debit card, the rights created by writing and delivering the cheque are not wholly dependent on contracts with financial institutions. The cheque has value even if it is dishonoured. By writing the cheque, I undertake that my bank will pay $50 when the cheque is presented and am liable to compensate you if it is dishonoured: *Cheques Act* 1986 (Cth), s 71.

Cheques are like cash because they are negotiable: *Cheques Act* 1986 (Cth), s 40. A cheque which is **payable to bearer** can be negotiated by delivery. So, if the cheque I wrote to you instructs my bank to pay you "or bearer" (like many cheques), you can transfer those rights by giving possession of the cheque to someone else. If the cheque is payable to you only (and not to bearer), it is a cheque **payable to order** and can be negotiated by delivery only if you **indorse** it first (by signing it). The indorser undertakes that the cheque will be paid when presented and is liable to compensate the holder if it is not: *Cheques Act* 1986 (Cth), s 73.

Crossed cheques are less negotiable than most. They bear two parallel lines drawn across the front, with or without the words "not negotiable" written between the lines. This is an instruction to the bank to pay the amount of the cheque only to another financial institution: see *Cheques Act* 1986 (Cth), s 54; *Commissioners of the State Savings Bank of Victoria v Permewan, Wright & Co Ltd* (1914) 19 CLR 457.

The holder of a cheque bears the rights associated with it: to receive payment from the bank when it is presented for payment or to receive compensation from the drawer or indorser if it is dishonoured. The holder accepts the risk that those rights might be worth less than the face value of the cheque. However, if there was also a significant risk that the holder might not obtain those rights because of the *nemo dat* principle, the cheque would not be fully negotiable and it would lose much of its utility. For this reason, cheques are partially excepted from that principle.

If a person receives a cheque in good faith, for value, and without notice that it has been dishonoured or that the person who transferred it had a defective title, he or she is a **holder in due course** (so long as the cheque appears to be complete and regular, is not stale, and is not crossed as "not negotiable"): *Cheques Act* 1986 (Cth), s 50. A holder in due course is excepted from the *nemo dat* principle and obtains the rights associated with the cheque, even though the transferor did not have those rights. According to section 49 of the *Cheques Act* 1986 (Cth):

> "A holder of a cheque who is a holder in due course: (a) holds the cheque free from any defect in the title of prior parties as well as from mere personal defences available to prior parties against one another; and (b) may enforce payment of the cheque against any person liable on the cheque."

This exception to *nemo dat* does not apply to a crossed cheque which bears the words "not negotiable" between the parallel lines across the cheque. The holder of the cheque does not receive a better title than the transferor: *Cheques Act* 1986 (Cth), s 55.

Option To Rescind

As discussed at page 322, if a person (called the plaintiff here for convenience) has a right to rescind a transaction and thereby recover an asset, he or she has a property right to that asset. Upon electing to rescind, legal or equitable ownership of the asset revests in the plaintiff, so long as it is possible to restore the parties to their pre-transaction positions (*restitutio in integrum*). Before electing to rescind, the plaintiff has a lesser property right to the recoverable asset. That lesser right, called an **option to rescind**, can be legal or equitable depending on whether the election to rescind will cause legal or equitable ownership to revert to the plaintiff. Equitable options to rescind are discussed in the next chapter under the heading, mere equities.

Durability of Options to Rescind

Unlike most other legal property rights, a legal option to rescind is always subject to the rights of a *bona fide* purchaser. For example, suppose I bought a bicycle from you and paid with a cheque, knowing that the cheque would be dishonoured. You have a right to rescind the sale because of my fraud. As discussed in Chapter 24, if you elect to rescind, legal ownership of the bicycle will revert to you. However, if I sell the bicycle to Olumide before you rescind, and he buys it in good faith without notice of your right to rescind, he will have priority.

This exception to *nemo dat* is found in every sale of goods statute in Australia. For example, section 23 of the *Sale of Goods Act* 1895 (WA) states:

> "When the seller of goods has a voidable title thereto, but his title has not been avoided at the time of the sale, the buyer acquires a good title to the goods, provided he buys them in good faith and without notice of the seller's defect of title."

This codifies the exception with respect to sales of goods. However, the exception is not limited to that situation. An option to rescind is, by nature, less durable than other legal property rights and always subject to the rights of a subsequent *bona fide* purchaser. This is true whether the purchaser acquires legal ownership under a sale or a lesser legal property right, such as a lease or mortgage. If the purchaser obtains ownership, the plaintiff's option to rescind is destroyed, since the purchaser's ownership is wholly incompatible with the plaintiff's rights. If the purchaser has acquired a lesser property right, the plaintiff may still be able to rescind and recover ownership, but subject to the purchaser's rights.

An option to rescind is less durable than other property rights because of the circumstances in which the option is created. Where a sale (or other disposition) is induced by fraud or duress, the plaintiff ought to be able to reverse the transaction and recover the asset sold. Since the plaintiff's intention to transfer the asset was defective, the buyer is unjustly enriched. However, until the plaintiff rescinds the sale, the buyer continues to be the legal owner of the asset and anyone dealing with the buyer will have no way of knowing that the sale was defective. People dealing with the buyer do have an opportunity to assess the quality of her or his title to the asset. However, the plaintiff also dealt with the buyer and had a greater opportunity to avoid the loss.

Options to Rescind and Buyers in Possession

Once the plaintiff rescinds the transaction, her or his less durable option to rescind is replaced by full legal ownership, subject to the normal priority rules. That ownership may still be at risk because of the exception for buyers in possession (discussed above). Returning to our previous example, suppose you elected to rescind the sale of your bicycle to me before I sold it to Olumide. Although legal ownership of the bicycle returned to you, I was still a buyer in possession and able to pass good title to Olumide: see *Newtons of Wembley Ltd v Williams* 1 QB 560.

The exception for buyers in possession will mean that, in many cases, it will not matter whether the plaintiff elected to rescind before or after the goods were resold to an honest buyer. However, before rescission, the exception to *nemo dat* is based on the fragile nature of an option to rescind and, after rescission, the exception is based on the circumstances of the resale. This distinction can be important.

Returning again to our previous example, suppose that I gave the bicycle to Yanson, who then sold it to Olumide (an honest buyer). The gift to Yanson does not affect your property rights and you are still entitled to rescind the sale to me. However, if you do not rescind before Yanson sells the bicycle to Olumide, your option to rescind will be destroyed. If you do rescind before that sale, legal ownership will revert to you and will have priority over Olumide's rights. This is because Yanson is not a buyer in possession and, therefore, Olumide cannot rely on that exception to *nemo dat*.

Native Title

As discussed in Chapter 19, when Britain acquired sovereignty over Australia, its indigenous people had property rights to the land under their traditional laws and customs. The change of sovereignty and introduction of English common law did not destroy those property rights. Instead, they were recognised and protected by the common law as native title.

Until 1975, native title was less durable than most property rights. Like an option to rescind (discussed above), it was routinely defeated by subsequent inconsistent rights. However, it was less durable for a different reason. Options to rescind are always subject to the rights of *bona fide* purchasers. The priority of native title is affected not by *bona fide* purchase, but by the lawful exercise of the Crown's power to grant inconsistent rights. In other words, the priority of an option to rescind depends on whether the recipient of an inconsistent right is a *bona fide* purchaser, while the priority of native title depends on whether the grantor of an inconsistent right acted lawfully.

The priority of native title has been improved greatly by two statutes: the *Racial Discrimination Act* 1975 (Cth) and the *Native Title Act* 1993 (Cth). These Acts recognise the importance of native title and give it the same status as other property rights to land. This discussion is divided into three parts, to deal with the priority of native title at common law, under the *Racial Discrimination Act*, and under the *Native Title Act*.

Common Law

Prior to 31 October 1975, when the *Racial Discrimination Act* came into force, the Crown had the power to destroy or impair native title by taking the land for its own use or by granting inconsistent rights. A grant of an estate in fee simple would completely destroy any native title to that land. As Kirby J said in *Fejo v Northern Territory* (1998) 195 CLR 96 at 155:

> "So fragile is native title and so susceptible is it to extinguishment that the grant of such an interest, without more, 'blows away' the native title forever."

The grant of a lesser interest (such as a pastoral lease) diminished native title to the extent of any inconsistency. As Kirby J said in *Wik Peoples v Queensland* (1996) 187 CLR 1 at 243:

"Only if there is inconsistency between the legal interests of the lessee (as defined by the instrument of lease and the legislation under which it was granted) and the native title (as established by evidence), will such native title, to the extent of the inconsistency, be extinguished."

Kirby J was talking about a pastoral lease, which was not an estate because it did not include a right to possession: see Chapter 16. It is not clear whether a true leasehold estate would extinguish native title completely. In *Mabo v Queensland (No 2)* (1992) 175 CLR 1 at 110, Deane J and Gaudron J said that native title would be "extinguished by an unqualified grant of an inconsistent estate in the land by the Crown, such as a grant in fee or a lease conferring the right to exclusive possession". However, *Mabo (No 2)* did not resolve that issue. As Kirby J said, in *Wik* at 225, "the effect of the grant of leasehold interests upon native title rights is not authoritatively decided".

The dissenting judges in *Wik Peoples v Queensland* thought that native title would be extinguished if the Crown granted a lease, because the Crown would thereby acquire a reversionary interest in the land. The Crown had used its radical title both to grant the lease and to acquire beneficial ownership of the land for the purpose of becoming a landlord. When the lease came to an end, the Crown would have a right to possess the land and not merely radical title. This follows an idea expressed by Brennan J, in *Mabo (No 2)* at 68:

"If a lease be granted, the lessee acquires possession and the Crown acquires the reversion expectant on the expiry of the term. The Crown's title is thus expanded from the mere radical title and, on the expiry of the term, becomes a plenum dominium."

In the *Wik* case, the majority of the judges either rejected this view or thought that it did not apply to a pastoral lease (which was not a true leasehold estate). As discussed at page 99, a reversion exists when a lease is granted by the holder of a fee simple, life estate, or greater leasehold estate. The reversion is not a new property right, but what is left of the greater estate when the lease is carved out of it. The landlord has a right to possession when the lease comes to an end, because he or she already has an estate that is no longer subject to the tenant's right to possession. In contrast, a lease granted by the Crown is not carved out of a greater estate, but created by an exercise of radical title. The right to remove the tenant at the end of the lease does not necessarily mean that the Crown has a right to possess the land. That depends on whether the Crown has otherwise acquired the land for its own use: see *Wik* at 127-129.

In *Western Australia v Ward* (2000) 170 ALR 159, the majority of the Federal Court of Australia decided that the grant of a true lease by the Crown extinguished native title, because the tenant's right to possession was necessarily inconsistent with native title. North J (dissenting) thought that native title was merely suspended during the term of the lease and would revive when the lease ended and the land was no longer subject to any inconsistent rights. Beaumont J and von Doussa J (the majority of the Court) said (at 183):

"A lease is only for a term of years, and is not permanent. The notion that native title can revive at the conclusion of the term of the lease is, in our view, inconsistent with the joint judgment in *Fejo* at CLR 131."

They were referring to *Fejo v Northern Territory* (1998) 195 CLR 96, where the High Court of Australia decided that native title is extinguished by the lawful grant of a fee simple estate and cannot revive even if the Crown later reacquires the land. However, a fee simple estate is a right to possess land indefinitely and, therefore, it is necessarily inconsistent with the existence of any native title, now and at any time in the future. It does not matter whether the estate lasts for ages or only for a short time. While it exists, the owner has a right which leaves no room for the survival of any native title.

In contrast, a leasehold estate is a right to possess land for a limited period of time. There is no inconsistency between the tenant's right to possession during the lease and the enjoyment of native title after the lease has ended. North J used the example of a lease granted to a shire for one day to hold a special event (at 330):

"The exclusive possession lease creates rights in the lessee which are temporarily inconsistent with some of the rights and interests dependent upon the existence of native title. The law could not hold that the inconsistent rights granted to the shire for one day bring to an end the native title of the Aboriginal community dating back hundreds of years."

Beaumont J and von Doussa J suggested (at 184) that, "If the grant of statutory rights is a grant only for a short finite period, the grant may not be inconsistent with the continuance of native title rights." However, as North J replied (at 352):

"[T]he only difference between a short and a long-term lease is the duration of the inconsistency. The nature of the inconsistency is the same, namely, in the case of a lease, the grant of exclusive possession to the lessee. In principle there is no distinction between the grant of a short-term interest or a long-term interest. The extinguishment consequences must follow in the same way in either case."

Regardless of whether the grant of a true lease necessarily destroyed native title, the underlying principle is not in doubt: a property right lawfully granted by the Crown took priority over native title. This was true whether or not the Crown intended to destroy native title. If there was any inconsistency between native title and the granted right, the latter right prevailed. This distinguished native title from other common law property rights to land.

It is true that the Crown has the power to expropriate property rights for its own use or to grant inconsistent rights to others: see Chapter 10. However, this requires an intention to expropriate and, normally, the payment of just compensation to the people whose property rights are taken. The mere grant of an inconsistent right would impair native title, but would not adversely affect other common law property rights. For example, in *O'Keefe v Malone* AC 365 and *O'Keefe v Williams* (1910) 11 CLR 171 (discussed at page 166), the Crown granted an estate to the plaintiff and then, by mistake, granted the same estate to the defendant. The second grant did not affect the first. The plaintiff, as holder of the first estate, had a right to possess the land and exclude the defendant from it.

The priority of inconsistent rights granted by the Crown depends on the order in which they are granted. At common law, native title does not enjoy this same priority. As the High Court said in *Western Australia v The Commonwealth* (1995) 183 CLR 373 at 439:

> "[A] grant cannot be superseded by a subsequent inconsistent grant made to another person. Nor can a right to use land, if granted validly by the Crown, be recalled prior to expiry unless the right is qualified by a power of recall contained in the terms of the grant or is conferred by statute. At common law, however, native title can be extinguished or impaired by a valid exercise of sovereign power inconsistent with the continued enjoyment or unimpaired enjoyment of native title."

Although property rights granted by the Crown are more durable than native title, this is not just because native title is not granted by the Crown. As discussed at page 224399, the Crown, as holder of radical title, has the power to grant property rights to land. Once that power is spent, it cannot be used again to grant inconsistent rights (unless the Crown expropriates the earlier right). Since native title existed when the British Crown first acquired sovereignty over Australia, the Crown had not yet exercised its power to grant rights to land subject to native title. It is the presence of that unexercised power which made native title fragile.

This last point is demonstrated by comparing native title with an estate acquired by adverse possession: see Chapter 8. Suppose the Crown granted a fee simple estate to Lionel and then Suzanne took possession of that land without Lionel's permission. After the limitation period expires (12 or 15 years), Suzanne holds a fee simple estate, which is similar to native title in two respects: the Crown has radical title to the land and the estate was not granted by the Crown. However, unlike native title, the Crown could not interfere with Suzanne's estate by granting inconsistent property rights. This is because the Crown has already used its radical title to grant a fee simple estate to Lionel and no longer has any power to grant further property rights to that land (without expropriation).

Racial Discrimination Act

When the *Racial Discrimination Act* 1975 (Cth) came into force, on 31 October 1975, native title became as durable as other common law property rights to land. As Brennan, Toohey, and Gaudron JJ said in *Mabo v Queensland* (1989) 166 CLR 186 at 218-219:

> "[I]f traditional native title was not extinguished before the *Racial Discrimination Act* came into force, a State law which seeks to extinguish it now will fail. It will fail because s 10(1) of the *Racial Discrimination Act* clothes holders of traditional native title who are of

the native ethnic group with the same immunity from legislative interference with their enjoyment of their human right to own and inherit property as it clothes other persons in the community."

Subsection 10(1) of the *Racial Discrimination Act* 1975 (Cth) states:

> "If, by reason of ... a law of the Commonwealth or of a State or Territory, persons of a particular race ... enjoy a right to a more limited extent than persons of another race, ... then, notwithstanding anything in that law, persons of the first-mentioned race ... shall, by force of this section, enjoy that right to the same extent as persons of that other race ..."

This protection applies to the "right to own property alone as well as in association with others", which is listed in Article 5 of the *International Convention on the Elimination of All Forms of Racial Discrimination*.

The Crown's use of its radical title to extinguish or diminish native title was unfairly discriminatory because native title was the only property right which could be adversely affected in this way and native title could be owned only by Aboriginal Australians and Torres Strait Islanders. Under the *Racial Discrimination Act*, the Crown is required to treat native title in the same manner as other property rights to land. Therefore, it cannot grant inconsistent rights without paying just compensation for what is, in effect, an expropriation of native title.

Although the *Racial Discrimination Act* is a Commonwealth statute and not a constitutional limit on the Crown's power, it prevails over inconsistent state law (by virtue of section 109 of the Constitution) and "binds the Crown in right of the Commonwealth, of each of the States, of the Northern Territory and of Norfolk Island": s 6. Therefore, after 31 October 1975, any Crown grant which interfered with native title, without paying just compensation, violated the *Racial Discrimination Act* and was invalid to the extent of the invalidity.

Native Title Act

The *Native Title Act* 1993 (Cth) was enacted for several different reasons. As discussed at page 230, it provides a mechanism for establishing the existence of native title. It also ensures that future dealings with land subject to native title will comply with the *Racial Discrimination Act* 1975 (Cth). In this part, we are concerned primarily with its effect on the priority of native title.

The *Native Title Act* provides a complete code for the priority of any native title that existed when it came into force. Section 11 states that "Native title is not able to be extinguished contrary to this Act." This is a form of special priority. It immunises native title from events that would destroy other property rights to land, such as adverse possession (see Chapter 8) or registration of inconsistent title (see Chapter 32). Native title can be impaired or extinguished, but only in compliance with the *Native Title Act*. Essentially, this means that governments must treat it with the same respect as other rights to land. They are allowed to expropriate native title if they follow the process set out in the Act and pay just compensation for their interference with it.

The *Native Title Act* organises actions that might adversely affect native title into three categories: past acts, intermediate period acts, and future acts.

Past acts include legislation enacted before 1 July 1993 and other government actions taken before 1 January 1994 that were "invalid to any extent" because of the existence of native title: s 228. Also included in this category is the subsequent exercise of rights granted before 1 January 1994, such as the exercise of an option to purchase or the renewal of a lease.

The existence of native title did not affect the government's power to act until the *Racial Discrimination Act* came into force. Therefore, past acts are those invalidated by the *Racial Discrimination Act*, because they adversely affected native title without properly expropriating it. This means that all past acts occurred after 31 October 1975.

Section 14 of the *Native Title Act* validates past acts of the Commonwealth government. This makes them legally effective, even though they contravened the *Racial Discrimination Act* when they occurred. The Commonwealth is required to compensate the holders of native title for the loss or impairment of their native title as a result of this validation of its past acts: ss 17, 18.

Section 15 describes the effect of validation on native title. Past acts are organised into four categories (A, B, C, and D, as defined by sections 229-232). Category A past acts extinguish native title completely. These are grants of freehold estates, grants of commercial, agricultural, pastoral, or residential leases, and the use of land for public works. Category B past acts are other types of leases, other than mining leases. These leases extinguish native title only to the extent that they are inconsistent with it. Category C past acts are mining leases and category D consists of all past acts that do not belong in the other three categories. Past acts in categories C and D take priority over native title, but do not extinguish it.

The validation of past acts gives them priority over native title, thus reversing the priority created by the *Racial Discrimination Act*. This means that validated past acts take priority over native title to the extent of any inconsistency between them. However, native title may be wholly extinguished even though it is only partially inconsistent with a past act. This is because life estates and leases are included in category A. For example, as discussed in Chapter 16, a pastoral lease might not give the tenant a right to possession. Although it was inconsistent with native title (or it would not be a past act), the inconsistency may be relatively minor. Nevertheless, the lease is validated and native title is wholly extinguished: ss 15, 237A.

States and territories are permitted to validate their past acts and, if they choose to do so, must compensate the holders of the native title adversely affected by the validation: ss 19, 20. Every state and territory, except Tasmania, has passed legislation validating past acts: *Native Title Act* 1994 (ACT); *Native Title (New South Wales) Act* 1994 (NSW); *Validation of Titles and Actions Act* 1994 (NT), *Native Title (Queensland) Act* 1993 (Qld); *Native Title (South Australia) Act* 1994 (SA); *Land Titles Validation Act* 1994 (Vic); and *Titles Validation Act* 1995 (WA).

Intermediate period acts are acts that took place between 1 January 1994 and 23 December 1996 (the day the *Wik* case was decided) and were invalid because of the existence of native title: s 232A. Before *Wik*, it was widely believed that pastoral leases were wholly inconsistent with native title, because they conferred rights to exclusive possession of land. Therefore, governments assumed that native title had been extinguished by pastoral leases granted before 1 January 1994 (either because they were validly granted before 31 October 1975 or because they contravened the *Racial Discrimination Act* and had been validated as past acts).

This incorrect assumption about the effect of a pastoral lease meant that governments dealt with land without realising that it was subject to native title. Those actions were invalid because they failed to meet the requirements in the *Native Title Act* 1993 (Cth) for future acts affecting native title. The *Native Title Amendment Act* 1998 (Cth) dealt with this problem by creating a new category of intermediate period acts. To qualify as an intermediate period act, it must relate to land that had previously been subject to an act (such as the grant of a lease) that created the false impression that native title had been extinguished.

Section 22A of the *Native Title Act* 1993 (Cth) validates the Commonwealth's intermediate period acts and the holders of native title affected by that validation are entitled to compensation. Section 22F permits states and territories to validate their intermediate period acts on the same basis and several of the state validation statutes listed above have been amended accordingly.

Validation of an intermediate period act has the same effect on native title as validation of a past act, with one important difference. The only agricultural and pastoral leases classified as category A intermediate period acts (which completely extinguish native title) are those which give the tenant a right to exclusive possession: s 232B. Other agricultural and pastoral leases (called non-exclusive leases) are category B intermediate period acts and only extinguish native title to the extent of any inconsistency: s 22B.

The category of **future acts** includes legislation enacted after 30 June 1993 and other acts taking place after 31 December 1993, but does not include past acts or legislation that validates past or intermediate period acts: s 233. Future acts may be valid or invalid (unlike past and intermediate period acts, which consist only of acts invalidated by the existence of native title). A future act can be an act which validly affects native title (other than validating legislation) or an act invalidated by the existence of native title (other than an past act).

A future act is valid only if done in compliance with the *Native Title Act* 1993 (Cth). That statute provides a code for dealing with land subject to native title. It creates a number of procedural safeguards, including rights to notice, negotiation, and arbitration. Generally speaking, future acts extinguish or impair native title only to the extent that they are inconsistent with it. If native title is impaired or extinguished by a future act, the government responsible for that act is liable to pay compensation.

Of course, the question whether a proposed dealing with land is a future act, that must comply with the *Native Title Act*, depends on whether that land is still subject to native title. This depends on previous dealings with that land and their legal effect. If native title never existed or was extinguished before 31 October 1975, the *Native Title Act* has no application (beyond regulating the process for determining whether native title exists, as discussed in Chapter 19). If native title survived past that date, it may have been extinguished later by the validation of a category A past act or category A intermediate period act. These questions may involve complex issues of fact and law.

Chapter Twenty-Nine

PRIORITY OF EQUITABLE PROPERTY RIGHTS

Equitable property rights are less durable than legal property rights. There are two main reasons for this. First and most importantly, all equitable property rights are subject to the defence of *bona fide* purchase, while most legal property rights are not. Secondly, a failure to protect equitable property rights can cause a loss of priority. In contrast, the carelessness of a legal owner normally does not affect the priority of her or his legal rights.

This chapter is divided into five main parts. The first looks at the nature of equitable property rights to understand why they are less durable than legal property rights. Second is a discussion of the defence of *bona fide* purchase for value without notice, while the third part looks at the meaning of notice. The fourth part deals with priorities between competing equitable property rights and the fifth provides a summary of the rules used to resolve priority disputes.

Nature of Equitable Property Rights

The priority of equitable property rights cannot be understood properly unless the nature of those rights is understood. As discussed in Chapter 13, equitable property rights are not carved out of legal rights, but imposed on the holders of rights. For example, if I hold a legal fee simple estate in trust for you, you have the entire beneficial use and enjoyment of the estate and I have only bare legal title and an onerous obligation to perform the trust. However, I am the sole legal owner of the estate, subject to an equitable obligation to let you have the beneficial use and enjoyment of my legal property right.

This is why the primary principle which determines the priorities of legal property rights, *nemo dat quod non habet*, does not have the same effect on equitable property rights. If I transfer my legal fee simple estate (which I hold in trust for you) to my friend, Simone, she gets everything I had to give: the entire legal fee simple estate. She does not receive a mere shell of the estate, with the equitable fee simple carved out of it. The important question is whether she is under an equitable obligation to carry out the trust.

In *Pilcher v Rawlins* (1872) 7 Ch App 259, an express trustee breached his trust by transferring trust property to a friend, who mortgaged it for £10,000. The mortgagees were *bona fide* purchasers without notice of the trust and, therefore, their mortgage had priority over the trust. This was because a court of equity had no reason to interfere with their legal title. James LJ said (at 268-269):

> "[A] purchaser's plea of purchase for valuable consideration without notice is an absolute, unqualified, unanswerable defence, and an unanswerable plea to the jurisdiction of this Court. Such a purchaser, when he has once put in that plea, may be interrogated and tested to any extent as to the valuable consideration which he has given in order to shew the *bona fides* or *mala fides* of his purchase, and also the presence or the absence of notice; but when once he has gone through that ordeal, and has satisfied the terms of the plea of purchase for valuable consideration without notice, then, according to my judgment, this Court has no jurisdiction whatever to do anything more than to let him depart in possession of that legal estate, that legal right, that legal advantage which he has obtained, whatever it may be."

The *nemo dat* principle did not assist the beneficiaries of the trust, because their trustee had legal title and the power to transfer it to his friend, who had the power to mortgage it (even though that was a breach of trust). The essential question was whether the mortgagees were entitled to enjoy the normal benefits of their legal property right or would be compelled by a court of equity to use it for the benefit of the trust beneficiaries. Since the mortgagees were *bona fide* purchasers, there was no reason to interfere with their legal rights.

Although the *nemo dat* principle is seldom mentioned in priority disputes involving equitable property rights, it does apply to all property rights. A person cannot give more than he or she has, regardless of whether it is legal or equitable.

As Lord Westbury C said, in *Phillips v Phillips* (1862) 45 ER 1164 at 1166:

> "I take it to be a clear proposition that every conveyance of an equitable interest is an innocent conveyance, that is to say, the grant of a person entitled merely in equity passes only that which he is justly entitled to and no more."

For example, in *Northern Counties of England Fire Insurance Co v Whipp* (1884) 26 Ch D 482 (discussed in the previous chapter), the defendant thought she had received a legal mortgage. However, the mortgagor had already mortgaged his land to the plaintiff and had only the equitable ownership of the land (an equity of redemption, discussed in Chapter 14). The mortgagor could not give the defendant a legal property right because he no longer had one to give. Therefore, the defendant received only an equitable mortgage of his equitable ownership.

The *nemo dat* principle will help determine the nature of the property rights held by each party to a priority dispute. However, it does not affect the outcome of many priority disputes involving equitable property rights. The owner of a legal property right, which is subject to an equitable property right, has the power to create conflicting legal or equitable property rights. If that occurs, it is necessary to use rules created by courts of equity to determine the priority of those conflicting rights.

This principle is demonstrated by the difference between a legal lease and an equitable lease. Suppose that I want to lease my house to you. As discussed in Chapter 21, I could create a legal lease (by executing a deed of lease or registering a lease) or an equitable lease (by making a contract to grant a lease). In either case, you obtain a leasehold estate. However, a legal lease is carved out of my fee simple: my legal right to possess the house has been transferred to you for a term of years. If I transfer the fee simple, the new owners can obtain only what I had, which is a fee simple estate with a leasehold estate already carved out of it.

In contrast, an equitable lease is impressed on the fee simple: I still have the right to possession at law, but am required by the rules of equity to use that right for your benefit for a term of years. If I transfer the fee simple, the new owners will obtain my legal right to possession and the question will be whether they are also required to use it for your benefit for the remainder of your equitable lease. This depends on whether they are *bona fide* purchasers.

Bona Fide Purchase

Effect of the Defence

The defence of *bona fide* purchase destroys or diminishes equitable property rights, leaving the purchasers to enjoy their legal property rights, free from interference by a court of equity. The effect on an equitable property right depends on the extent of its inconsistency with the new legal right. For example, if I held a fee simple estate in trust for you and sold that estate to a *bona fide* purchaser, the trust would be destroyed since it is wholly inconsistent with the purchaser's right to the full use and enjoyment of the land for an indefinite period of time. However, if I leased or mortgaged the estate to a *bona fide* purchaser, your trust would survive, subject to the rights of the tenant or mortgagee.

Once an equitable property right is destroyed or diminished by the defence of *bona fide* purchase, it does not revive (with one exception, discussed below). This is true even if the purchasers later discover that the sale was a dishonest breach of trust, which caused a great loss to the trust beneficiaries. They are free to continue to use and enjoy their legal property right and can sell that right to other people who know about the breach of trust. Otherwise, the defence of *bona fide* purchase would fail to protect them adequately. A publicised breach of trust would destroy the market value of the property if the *bona fide* purchasers were unable to sell it free of the trust.

The exception to this rule occurs when property is transferred back to the trustees who wrongly caused the destruction of their trust (or to anyone who dishonestly helped them breach their trust). The trust, which was destroyed by the defence of *bona fide* purchase, revives. This prevents trustees from ridding themselves of equitable property rights by selling the trust property to *bona fide* purchasers and repurchasing it (themselves or with the help of dishonest friends).

Elements of the Defence

The defence of *bona fide* purchase consists of four different elements: (1) *bona fide*, (2) purchase, (3) for value, and (4) without notice. It is not entirely clear who bears the onus of proving these elements. Since *bona fide* purchase is a defence to a claim to enforce an equitable property right, it might be assumed that the purchaser bears the burden of establishing the defence. This seems to be the case with regard to property rights to land. In *Re Nisbet & Potts' Contract* [1906] 1 Ch 386 at 403 (concerning notice of a restrictive covenant), Collins MR said that "the burden is upon the person who takes the land to shew that he has acquired it under such conditions as to defeat the right as against him, namely, that he has acquired it for value and without notice".

With regard to banks having notice of trusts, the rule seems to be different. If a bank has received money, which is deposited or withdrawn in breach of trust, and it is sued over its involvement in the breach of trust, the plaintiff bears the onus of showing that the bank acted in bad faith or with notice of the trust: *Thomson v Clydesdale Bank Ltd* [1893] AC 282; *Union Bank of Australia Ltd v Murray-Aynsley* [1898] AC 693.

Bona Fide

Bona fide means "good faith". Some people question whether this element has any separate work to do. Can a person who satisfies the other elements of the defence, by purchasing for value without notice of an existing equitable property right, be acting in bad faith? This might be the case if the purchase was part of a criminal or other illegal enterprise. Even though the purchasers paid value and knew nothing of the existing equitable property right, a court of equity may say that they lacked the good faith necessary to claim the defence: see *Midland Bank Trust Co Ltd v Green* [1981] AC 513 at 528. Normally, however, this requirement is satisfied by proof of the other elements of the defence.

Purchase

It may seem that requiring both "purchase" and "for value" is redundant. However, both have separate work to do and are necessary. "Purchase" is a legal term of art. At one time, it was used to refer to the acquisition of legal title other than by inheritance. In other words, property was either inherited or purchased. It now refers to the acquisition of legal title. Someone who acquires an equitable property right cannot claim the defence.

For Value

"For value" means that the purchasers gave valuable consideration, in money or money's worth, in exchange for the purchased property right.

At one time, marriage was sufficiently valuable consideration for this purpose. It is not necessary that the purchasers paid full market value for the property. People who make great deals and obtain property for bargain prices can still claim the defence. If the consideration is very low in relation to the true market value of the property, this may raise an inference that the purchasers had notice of the conflicting equitable property right or lacked good faith. It could also indicate that the transaction was part sale and part gift.

Without Notice

Did the purchasers have notice of the equitable property right? This is the issue that is most often contested and most likely to defeat the defence. It is important to note that the requirement is absence of notice rather than absence of knowledge. Even if the purchasers did not know about the inconsistent right, they will have notice of it if they should have known about it. Notice is relevant to a number of priority issues and is explored in some detail below.

For the defence of *bona fide* purchase, the important issue is whether the purchasers had notice of a conflicting equitable property right when they acquired their legal property right. The relevant time is when legal title passed to the purchasers. However, there is an exception. If they acquired an equitable property right in good faith, for value, and without notice of the inconsistent right, they can later replace it with the equivalent legal property right and use the defence of *bona fide* purchase, even though they acquired notice of the inconsistent right before getting the legal right: *Blackwood v London Chartered Bank of Australia* (1874) LR 5 PC 92 at 111.

This is an odd rule because the purchasers did not have priority when they held equitable title (since an older equitable right usually takes priority over a newer equitable right, as discussed below). They obtained priority only by getting legal title and becoming *bona fide* purchasers, and yet they did not meet the normal requirement of absence of notice. Nevertheless, it is an established rule of equity that an equitable owner, who discovers a prior equitable property right, may be able to obtain priority over it by getting legal title. As Lindley LJ said, in *Bailey v Barnes* [1894] 1 Ch 25 at 36:

> "Equitable owners ... may struggle for the legal estate, and he who obtains it, having both law and equity on his side, is in a better position than he who has equity only. The reasoning is technical and not satisfactory; but, as long ago as 1728, the law was judicially declared to be well settled and only alterable by Act of Parliament."

Legal title obtained in this way is sometimes called the *tabulam in naufragio*, meaning "the plank in the shipwreck". The metaphor was used to describe a situation in which there were two or more equitable mortgagees and the mortgaged assets were insufficient to pay everyone. According to Megarry and Wade, *The Law of Real Property* (5th ed, 1984) p 1006:

"The insufficiency of the security was the 'shipwreck' and the legal estate was the 'plank' which any equitable mortgagee might seize without concern for the others."

So long as the equitable mortgage was obtained in good faith, for value, and without notice of prior equitable mortgages, the mortgagee was entitled to the defence of *bona fide* purchase if he or she could obtain a legal mortgage. The rule is not limited to mortgages, but can apply to any equitable property rights. However, it cannot be used by someone who acquires legal title with notice that the transfer is a breach of trust: *Mumford v Stohwasser* (1874) LR 18 Equity 556.

Notice

When we ask whether somebody had notice of something, we are asking a specific question: did that person have notice of a particular fact at a particular time? That depends on why we are asking. We cannot frame the specific question until we know why it matters. If notice is relevant in a priority dispute, we want to know whether a person had notice of an existing property right when he or she acquired a conflicting property right.

There are three kinds of notice: actual, constructive, and imputed.

Actual Notice

A person has actual notice of something if it is brought to her or his attention at some point. Actual notice includes, but is not limited to, knowledge. For example, in *Re Montagu's Settlement Trusts* [1987] Ch 264, the tenth Duke of Manchester was informed of the terms of a trust by his solicitors. Years later, he received and sold trust assets in breach of that trust. Although he knew the terms of the trust at one point, he had forgotten them and, therefore, did not have knowledge of the breach of trust. As Vinelott J said, in *Eagle Trust plc v SBC Securities Ltd* [1993] 1 WLR 484 at 494:

> "A man may have actual notice of a fact and yet not know it. He may have been supplied in the course of a conveyancing transaction with a document and so have actual notice of its content, but he may not in fact have read it; or he may have read it some time ago and have forgotten its content."

A warning that a property right might exist is actual notice of that right. For example, suppose you want to acquire a right to land, search the land titles register, and discover a **caveat**. As discussed at page 481, a person claiming an equitable property right to land in a Torrens system can protect that right by lodging a caveat on the title. Finding the caveat gives you actual notice of the claimed right. However, you still do not know if the caveator really does have the property right he or she claims.

Constructive Notice

As the adjective implies, constructive notice is not actual notice. It is a situation in which someone is treated as if he or she had notice. People have constructive notice of things they would have discovered if they had performed the searches that a reasonable person would have performed in the circumstances. What is reasonable depends on two main factors:

1) .....the nature of the transaction; and
2) .....the facts discovered during that transaction.

Nature of the Transaction

The kinds of searches and the extent of the searches performed by a reasonable buyer (or tenant, mortgagee, etc) will depend on the value and nature of the property rights involved. The purchase of a fee simple estate calls for more diligence than the lease of a vacation house for two weeks. People take more care when they charter a ship than when they hire a car. If buyers fail to perform the usual title searches performed by a reasonable person in that situation, and those searches would have uncovered a property right, they will have constructive notice of that right.

In *Joseph v Lyons* (1884) 15 QBD 280, the plaintiff had an equitable charge on Manning's jewellery. Manning pledged some of that jewellery to the defendant pawnbroker for a loan of £70. The defendant's legal security right had priority over the plaintiff's equitable security right, because the defendant was a *bona fide* purchaser. He had no knowledge or actual notice of the plaintiff's right. Although he would have discovered it if he had searched the register of bills of sale, most pawnbrokers did not search that register when accepting a pledge. Since a reasonable pawnbroker would not have discovered the plaintiff's mortgage, the defendant did not have constructive notice of that right.

The conduct of reasonable buyers is affected by statute, especially when the transaction concerns property rights to land. If the land is registered in a Torrens system, reasonable buyers will rarely explore the history of the title to the land they are buying. As discussed at page 463, Torrens statutes protect buyers from the effects of notice. In most cases, reasonable buyers will be content with a search of the current state of the title, any registered documents which affect the title (such as a lease, easement, or restrictive covenant), the rights of any tenants in possession of the land, and incidental matters affecting the land (such as the local zoning laws, environmental hazards, property taxes, and utilities).

Buyers of land outside the Torrens system need to trace the history of their seller's title to ensure that they will obtain good title, which is not adversely affecting by conflicting property rights they are unwilling to accept. If buyers were expected to trace title back to the original Crown grant, the legal costs of the purchase could be very expensive and out of proportion to the value of the property rights acquired. Also, it might be impossible for the seller to produce the entire chain of documents needed for that investigation.

To deal with this problem, every state (except South Australia) has a statutory definition of the period of **commencement of title**. That period is 30 years, except in Tasmania, where it is 20 years: *Conveyancing and Law of Property Act* 1884 (Tas), s 35. These definitions accomplish two things. First, they limit the seller's obligation to provide title documents to the buyer. For example, section 44 of the *Property Law Act* 1958 (Vic) states:

> "Thirty years shall be the period of commencement of title which a purchaser of land may require instead of an earlier title commencing with the Crown grant."

A seller may need to produce documents that are more than 30 years old, if they are needed to trace title back to the beginning of the commencement period. For example, suppose that I bought (non-Torrens) land in Victoria from Murray 12 years ago and sold it to you. You would need the transfer document which proves that I acquired the estate I am selling to you. However, that document is only 12 years old and you need to trace title back 30 years. If Murray acquired the land 40 years ago, I would need produce the document which transferred title to him, even though it was made before the period for commencement of title.

Secondly, the statutory definition of a period for commencement of title protects purchasers from constructive notice of things they would have discovered if they had searched title to an earlier date. For example, section 237 of the *Property Law Act* 1974 (Qld) states:

> "A purchaser shall not be deemed to be or ever to have been affected with notice of any matter or thing of which, if the purchaser had investigated the title or made enquiries in regard to matters prior to the period of commencement of title fixed by this Act, or by any other statute, or by any rule of law, the purchaser might have had notice, unless the purchaser actually makes such investigation or enquiries."

Facts Discovered During the Transaction

If buyers receive information that would cause a reasonable person to conduct additional searches, they have constructive notice of any rights that would be discovered by those searches. A buyer, who has reason to suspect the possible existence of inconsistent rights, cannot safely close her or his eyes and rely on the fact that all the standard searches have been made.

Jared v Clements [1902] 2 Ch 399 was a case involving actual rather than constructive notice. However, it demonstrates what can happen when a buyer uncovers information that would not have been discovered by the usual searches. The plaintiff had an equitable mortgage on Taylor's leasehold estate. Taylor became bankrupt for a year and later sold his estate to the defendant. Taylor's solicitor, Parr, failed to disclose the plaintiff's mortgage when he prepared a list of title documents for the defendant's solicitors. However, they discovered it when they searched the bankruptcy files. Parr then promised to pay off the mortgage and the sale was completed. Unfortunately, he forged a discharge of the mortgage and absconded with the money instead.

As Byrne J said (at 403), if the defendant's solicitors had not searched the bankruptcy files, "the mortgage would probably never have been disclosed, and the purchaser could then have claimed to be a purchaser for value without notice". Since that was not a typical search, the defendant would not have had constructive notice of the mortgage. However, the defendant could not be a *bona fide* purchaser once he received actual notice of it.

Although *Jared v Clements* concerned actual notice, the acquisition of information can also expand a purchaser's constructive notice. If certain information would cause reasonable buyers to conduct an unusual search, then a purchaser with that information will have constructive notice of anything that would be discovered by that search. For example, if reasonable buyers would search the bankruptcy files if they discovered that the seller had recently been bankrupt, then a buyer with that knowledge would have constructive notice of the information contained in those files.

Failure to Search

A buyer is not negligent because he or she fails to conduct the searches that a reasonable buyer would make. There is no duty to search and no wrong is committed by failing to search. The conduct of a reasonable buyer is relevant only to the question of notice. It does not otherwise affect a buyer's entitlement to the defence of *bona fide* purchase.

Buyers are free to dispense with the normal searches and trust the seller's promise to transfer good title. They will take title subject to any property rights that would have been discovered by the normal searches. However, they may be happy to take that risk (especially if the seller is trustworthy and able to pay compensation for breach of the contract of sale).

The failure to search does not mean that a buyer has notice of all possible rights to the purchased asset. The buyer has constructive notice of the rights that would have been discovered by the searches made by a reasonable buyer in the circumstances. If a right would not have been discovered by a reasonable buyer, it will not affect an unreasonable buyer.

In *Smith v Jones* [1954] 1 WLR 1089, Jones bought a farm at an auction. He knew that Smith had leased the farm and inspected the tenancy agreement before the sale. Later, Smith claimed that the written tenancy agreement did not reflect the actual agreement between him and his original landlord. He claimed that he had an equitable right to rectify the lease (see page 325) and that Jones was bound by that right. Upjohn J rejected Smith's claim and said (at 1093) that, in any event, it "was barred by the plea of bona fide purchaser of value without notice".

A buyer of land has constructive notice of the rights of a tenant in possession of that land. As the Privy Council advised, in *Barnhart v Greenshields* (1853) 14 ER 204 at 209:

> "[T]he possession of the tenant is notice that he has some interest in the land, and ... a purchaser having notice of that fact, is bound, according to the ordinary rule, either to inquire what that interest is, or to give effect to it, whatever it may be."

Therefore, Jones had constructive notice of any rights that he would have discovered through a proper inquiry into Smith's rights as a tenant. However, when Jones bought the farm, Smith was unaware of the mistake in the written tenancy agreement and, if asked, would have said that it correctly represented his rights. Since Jones would not have discovered Smith's right to rectification, even if he had made the proper inquiries, he did not have constructive notice of it. His failure to make those inquiries did not affect his status as a *bona fide* purchaser.

Imputed Notice

You have imputed notice of something when someone else has notice of it and you are treated as having the same notice. In other words, the other person's notice is imputed to you. Generally speaking, an agent's notice is imputed to her or his principal, unless the agent is acting fraudulently with the intention to harm the principal. For example, a solicitor's notice is imputed to her or his clients, a business partner's notice is imputed to her or his fellow partners, and a corporation is imputed to have the same notice as its directors and officers.

Notice is imputed because of the agency relationship between the parties and not because of the actual communication between them. For example, if you hire a solicitor to complete a purchase of land, and he or she receives notice of a restrictive covenant affecting that land, that notice will be imputed to you. You cannot claim to be a *bona fide* purchaser, without notice of the covenant, even if the solicitor failed to report it to you.

Imputed notice may be based on actual or constructive notice. For example, it does not matter whether your solicitor has actual or constructive notice of an equitable property right. In either case, that notice will be imputed to you.

Of course, solicitors may deal with many transactions for many different clients over many years. While working for each client, he or she may receive notice of equitable property rights. If that notice was imputed to all of the solicitor's clients from then on, he or she would soon be out of a job. To deal with this problem, most jurisdictions have a statute that restricts imputed notice to notice acquired by a purchaser's agent "in the same transaction with respect to which a question of notice to the purchaser arises": *Law of Property Act* 1936 (SA), s 117.

These statutes solve the problem (faced by solicitors and others) that arises when one agent acts for many principals. They also solve the problem of one principal with many agents. A large corporation may employ many different officers, managers, solicitors, and other agents to acquire property rights. The corporation will have imputed notice of everything its agents know or ought to know. If imputed notice was not restricted by statute to notice acquired by an agent in the same transaction, notice acquired by an agent during one transaction could adversely affect the priority of property rights being acquired by the corporation in unrelated transactions involving other agents.

The statutory restriction on imputed notice might not help trustees who administer many different trusts for many different beneficiaries (although it will help a trustee company that employs managers and other agents). Trustees are not agents for their beneficiaries and their notice is not imputed to their beneficiaries. However, many questions of priority depend on whether the trustees had notice of conflicting property rights. The priority of property rights acquired for a trust might be adversely affected by notice that a trustee had acquired while managing an unrelated trust. Most states provide a statutory solution to this problem. For example, section 68 of the *Trustees Act* 1962 (WA) states:

> "A trustee acting for the purposes of more than one trust shall not, in the absence of fraud, be affected by notice of any instrument, matter, fact or thing in relation to any particular trust, if he has obtained notice thereof merely by reason of his acting or having acted for the purposes of another trust."

Essentially, the statute divides the mind of a trustee into separate compartments for each of the trusts being administered. A trustee could have actual knowledge of a fact for one trust and, at the same time, have no notice of that fact for another trust.

Knowledge and Notice

With this discussion of the three types of notice, it is easy to lose sight of the important distinction between knowledge and notice. Very simply, knowledge is what a person knows, while notice is what a person ought to know. In many situations, there will be no need to draw a distinction between the two. For example, the defence of *bona fide* purchase is not available to someone who knew or ought to have known about the equitable property right in dispute.

In some situations, the distinction between knowledge and notice will be very important. For example, if I receive assets knowing that they were transferred to me in breach of trust, I have acted dishonestly. I am guilty of wrongly assisting that breach of trust and may be liable to compensate the trust beneficiaries for losses caused by that breach. However, if I receive those assets merely with notice of the breach of trust, I am probably not dishonest, but merely careless. Although I am not a *bona fide* purchaser, I am not a wrongdoer.

Generally speaking, courts prefer to deal with cases on the basis of notice, rather than knowledge, whenever the distinction is irrelevant. A conclusion that someone ought to have known better is not a statement about her or his honesty. Lawyers tend to avoid allegations of actual knowledge (and the inference of dishonesty) unless liability depends on that fact.

The distinction between knowledge and notice does not correspond precisely to the distinction between dishonesty and carelessness. It is possible for a person to be dishonest even though he or she does not have knowledge of a breach of trust or other wrong. There are cases where a person suspects the truth and chooses not to investigate. As Tadgell JA, in *Macquarie Bank Ltd v Sixty-Fourth Throne Pty Ltd* [1998] 3 VR 133 at 143:

> "[T]o abstain deliberately from reasonable enquiry for fear of what the enquiry will reveal, to choose to shut one's eyes to the obvious — to assume a state of 'wilful blindness' — or otherwise to generate a state of contrived ignorance, may of course be dishonest."

If a person is wilfully blind, notice can amount to dishonesty. Some courts refer to this state of mind as "constructive knowledge" to distinguish it from notice. The important feature, which amounts to dishonesty, is that the person deliberately refrained from making inquiries for the purpose of avoiding knowledge. As Tadgell JA said (at 146), "wilful blindness connotes a form of designed or calculated ignorance". In contrast, honest people have notice of things because they carelessly failed to do the searches expected of a reasonable person in that situation.

Competing Equitable Property Rights

When an older equitable property right conflicts with a newer legal property right, the resolution of the dispute will depend on whether the holder of the newer right is a *bona fide* purchaser for value, without notice of the older right. However, this defence does not apply to a conflict between two equitable property rights. The holder of the newer right does not have legal title and cannot claim to be a purchaser (in the technical sense), even if he or she acquired the equitable right in good faith, for value, and without notice of the older right. As discussed below, these same factors are relevant, but there is no defence of *bona fide* purchase.

First in Time

The starting point in a competition between two equitable property rights is the equitable maxim, *qui prior est tempore potior est jure* (he or she who is first in point of time is preferred in law). The older equitable right has priority over the newer equitable right, unless some other factor causes the older right to be postponed to the newer right (as discussed below).

In *Rice v Rice* (1854) 61 ER 646 at 648, Kindersley VC said that, "in a contest between persons having only equitable interests, priority of time is the ground of preference last resorted to". In other words, he regarded the order of creation as a factor to be used only if competing rights "are *in all other respects* equal". However, this was overruled by higher courts. As Lord Wright advised, in *Abigail v Lapin* [1934] AC 491 at 504:

> "The opinion of the Vice-Chancellor no doubt has not been approved in so far as he says that priority in time is only taken as the test where the equities are otherwise equal: it is now clearly established that prima facie priority in time will decide the matter unless, as laid down by Lord Cairns LC in *Shropshire Union Rys and Canal Co v The Queen* [(1875) LR 7 HL 496], that which is relied on to take away the pre-existing equitable title can be shown to be something tangible and distinct having grave and strong effect to accomplish the purpose."

The person who holds the older right has a vested property right and a court should not interfere with that right without a good reason.

Therefore, two competing equitable property rights take priority according to the order in which they were created, unless there is some substantial reason for changing that priority.

Postponing the Older Right

Reasons for Postponing the Older Right

In some situations, an older equitable right will be postponed to a newer equitable right. Generally speaking, this occurs when the holder of the older right has failed to protect it properly and has thereby made it easier for the legal owner of the asset to deal with it as if that equitable right did not exist. The older right is postponed because:

1) .....the newer right was acquired in the belief that the older right did not exist; and
2) .....the holder of the older right contributed to that belief in some way.

This basis for reversing the priority of two equitable property rights is similar to estoppel: see Chapter 23.

Rice v Rice (1854) 61 ER 646, provides a good example. Land was sold and the buyer received legal title and the title documents, including a statement that the purchase price had been paid in full. In fact, he still owed part of the purchase price to the sellers. The buyer then deposited the title deeds with a lender as security for a loan. The sellers had an equitable vendors' lien to secure payment of the purchase price and the lender had an equitable mortgage to security payment of the loan: see Chapter 21.

The buyer's legal title was subject to two equitable security rights. The vendors' lien arose first and would have taken priority over the equitable mortgage, except for one factor. By giving the buyer the title documents and a written statement that the full purchase price had been paid, the sellers created the impression that their vendors' lien did not exist. As Kindersley VC said (at 650), "they voluntarily armed the purchaser with the means of dealing with the estate as the absolute legal and equitable owner, free from every shadow of incumbrance or adverse equity". The lender relied on that false belief when he accepted an equitable mortgage as security for the loan. Therefore, the vendors' lien was postponed to the mortgage.

Reasons for Not Postponing the Older Right

There are two situations in which an older equitable property right will never be postponed to a newer equitable property right:

1) .....when the newer right is acquired with notice of the older right; and
2) .....when the newer right is acquired as a gift.

Notice

If the holders of the newer right had knowledge of the older right, they did not rely on a belief that the older right did not exist. If they had notice of the older right, they would have discovered it if they had made the proper searches. Either way, the holder of the older right was not responsible for misleading them and there is no reason to postpone the older right to the newer right: see *Moffett v Dillon* [1999] 2 VR 480.

Gifts

The donee of a gift cannot complain if it turns out to be less valuable than anticipated. For example, suppose that you became a beneficiary of a trust created by a will or family trust settlement. You then discovered that the trust assets are subject to an older equitable mortgage and, therefore, your share of the trust is much less valuable than you thought. If your share was a gift, you are not harmed by the existence of that mortgage. You are still better off than you would be without the trust. There is no reason to interfere with the property rights of the equitable mortgagee to increase the value of the gift to you.

If the newer of two equitable property rights is received as a gift, it will never gain priority over the older right. However, it does not matter whether the older right was a gift. The older right is a vested property right, created properly without infringing on the property rights of others. Whether received as a gift or in exchange for value, it is entitled to the same protection from interference as other property rights of the same kind. When the newer, inconsistent right is created, the question arises: is there a reason to postpone the older right to the newer right? In other words, should a court destroy or diminish the older right for the benefit of the holders of the newer right? The fact that the older right was received as a gift is not relevant to this issue.

Similarity to Bona Fide Purchase

An older equitable property right will not be postponed to a newer one, unless the newer right was acquired in good faith, for value, and without notice of the older right. This looks a lot like the defence of *bona fide* purchase. However, these factors are not elements of a defence, but the minimum conditions needed for making a claim that the prior equitable right should be postponed. There must be some additional reason for postponing the older right.

Normally, in a contest between two equitable property rights, the older right will not be postponed to the newer right unless the holder of the older right has done something to cause the holder of the newer right to believe that the older right did not exist. In contrast, if the newer property right is legal, its holder can use the defence of *bona fide* purchase to obtain priority. That defence does not depend on fault. An equitable property right can be destroyed by the defence of *bona fide* purchase even though its holder has done everything expected of a reasonable owner in the circumstances.

Two kinds of equitable property rights are treated differently than the rest: the interests of beneficiaries under express trusts and "mere equities". The former are less likely to be postponed to subsequent equitable property rights and the latter are more likely to be.

Express Trusts

Generally speaking, the rights of beneficiaries of express trusts are not postponed to newer equitable rights, even if the beneficiaries take no steps to protect their interests. For this reason, the equitable ownership created by an express trust is more durable than other equitable property rights. The trust might be postponed if the beneficiaries took positive steps to mislead others to believe that it did not exist. However, it will not be postponed just because they carelessly failed to protect their rights: *Shropshire Union Railways and Canal Co v The Queen* (1875) LR 7 HL 496 at 506-507; *Abigail v Lapin* [1934] AC 491 at 505.

This difference in durability can be explained by the relationship between express trustees and their beneficiaries. Those trustees have onerous equitable obligations to look after the interests of their beneficiaries. When dealing with trust assets, they must observe a high standard of care and serve the beneficiaries loyally. The beneficiaries are entitled to rely on the trustees to look after their best interests and are not blamed for failing to protect themselves from a breach of trust.

Other equitable property rights do not involve the same duties of loyalty and care. For example, as discussed in Chapter 21, the seller of land holds it on constructive trust for the buyer and, during the transaction, vendors' and purchasers' liens may arise to secure payment or refund of the purchase price. Although the parties must obey the contract and deal with each other in good faith, they are dealing at arms length. One party is not obliged to look after the best interests of the other party. They are both expected to protect their own interests and risk losing the priority of their equitable property rights if they fail to take steps to protect them adequately. The same is true of other equitable property rights, such as equitable leases and mortgages and restrictive covenants.

It should be noted that this preferential treatment is accorded only to the beneficiaries of express trusts. Interests arising under constructive or resulting trusts are usually treated like other equitable property rights. This is because most constructive and resulting trustees have not undertaken the onerous duties of care and loyalty expected of express trustees.

Mere Equities

While express trusts are more durable than average, some equitable property rights are less durable than average. They are called "mere equities" and are always postponed to newer equitable property rights acquired for value, in good faith, and without notice of them. Unlike other equitable property rights, postponement of a mere equity does not depend on the conduct of the right holder. Mere equities are routinely postponed to subsequent equitable property rights in the same way that all equitable property rights are subject to the defence of *bona fide* purchase.

This area of law is complicated by the fact that the phrase "mere equity" has no clearly accepted meaning. Three issues are discussed here:

1) .....what are mere equities;
2) .....what priority do they have; and
3) .....why are some property rights classified as mere equities?

What are Mere Equities?

When used to describe a right, the term "mere equity" tells us only that it is equitable. It does not indicate whether the right is personal or property nor does it provide any other clues about its nature.

In "Property and Unjust Enrichment: Categorical Truths" [1997] *New Zealand Law Review* 623 at 638, Peter Birks described it as a "horribly evasive phrase" and noted that, "No one has yet had the nerve to speak of 'a mere common law'."

"Mere equity" has (at least) two distinct meanings. First, it is often used to describe equitable personal rights. On those occasions, the adjective "mere" is used to indicate that the right is only personal and not property. Secondly, it is also used to describe equitable property rights which are less durable than most. In that context, the adjective indicates that the right is less deserving of protection than other equitable property rights. We are concerned here with mere equities of the second type, but it is helpful to begin by distinguishing them from mere equities of the first type.

Personal Rights

As discussed in Chapter 2, property rights have two essential characteristics: first, they are rights to things and, secondly, they are enforceable generally against other members of society. If a right lacks either quality it is, by definition, a personal right.

It is possible to create personal rights to things. For example, a lodger in a private home normally has only a personal right (called a **licence**) to reside in the home: see Chapter 18. Unlike a tenant, the lodger cannot enforce her or his right generally against other members of society. Although the licence is a right to use the home, it is enforceable only against the home owner who created it. If the home is sold, mortgaged, or leased, the licence does not create a priority problem, because it is not enforceable against the holder of the new property right. The lodger might have a personal right to be compensated by the home owner for breach of the licence, but the new property right will not be affected by the lodger's rights.

This basic principle applies to legal and equitable personal rights. However, equitable personal rights are often called "mere equities". This label creates confusion since it does not tell us whether the right is personal or property. If the mere equity is personal, there is no priority dispute.

For example, in *National Provincial Bank Ltd v Ainsworth* [1965] AC 1175, a husband was the sole legal owner of the family home. He deserted his wife, leaving her in possession of the home. He then mortgaged the home to the bank and failed to pay the mortgage loan. The bank wanted to enforce the mortgage and take possession of the home. However, the wife claimed that she had an equitable right to stay in the home (called a **deserted wife's equity**) and that the bank's mortgage was subject to her right, because the bank had notice of it. In other words, the bank was not a *bona fide* purchaser.

The bank was entitled to possession of the home, even though it had notice of the wife's rights. However, this case tells us nothing about the priorities of mere equities, because the wife's mere equity was a personal right enforceable only against her husband. At one time, a husband had an obligation to provide a home for his wife. She did not have a property right to any particular home, but her husband was not allowed to evict her unless he provided her with suitable alternative accommodation. Since a deserted wife's equity could be enforced only against her husband, it could not affect the bank's property right to the home. Notice was irrelevant. As Lord Wilberforce said (at 1253), it was "a fallacy that, because an obligation binds a man's conscience, it therefore becomes binding on the consciences of those who take from him with notice of that obligation".

National Provincial Bank Ltd v Ainsworth was decided before courts began to declare that a spouse could have a constructive trust of the family home, based on contributions to the family and detrimental reliance on the expectation of obtaining that right: see Chapter 23. In the Court of Appeal, Lord Denning MR attempted to develop the deserted wife's equity to protect wives better, by making that right binding on others. This is similar to what he tried to do with licences: see Chapter 18. Although personal rights can evolve into property rights, the House of Lords rejected this attempt to convert the deserted wife's equity into a property right. The development of the constructive trust made it unnecessary to do so.

Property Rights

If an equitable property right is classified as a mere equity, it does not cease to be a property right. Like all property rights, a mere equity may conflict with other property rights and, if it does, its priority becomes an issue. Its status as a mere equity will affect its priority in one situation (discussed below) and may affect the right to lodge a caveat to protect it: see page 484. However, there does not appear to be any other significant difference between mere equities and other equitable property rights.

An equitable property right is classified as a mere equity if it is created either by a right to **rescission** or by a right to **rectification**: see page 325. This classification comes from a comment made by Lord Westbury C, in *Phillips v Phillips* (1862) 45 ER 1164 at 1167. He was describing the situations in which one equitable right might be postponed to another and said that this would occur if:

1) .....the older right was "an equity as distinguished from an equitable estate — as for example, an equity to set aside a deed for fraud, or to correct it for mistake"; and
2) .....the newer right was acquired "for valuable consideration without notice" of the older right.

There do not appear to be any other property rights classified as mere equities (but others could arise in the future).

As discussed at page 324, if someone is entitled to rescind a transaction and thereby recover an asset, he or she has a property right to the recoverable asset. That property right can be called an **option to rescind**. It is legal if the right to rescind is legal and equitable if the right to rescind is equitable. A right to rescind can be legal if the transaction is voidable for fraud or duress (or by statute) and it is possible to restore both parties to their pre-transaction positions (*restitutio in integrum*). The right is equitable if the transaction is voidable only under the rules of equity. Courts of equity permit rescission for a wider variety of reasons (including undue influence and mistake) and when it is no longer possible to achieve complete *restitutio in integrum*. Also, the right to rescind will create equitable rights if recovery of legal title requires the assistance of a court of equity.

Like options to rescind, rights to rectification can also create property rights. If someone is entitled to rectify a document (by correcting a mistake in it) and thereby recover an asset, he or she has a property right to the recoverable asset. The right to the recoverable asset is always equitable, because the right to rectify documents is equitable.

It is important to remember that rights to rescind or rectify do not always create property rights. As discussed in Chapter 24, rescission and rectification often affect only personal rights. They create property rights only when the exercise of the right will lead to the recovery of property from the other party. Whether personal or property, equitable rights to rescission or rectification are often called mere equities.

Priority of Mere Equities

Normally, in a competition between two equitable property rights, the older right will be postponed to the newer right only if the holder of the older right is responsible for misleading the holder of the newer right to believe that the older right does not exist. In contrast, mere equities will always be postponed to newer equitable property rights acquired for value, in good faith, and without notice of them. In other words, postponement of a mere equity does not depend on the fault of its holder.

In this respect, a mere equity is similar to a legal option to rescind. As discussed in the previous chapter, legal options to rescind are less durable than most legal property rights, because they are subject to the defence of *bona fide* purchase. A mere equity is less durable than most equitable property rights, because it is subject to all conflicting property rights acquired for value, in good faith, and without notice of it. Other equitable property rights are subject to the defence of *bona fide* purchase, but postponed to other equitable property rights only if the conduct of the right holders justifies the postponement.

In *Latec Investments Ltd v Hotel Terrigal Pty Ltd* (1965) 113 CLR 265, the High Court of Australia confirmed that mere equities are less durable than other equitable property rights. Terrigal was the registered legal owner of a hotel. It granted a registered mortgage to Latec and defaulted on the mortgage loan. Latec had the power, as mortgagee, to sell the hotel to pay the mortgage debt, but it used that power fraudulently to sell the hotel to its subsidiary company, Southern Hotels Pty Ltd. Southern became the registered legal owner and granted an equitable charge to MLC Nominees Ltd.

Southern was a party to, or at least had notice of, Latec's fraud and was not a *bona fide* purchaser. Therefore, Terrigal had an equitable right to rescind Latec's sale to Southern and recover legal title (subject to Latec's mortgage). However, MLC had acquired its equitable charge for value, in good faith, and without notice of Terrigal's option to rescind. Therefore, MLC's charge took priority over Terrigal's option to rescind. Terrigal was entitled to rescind the sale and recover legal ownership of the hotel, but the land would still be subject to MLC's equitable charge.

The High Court confirmed that Terrigal had an equitable property right to the hotel because it could recover that hotel by exercising its right to rescind the sale to Southern. That property right arose when legal title was transferred to Southern and was older than MLC's equitable charge. However, the competition between those two equitable property rights was not decided on the basis of order of creation. Terrigal's option to rescind was treated as a mere equity and MLC's charge had priority.

It is important to note that MLC's equitable charge had priority because it was acquired for value and without notice of Terrigal's option to rescind. Terrigal's right would not have been postponed if MLC had acquired its right either as a gift or with notice of it. Treating Terrigal's right as a mere equity, for the purpose of the priority dispute, does not mean that it was being treated as a personal right, which could not possibly affect MLC. Its status as a mere equity simply meant that it was less durable than other equitable property rights.

It is not clear whether a mere equity could ever take priority over an older equitable property right, but it is unlikely that this situation will ever arise. For example, suppose that you sell land to me in circumstances that entitle you to rescind the sale and recover the land. Before you elect to rescind, I grant an equitable mortgage to Margot. This is a priority dispute between an older mere equity and a newer equitable property right. Change the order, so that you grant the mortgage to Margot and then sell the land to me. Your right to rescind is now the newer right, but it does not conflict with the older mortgage to Margot. If you rescind the sale, you will be returned to your pre-sale position, holding title subject to Margot's mortgage.

Whatever combinations of rights are imagined, it is impossible to create a situation in which a newer option to rescind conflicts with an older equitable property right. The option to rescind is designed to restore the *status quo ante*, in which the asset in question is subject to the older right. The same is true of property rights recoverable through rectification. Unless a new form of mere equity is developed, this priority dispute will not arise.

Why Classify Property Rights as Mere Equities?

It is not entirely clear why equitable options to rescind and property rights created by rights to rectification are classified as mere equities. Why are they less durable than other equitable property rights? There are five characteristics which might distinguish them from other equitable property rights:

1) .....they depend on the exercise of judicial discretion;
2) .....they are created by unjust enrichment;
3) .....their holders must make an election to exercise them;
4) .....they are harder to discover than other equitable property rights; and
5) .....their holders are less likely to protect them.

The last factor seems to provide the best explanation for the reduced durability of property rights dependent on rescission or rectification. However, it is worth considering all five factors briefly.

First, HWR Wade said (in a note in the [1955] *Cambridge Law Journal* 158 at 160) that rights to rescind and rectify might be treated differently because they are discretionary equitable remedies:

> "The dividing line between equitable interests and mere equities is perhaps the discretionary character of the latter. Equitable claims to set aside deeds, or to secure their rectification, or to reopen a foreclosure, are at the discretion of the court in a way which does not apply to equitable titles such as those of beneficiaries under a trust or a mortgagor's equity of redemption. It is natural that the court should be unwilling to exercise its discretion to the detriment of an innocent purchaser even though he lacks the armour of a legal estate."

The difficulty with this basis of distinction is that specific performance is also regarded as a discretionary equitable remedy. Yet, when specific performance of a contract entitles a person to receive a property right, he or she acquires that right in equity. As discussed at page 263, a specifically enforceable sale contract creates a constructive trust for the buyer and a specifically enforceable contract to grant a mortgage, lease, easement, etc, creates an equitable version of the promised property right. These rights are not classified as mere equities, but have the durability of a normal equitable property right.

The second possible basis for distinction is that property rights dependent on rescission or rectification are both created by unjust enrichment. That may justify different treatment. For example, rights created by unjust enrichment are subject to the defence of change of position, while other rights are not. Are property rights created by unjust enrichment less durable by nature? If so, the law is inconsistent, because unjust enrichment also creates resulting and constructive trusts, which are no less durable than other equitable property rights: see Chapter 24.

Thirdly, the distinction might have something to do with the optional character of the rights regarded as mere equities. The holder of an option to rescind must choose whether to rescind the transaction or not. The transaction is valid pending that election. However, as discussed at page 327, a right to rectification is not conditional upon the holder's election to rectify. Of course, the holder must choose whether to enforce the right, but this is true of almost every right. Also, the holder of an **option to purchase** must elect whether to exercise that option. Yet, as discussed at page 264, if the exercise of the option will create a specifically enforceable contract of sale, the option is an equitable property right and not a mere equity.

Fourthly, it is true that rights dependent on rescission or rectification are harder to discover than other equitable property rights. For example, in *Smith v Jones* [1954] 1 WLR 1089 (discussed above), Jones did not have constructive notice of Smith's right to rectify a lease, because he would not have discovered it if he had made all the proper enquiries. However, this difficulty is linked not to the nature of the property right, but to the fact that Smith was unaware of his right at the time. Other equitable property rights, such as trusts and options to purchase, are not more visible by nature. They are easier to discover because trustees and other right holders take steps to protect those rights from competing property rights.

This leads to the fifth and perhaps most convincing reason for classifying property rights dependent on rescission or rectification as mere equities: the holders of those rights are unlikely to take steps to protect them. Those rights exist because someone transferred a property right by mistake, under undue influence, or under some other condition that impaired her or his judgment. That person will probably be unaware of the defect in the transaction until he or she discovers the mistake or is freed of the undue influence or other factors which justify equitable intervention. Until he or she wakes up and takes steps to rescind or rectify the transaction, it will be almost impossible for other people to discover that right.

In a competition between two equitable property rights, the older right will be postponed if its holders failed to take adequate steps to protect it. In other words, the older right will lose priority only because its holders are at fault for misleading others to believe that it does not exist. If that same rule also applied to rights dependent on rescission or rectification, they would hardly ever be postponed, because we cannot blame people for failing to protect rights that they do not know they have (although this was done in *Barry v Heider* (1914) 19 CLR 197). The effect would be enhanced priority.

For this practical reason, the priority of property rights dependent on rescission or rectification cannot depend on the conduct of the right holders. Those rights are made less durable to facilitate the integrity of the market place and the security of property rights. People are entitled to assume that transactions are valid if they appear to be valid. If they acquire a competing property right (whether legal or equitable) for value, in good faith, and without notice of the invalidity of an earlier transaction affecting the same assets, they obtain priority over any property rights created by that invalidity.

Resolving Priority Disputes

Many property rules are designed to help people avoid priority disputes. For example, if property rights are easy to find (because they are registered or created by formal documents), people are less likely to acquire inconsistent rights. However, no system is perfect and priority disputes are bound to arise. So, another important goal of property law is to make it easy for people to resolve those disputes peacefully, quickly, and inexpensively. This is possible only if priority rules are made plain and easy to apply.

Fortunately, most priority disputes can be resolved by the mechanical application of fairly simple rules. This does not mean that this is a simple area of law. The choice of priority rules continues to be a subject of debate and reappraisal, because those rules must balance conflicting interests in the security and marketability of property rights. However, the goal is to reduce this complexity to a set of basic propositions that can be used to determine (with ease and certainty) which of two competing rights has priority.

In this final part of the chapter, the basic rules for resolving priority disputes are summarised. It briefly describes the steps needed to determine which of two competing rights has priority. Of course, stating the rules is easier than applying them. There will be disputes over the relevant facts (such as whether a buyer had notice of a conflicting right) and the proper application of the law, in addition to areas of legal uncertainty.

Identify the Competing Rights

The first step is to identify the nature of the two rights involved and the order of their creation. This requires an application of the principles discussed in Parts III and IV: what sort of right is claimed and how (and when) was that right created? Once the rights are identified, it is possible to determine whether and to what extent they are inconsistent with each other. It is then possible to say whether there is a priority dispute and, if so, what will happen to the losing property right: destruction or impairment.

If there is a priority dispute, it is necessary to select the priority rules that will be used to resolve it. As discussed above and in the previous chapter, this depends on whether the rights are legal or equitable and on the order in which they were created.

Where the Older Right is Legal

If the older right is legal, the resolution of the dispute will depend primarily on the application of the *nemo dat* principle and the exceptions to it (discussed in the previous chapter). The older right will have priority unless an exception to *nemo dat* applies. The exceptions relate either to the nature of the transaction which created the newer right (such as a sale by an apparent agent or in market overt) or to the nature of the older right (because currency, legal options to rescind, and native title are less durable than other legal property rights). Except for native title, postponement of the older right is possible only if the newer right is created for value, in good faith, and without notice of the older right.

Where the Older Right is Equitable

And the Newer Right is Legal

If the older right is equitable and the newer right is legal, the resolution of the dispute depends primarily on the defence of *bona fide* purchase. Did the holders of the legal right acquire it in good faith, for value, and without notice of the older equitable right. If so, the legal right has priority. If not, the legal right is subject to the equitable right.

And the Newer Right is Equitable

If both rights are equitable, the starting point is *qui prior est tempore potior est jure* (he or she who is first in point of time is preferred in law). The older right will have priority unless there is some good reason to postpone it to the newer right. To decide whether it should be postponed, look first at the newer right. Was it acquired for value, in good faith, and without notice of the older right? If not, there is no reason to postpone the older right and the dispute is resolved. If so, then it is at least possible to postpone the older right.

If postponement is possible, look at the older right to see if it should be postponed. If the older right is a mere equity, it will be postponed to the newer right. If the older right is not a mere equity, then postponement will depend on the conduct of its holders. If the older right is an express trust, it will be postponed only if the beneficiaries did something to mislead the holders of the newer right to believe that the trust did not exist. If the older right is any other equitable property right, postponement may be justified if its holders failed to take reasonable steps to protect it.

Registration

This part of the book concerns the common law and equitable priority rules, as they exist today with some statutory modifications. However, the registration of property rights has a significant effect on those rules. This is especially true of the Torrens system, discussed in Chapter 32. Therefore, an understanding of priorities is incomplete without Part VI.

Conversely, an understanding of the common law and equitable priority rules is an essential prerequisite to understanding the priorities of property rights in a registration system. It is difficult to understand the effect of registration without understanding those rules. Also, in every registration system, there are unregistered rights which continue to be subject to them.

Part VI
Registration of Property Rights to Land

Chapter Thirty

REGISTRATION

■■■

Most aspects of the law of property are explored in the first five Parts of this book: the nature of property, the various kinds of property rights recognised in Australia, how those rights are created, and priorities among competing rights. However, the picture is incomplete without an introduction to the registration of property rights. The creation of property rights by registration is discussed above in Chapter 21 and explored further in Chapter 32. Most of this Part is about the effect of registration on priorities.

There are many different registration systems in Australia, which affect a wide variety of property rights. A brief description of each system would have little value. Instead, the remaining chapters are spent introducing the two main systems for registering property rights to land. This is because most property rights to land are registered, while most other property rights are not.

Variety of Registers

The various systems for registering property rights can be divided into two main groups: some are designed for the state regulation of property and others for the protection of property. The first category consists of laws which require the registration of things, such as cars, boats, firearms, cats, and dogs. They are created to control ownership, help law enforcement officers identify owners, and raise revenue through licence fees. This type of registration is regarded as a burden of ownership. Although these registers may help owners recover stolen cars or lost pets, they do not modify property rights to those things.

Registration systems in the second category are designed to protect property rights from competing claims. They modify the common law and equitable priority rules and thereby reduce the number of priority disputes and the cost of avoiding such disputes. The registration systems discussed in this book are of this type.

A large number of registration systems fall in this second category. Whether a property right should be registered and where it should be registered depend on the nature of the right and the nature and location of the thing subject to that right. Most personal property rights are not registered. The main exceptions are intellectual property rights and security rights. Circuit layouts, designs, patents, plant breeders' rights, and trade marks are protected by registers provided by the Commonwealth: see Chapter 17. Security rights to most other types of personal property are protected by registers maintained by state and territorial governments.

In each state and territory, property rights to land are protected (or affected) by several different registers. The most important is the Torrens registration system, which is used primarily for the protection of property rights to privately owned land. There are separate registers for land outside the Torrens system and for mineral rights, native title, and an assortment of other rights.

For example, in South Australia, the Torrens system is established by the *Real Property Act* 1886 (SA), while rights to land outside that system can be registered under the *Registration of Deeds Act* 1935 (SA). The Director of Mines maintains registers of mineral rights under the *Mining Act* 1971 (SA), *Opal Mining Act* 1995 (SA), and *Petroleum Act* 1940 (SA) (see Chapter 16), and native title and native title claims can be registered under the *Native Title (South Australia) Act* 1994 (SA) and *Native Title Act* 1993 (Cth). Other registers which can affect property rights to land in South Australia include the State Heritage Register, under the *Heritage Act* 1993 (SA), the Register of Historic Shipwrecks, under the *Historic Shipwrecks Act* 1981 (SA), and the register of water licences and permits granted under the *Water Resources Act* 1997 (SA).

This list of South Australian registers is not exhaustive and does not include registers designed primarily for the protection of personal property rights. Similar lists could be compiled for other states and territories. Even with the exclusion of personal property registers, it is still not practical to discuss each registration system in detail. Instead, Part VI discusses the general principles of the two main registration systems used in each state and territory.

The **deeds registration system** is discussed in the next chapter. It is used not to create property rights, but to modify the common law and equitable priority rules which would otherwise apply to those rights. Property rights to land in that system are created without registration, in the normal ways discussed in Part IV. Documents which create those rights can be registered to protect them from competing rights.

The **Torrens system** is discussed in Chapter 32. It has a greater impact on the law of property for two main reasons. First, it requires that most legal property rights be created by registration. Secondly, it modifies the common law and equitable priority rules to a greater extent than does a deeds registration system.

Most registration systems designed to protect property rights follow one of these two models. Many systems leave the creation of property rights alone and use registration solely for the purpose of ordering priorities between competing rights (like the deeds registration system). Others attempt a more fundamental change by making the existence of property rights dependent on registration (like the Torrens system).

An understanding of the general principles of the deeds registration and Torrens systems will make it easier to understand any registration system designed to protect property rights. When dealing with any system, it is important both to identify the basic structure of that system and to pay close attention to the particular provisions of the statute which created it.

Importance of Registration

The common law and equitable priority rules, discussed in Part V, reveal why registration is used to protect property rights. Since no one can give what he or she does not have (*nemo dat quod non habet*), you can buy something in good faith and not get the ownership for which you bargained. The risk is small and acceptable for most purchases. Not much money is at stake and you are happy to rely on the seller's promise that you will get good title. However, when spending many thousands of dollars on a home, you want greater assurance that you will get everything you purchased.

The defence of *bona fide* purchase can create problems for both owners and buyers. Owners of equitable property rights can lose those rights, through no fault of their own, to people who acquire the legal title for value without notice of them. Buyers, who think they have acquired full beneficial ownership, can discover that their legal title is subject to prior equitable interests of which they had notice, but no knowledge.

These risks increase the legal costs of acquiring property rights. The searches needed to confirm the absence of competing rights can be time consuming, technical, and expensive. For many transactions, those expenses are hard to avoid because buyers will have notice of rights that competent legal advisors would have discovered. Yet, even a competent legal advisor can fail to discover defects in title.

Registration systems alleviate these problems. The holders of property rights can provide notice of those rights to the public by registering them in a searchable database. This protects equitable property rights from destruction by *bona fide* purchasers and helps everyone avoid time consuming and costly priority disputes. Since registered rights are easily discovered, searches for competing property rights are less expensive and more effective.

Most registration systems go further than this and make the priority of property rights dependent on the order of registration. This accomplishes two things. First, it provides a powerful incentive to register property rights, thereby disclosing them publicly. Secondly, buyers who register their property rights are less unlikely to be disturbed by competing unregistered rights. This means greater security of title. Of course, no system is perfect. Unregistered property rights do exist in both the deeds registration and Torrens systems and can take people by surprise. However, the problem is greatly reduced by registration.

If registration is so helpful, why are so few property rights registered? Think of all the things you have. A few things (like your cat or car) might be registered as required by law. However, unless you own some land, it is unlikely that you have registered any property rights for the purpose of protecting them from competing claims. You may have a few shop receipts, but are otherwise content to rely on your possession as proof of ownership: see page 50.

Registration systems are expensive to create and maintain and create additional transaction costs. Buyers must search the register for competing rights and then register their own newly acquired rights. Those costs are justified only if they produce greater savings by reducing both the cost of searching for competing rights and the risk of losing priority. For most property rights, the additional cost of registration cannot be justified.

Registration is used in situations where the benefits outweigh the costs. This will be true when the market values of the property rights registered tend to be high and, therefore, the consequences of losing priority could be ruinous. It is also true when property rights are not easily discovered, thus increasing both the risk of losing priority and the cost of avoiding that risk. While possession is readily observable, most other property rights are not. Therefore, registration becomes more desirable as the possibility of non-possessory property rights increases.

Land is registered for both these reasons. It is the greatest investment most people make and a loss of priority could well lead to bankruptcy. Also, non-possessory property rights to land are common. Many rights, such as easements, restrictive covenants, mineral rights, and mortgages, would be easy to overlook without registration. In contrast, most goods are much less expensive, possessed by their owners, and free of other property rights.

Registers of personal property rights exist where those rights are likely to be highly valuable or non-possessory. For example, ships are registered, under the *Shipping Registration Act* 1981 (Cth), because there is a lot of money at stake and it is likely that non-possessory security rights will be used to finance their acquisition. Most intellectual property rights get registered simply because they are non-possessory and otherwise difficult to verify. Personal property security rights are registered for the same reason: the vast majority of them are non-possessory.

Chapter Thirty-One

DEEDS REGISTRATION SYSTEM

What is a Deeds Registration System?

There are many different systems for registering property rights to land. They can be divided into two groups: Torrens systems and others. The other systems are often called deeds registration systems. However, there are many different kinds of non-Torrens systems and they cannot all be described accurately as deeds registration systems. Nevertheless, there is no established terminology for describing different kinds of non-Torrens systems and it is convenient to group them together under one familiar label.

There are two fundamental characteristics of Torrens systems which distinguish them from other land registration systems. First, in a Torrens system, most legal property rights are created by registration. In other systems, most legal property rights are created by deed. Secondly, in a Torrens system, a registered property right has priority over all unregistered property rights, subject to a limited number of exceptions. In other systems, the priority of property rights can be preserved or enhanced by registration, but may still be affected by unregistered rights.

Some registration systems have some of the attributes of a Torrens system. For example, the *Land Act* 1994 (Qld) creates a system for registering leases granted by the Crown and other property rights to Crown land. Like a Torrens system, legal property rights are created by registration: ss 301, 302. However, unlike a Torrens system, registration does not confer priority over most unregistered property rights. Without that protection, it is not a Torrens system, but more like a deeds registration system.

What can be Registered?

Despite the name, deeds registration systems are not limited to the registration of deeds. Many registered documents are deeds, because that is the normal way to create a legal property right to land (outside a

Torrens system): see page 249. However, property rights to land can be created by other documents, such as specifically enforceable contracts to sell estates or grant mortgages. Many deeds registration systems allow for the registration of a variety of documents.

Each registration system specifies the documents that can be registered in that system. The discussion of this issue is easier if we distinguish between two different kinds of non-Torrens registration systems. First, there are systems that were originally intended to apply generally to all privately-owned land. Secondly, there are systems designed for the registration of specific kinds of property rights, such as mineral rights. These are discussed here under the headings, **general registration systems** and **specific registrations systems**, respectively. However, these terms do not have any special legal meaning and are used here merely for convenience.

General Registration Systems

Each state has a general deeds registration system that was originally designed for the registration of a wide variety of property rights to land. Those systems were established across Australia in the first half of the 19th century and continue to exist under the *Conveyancing Act* in New South Wales, the *Property Law Act* in Queensland and Victoria, and the *Registration of Deeds Act* in the Australian Capital Territory, South Australia, Tasmania, and Western Australia.

During the second half of the 19th century, each state enacted a Torrens system of land registration, which was intended to replace the general deeds registration system. Every Crown grant of a fee simple estate, made after the creation of the Torrens system, is registered in that system. Crown grants of leasehold estates are also registered in the Torrens system, except in Queensland and Tasmania. In addition, the Torrens statutes provided a mechanism for converting land from the deeds registration to the Torrens system. The goal was (and is) the eventual elimination of the general deeds registration system, so that all freehold (and in some states leasehold) land will be registered in a Torrens system. That process is complete in Queensland and the Northern Territory and nearing completion in other states.

Victoria provides a good example of the progression from deeds registration to Torrens. Early European settlement meant that there were a large number of Crown grants made before the introduction of the Torrens system in 1862. Since that time, all Crown grants of freehold and leasehold estates have been registered in the Torrens system and people holding estates granted before 1862 have had the option to bring their land into that system. Since 1999, it is no longer possible to register documents in the deeds registration system: *Transfer of Land (Single Register) Act* 1998 (Vic), s 22. The deeds registration system continues to exist. However, if someone wants to register a property right to land in the deeds registration system, it will be necessary to bring that land into the Torrens system. In every state, the general deeds registration system permitted the registration of a wide variety of documents affecting estates that were first granted by the Crown before the introduction of the Torrens system and have remained outside that system. For example, the *Registration of Deeds Act* 1935 (SA) permits the registration of deeds, conveyances, contracts, wills, and judgments affecting property rights to land, but excludes leases up to three years and does not affect land in South Australia's Torrens system: ss 9, 10. It is conceivable that a document (such as a restrictive covenant) could affect land in both systems. However, registration of that document in the deeds registration system will not affect property rights to land in the Torrens system (and vice versa).

Land which is not in a Torrens system is sometimes called **general law land** or **old system land**. However, both labels can be misleading. First, the general law of property applies to Torrens and non-Torrens land alike. Torrens modifies certain laws (such as the manner in which legal property rights are created, the form of legal mortgages, and the priority of legal property rights), but the same principles otherwise apply. Secondly, it is true that the general deeds registration system in each state is being replaced by a Torrens system and is therefore the "old system". However, that does not make Torrens a new system. The first Torrens system was introduced in South Australia in 1858 and it has long been an established feature of property law in Australia (and elsewhere). Also, there are now many non-Torrens registration systems for registering specific kinds of property rights to land. Most of these are newer than the Torrens system and intended to coexist with it.

Specific Registration Systems

In Australia, a Crown grant of a new freehold estate will get registered in a Torrens system. This is also true of most Crown leases, except in Queensland and Tasmania. However, that leaves a large number of property rights, granted by the Crown, which do not get registered in a Torrens system. In Queensland, Crown leases are registered under the *Land Act* 1994 (Qld) and, in every jurisdiction except the Australian Capital Territory, mineral rights (discussed in Chapter 16) are registered in special registers created for that purpose. For example, there are several registers established under the *Mining Act* (NT) for registering different mineral rights in the Northern Territory: see reg 29 of the *Mining Regulations* (NT).

Effect of Registration

Creation of Property Rights

Most deeds registration systems do not change the way in which property rights are created. The execution of a document creates the legal or equitable property right (as discussed in Chapter 21) and registration affects its priority (as discussed below). This means that registration of a document will not cure its defects. If the document is a forgery or contains an error, registration does not fix the problem.

For example, suppose that I want to transfer my fee simple estate to you and execute a deed of transfer. Unfortunately, I do not own that estate, because one of the documents in my chain of title is a forgery. The *nemo dat* principle (discussed in Chapter 28) means that I cannot transfer what I do not have and you do not acquire that estate.

Registration of the deed will not change that fact. However, registration may have value, because it will preserve the priority of any rights you did acquire from me, such as my adverse possession of the land: see Chapter 8.

All the general deeds registration systems operate in this manner and so do some specific registration systems. For example, under section 160 of the *Mining Act* 1992 (NSW), a "legal or equitable interest in" a mineral lease or licence is created by execution of a document. That interest may be registered under section 161, but "registration of an interest under this section is not to be taken to be evidence of the existence of the interest". In other words, if the document is ineffective to create an interest in a mining right, registration will not help.

Some deeds registration systems make the creation of the right conditional on registration. As discussed above, the *Land Act* 1994 (Qld) is like a Torrens system, because registration is the event which creates or transfers a legal lease or licence: ss 301, 302. This means that registration of a document in that system can create a property right, even though the document might be ineffective to create that right at common law.

In several other systems, registration of a document is an essential condition for creating the intended property right, but does not give the document any greater effect than it would otherwise have had. For example, section 70 of the *Mineral Resources Development Act* 1990 (Vic) states that a "document ... is ineffective for creating, assigning or affecting any interest in or conferred by a licence ... until it is registered". However, that section goes on to say that:

"The approval or registration of a document does not give any right, interest or dealing that is evidenced by that document any force or effect that the right, interest or dealing would not have had if this Part had not been enacted."

If registration is required to create a property right or make a document fully effective to create that right, the unregistered document can create an equitable version of that right. As discussed at page 273, if a person has the power to obtain a property right by registration, equity treats the transaction as complete and regards that person as the equitable owner of that right before registration occurs: see *Corin v Patton* (1990) 169 CLR 540. In many cases, an equitable property right will already exist, because the parties made a specifically enforceable contract to transfer that right: see page 25900.

Priorities

Practical Effects of Registration

Most deeds registration systems alter the common law and equitable priority rules, discussed in Part V. Some do not. For example, the *Mineral Resources Development Act* 1990 (Vic) does not create any special priority rules and states that registration of a document does not enhance its "force or effect" (in section 70, quoted above).

A system which does not alter priority rules can still affect the outcome of priority disputes, in two ways. First, people will have constructive notice of documents registered in that system, if reasonable buyers in their situation would search the register. This will stop most people from obtaining priority over older equitable property rights that are registered. Note that registration is not notice to the whole world, but only to those people who should search the register. Therefore, it is possible for people to acquire property rights without notice of registered documents.

Secondly, suppose that two conflicting equitable property rights were created and the newer right was acquired for value, in good faith, and without notice of the older right. As discussed in Chapter 29, this raises the question whether the older right should be postponed to the newer right. In many cases, this will depend on whether the holders of the older right took adequate care to preserve it. Registration of the document which created the older right may show that its holders did take adequate care and, therefore, it should not be postponed.

Order of Registration

Most deeds registration systems make the priority of documents depend on the order of registration, instead of (or in addition to) the factors which determine priority at common law or in equity. For example, section 184G of the *Conveyancing Act* 1919 (NSW) states:

> "All instruments (wills excepted) affecting, or intended to affect, any lands in New South Wales which are executed or made bona fide, and for valuable consideration, and are duly registered ... shall have and take priority not according to their respective dates but according to the priority of the registration thereof only."

Other systems achieve the same effect using different language. For example, section 10 of the *Registration of Deeds Act* 1935 (SA) states that a document is "fraudulent and void at law and in equity against any subsequent registered purchaser, mortgagee or party for or upon valuable consideration", unless that document is registered first. The words "fraudulent and void" suggest that a failure to register has very serious consequences. However, the statute does not invalidate the unregistered document, but only makes it unenforceable against a newer document which is registered first. In other words, priority between those two documents depends on order of registration.

In most deeds registration systems, the priority provided by registration is available only if certain conditions are met (such as good faith and the giving of value). The conditions vary from system to system. This is discussed below under the heading, "entitlement to priority". We now consider the effect of priority based on the order of registration.

What does it mean when a registered document has priority over an unregistered or subsequently registered document? Simply put, it means that the rights created by the first registered document prevail over the rights created by the other document, if they conflict. However, it can be confusing trying to determine the outcome of a priority dispute when the two documents create different kinds of rights (such as a legal mortgage versus an equitable lease) or when one document will only create rights if it has priority over the other. A simple way to determine their priority is to:

1) .....treat the first registered document as if it was executed first; and
2) .....treat the other document as if it was executed with notice of the first registered document; and then
3) .....apply the common law and equitable priority rules discussed in Part V.

For example, suppose that I granted a legal mortgage to Deb and then granted an equitable mortgage to Katy. If Katy registered her mortgage first, it would have priority over Deb's mortgage. The outcome would be the same if the equitable mortgage to Katy was executed first, Deb acquired her mortgage with notice of Katy's mortgage, and neither mortgage was registered. In that case, the equitable priority rules would give Katy's mortgage priority, because Deb would not be a *bona fide* purchaser.

This approach was used in *Blackwood v London Chartered Bank of Australia* (1871) 10 SCR (NSW) (Equity) 56, in a competition between two equitable mortgages. The defendants registered their newer mortgage first. Stephen CJ said (at 84):

> "The equities of each mortgagee here being equal, the superior title of the plaintiffs has rested solely on their priority in respect of time. But, by our Registration Act, all instruments whatsoever affecting or intended to affect real or leasehold estates take priority, not according to their dates, but according to the priority of their registration. ... The effect of registration is, therefore, by express provision, to reverse the order of priority; and thus, as between these parties, to confer on the defendants' security an efficacy countervailing that of the plaintiffs'. In other words, to compel the Court to regard the second as if it were the earlier instrument."

When priority depends on the order of registration, the registration of a document can have unexpected consequences. It can produce exceptions to the *nemo dat* principle or cause destroyed equitable property rights to revive. For example, in *Boyce v Beckman* (1890) 11 LR (NSW) (L) 139, the Crown granted a fee simple estate to William O'Donnell, who transferred it to William Sparke. Sparke sold part of that land to Elizabeth Boyce in 1845 and sold the rest of it to John Turner in 1852. The deed of transfer to Turner said that it included "all or any other lots forming a portion of the said grant to William O'Donnell to which he the said William Sparke is entitled". This clause was supposed to give Turner every part of the land that had not been transferred to Boyce.

When Sparke executed the deed of transfer to Turner, he no longer owned the land he had transferred to Boyce. According to the *nemo dat* principle, he could not give Turner more than he had and the deed could not affect Boyce's land. However, Turner's deed was registered before Boyce's and this changed the legal effect of both deeds. Turner's deed had to be read as if it was executed before Boyce's. At that point, Sparke owned all of the land he had received from O'Donnell and, therefore, it would cause all of that land to be transferred to Turner. In other words, the registration of Turner's deed (in 1852) created an exception to the *nemo dat* principle, because it caused land which belonged to Boyce (since 1845) to be transferred to Turner, without her consent.

Normally, registration in a deeds registration does not create an exception to the *nemo dat* principle. For example, suppose that I believe I am the legal owner of land. However, the transfer to me was invalid for some reason and Damien is its true legal owner (having received a proper deed of transfer from its previous owner). I then execute a deed purporting to transfer the land to Eliza and she registers that deed before Damien registers his deed. Priority is unaffected by that registration. Since I was never the owner of the land, I cannot transfer it to Eliza. Her deed is a nullity and would have no effect even if it had been executed before Damien's deed and he had obtained his deed with notice of her deed.

The registration of documents can also revive equitable property rights that were previously destroyed by the defence of *bona fide* purchase. In *Moonking Gee v Tahos* (1960) 80 WN (NSW) 1612, George Tahos made a contract to sell his land to Moonking Gee (the plaintiff). Three months later, Tahos made another contract to sell the same estate to Yuk Win (the defendant) for more money. Tahos transferred his legal estate to the defendant on 6 March, the plaintiff registered his contract of sale on 12 March, and the defendant registered his deed of transfer on 23 March.

Before 6 March, Tahos was the legal owner of the land, subject to two equitable property rights created by the two contracts of sale: a constructive trust for the plaintiff, followed by a constructive trust for the defendant. As the older trust, the plaintiff's right would have priority over the defendant's. On 6 March, the defendant acquired legal title as a *bona fide* purchaser. He did not have constructive notice of the plaintiff's contract because it was not yet registered. Therefore, the plaintiff's equitable property right was destroyed and the defendant held the land free of it until 12 March.

When the plaintiff registered his contract on 12 March, that document acquired priority over the deed of transfer to the defendant. In other words, the contract was then treated as if the defendant had notice of it when he obtained legal title. The plaintiff's equitable interest revived and the defendant held his legal estate on constructive trust for him. The defendant was required to transfer the land to the plaintiff on receipt of the balance of the purchase price which the plaintiff still owed to Tahos.

Property Rights that Cannot be Registered

Many deeds registration systems exclude the registration of certain documents that can affect property rights to land in those systems. For example, short leases are excluded from the general deeds registration systems in most states, for two reasons. First, a person wanting to buy land will know that it is occupied and can easily discover the rights that the occupants are claiming. Secondly, the registration of a large number of short leases would clog the system: see pages 249–250. In Queensland, South Australia, and Victoria, leases up to three years are excluded and, in Tasmania and Western Australia, leases up to 14 years are excluded if they are made in good faith for a **rack rent** (the full market rental value of the land).

Also, as discussed in Part IV, property rights can be created without the use of documents. For example, I might hold my house on constructive trust for my de facto spouse, because she contributed to our family with the expectation of sharing it (see Chapter 23) or on resulting trust for her because she contributed to the purchase price (see Chapter 24). My brother might have an equitable mortgage over the house, because he loaned money to me in exchange for a deposit of my title deeds (see Chapter 21) or I might hold the house on constructive trust for my employer because I accepted bribes and used the money to buy it (see Chapter 25). Freehold estates can be created by adverse possession (see Chapter 8) and short leases can be created informally (see Chapter 21).

In most deeds registration systems, the priority of a property right, which is created without a document or by an unregisterable document, is not affected by the registration of a document which creates a conflicting right. This is because most systems deal only with priorities between registerable documents. If the holder of a right cannot register a document, he or she is not adversely affected by a failure to register: see *White v Neaylon* (1886) 11 App Cas 171.

The exception for rights created without documents can create anomalies. For example, suppose I mortgage my land to you and then make a contract to lease it for 20 years to Liz (who has no notice of your mortgage). If Liz registers her contract and you do not register your mortgage, will registration affect the relative priorities of your rights? If you have a legal mortgage (created by deed) or an equitable mortgage (created by a specifically enforceable written contract), Liz's equitable lease will have priority over your mortgage. However, if you have an equitable mortgage created by part performance of an oral contract of mortgage (as discussed at page 264), registration will not affect priority. The normal equitable rules will be used to determine priority between your conflicting equitable rights. Since your mortgage is older, it should have priority unless you failed to protect it adequately or otherwise misled Liz to believe it did not exist: see page 415. It seems odd that the least formal method of creating the mortgage should produce the most durable property right in that situation.

Some deeds registration systems have the capacity to deal with undocumented property rights. They allow people to lodge **caveats**, which provide warnings of the existence of unregistered property rights and prevent the registration of other documents that might create conflicting rights. For example, section 183 of the *Mineral Resources Development Act* 1995 (Tas) states:

> "Any person with an interest in a mineral tenement may lodge with the Registrar a caveat forbidding the approval of any transfer or other dealing affecting that mineral tenement."

Caveats are used in Torrens systems to protect unregistered property rights and are discussed further in the next chapter.

Entitlement to Priority

In most deeds registration systems, the priority of documents is not based solely on the order of registration. Usually, a registered document will not prevail over an older unregistered document unless certain other conditions are met. For example, section 184G of the *Conveyancing Act 1919* (NSW) (quoted above) states that the order of registration will determine priority only if the document is "made bona fide, and for valuable consideration". The two most common requirements relate to value and notice. These are discussed below. Also discussed is the effect of fraud.

Value

Deeds registration systems can be used by donees of gifts (such as the beneficiaries of a will or trust) to protect the priority of their property rights. Registration of the deed will ensure that the gift is not destroyed or impaired by the subsequent creation and registration of a conflicting property right. However, in most systems, registration of a deed by a donee will not give that deed priority over older, unregistered documents. The advancement of priority through registration is available only to people who give value for their property rights.

The requirement of value is stated in different ways in different systems. For example, section 3 of the *Registration of Deeds Act* 1856 (WA) states that unregistered documents "shall (as against any subsequent bona fide purchaser or mortgagee ... for valuable consideration) be absolutely null and void". In other words, an older, unregistered document will not be postponed to a newer, registered document, unless the newer property right was acquired for value.

Section 9 of the *Registration of Deeds Act* 1935 (Tas) uses different language to achieve the same effect. It states that:

> "All instruments which are executed or made in good faith and for valuable consideration, and are registered under the provisions of this Act, shall have and take priority, not according to their respective dates, but according to the priority of the registration thereof only."

Although this seems to suggest that the benefits of registration are available only for documents acquired for value, that is not true. Donees are permitted to register their deeds and obtain the protection of that registration. However, registration of a deed will not give it priority over older documents, unless the deed was obtained for value.

In every state, the general deeds registration system will not permit a donee to use registration to obtain priority over an older document. This is also true of some specific deeds registration systems: see, eg, *Mining Regulations* 1981 (WA), reg 103. In contrast, the *Land Act* 1994 (Qld) (which is used to register Crown leases and other property rights to Crown land) expressly removes the requirement of value. Section 300 states: "The benefits of this division apply to a document whether or not valuable consideration has been given." This same statement is also found in Queensland's Torrens statute (which applies only to freehold land).

The *Mining Act* 1992 (NSW) is silent on the question of value. Section 161 states:

"For the purposes of any legal proceedings concerning an authority: (a) a registered interest has priority over an interest that is not registered, and (b) an earlier registered interest has priority over a later registered interest."

With no mention of value (or notice), does this mean that the donees of a gift can register their interest and thereby obtain priority over older interests? Traditionally, courts were reluctant to take away vested property rights without clear justification. In the absence of a clear statement (like the quotation from section 300 of the *Land Act* 1994 (Qld), above), a court was inclined to interpret the statute in a way which preserves property rights from destruction by donees.

As discussed in the next chapter, most Torrens systems do not state clearly whether donees can use registration to obtain priority over unregistered property rights. Many courts have decided that they cannot. However, the New South Wales Court of Appeal has said that they can: *Bogdanovic v Koteff* (1988) 12 NSWLR 472. This may indicate that a court in New South Wales would interpret section 161 of the *Mining Act* 1992 (NSW) in a similar way and let the order of registration determine priority, regardless of value.

Notice

In many deeds registration systems, a registered document will not be entitled to priority over an older unregistered document, unless the registered document was "made and executed bona fide and for a valuable consideration": *Property Law Act* 1958 (Vic), s 6. This refers to the buyer's good faith and not the seller's. Otherwise, registration would offer little protection, because an honest buyer could not be sure that the seller was acting properly. As Hood J said, in *Davidson v O'Halloran* [1913] VLR 367 at 373, "no vigilance can protect a transferee from an improper motive acting on the mind of the transferor".

Normally, a document will not be made in good faith if the buyer had notice of an older conflicting right: see Chapter 29. In *Midland Bank Trust Co Ltd v Green* [1981] AC 513 at 528, Lord Wilberforce said:

"I think that it would generally be true to say that the words 'in good faith' relate to the existence of notice. Equity, in other words, required not only absence of notice, but genuine and honest absence of notice."

Therefore, if a buyer has notice of an older, unregistered property right when the document is executed, registration of that document will not give it priority over the older right. Notice obtained after execution, but before registration, does not prevent the buyer from registering the document for the purpose of obtaining priority. Since the document was made in good faith and for value, it is entitled to priority if it is registered before the older document.

Some registration systems confer priority on registered documents, even if they were obtained with notice of conflicting unregistered documents. For example, section 10 of the *Registration of Deeds Act* 1935 (SA) does not require that a registered document be made in good faith and states that it is entitled to priority over an older unregistered document, even though the buyer had notice of the older document. Section 298 of the *Land Act* 1994 (Qld) states that the priority of registered documents (by order of registration) "is not affected by actual, implied or constructive notice."

Fraud

Registration of a document will not give it priority if that document was obtained by fraud. People are not supposed to make fraudulent use of registration systems to gain priority. Of course, the effect of this basic principle depends on what is meant by "fraud". Normally, we use that word to describe dishonest conduct. However, lawyers sometimes speak of **equitable fraud** or **constructive fraud** when describing the conduct of people who were not dishonest, but had notice of facts that would indicate that their conduct was improper.

In this context, it is usually regarded as fraud if a person acquires a property right, knowing that it is inconsistent with another property right. As discussed at page 413, there is an important distinction between knowledge and notice. Normally, notice of a conflicting right does not involve dishonesty, but knowledge does. Also, a person may be dishonest if he or she is willfully blind. That term is used to describe a situation in which a person suspects the truth and chooses not to investigate further.

The deeds registration systems, which confer priority on documents regardless of notice, do not make any reference to knowledge. Therefore, they will not assist a person who obtained a property right with knowledge of an older, conflicting property right (or suspicion of its existence). In contrast, most Torrens systems say that knowledge of an unregistered interest is not itself fraud. This is discussed further in the next chapter.

Chapter Thirty-Two

TORRENS SYSTEM

Introduction

The Torrens system of land title registration is an important part of Australian property law. As discussed in the previous chapter, it was first introduced in South Australia in 1858 and has since been adopted across Australia and in many jurisdictions around the world, including New Zealand and the provinces of western Canada. It is commonly called the Torrens system after Robert Torrens, the South Australian politician primarily responsible for its enactment. However, the statutes that create Torrens systems go by different names in different places. It is called the *Land Title Act* in Queensland, the *Land Titles Act* in the Australian Capital Territory and Tasmania, the *Real Property Act* in New South Wales, the Northern Territory, and South Australia, and the *Transfer of Land Act* in Victoria and Western Australia.

A German lawyer, Ulrich Hübbe, contributed to the development of the Torrens system, using principles borrowed from the Hanseatic registration system in Hamburg: see Murray Raff, *German Real Property Law and the Conclusive Land Title Register* (University of Melbourne PhD thesis, 1999). This was a marked departure from the common law of real property and the development of the Torrens system has been influenced by the reluctance of common law judges to accept it. An example of that reluctance is the dissenting opinion of Rinfret, the Chief Justice of Canada, in *Canadian Pacific Railway Co Ltd v Turta* [1954] SCR 427 at 429. He said that giving full effect to a Torrens statute "would create an intolerable situation" and continued:

> "Interpreted as suggested ... , the statute would do away with all traditional principles of law and equity. Indeed, I am not sure that it does not boast of such intention ... And, if it were so, I confess that the statute in question would not fill me with enthusiasm."

Limits of Deeds Registration

The Torrens system was designed to replace the general deeds registration system (discussed in the previous chapter) and remedy its limitations. There are two main problems that deeds registration does not cure. First, it is a system for registering documents and is subject to the frailties of those documents. Registration of a document will not create good title if there is a defect in the document or in the chain of title leading to that document. Therefore, a person proposing to deal with land cannot rely solely on the register, but must search the history of title to confirm the validity of every document in the chain.

Secondly, registration does not give a document priority over all unregistered property rights. Registration does not affect the priority of rights created without documents and, in most systems, the priority of a registered document depends on the absence of notice. If the document was obtained by someone with constructive notice of an unregistered property right, it will be subject to that right. Therefore, a search of the deeds register is inadequate. It is necessary to conduct further searches to confirm the absence of conflicting unregistered property rights.

Goals of the Torrens System

The limits of the deeds registration system meant that transfers of land were slow, expensive, and often unable to create certainty of title. The Torrens system was intended to alleviate those problems, by enabling people to rely on one register to discover all the property rights that might adversely affect them. Ideally, the register would present an accurate picture of property rights to land: every property right would be there and every property right there would truly exist. Although it is impossible to achieve this goal, the Torrens system makes significant progress in that direction, with two major changes to the common law:

1) .....most legal property rights are created by registration and not by the execution of a document; and
2) .....the defence of *bona fide* purchase is expanded to allow people who register property rights, without fraud, to take free of unregistered property rights, even if they have notice or knowledge of those rights.

Rights Created by Registration

First and most importantly, Torrens is a system for registering property rights, not documents. Most legal property rights are created by registration and not by execution of a document. There is no need to confirm the validity of a chain of title, because legal title does not depend on that chain. In a Torrens system, the source of legal title is registration.

This means that registration in a Torrens system is another exception to the *nemo dat* principle, since a person can thereby acquire a property right without the consent of its previous owner. To deal with this problem, most Torrens systems have an **assurance fund** to compensate people who lose their property rights because of Torrens principles (or because of errors made by the people operating the system). As discussed in Chapter 28, the law has long struggled to set the proper balance between the protection of property and the protection of commercial transactions. Since Torrens systems tip the balance in favour of protecting transactions, most jurisdictions provide compensation to those who lose their property as a result.

Priority Over Unregistered Rights

It is impossible to make every property right depend on registration. People will always make informal arrangements with each other about the use of their things, including their land, and the law cannot refuse to recognise that practical reality. Also, as discussed in Part IV, property rights are created in various ways: usually by intention, but also in response to other events, such as detrimental reliance, unjust enrichment, or wrongdoing. The law responds to these different events in order to create a more complete system of justice. The justifications for creating property rights are not any different in a Torrens system. That system must cope with the problems of ordinary people and not vice versa.

The existence of unregistered property rights means that a Torrens register may not be an accurate reflection of property rights to land. This creates a priority problem: in what circumstances should a newly acquired registered right be subject to an older unregistered right? If notice was the standard, the Torrens system would be little better than the deeds registration system it replaced (and probably not worth the costs of changing). People dealing with Torrens land would still need to conduct extensive searches for conflicting rights. Therefore, a person who obtains a registered property right, without fraud, holds it free of most unregistered property rights, regardless of notice.

Of course, the destruction of unregistered property rights creates additional problems. The Torrens system deals with them in two main ways. First, it exempts certain unregistered rights (such as short leases) from destruction. A person dealing with land is expected to search for those rights because they are either too important to destroy or easily discoverable. Although this makes it necessary to look beyond the Torrens register, the searches are still far less onerous than those required under a deeds registration system.

Secondly, a person with an unregistered property right to Torrens land can protect it by lodging a **caveat** in the Torrens register. This warns people searching the register about the existence of the right and prevents the creation of conflicting registered property rights.

Outline of the Chapter

This chapter deals with the essential principles of Torrens systems in Australia and uses terms and describes procedures that are typical of most of them. However, there are variations from place to place. Most of the differences are superficial, but those that are more substantial are discussed below.

The remainder of the chapter is divided into three main parts:

1) .....creation of property rights;
2) .....registered property rights; and
3) .....unregistered property rights.

The first part discusses the creation of registered and unregistered property rights in a Torrens system. The second part deals with the priority of registered rights over both registered and unregistered rights. This concerns the principle of indefeasibility of title and the exceptions to that principle. The third part concerns the protection of unregistered rights (with caveats) and priorities between conflicting unregistered rights.

Creation of Property Rights

The most important characteristic of a right is whether it is personal or property, primarily because this helps determine whether it is enforceable against specific persons or generally against other members of society: see Chapter 2. Another important characteristic is whether a right is legal or equitable. This used to have much greater importance when those two systems of law were administered by separate courts. However, it is still important in property law, because it helps determine the priority of a property right. As discussed in Part V, legal rights tend to be more durable than equitable rights.

In a Torrens system, another important characteristic of property rights is whether they are registered and unregistered. Although this is important in all registration systems, it has special significance in a Torrens system, because registration both creates rights and determines their priorities.

As a general rule, property rights to Torrens land are legal if they are registered and equitable if they are unregistered. In other words, legal property rights are created by registration and equitable property rights are created in other ways. This is because Torrens systems were designed to make the register an accurate reflection of legal property rights only. Of course, this makes it necessary to find other ways to protect unregistered equitable property rights (as discussed below). This is one of the criticisms of the Torrens system.

There are at least four exceptions to this general rule in most Torrens systems: two legal property rights can be created without registration (adverse possession and informal leases) and two equitable property rights can be registered (options to purchase and restrictive covenants). This rule and these exceptions are explored below.

Registered Property Rights

In each jurisdiction, the Torrens system is administered by a public official and her or his deputies and assistants. That official is called the Registrar-General, Registrar of Titles, or Recorder of Titles, depending on the jurisdiction, but is referred to here simply as the **Registrar**.

The Registrar is responsible for the **register** of land titles, which consists of the registered documents and other records affecting Torrens land in a state or territory. The register might be kept in different forms, including paper documents, microfilm, and computer records.

Bringing Land into the System

There are three ways to bring land into a Torrens system:

1)......registration of an estate granted by the Crown;
2)......a change from deeds registration to Torrens; and
3)......registration of Crown land.

The first and usual method is by registration of a Crown grant of an estate, made in the appropriate form. Usually, the grant is of a fee simple estate but, in every jurisdiction except Queensland and Tasmania, land can be brought into the Torrens system by registering a Crown lease.

Secondly, land registered in a deeds registration system can be brought into the Torrens system by its owners or other interested parties. As discussed in the previous chapter, this method applies to estates granted by the Crown before the advent of the Torrens system. The process of converting land from deeds registration to Torrens is complicated by two main problems. First, a chain of documents creating apparent legal title may be defective. Therefore, registration of that title could create ownership where none existed before. Secondly, unregistered property rights may exist and be destroyed by Torrens priority principles. Torrens statutes contain procedures to deal with these problems, except in jurisdictions (such as Queensland) where they are no longer needed because the conversion from deeds registration to Torrens is complete.

Thirdly, in several states, it is possible for the government to bring land into the Torrens system without granting an estate to anyone. In Western Australia, this produces a "certificate of Crown land title"; in New South Wales, the state is registered "as the proprietor of the land", and in Tasmania, "the Crown shall be registered as the proprietor of the land for an estate in fee simple". Also, in Queensland, "The State may ... acquire, hold and deal with lots."

It may seem odd that, in Tasmania, the Crown can hold an estate even though it cannot have a tenure relationship with itself. However, this may also happen because of the abolition of escheat in every state, except Western Australia. As discussed in Chapter 12, if the holder of a fee simple estate dies intestate without heirs, the estate is transferred to the Crown as *bona vacantia* (ownerless goods). Since this does not remove the land from the Torrens system, the estate would continue to exist with the Crown as proprietor.

Folios and Certificates of Title

When a parcel of land is brought into the Torrens system, the Registrar creates a **folio** for the documents and records concerning that land. Each document accepted for registration is given a distinctive reference number and recorded in the folio. The Registrar creates a **certificate of title** for that land, which describes the parcel of land (by reference to a plan or survey), the estate granted, and the people to whom it was granted.

A person holding a registered property right is called the **registered proprietor** of that right. It is common to refer to the owner of a fee simple estate as the registered proprietor. However, a person who holds a lesser registered property right can also be called the registered proprietor of that right. For example, a person who has a registered mortgage can be called a registered mortgagee or the registered proprietor of a mortgage.

The Register issues the certificate of title to the registered proprietor. However, in many jurisdictions, the certificate issued to the registered proprietor is called the **duplicate certificate of title** (or **DCT**), because the original is kept in the folio. The certificate of title (or DCT) is an important document, because it must be returned to the Registrar if the registered proprietor wishes to deal with the land. Therefore, it can be pledged as security for a loan (creating an equitable mortgage, as discussed at page 266). However, it is not a perfect form of security, since the Registrar will allow the registered proprietor to deal with the land if he or she makes a declaration that the certificate was lost or destroyed.

People searching the register can obtain copies of the certificate of title and other documents affecting the land. They can also obtain certified copies of those documents, which can be used as evidence in court. A certified copy of a certificate of title is often called a **certified copy of title** and should not be confused with the certificate of title or DCT.

Dealing with Land

If a registered proprietor wishes to transfer legal ownership of the land or grant some registered property right to it (such as a mortgage, lease, or easement), he or she must execute a document in the form prescribed by the Torrens statute. The document is submitted to the Registrar, together with the certificate of title (or DCT) and the appropriate fee. If acceptable, the document is registered and the folio and certificate of title are amended accordingly.

If the estate granted by the Crown is transferred, the certificate of title is cancelled and a new certificate of title is issued to the new registered proprietors. If lesser property rights are created (such as leases, mortgages, or easements), they are endorsed on the existing certificate in the order in which they are registered. These lesser rights are often called **encumbrances** (although that term is sometimes used to refer just to security rights, such as mortgages, liens, and charges). A person searching the title can see what document was registered (such as a mortgage to a certain bank) and what identification number was assigned to it by the Registrar. It is then possible to obtain a copy of the document itself.

Torrens systems do not permit the registration of every document that creates property rights to land. It must be in the proper form prescribed by the Torrens statute or it will not be accepted by the Registrar. Every statute provides for the registration of transfers, mortgages, leases, and easements. Only half of the jurisdictions provide specifically for the registration of profits à prendre (Australian Capital Territory, New South Wales, Queensland, and Tasmania). However, since a profit à prendre is a legal property right, it can be registered in other states by registering a transfer of that right.

Trusts

Every Torrens statute prohibits the registration of all or at least most trusts (introduced in Chapter 13). As legal owners of the property rights held in trust, the trustees will be the registered proprietors of those rights. However, the beneficiaries of trusts are not permitted to register their interests. Section 162 of the *Real Property Act* (NT) is fairly typical. It states that:

> "[T]he Registrar-General shall not make an entry in the Register of the particulars of a trust and shall not register an instrument under this Act that declares or contains trusts relating to land under this Act."

However, in the Northern Territory, the Registrar is required to record on certificates of title the particulars of any trusts for public purposes that are contained in the original grants from the Crown. Similar provisions are found in section 161 of the *Real Property Act* 1886 (SA), and section 55 of the *Transfer of Land Act* 1893 (WA).

In most jurisdictions, trust documents can be deposited with the Registrar "for safe custody" and, in Queensland and Tasmania, registered proprietors can be described in certificates of title as trustees: *Land Title Act* 1994 (Qld), s 109; *Land Titles Act* 1980 (Tas), s 132. However, these things do not affect registered property rights in any way. A trust document is not part of the register and the trust is not a registered property right.

Mortgages

As discussed at page 125, a registered mortgage of Torrens land differs from a common law mortgage. It is not a transfer of the fee simple estate to the mortgagee, but a statutory charge on the land. The Torrens mortgagee has the same basic rights as a common law mortgagee to use the land as security for payment of a debt. If the mortgagor fails to pay the debt, the mortgagee can take possession of the land, foreclose their interest in it, or sell it to pay the debt. However, Torrens mortgagors continue to be the registered proprietors of the fee simple, with the registered mortgage endorsed on their certificate of title. In contrast, common law mortgagors have only an equity of redemption.

Although Torrens mortgagors retain the legal fee simple estate, it is still common to speak of their **equity of redemption**: see *Re Forrest Trust* [1953] VLR 246. They have a right to redeem the mortgage, even after they default on the loan. On payment of the money due to the mortgagee, they have a right to have the mortgage discharged from their certificate of title. The value of their interest in Torrens land (calculated by subtracting the amount due under the mortgage from the market value of the land) is still referred to as equity.

The difference between a Torrens and a common law mortgage creates minor differences in the ways those mortgages are enforced. In the both cases, a mortgagee who wants to foreclose on the mortgage needs to get a court order. At common law, the order for final foreclosure destroys the equity of redemption and entitles the mortgagee to the full beneficial ownership of the fee simple estate (which the mortgagee obtained as security when the mortgage was granted). Foreclosure of a Torrens mortgage means that the legal fee simple estate is transferred from the mortgagor to the mortgagee by cancellation of the mortgagor's certificate of title and issuing a new certificate to the mortgagee.

The difference between the two types of mortgages affects powers of sale in a similar way. In both cases, the sale is authorised by a court order. A common law mortgagee completes the sale by transferring the fee simple estate to the buyer. A Torrens mortgagee completes the sale by exercising a power to transfer the mortgagor's estate. When the transfer is registered, legal ownership will pass directly from the mortgagor to the buyers.

It is possible to create a common law mortgage in a Torrens system by transferring the fee simple estate to the mortgagee as security for a debt: see, eg, *Abigail v Lapin* [1934] AC 491. The mortgagee becomes the registered proprietor of the fee simple estate and the mortgagor has an unregistered equity of redemption. However, there is an important difference between this arrangement and a normal common law mortgage. Someone who examines a common law mortgagee's title documents will see that title was acquired through a deed of mortgage and will know that the mortgagee has only a security interest unless that mortgage is accompanied by an order for foreclosure.

In contrast, when a common law mortgage is created in a Torrens system, people searching the register will have no way of knowing that the registered proprietor of a fee simple estate is really just a mortgagee. They will assume that the mortgagee has beneficial ownership of the land and not merely a security right. Therefore, the mortgagor's equity of redemption is especially vulnerable to the mortgagee's abuse of power. People wanting to mortgage Torrens land should either use the proper form of Torrens mortgage or make an equitable mortgage by deposit of the certificate of title.

Leases

Leases can be created in several different ways. Most legal leases are created by registration, but some short legal leases and all equitable leases are created without registration, as discussed below. The method of registering a lease depends on whether it is granted by the Crown or by the holder of another estate.

In most jurisdictions, the registration of a Crown lease will lead to the creation of a new folio of the register and a new certificate of title for the leasehold estate. However, if the Crown is already the registered proprietor of the land, it is possible to register the lease in the existing folio and endorse it on the Crown's certificate of title.

When the registered proprietor of a fee simple estate grants a lease, it will be registered in the existing folio and endorsed on the existing certificate of title. This also occurs when a folio has been created for a life or leasehold estate and the registered proprietor of that estate grants a lease or sublease.

In some jurisdictions, the Registrar may create a new folio for a lease granted by the registered proprietor of a greater estate. For example, suppose that I am the registered proprietor of a fee simple estate and grant a 25 year lease to you. When you register that lease, it will be recorded in the existing folio and endorsed on my certificate of title. The Registrar might also decide to create a new folio for your leasehold estate. The advantage of the separate folio is that property rights which attach only to your estate can be registered in that folio. If you mortgage your leasehold estate or grant a sublease, easement, or any other property rights to it, they will not appear on my certificate of title.

If the Registrar does not create a separate folio for your lease, then any property rights you create will be recorded in the folio for my fee simple estate and endorsed on the certificate of title for my estate. Although this may lead to a large number of endorsements on that certificate of title, it will be clear that some endorsements relate only to your lease. For example, if you mortgage your lease, the registered mortgage will be recorded in the folio and endorsed on the certificate of title as a mortgage of your registered lease (with a reference to the registration number of your lease).

In the Northern Territory, Queensland, and South Australia, all leases can be registered. In the Australian Capital Territory, registration is available for all leases except periodic tenancies. Other states provide for the registration of leases greater than three years. However, Tasmania is the only state that makes it clear that a "lease for a term of 3 years or less is not registrable": *Land Titles Act* 1980 (Tas), s 64.

Section 53 of the *Real Property Act* 1900 (NSW) states that "the proprietor shall execute a lease in the approved form" if he or she wants to lease land "for a life or lives or for any term of years exceeding three years". This is understood to mean that registration is the only way to create a legal lease longer than three years, but it can also be used to create shorter leases: see *Parkinson v Braham* (1961) 62 SR (NSW) 663.

In Victoria and Western Australia, the Torrens statute does not say that leases over three years "shall" be in a certain form, but that a landlord "may" use that form to create that lease: *Transfer of Land Act* 1958 (Vic), s 66; *Transfer of Land Act* 1893 (WA), s 91. This implies (and is generally understood to mean) that registration may not be used to create shorter leases.

In the Australian Capital Territory, "A lease in registrable form for a life or lives or a term that expires on a date specified in the lease, may be registered under this Act": *Land Titles Act* 1925 (ACT), s 82. As in Victoria and Western Australia, the use of the word "may" implies that other leases (periodic tenancies) may not be registered.

The inability to register short leases does not create a problem because those leases are given special priority (as discussed below) even though they are unregistered. There are three reasons for this. First, it avoids the problem of the registration system being overwhelmed by the volume of short leases submitted for registration. Secondly, many periodic and short-term tenants do not bother to register their leases. If the Torrens system did not recognise the validity of unregistered short leases, many tenants would be at risk of losing their property rights in priority disputes. Thirdly, leases of three years or less were given special treatment by the common law and by deeds registration systems. They could be created informally at common law and were exempt from registration in most systems: see Chapters 21 and 31. By allowing established practices to continue, the disruption caused by the introduction of the Torrens system was reduced.

Options to Purchase

An option to purchase land can be an equitable property right: see page 263. The option holder has the right to make a contract to buy land on certain terms. Essentially, the seller has made an offer to sell and the buyer has a specified amount of time in which to accept that offer. If the exercise of the option will create a specifically enforceable contract of sale, then the option is an equitable property right (which will become a constructive trust when the contract is made).

Options to purchase can be granted independently, but are often attached to leases. For example, I might lease my house to you for five years and give you an option to purchase that house at a specified price at any time during the lease. The terms of the option would normally be included in our lease documents.

Leases often contain **options to renew** them. During the term of the lease, the tenant may have the option to obtain one or more additional terms. If the exercise of the option will create a specifically enforceable contract of lease (and therefore an equitable lease), the option to renew is also an equitable property right.

An option to renew is the same kind of property right as an option to purchase. In both cases, the option holder has the power to buy an estate in land and that power is regarded by courts of equity as a lesser property right to the land. The only difference between them is the duration of the estate that will be acquired when the option is exercised: leasehold or freehold. This is a difference of degree, not kind.

Torrens systems do not provide for the separate registration of options to purchase or renew. However, they are often contained in leases that get registered. This will make the option a registered property right, although there is some doubt about the status of options to purchase in some states.

In *Mercantile Credits Ltd v Shell Co of Australia Ltd* (1976) 136 CLR 326, a 10 year lease, registered under the *Real Property Act* 1886 (SA), contained options to renew the lease for three further terms of five years each. The court decided that the options were registered property rights, which had priority over a mortgage registered after the lease. If the option was exercised, it would produce a new unregistered lease (which could be registered as a new lease or as an extension of the old lease). However, the property right to obtain that lease was registered and obtained the benefits of that registration.

Section 117 of the *Real Property Act* deals with the contents of registered leases and says that "a right for or covenant by the lessee to purchase the land therein described may be stipulated in such lease, and shall be binding". Even though this does not mention options to renew, the court decided that an option to renew would be a registered property right, because it was so closely connected to the registered leasehold estate. However, some of the judges doubted whether this also applied to options to purchase, in the absence of statutory authority. Stephen J said (at 351):

"Were it not for s 117 it would be doubtful whether an option to purchase might properly be included in a registered memorandum of lease ... Such an option is of its nature unrelated to the tenant's estate or interest under the lease."

There are three other Torrens statutes which say that an option to purchase may be included in a registered lease: the *Land Titles Act* 1925 (ACT), section 83, *Real Property Act* 1900 (NSW), section 53, and *Real Property Act* (NT), section 117. Other statutes are silent on this issue. However, in every jurisdiction, options to purchase should be treated in the same way as options to renew: DJ Whalan, *The Torrens System in Australia* (1982) p 118. In both cases, the tenant has a legal right to possession of land and an equitable right to extend that right (either for a term or indefinitely). It is common knowledge that registered leases may contain either or both options and there is no reason to regard one as a registered property right and the other as unregistered.

The registration of an option to purchase or renew does not convert it into a legal property right. It is property only because its exercise will produce a contract that can be specifically enforced according to the rules of equity. If, for any reason, its exercise will not produce a specifically enforceable contract, the option is not a property right: see *Travinto Nominees Pty Ltd v Vlattas* (1973) 129 CLR 1; *Re Eastdoro Pty Ltd (No 2)* [1990] 1 Qd R 424. In that situation, the registration of the lease has no effect on the option. If an option is not a property right, registration will not make it property, because it will not make the contract (obtained by exercising the option) specifically enforceable.

Restrictive Covenants

As discussed in Chapter 16, restrictive covenants can be created by contracts between neighbouring land owners or as part of development schemes. If a covenant restricts the use of land for the benefit of nearby land (such as a promise not to build higher than 15 metres), that restriction may be enforceable as an equitable property right. This is because courts of equity would enforce those kinds of restrictions by granting injunctions against the person who made the covenant and against anyone who acquired the land with notice of the covenant.

The first Torrens systems did not have provisions to deal with restrictive covenants: see DJ Whalan, *The Torrens System in Australia* (1982) pp 109-114. This is probably because they were being enacted in Australia at roughly the same time that restrictive covenants were being developed in England. When Australian courts began recognising restrictive covenants, Registrars began noting them in folios without statutory authority. There are still no provisions dealing specifically with restrictive covenants in the *Land Titles Act* 1925 (ACT) or *Real Property Act* 1886 (SA).

In New South Wales, a person entitled to the benefit of a restrictive covenant can protect it by lodging a "caveat prohibiting the Registrar-General from granting an application to extinguish a restrictive covenant": *Real Property Act* 1900 (NSW), s 74F. In the Northern Territory, the Registrar is required to note restrictive covenants in favour of the Crown in the folio and on the certificate of title: *Real Property Act* (NT), ss 47, 49. Section 97A of the *Land Title Act* 1994 (Qld) permits the registration of restrictive covenants in favour of "the State or a local government". Tasmania, Victoria, and Western Australia provide mechanisms for registering all restrictive covenants: see, eg, *Transfer of Land Act* 1893 (WA), ss 129A and 136D.

The restrictive covenant is an equitable property right without an equivalent legal right. Registration does not convert it into a legal property right. That is made clear in Victoria and Tasmania. Section 88 of the *Transfer of Land Act* 1958 (Vic) states that "a recording in the Register of any such restrictive covenant ... shall not give it any greater operation than it has under the instrument or Act creating it". Section 102 of the *Land Titles Act* 1980 (Tas) is similar. Registration of a restrictive covenant enhances its priority, but does not otherwise change the nature of the right.

Effect of Registration

As discussed above and in Chapter 21, most legal property rights to Torrens land are created not by the execution of a document, but by its registration. This changes the common law rule that most legal property rights are created by executing a deed. Each Torrens statute contains a provision similar to section 40 of the *Transfer of Land Act* 1958 (Vic):

> "(1) Subject to this Act no instrument until registered as in this Act provided shall be effectual to create vary extinguish or pass any estate or interest or encumbrance in on or over any land under the operation of this Act, but upon registration the estate or interest or encumbrance shall be created varied extinguished or pass in the manner and subject to the covenants and conditions specified in the instrument or by this Act prescribed or declared to be implied in instruments of a like nature.
>
> (2) Every instrument when registered shall be of the same efficacy as if under seal and shall be as valid and effectual to all intents and purposes as a deed duly executed acknowledged or other the appropriate form of document."

Like the equivalent provisions in other jurisdictions, this section does two main things. First, it means that the execution of a document will not create a legal property right in a Torrens system, even though it would create that right at common law. Secondly, the registration of a document will create a legal property right according to its terms. This means that legal property rights can be created by the registration of documents that would not create property rights at common law (such as forgeries or otherwise defective documents).

For example, suppose that I want to transfer my house to you. I will need to execute a transfer of land in the prescribed form and cause it to be registered. If I execute the transfer and deliver it to you, together with my certificate of title, you do not thereby acquire any legal property rights (other than possession of those documents). As discussed below, you would have the equitable ownership of my house (because you have the power to obtain legal ownership), but you would not get legal ownership until the transfer was registered.

Unregistered Property Rights

Most Torrens statutes create the false impression that registration is the only way to create property rights to land in that system. This is because they say that documents are ineffective to create any property rights whatsoever until they are registered (like section 40 of the *Transfer of Land Act* 1958 (Vic), quoted above). However, those statements mean only that registration is the only way to create most legal property rights. Some legal rights and all equitable rights are unaffected by that limitation. There are two reasons for this: Torrens statutes affect neither the creation of property rights without documents nor the creation of equitable property rights with documents.

Rights Created Without Documents

Torrens statutes say that documents do not create property rights until registered, but say nothing about the creation of property rights without documents. Legal rights to possession can be created without documents in two ways: adverse possession (discussed in Chapter 8) and informal leases of up to three years (discussed at page 250). There are many different ways to create equitable property rights without using documents: see Part IV.

Adverse Possession

If a person takes possession of land, he or she thereby acquires a legal right to possession, which is enforceable against everyone else in society, except someone with a better right to possession. For convenience, the person with a better right to possession is called the owner here, but he or she may be the owner of the fee simple, a tenant, or merely a person who had prior possession of the land. Possession without permission of the owner is called adverse possession. Since this legal property right is created without documents, the Torrens system does not interfere with its creation.

If possession is adverse, the owner has to recover possession or start legal proceedings for that purpose within the **limitation period** (15 years in South Australia and Victoria and 12 years in other states). If the owner fails to do so, her or his right to possession is extinguished by the *Limitation Act* or *Limitation of Actions Act*. There are exceptions. The limitation period is extended for people who lack legal capacity and the Crown has a longer limitation period or is exempt entirely (depending on the jurisdiction).

If the owner's right to possession is barred by the limitation statute, the adverse possessor then has the best right to possession. This is equivalent to ownership and, in every state, the Torrens statute permits the adverse possessor to apply to become the registered proprietor of the owner's estate.

In the Australian Capital Territory and Northern Territory, the limitation statutes do not apply to possession of Torrens land. Section 69 of the *Land Titles Act* 1925 (ACT) states:

> "No title to land adverse to or in derogation of the title of the registered proprietor shall be acquired by any length of possession by virtue of any statute of limitations relating to real estate, nor shall the title of any such registered proprietor be extinguished by the operation of any such statute."

Section 251 of the *Real Property Act* (NT) is similar. The adverse possessor has an unregistered legal property right, since that right to possession is enforceable against everyone except the owner. However, that right never becomes ownership in the territories, because it cannot affect the right of the registered proprietor to recover possession.

Informal Leases

At common law, a lease can be created informally, without documents, if the tenant takes possession of the land. A person who has possession with permission of the owner is at least a tenant at will. If the tenant pays rent, then (in the absence of evidence to the contrary) the common law assumes that a periodic tenancy has been created, with the period matching either the frequency of rental payments or the local custom. However, the tenant can have a legal lease for a fixed term of up to three years, if the arrangement can be proved and the rent is set at full market value.

Since informal leases are created without documents, the Torrens system does not prevent them from arising. They exist as unregistered legal estates.

Rights Created With Documents

The courts have interpreted Torrens statutes in a way that leaves the creation of equitable property rights more or less unchanged. The leading case is *Barry v Heider* (1914) 19 CLR 197. Mrs Heider claimed an equitable mortgage of Mr Barry's land, based on an unregistered transfer from Barry to Mr Schmidt and an unregistered mortgage from Schmidt to Heider. Barry argued that this was not possible, because the Torrens statute made documents inoperative until they were registered.

The High Court of Australia rejected Barry's argument. Torrens statutes recognise the existence of unregistered property rights created by unregistered documents. They prohibit the registration of trusts (but allow the deposit of trust documents) and permit people to lodge caveats to protect unregistered property rights created by documents. Isaacs J (at 213) said of the Torrens statutes in Australia that:

> "They have long, and in every State, been regarded ... as giving greater certainty to titles of registered proprietors, but not in any way destroying the fundamental doctrines by which Courts of Equity have enforced, as against registered proprietors, conscientious obligations entered into by them."

In other words, Torrens statutes do not affect the creation of equitable property rights. If someone makes a specifically enforceable contract to transfer land or grant a mortgage, that property right will be created in equity: see page 263. Therefore, Barry's contract of sale could create a constructive trust for Schmidt and Schmidt's contract of mortgage could create an equitable mortgage of that trust for Heider.

Although *Barry v Heider* tells us that unregistered documents can create equitable property rights, the documents in that case were not effective to create those rights directly. This is because the sale to Schmidt had been induced by his fraud and was rescinded by Barry. Since the contract of sale was never specifically enforceable, Schmidt did not have a property right to Barry's land and had nothing to mortgage to Heider. Even if it had been specifically enforceable when it was made, Barry's rescission of the contract would have destroyed Schmidt's interest in the land and Heider's mortgage of that interest. However, Heider had an equitable mortgage created by estoppel (discussed in Chapter 23): Barry had represented to Heider that Schmidt was the beneficial owner of the land and she had relied on that representation to her detriment.

Contracts

As discussed at page 263, a contract to transfer a property right to land will create that right in equity if the contract is specifically enforceable. This is how most unregistered leases are created. Most landlords and tenants will make a written lease contract (often called a tenancy agreement). Although that contract cannot be registered, it will create an equitable lease when it is signed. If the parties then execute a lease in the appropriate form and register it, this will create a legal lease, which will replace the equitable lease created by the contract.

Normally, contracts to transfer property rights to land are not enforceable unless they are made in writing (or there is sufficient part performance of the contract, as discussed at page 265). However, if a registered proprietor makes an oral contract to transfer a property right and then executes a document for registration of that right, the document will fulfil the writing requirement and the contract will become specifically enforceable.

For example, suppose that we make an oral agreement that I will grant an easement to you. The contract is not specifically enforceable without writing and no property rights are created. If I execute the document that will enable you to register the easement, there is sufficient written evidence of the contract and it becomes specifically enforceable. At that point, an equitable easement is created (which will be replaced by a legal easement if the document is registered).

Trusts

Even in the absence of a contract, documents can create trusts. Of course, many trusts are created without documents, but an express trust of land must be manifest in writing: see page 251. Therefore, if a settlor executes a deed of trust or signs some other document setting out the terms of the trust, a trust will arise even though that document cannot be registered.

Constructive trusts are often created by contracts of sale (as discussed above), but can also be created simply by the execution and delivery of transfer documents. Suppose that I intend to give my house to you. My intention will not create a property right for you, nor will my execution of a transfer of land. However, if I deliver the transfer and my certificate of title to you, you will become the equitable owner of the house because you have the power to obtain legal ownership by registration: *Corin v Patton* (1990) 169 CLR 540. Equity treats the gift as complete and I will hold my house in trust for you until you become the registered proprietor: see Chapter 21.

All of this means that, despite the plain wording of Torrens statutes, documents routinely create property rights to Torrens land without being registered. This is one of the complaints about Torrens systems. The statutes are not "user friendly", because they do not convey an accurate impression of how those systems actually operate. The *Land Title Act 1994* (Qld) is the most modern Torrens statute in Australia and was designed to deal with this problem. Section 181 states simply that "An instrument does not transfer or create an interest in a lot at law until it is registered." This makes it clear that documents do not create legal property rights before they are registered, but are capable of creating equitable property rights.

Registered Property Rights

In this part of the chapter, we consider the priority of registered property rights. It is divided into four separate sections:

1) .....priority between registered rights;
2) .....priority over unregistered rights (indefeasibility);
3) .....survival of unregistered rights (exceptions to indefeasibility); and
4) .....creation of new unregistered rights (the *in personam* exception).

The priority between registered rights is relatively straightforward, while the issues surrounding the priority of registered rights over unregistered rights are more complex. The second section introduces the general principle of indefeasibility, which gives registered rights priority over older unregistered rights. This is followed by a discussion of the various exceptions to the general principle, which permit older unregistered rights to survive and take priority over newer registered rights. The fourth section concerns the ways in which registered rights can be diminished or destroyed by the creation of new unregistered rights.

Priority Between Registered Rights

In every Torrens system, documents are registered in the order in which they are submitted to the Registrar (provided they are properly registerable) and registered rights take priority according to the order of registration. For example, section 53 of the *Transfer of Land Act* 1893 (WA) states:

> "(1) The Registrar shall register an instrument presented for registration in the order, and from the time, of its presentation.
>
> (2) Instruments purporting to affect the same estate or interest have priority as between each other according to the time of registration and not according to the date of the instrument, notwithstanding any actual or constructive notice."

Rights Attached to Different Estates

Note that the order of registration determines the priority of documents "purporting to affect the same estate or interest" in land. This sets the priority of two registered property rights that are attached to the same estate, but does not affect the priority between a property right and the estate to which it is attached. For example, suppose that I am the registered proprietor of a fee simple estate and mortgage it to Maureen and then lease it to Helen. The priority between Maureen's mortgage and Helen's lease will depend on the order in which they are registered. However, the transfer of land, which created my fee simple estate, was registered before either of them. Although that gives me a right to exclude others from the land, it does not take priority over Maureen's mortgage or Helen's lease.

In one sense, my transfer, Maureen's mortgage, and Helen's lease all purport to affect the same estate. However, the transfer is the document that created my estate, while the mortgage and lease are documents that affected it. My estate is not in competition with any rights that attach to and depend on it, but those dependent rights are, potentially, in conflict with each other. In a Torrens system, the order of registration is used as the primary basis for determining priority among the various rights that can become attached to the same estate.

Suppose that Helen mortgaged her leasehold estate to Wayne and that documents were registered in the following order: transfer to me, lease to Helen, mortgage to Maureen, and mortgage to Wayne. The only two rights in direct conflict are the lease to Helen and mortgage to Maureen, because they are attached to the same estate. Wayne's mortgage is attached to Helen's lease and depends on the continued existence of that estate. If I failed to pay my debt to Maureen and she foreclosed on the mortgage, she would obtain the fee simple estate, subject to Helen's lease and Wayne's mortgage of that lease. It does not matter that Wayne's mortgage was registered after Maureen's, because they do not purport to affect the same estate.

At common law, any conflict between Maureen and I, Helen and I, or Helen and Wayne would not be regarded as a priority dispute: see Chapter 27. The conflict is not resolved by determining whose rights have priority, but by deciding what rights were created and whether someone has failed to perform the obligations which correspond to those rights.

In a Torrens system, these sorts of disputes can look like priority disputes, because forgeries can create property rights (as discussed below). For example, suppose that I did not grant a mortgage to Maureen, but someone impersonated me and forged it. If Maureen is innocent of the fraud and gave value for the mortgage, it will be enforceable when it is registered. Since Maureen and I did not deal directly with each other, it looks like a priority dispute between two conflicting property rights to the same land. However, this is not a competition between two independent rights attached to the same estate. Maureen's mortgage is attached to my estate and I cannot claim priority on the basis that my transfer was registered first (although Helen's lease will have priority on that basis).

Unlike other Torrens statutes, the *Land Title Act* 1994 (Qld) does not say that the order of registration determines the priority of documents "purporting to affect the same estate or interest". Section 178 says that "Registered instruments have priority according to when each of them was lodged and not according to when each of them was executed." A plain reading of this would indicate that my estate would have priority over Maureen's mortgage, because my transfer was registered before her mortgage. However, this interpretation would be absurd, since it would mean that registered property rights would not bind the estate to which they attached. This section must have the same effect on priorities as the corresponding sections in other jurisdictions.

Variation of Priority

In many Torrens systems, it is possible to vary the priority of registered rights by agreement. For example, section 56 of the *Real Property Act* 1886 (SA) states that, "The Registrar-General may, on application in the appropriate form, vary the order of priority between two or more registered mortgages or encumbrances." The variation is endorsed on the documents affected and on the certificate of title.

Priority Over Unregistered Rights (Indefeasibility)

Torrens statutes are designed to provide registered proprietors with security of title. A registered property right is supposed to have priority over all unregistered property rights, except as provided by statute. This is often called "indefeasibility of title". However, the term can be misleading, because it suggests that a registered title cannot be annulled or defeated. The protection of the Torrens system does not prevent the creation of newer registered or unregistered rights, which might diminish or destroy an "indefeasible" registered right. As discussed below, this can happen without the consent, knowledge, or involvement of the registered proprietor.

The principle of indefeasibility is like the defence of *bona fide* purchase for value without notice. Registration of a property right gives it priority over older unregistered rights, but does not prevent the creation of newer rights. Also, there are numerous exceptions to the principle of indefeasibility, which permit older unregistered rights to have priority over newer registered rights. As discussed below, some unregistered rights have special priority and some registered proprietors are not allowed to claim the priority normally accorded to registered rights. Therefore, the term "indefeasibility" is simply shorthand for the set of priority rules in a Torrens system, which permit registered rights to gain priority over older unregistered rights.

Indefeasibility Provisions

Indefeasibility is the combined effect of a number of rules which add to or detract from the priority of registered property rights. Therefore, the principle of indefeasibility depends on, and is defined by, a number of different sections in each Torrens statute. They provide three basic forms of protection for registered property rights: priority over unregistered rights, protection from the effects of notice, and protection from interference with possession. They then qualify this protection by creating a number of exceptions to it.

Priority over Unregistered Rights

The primary indefeasibility provisions give registered property rights priority over all unregistered rights (subject to a number of exceptions). For example, section 42 of the *Real Property Act* 1900 (NSW) states:

> "Notwithstanding the existence in any other person of any estate or interest which but for this Act might be held to be paramount or to have priority, the registered proprietor for the time being of any estate or interest in land recorded in a folio of the Register shall, except in case of fraud, hold the same, subject to such other estates and interests and such entries, if any, as are recorded in that folio, but absolutely free from all other estates and interests that are not so recorded ..."

Other Torrens statutes use different language to achieve the same effect. For example, the *Land Titles Act* 1980 (Tas) is one of the few Torrens statutes that actually uses the word "indefeasible". Section 40 states that "the title of a registered proprietor of land is indefeasible" and defines "indefeasible" to mean "subject only to such estates and interests as are recorded on the folio of the Register or registered dealing evidencing title to the land." Section 184 of the *Land Title Act* 1994 (Qld) states that:

> "A registered proprietor of an interest in a lot holds the interest subject to registered interests affecting the lot but free from all other interests."

Protection from Notice

Torrens statutes also protect registered proprietors from the effects of notice. For example, section 134 of the *Transfer of Land Act* 1893 (WA) says that, except in the case of fraud, people dealing with the registered proprietor are not "affected by notice actual or constructive of any trust or unregistered interest any rule of law or equity to the contrary notwithstanding". These provisions relieve people, who wish to acquire registered property rights, of the burden of having to investigate whether the current registered proprietor has a valid title free of unregistered property rights.

Protection from Interference

A person who acquires a registered estate wants to hold it free from interference by people with competing claims to the land. The statutory priority over unregistered rights should be sufficient for this purpose. However, Torrens statutes also provide additional protection for registered rights to possession.

The *Land Title Act* 1994 (Qld) provides the simplest and fullest protection from interference with possession. Section 184 states that "the registered proprietor ... is liable to a proceeding for possession of the lot or an interest in the lot only if the proceeding is brought by the registered proprietor of an interest affecting the lot".

Other statutes provide protection for registered proprietors who acquire their rights in good faith and for value. They are not "subject to an action of ejectment or for recovery of damages or for deprivation of the estate or interest", even though they acquired their registered rights from a registered proprietor who "was registered as proprietor through fraud or error": *Transfer of Land Act* 1958 (Vic), s 44. This confirms that registered rights are not dependent on a chain of title. Many of the problems that cause defective chains of title in deeds registration systems are irrelevant in a Torrens system.

Exceptions to Indefeasibility

These three provisions establish the basic concept of indefeasibility, which gives registered property rights priority over all older unregistered rights. Every Torrens statute then cuts down that priority, by placing qualifications on the right to claim it and by exempting some unregistered rights from it. These are discussed below. The true priority of a registered right depends on the combined effect of the basic protection provided by statute and the various exceptions to that protection.

Immediate and Deferred Indefeasibility

For many years, lawyers and judges debated whether an indefeasible title could be created by the registration of a forged or otherwise invalid document. There was no doubt that it would produce a legal property right. The issue was whether the registration could be cancelled at the request of the registered proprietor adversely affected by it.

There are two theories: indefeasibility is either immediate or deferred. **Immediate indefeasibility** means that registration based on an invalid document is entitled to the same priority as any other registered property right. **Deferred indefeasibility** means that the registration can be cancelled, but that its cancellation will not affect the indefeasibility of any subsequently registered property rights. Following *Gibbs v Messer* [1891] AC 248, the theory of deferred indefeasibility was dominant in Australia for the first half of the 20th century, but immediate indefeasibility has since prevailed in New Zealand and Australia: see *Frazer v Walker* [1967] 1 AC 569. Some doubts lingered over whether immediate indefeasibility applied everywhere in Australia, but those have been laid to rest: see *Pyramid Building Society v Scorpion Hotels Pty Ltd* [1998] 1 VR 188.

The difference between the two theories is best illustrated with an example. Suppose that Geoff was the registered proprietor of a fee simple estate and that I impersonated him and sold it to Harold, who mortgaged it to Sally. I forged a transfer of land to Harold, he executed a mortgage to Sally, and those documents were registered. Sally loaned the purchase price to Harold, who paid it to me just before I left the country. Geoff was then surprised to discover that his land is owned by Harold and mortgaged to Sally. All three are innocent victims of my fraud.

Immediate indefeasibility means that Harold and Sally have indefeasible titles and that Geoff must look to the assurance fund for compensation (since he will probably have trouble getting any money from me). Deferred indefeasibility means that Harold's title can be cancelled and Geoff can recover his fee simple estate. However, Sally's mortgage was created by a valid document and she relied on the fact that Harold was recorded in the register as the registered proprietor (when her mortgage was registered). Therefore, her mortgage is indefeasible and Geoff recovers the land subject to it.

Under deferred indefeasibility, Geoff could obtain compensation from the assurance fund to pay Sally and discharge her mortgage (if Harold was unable to pay the loan). However, Harold would not be so fortunate. He was not deprived of an interest in land, but was tricked into paying me a large sum of money. His loss was not caused by the Torrens system. Unless he could recover his money from me, he could be ruined financially.

This may have been a factor which led courts to adopt the theory of immediate indefeasibility. Better to let Harold keep the land and compensate Geoff than to let Geoff recover his land and send Harold into bankruptcy. However, it would make more sense to restore the land to Geoff and compensate Harold. The land may mean a great deal to Geoff. It may have been his home for years, the family farm for generations, or the site of his successful business. In contrast, Harold's interest in the land is new and much less substantial. Compensation might be cold comfort for Geoff, yet it would restore Harold fully to the position he occupied just a short time ago. However, it is too late for that solution. Immediate indefeasibility is well and truly established and the law must now devise ways to cope with some of the difficulties and inconsistencies it has created. These are discussed below.

Survival of Unregistered Rights (Exceptions to Indefeasibility)

When we say that a title is indefeasible, we mean only that it has priority over older unregistered property rights. Indefeasibility does not prevent the creation of newer rights. *Barry v Heider* (1914) 19 CLR 197 (discussed above) is an example of that. Mr Barry was a registered proprietor and, as a result of his conduct, Mrs Heider acquired a newer equitable mortgage over his land by estoppel. This was not a priority dispute and had nothing to do with indefeasibility of title. The issue was whether a property creating event (detrimental reliance) had occurred.

Therefore, to assess the indefeasibility of a registered property right, it is necessary to divide potentially conflicting unregistered rights into two groups: those created before its registration and those created on or after its registration. Sometimes, a new unregistered right (not affected by indefeasibility) can be mistaken for a pre-existing unregistered right (which may be destroyed by indefeasibility). That is especially true of unregistered rights that arise at the same time as a registered right, partly because of events that occurred before registration. This is discussed further below.

In this part of the chapter, we are concerned with the four main exceptions to indefeasibility, which permit unregistered property rights to survive the registration of conflicting rights:

1).....the Torrens statute expressly states that it will take priority;
2).....another statute protects it from destruction by the Torrens statute;
3).....the conflicting registered property right is acquired as a gift; or
4).....the registered proprietor is guilty of fraud.

Note that the first two exceptions are linked to the nature of the unregistered property right and the last two exceptions are linked to the nature of the transaction which led to the registration of a conflicting property right.

Express Exceptions

Each Torrens statute contains a list of specific exceptions to indefeasibility of title. The most important exception is fraud, discussed below. We are concerned here with specific unregistered property rights that are not adversely affected by the registration of a document creating a newer conflicting property right. The list of unregistered rights expressly saved from destruction varies from place to place. The specific exceptions found in each system are not discussed here in detail. This section deals generally with the exceptions common to most Torrens systems:

1).....prior certificates of title;
2).....misdescription of boundaries;

3) .....adverse possession;
4) .....short leases; and
5) .....easements.

Prior Certificates of Title

Torrens statutes provide for the unlikely event that two separate folios are created for the same land. The registered proprietors of the estates and other property rights registered in each folio will each have a claim to indefeasibility of title. The Torrens system resolves these conflicts by giving priority to the older of the two conflicting folios in existence when the conflict first arose. In other words, if a folio is created, that includes land already contained in another (uncancelled) folio, the older folio will take priority.

This does not mean that the person with the oldest title will prevail. The conflict might not be discovered until long after it first arose. Therefore, the current registered proprietors could be an entirely different group of people than the proprietors who first held conflicting titles in separate folios. Priority is not given to the oldest title then in existence, but to the title that can be traced back to the older of the two folios that existed when the conflict first arose. This is the one situation in which priority in a Torrens system depends upon a chain of title.

Misdescription of Boundaries

A problem can occur when the boundaries of land are described incorrectly, causing land that belongs in one folio to be included in another. This error is rare, but the risk is greatest when land is first brought into the Torrens system. Registration gives the new registered proprietor an indefeasible title, but an exception is made for the extra portions wrongly included in that folio. For example, section 40 of the *Land Titles Act* 1980 (Tas) states:

> "The title of a registered proprietor of land is not indefeasible ... so far as regards any portion of land that may be erroneously included in the folio of the Register or registered dealing evidencing the title of that registered proprietor by a wrong description of parcels or boundaries."

By "wrong description", Torrens statutes are creating an exception only for errors made describing the physical boundaries of estates. It does not apply to an error describing the nature of an estate or the rights contained within it. For example, in *Canadian Pacific Railway Co Ltd v Turta* [1954] SCR 427, a person registered a transfer of land, which excluded "all coal and petroleum". By mistake, the Register created a certificate of title which excluded only the coal. The person adversely affected by the error argued that this was a wrong description of the land. The court rejected that argument. The exception applied only to a wrong description of physical boundaries, which caused land to be included in a folio, when it belonged in the folio relating to adjacent land.

In every jurisdiction except Queensland and Tasmania, the exception does not apply to a registered proprietor who acquired title to the extra land for value. For example, suppose that my title includes land by mistake because of a wrong description of the boundary. If I sell or mortgage the land to you and you obtain registration, intending to acquire property rights to the entire parcel described in my certificate, you will get an indefeasible title to the portion included by mistake.

Adverse Possession

People in possession of land often receive special treatment in a Torrens system. As discussed below, all Torrens systems confer priority on people in possession under short leases. Some systems also confer priority on people who possess land adversely to the current registered proprietor. These exceptions to indefeasibility are justified, because possession is easily discovered by anyone wishing to acquire a right to the land.

In every system, the adverse possessor has a legal property right, which is enforceable against everyone except a person with a better right to possession. Except in the territories, adverse possession of Torrens land for a sufficient length of time can become ownership. The registered proprietor's right to recover possession will be barred by the statute of limitations: see above and Chapter 8.

In Tasmania, Victoria, and Western Australia, the rights of adverse possessors are not affected by the registration of conflicting property rights. For example, if I have been in adverse possession of land in Perth for four years when you become the registered proprietor of that land, you will have only eight years to recover possession from me. If you fail to do so, I will have had possession for the full limitation period and your right to possession will be extinguished.

In Queensland, this exception to indefeasibility applies only to "the interest of a person who, on application, would be entitled to be registered as owner of the lot because the person is an adverse possessor": *Land Title Act* 1994 (Qld), s 185. In other words, the adverse possessor's rights will take priority over the rights of a new registered proprietor only if adverse possession had continued for at least 12 years before registration occurred. Otherwise, the new registered proprietor's rights are unaffected (unless they are extinguished by a further 12 years of adverse possession).

The exception for adverse possessors is even more limited in South Australia. It applies only to people who had adverse possession of land for 15 years before the land was brought into the Torrens system: *Real Property Act* 1886 (SA), s 69. In all other cases, the rights of an adverse possessor are subject to the rights of registered proprietors.

In the Australian Capital Territory, New South Wales, and the Northern Territory, adverse possession is not an exception to indefeasibility of title. New South Wales is the only jurisdiction of the three that allows an adverse possessor to become the registered proprietor. However, that application cannot extinguish a registered property right unless the full 12 year limitation period has passed since that right was registered. For example, suppose that I have been in adverse possession of land for 30 years. Although I have been entitled to apply to become the registered proprietor for the last 18 years, my rights will not affect a new registered proprietor. If you register a fee simple estate, you will have a better right to possession for the next 12 years.

Short Leases

All Torrens statutes give some unregistered leases priority over registered property rights. Therefore, it is important for people buying rights to Torrens land to determine whether there are any tenants in possession and what rights they have.

This exception to indefeasibility varies from place to place. The following unregistered leases will survive registration of a conflicting property right:

1) .....leases up to one year, in the Northern Territory and South Australia;
2) .....leases up to three years, in the Australian Capital Territory, New South Wales, Queensland, and Tasmania;
3) .....leases up to five years in Western Australia; and
4) .....leases of any duration in Victoria.

In the Northern Territory, South Australia, Victoria, and Western Australia, the exception applies only to tenants in possession of the land. Therefore, if the tenant has an equitable lease, but has not yet taken possession, a newer registered right will have priority. This limit makes sense. The exception for unregistered leases is justified because a tenant's rights can be discovered by inspecting the land. It is much harder for people dealing with the land to discover an unregistered lease if the tenant is not in possession.

In Tasmania, this exception to indefeasibility applies to any periodic tenancy, informal leases up to three years (at full market rent) where the tenant is in possession, and any equitable lease. However, the exception for equitable leases does not apply "against a bona fide purchaser for value without notice of the lease who has lodged a transfer for registration": *Land Titles Act* 1980 (Tas), s 40.

Nowhere in Australia does the exception for unregistered leases correspond exactly to the restrictions on registering leases (discussed above). In other words, every jurisdiction gives priority to some unregistered leases that could be registered. This mismatch has been criticised. The register would provide a more accurate reflection of property rights if everyone, who could register a lease, would lose priority if they failed to do so. However, the protection of tenants in possession of land is based on the recognition that people do make informal arrangements about the use of land. Many tenancies would be at risk if those arrangements were not given priority over registered rights. Since they are easy to discover and do not detract greatly from the value of land, the limited protection given to unregistered leases is a reasonable intrusion on the rights of registered proprietors. The permission to register short leases provides an additional advantage to tenants, but is not itself a reason to limit the protection of unregistered leases.

Easements

Every Torrens statute provides some protection for unregistered easements. Some statutes limit this exception. For example, section 185 of the *Land Title Act* 1994 (Qld) protects unregistered easements that were in existence when the land was first brought into the Torrens system or were registered and then later removed from the register by mistake.

Other statutes protect all unregistered easements. For example, section 42 of the *Transfer of Land Act* 1958 (Vic) gives priority to "any easements howsoever acquired subsisting over or upon or affecting the land".

An unlimited exception to indefeasibility is difficult to justify. Since easements are non-possessory rights to land, they can be very difficult to discover. It is easy to understand why public easements (for utilities or public rights of way) are given priority. The greater public good provides a justification for limiting the rights of private land owners. However, why should the holder of a private easement over her or his neighbour's land be spared the bother and expense of registering it?

Other Statutes

The priority rules created by a Torrens statute may be affected by other statutes. A Torrens statute is a state or territorial government's declaration that titles to land are indefeasible under certain conditions. However, that cannot bind the Commonwealth nor can it prevent the state or territory from making other laws which detract from the indefeasibility it has created. The issue is one of statutory interpretation: does another statute conflict with the Torrens statute and, if so, which prevails?

Commonwealth laws take priority over state laws according to section 109 of the Constitution. Therefore, a state rule, that registered property rights have priority over unregistered property rights, cannot impair unregistered rights created or protected by Commonwealth legislation. For example, section 11 of the *Native Title Act* 1993 (Cth) states that "Native title is not able to be extinguished contrary to this Act": see Chapter 28. Therefore, the registration of a conflicting property right will not affect native title unless it is permitted to do so by the *Native Title Act*.

When there is a conflict between a Torrens statute and another state or territorial law, its resolution depends on the legislature's intention. Was the conflicting law supposed to affect property rights even though that might interfere with indefeasible titles created under the Torrens statute? In *Miller v Minister of Mines* [1963] AC 484, the Privy Council advised that a mining licence granted under New Zealand's *Mining Act* had priority over an estate registered under its Torrens statute, the *Land Transfer Act*. Lord Guest said (at 498):

> "It is not necessary ... that there should be a direct provision overriding the provisions of the Land Transfer Act. It is sufficient if this is proper implication from the terms of the relative statute."

Hopefully the conflicting statute will make this clear. For example, section 16 of the *Mining Act* 1971 (SA) states that, "Notwithstanding the provisions of any other Act or law, or of any land grant or other instrument, the property in all minerals is vested in the Crown." Therefore, there is no doubt that a fee simple estate, registered under the *Real Property Act* 1886 (SA), will not include mineral rights, even though that estate extends underground and no exception for mineral rights appears on the certificate of title: see Chapters 12 and 16.

This exception to indefeasibility has been criticised because it permits the creation of unregistered rights that will adversely affect registered proprietors and yet may be hard to find: see *Quach v Marrickville Municipal Council* (1990) 22 NSWLR 55. Some conflicting rights (such as mineral rights) are registered in other systems (discussed in the previous chapter), but it is possible for rights to exist and prevail over indefeasible titles, even though they are not listed in any public register. With so many statutes that might affect interests in land, it is not always easy to know where to look for those rights.

Donees

The *Land Title Act* 1994 (Qld) is the only Torrens statute which states clearly that registration of a gift of land produces an indefeasible title. According to section 180, an indefeasible title can be created by registration of a document "whether or not valuable consideration has been given".

In other jurisdictions, courts have had to decide whether donees of registered property rights are entitled to priority over older unregistered rights. In New South Wales, a registered right is indefeasible, regardless of whether the registered proprietor gave value for that right: *Bogdanovic v Koteff* (1988) 12 NSWLR 472. In South Australia and Victoria, the registration of a right received as a gift does not affect older unregistered rights: *Biggs v McEllister* (1880) 14 SALR 86; *Rasmussen v Rasmussen* [1995] 1 VR 613. In other states, the issue is not resolved, but it is commonly assumed that the law is the same as in South Australia and Victoria.

The exception for the registration of gifts is sometimes called the **volunteer exception**, although this can be confusing, because the term "volunteer" can mean different things in different legal contexts. This priority rule follows the position, taken by the common law, equity, and most deeds registration systems, that there is no reason to give a donee priority over older unregistered rights. He or she is not harmed if the gift turns out to be less valuable than expected. There is no reason to destroy vested property rights to enhance its value, in the absence of a clear statutory direction to do so.

In *King v Smail* [1958] VR 273, a husband and wife were the registered proprietors of land as joint tenants. The husband became bankrupt and all his property, including his interest in the land, was assigned to a trustee in bankruptcy. The husband then transferred his interest in the land to his wife, who became the sole registered proprietor. Since her registered title was received as a gift, it was subject to the trustee's older unregistered right to the husband's share of the land.

Adam J noted (at 276) that the primary indefeasibility provision, which gives registered titles priority over unregistered rights, "draws no distinction between persons becoming registered proprietors for value and mere volunteers". However, the statute "is to be read as a whole" and this provision "should be read subject to qualifications required of necessity or by implication to give effect to the scheme of legislation". He noted that several other rights are available only to purchasers for value, such as the protection from interference with possession and the right to compensation from the assurance fund.

He said (at 277) that the provision protecting registered proprietors from the effect of notice was "strong confirmation of the view that mere volunteers are outside the contemplation of the indefeasibility provisions". Section 43 of the *Transfer of Land Act* 1958 (Vic) states that registered proprietors are not "affected by notice actual or constructive of any trust or unregistered interest". However, at common law and equity, a donee takes subject to older property rights regardless of notice. Therefore, protection from the effect of notice will not enhance her or his position: see *IAC (Finance) Pty Ltd v Courtenay* (1963) 110 CLR 550 at 572. If Torrens statutes wanted to confer priority on donees, they should say that registered proprietors are not affected by trusts and unregistered interests and not merely that they are not affected by notice of those rights.

In the Northern Territory and South Australia, the *Real Property Act* provides even more support for the view that registration of a gift does not confer priority over older unregistered rights. Section 71 expressly preserves the priority of unregistered rights of any people with whom the registered proprietor has had dealings and any beneficiaries of trusts, but goes on to state that:

> "no unregistered estate, interest, power, right, contract, or trust shall prevail against the title of a registered proprietor taking *bona fide* for valuable consideration, or of any person *bona fide* claiming through or under him."

This protection of registered proprietors who give value for their rights suggests that the *Real Property Act*, when read as whole, is not supposed to destroy or impair unregistered rights in favour of donees.

The priority given to donees in New South Wales and Queensland may create difficulties, especially when combined with immediate indefeasibility (discussed above) and the narrow definition of Torrens fraud (discussed below). The registration of a forgery can give a donee a good title. Suppose that a modern day Robin Hood decided to register a large number of forgeries transferring houses in Sydney to the poor and homeless. The recipients of that generosity would be entitled to keep those homes and evict their former owners.

Although this example is far fetched, it is not hard to think of ways to abuse a Torrens system that confers indefeasible titles on donees. A gift to a friend or relative could destroy a trust for a de facto spouse or someone who transferred her or his land by mistake or under undue influence. In *Bogdanovic v Koteff* (1988) 12 NSWLR 472, a trust of a home was destroyed simply because the registered proprietor died and title passed to his son. Although courts and legislatures can find other ways to deal with these problems, it would be simpler just to preserve unregistered property rights, unless conflicting rights are acquired for value.

The main counter argument is that registration ought to create certainty of title, even for donees. However, anyone who buys land from a donee (or accepts a mortgage, lease, or other right for value) will obtain indefeasible title by registration. If a donee relies on her or his apparent ownership of land received as a gift and thereby suffers a detriment, her or his interests can be protected through estoppel: see Chapter 23.

Fraud

A title is not indefeasible if the registered proprietor obtained it fraudulently. Although the registration is effective to create legal title, it does not have priority over older unregistered rights and can be cancelled to restore title to the previous registered proprietor.

Whose Fraud?

Fraud affects the priority of a registered property right only if the registered proprietor (or her or his agent) was guilty of fraud when that right was acquired. The fraud of previous registered proprietors or other people involved in the transaction is irrelevant, unless the registered proprietor knew about or suspected their fraud. As Lord Lindley said, in *Assets Co Ltd v Mere Roihi* [1905] AC 176 at 210:

> "[T]he fraud which must be proved in order to invalidate the title of a registered purchaser for value ... must be brought home to the person whose registered title is impeached or to his agents. Fraud by persons from whom he claims does not affect him unless knowledge of it is brought home to him or his agents."

The fraud of an agent can be attributed to the registered proprietor in the same way that an agent's notice can be imputed to her or his principal: see page 412. If the agent helped the registered proprietor acquire the title in question, and was guilty of fraud in the course of that transaction, that fraud will be attributed to the proprietor and prevent her or him from claiming an indefeasible title. However, if the registered proprietor was also a victim of the agent's fraud, it might not affect her or his rights.

What is Torrens Fraud?

The concept of fraud is defined narrowly in Torrens systems. As Lord Lindley said in *Assets Co Ltd v Mere Roihi* (above at 210), "by fraud in these Acts is meant actual fraud, ie, dishonesty of some sort, not what is called constructive or equitable fraud". Torrens fraud occurs when someone acquires a registered property right by means of deceptive or otherwise wrongful conduct, but only if he or she participated in that conduct or knew or suspected it had occurred when registration was obtained. Mere notice of wrongdoing is not fraud in this context. As Lord Lindley said (at 210):

> "The mere fact that he might have found out fraud if he had been more vigilant, and had made further inquiries which he omitted to make, does not of itself prove fraud on his part. But if it be shewn that his suspicions were aroused, and that he abstained from making inquiries for fear of learning the truth, the case is very different, and fraud may be properly ascribed to him."

Every Torrens statute, except the *Land Title Act* 1994 (Qld), states that mere knowledge of the existence of an unregistered property right is not fraud. For example, section 72 of the *Real Property Act* (NT) states:

"Knowledge of the existence of any unregistered estate, interest, contract, or trust shall not of itself be evidence of want of bona fides so as to affect the title of any registered proprietor."

Since it is not fraud if a registered proprietor knows that an unregistered right exists, it cannot be fraud to register a document knowing that this will destroy the unregistered right. Otherwise, the section about knowledge would be meaningless. As Walters J said, in *RM Hosking Properties Pty Ltd v Barnes* [1971] SASR 100 at 103:

"I think that in enacting the section, the legislature meant that a bona fide purchaser might disregard the fact of there being an unregistered interest and need not take into consideration the rights of persons claiming under that unregistered interest."

In that case, the registered proprietor obtained title knowing that a tenant had possession of the land under an unregistered lease. Since the lease was longer than a year, it was not an express exception to indefeasibility under the *Real Property Act* 1886 (SA). The registered right took priority and the registered proprietor was entitled to possession of the land.

Something more than knowledge is required before the registered proprietor will be guilty of Torrens fraud. For example, if I buy land from Catherine, knowing that she holds it in trust for Jessica, I am not, for that reason alone, guilty of fraud. I am free to register the transfer of land and obtain title free of that trust. It is not up to me to protect Jessica's interests or inquire whether Catherine is acting properly. However, if I know or suspect that Catherine is selling the land to me in breach of trust, I will be guilty of fraud and hold the land in trust for Jessica.

Loke Yew v Port Swettenham Rubber Co Ltd [1913] AC 491 was similar to the *RM Hosking Properties* case and yet the registered proprietor was guilty of fraud. A company bought land knowing that it was subject to an unregistered lease. The vendor refused to sell unless the company promised to respect the tenant's rights. The company's agent made that promise, but had no intention of keeping it. This was a fraudulent misrepresentation and, therefore, the lease had priority over the company's registered title.

A person is guilty of fraud if he or she submits a document for registration, knowing that it was not executed properly. In *Australian Guarantee Corp Ltd v De Jager* [1984] VR 483, a home owned jointly by a husband and wife was mortgaged to Australian Guarantee Corp (AGC). The wife's signature on the mortgage was forged by her husband's business partner. AGC did not know about the forgery, but its employee knew that the person who signed the mortgage, as the witness to the wife's signature, did not see her sign it. Since that knowledge was attributed to AGC, its registration of that document was fraud and the mortgage did not affect the wife's interest in the land. Tadgell J said (at 497-498):

"A system of land title by registration, such as the Torrens system is, plainly depends on the good faith of those presenting instruments for registration... To lodge an instrument for registration in the knowledge that the attesting witness had not been present at execution must deprive the lodging party of an honest belief that it is a genuine document on which the Registrar can properly act."

The *Land Title Act* 1994 (Qld) does not contain the standard Torrens provision that knowledge of an unregistered property right is not fraud. The corresponding provision (in section 184) states that "the registered proprietor ... is not affected by actual or constructive notice of an unregistered interest affecting the lot", but not "if there has been fraud by the registered proprietor". Since fraud is not defined in the statute, it may have a broader meaning in Queensland than in other Torrens systems. Notice will not affect a registered proprietor, but knowledge that registration will destroy an unregistered interest could be regarded as fraudulent.

Fraud After Registration

In *Bahr v Nicolay* (1988) 164 CLR 604, it was suggested that a registered property right can lose its indefeasibility if a person acts fraudulently after he or she becomes a registered proprietor. The Bahrs sold land to Nicolay for $32,000 and took a lease back from him for three years, with an option to purchase the land for $45,000. Nicolay became the registered proprietor, but the lease was not registered. The Bahrs made this arrangement to raise money to improve the land. Essentially, they were the beneficial owners of the land and Nicolay held the fee simple as security for a loan. It was similar to a common law mortgage.

Nicolay sold the land to the Thompsons (for $40,000), who acknowledged the agreement between the Bahrs and Nicolay and later wrote to the Bahrs confirming that they would honour their option to purchase. However, when the Bahrs exercised that option, the Thompsons refused to sell. The High Court ordered specific performance of the contract of sale (after the lower courts had refused to do so).

Since the option to purchase was an older unregistered right, which was not expressly excepted from indefeasibility, the difficulty is understanding how it could survive registration of the transfer to the Thompsons. The best explanation is that it did not. Instead, the conduct of the Thompsons gave the Bahrs a new right to purchase the land (as discussed below). However, two of the judges suggested that the case could also be understood on the basis of fraud.

Mason CJ and Dawson J compared *Bahr v Nicolay* to *Loke Yew v Port Swettenham Rubber Co Ltd* [1913] AC 491 (discussed above) and said (at 615):

> "[T]here is no difference between the false undertaking which induced the execution of the transfer in *Loke Yew* and an undertaking honestly given which induces the execution of a transfer and is subsequently repudiated for the purpose of defeating the prior interest. The repudiation is fraudulent because it has as its object the destruction of the unregistered interest notwithstanding that the preservation of the unregistered interest was the foundation or assumption underlying the execution of the transfer."

With great respect, there is a world of difference between the two situations. In *Loke Yew*, the registered proprietor obtained title by lying to the vendor. In *Bahr v Nicolay*, the Thompsons honestly made a promise and later changed their minds. If the Thompsons are guilty of fraud, then every intentional breach of contract is fraud. This cannot be right. The repudiation of a promise soon after it is made indicates fraud, but only because it suggests that the person never intended to keep the promise. However, if a person chooses not to perform a contract honestly made, he or she is guilty of breach of contract, nothing more.

Also, when the Thompsons registered the transfer without fraud, they obtained an indefeasible title, free of the Bahrs' older unregistered property right. It cannot be wrong to refuse later to recognise a right that no longer exists. The extinguished right cannot be recreated by a denial of its existence. If property rights could be created in this way, a very wide door would be opened in the wall of indefeasibility. Honest registered proprietors could find themselves subject to older unregistered rights simply because they refuse to give effect to them.

Fortunately, this view of fraud did not prevail in the High Court. It had been put forward by Mason CJ and Dawson J as an alternative approach and was rejected by Wilson J and Toohey J. The court held that the Bahrs had a right to purchase the land because the Thompsons had accepted an undertaking to resell it to them. This right did not depend on fraud and is discussed below.

Creation of New Unregistered Rights (the In Personam Exception)

Indefeasibility of title provides a registered proprietor with powerful protection from older unregistered rights. However, with one important exception (discussed below), it does not affect the creation of new property rights to land. Registered proprietors are free to create property rights to their land. Property rights can also arise without their consent, in response to events such as detrimental reliance, unjust enrichment, and wrongdoing: see Part IV. When a property right is created by registration, older conflicting unregistered rights are destroyed (subject to exceptions), but new property rights may be created from that moment on.

This principle, that indefeasibility of title does not prevent the creation of rights, is sometimes called the "*in personam* exception" to indefeasibility. This phrase was coined following a comment made by Lord Wilberforce in *Frazer v Walker* [1967] 1 AC 569 at 585. After setting out the principle of immediate indefeasibility, he said that "this principle in no way denies the right of a plaintiff to bring against a registered proprietor a claim in personam, founded in law or in equity, for such relief as a court acting in personam may grant".

The phrase "*in personam* exception" is unfortunate for two reasons. First, it is not really an exception to indefeasibility of title. It refers not to the survival of older unregistered rights, but to the creation of newer unregistered rights. Indefeasibility of title is about the priority of rights and has (almost) nothing to do with their creation. The *in personam* exception is an "exception" to indefeasibility only because a registered right can be affected by the creation of a new right. For example, when a trust attaches to a fee simple estate, the registered proprietors, as trustees, are no longer free to use that estate for their own benefit. In this same sense, registration of a document is also an "exception" to indefeasibility.

Secondly, this "exception" is not limited to the creation of personal rights. Registered proprietors often create personal rights to use their land (such as a licence to stay in the guest room for the weekend), but they also create unregistered property rights, through tenancy agreements, contracts of sale, equitable mortgages and the like. Both fall within the *in personam* exception.

This part of the chapter is about the creation of unregistered property rights to Torrens land. Of course, there is no need to repeat what is written above on this subject. The cases that discuss the *in personam* exception are concerned with a particular situation: the creation of new equitable property rights, by operation of law, at the time of registration or shortly thereafter.

It is easy to mistake this situation for a true exception to indefeasibility (in which an older unregistered right survives registration). There are four reasons for this. First, these rights can arise without the consent of the new registered proprietors and interfere with their enjoyment of their new registered rights. Secondly, they arise on or shortly after registration, making it look like the registered proprietors did not obtain the full benefits of registration. Thirdly, some of the events which lead to the creation of new unregistered rights can occur before registration, so it looks like those rights existed before registration. Fourthly, unregistered rights can arise in favour of previous owners of the land. If the new registered proprietors are required to make restitution to the previous registered proprietors, then the effect of registration will be undone.

These issues are considered here under three separate headings: the creation of rights, events before registration, and restitution of unjust enrichment.

Creation of Rights

There is another reason why the label "*in personam* exception" is unfortunate. Since there is no counterpart in other areas of property law, it gives the false impression that it concerns rights found only in the Torrens system. However, with the exception of Torrens mortgages and the requirement of registration, the nature and creation of property rights to land are more or less unaffected by Torrens statutes. The rights, which might be seen as falling within the *in personam* exception, are created in the normal ways discussed in Part IV.

There is a strong desire to turn to the *in personam* exception, when there is no real exception to indefeasibility and the outcome seems unfair. However, hardship and perceived unfairness do not give courts authority to create new rights in new ways to overcome perceived deficiencies of a Torrens system. The creators of those systems knew that people would lose property rights because of them and created assurance funds to compensate them.

Someone who claims a new unregistered right to Torrens land needs to prove that the right was created in a manner recognised by Australian property law. It is not enough to plead unfairness. As Hansen J said in *Koorootang Nominees Pty Ltd v ANZ Banking Group Ltd* [1998] 3 VR 16 at 125:

> "I have some difficulty with the notion that a person can defeat a registered proprietor's interest merely by persuading the court that, viewing the circumstances of the case as a whole, the registered proprietor has been guilty of unconscionable conduct. The danger of taking such an approach without linking the suggested unconscionable conduct to a recognised cause of action or right to relief at law or in equity is that the court may fall into the error of applying a subjective view of what the 'fair result' ought to be."

In some cases, a new unregistered right is recognised by the court, but a diversity of opinion among the judges makes it difficult to identify the events that created it. For example, in *Bahr v Nicolay* (1988) 164 CLR 604, the new registered proprietors (the Thompsons) held their land subject to an option to purchase granted by the previous registered proprietor (Nicolay) to the tenants (the Bahrs). As discussed above, there was a suggestion that the option survived registration under the fraud exception. However, the majority of opinion was that the option was a new unregistered right created by the Thompsons' dealings with Nicolay.

The contract of sale from Nicolay to the Thompsons contained a clause that "the Purchaser acknowledged that an agreement exists between" the Bahrs and Nicolay. The case turned on the effect of that written acknowledgement. Mason CJ and Dawson J decided (at 618-619) that this revealed an intention to create an express trust for the Bahrs. As discussed at page 252, it is not necessary that people realise they are creating a trust, so long as it is certain that they intended to create the relationship which equity recognises as a trust. Since the acknowledgement was in writing, it satisfied the formal requirements for creating trusts of land.

Wilson J and Toohey J (at 638) and Brennan J (at 653) took a different approach. Nicolay sold the land to the Thompsons on the basis that they would honour the Bahrs' option to purchase the land. Their acknowledgement of that option was a contractual obligation to sell the land to the Bahrs if the option was exercised. Since that obligation was specifically enforceable, the Thompsons held the land on constructive trust for the Bahrs. The only wrinkle, which made this case difficult, was that there were three different parties: the Thompsons' promise, to sell the land to the Bahrs, was made to Nicolay.

Events Before Registration

As Mason CJ and Dawson J said in *Bahr v Nicolay* (1988) 164 CLR 604 at 613, new equitable rights can arise "from conduct of the registered proprietor before registration ... so long as the recognition and enforcement of that equity involves no conflict with" the Torrens statute. In that case, the significant event occurred before registration, when the Thompsons acknowledged the Bahrs' rights. Before registration, the Bahrs had an option to purchase granted by Nicolay, which could not survive registration as an exception to indefeasibility. However, the transaction between Nicolay and the Thompsons recreated that option at the moment of registration.

There are a number of ways in which unregistered rights can arise, at the moment of registration, in response to events that took place before registration. For example, suppose that you contributed to the purchase price of a house in my name, without intending to make a gift to me. As discussed at page 331, when I become the sole registered proprietor of the house, I will hold it on resulting trust for both of us in proportion to our contributions. That trust depends on events which occurred before the transfer to me. However, it did not arise until I obtained ownership of the land from the vendor.

A similar situation could occur if we were domestic partners and you contributed to the relationship and made sacrifices for years relying on the belief that you would acquire an interest in the family home one day. If this enabled me to save enough money to buy a home in my own name, a constructive trust would arise when I became the registered proprietor. That trust would be responding to detrimental reliance that occurred before registration: see Chapter 23.

Suppose that I accepted bribes to betray my duty to you and used that money to buy Torrens land. As soon as I acquired the land, I would hold it on constructive trust for you, because it represents the profit of wrongdoing that occurred before registration: see *Attorney-General for Hong Kong v Reid* [1994] 1 AC 324 (discussed in Chapter 25).

In these examples, the trust arose when I became the registered proprietor, because a court of equity would say that I am not allowed to keep the land for my own benefit. It does not exist earlier, when the relevant events occurred, because the vendor was still the owner of the land and unaffected by our dealings with each other. In other words, most of the events which created the trust occurred before registration, but the last significant event (my becoming the registered proprietor), occurred upon registration. That is when the trust of my legal estate would arise (although I might hold money, bank accounts, and my rights under the contract of sale in trust for you before registration).

In most cases, property rights are created by events involving the conduct of the new registered proprietor. As quoted above, Mason CJ and Dawson J specifically referred to the "conduct of the registered proprietor before registration" as the source of the property right in *Bahr v Nicolay*. However, unregistered property rights can arise even though the registered proprietor had no involvement in the events that created them. If, for example, I purchased a house in your name, without intending to make a gift to you, you would hold that house on resulting trust for me, even if you did not know you were its registered proprietor. This is because the event which created that trust, your unjust enrichment at my expense, does not depend on your intentions, representations, wrongdoing, or other conduct.

In the vast majority of cases, the creation of unregistered rights will involve the conduct of the registered proprietor in some way. This makes it easy to overlook the few cases in which it does not. Unfortunately, the *Land Title Act* 1994 (Qld) seems to do just that. Section 185 creates an express exception to indefeasibility for "an equity arising from the act of the registered proprietor". This suggests that equitable property rights will not arise unless the registered proprietor does something to create them. However, a solution is to recognise that unregistered rights, created on or after registration, are not exceptions to indefeasibility and are unaffected by it. Therefore, as in other jurisdictions, they arise without being expressly excepted from indefeasibility.

Restitution of Unjust Enrichment

Unregistered property rights can arise to effect restitution of unjust enrichment. For example, if a registered right is obtained by mistake or undue influence, the registered proprietor might hold it in trust for its previous owner. This has the effect of reversing the transaction and restoring title to the previous registered proprietor. The creation of an unregistered right for this purpose appears to be a direct assault on the principle of indefeasibility. There is a conflict between the desire to prevent unjust enrichment and the need for security of title. Unfortunately, the courts have not yet resolved this conflict satisfactorily.

Rights Consistent with Indefeasibility

There are cases where there is no conflict between restitution and security of title, because the right to restitution does not impeach a registered title. For example, suppose that you transfer land to me to hold on express trust for your family and that trust fails for some reason. I will hold the land on resulting trust for you, because you did not intend to make a gift to me and I would be unjustly enriched if I was allowed to keep it for myself.

Although the express trust failed, there was nothing wrong with the transfer of legal title to me. You wanted me to be the registered proprietor for a particular purpose. The failure of that purpose means that I must return the land to you, but the resulting trust (which compels me to return it) does not interfere with the indefeasibility of the legal title you transferred to me.

Rights that Detract from Indefeasibility

In some cases, the right to restitution seems to be in direct conflict with the principle of indefeasibility. This is because the reason for restitution is a defect in the decision to transfer the registered property right. That decision was caused by mistake, duress, undue influence, or the exploitation of weakness and, therefore, the transfer can be set aside and registered title can be restored to the previous registered proprietor.

For example, in *Taitapu Gold Estates Ltd v Prouse* [1916] NZLR 825, the plaintiffs transferred more land than intended to the defendants, by mistake. According to their contract, the plaintiffs were supposed to retain the minerals under the land being sold. However, this was not excepted from the transfer that was registered, thereby giving the defendants legal title to those minerals. The defendants held those minerals in trust for the plaintiffs, even though they had obtained registration without fraud. The defendants were unaware of the mistake when they registered the transfer, but they did not expect to receive the mineral rights and would be unjustly enriched if they retained them.

Tutt v Doyle (1997) 42 NSWLR 10 was similar. The Doyles subdivided their land and sold a lot to the Tutts. The survey pegs were set in the wrong place and, when the land was surveyed and the plan and transfer were registered, the Tutts received a larger lot than the Doyles intended. Mr Tutt was aware of the mistake when those documents were registered. This was not Torrens fraud (since the documents were genuine), but the Tutts were not allowed to take advantage of the Doyles' mistake. The Doyles were entitled to restitution of the extra portion they had transferred by mistake.

In *Garcia v National Australia Bank Ltd* (1998) 194 CLR 395, the Garcias were directors and shareholders of a company and mortgaged their home to the bank to guarantee the company's debt to the bank. Mr Garcia had pressured Mrs Garcia to grant the mortgage and had failed to explain the extent of the guarantee secured by the mortgage. Therefore, she was entitled to rescind them.

The bank was not guilty of fraud, but could not enforce the mortgage against Mrs Garcia, because "the lender is to be taken to have understood that, as a wife, [she] may repose trust and confidence in her husband in matters of business and therefore to have understood that the husband may not fully and accurately explain the purport and effect of the transaction to his wife": at 409. The bank could not enforce the mortgage because it neither explained the transaction to her nor ensured that she received independent advice.

The bank was not guilty of fraud or bad faith, but knew that Mrs Garcia was married and, therefore, should have known that there was a risk that Mr Garcia might unduly influence her or mislead her to grant the mortgage. In other words, the bank had constructive notice of her defective intention to grant the mortgage.

Why did registration in these cases not produce an indefeasible title? The equitable property right to the recoverable land is not an older right, which survives registration, but a new right created by the unjust enrichment caused by that registration. Before registration, the plaintiffs were registered proprietors with legal title. After registration, they had an equitable right to rescind or rectify the transaction and recover land. This gave them a new equitable property right to the recoverable land, as discussed in Chapter 24.

The difficulty with this answer is that these new equitable property rights, created by unjust enrichment, have the effect of undoing registrations. They directly interfere with indefeasibility of title. Courts have said repeatedly that the *in personam* exception cannot be used to destroy indefeasibility. In *Frazer v Walker* [1967] 1 AC 569 at 585, Lord Wilberforce said that the principle of indefeasibility "must always remain paramount" and, therefore, any claims against the registered proprietor, which are prohibited by the indefeasibility provisions of a Torrens statute, "may not be maintained". Mason CJ and Dawson J said the same thing in *Bahr v Nicolay* (1988) 164 CLR 604 at 613.

Forgery and Fraud

A further difficulty is created by an apparent inconsistency. Indefeasibility does not protect a registered proprietor who had notice that registration was obtained by mistake, duress, undue influence, or exploitation of weakness. However, it does protect a registered proprietor who had notice that the registered document was a forgery or obtained by fraud.

If a person obtained registration, knowing or suspecting that the document was a forgery or obtained by fraud or other wrongdoing, the fraud exception would apply. As Tadgell JA said, in *Macquarie Bank Ltd v Sixty-Fourth Throne Pty Ltd* [1998] 3 VR 133 at 143, it is dishonest "to choose to shut one's eyes to the obvious — to assume a state of 'wilful blindness' — or otherwise to generate a state of contrived ignorance": see Chapter 29. However, a merely careless failure to make the normal inquiries, that would have revealed the forgery or fraud, is not dishonest: see *Pyramid Building Society v Scorpion Hotels Pty Ltd* [1998] 1 VR 188.

Immediate indefeasibility means that a title cannot be impeached by fraud or forgery unless the registered proprietor participated in, knew about, or suspected the wrongdoing. Dishonesty is required. If restitution of unjust enrichment was available in cases where an honest registered proprietor had notice of the wrong, the policy of the Torrens system would be undermined. The difficulty is that this argument applies with equal force to cases where the registered proprietor had notice of mistake, duress, undue influence and the like. The only real distinction is not logical, but practical: the assurance fund will compensate victims of fraud or forgery, but not transferors who were mistaken or unduly influenced.

Unregistered Property Rights

Despite the importance of registration in a Torrens system, unregistered property rights to land continue to exist as very important parts of the law of real property in Australia. In truth, the Torrens system has had little effect on the creation of equitable property rights, except as a consequence of its effect on the creation of legal property rights. Since most legal property rights to Torrens land are created by registration, many events that would have created legal rights at common law will create equitable rights in a Torrens system. Also, the Torrens form of mortgage means that mortgagors have legal ownership instead of an equity of redemption.

Since equitable property rights cannot be registered in a Torrens system, there are two important questions to consider: how do we protect them and what priority rules apply when such rights conflict with each other?

Protection of Unregistered Property Rights (Caveats)

In most cases, a person claiming an unregistered property right to Torrens land can lodge a caveat to protect that right. The caveat must be signed by the caveator (or her or his agent) and be supported by a declaration that the caveator has the right claimed. Three issues are discussed here: the effect of a caveat, the right to lodge a caveat, and compensation for lodging a caveat improperly.

Effect of a Caveat

A caveat is not the same as registration. It does not change the nature of the unregistered right it protects nor does it give that right priority over older rights. Caveats do two things. They provide people searching the register with notice of unregistered rights and they prevent the registration of conflicting rights.

When a caveat is lodged, the Registrar will notify the registered proprietors, who can require the caveator to take legal action to establish the existence of the unregistered right. If the caveator fails to do so within the prescribed time, the caveat will lapse and be removed from the register. If the registered proprietors do nothing, the caveat will remain in the register.

A caveat might prohibit the registration of all documents affecting the land or only certain dealings with the land. It does not prevent people from lodging other caveats claiming other unregistered property rights. If someone is unable to register a document because of a caveat, he or she can apply to the court to have the caveat removed.

Right to Lodge a Caveat

As a general rule, a caveat can be lodged by anyone claiming an unregistered property right to land in the Torrens system. For example, section 89 of the *Transfer of Land Act* 1958 (Vic) states that:

> "Any person claiming any estate or interest in land under any unregistered instrument or dealing or by devolution in law or otherwise or his agent may lodge with the Registrar a caveat in an appropriate approved form forbidding the registration of any person as transferee or proprietor of and of any instrument affecting such estate or interest either absolutely or conditionally ..."

There are exceptions to the general rule. Some people can lodge caveats, even though they do not have an unregistered right, and some people cannot lodge caveats, even though they do.

People Without Unregistered Property Rights

There are three groups of people entitled to lodge caveats even though they do not have unregistered property rights to land:

1)......Registrars;
2)......registered proprietors; and
3)......(in some jurisdictions) the settlors of trusts.

The first and perhaps most important exception is made for the Registrar. He or she can lodge caveats to protect the rights of others: see, eg, *Real Property Act* 1900 (NSW), s 12; *Land Title Act* 1994 (Qld), s 17. This might be done for a variety of reasons. For example, the Registrar might want to protect the unregistered right of a person under a disability, prevent improper dealings with documents, or stop registrations when problems arise, such as a misdescription of land.

Secondly, a registered proprietor can lodge a caveat to protect her or his registered right, if there is a danger that it might be destroyed or impaired by improper dealings. Strictly speaking, this is not authorised by most Torrens statutes. They permit people to lodge caveats to protect unregistered property rights and not to protect registered rights. This is why Richmond J said, in *Re Haupiri Courts Ltd (No 2)* [1969] NZLR 353 at 357, that:

> "A registered proprietor cannot lodge a *caveat* against dealings merely because he is the registered proprietor. He must go further and establish some set of circumstances over and above his status as registered proprietor which affirmatively gives rise to a distinct interest in the land."

There is no conceptual difficulty if the registered proprietor of a property right lodges a caveat to protect an additional unregistered right. For example, the registered proprietor of a lease might caveat an option to purchase not contained in that lease. However, a fee simple estate is the greatest possible interest in land that a person (other than the Crown) can hold. Therefore, any possible right to land held by the registered proprietor of that estate would be included in it.

Nevertheless, courts have long permitted registered proprietors to lodge caveats to protect their own registered rights from destruction. This risk arises when someone obtains the documents needed to transfer the land, but is not supposed to use them. For example, in *Barry v Heider* (1914) 19 CLR 197 (discussed above), Barry lodged a caveat over his own land to prevent Schmidt from registering the transfer he had obtained by fraud. In *J & H Just (Holdings) Pty Ltd v Bank of NSW* (1971) 125 CLR 546 at 553, Barwick CJ said that it is appropriate for registered proprietors to lodge a caveat if they create an equitable mortgage by giving the certificate of title and an executed transfer to the mortgagee: "This would be a means of safeguarding themselves against an abuse of authority which they had given to the mortgagee."

In New South Wales and Queensland, there is statutory authority for this practice. Section 122 of the *Land Title Act* 1994 (Qld) states that "A caveat may be lodged by ... the registered owner of the lot." According to section 74F of the *Real Property Act* 1900 (NSW):

> "Any registered proprietor of an estate or interest who, because of the loss of a relevant certificate of title or some other instrument relating to the estate or interest or for some other reason, fears an improper dealing with the estate or interest by another person may lodge with the Registrar-General a caveat prohibiting the recording of any dealing affecting the estate or interest."

Thirdly, settlors, who create trusts of Torrens land, can lodge caveats over that land in the Australian Capital Territory, Northern Territory, South Australia, and Tasmania. When a trust is created, the trustees have legal title to the asset held in trust and the beneficiaries are the equitable, beneficial owners of it: see page 111. However, the settlor who created the trust has no further interest it (as settlor). He or she could be a trustee or beneficiary of the trust created and have rights to the trust assets in those capacities, but has no further rights as the settlor.

The beneficiary of a trust will have an unregistered property right and be entitled to lodge a caveat to protect it. However, the trust beneficiaries may include young children or even the unborn children that people might have in the future. It is helpful to permit the settlor to lodge a caveat to protect their rights.

People With Unregistered Property Rights

There are two situations in which people might not be allowed to lodge caveats to protect their unregistered property rights:

1) .....if the right was once protected by a caveat, that was removed from the register; or
2) .....if the right is a "mere equity" to recover land in Victoria.

First, if a caveat is removed from the register, the caveator is not permitted to lodge another caveat protecting the same right, without court approval or the consent of the registered proprietor. This does not apply in Tasmania, except to caveats that forbid bringing land into the Torrens system: *Land Titles Act* 1980 (Tas), s 14.

These prohibitions are designed to prevent abuse of the Torrens system. The registered proprietor or someone adversely affected by a caveat can give notice to the caveator to take proceedings to prove the validity of her or his claim. If the caveator fails to act in time, the caveat lapses and is removed from the register. If the caveator was then permitted to lodge another caveat claiming the same right, he or she could prevent the registration of documents indefinitely, without ever proving the existence of the right claimed. Although compensation is available for lodging caveats without reasonable cause (as discussed below), this might not help if the caveator actually has the unregistered right claimed in the caveat.

This rule means that a person might have an unregistered property right and be unable to lodge a caveat to protect it. This could cause hardship if notice to prove the caveat was delivered to the address specified in the caveat and the caveator had moved or was interstate at the time (which is why caveators use their solicitors' addresses). If the unregistered right still survived, he or she would need a court order to lodge a new caveat. However, the onus is on the caveator to protect her or his rights diligently.

Secondly, in *Swanston Mortgage Pty Ltd v Trepan Investments Pty Ltd* [1994] 1 VR 672, the Supreme Court of Victoria decided that people cannot lodge caveats to protect mere equities. As discussed at page 418, the term "mere equity" is used to describe both personal and property rights. It is true that people cannot lodge caveats to protect personal rights. However, the Court was talking about a property right to rescind a transaction and thereby recover land.

In that case, a registered proprietor defaulted on its mortgage and the mortgagee exercised its power to sell the land. The proprietor lodged a caveat against its own title, prohibiting the registration of any transfer by the mortgagee, claiming that sale was voidable, because the mortgagee had exercised its power improperly. The court ordered the Registrar to remove the caveat, because the proprietor did not have an equitable interest in the land.

It is no doubt true that the registered proprietors of a fee simple estate do not have an equitable interest in their land. They have no rights beyond their registered legal estate. However, as discussed above, the High Court of Australia has approved the practice of registered proprietors lodging caveats when there is a risk that improper dealings will destroy or impair their registered rights. Unfortunately, the Court in Victoria did not refer to those cases and so it is not clear whether this case accurately reflects the law in Victoria.

Nevertheless, the present concern is the Court's suggestion that the mortgagor would not have been entitled to lodge a caveat even if the land had been transferred to a new registered proprietor. The Court referred to *Latec Investments Ltd v Hotel Terrigal Pty Ltd* (1965) 113 CLR 265: see page 420. In that case, the mortgagee had used its power fraudulently to transfer the land to a related company. The new registered proprietor was a party to the fraud and the mortgagor was entitled to rescind the sale and recover the land. However, someone then acquired an equitable charge over the land for value, in good faith, and without notice of the mortgagor's right to rescind the transfer. Therefore, the land would remain subject to that charge after the mortgagor recovered title.

In the *Latec* case, the High Court said that the equitable charge had priority over the mortgagor's right to rescind the transfer, because the latter right was a mere equity. However, this did not mean that it was only a personal right. There was no doubt that the mortgagor had a property right, which would take priority over newer property rights acquired by donees or by people with notice of it. The term "mere equity" was used to indicate that the right was less durable than most equitable property rights and would lose priority to conflicting equitable rights acquired for value and without notice of it.

The mortgagor's right to lodge a caveat was not discussed in *Latec*. The court in *Swanston* suggested that the mortgagor in *Latec* would not have had that right. However, this suggestion was made without considering another case in which the High Court of Australia said that the mortgagor did have that right: *Breskvar v Wall* (1971) 126 CLR 376. In that case, the mortgagors signed a blank transfer of land as security for a loan. The equitable mortgagee inserted the name of his grandson in the transfer and registered it. The grandson was a party to the mortgagee's fraud and the mortgagors were entitled to rescind the transfer. However, the grandson sold the land to innocent buyers and their equitable property right (a constructive trust created by a specifically enforceable contract of sale) had priority over the mortgagors' right to rescission.

In *Breskvar v Wall*, the mortgagors lodged a caveat claiming a right to rescind the transfer to the grandson. However, it was lodged after the sale to the innocent buyers and did not affect them. Not only was this caveat permitted, but the High Court criticised the mortgagors for not lodging it earlier. Walsh J said (at 409) that "their failure at the relevant time to place upon the register any notice of any interest retained by them in the land" was a factor which enabled the mortgagee and his grandson to mislead the innocent buyers.

Since the judgment in the *Swanston* case does not mention the relevant judgments of the High Court of Australia, it is doubtful whether it accurately sets out the law in Victoria. However, the Registrar in Victoria may be bound by that decision and be required to reject caveats claiming an interest in land arising from a right to rescind or rectify a transfer. However, it should not affect the law in other jurisdictions, where the Registrars would be bound by the law set by the High Court. Also, lower courts in other states have also said that mortgagors are permitted to lodge caveats to prevent their mortgagees from exercising their powers improperly: see *Sinclair v Hope Investments Pty Ltd* [1982] 2 NSWLR 870 and *Re McKean's Caveat* [1988] 1 Qd R 524.

Compensation for Lodging a Caveat Improperly

A person, who lodges a caveat without reasonable cause, can be required to pay compensation for any losses caused by that caveat: see, eg, *Transfer of Land Act* 1893 (WA), s 140. The damages could be considerable, especially if the caveat delayed or prevented a major real estate development project. This rule is designed to reduce abuse of the Torrens system.

The caveator is not liable just because he or she does not have the interest claimed. Torrens statutes authorise the lodgement of caveats by people claiming unregistered property rights and not just by people who have them. However, the caveator must reasonably believe that he or she has that property right, based on proper legal advice. If the belief is not honestly and reasonably held, the caveator may be liable: see *Bedford Properties Pty Ltd v Surgo Pty Ltd* [1981] 1 NSWLR 106.

Priority Between Unregistered Property Rights

Torrens systems set rules to determine the priority of an unregistered right that conflicts with a registered right. However, they do not deal with conflicts between two unregistered rights. Therefore, it is necessary to use the priority rules of common law and equity (discussed in Part V) to resolve the dispute.

Legal Rights

As discussed above, people can have unregistered legal rights to possess land in a Torrens system, either adversely or under an informal lease.

Adverse Possession

Since adverse possessors do not give value for their rights, they cannot use the defence of *bona fide* purchase for value to defeat older equitable property rights. For example, an adverse possessor would be subject to a restrictive covenant affecting the land (regardless of notice). Adverse possession, for the duration of the limitation period, destroys only the rights of people wrongly excluded from the land, who have failed to commence legal action to enforce their rights within the time prescribed by statute: see Chapter 8. Other rights (including rights to possession at some future time) are unaffected.

Of course, if the adverse possessor applies for and obtains a registered estate, the principle of indefeasibility can destroy unregistered rights that were unaffected by the adverse possession. This is why Torrens statutes include procedures designed to protect those rights. For example, section 103 of the *Land Title Act* 1994 (Qld) requires that notice be given to people likely to be affected, and section 104 allows them to lodge caveats to protect their rights.

Informal Leases

As discussed above, most unregistered leases are equitable, created by contracts to grant leases. However, tenants can have unregistered legal leases created informally. If they are *bona fide* purchasers for value, their legal leasehold estate will take priority over older unregistered equitable property rights: see Chapter 29. This will not destroy those rights completely, since informal leases cannot be longer than three years. However, the tenants' right to possession will take priority for the duration of the lease.

Informal leases are not affected by subsequent unregistered rights because of the *nemo dat* principle, discussed in Chapter 28. In any event, the tenant's possession of the land provides notice of her or his rights to anyone dealing with that land. Although registration of a property right is an exception to the *nemo dat* principle and is not affected by notice, most informal leases have priority over registered rights as express exceptions to indefeasibility (discussed above).

Equitable Rights

When two unregistered equitable rights to Torrens land are in conflict, the dispute is resolved according to the normal priority rules of equity, discussed in Chapter 29. Normally, the older right will have priority over the newer right. However, if the newer right was acquired for value, in good faith, and without notice of the older right, there is a possibility that the older right will be postponed to the newer right. Mere equities are always postponed in that situation. Other equitable property rights are postponed only if the holder of the right is responsible for causing the holder of the newer right to believe that the older right did not exist.

The beneficiaries of express trusts are not expected to take active steps to preserve their interests. Therefore, their rights will be postponed only if they actively misled the holder of the newer right in some way. Other equitable property rights might be postponed if their holders failed to take reasonable steps to protect them. In a Torrens system, this issue can be affected by the presence or absence of caveats.

Caveats

Caveats can affect the priorities of conflicting unregistered rights in two ways. First, a caveat can provide notice of the existence of a right. Secondly, the failure to lodge a caveat might be regarded as a reason for postponing an older equitable property right to a newer one.

Notice

One of the purposes of a caveat is to provide notice of the existence of an unregistered property right to Torrens land. However, a caveat is notice not to the whole world, but merely to those people who search the register or should search the register. If people search the register and discover a caveat, they will have actual notice of the right claimed in the caveat and cannot claim priority for any unregistered rights they obtain thereafter: see *Moffett v Dillon* [1999] 2 VR 480.

If people do not search the register, they will have constructive notice of its contents only if a reasonable person in their position would have searched the register. This depends on normal practices of people in the same area or business. People who acquire unregistered property rights, with constructive notice of an older right, cannot claim priority over that right.

Failure to Caveat

As discussed above and in Chapter 29, an older equitable property right may be postponed to a newer right if the holders of the older right failed to take reasonable precautions to protect their interests. The failure to lodge a caveat to protect an unregistered right is a factor to be considered. If a reasonable person in that position would have lodged a caveat, then the failure to do so may result in the postponement of that right.

In many cases, the failure to caveat is not the main reason for postponing the older right to the newer right. The holders of the older right created a situation in which the registered proprietor could pretend to be the beneficial owners of the land, free of the older right. If they had lodged a caveat, the problem would have been avoided. However, the failure to caveat was not otherwise significant, because other conduct justified the postponement.

For example, in *Heid v Reliance Finance Corp Pty Ltd* (1983) 154 CLR 326, Mr Heid sold land to a company for $165,000 and the land was transferred to the company, but he received only $15,000. The remainder was secured by two unregistered equitable property rights: a mortgage for $50,000 and an unpaid vendor's lien for $100,000. However, Heid signed a transfer, which said that the entire $165,000 had been paid, and then relied on the company's agent to look after his rights. Instead, the company granted equitable mortgages for $140,000 to people who had no notice of Heid's rights.

Heid's mortgage and lien were postponed to the subsequent mortgages, because he had enabled the company to pretend to be the beneficial owner of the land, free of his security rights. If Heid had lodged a caveat in time, the conflict could have been avoided, but, as Gibbs CJ said (at 338), his "failure to lodge any caveat ... was not in itself fatal to his case". The outcome of the priority dispute would have been the same even if the failure to caveat was completely ignored. Therefore, cases like this tell us very little about the effect of a failure to caveat.

There are cases in which the failure to caveat was sufficient to cause postponement of an equitable property right. In *Person-to-Person Financial Services Pty Ltd v Sharari* [1984] 1 NSWLR 745, Mr Tredgolde had an unregistered second mortgage, but did not lodge a caveat to protect it. A finance company searched the register and found the registered first mortgage. It then loaned $10,000 to the registered proprietors in exchange for an unregistered mortgage. This was a third mortgage, but the company believed it was a second mortgage. Tredgolde's mortgage was postponed to the company's, because he had failed to lodge a caveat (and thereby contributed to the company's mistaken belief). McLelland J said that it was the normal practice of solicitors in New South Wales either to register a mortgage or to lodge a caveat to protect it. Tredgolde's failure to take any reasonable steps to protect his interest justified its postponement.

In other cases, the failure to caveat was not unreasonable, because the unregistered property right was protected in other ways. For example, in *J & H Just (Holdings) Pty Ltd v Bank of NSW* (1971) 125 CLR 546, the equitable mortgagee had possession of the certificate of title. This protected its interest because the Registrar would not register documents without the certificate of title (or a false declaration that it had been lost) and another mortgagee dealing with the land would expect to receive or at least see the certificate.

In *Heid v Reliance Finance Corp* (above at 337), Gibbs CJ said that it was reasonable for registered proprietors to give transfer documents to their own solicitors, without lodging a caveat. People are entitled to rely on their solicitors to perform their fiduciary duty to protect their clients' best interests (just as beneficiaries are entitled to rely on their trustees). If solicitors breach their duty and create conflicting unregistered rights, their clients are not blamed for failing to protect themselves. In contrast, it is not reasonable to trust the other party to a transaction to look after those interests.

In *Jacobs v Platt Nominees Pty Ltd* [1990] VR 146, Ms Jacobs paid $500,000 to acquire an option to purchase a motel for $16 million from her parents' company. Her solicitors advised her to lodge a caveat, but she refused because she did not want to upset her father. The company sold the land without her consent, but the buyers did not get priority over her option. Although she had failed to take the normal precaution of lodging a caveat, the court said she was justified relying on her mother to protect her interests. This does seem odd, since the mother's company was on the other side of the transaction and she did not owe a fiduciary duty to look after her adult daughter's best interests. There is a better explanation for this outcome. The buyer searched the register only after it made the contract to buy the land and took no further steps after the search. In other words, the buyer did not rely on Jacobs' failure to caveat.

Failure to Search the Register

How is the presence or absence of a caveat relevant, when someone acquires a newer equitable property right without searching the register? First, if the older right is protected by a caveat, it is likely that the newer right was acquired with constructive notice of the older right. In that case it cannot gain priority over the older right. In any event, the caveat protects the older right by preventing the registration of documents (but not the creation of conflicting equitable rights). This may mean that the older right will not be postponed because its holders have taken sufficient steps to protect their interests.

Secondly, if there is no caveat and no search of the register, then the failure to caveat had nothing to do with the mistaken belief that the older right does not exist. It provides no reason for postponing the older right. Also, the failure to search should not affect the claim that the newer right deserves priority. In *Abigail v Lapin* [1934] AC 491, Abigail took an equitable mortgage without searching the register. The Lapins had an older equity of redemption and did not lodge a caveat to protect it. Their interest was postponed to Abigail's because they enabled the registered proprietors to pretend to be the beneficial owners of the land. Although a caveat might have preserved the priority of the older right, the failure to caveat and failure to search the register did not otherwise affect the priority of the conflicting unregistered rights.

Possible Reform

A common criticism of the Torrens system is that it does not deal with equitable property rights adequately. Although they are accepted as integral parts of real property law, most cannot be registered in the Torrens systems which regulate most privately owned land in Australia. Therefore, Torrens systems fall well short of their goal of providing complete and accurate reflections of property rights to land. Also, most equitable property rights are far more vulnerable to destruction in a Torrens system than in a deeds registration system (since few are expressly excepted from indefeasibility).

Caveats were designed originally to provide temporary protection for unregistered rights and may not be the best way to protect them for long periods. If someone serves notice on a caveator to prove a claim to the land, he or she must commence court proceedings or lose the protection of the caveat. Also, caveats do not give equitable rights priority over older unregistered rights. They merely help preserve the status quo. Therefore, many priority disputes are resolved using the rules of common law and equity, without any help from the Torrens system. In contrast, most deeds registration systems confer the full benefits of registration on both legal and equitable property rights.

In response to these concerns, Canadian provinces have modified their Torrens systems to make caveats more like registration. Caveats are accepted as permanent forms of protection for unregistered property rights. A right protected by caveat is entitled to the same priority as a right obtained by registration. It will have priority over other unregistered and subsequently registered rights (subject to the usual exceptions for fraud and the like) and the caveator has the same protection from notice. In other words, someone can lodge a caveat, with knowledge of a conflicting unregistered right, and thereby obtain priority over that right.

There is now only one substantial difference between registration and caveats in Canada. Registration creates the property right, whereas caveats merely protect existing property rights. Therefore, a caveat will not help a caveator who does not have the right claimed. Several Canadian provinces are considering the adoption of a modified Torrens system that would treat most property rights in the same manner. A grant or transfer of a fee simple estate would still produce a certificate of title, but all other property rights could be recorded on that title and receive Torrens-style priority: see the Alberta Law Reform Institute, *Proposals for a Land Recording and Registration Act for Alberta* (1993).

As with all law reform, there are advantages and disadvantages to these proposals. However, they could help move the Torrens system closer to its ideal of a register that accurately reflected all property rights to land. In hindsight, it was a mistake to attempt to exclude equitable interests from the Torrens system. The German registration system, which provided a model for Ulrich Hübbe and Robert Torrens, did not have to cope with the duality of common law and equity that permeates the Commonwealth. Australian property law is constructed on that duality and the Torrens system will not be complete until it accepts that fact, not just grudgingly, but freely and openly.

BIBLIOGRAPHY

Aboriginal Land Rights Commission (NT), *Second Report* (Canberra, 1975)

Aitken, L, "Applications in Equity: Removal of Tenant's Fixtures?" (1999) 73 *Australian Law Journal* 834

Alexander, G, "Critical Land Law" in Bright and Dewar, *Land Law Themes and Perspectives* (1998) 52

American Law Institute, *Restatement of the Law of Restitution* (St Paul, 1937)
— *Restatement of the Law of Trusts, Second* (St Paul, 1959)

Ames, JB, "The Origin of Uses and Trusts" in *Select Essays in Anglo-American Legal History* (1908) 737

Atiyah, PS and Adams, JN, *The Sale of Goods* (9th ed, London, 1995)

Austin, RP, "The Melting Down of the Remedial Trust" (1988) 11 *University of New South Wales Law Journal* 66

Baker, JH, "The Use upon a Use in Equity 1558-1625" (1977) 93 *Law Quarterly Review* 33
— "Property in Chattels" (1978) 94 *Selden Society* 209
— *An Introduction to English Legal History* (3rd ed, London, 1990)

Baker, PV, "Land as Donatio Mortis Causa" (1993) 109 *Law Quarterly Review* 19

Barker, K, "Bona Fide Purchase as a Defence to Unjust Enrichment Claims: A Concise Restatement" [1999] *Restitution Law Review* 75

Bartlett, R, "*Mabo*: Another Triumph for the Common Law" (1993) 15 *Sydney Law Review* 178

Barton, JL, "The Medieval Use" (1965) 81 *Law Quarterly Review* 562
— "The Statute of Uses and the Trust of Freeholds" (1966) 82 *Law Quarterly Review* 215

Battersby, G, "Informally Created Interests in Land" in Bright and Dewar, *Land Law Themes and Perspectives* (1998) 487

Bell, AP, *Modern Law of Personal Property in England and Ireland* (London, 1989)
— "Bona Vacantia" in Palmer and McKendrick, *Interests in Goods* (2nd ed, 1998) 207

Bhuta, N, "*Mabo, Wik,* and the Art of Paradigm Management" (1998) 22 *Melbourne University Law Review* 24

Bird, H, "A Critique of the Proprietary Nature of Share Rights in Australian Publicly Listed Corporations" (1998) 22 *Melbourne University Law Review* 131

Birks, P, *An Introduction to the Law of Restitution* (rev ed, Oxford, 1989)
— "An Unacceptable Face of Human Property" in P Birks, ed, *New Perspectives in the Roman Law of Property: Essays for Barry Nicholas* (1989) 61
— *Restitution — the Future* (Sydney, 1992)
— "Mixing and Tracing: Property and Restitution" (1992) 45 *Current Legal Problems* 69
— "Restitution and Resulting Trusts" in Goldstein, S, *Equity and Contemporary Legal Developments* (1992) 335
— "Property in the Profits of Wrongdoing" (1994) 24 *University of Western Australia Law Review* 8
— ed, *The Frontiers of Liability* (Oxford, 1994) 2 volumes
— "Proprietary Rights as Remedies" in Birks, ed, *The Frontiers of Liability*, Vol 2 (1994) 214
— "Equity in the Modern Law: An Exercise in Taxonomy" (1996) 26 *University of Western Australia Law Review* 1
— "Trusts Raised to Reverse Unjust Enrichment: the *Westdeutsche* case" [1996] *Restitution Law Review* 3
— ed, *Privacy and Loyalty* (Oxford, 1997)
— ed, *The Classification of Obligations* (Oxford, 1997)
— "Definition and Division: A Meditation on *Institutes* 3.13" in Birks, ed, *Classification of Obligations* (1997) 1
— "Property and Unjust Enrichment: Categorical Truths" [1997] *New Zealand Law Review* 623
— "Before We Begin: Five Keys to Land Law" in Bright and Dewar, *Land Law Themes and Perspectives* (1998) 457
— "Mixtures" in Palmer and McKendrick, *Interests in Goods* (2nd ed, 1998) 227
— "Equity, Conscience, and Unjust Enrichment" (1999) 23 *Melbourne University Law Review* 1
— "The Law of Restitution at the End of an Epoch" (1999) 28 *University of Western Australia Law Review* 13

Birks, P and Rose, F, eds, *Restitution and Equity* (London, 2000)

Blackstone, W, *Commentaries on the Laws of England* (15th ed, London, 1808)

Bordwell, P, "Property in Chattels" (1916) 29 *Harvard Law Review* 374

Bradbrook, AJ, MacCallum, SV and Moore, AP, *Australian Property Law Cases and Materials* (Sydney, 1996)

Bradbrook, AJ, MacCallum, SV and Moore, AP, *Australian Real Property Law* (2nd ed, Sydney, 1997)

Brereton, P, "The Rights Between Co-Owners of Land" (1995) 69 *Australian Law Journal* 316

Bright, S, "Of Estates and Interests: A Tale of Ownership and Property Rights" in Bright and Dewar, *Land Law Themes and Perspectives* (1998) 529

Bright, S and Dewar, J, eds, *Land Law Themes and Perspectives* (Oxford, 1998)

Brooke-Taylor, JDA, "Racial and Religious Restrictive Covenants" (1978) 42 *Conveyancer and Property Lawyer* 24

Bryan, M, "Constructive Trusts: A New Zealand Development" (1990) 106 *Law Quarterly Review* 212
— "The Meaning of Notice in Tracing Claims" (1993) 109 *Law Quarterly Review* 368
— "Constructive Trusts and Unconscionability in Australia: On the Road to Unattainable Perfection" (1994) 8 *Trust Law International* 74
— "Parents as Fiduciaries: A Special Place in Equity" (1995) 3 *International Journal of Children's Rights* 227
Buckle, *Natural Law and the Theory of Property — Grotius to Hume* (Oxford, 1991)
Burrows, AS, *Essays on the Law of Restitution* (Oxford, 1990)
— *The Law of Restitution* (London, 1993)
— *Remedies for Torts and Breach of Contract* (2nd ed, London, 1994)
Burrows, AS and McKendrick, E, *Cases and Materials on the Law of Restitution* (Oxford, 1997)
Butt, P, "System Stands on Shaky Foundations" (1992) 27(11) *Australian Law News* 12
— *Land Law* (3rd ed, Sydney, 1996)
Cane, P, *The Anatomy of Tort Law* (Oxford, 1997)
Carroll, R, ed, *Civil Remedies: Issues and Developments* (Sydney, 1996)
Carter, R, "Does Indefeasibility Protect the Title of a Volunteer?" (1985) 49 *Saskatchewan Law Review* 329
Certoma, L, *The Law of Succession in New South Wales* (3rd ed, Sydney, 1997)
Chambers R, "Restitution, Trusts and Compound Interest" (1996) 20 *Melbourne University Law Review* 1192
— *Resulting Trusts* (Oxford, 1997)
— "Tracing, Trusts and Liens" (1997) 11 *Trust Law International* 86
— "Proprietary Interests in Commercial Transactions" (1998) 18 *Oxford Journal of Legal Studies* 363
— "Conditional Gifts" in Palmer and McKendrick, *Interests in Goods* (2nd ed, 1998)
— "Indefeasible Title as a Bar to a Claim for Restitution" [1998] *Restitution Law Review* 126
— "Constructive Trusts in Canada" (1999) 37 *Alberta Law Review* 173
— "Resulting Trusts in Canada" (2000) 38 *Alberta Law Review* 378
Chin NY, see Nahan
Churchill, J, "Patenting Humanity: The Development of Property Rights in the Human Body and the Subsequent Evolution of Patentability of Living Things" (1994) 8 *Intellectual Property Journal* 249
Cohen, F, "Dialogue on Private Property" (1954) *Rutgers Law Review* 357
Cope, M, *Constructive Trusts* (Sydney, 1992)
Cornish, WR, Nolan, R, O'Sullivan, J and Virgo, G, *Restitution Past, Present and Future: Essays in Honour of Gareth Jones* (Oxford, 1998)

Costigan, GP, "The Classification of Trusts as Express, Resulting, and Constructive" (1914) 27 *Harvard Law Review* 437

Crilley, D, "A Case of Proprietary Overkill" [1994] *Restitution Law Review* 57

Critchley, P, "Instruments of Fraud, Testamentary Dispositions, and the Doctrine of Secret Trusts" (1999) 115 *Law Quarterly Review* 631
— "Taking Formalities Seriously" in Bright and Dewar, *Land Law Themes and Perspectives* (1998) 507

Dal Pont, GE and Chalmers, DRC, *Equity and Trusts in Australia and New Zealand* (Sydney, 2000)

Davies, JD, "Informal Arrangements Affecting Land" (1979) 8 *Sydney Law Review* 578
— "The Re-Awakening of Equity's Conscience: Achievements and Problems" in Goldstein, *Equity and Contemporary Legal Developments* (1992) 46
— "Informally Created Trusts of Land and Some Alternatives to Them" (1990) 106 *Law Quarterly Review* 539

Dodds, J, "The New Constructive Trust: An Analysis of its Nature and Scope" (1988) 16 *Melbourne University Law Review* 482

Dodds Streeton, J and Langford, R, *Aspects of Real Property and Insolvency Law* (Adelaide, 1994)

Duncan, WD and Willmot, L, *Mortgages Law in Australia* (2nd ed, Sydney, 1996)

Duggan, AJ, "Unconscientious Dealing" in Parkinson, *The Principles of Equity* (1996) 121
— "Is Equity Efficient?" (1997) 113 *Law Quarterly Review* 601

Eekelaar, J, "Non-marital Property" in Birks, *The Frontiers of Liability* (Vol 2, 1994) 204

Edgeworth, B, "Tenure, Allodialism and Indigenous Rights at Common Law: English, United States and Australian Land Law Compared After *Mabo v Queensland*" (1994) 23 *Anglo-American Law Review* 397

Eleftheriadis, P, "The Analysis of Property Rights" (1996) 16 *Oxford Journal of Legal Studies* 683

Elias, G, *Explaining Constructive Trusts* (Oxford, 1990)

Enonchong, N, "Title Claims and Illegal Transactions" (1995) 111 *Law Quarterly Review* 135

Evans, S, "Rethinking Tracing and the Law of Restitution" (1999) 115 *Law Quarterly Review* 469

Fehlberg, B, "The Husband, the Bank, the Wife and her Signature" (1994) 57 *Modern Law Review* 467

Fisher, S, *Commercial and Personal Property Law* (Sydney, 1997)

Ford, HAJ and Lee, WA, *Principles of the Law of Trusts* (3rd ed, Sydney, 1996)

Fouts, R, *Next of Kin: What My Conversations with Chimpanzees have Taught Me about Intelligence, Compassion, and Being Human* (London, 1997)

Fox, DM, "Property Rights and Electronic Funds Transfers" [1996] *Lloyds Maritime and Commercial Law Quarterly* 456
— "Bona Fide Purchase and the Currency of Money" (1996) 55 *Cambridge Law Journal* 547
— "Common Law Claims to Substituted Assets" [1999] *Restitution Law Review* 55

French, RS, "The Role of the Native Title Tribunal" in Bartlett, *Native Title Legislation in Australia* (1994) 73

Friedman, M, *Capitalism and Freedom* (Chicago, 1962)

Fulcher, J, "Sui Generis History? The Use of History in Wik" in Hiley, *The Wik Case: Issues and Implications* (1997) 51

Gardner, S, "The Proprietary Effect of Contractual Obligations under *Tulk v Moxhay* and *De Mattos v Gibson*" (1982) 98 *Law Quarterly Review* 279
— "Equity, Estate Contracts and the Judicature Acts: *Walsh v Lonsdale* Revisited" (1986) 7 *Oxford Journal of Legal Studies* 60
— *An Introduction to the Law of Trusts* (Oxford, 1990)
— "New Angles on Unincorporated Associations" [1992] *Conveyancer* 41
— "Rethinking Family Property" (1993) 109 *Law Quarterly Review* 263
— "The Element of Discretion" in Birks, *The Frontiers of Liability* (Vol 2, 1994) 186
— "A Detail in the Construction of Gifts to Unincorporated Associations" [1998] *Conveyancer* 8
— "The Remedial Discretion in Proprietary Estoppel" (1999) 115 *Law Quarterly Review* 438

Glover, J, "Equity, Restitution and the Proprietary Recovery of Value" (1991) 14 *University of New South Wales Law Journal* 247

Goddard, D, "Equity, Volunteers and Ducks" [1988] *Conveyancer* 19

Goff, R and Jones, G, *The Law of Restitution* (5th ed, London, 1998)

Goldstein, S, *Equity and Contemporary Legal Developments* (Jerusalem, 1992)

Goode, RM, "Ownership and Obligation in Commercial Transactions" (1987) 103 *Law Quarterly Review* 433
— "Property and Unjust Enrichment" in Burrows, *Essays on the Law of Restitution* (1991) 215
— "Charges Over Book Debts: A Missed Opportunity" (1994) 110 *Law Quarterly Review* 592
— *Commercial Law* (2nd ed, London, 1995)

Goodhart, W and Jones, G, "The Infiltration of Equitable Doctrine into English Commercial law" (1980) 43 *Modern Law Review* 489

Grantham, RB, "Doctrinal Bases for the Recognition of Proprietary Rights" (1996) 16 *Oxford Journal of Legal Studies* 561
— "The Doctrinal Basis of the Rights of Company Shareholders" (1998) 57 *Cambridge Law Journal* 554

Grantham, RB and Rickett, CEF, "Restitution, Property and Ignorance — A Reply to Mr Swadling" [1996] *Lloyds Maritime and Commercial Law Quarterly* 463
— "Restitution, Property and Mistaken Payments" [1997] *Restitution Law Review* 83
— "Property and Unjust Enrichment: Categorical Truths or Unnecessary Complexity" [1997] *New Zealand Law Review* 668

Gray, K, "Property in Thin Air" (1991) 50 *Cambridge Law Journal* 252
— *Elements of Land Law* (2nd ed, London, 1993)
— "Equitable Property" (1994) 47 *Current Legal Problems* 157

Gray, K and Gray, SF, "The Idea of Property in Land" in Bright and Dewar, *Land Law Themes and Perspectives* (1998) 15

Guest, AG, ed, *Benjamin's Sale of Goods* (5th ed, London, 1997)

Gummow, WMC, "Unjust Enrichment, Restitution and Proprietary Remedies" in Finn, *Essays on Restitution* (1990) 47

Gyles, RV, "Indefeasibility and Actions In Personam" (1972) 46 *Australian Law Journal* 644

Hackney, J, *Understanding Equity and Trusts* (London, 1987)

Hardingham, IJ, "Equitable Liens for the Recovery of Purchase Money" (1985) 15 *Melbourne University of Law Review* 65

Hardman, FW, "The Law of Escheat" (1888) 4 *Law Quarterly Review* 318

Harris, DR, "The Concept of Possession in English Law" in Guest, *Oxford Essays in Jurisprudence* (1961) 69

Harris, JW, "Ownership of Land in English Law" in MacCormick and Birks, *The Legal Mind* (1986) 143

— "Who Owns my Body?" (1996) 16 *Oxford Journal of Legal Studies* 55

Hayton, DJ, "Remedial Constructive Trusts of Homes; an Overseas View" [1988] *Conveyancer* 259

— "Constructive Trusts: Is the Remedying of Unjust Enrichment a Satisfactory Approach?" in Youdan, *Equity, Fiduciaries and Trusts* (1989) 205

— "Equitable Rights of Cohabitees" in Goldstein, *Equity and Contemporary Legal Developments* (1992) 590

— *The Law of Trusts* (2nd ed, London, 1993)

— "Constructive Trusts of Homes — A Bold Approach" (1993) 109 *Law Quarterly Review* 485

— "Uncertainty of Subject-Matter of Trusts" (1994) 110 *Law Quarterly Review* 335

— "Equity's Identification Rules" in Birks, *Laundering and Tracing* (1995) 1

Hepburn, S, *Principles of Property Law* (Sydney, 1998)

Hiley, G, ed, *The Wik Case: Issues and Implications* (Sydney, 1997)

Hill, J, "Formalities Relating to Gifts" (1993) 56 *Modern Law Review* 542

Ho, HL, "Some Reflections on 'Property' and 'Title' in the Sale of Goods Act" (1997) 56 *Cambridge Law Journal* 571

Hohfeld, WN, "Fundamental Legal Conceptions as Applied to Judicial Reasoning" (1917) 26 *Yale Law Journal* 710

Holdsworth, WS, *A History of English Law* (London, 1903-1924)

Honoré, T, "Ownership" in AG Guest, *Oxford Essays in Jurisprudence* (1961); reprinted in T Honoré, *Making Law Bind* (Oxford, 1987) 161

Hookey, J, "Settlement and Sovereignty" in Hanks and Keon-Cohen, *Aborigines and the Law* (1984)

Howell, J, "The Doctrine of Notice: An Historical Perspective" [1997] *Conveyancer* 431

— "Deeds Registration in England: A Complete Failure?" (1999) 58 *Cambridge Law Journal* 366

Hubert, J, in "Dry Bones or Living Ancestors? Conflicting Perceptions of Life, Death and the Universe" (1992) 1 *International Journal of Cultural Property* 105

Hudson, AH, "Is Divesting Abandonment Possible at Common Law?" (1984) 100 *Law Quarterly Review* 110
— "Mental Incapacity in the Law of Contract and Property" [1984] *Conveyancer* 32
— "Mental Incapacity Revisited" [1986] *Conveyancer* 178
— "Abandonment" in Palmer and McKendrick, *Interests in Goods* (2nd ed, 1998) 595
— "Money Claims for Misuse of Chattels" in Palmer and McKendrick, *Interests in Goods* (2nd ed, 1998) 837

Hughson, M, Neave, M and O'Connor, P, "Reflections on the Mirror of Title: Resolving the Conflict Between Purchasers and Prior Interest Holders" (1997) 21 *Melbourne University Law Review* 460

Hunter, P, "The Wik Decision: Unnecessary Extinguishment" (1997) 3 *Native Title News* 1

Ing, ND, *Bona Vacantia* (London, 1971)

Jackson, "The Legal Effects of the Passing of Time" (1970) 7 *Melbourne University Law Review* 407
— "The Animus of Squatting" (1980) 96 *Law Quarterly Review* 333

Jaffey, P, "Restitutionary Damages and Disgorgement" [1995] *Restitution Law Review* 30

Jones, A, "Identification of Improperly Appropriated Trust Money — Mixing and Maxwell" [1996] *Conveyancer* 129

Jones, NG, "Uses, Trusts, and a Path to Privity" (1997) 56 *Cambridge Law Journal* 175

Jordan, F, *Chapters on Equity in New South Wales* (6th ed by FC Stephen, 1947)

Kreltszheim, D, "Tracing Electronic Cash: Fraud and the Electronic Transfer and Storage of Value" (1999) 27 *Australian Business Law Review* 112

Kremer, B, "An 'Unruly Horse' in a 'Shadowy World'?: The Law of Illegality after *Nelson v Nelson*" (1997) 19 *Sydney Law Review* 240

Kull, A, "Restitution and the Noncontractual Transfer" (1997) 11 *Journal of Contract Law* 93

Langbein, JH, "The Contractarian Basis of the Law of Trusts" (1995) 105 *Yale Law Journal* 625

Langford, R, "The *In Personam* Exception to Indefeasibility of Title" in Dodds Streeton and Langford, *Aspects of Real Property and Insolvency Law* (1994) 91

Laski, HJ, *A Grammar of Politics* (5th ed, London, 1967)

Law Commission (UK), *Transfer of Land: Passing of Risk from Vendor to Purchaser* (Working Paper No 109, 1988)
— *Transfer of Land: Risk of Damage After Contract for Sale* (Law Com No 191, 1990)
— *The Law of Trusts: The Rules Against Perpetuities and Excessive Accumulations* (LCCP No 133, 1993)

Law Reform Commission (Australia), *Personal Property Securities* (Interim Report No 64, 1993)

Law Reform Commission (NSW), *Unilateral Severance of a Joint Tenancy* (Report No 73, 1994)

Law Reform Commission (WA), *Report on Joint Tenancy and Tenancy in Common* (Report No 78, 1994)

Law Reform Institute (Alberta), *Proposals for a Land Recording and Registration Act for Alberta* (Report No 69, 1993)

Lawson, FH and Rudden B, *The Law of Property* (2nd ed, Oxford, 1982)

Litman, MM, "The Emergence of Unjust Enrichment as a Cause of Action and the Remedy of Constructive Trust" (1988) 26 *Alberta Law Review* 407

Lucy, WNR and Mitchell C, "Replacing Private Property: The Case for Stewardship" (1996) 55 *Cambridge Law Journal* 566

MacMillan, C, "The European Court of Justice Agrees with Maitland: Trusts and the Brussels Convention" [1996] *Conveyancer* 125

Macpherson, CB, ed, *Property: Mainstream and Critical Positions* (Toronto, 1978)

Magnusson, R, "Proprietary Rights in Human Tissue", in Palmer and McKendrick, *Interests in Goods* (2nd ed, 1998) 25

Mann, FA, *The Legal Aspect of Money* (5th ed, Oxford, 1992)

Mansell, M, "Australians and Aborigines and the *Mabo* Decision: Just Who Needs Whom the Most?" (1993) 15 *Sydney Law Review* 168

Maitland, FW, *Equity* (rev ed, Cambridge, 1936)

Marshall, G, "Rights, Options and Entitlements" in Simpson, *Oxford Essays in Jurisprudence* (Second Series, 1973) 228

Martin, JE, *Hanbury & Martin Modern Equity* (15th ed, London, 1997)
— "Fusion, Fallacy and Confusion; A Comparative Study" [1994] *Conveyancer* 13
— "Certainty of Subject Matter: A Defence of *Hunter v Moss*" [1996] *Conveyancer* 223

Mason, K and Carter, JW, *Restitution Law in Australia* (Sydney, 1995)

Matthews, P, "The Constitution of Disclaimed Trusts Inter Vivos" [1981] *Conveyancer* 141
— "Whose Body? People as Property" (1983) 36 *Current Legal Problems* 193
— "Resulting Trusts and Subsequent Contributions" (1994) 8 *Trust Law International* 43
— "The Legal and Moral Limits of Common Law Tracing" in Birks, *Laundering and Tracing* (1995) 23

Maudsley, RH, "Proprietary Remedies for the Recovery of Money" (1959) 75 *Law Quarterly Review* 234
— "Incompletely Constituted Trusts" in Pound, Griswold, and Sutherland, *Perspectives of Law: Essays for Austin Wakeman Scott* (1964) 240

Maxton, JK, "*De Facto* Spouses and the Presumption of Advancement" (1986) 12 *New Zealand Universities Law Review* 79

McBride, N, "On the Classification of Trusts" in Birks and Rose, *Restitution and Equity* (2000) 23

McCormack, G, "Mistaken Payments and Proprietary Claims" [1996] *Conveyancer* 86

McDonald, B, "Constructive Trusts" in Parkinson, *The Principles of Equity* (1996) 709

McInnes, MP, "Advancement, Illegality and Restitution" (1997) 5 *Australian Property Law Journal* 1
— "Unjust Enrichment and Constructive Trusts in the Supreme Court of Canada" (1998) 25 *Manitoba Law Journal* 513
— "Reflections on the Canadian Law of Unjust Enrichment: Lessons From Abroad" (1999) 78 *Canadian Bar Review* 416

McKendrick, E, "Tracing Misdirected Funds" [1991] *Lloyds Maritime and Commercial Law Quarterly* 378
— "Restitution, Misdirected Funds and Change of Position" (1992) 55 *Modern Law Review* 377
— "Unascertained Goods: Ownership and Obligation Distinguished" (1994) 110 *Law Quarterly Review* 509
— "Restitution and the Misuse of Chattels — The Need for a Principled Approach" in Palmer and McKendrick, *Interests in Goods* (2nd ed, 1998) 897

McRae, H, Nettheim, G and Beacroft, L, *Indigenous Legal Issues* (2nd ed, Sydney, 1997)

Meagher, RP, Gummow, WMC and Lehane, JRF, *Equity Doctrines and Remedies* (3rd ed, Sydney, 1992)

Meagher, RP and Gummow, WMC, *Jacobs' Law of Trusts in Australia* (6th ed, Sydney, 1997)

Mee, J, "Trusts of the Family Home: The Irish Experience" [1993] *Conveyancer* 359
— "Undue Influence, Misrepresentation and the Doctrine of Notice" (1995) 54 *Cambridge Law Journal* 536
— *The Property Rights of Cohabitees* (Oxford, 1999)

Megarry, RE, "The Statute of Uses and the Power to Devise" (1941) 7 *Cambridge Law Journal* 354
— "Mere Equities, the Bona Fide Purchaser and the Deserted Wife" (1955) 71 *Law Quarterly Review* 480

Megarry, RE and Wade, HWR, *The Law of Real Property* (5th ed, London, 1984)

Mendes da Costa, D, "Co-ownership Under Victorian Law" (1961) 3 *Melbourne University Law Review* 137

Millett, PJ, "The Quistclose Trust: Who Can Enforce It?" (1985) 101 *Law Quarterly Review* 269
— "Tracing the Proceeds of Fraud" (1991) 107 *Law Quarterly Review* 71
— "Bribes and Secret Commissions" [1993] *Restitution Law Review* 7; reprinted in Birks, *The Frontiers of Liability* (Vol 1, 1994) 51
— "Equity — The Road Ahead" (1995) 9 *Trust Law International* 35

Millett, PJ, "Equity's Place in the Law of Commerce" (1998) 114 *Law Quarterly Review* 214
— "Restitution and Constructive Trusts" in Cornish, *Restitution Past, Present and Future: Essays in Honour of Gareth Jones* (1998) 199
— "Restitution and Constructive Trusts" (1998) 114 *Law Quarterly Review* 399

Milsom, SFC, *Historical Foundations of the Common Law* (2nd ed, London, 1981)

Mitchell, C, *The Law of Subrogation* (Oxford, 1994)
— "Subrogation, Tracing and the *Quistclose* Principle" [1995] *Lloyds Maritime and Commercial Law Quarterly* 451
— "*Westdeutsche* in the House of Lords" (1996) 10 *Trust Law International* 84
— "Tracing Trust Funds into Insurance Proceeds" [1997] *Lloyds Maritime and Commercial Law Quarterly* 465

Moore, JP, "Equity, Restitution and in personam claims under the Torrens system" (1998) 72 *Australian Law Journal* 258

Morgan, EM, "Presumptions" (1937) 12 *Washington Law Review* 255

Moriarty, S, "Tracing, Mixing and Laundering" in Birks, *Laundering and Tracing* (1995) 73

Morris, ML, "Rediscovering the Resulting Trust: Modern Maneuvers for a Dated Doctrine?" (1983) 17 *Akron Law Review* 43

Mortimer, D, "Property Rights in Body Parts: The Relevance of *Moore's* Case in Australia" (1993) 19 *Monash Law Review* 217

Munzer, SR, *A Theory of Property* (Cambridge, 1990)

Nahan, NY (nee Chin), "Undue Influence and Third Parties" (1992) 5 *Journal of Contract Law* 108
— "Relieving Against Forfeiture: Windfalls and Conscience" (1995) 25 *University of Western Australia Law Review* 110
— "Rescission: A Case for Rejecting the Classical Model?" (1997) 27 *University of Western Australia Law Review* 66

National Health and Medical Research Council, *Statement on Human Experimentation and Supplementary Notes* (1992)

Neave, MA, "Living Together — The Legal Effects of the Sexual Division of Labour in Four Common Law Countries" (1991) 17 *Monash Law Review* 14

Neave, MA, Rossiter, CJ and Stone, MA, *Sackville and Neave: Property Law Cases and Materials* (6th ed, Sydney, 1999)

Nicholas, B, *An Introduction to Roman Law* (Oxford, 1962)

Nolan, R, "Change of Position" in Birks, *Laundering and Tracing* (1995) 135
— "Our Money on Your Life" (1997) 56 *Cambridge Law Journal* 491
— "Dispositions Involving Fiduciaries: The Equity to Rescind and the Resulting Trust" in Birks and Rose, *Restitution and Equity* (2000) 119

Oakley, AJ, "The Precise Effect of the Imposition of a Constructive Trust" in Goldstein, *Equity and Contemporary Legal Developments* (1992) 427

Oakley, AJ, *Constructive Trusts* (3rd ed, London, 1997)
— "Proprietary Claims and their Priority in Insolvency" (1995) 54 *Cambridge Law Journal* 377
— *Parker & Mellows: The Modern Law of Trusts* (7th ed, London, 1998)
— "Restitution and Constructive Trusts: A Commentary" in Cornish, *Restitution Past, Present and Future: Essays in Honour of Gareth Jones* (1998) 219

Oditah, F, "Assets and the Treatment of Claims in Insolvency" (1992) 108 *Law Quarterly Review* 459

O'Connor, P, "Aboriginal Land Rights at Common Law: *Mabo v Queensland*" (1992) 18 *Monash Law Review* 251
— "Happy Partners or Strange Bedfellows: The Blending of Remedial and Institutional Features in the Evolving Constructive Trust" (1996) 20 *Melbourne University Law Review* 735

O'Keefe, P, "Maoris Claim Head" (1992) 1 *International Journal of Cultural Property* 393

O'Sullivan, D, "Partial Rescission for Misrepresentation in Australia" (1997) 113 *Law Quarterly Review* 16

O'Sullivan, T, "Defending a Liquidator's Claim for Repayment of a Voidable Transaction" (1997) 9 *Otago Law Review* 111

Palmer, NE, "The Abolition of Detinue" [1981] *Conveyancer* 62
— *Bailment* (2nd ed, Sydney, 1991)

Palmer, NE and Hudson, A, "Damages for Distress and Loss of Enjoyment in Claims Involving Chattels" in Palmer and McKendrick, *Interests in Goods* (2nd ed, 1998) 867

Palmer, NE and McKendrick, E, *Interests in Goods* (2nd ed, London, 1998)

Parkinson, JE, *Corporate Power and Responsibility* (Oxford, 1993)

Parkinson, P, "Beyond *Pettkus v Becker*: Quantifying Relief for Unjust Enrichment" (1993) 43 *University of Toronto Law Journal* 217
— *The Principles of Equity* (Sydney, 1996)
— "The Conscience of Equity" in Parkinson, *The Principles of Equity* (1996) 28

Parkinson, P and Wright, D, "Equity and Property" in Parkinson, *The Principles of Equity* (1996) 53

Patterson, D, ed, *A Companion to Philosophy of Law and Legal Theory* (Oxford, 1996)

Penner, JE, "The 'Bundle of Rights' Picture of Property" (1996) 43 *University of California Los Angeles Law Review* 711
— *The Idea of Property in Law* (Oxford, 1997)
— "Basic Obligations" in Birks, *The Classification of Obligations* (1997) 91
— *The Law of Trusts* (London, 1998)

Pettit, PH, "Farewell Section 40" [1989] *Conveyancer* 431
— *Equity and the Law of Trusts* (7th ed, 1993)

Phillips, J, "Equitable Liens — A Search for a Unifying Principle" in Palmer, N and McKendrick, E, *Interests in Goods* (2nd ed, 1998) 975

Pollock, F and Maitland FW, *The History of English Law* (2nd ed by SFC Milsom, Cambridge, 1968)

Posner, RA, *Economic Analysis of Law* (5th ed, New York, 1998)

Priestley, LJ, "The Romalpa Clause and the Quistclose Trust" in Finn, *Equity and Commercial Relationships* (1987) 217

Proksch, L, "Rescission on Terms" [1996] *Restitution Law Review* 71

Radin, MJ, "Property and Personhood" (1982) 34 *Stanford Law Review* 957

Raff, M, "Environmental Obligations and the Western Liberal Property Concept" (1998) 22 *Melbourne University Law Review* 657
— *German Real Property Law and the Conclusive Land Title Register* (University of Melbourne PhD thesis, 1999)

Reeve, A, "Property" in Goodin and Pettit, *A Companion to Contemporary Political Philosophy* (1993) 558

Reich, CA, "The New Property" (1964) 73 *Yale Law Journal* 733

Richardson, N, "De Facto Property Disputes in New Zealand" (1996) 7 *Canterbury Law Review* 369
— "Floating Trusts and Mutual Wills" (1996) 10 *Trust Law International* 88

Rickett, CEF, "Unincorporated Associations and their Dissolution" (1980) 39 *Cambridge Law Journal* 88
— "Mutual Wills and the Law of Restitution" (1989) 105 *Law Quarterly Review* 534
— "No Donatio Mortis Causa of Real Property — A Rule in Search of a Justification?" [1989] *Conveyancer* 184
— "Different Views on the Scope of the *Quistclose* Analysis: English and Antipodean Insights" (1991) 107 *Law Quarterly Review* 608
— "Extending Equity's Reach through the Mutual Wills Doctrine?" (1991) 54 *Modern Law Review* 581
— "Loans for Purposes: Implied Contract, Express Trust or Pure Unjust Enrichment?" [1992] *Lloyds Maritime and Commercial Law Quarterly* 3
— "Trusts and Insolvency. The Nature and Place of the Quistclose Trust" in Waters, *Equity, Fiduciaries and Trusts 1993* (1993) 325
— "Mutual Wills, Restitution and Constructive Trusts — Again" [1996] *Conveyancer* 136

Riddall, JG, *The Law of Trusts* (5th ed, London, 1996)

Roberts, S, "More Lost Than Found" (1982) 45 *Modern Law Review* 683

Robertson, A, "Situating Equitable Estoppel Within the Law of Obligations" (1997) 19 *Sydney Law Review* 32

Robinson, S, *Transfer of Land in Victoria* (Sydney, 1978)

Rose, F, *Failure of Contracts* (Oxford, 1997)

Rose-Ackerman, S, "Inalienability and the Theory of Property Rights" (1985) 85 *Columbia Law Review* 931

Rotherham, C, "The Metaphysics of Tracing: Substituted Title and Property Rhetoric" (1996) 34 *Osgoode Hall Law Journal* 321
— "The Recovery of the Profits of Wrongdoing and Insolvency: When is Proprietary Relief Justified" [1997] *Company and Finance Insolvency Law Review* 43

Sackville, R, "Property, Rights and Social Security" (1978) 2 *University of New South Wales Law Journal* 246

Sarmas, L, "A Step in the Wrong Direction: The Emergence of Gender 'Neutrality' in the Equitable Presumption of Advancement" (1994) 19 *Melbourne University Law Review* 758

Scane, RE, "Relationships 'Tantamount to Spousal', Unjust Enrichment, and Constructive Trusts" (1991) 70 *Canadian Bar Review* 260

Schlatter, R, *Private Property: The History of an Idea* (London, 1951)

Schultz, J, "Judicial Acceptance of Immediate Indefeasibility in Victoria" (1993) 19 *Monash Law Review* 326

Scott, AW, "The Right to Follow Money Wrongfully Mingled with Other Money" (1913) 27 *Harvard Law Review* 125
— "The Nature of the Rights of the Cestui Que Trust" (1917) 17 *Columbia Law Review* 269
— "Conveyances upon Trusts Not Properly Declared" (1924) 37 *Harvard Law Review* 653
— "Resulting Trusts Arising upon the Purchase of Land" (1927) 40 *Harvard Law Review* 669

Scott, AW and Fratcher, WF, *The Law of Trusts* (4th ed, Boston, 1989)

Sedjo, RA, "Property Rights, Genetic Resources, and Biotechnological Change" (1992) 35 *Journal of Law and Economics* 199

Sheridan, LA, *Keeton & Sheridan's The Law of Trusts* (12th ed, Chichester, 1993)

Sherwin, EL, "Constructive Trusts in Bankruptcy" [1989] *University of Illinois Law Review* 297

Simpson, AWB, *Oxford Essays in Jurisprudence* (Second Series, Oxford, 1973)
— *A History of the Land Law* (2nd ed, Oxford, 1986)

Smart, PSJ, "Holding Property for Non-Charitable Purposes: Mandates, Conditions and Estoppels" [1987] *Conveyancer* 415

Smith, JC, "*Lister v Stubbs* and the Criminal Law" (1994) 110 *Law Quarterly Review* 180

Smith, LD, "The Province of the Law of Restitution" (1992) 71 *Canadian Bar Review* 672
— "Breach of Confidence — Constructive Trusts — Punitive Damages — Disgorgement of the Profits of Wrongdoing" (1994) 73 *Canadian Bar Review* 259
— "Disgorgement of the Profits of Breach of Contract: Property, Contract and 'Efficient Breach'" (1994) 24 *Canadian Business Law Journal* 121
— "Tracing, 'Swollen Assets' and the Lowest Intermediate Balance" (1994) 8 *Trust Law International* 102

Smith, LD, "Bailment with Authority to Mix — and Substitute" (1995) 111 *Law Quarterly Review* 10
— "Tracing into the Payment of a Debt" (1995) 54 *Cambridge Law Journal* 290
— *The Law of Tracing* (Oxford, 1997)
— "Tracing Into Life Assurance Proceeds" (1997) 113 *Law Quarterly Review* 552
— "Constructive Trusts — Unjust Enrichment — Breach of Fiduciary Obligation" (1997) 76 *Canadian Bar Review* 539
— "Constructive Trust for Breach of Fiduciary Obligations" (1998) 114 *Law Quarterly Review* 14
— "Constructive Trusts and Constructive Trustees" (1999) 58 *Cambridge Law Journal* 294
— "Tracing in Bank Accounts: The Lowest Intermediate Balance Rule on Trial" (2000) 33 *Canadian Business Law Journal* 75
— "Unjust Enrichment, Property, and the Structure of Trusts" (2000) 116 *Law Quarterly Review* 412

Spender, P, "Guns and Greenmail: Fear and Lothing After *Gambotto*" (1998) 22 *Melbourne University Law Review* 96

Stapledon, G, *Institutional Shareholders and Corporate Governance* (Oxford, 1996)

Stevens, D, "Restitution, Property and the Cause of Action in Unjust Enrichment: Getting by with Fewer Things" (1989) 39 *University of Toronto Law Journal* 258, 325

Stevens, J, "Finders Weepers — Landowners Keepers" [1996] *Conveyancer* 216

Stone, HF, "Resulting Trusts and the Statute of Frauds" (1906) 6 *Columbia Law Review* 326

Sunnucks, JHG, Ross Martyn, JG and Garnett, KM, *Williams, Mortimer and Sunnucks on Executors, Administrators and Probate* (London, 1993)

Swadling, WJ, "The Proprietary Effect of a Hire of Goods" in Palmer and McKendrick, *Interests in Goods* (2nd ed, 1998) 491
— "A New Role for Resulting Trusts?" (1996) 16 *Legal Studies* 110

Sykes, EI and Walker, S, *The Law of Securities* (5th ed, Sydney, 1993)

Tan, PL, Webb, EA and Wright, D, *Land Law* (Sydney, 1997)

Tehan, M, "The Wik Peoples v Queensland" (1997) 21 *Melbourne University Law Review* 343

Thomas, TC, "Conditions in Favour of Third Parties" (1952) 11 *Cambridge Law Journal* 240

Tilbury, MJ, *Civil Remedies* (Sydney, 1990-3) 2 volumes
— "Relief Against Forfeiture" in Parkinson, *The Principles of Equity* (1996) 309
— "Restitutionary Damages" in Carroll, *Civil Remedies: Issues and Developments* (1996) 2

Tooher, JG, Dwyer, BM and Teh, GL, *Introduction to Property Law* (3rd ed, Sydney, 1997)

Tory, JC, "Informally Created Interests in Land" (1981) 39 *University of Toronto Faculty Law Review* 55

Trindade, F and Cane, P, *The Law of Torts in Australia* (3rd ed, Sydney, 1999)

Tyler, ELG, "The Presumption of Advancement in Relation to Personalty" (1966) 30 *Conveyancer* 223

Tyler, ELG and Palmer, NE, *Crossley Vaines' Personal Property* (5th ed, London, 1973)

Ulph, J, "Title Obligations and Barber: Too Many Short Cuts?" [1997] *Lloyds Maritime and Commercial Law Quarterly* 12

— "The Proprietary Consequences of an Excess Delivery" [1998] *Lloyds Maritime and Commercial Law Quarterly* 4

Underkuffler, LS, "On Property: An Essay" (1990) 100 *Yale Law Journal* 127

— "The Perfidy of Property" (1991) 70 *Texas Law Review* 293

Vines, P, "Resting in Peace? A Comparison of the Legal Control of Bodily Remains in Cemeteries and Aboriginal Burial Grounds in Australia" (1998) 20 *Sydney Law Review* 78

Virgo, G, *The Principles of the Law of Restitution* (Oxford, 1999)

Voumard, *The Sale of Land* (4th ed, Sydney, 1986)

Wade, HWR, "Husband and Wife — Deserted Wife's Right to Matrimonial Home — Equitable Interests and 'Mere Equites'" [1955] *Cambridge Law Journal* 158

— "Real Property — Title in Ejectment — Possession" [1956] *Cambridge Law Journal* 177

Waldron, J, *The Right to Private Property* (Oxford, 1988)

— "Property Law" in Patterson, *A Companion to Philosophy of Law and Legal Theory* (1996) 3

— "The Normative Resilience of Property" (1998) 9 *Otago Law Review* 195

Waters, DWM, *The Constructive Trust* (London, 1964)

— *Law of Trusts in Canada* (2nd ed, Toronto, 1984)

— "The Constructive Trust in Evolution: Substantive and Remedial" in Goldstein, *Equity and Contemporary Legal Developments* (1992) 457

— *Equity, Fiduciaries and Trusts 1993* (Toronto, 1993)

— "The Nature of the Remedial Constructive Trust" in Birks, *The Frontiers of Liability* (Vol 2, 1994) 165

Watts, P, "Bribes and Constructive Trusts" (1994) 110 *Law Quarterly Review* 178

— "Restitution — A Property Principle and a Services Principle" [1995] *Restitution Law Review* 49

Wendrich, C, "Who Should Profit from an Academic Degree Upon Marital Breakdown? Comparing Manitoba Common Law and the German Civil Code" (1997) 25 *Manitoba Law Journal* 267

Whalan, DJ, *The Torrens System in Australia* (Sydney, 1982)

Wheeldon, S, "Reflections on the Concept of 'Property' with Particular Reference to Breach of Confidence" (1997) *Auckland University Law Review* 353

Wheeler, S, *Reservation of Title Clauses* (Oxford, 1991)

White, PD, "The Illusion of the Mere Equity" (1967) 5 *Sydney Law Review* 499

Williams, GL, "The Three Certainties" (1940) 4 *Modern Law Review* 20

Williams, TC, "The Terms Real and Personal in English Law" (1888) 4 *Law Quarterly Review* 394

Willmot, L, *De Facto Relationships Law* (Sydney, 1996)

Woodman, RA, "The Torrens System in New South Wales: One Hundred Years of Indefeasibility of Title" (1970) 44 *Australian Law Journal* 96

Worthington, S, "Proprietary Restitution — Void, Voidable and Uncompleted Contracts" (1995) 9 *Trust Law International* 113
— *Proprietary Interests in Commercial Transactions* (Oxford, 1996)
— "Proprietary Remedies: The Nexus between Specific Performance and Constructive Trusts" (1996) 11 *Journal of Contract Law* 1
— "The Proprietary Consequences of Contract Failure" in Rose, *Failure of Contracts* (1997) 67

Wright, "*Sinclair v Brougham*" (1938) 6 *Cambridge Law Journal* 305

Wright, RB, "North Carolina Eliminates Presumption of Purchase Money Resulting Trust for Wives" (1983) 61 *North Carolina Law Review* 576

Yeung, K, "When Does a Company Acquire Knowledge?" [1997] *Corporate, Finance & Insolvency Law Review* 67

Youdan, TG, "The Mutual Wills Doctrine" (1979) 29 *University of Toronto Law Journal* 390
— "Informal Trusts and Third Parties: A Response" [1988] *Conveyancer* 267
— *Equity, Fiduciaries and Trusts* (Toronto, 1989)
— "The Fiduciary Principle: The Applicability of Proprietary Remedies" in Youdan, *Equity, Fiduciaries and Trusts* (1989) 93
— "Equitable Transformations of Family Property Law" in Goldstein, *Equity and Contemporary Legal Developments* (1992) 517
— "Writing on the Law of Trusts" (1992) 12 *Oxford Journal of Legal Studies* 275
— "Resulting and Constructive Trusts" [1993] *Law Society of Upper Canada Lectures* 169

Ziff, BH, *Principles of Property Law* (3rd ed, Toronto, 2000)

Zimmermann, R, *The Law of Obligations: Roman Foundations of the Civilian Tradition* (Oxford, 1996)

INDEX

abandonment, 10, 48, 69, 192, 368
abatement, 279
aboriginal laws and customs, 219-220
aboriginal relic, 19, 20
aboriginal title — *see also* native title
absence of term, 79
accession, 362-364
accessories, 362-370
accommodation, 149
account of profits, 176, 350
accretion, 359-361
accrual of cause of action, 68
action to recover goods, 59
action to recover land, 59, 67
actual authority, 385
actual notice, 409
actus reus, 58
ademption, 279
administrator, 277
advancement, presumption of, 330
adverse possession, 58, 68-71, 98, 250, 399, 440, 457, 467, 486-487
advertisement, 189
aeroplane, 46
agency, 385
    apparent, 382, 385-387
agreement as to shared rights, 130
    severance, 141
agricultural fixture, 367
air space, 89
airport, 47
alienability, 10, 80
allocating rights, 358-359
allodial title, 86, 225
allodium, 86
ameliorating waste, 103
animals, 38, 48, 358
animus possidendi, 48

annexation
    degree of, 365
    object of, 365-366
apparent agency, 382, 385-387
apparent authority, 385-386
apparent gift, 329-332
archeology, 20
artistic work, 25, 176
ascertained goods, 244
assessment lease, 171
assets, right to, 198
assignment of intangible property, 246
assignment of lease, 94
assurance fund, 446
attribution of authorship, 178
authority
    actual, 385
    apparent, 385-386
    representations of, 383-384
automated banking machine, 391

bailment, 52, 53, 60
bank account, 11, 115, 122, 245, 340-341
bank draft, 391
bankruptcy, 117, 118, 320, 381, 470
bar the entail, 92
bare licence, 206
bare trust, 116
bargain and sale, 248
beach, 32
bearer bond, 391
bee, 48
beneficial interest, 111
beneficial ownership, 86, 110-111, 126, 306-310, 396
beneficiary
    estate, of, 278
    transfer of estate to, 278-279
    trust, of, 110-111, 252

benefit to land, 150
benefits of wrongdoing, 345-346
bequest, 41, 280
bicentennial, 26
bill of exchange, 391
bill of sale, 51, 120, 128, 242, 243, 256
blind trust, 114
blood, 20, 21, 22
boat, 46, 132
bona fide purchase, 160, 246, 257, 324, 338, 378, 379-380, 403-408, 416, 431, 439, 462, 487
bona vacantia, 91, 284, 288-289, 370, 449
bond, 194
book, 7, 25, 33, 45, 50, 56, 77
boundary of estate, 359-361
   misdescription, 466-467
breach of confidence, 25, 187, 189-191, 234, 348, 349
breach of contract, 258-259, 348, 349
breach of duty, 55-58
breach of fiduciary duty, 22, 234, 348, 349, 350
breach of trust, 350
breach of warranty of authority, 385
bread, 38, 356
bribes, accepting, 41, 351, 440, 478
British Empire, 222
British sovereignty, 222-225, 227, 395
broadcast, 177
building scheme, 163-164
bundle of rights, 28, 79-80
burial right, 17, 19, 207
business name, 184, 186-187
business trust, 194
buyer in possession, 382, 387, 388, 394

cafe, 47
capital, 79
car, 38, 46, 64, 356
carelessness, 380-381
cat, 48
cave, 89
caveat, 408, 440, 455, 481-486
   failure to caveat, 488-489
   lapse, 484
   improperly lodged, 486
   notice, 487-488

   right to lodge, 482-486
   search, 488-490
certainty of intention, 252-253
certainty of object, 109, 252
certainty of subject, 109, 252
certainty of words, 253
certificate of title, 449
certified copy of title, 450
cestui que trust, 112
cestui que use, 112
chain of title, 435, 466
Chancery, 39, 105, 106, 124, 160
change of position, 315
charge, 117
   equitable, 121-122, 128
   fixed, 121
   floating, 121
   statutory, 123
charitable trust, 110
charter of feoffment, 247
chattel, 4, 38
chattel lease, 53
chattel mortgage, 120, 243
chattel real, 39, 92, 280
cheque, 245, 283, 391-393
   crossed, 392
   dishonoured, 392
   holder in due course, 393
   indorsing, 392
   nemo dat exception, 391-393
CHESS, 247
child, 14, 18
   gift to, 330
   organs, 22
   remainder to, 101, 109
   trust for, 113-114, 484
chimpanzee, 16
chose in action, 41, 196
chose in possession, 41
circuit layouts, 180-181, 429
civil wrong, 344
Clayton's rule, 340-341
codicil, 276, 280
coins, 46, 245
collective property, 32, 33
colony, 222
commencement of title, 410
commercial lease, 92
commingling, 339-341, 370-374

commixtio, 373
common intention constructive trust, 303-306
common law, 84, 105
common law estoppel, 292
common law liens, 119-120, 128, 267-268
common law rescission, 319
common ownership, 371, 373, 374
common property, 32, 33
communal rights, 220-221
company, 193-194
    shares in, 41, 193-203, 258-259
compensation, 59-61, 103, 107, 190, 234, 258, 344, 486
competing rights, 50, 55-66, 377-378
competition, 28
completion of gift, 272
compulsory licence, 182
computer program, 25, 177
conditional sale, 53, 117, 121, 126, 128, 388
confidential information, 25, 175, 176, 187-193
confusio, 373
consent
    mixture by, 371
    mixture without, 371-374
    possession acquired by, 52-53
    possession acquired without, 53
    right to possession acquired by, 63
    rights created by, 41, 132, 234, 236
consideration, 406-407
consignment, 386
continuing ownership, 371, 373, 374
constructive fraud, 443
constructive knowledge, 414
constructive notice, 409-412
constructive trust, 111, 237, 261, 262, 273-274, 286, 301, 334, 351, 353-354, 419, 422, 440, 459, 478
    common intention, 303-306
Consumer Credit Code, 127
consumer protection, 321
contingent remainder, 100
contract of lease, 459
contract of sale
    of goods, 240, 243-244, 262-263, 302
    of human tissue, 21
    of land, 270-271, 302

contractual licence, 206-207
contribution to purchase, 331-332
control, 45-48
conversion, 22, 39, 56, 57, 60, 63, 132, 348
co-ownership, 129-143
copyhold estate, 85
copyright, 25, 26, 41, 45, 50, 176-178
cornea, 22
corporation, 135, 193-194
    shares in, 41, 193-203, 258-259
corporeal rights, 40
corpse, 16-20, 22
co-tenancy, 129-143, 374
court of equity, 40, 105
Courts
    Chancery, 39, 104, 105, 106, 124, 160
    common law, 39, 40, 105
    Common Pleas, 39
    ecclesiastical, 17
    High Court of Justice, 40
    King's Bench, 39
    manorial, 105
    superior, 40
covenant, 156
    freehold, 157
    leasehold, 156, 225
    quiet enjoyment, 166
    restrictive, 108, 145, 156-164, 257
crane, 89
creation of rights, 41-42, 233-237
    deeds registration, 435-436
    easement, 154-155, 209
    equitable charge, 254-256
    equitable property rights, 250-257
    legal property rights, 240-250
    licence, 208-210
    restrictive covenant, 257
    shared ownership, 136-140
    Torrens system, 249, 448-459, 475-481
    trust, 237, 252-254
creation of things, 355-361
credit card, 117, 391
creditor protection, 320, 323
crime, 58, 233
    proceeds of, 345-346
    property used to commit, 346
crocodile, 217, 218, 226
crops, 147
crossed cheque, 392

Crown
  allodial title, 86
  corporation, 202
  grant, 97, 169, 226, 434, 448
  land, 19, 33
  lease, 395-402, 435, 441, 448, 452
  minerals, right to, 90, 169-170
  pastoral lease, 97, 167, 395
  profits à prendre granted by, 146
  radical title, 86, 224-225, 226
  right to land, 86-87
  sovereignty, 86, 222-225, 395
  tenure, 83
currency, 244, 245
custody, 66
customer list, 188

damages, 60, 107, 176, 212, 258
  disgorgement, 350
  exemplary, 62, 212
  punitive, 62, 212
  restitutionary, 350
de facto relationship, 299-300
  breakdown, 297-311, 320
de facto spouse
  body of spouse, right to, 17
  mutual wills, 287-288
  resulting or constructive trust, 111, 301, 440, 478
dead body, 16-20, 22
death
  order of, 135-136
  ownership of assets, 297
  succession on, 236, 275-289
  survivorship, 134-136
debenture, 121, 194, 255
debit card, 391
debt, 117
debtor, 117
debtor's prison, 82
deceit, 349
declaration of severance, 141-142
declaration of trust, 252
deed, 51, 242, 243, 248, 251, 255, 322, 433
  estoppel by, 292
deeds registration, 249-250, 430, 433-443, 445-446
  conversion to Torrens system, 434-435, 449
  creation of rights, 435-436
  priority, 436-443
defamation, 184, 348
deferred indefeasibility, 464-465

defrauding creditors, 320
degree of annexation, 365
delivery, 52, 190, 240, 241-242
demise, 92
deserted wife's equity, 418
Design Office, 180
designs, 25, 179-180, 429
destruction of four unities, 140-141
destruction of premises, 361
detinue, 57, 60, 348
detrimental reliance, 236, 291-311, 303-306, 447
development scheme, 163-164
devise, 280
direct enforcement, 59, 344
disability, 68
discretionary trust, 111
disgorgement, 344
disgorgement damages, 350
dishonesty, 414, 481
dishonoured cheque, 392
dispute as to priority, 423-425
dividend, 197-198
divorce or separation, 297-311
doctor and patient, 188
document of transfer, 240, 242-243, 246
dog, 38, 45
dolphin, 16
domestic animal, 48, 358
domestic relationship, 299-300
  breakdown, 297-311
dominant tenement, 149-151
dominium, 84
donatio mortis causa, 279, 281-284, 288
donee, 271, 441, 442
donor's intention, 332
dramatic work, 25, 177
driver's licence, 205
duplicate certificate of title, 449
duress, 316, 319, 419, 480
duty of confidence, 187, 188-189

easement, 46, 145, 149-156, 209, 249, 459, 468-469
  benefit to land, 150
  by prescription, 154-155
  changes in use, 156
  cost of maintaining, 154

easement — *continued*
   creation of, 154-155
   in gross, 150
   less than possession, 152-153
   negative, 152
   of necessity, 154
   positive, 151-152
   restrictive covenant compared, 157
   Torrens system, 468-469
   utilities, 150
education, 15
eggs, 36, 356
Egyptian mummy, 19
ejectment, 39, 59, 64, 92
EL (eligible layout) right, 180-181
electronic funds transfer, 391
emblement, 147
embryo, 21, 23-24
employee and employer, 65-66
encumbrance, 121-123, 450
   statutory, 123
endangered species, 82
enforcement, 59
   direct, 59, 344
   licence, 210-215
   right to vote, 199-200
enrichment, 314-315
equitable charge, 121-122, 128, 252, 254-256
equitable estoppel, 292, 293, 295, 303, 305
equitable fraud, 443
equitable lease, 263, 440
equitable lien, 122, 128, 267, 268-271, 335-337, 415
   trust compared, 336-337
equitable mortgage, 121, 128, 256, 263, 438, 449, 458, 485
equitable options, 325
equitable rescission, 319, 323-324
equitable right (or interest), 39-40, 105-116, 250-257
   formalities, 250-252
   nature of, 115-116, 403-405
   priority, 403-425, 487
equitable tenant in common, 139-140, 300-301, 331-332, 353-354
equitable waste, 104
equitable wrongs, 234
equity, 39, 105, 107-108, 124
   mere, 325, 417-423, 484-485, 487
   negative, 125
   shared rights, 139-140

equity of redemption, 124, 125, 193, 380, 451
erosion, 359-361
error, 325-327, 435
escheat, 90, 91, 98, 112, 280, 288, 289
estate, 89-104
   copyhold, 85
   Crown grant, 97, 226
   fee simple, 90-91, 98, 99, 112, 225-226, 434, 448, 451
   fee tail, 91-92
   leasehold, 92-96, 225, 263, 434
   life, 92, 99, 367
   per autre vie, 92
   perpetual lease, 97-98, 165
   privity of, 156, 225
   restrictive covenant compared, 156-157
estoppel, 207, 291-297, 471
   common law, 292
   consequences, 295-297
   creation of, 293-294
   deed, by, 292
   equitable, 292, 293, 295, 303, 305
   negligence, by, 385
   nemo dat exception, 382, 383-385
   promissory, 293
   proprietary, 293
European settlement, 222
events creating rights, 27, 41-42, 234
excludability, 10-11
executing the use, 112
execution
   deed, 248
   liability to, 79, 82
execution creditor, 117
executor, 276-277
exemplary damages, 62, 212
exploitation of disadvantage, 319, 481
exploration licence, 170, 171-172, 205
exploration permit, 171
express trust, 111, 237, 252-254, 272-273, 286, 329, 416-417
extinguishment
   native title, 165, 229, 395-402
   right to possession, 71, 165
extraterrestrial, 16

factor, 386
failure of consideration, 316
failure of trust, 328-329
failure to caveat, 488-489
failure to disclose, 319

failure to protect ownership, 384-385
failure to search, 411-412
fair trading, 321
family property, 297-311, 381
family provision, 284, 289, 320
fee simple, 90-91, 98, 99, 112, 225-226, 434, 448, 451
fee tail, 91-92
fence, 46, 68, 154
feoffee, 247
feoffee que use, 112
feoffment, 112, 247
feoffor, 247
feudal incidents, 112
feudal services, 85-86
feudalism, 83-84
fictional ownership, 179
fiduciary, 22, 126
FIFO (first in, first out), 340
fine, 345
firearm, 23
first in time priority, 414-415, 424
fish, 48
fishing right, 217
fixed charge, 121
fixed term lease, 94
fixture, 362, 364-370
    agricultural, 367
    degree of annexation, 365
    object of annexation, 365-366
    permanent, 366-368
    removal of, 368
    security rights, 369-370
    tenant's, 366-368
floating charge, 121
fluids, 48
    bodily, 21
    mixture, 373
    possession of, 48
foetus, 24
folio, 449, 452, 466
foreclosure, 120, 125, 380, 451
forestry right, 147
forfeiture, 345-347, 352-354
forfeiture order, 346
forfeiture rule, 352
forgery, 435, 480-481
formalities, 240
fossicking permit/licence, 171

fossil, 20
four unities, 130-131
    destruction of, 140-141
frankalmoign, 85
fraud, 304, 319, 322, 349, 419, 420, 443, 483
    Torrens system, 472-475, 480-481
fraudulent and void document, 437
fraudulent misrepresentation, 318
free acceptance, 315
free and common socage, 85
free market, 35, 36
freedom of information, 25-29
freehold covenant, 157
freehold estate, 90-92, 283, 440
freeway, 33
frisbee, 176
future act, 401-402
future estate, 99
future goods, 244
future interests, 99-104
future possession, right to, 58
future property, 256

gage, 124
gap in seisin, 113
garden, 46, 68, 69, 133, 147
general law land, 435
general purpose lease, 173
general registration system, 434-435
gift, 53, 78, 209, 241, 416, 470-471
    abatement, 279
    ademption, 280
    apparent, 329-332
    completion, 272
    conditional, 281
    donatio mortis causa, 279, 281-284
    incomplete, 271-274
    lapse, 280
gold, 89, 169
good faith, 126
good will, 184
goods, 38
    ascertained, 244
    creation of, 356-357
    future, 244
    specific, 244
    specification, 356
    transfer of rights, 241-244
    ascertained, 244
government owned property, 32

government secret, 187
grant
    Crown, 97, 169, 226, 434, 448
    licence coupled with, 207
granular mixtures, 373-374
grave, 208
grazing licence, 164, 167, 205
guardian, 18
    gift to child, 330
gun, 23, 429

hair, 10, 21
half secret trust, 284
harm, duty to prevent, 79, 81-82
head, 19
heir, 90
heir of the body, 91
heritage site, 132, 161
hire purchase, 53, 78, 121, 128, 369-370, 388
historical site, 161
holder in due course, 393
homicide, 140, 351-354
Houdini, 196
house, 47, 78, 152, 153, 209, 214
household goods, 47
human tissue, 16-24
    dead, 16-20
    living, 20-24
hunting, 217-218, 226
hypothecation, 121

illegal or immoral purpose, 161
immediate indefeasibility, 464-465, 481
immoveables, 38
imperialism, 87
implied permission, 69
implied trust, 237
imported goods, 186, 346
improvements, 359
imputed notice, 412-413
in personam exception, 475-481
in personam right, 7, 8, 39, 106, 110
    sharing, 130
in rem right, 7, 8, 39, 106, 110
incapacity, 108, 113
incident of residuary, 78, 79
income, right to, 79
incomplete gift, 271-274

incontrovertible benefit, 315
incorporeal rights, 40
indefeasibility, 462-465
    deferred, 464-465
    exceptions, 463, 465-475
    immediate, 464-465, 481
indorsing cheque, 392
infant, 18
    stillborn, 19
informal lease, 250, 457-458, 487
information, 24-29
    confidential, 25, 175, 176, 187-193
infringing copy, 179
injunction, 59, 103, 107, 160, 176, 190
    mandatory, 161, 210
    prohibitive, 210
innocent misrepresentation, 319
innocent purchaser, 379-380
insect, 47
insolvency, 117
insurance contract, 320
intangibles, 40-41, 50, 175-203
    transfer, 246-247
integrated circuit, 180
intellectual property, 25, 175, 348
intention
    certainty of, 252-253
    contract of sale, 260-261
    criminal, 58
    defective, 261
    profit à prendre, 148
    to benefit, 328-332
    to commit wrong, 349-350
    to create right, 209-210, 254-255
    to create trust, 252-253, 301-302, 332
    to possess, 48-49
    to transfer, 241, 242
intentional transfer, 236, 239-274
inter vivos, 239, 275-276, 279, 281-282, 286
interference with possession, 55-58
    protection from, 463
intermediate period act, 401
intestacy, 276, 284, 288
    partial, 276
invention, 25
    patentable, 181

jewellery, 47, 52, 63, 65
joint tenancy (ownership), 129-143, 371
    creation, 137-140
    severance, 140-142

joint tenant (owner), 129-143, 297, 307, 310, 353
joyride, 56, 60
judgment creditor, 82, 117
jus accrescendi, 129
jus tertii, 61, 64

key, 46
kidney, 10, 21, 22
killing, 140, 351-354
knowledge
    constructive, 414
    notice distinguished, 413-414

laches, 318
land, 38-39, 45
    Crown right to, 86-87
    native title, 217-230
    physical changes to, 359-361
    possession, 46, 64
    restrictive covenants attached to, 162-164
    title, 51
    Torrens system — *see also* Torrens system
    transfer, 247-250
landlord, 93-94, 225, 263, 459
lapse of gift, 280
law merchant, 243
lease, 90, 92-96
    assessment, 171
    assignment of, 94
    chattel, 53
    combinations, 96
    Crown grant, 97, 226, 395-402
    duration, 94-96
    equitable, 263
    fixed term, 94
    freeholding, 93
    general purpose, 173
    informal, 250, 457-458, 487
    land, 39
    mineral, 171
    mining, 173
    opal development, 173
    option, 96
    pastoral, 97, 98, 213, 395
    periodic, 94-95
    perpetual, 97-98, 165
    petroleum, 173
    retention, 171
    short, 249-250, 439, 468
    sublease, 94, 95, 130
    Torrens system, 452-453
lease and release, 248
leasehold covenant, 156, 225

leasehold estate, 90, 92-96, 225, 263, 434
    restrictive covenant compared, 156-157
legacy, 280
legal right (or interest), 39-40, 105
legal tender, 245
lessee, 53
lessor, 53
letters patent, 181
libel, 184
licence, 98, 130, 147, 149, 205-215, 418
    bare, 206
    compulsory, 182
    contractual, 206-207
    coupled with an interest, 207-208, 213
    driver's, 205
    exploration, 171, 205
    fossicking, 171
    grazing, 164, 167, 205
    mere, 206
    mining, 173
    occupation, 164, 166
    opal prospecting, 171
    pastoral right, 164, 166
    plant breeder's right, 183
    production, 173
    prospecting, 171
    special prospecting, 171
lien, 117, 119-120, 267-271, 307
    common law, 119-120, 128, 267-268
    effect of, 270-271
    equitable, 122-123, 128, 267, 268-271, 335-337, 415
    general, 120
    particular, 119
    possessory, 119-120
    purchaser's, 122, 267-268
    vendor's, 122, 267, 268, 415, 488
life estate, 92, 99, 367
life in being, 101
life tenant, 92, 367
limitation period, 67-68, 457
literary work, 25, 177
livery of seisin, 247-248
lock, 46, 68, 69
lodger, 418
lost and found, 65
lowest intermediate balance rule, 339

mail, 61
mandatory injunction, 161

manslaughter, 352
Maori warrior, 19
market overt, 382, 389-390
marriage breakdown, 297-311
Martian, 16
master and servant, 65-66
medical school, 19
mens rea, 58
mercantile agent, 386-387
mere equity, 325, 417-423, 484-485, 487
mere expectancy, 303
mere licence, 206
merger, 151
Meriam people, 217, 218
mesne lord, 84
milk bar, 98
mineral claim, 171
mineral development permit, 171
mineral lease, 171
mineral rights, 89-90, 145, 168-173, 213, 430, 469
miner's right, 170, 171
mining lease, 173
mining licence, 173
misappropriation of reputation, 184, 185
misdescription of boundaries, 466-467, 482
misleading advertising, 190
misrepresentation, 318, 319
mistake, 41, 55, 316, 318, 319, 325, 420, 423, 468, 480
mixture, 370-374
   by consent, 371
   fluid, 373-374
   granular, 373-374
   tracing through, 339-341
   without consent, 371-374
   wrongful, 372-373
money, 244-246
   nemo dat exception, 390-393
   transfer, 245-246
money had and received, 350
monopoly, 181, 182
moral right, 178
mortgage, 117, 120-121, 124-126, 128, 380
   chattel, 120, 243
   common law, 120, 128, 451

   equitable, 121, 128, 256, 263, 404, 438, 440, 449, 458, 485
   equity of redemption, 124, 125, 380, 451
   foreclosure, 125, 380, 451
   fraud, 348-349
   oral, 266
   registered, 449
   Torrens, 123, 128, 451-452
   trust compared, 125-126
   unregistered, 458
mortgagee, 124, 126
   registered, 449
mortgagor, 124
movables, 38
movie, 25, 176
mummy, 19
murder, 351-354
museum, 19
musical work, 25, 177
mutual fund, 114
mutual mistake, 319
mutual wills, 279, 287-288
name of business, 184, 186-187
native title, 32, 33, 51, 98, 165, 217-230, 430, 469
   Act, 230, 395, 399-402
   Crown leases and, 395-402
   extinguishment, 165, 229, 395-402
   inconsistent rights, 395-402
   loss of, 229
   proof of, 226-230
   sovereignty and, 222-225, 227, 395
   tenure and, 225-226
   transfer, 227-228
natural person, 194
natural vegetation, 146
negative easement, 152
   restrictive covenant compared, 157
negative equity, 125
negligence, estoppel by, 385
negligent driving, 352
negligent misrepresentation, 319
negotiable instrument, 391, 392
nemo dat, 379-381, 403-405, 424, 431, 435, 438, 439, 446, 487
   exceptions, 381-402, 424
new goods, 356-357
news, 28
noise, 58, 152

non-possessory right (or interest), 145-173
  sharing, 130-131
non-voluntary transfer, 316-317
notes and coins, 245
notice, 408-414
  actual, 408
  constructive, 409-412
  deeds registration, 442-443
  imputed, 412-413
  knowledge distinguished, 413-414
  nemo dat exception, 382, 383
  protection from, 463
notional estate, 289
nova species, 356, 357
novation, 159
nuisance, 27, 58

object of annexation, 365-366
obtaining possession, 51-53
occupation, 164, 166
occupation licence, 164, 166
old system land, 435
opal, 171, 173
  development lease, 173
  prospecting block, 171
  prospecting licence, 171
open market, 389-390
operation of law, 236
  transfer on death by, 284-289
oppression remedy, 199
option, 194
option to purchase, 53, 96, 194, 263-264, 388, 422, 453-455
option to renew, 96, 264, 454
option to rescind, 324, 393-395, 419
oral mortgage, 266
organ for transplant, 20, 22-23
ova, 20, 21, 23-24
overholding tenant, 58, 95
overlap of torts, 57
ownership, 50, 120-121
  beneficial, 86, 110-111, 126, 306-310, 396
  common, 371, 373, 374
  continuing, 371, 373, 374
  co-ownership, 129
  equitable, 105
  failure to protect, 384-385
  joint, 129, 371
  legal, 105
  possession distinguished, 50, 77-79
  responsibilities, 80-82

painting, 358
parent, 18
  gift to child, 330
  trust for child, 113-114
park, 32, 46, 47, 152
part performance, 255, 264-266
partial intestacy, 276
partition of co-tenancy, 142-143
partner, domestic, 299-300, 478
partnership, 194
passing off, 25, 184, 185
past act, 400
pastoral lease, 97, 98, 164, 213, 395
pastoral right, 145, 164-168
  licence, 166
  possession, 165-167
  property, 167-168
patent, 50, 181-182, 246, 429
patentable invention, 181
pawn, 119
pawnbroker, 119
PBR (plant breeder's right), 183-184, 246, 429
PCT (Patent Cooperation Treaty), 182
pecuniary penalty order, 346
pension fund, 114
perfectionary trust, 326
performance
  part, 255, 264-266
  specific, 107, 161, 210, 212, 257-266, 270, 422
periodic tenancy, 94-95
permanent damage to goods, 57
permanent fixture, 366-368
permanent possession of land, 217, 225
permission, 69-70
permissive waste, 103
permit
  exploration, 171
  fossicker's, 171
  mineral development, 171
  precious stones prospecting, 171
  prospecting, 171
perpetual lease, 97-98, 165
perpetuities, rule against, 100-102
person, 16
personal action, 38
personal property, 38-39
personal representative, 277

personal right, 7, 8, 15, 208
personal secret, 25, 187
personalty, 38
petroleum, 90, 169, 171, 173
petroleum lease, 173
petty patent, 182
photograph, 27, 178
physical changes creating rights, 236, 355-374
pigeon, 48
pigeon hole, 76
plank in the shipwreck, 407, 408
plant breeder's right, 183-184, 246, 429
plant variety, 25, 183
pledge, 117, 119, 128, 255
plutonium, 23
positive easement, 151-152
   restrictive covenant compared, 157
possession, 40-41, 45-53, 68-69
   acquired by consent, 52-53
   acquired without consent, 53
   adverse, 58, 68-71, 98, 250, 399, 440, 457, 467, 486-487
   animals, 48
   animus possidendi, 48
   competing claims, 50, 55-66
   control, 45-48
   delivery of, 241-242
   factual, 45
   fluids, 48
   goods, 50
   illegal, 49
   importance of, 49-50
   intention, 48-49
   interference with, 55-58
   keys, 46
   land, 98-99, 250
   obtaining, 51-58
   ownership distinguished, 50, 77-79
   pastoral right, 165-167
   permanent, 217, 225
   permission, with, 69-70
   right to, 40-41, 50, 118-119
   stolen goods, 49
   title distinguished, 51
   unity of, 130-131
possessory securities, 118-120
possessory title, 51
postponing older right, 415-416
power to rescind, 324
precious stones, 171, 173
   claim, 173
   prospecting permit, 171

pre-emptive right, 264
preferred creditor, 117
prerogative, 169
prescription, easement by, 154-155
presumption against wrongdoer, 339
presumption of advancement, 330-331
presumption of resulting trust, 329-331
primate, 16
primer seisin, 112
principal and agent, 385
prior art base, 181
priority
   deeds registration, 436-443
   dispute resolution, 423-425
   equitable rights, 403-425
   first in time, 414-415, 424
   legal rights, 379-402
   mere equities, 420-421
   postponing older right, 415-416
   rules, 377
   Torrens system, 460-465
private property, 33, 34-36
privity of contract, 158-160
privity of estate, 156, 225
pro rata, sharing, 340
probate, 277
proceeds of crime, 345-346
production licence, 173
professional qualifications, 15
profit, 176, 344-351
profit à prendre, 145, 146-149, 172, 249, 265
   licence coupled with, 207
   restrictive covenant compared, 157
   sale of goods contract compared, 147-148
prohibitive injunction, 210
promissory estoppel, 293
promissory note, 391
propagating material, 183
property
   collective, 32, 33
   common, 32, 33
   future, 256
   ownerless, 91, 289, 449
   personal, 38-39
   private, 33, 34-36
   quasi, 28, 29
   real, 38-39
   right (or interest), 7-12, 196, 208, 236
proprietary company, 195

proprietary estoppel, 293
prospecting licence, 171
prospecting permit, 171
protective trust, 114
proxy, 199
public policy, 317
public trustee, 277, 278
published edition, 179
punishment, 62, 345
punitive damages, 62, 212
purchase, 406
   bona fide, 160, 324, 378, 379-380, 403, 405-408, 416, 431, 439, 487
purchaser's lien, 122, 267-268, 269

quasi easement, 154
quasi property, 28, 29
quiet enjoyment, 166

racial discrimination, 226, 398-399, 400
rack rent, 439
radical title, 86, 224-225, 226
real action, 39
real property, 38-39
realty, 38
recaption, 59
receiver, 82
recorder of titles, 448
rectification, 325-327, 419, 422
redistribution of family assets, 297-311
register, 429-430
   business names, 187
   failure to search, 489-490
   search, 488
registered right (or interest), 448-456
   priority, 460-465
registered proprietor, 449
registered title, 51
registrable plant variety, 183
Registrar, 448
registration of right to land, 425, 429-432, 445-446
   creation of rights, 435-436, 448-459
   deeds registration, 249-250, 430, 433-443
   general registration system, 434-435
   priority, 436-443
   specific registration system, 434, 435
   Torrens system — see also Torrens system

registration of transfer, 240, 243, 246-247
relativity of property rights, 63-66
reliance on apparent authority, 382, 385-387
reliance on expectation, 272, 303-306
relic, 19
relief, 112
relief from forfeiture, 354
remainder, 99, 100
   contingent, 100
remainderman (or person), 100
rent, 93
   rack rent, 439
representation, 293-294
   authority, of, 383-384
   detrimental reliance on, 294
reputation, 176, 184-187
rescission, 23, 318-325, 419, 422
   common law, 319, 322-323
   equitable, 319, 323-324
   option to rescind, 324, 393-395, 419
   property rights before, 324-325
   property rights created by, 322-324
   statutory, 320-321, 323
residential tenancy, 368
residuary beneficiary, 280
residuary estate, 280
restitutio in integrum, 318, 319, 322, 323, 333, 393, 419
restitution, 61-62, 103, 190, 234, 258, 344-345
   indefeasibility and, 479-481
   specific, 61
   unjust enrichment, 308, 313, 317-341, 479-481
   victim, to, 347-351
   waste, 103
   wrongdoing, 344-345
restitutionary damages, 350
restitutionary trust, 326
restraining order, 347
restrictive covenant, 108, 145, 156-164, 193, 257, 455
   attaching to land, 162-164
   creation, 257
   development schemes, 163-164
   easements compared, 157
   estate compared, 156-157
   profit à prendre compared, 157
   Torrens system, 455
resulting trust, 111, 237, 316, 327-335, 422
   presumption of, 329-331

resulting use, 329
retention lease, 171
reversion, 93
reversionary right, 78, 396
reverse engineering, 180
right
   burial, 17, 19, 207
   EL (eligible layout), 180-181
   miner's, 170, 171
   moral, 178
   personal, 7, 208
   property, 7-12, 196, 208
   shareholder, 198-203
   voting, 198-203
right in personam, 7, 8, 39, 106, 110
   sharing, 130
right in rem, 7, 8, 39, 106, 110
right of first refusal, 264
right of way, 11, 41, 149
right to possession, 40-41, 62-66, 118-119
   competing rights, 50, 55-66
   enforcement, 59
   extinguishment, 71
   interference with, 56
   land, 98-99
   obtaining, 63
Romalpa clause, 357
royal prerogative, 90, 169
royalties, 349

sale, 53, 78
sale of goods, 41, 262-263, 320-321
   profit à prendre compared, 147-148
sale of land, 262
salvage, 47
scaffolding, 89
scientific advances, 175, 181-184
seal, 248
search, 411-412, 488-490
seashell, 236
secret
   government, 187
   invention, 182
   personal, 25, 187
   trade, 25, 187, 188
secret trust, 279, 284-287
secured creditor, 117, 126
securities, 194-195
security right (or interest), 117-128, 369-370
seeds, 183, 356

seisin, 90, 92
self help, 59
seller in possession, 382, 387
settlement, trust, 252
settlor, 111, 252
servient tenement, 146, 149
   ownership, 150-151
severance of joint tenancy, 140-142
share (corporate), 41, 175, 193-203, 247, 258-259
share certificate, 195-196
shared rights, 129-143
   agreement regarding use, 130
   creation of, 136-140
   four unities, 130-131, 140-141
   non-possessory rights, 130-131
   statutory rights, 134
shareholder rights, 198-203
sharing pro rata, 340
ship, 47, 432
shipwreck, 47, 430
shop, 47
shoreline, 359-361
short lease, 249-250, 439, 468
silver, 89, 169, 373
skeleton, 19
slander, 184
slavery, 15, 18
socage, 85
software, 177
soil, 146, 147
sovereignty, 86, 222-225, 227
space, 89
special property, 17
special prospecting licence, 171
specific goods, 244
specific performance, 107, 161, 210, 212, 257-266, 270, 422
specific registration system, 434, 435
specific restitution, 61
specification (of invention), 182
specification (specificatio), 356, 362, 363
spendthrift trust, 114
sperm, 20, 21, 23-24
spouse
   gift to, 330
   mutual wills, 287-288
   resulting or constructive trust, 111, 301, 419

spy, 349
standard patent, 182
state owned property
statutory encumbrance, 123, 128
statutory rights, 105
statutory trust, 111, 237
statutory wrongs, 234
stillborn child, 19
stock, 194
stolen goods, 49, 379-390
storage charge, 119
sub-bailment, 52, 120
subinfeudation, 83
    abolition, 84-85
sublease, 94, 95, 130
subtenancy, 94, 95
subtenant, 94
succession, 236, 275-289
superannuation fund, 114
survey, 360
survivorship, 129, 134-135
    corporations, 135
    no survivorship, 136
    order of death, 135-136
suspicion, 413-414, 443, 472-473

tabula in naufragio, 407
tangible, 40-41
taxonomy, 37-42, 235, 236
telephone, 32
television, 189, 338
tenancy, 70
    at sufferance, 95
    at will, 70, 95-96
    fixed term, 94
    in common, 129-143
    joint, 129-143
    periodic, 94-95
tenancy agreement, 459
tenant, 93-94, 263, 459
    at will, 250
    in chief, 83
    in demesne, 84
    joint, 129-143, 297, 307, 310, 353
    life, 92, 367
    leasehold, 93
    overholding, 58, 95
tenant's fixture, 366-368
tennis, 46, 76
tenure, 83-87
    native title and, 225-226

terra nullius, 86, 222, 223, 225, 226, 229
testamentary disposition, 239, 275-284, 286
testamentary trust, 281
testator (testatrix), 276
theft, 245-246
Thomas, Dylan, 241
threat to kill, 322
three certainties, 252, 257
title, 51
    commencement of, 410
    unity of, 131
title documents, 51, 255, 409, 410
Torrens mortgage, 123, 128
Torrens system, 51, 123, 430, 433, 434, 435, 442, 445-491
    adverse possession, 457, 467, 486-487
    assurance fund, 446
    bringing land into the system, 448-449
    caveat, 408, 455, 481-490
    certificate of title, 449, 450, 451, 452
    certified copy of title, 450
    conflict with another statute
    constructive trusts, 263, 459
    creation of rights, 249, 448-459, 475-481
    Crown grant, 448
    Crown lease, 448, 452
    DCT, 449, 450
    donee, 470-471
    duplicate certificate of title, 449
    easement, 249, 459, 468-469
    encumbrance, 450
    equitable right (or interest), 403-425
    exceptions to indefeasibility, 463, 465-475
    failure to caveat, 488-489
    folio, 449, 452, 466
    forgery, 480-481
    fraud, 472-475, 480-481
    gift, 470-471
    in personam exception, 475-481
    indefeasibility, 462-465
    lapse of caveat, 484
    lease, 249, 452-453
    mere equity, 484-485
    misdescription, 466-467, 482
    mortgage, 123, 128, 249, 451-452
    no survivorship, 136
    notice, 409
    option to purchase, 453-455
    option to renew, 454
    prior certificate or folio, 466

Torrens system — *continued*
  priority, 460-465
  recorder of titles, 448
  register, 448
  Registrar, 448
  registration, 249
  restrictive covenant, 455
  search of register, 488-490
  short lease, 249-250, 468
  statutes affecting, 469-470
  trust, 450-451, 459
  unregistered right (or interest), 446-447, 456-459, 481-491
  volunteer, 470
torts, 55-57, 233-234, 344
total destruction of premises, 361
tourist fossicking, 171
tracing, 317, 337-241, 362
trade mark, 25, 26, 184, 185-186, 346, 430
trade practices, 28, 321, 323
trade secret, 25, 187, 188
trading trust, 114
traditional laws and customs, 219-220
transfer
  death, on, 275-289
  goods, 241-244
  intangibles, 246-247
  intentional, 239-274
  inter vivos, 239, 275-276, 279, 281-282
  land, 247-250
  money, 244-246
  non-voluntary, 316-317
  operation of law, by, 236, 284-289
  testamentary, 275-284
  unregistered, 458
trees, 147, 148
trespass, 55, 56, 57, 63, 89, 132, 151, 348
trover, 56, 63
trust, 108-115, 193
  bare, 116
  beneficiary of, 110-111, 252
  blind, 114
  breach of, 350
  business, 194
  certainty of objects, 109
  certainty of subject matter, 109
  charitable purpose, 110
  classification, 334-335
  common intention constructive, 303-306
  constitution of, 108, 253-254, 285-286
  constructive, 111, 237, 261, 262, 273-274, 286, 301, 309, 334, 351, 353-354, 419, 422, 440, 459, 478
  creation of, 237, 251-252, 259-261
  declaration of, 252
  development of, 111-113
  discretionary, 111
  express, 111, 237, 252-254, 272-273, 286, 329, 416-417
  half secret, 284
  implied, 237
  incompletely constituted, 253
  modern uses of, 113-115
  mortgage compared, 125-126
  non-charitable purpose, 110
  object of, 108, 109-110, 252
  perfectionary, 326
  protective, 114
  restitutionary, 326
  resulting, 111, 237, 316, 327-335, 422
  secret, 279, 284-287
  settlement, 252
  specifically enforceable contract, created by, 259-262
  spendthrift, 114
  statutory, 111, 237
  subject of, 108-109, 252
  testamentary, 281
  Torrens system, 450-451, 459
  trading, 114
  types, 111
  unit, 114
trustee, 108
  beneficiary, as, 110
  fiduciary duty, 126
trustee in bankruptcy, 82, 117, 242

unascertained goods, 244
uncertainty, 309-311
unconscionability, 306-311
undivided shares, 130
undue influence, 316, 319, 420, 423, 480
unfair competition, 28
unilateral declaration of severance, 141-142
unit trust, 114
unity of interest, 131
unity of possession, 130-131
unity of time, 131
unity of title, 131

unjust enrichment, 41, 132, 133-134, 234, 236, 302, 313-341, 362, 422, 447
   restitution of, 308, 313, 317-341, 479-481
   types, 314-317
   unjust factors, 315-317
unlawful killing, 140, 351-354
unpaid vendor's lien, 122, 267, 268, 488
unregistered documents, 441
unregistered rights, 446-447, 456-459, 481-491
   priority, 462-465, 486-490
   protection, 481-486
   survival, 465-475
unregistrable rights, 439-440
unsecured creditor, 117
urine, 21
use, 112
use upon a use, 112
utility easements, 150

vacation house, 46
valuable consideration, 195, 406-407
value, 11, 441-442
vendor's lien, 122, 267, 268, 415, 488
vested in interest, 99, 276
vested in possession, 99
victim, 343
   restitution to, 347-351
video recorder, 82

voidable transaction, 318, 323
voluntary waste, 103
volunteer exception, 470
voting right, 198-203

wait and see rule, 102
wardship, 112
waste, 58, 81, 102-104
   ameliorating, 103
   compensation for, 103
   equitable, 104
   injunction against, 103
   permissive, 103
   restitution, 103
   voluntary, 103
water, 147
whale, 16
wild animal, 146, 358
wilful blindness, 414, 481
will, 41, 276, 279-281
   mutual, 279, 287-288
   witnessing, 280
William the Conqueror, 83
words of severance, 137
writing requirement, 249, 251
wrongdoer, presumption against, 339
wrongdoing, 41, 132-133, 233-234, 236, 343-354, 447
wrongful mixture, 372-373

zoo, 33